DEMENTIA PRAECOX

OR

THE GROUP OF SCHIZOPHRENIAS

MONOGRAPH SERIES ON SCHIZOPHRENIA NO. 1

DEMENTIA PRAECOX OR THE GROUP OF SCHIZOPHRENIAS

By

EUGEN BLEULER

Translated by JOSEPH ZINKIN, M.D.

Foreword by NOLAN D. C. LEWIS, M.D.

INTERNATIONAL UNIVERSITIES PRESS

NEW YORK NEW YORK

SUMMER, 1908 (p.2)

First Printing, 1950
Second Printing, 1952
Third Printing, 1955
Fourth Printing, 1958
Fifth Printing, 1961

Manufactured in the United States of America

FOREWORD

Eugen Bleuler (1857-1939) is universally well known for his outstanding contributions to psychiatric knowledge. Among his numerous original works which have vitalized this field, are the psychology of dementia praecox (schizophrenia), including the phenomena of ambivalence, and of autistic thinking; the delineation of the "schizoid" and "syntonic" personality types, the *Text Book of Psychiatry* and some later biophilosophical theories.

A great deal of Bleuler's work has been translated into English, including the *Text Book*, his monograph on negativism and several papers on different psychiatric topics, but his most important work, the large monograph on dementia praecox which appeared in 1911 as a volume of *Aschaffenburg's Handbuch*, under the title of *Dementia Praecox oder die Gruppe der Schizophrenien* has not been translated previously into English nor apparently into any other language. This has been an unfortunate neglect, as many students, unable to read the German language with facility, have had to depend upon quotations, digests and second hand expositions of its important contents.

The *Text Book* which has been available in English for several years contains much material on schizophrenia including the analysis of symptoms and excellent descriptions of the course of this group of disorders. In his original work he considered the fundamental symptoms to represent a splitting of the personality which he designated "schizophrenia." With the development of the concept of schizophrenia he introduced the term "ambivalence," and otherwise elucidated and revised the whole problem of this disorder of the thought processes.

In his epoch-making monograph he pointed out the particular expressions of affect and emphasized the specific loosening of the associations as being characteristic of the disorder, as well as the phenomenon of autistic thinking. The manifestation of this loosening of the associations he described as a group of basic symptoms which were always present in true schizophrenia. Bleuler's views were accepted generally in America, but his analysis of the symptoms into primary and secondary groups has seldom been used in a practical way to the extent which it deserves.

The present translation of Bleuler's monograph, which is his major contribution to psychiatry, will be welcome to all students in this discipline, as it will bring to them the original details of a splendid work which is not only of historical value, but also of immediate practical importance. The translator and the publishers have rendered psychiatry a valuable service.

Nolan D. C. Lewis
Psychiatric Institute
Columbia University

TRANSLATOR'S PREFACE

It is one of the curiosities of psychiatric work in our time that one of the most valuable monographs in psychiatric literature has remained, for thirty years, untranslated from the original German. Although during this period practically every psychiatric bibliography made reference to Bleuler's monograph, often praising it as an outstanding work, very few psychiatrists, at least of my generation, had any personal knowledge of the Bleulerian text. Most, if not all, references to the Swiss work were second-hand; hence the frequent misunderstanding of what our author really had to say. The contents of the volume remained buried in its German text and few libraries in this country even possess a copy.

In asking many outstanding psychiatrists whether they would be interested in a translation of Bleuler's work, I almost invariably encountered the belief that it had long been translated. Everyone supposed that someone else had really read it. For years it had been Dr. Gregory Zilboorg's hope that someone would translate this classic work, and he often stressed the need for an English translation. He was apparently one of the relatively few who had read and studied the work in German. I want to thank him especially for the interest he showed in the translation and for his powerful advocacy of the need for it to some of the rather reluctant American publishers. It was he who said of Bleuler's monograph that, "it was the classic work of twentieth century psychiatry." I trust he will be pleased that it was this comment in his *History of Medical Psychology* which made me feel that it was more than a worthwhile effort to undertake this translation.

I wish to acknowledge my debt to Dr. N. D. C. Lewis, of the Psychiatric Institute of New York, for his encouragement, as well as for the several interesting conversations we had concerning Bleuler and European psychiatry of his period. It was he who took the trouble to read the manuscript and to submit it to some of his colleagues. Dr. Paul Hoch of the same Institute took time off from a very busy schedule to read the manuscript. As a former pupil of Eugen Bleuler, he was extremely interested in seeing an English translation of the work of his old teacher. Dr. Hoch's kindness is more than appreciated.

I am most grateful, also, to Dr. V. T. Davis, my old chief at the Neuropsychiatric Division of the United States Marine Hospital, Ellis Island, New York, and to Dr. Robert H. Felix, chief of the Division of Mental Hygiene, United States Public Health Service, as well as to the other members of the Service. They showed great interest in and understanding of this valuable classic work, and thus aided and encouraged me.

I also wish to express my appreciation for their valuable co-operation to Gerda Corvin, Lottie Maury and Milan Stoeger.

Finally, I wish to thank, in print, a silent co-partner, my wife, Lillian W. Zinkin, who assisted me in the actual work of the translation, in the reading and correction of the long manuscript, and who bore the burden of reading proof. I really owe her a great deal more in this enterprise than these words of thanks can express.

New York, N. Y. 1949 — Joseph Zinkin, M. D.

CONTENTS

AUTHOR'S PREFACE

Our knowledge of the disease group which Kraepelin established under the name of Dementia Praecox is too recent to warrant a complete description. The whole complex is still too fluid, incomplete, tentative. Since it would be rather tedious to draw attention to all the reservations implied by this fact, I hope I am justified in assuming that the reader will bear this in mind.

An additional difficulty arises with regard to the chapters on psychopathology, that is the embryonic state of contemporary psychology. We do not even have the necessary terminology for the new psychological concepts. All the terms we employ may have various meanings. Whoever does not take the trouble to follow the thought of the author closely, will soon come to understand a specific term in a sense other than the one intended by the author, and thus develop a wrong picture of the basic issue. If in spite of these difficulties, I attempt to clarify some psychological connections and concepts, I do not do so merely because each new fact is of value in itself, but mainly because in the present state of our knowledge it appears that in this way new insight can be obtained into the nature of the psychoses.

Consequently, the various aspects of this disease will receive rather uneven consideration. The principles clearly understood by every psychiatrist may simply be stated, whereas less familiar points must receive their introduction, discussion and exemplification. Hence, I had to sacrifice the aesthetic to the practical purposes of this work. Also, repetitions could hardly be avoided since, in view of the complexity of the human psyche, similar processes are bound to appear in the most diverse connections.

The whole idea of dementia praecox originates with Kraepelin. Almost exclusively to his work we also owe the grouping and description of the separate symptoms. It would be too tedious to acknowledge our debt to him in each and every instance, and I hope that this remark will serve for all subsequent omissions. An important aspect of the attempt to advance and enlarge the concepts of psychopathology is nothing less than the application of Freud's ideas to dementia praecox. I feel certain that every reader realizes how greatly we are indebted to this author, without my mentioning his name at each appropriate point of the discussion. Also,

I wish to thank my co-workers in Burgholzli of whom I mention only Riklin, Abraham, and particularly Jung. It would be impossible to state precisely who contributed this or that idea or observation.

It seemed of little value to review the literature completely, since this would be almost impossible in view of the fact that practically the entire psychiatric literature would have to be included; to some extent, almost every systematic work on psychiatry has touched upon what we have come to consider the dementia praecox question. Only the more recent publications are of some value; many of these are interesting only inasmuch as they reveal how erroneously an excellent concept can be understood.

In my opinion, it is inconsiderate to the reader to acknowledge priority for each less important point; I have acted accordingly.

This work was completed in the summer of 1908, but later publications provided opportunities for further additions and amendments.

Numbers in brackets refer to the appended bibliography.

GENERAL INTRODUCTION

Historical Background

The observation that an acute disease may result in permanent damage to the affected organ has had far greater significance in psychiatry than in any other field of medicine. Our mental institutions have always been filled with the victims of the so-called "secondary" incurable maladies. Thus it has become a vital question which of the acute forms of disease terminate in incurable states and which do not. Up to now, all the described acute forms of "simple psychoses" could either end in recovery or lead to "secondary" forms. Kraepelin finally succeeded in isolating a number of symptoms which were present in maladies with very poor prognoses while absent in other disease-groups. The psychoses characterized by the presence of these symptoms were subsumed under the term Dementia Praecox. There were always some cases, however, which exhibited these symptoms, yet seemed to recover. Nevertheless, the knowledge had been gained that a certain symptom-group indicated a tendency to result in deterioration (dementia). On the other hand, other acute diseases in which these same symptoms were lacking never seemed to terminate in secondary deterioration. These were subsumed under the term of Manic-depressive Psychoses. From a practical and theoretical point of view, this classification offered a great advantage since it provided a basis on which to make predictions in a large number of cases as to acute attacks, and terminal state.

By the presence of the symptom-complex so selected and defined, the great group of dementia praecox is characterized as a unit. Kraepelin's conception is still being opposed by many; some are baffled by the manifold external clinical manifestations presented by this disease, others cannot be content with the concept of a disease which originally seemed to be defined in terms of the course peculiar to it, while at the same time including cases with both good and bad outcome. However, a closer examination shows that, in fact, all these cases have much in common, that they are clearly marked off from other types of mental disease. This certainly constitutes a vast advance from all earlier attempts to define this disease-group. Although this disease does not always result in complete deterioration, on closer scrutiny each case nevertheless reveals some significant residual symptoms common to all. Thus, apart from identical symptomatology, we also find identical end results—not quantitatively, but qualitatively—namely, in terms of the direction in which the disease develops. Other psychoses neither show the same symptomatology nor the same outcome. Conversely, all the psychoses heretofore considered as secondary show the same general symptom complex. In the present state of our knowledge, therefore, the delineation of this disease-group is not only permissible, it is mandatory.

Furthermore, it has been established that all those forms of deterioration that begin without any prominently acute phase, but slowly and insidiously, have identical symptoms and can at no time be differentiated from the so-called "secondary" types. Thus we must include in this disease all those types known under a wide variety of names, such as "primary deterioration," "deteriorating paranoia," etc., etc.

Up to now, all attempts to classify these cases into subdivisions or groups in accordance with their external clinical pictures have failed completely.

Under the term dementia praecox or schizophrenia we thus subsume a group of diseases which can be clearly distinguished from all the other types of diseases in Kraepelin's system. They have many common symptoms and similar prognoses. Nevertheless, their clinical pictures may be extremely varied. This concept may be of temporary value only inasmuch as it may later have to be reduced (in the same sense as the discoveries of bacteriology necessitated the subdivision of the pneumonias in terms of the various etiological agents). Nevertheless we believe that an advance has been made which is even greater than the progress made by the discovery of the etiology of general paresis. The latter syndrome too was for a long time obscured by many other symptom-pictures. We feel that the dementia praecox problem involves much more deeply the entire complex of the systematics of all the psychoses than the problem of general paresis ever did in its day. Those facts which still remain obscure no longer involve the main bulk of the cases of dementia praecox but rather only the exceptional or difficult ones, such as the fever-psychoses which up to now have defied the closer study by the expert. For the first time, we have definitions that permit us to arrive at some common understanding. In addition, we know where our present knowledge and means of investigation do not enable us to draw sharp delineations.

The development of the concept of dementia praecox constitutes a considerable part of the whole development of theoretical psychiatry. One can hardly be described without the other. Therefore it is quite impossible to attempt a complete discussion of the genesis of the dementia praecox concept. The cradle of the idea is the Fifth Edition of Kraepelin's *Psychiatry* (1896).

Of course, it was known for a long time that some acute psychoses improved, while others tended to become chronic. It had also been observed and known for a long time that simpler deteriorating cases could progress to such a state without exhibiting acute symptoms. Already Esquirol had separated "acquired or accidental" idiocy from the hereditary or congenital. He had noted the stereotyped behavior of some of his patients. Furthermore, it was known for a long time that mainly young persons were affected by such deteriorating processes. It was for this reason that Morel coined the name "démence précoce" (dementia praecox). However, no single unifying denominator could be discovered in the chaos of the variegated clinical pictures of the deteriorating process. A great obstacle to this end was the rather naive belief (very widely held during the middle of the last century) that the psychoses, or rather the psychosis, must have a very definite course which was ordinarily supposed to be initiated by a melancholic state.

This notion also marred Kahlbaum's theories which in other respects signified an essential advance. Naturally, several astute minds, even before him, had already known that the old names, such as melancholia, insanity, mania, deliria, merely designated symptom-pictures. However, one was unable to isolate true disease processes; therefore symptomatological entities were treated as if they corresponded to real diseases. Kahlbaum was the first to make a conscious attempt at sorting out disease processes from this complex of symptoms.

In 1863, in his *Grouping of Psychic Diseases*, he drew attention to the catatonic symptom complex, but it was only in the following year that he described the disease more accurately under this name—and finally established it definitely in his monograph of 1874. According to him catatonia passes through the stages of melancholia, mania, stupor, confusion, and finally dementia (analogous to what he termed Vesania typica). Any of these various stages might be absent and cure could set in at any stage except the last. The author characterized the disease (corresponding to general paresis) by a group of bodily symptoms which we now consider to be catatonic manifestations.

Since that period, catatonia as a disease process has never disappeared from the literature although it was often vigorously attacked. Only a few authors accepted the concept of catatonia as a "disease process;" the majority of German psychiatrists rejected it, mainly for the very obvious reason that a typical course as postulated by Kahlbaum was the exception rather than the rule, and furthermore because the concept did not seem sufficiently delimited in any direction.

In 1871, Hecker, at Kahlbaum's suggestion, described hebephrenia which Kahlbaum then lined up with his catatonic group, and thereafter he enlarged the entire group to include the heboid which itself is no more than a milder form of hebephrenia manifesting itself chiefly by changes of character. Schuele, at an early date, was able to describe catatonia as "a hebephrenia in conjunction with tension neurosis."

In contrast to Kahlbaum, many authors brought the deteriorating (dementing) psychoses into closer connection with the degenerations, familial as well as individual. Earlier Morel had raised the question of the causal significance of heredity. A defective brain was therefore believed especially predisposed to this disease (catatonia).

Somewhat later than catatonia and hebephrenia, simple deterioration (which had been often diagnosed in practice but rarely described) was more carefully studied by Pick (573), 1891 and especially by Sommer (725). It was the latter who three years later offered an excellent description not only of the catatonic clinical syndrome, but also of the various primary dementias in which he included hebephrenia. Thus he enlarged the concept in a proper way since he included the deteriorating paranoid syndromes in the concept of "primary dementia." Yet, in his final classification, he still separates catatonia and these types of deterioration.

Kahlbaum's ideas and classification found little support outside Germany. Even Séglas and Chaslin, who had been the first to take a deeper interest in the question of catatonia, came to the conclusion that it was a symptom complex, not a disease proper. In England the subject was not given attention till still later.

In 1896, Kraepelin included the "deteriorating psychoses" in a group of diseases which he believed were essentially metabolic disturbances. The term, dementia praecox (which he had taken up again), he applied at first only to the hebephrenias and to what other authors had termed the primary "dementing" (deteriorating) syndromes. He called primary catatonia all forms with prevalently catatonic symptoms, while under the name, dementia paranoides, he described a none too frequent form with a rapid efflorescence of hallucinations and confused delusions, with relatively intact external deportment, and with an early arrest of the whole process. Three years later he subsumed the whole deteriorating group under the term, dementia praecox. Catatonia retained its usual meaning; that which was previously called dementia praecox was now included mainly under hebephrenia while—and this was the most important step—he included, as the paranoid form of dementia praecox, the formerly so-called paranoia hallucinatoria or phantastica.

Since that time, the scope of the concept of dementia praecox has remained essentially the same. There has been only one further development. Kraepelin retreated somewhat from his earlier position in which he had emphasized most strongly that the course of the disease always ended in deterioration. He now considered the many cases which, for all practical purposes at least, could be cured permanently or arrested for very long periods, as also belonging to the dementia praecox group.[1]

For a long time, psychiatric discussion revolved around symptoms rather than around Kraepelin's concept; at present, however, there seems to be a tendency to disregard these same catatonic symptoms in favor of the study and discussion of the disorders of association and affectivity.

Hand in hand with the elaboration of the dementia praecox concept other disease-entities were defined, particularly the manic-depressive psychosis. In this way, dementia praecox was thrown into bold relief; and its delimitations were no longer drawn unilaterally from within but also solidly from without.

The Name of the Disease

Unfortunately we could not shirk the uncomfortable duty of coining a new name for this disease. But the present one seems too awkward. It only designates the disease, not the diseased; moreover it is impossible to derive from it an adjective denoting the characteristics of this illness, although an exasperated colleague has used "praecox symptom." Without such a new term, a thorough work on differential diagnosis would be hard to write and even harder to read.

But there is a far more important and practical reason why it seems so unavoidable to me to propose a new designation beside the older one. The older form is a product of a time when not only the very concept of dementia, but also that of precocity, was applicable to all cases at hand. But it hardly fits our contemporary ideas of the scope of this disease-entity. Today we include patients whom we would neither call "demented" nor exclusively victims of deterioration early in life.

In view of the fact that Kraepelin described in classical fashion exactly what he proposed to signify by the term, we might as well regard the original meaning of the term "dementia praecox" as irrelevant. After all we speak of "melancholia" today without being disturbed by ancient ideas of "black bile." It is no credit to the science of psychiatry that this is no longer the case. By its very name Kraepelin's "periodic psychosis" has closed many a door which was open to the term "manic-depressive insanity" because there were psychiatrists who under no circumstances could bring themselves to designate as "periodic" a disease which under certain conditions manifests itself only in a few attacks, or

1. Since this was first written, Kraepelin has again narrowed down his conception of this disease group in favor of the manic-depressive psychosis.

perhaps even as only one isolated attack in the course of a whole life time.

As for the designation, "dementia praecox," matters are a great deal worse. There is hardly a single psychiatrist who has not heard the argument that the whole concept of dementia praecox must be false because there are many catatonics and other types who, symptomatologically, should be included in Kraepelin's dementia praecox, and who do not go on to complete deterioration. Similarly, the entire question seems to be disposed of with the demonstration that in a particular case deterioration has not set in precociously but only in later life. Then again, the concept of dementia praecox is often identified with that of a certain form of psychosis in young people; and since it can be demonstrated easily enough that there are many other diseases characteristic of puberty, inclusion of all of them in one concept is considered incorrect. This situation is found at its worst in England where (as far as I am familiar with the discussions of the problem there) the great majority of psychiatrists seem to have clung to the literal sense of the term, dementia praecox, and either have ignored or not understood the basic concept of this disease-entity.

Thus we are left with no alternative but to give the disease a new name, less apt to be misunderstood. I am well aware of the disadvantages of the proposed name but I know of no better one. It is really quite impossible to find a perfect name for a concept which is still developing and changing. I call dementia praecox "schizophrenia" because (as I hope to demonstrate) the "splitting" of the different psychic functions is one of its most important characteristics. For the sake of convenience, I use the word in the singular although it is apparent that the group includes several diseases.

Similar ideas may have led to the suggestions made by Zweig and Gross (278). Zweig called the disease "dementia dessecans"; Gross called it "dementia sejunctiva." But as we have already indicated, the term "dementia" is most inappropriate.[2] Regarding the term "dementia sejunctiva," it must be noted that the concept of sejunction as used by Wernicke is not defined precisely enough to characterize the disease adequately and properly. Moreover, other authors[3] define sejunction in even vaguer terms so that only fruitless discussion would result from its adoption.

Paris has proposed the term, "psychose catatonique dégénérative." We cannot accept this designation since, in this connection, we reject

2. For the same reasons we cannot accept such terms as "dementia primitiva" (Italian psychiatrists, Sommer), "dementia simplex" (Rieger), "dementia apperceptiva" (Weygandt). Nor do I find Brugias' "parademmentia" acceptable.

3. Gross and Weber (798, p. 822).

the idea of degeneration and regard the catatonic symptoms as not essential. Such terms as "dementia paratonica progressiva," "paratonia progressiva" (Bernstein), or "amblythymia," "amblynoia simplex et catatonica" [Evensen (211)] are entirely too one-sided. The designation, "adolescent insanity" (Conaghey) is unsuitable in every way. Recently Wolff has proposed "dysphrenia." But this term has already been employed in another sense; it also has such a wide meaning that the temptation to misinterpret it becomes too great.

The Definition of the Disease

By the term "dementia praecox" or "schizophrenia" we designate a group of psychoses whose course is at times chronic, at times marked by intermittent attacks, and which can stop or retrograde at any stage, but does not permit a full *restitutio ad integrum.* The disease is characterized by a specific type of alteration of thinking, feeling, and relation to the external world which appears nowhere else in this particular fashion.

In every case we are confronted with a more or less clear-cut splitting of the psychic functions. If the disease is marked, the personality loses its unity; at different times different psychic complexes seem to represent the personality. Integration of different complexes and strivings appears insufficient or even lacking. The psychic complexes do not combine in a conglomeration of strivings with a unified resultant as they do in a healthy person; rather, one set of complexes dominates the personality for a time, while other groups of ideas or drives are "split off" and seem either partly or completely impotent. Often ideas are only partially worked out, and fragments of ideas are connected in an illogical way to constitute a new idea. Concepts lose their completeness, seem to dispense with one or more of their essential components; indeed, in many cases they are only represented by a few truncated notions.

Thus, the process of association often works with mere fragments of ideas and concepts. This results in associations which normal individuals will regard as incorrect, bizarre, and utterly unpredictable. Often thinking stops in the middle of a thought; or in the attempt to pass to another idea, it may suddenly cease altogether, at least as far as it is a conscious process (blocking). Instead of continuing the thought, new ideas crop up which neither the patient nor the observer can bring into any connection with the previous stream of thought.

Primary disturbances of perception, orientation, or memory are not demonstrable. In the severest cases emotional and affective expressions seem to be completely lacking. In milder cases we may note only that the degree of intensity of the emotional reactions is not commensurate with the various events that caused those reactions. Indeed, the intensity of the affective reactions may range from a complete lack of emotional expression to extremely exaggerated affective responses in relation to different thought-complexes. The affectivity can also appear to be qualitatively abnormal; that is, inadequate to the intellectual processes involved.

In addition to the often discussed signs of "deterioration," many other symptoms are present in a majority of the hospital cases. We find hallucinations, delusions, confusion, stupor, mania and melancholic affective fluctuations, and catatonic symptoms. Many of these accessory symptoms and symptom-complexes betray a specific schizophrenic character so that their presence may be utilized in diagnosing the disease. Outside the hospital, there are schizophrenics in whom accessory symptoms are less apparent, or absent altogether.

At the present time, we divide dementia praecox tentatively into four subdivisions:

1. *Paranoid.* Hallucinations or delusions continuously hold the forefront of the clinical picture.
2. *Catatonia.* Catatonic symptoms dominate continuously, or for rather long periods of time.
3. *Hebephrenia.* Accessory symptoms appear but do not dominate the picture continually.
4. *Simple Schizophrenia.* Throughout its whole course only the specific, basic symptoms can be found. [4]

The theoretical delimination of schizophrenia from other groups of psychoses is fairly unequivocal, as a review of the symptoms appearing in other diseases will quickly demonstrate.

The *organic psychoses*, comprising those that are considered manifestations of a diffuse disintegration of the cerebral cortex (dementia paralytica, dementia senilis, and in a certain sense, Korsakow's psychosis) show the following characteristics:

Intellectual aspect: Slow and unclear perceptions; inability to grasp complex problems completely, that is, only those associations are formed which have an immediate connection with the momentary drive; memory disturbances, more acute in dealing with recent events than with older ones. Orientation in time, space, and situation is strongly impaired.

Intermediary region: Attention is disturbed but the habitual type is usually affected earlier and more strongly than the maximal one.

Affect: all the emotions are preserved and correspond qualitatively

4. For more details see Section II.

to the thought content, but they are "superficial" and inconstant, incapable of giving a definite permanent direction to any drive. None of these symptoms is characteristic of dementia praecox.

Epileptic conditions:

Intellectual aspect: Apperception, if altered at all, is slowed and fuzzy. Associations of ideas gradually contract in a manner similar to the organic psychoses, but are markedly egocentric. Flow of thoughts is slowed and halting with an ensuing difficulty to break away from one idea or theme. There is a tendency to unnecessary detail (circumstantiality in speech and action) as well as to a specific type of perseveration. Memory disturbances appear late and are much more diffuse than in organic diseases. Amnesias appear to have physical causes.

Affectivity: all affects seem qualitatively adequate to the intellectual thought content but intensified, in marked contrast to the organic psychoses; they are lasting, can be diverted with great difficulty only and are thoroughly consistent at any given moment (epileptic delirium).

Motor States: singing, hesitating type of speech. Epileptic convulsive attacks can appear in many other diseases, particularly in schizophrenia. What is characteristic of epilepsy is not the individual attack but its repetition over many years, and the clinical mental picture accompanying it. Dementia praecox does not exhibit any of these symptoms.

The many disorders we call *idiocy* have the following in common: They begin in early life or even in the intra-uterine state, and do not show considerable progressive changes. Affectivity is unusually varied, but does not differ essentially from that of the healthy person. The range of this variability is, if anything, even wider than that of normal individuals. There is no flattening of affect. Associations are limited to what is most obvious intellectually. In dementia praecox we have a different kind of associative disturbance, as well as a typical affect disturbance.

Paranoia: The construction, from false premises, of a logically developed and in its various parts logically connected, unshakable delusional system without any demonstrable disturbance affecting any of the other mental functions and, therefore, also without any symptoms of "deterioration," if one ignores the paranoiac's complete lack of insight into his own delusional system. In dementia praecox, the delusions themselves, whenever they are present, usually show crude, but always at least subtle, violations of obvious logical consistency. In addition, the other symptoms of dementia praecox are present.

Chronic alcoholism: Intellectually: quick, superficial trains of thought, and a strong urge to round out the ideas, especially in regard to their causal relationships. There is, in particular, a marked touchiness for any personal insinuations and great readiness to produce excuses.

Affectivity: easily mobilized, short lived, labile. Correspondingly, attention is always directed to the momentary, and lacking in endurance. Signs of organic disturbance (brain-atrophy) often appear in more advanced stages; thus it presents a picture which, in all details, is the opposite of that of schizophrenia. (However, combinations of both diseases are very frequent).

Delirium tremens: Accompanied by a definite type of hallucinations; a characteristic delirious state with capacity for being "called back." Varying, but at any given moment consistent affectivity, with an undercurrent of "gallows-humor" (Galgenhumor).

Alcoholic Delusional States: Cf. Sect. V this volume.

Amentia: The Kraepelinean amentia has a very characteristic disturbance of perception and apperception. But there are also many other types which have as yet found no adequate description.

Fever Psychoses: cannot be briefly described, primarily because they have not yet been sufficiently studied.

Manic-depressive forms: The essential character of this disease lies in a generally heightened or depressed psychic "tonus" regarding affectivity, association and mobility (pathological euphoria, flight of ideas, pressure of activity on the one hand; depression, blocking of thought, general motor inhibition on the other). Specific symptoms of other groups of diseases are absent, like deterioration in the sense used in schizophrenia. What one ordinarily calls deterioration in manic-depressive insanity is emotional incontinence or depressive thought blocking or additional dementia due to cerebral atrophy. Not rarely do we find, in cases of dementia praecox, positive symptoms of manic-depressive insanity, but these are complicated by the specific characteristics of dementia praecox.

Hysteria (as in dementia praecox): Essential symptoms and particularly the course of the illness may be explained in terms of psychogenic factors as an exaggeration of certain affectively-charged ideas. However, deterioration and specifically schizophrenic symptoms are lacking. In dementia praecox, we may find many hysterical symptoms but these exhibit a marked schizophrenic coloring, seem caricatured, and appear in combination with the specific symptoms of this disease.

In these two diseases, manic-depressive psychosis and hysteria, and in a certain sense perhaps also in paranoia, we are so far acquainted only with symptoms which may just as well appear in dementia praecox. The difference between these psychoses and dementia praecox consists essentially in a plus on the side of dementia praecox. All other psychotic states manifest specific symptoms which do not appear in dementia praecox.

SECTION I

SYMPTOMATOLOGY

INTRODUCTION

Certain symptoms of schizophrenia are present in every case and at every period of the illness even though, as with every other disease symptom, they must have attained a certain degree of intensity before they can be recognized with any certainty. Here, of course, we are discussing only the large symptom-complexes as a whole. For example, the peculiar association disturbance is always present, but not each and every aspect of it. Sometimes the anomalies of association may manifest themselves in "blocking," or in the splitting of ideas; at other times in different schizophrenic symptoms.

Besides these specific permanent or fundamental symptoms, we can find a host of other, more accessory manifestations such as delusions, hallucinations or catatonic symptoms. These may be completely lacking during certain periods, or even throughout the entire course of the disease; at other times, they alone may permanently determine the clinical picture.

As far as we know, the fundamental symptoms are characteristic of schizophrenia, while the accessory symptoms may also appear in other types of illness. Nevertheless, even in such cases close scrutiny often reveals peculiarities of genesis or manifestation of a symptom, which are only found in schizophrenia. We can expect that gradually we will come to recognize the characteristic features in a great number of these accessory symptoms.

A description of the symptoms can be based only on clear-cut cases. But it is extremely important to recognize that they exist in varying degrees and shadings on the entire scale from pathological to normal; also the milder cases, latent schizophrenics with far less manifest symptoms, are many times more common than the overt, manifest cases. Furthermore, in view of the fluctuating character which distinguishes the clinical picture of schizophrenia, it is not to be expected that we shall be able to demonstrate each and every symptom at each and every moment of the disease.

CHAPTER I

THE FUNDAMENTAL SYMPTOMS

The fundamental symptoms consist of disturbances of association and affectivity, the predilection for fantasy as against reality, and the inclination to divorce oneself from reality (autism). Furthermore, we can add the absence of those very symptoms which play such a great role in certain other diseases such as primary disturbances of perception, orientation and memory, etc.

A. The Simple Functions

1. The Altered Simple Functions

(*a*) *Association*

In this malady the associations lose their continuity. Of the thousands of associative threads which guide our thinking, this disease seems to interrupt, quite haphazardly, sometimes such single threads, sometimes a whole group, and sometimes even large segments of them. In this way, thinking becomes illogical and often bizarre. Furthermore, the associations tend to proceed along new lines, of which so far the following are known to us: two ideas, fortuitously encountered, are combined into one thought, the logical form being determined by incidental circumstances. Clang-associations receive unusual significance, as do indirect associations. Two or more ideas are condensed into a single one. The tendency to stereotype produces the inclination to cling to one idea to which the patient then returns again and again. Generally, there is a marked dearth of ideas to the point of monoideism. Frequently some idea will dominate the train of thought in the form of blocking, "naming," or echopraxia. In the various types of schizophrenia, distractibility does not seem to be disturbed in a uniform manner. A high degree of associational disturbance usually results in states of confusion.

As to the time element in associations, we know of two disturbances peculiar to schizophrenia—pressure of thoughts, that is, a pathologically increased flow of ideas, and the particularly characteristic "blocking."

A young schizophrenic who had first appeared as either paranoid or hebephrenic and then some years later became markedly catatonic, wrote the following spontaneously:

The Golden Age of Horticulture.

"At the time of the new moon, Venus stands in Egypt's August-sky and illuminates with her rays the commercial ports of Suez, Cairo, and Alexandria. In this historically famous city of the Califs, there is a museum of Assyrian monuments from Macedonia. There flourish plantain trees, bananas, corn-cobs, oats, clover and barley, also figs, lemons, oranges, and olives. Olive-oil is an Arabian liquor-sauce which the Afghans, Moors and Moslems use in ostrich-farming. The Indian plantain-tree is the whiskey of the Parsees and Arabs. The Parsee or Caucasian possesses as much influence over his elephant as does the Moor over his dromedary. The camel is the sport of Jews and Arabs. Barley, rice, and sugar-cane called artichoke, grow remarkably well in India. The Brahmins live as castes in Beluchistan. The Circassians occupy Manchuria in China. China is the Eldorado of the Pawnees."

A hebephrenic patient, ill for fifteen years but still able to work and still full of ambitions, gave me the following oral[1] answer to the question, "Who was Epaminondas?":

"Epaminondas was one of those who are especially powerful on land and on sea. He led mighty fleet maneuvers and open sea-battles against Pelopidas, but in the second Punic War he was defeated by the sinking of an armed frigate. With his ships he wandered from Athens to Hain Mamre, brought Caledonian grapes and pomegranates there, and conquered the Beduins. He besieged the Acropolis with gun-boats and had the Persian garrisons put to the stake as living torches. The succeeding Pope Gregory VII . . . eh . . . Nero, followed his example and because of him all the Athenians, all the Roman-Germanic-Celtic tribes who did not favor the priests, were burned by the Druids on Corpus Christi Day as a sacrifice to the Sun-God, Baal. That is the Stone Age. Spearheads made of bronze."

These two performances indicate a moderate degree of schizophrenic association disturbance. Though they stem from two patients whose clinical picture is diametrically different, yet they are amazingly similar. In these patients, the most important determinant of the associations is completely lacking—the concept of purpose. The first patient apparently desires to describe oriental gardens, as such an odd idea for a plain, simple clerk who had never left his native land but idled in a hospital ward for years. The second patient formally adheres to the question put to him, but in fact never speaks of Epaminondas; actually he covers a much larger group of ideas.

1. The fact that the peculiarities of the associative process usually manifest themselves in the identical fashion, regardless of whether they are expressed in oral or written form, is certainly of great, if as yet unrealized, significance to the theory of associative thinking.

This means that thoughts are subordinated to some sort of general idea, but they are not related and directed by any unifying concept of purpose or goal. It looks as though ideas of a certain category (in the first case pertaining to the Orient, in the second, to data of ancient history) were thrown into one pot, mixed, and subsequently picked out at random, and linked with each other by mere grammatical form or other auxiliary images. Still, certain sequences of the ideas are more closely linked to each other by some sort of common thread which, however, proves too loose to provide a logically useful connection. (Fleet-maneuvres—sea-battle—armed frigate; Acropolis—Persian garrison—burning—living torches—Nero; priests—Druids—Corpus Christi Day—Sun-God Baal, etc.)

In analyzing the disturbances of association, we must realize the influences which actually guide our thinking. Associations formed in terms of habit, similarity, subordination, causality, etc., of course will never generate truly fertile thoughts. Only the goal-directed concept can weld the links of the associative chain into logical thought. However, what we mean by a goal-directed concept is not just one single idea, but an infinitely complicated hierarchy of ideas. If we work out a particular theme, the first goal is to give permanent formulation to a part-idea for which, usually, a sentence will serve as a symbol. A further, more generalized goal is the construction of a paragraph which again will be subordinated to a chapter and so forth.

The main objective, which is the greatest possible fertilization of his land, must forever be present in the mind of a farmer at work. Even though at any given moment this idea may not be in focal awareness of his thoughts, this main objective will determine his associations. For, if he were persuaded that the work he is doing will not serve his main purpose, he would drop it at once. A number of minor, secondary goals subordinate themselves to the idea of the main goal. If, at a certain time, he prepares to sow, he must consider other activities which may conflict with sowing, such as eating, and sleeping, weather and time, etc. In addition, all activities which comprise the final act of sowing—like getting the seed, going to the field, spreading the seed—all of these have their special, part-goals. The concepts of these part-goals and their interrelation must constantly rule his actions and therefore, more immediately, his associations.

Not only our goal-concept, but also the supposedly simpler, subordinate ideas with which we ordinarily operate, are composed of numerous elements which change according to context. The idea of water is quite different depending on whether it refers to chemistry, physiology, navigation, landscape, inundation, or source of power. Each of these special ideas becomes connected with the other ideas by a quite different set of threads. No healthy person thinks of crystal water when his house is being swept away by a flood; nor will he think of water as a medium of transportation when he is thirsty.

Naturally, even the most limited idea of water is composed of various concepts such as fluid, evaporable, cold, colorless, etc. But in the normal mind only those part concepts dominate the picture that belong to a given frame of reference. The others exist only potentially, or at least retreat into the background so that we cannot even demonstrate their influence.

The direction of our associations is determined not by any single force but by an almost infinite number of influences. In the thought processes of schizophrenia, however, all the associative threads indicated here, whether singly or in haphazard groupings, may remain totally ineffective.

A few more examples may illustrate this:

"Dear Mother: Today I am feeling better than yesterday. I really don't feel much like writing. But I love to write to you. After all, I can tackle it twice. Yesterday, Sunday, I would have been so happy if you and Louise and I could have gone to the park. One has such a lovely view from Stephan's Castle. Actually, it is very lovely in Burgholzli. Louise wrote Burgholzli on her two last letters, I mean to say on the envelopes, no, the 'couverts' which I received. However, I have written Burgholzli in the spot where I put the date. There are also patients in Burgholzli who call it 'Holzliburg.' Others talk of a factory. One may also regard it as a health-resort.

"I am writing on paper. The pen which I am using is from a factory called 'Perry & Co.' This factory is in England. I assume this. Behind the name of Perry Co. the city of London is inscribed; but not the city. The city of London is in England. I know this from my school-days. Then, I always liked geography. My last teacher in that subject was Professor August A. He was a man with black eyes. I also like black eyes. There are also blue and gray eyes and other sorts, too. I have heard it said that snakes have green eyes. All people have eyes. There are some, too, who are blind. These blind people are led about by a boy. It must be very terrible not to be able to see. There are people who can't see and, in addition, can't hear. I know some who hear too much. One can hear too much. There are many sick people in Burgholzli; they are called patients. One of them I like a great deal. His name is E. Sch. He taught me that in Burgholzli there are many kinds, patients, inmates, attendants. Then there are some who are not here at all. They are all peculiar people. . . ."

A non-schizophrenic informant would tell us what in his immediate environment affected him; what may have made him feel comfortable or uncomfortable; or, perhaps, something that might interest his reader. There is complete absence of any such purpose here. The common denominator of all of the patient's ideas rests in the fact that they are present in his awareness, but not because they have any close relation to him. In this respect, the thinking is even more scattered than that of "Horticulture," or of "Epaminondas." On the other hand, it is better co-ordinated as to details. Whereas in the other examples coherence of details was the exception, and only referred to small groups, in this letter we do not find any sudden breaks. In this respect, the "laws of association" remain in force. In an experimental set-up which would exclude the idea of a main purpose, these associations would even have to be considered perfectly valid: London—geography-lesson—geography-teacher—his black eyes—gray eyes—green snake-eyes—human eyes—blind people—their companions—horrible fate, etc. Although nearly all the ideas expressed are correct, nevertheless the letter is meaningless. The patient has the goal of writing, but nothing to write about.

A hebephrenic wishes to sign her name "B. Graf" in the customary position at the end of a letter. She writes "Gra;" then another word beginning with "Gr" comes to her mind; whereupon she changes the "a" to "o," affixes "s," and then repeats the word "Gross" twice over. Thus, the whole complex of concepts which was at the root of the purpose of signing her name, has all at once become completely ineffective, with the exception of the first two letters, "Gr." In this way the patients may lose themselves in the most irrelevant side-associations, and a uniform chain of thought does not come about. This symptom has also been called "*Vorbeidenken*" (a sort of non-sequitur thinking, skimming past things).

To the question: "What was your father?", a patient answers "Johann Friedrich." He understood that the question concerned his father but the inquiry about his father's occupation did not influence his retort; instead, he answered the unasked question as to his father's name. If such cases are investigated more closely, we usually find that the patient grasped the question as such but that the corresponding concepts were never elaborated in his mind.

A hebephrenic demanded his release from the hospital by petitioning the Government as follows: "You are invited to carry out my release and to announce this fact in public notices in the newspapers of May, 1905. Otherwise you will be discharged from your position in accordance with my traditional rights. You may continue to exercise your offices until the new election. Respectfully . . ."

This patient, at one time actually a member of the city council, did not have the delusion that he could give orders to the Government or depose its officials; it was only while he was writing that anything not fitting into his concept seemed to have dropped out of his thoughts.

Another hebephrenic writes: "The mountains which are outlined in the swellings of the oxygen are beautiful." This is a description of a walk the patient had taken in which chemical terms do not fit. Obviously, something about "fresh-air" floated into his mind because in the next sentence the patient begins very abruptly to talk about his health.

A similar example: "Are you very unhappy?"—"No".—"Is something weighing heavily on your mind?"—"Yes. Iron is heavy."—"Heavy" is here suddenly conceived in its physical sense.

A table usually standing near a patient's bed is taken away one day. He says: "Farewell, I am Christ!", leans back like someone dying, and bows his head. Usually, the patient does not consider himself to be Christ. The part thought is that something has been taken away from him as when a person takes his leave, and this is at once associated with the taking away of the table. To the normal person these two concepts are worlds apart. But the patient's associations were influenced, only by the *tertium comparationis,* the taking away, a notion which in no way fits the specific case. The leave-taking, obviously in reference to the table, arouses in him the image of Jesus. For this patient, the enormous differences between Jesus' farewell and his bidding farewell to a table, do not come into play. However, not only the association Jesus occurs, but the minimal similarity of the patient's situation with that of Christ suffices, at least for a short time, to make him identify himself with Christ. But even here a number of intermediate concepts were lost, concepts distinguishing Jesus' farewell to the Apostles, from His farewell on the Cross. (Other operative elements responsible for evoking the idea of Jesus could not be demonstrated in this case.)

Where the fragments are of a more secondary nature, the associations do not become entirely senseless, but they still appear odd, bizarre, distorted, even if they are correct in the main. If, for example, Brutus is called "an Italian," this is correct, except for the historical period suggested by this ethnic term. But it is unusual that the more general term, "Italian" should be substituted for the more precise concept "Roman." The author of the "Golden Age of Horticulture" answered the question: "Where is Egypt?" with, "between Assyria and the Congo." This answer, correct as to content, is unusual because of the definition of location in terms of one African and one Asiatic country; and even more so because of the connection between one of the oldest and one of the most modern states. In respect to place as well as time, part concepts, which are normally never missing, have become ineffective. During an experiment a patient associates "threads" to the stimulus word, "heart," because "two hearts are linked as by a thread." A hebephrenic defines "hay" as a "means of maintenance of the cow." The end of a letter reads, "Please give my regards to my other sisters and brothers, sisters-in-law, and your children. Not only God's wrath and punishment, but also His love and the grace of our Lord Jesus Christ be with all of us, also with you, and you shall come to me." Here all the transitions from one idea to another can be easily explained by the circumstances and the feelings dominating the patient. Each sentence expresses an idea which could easily have closed her letter; and each is understandably related to the one before. Yet it all sounds so bizarre that one could not think of ascribing it to a manic flight of ideas, much less to healthy thinking.

In some cases, all the threads between thoughts are torn. Unless new paths are found, we have stupor or blocking. Frequently the patient drops a thought in an entirely matter-of-course way, only to proceed to quite a different one that has no recognizable associative connection with the previous one.

In the following fragment of an "Autobiography" the sudden leaps are marked by the symbol (*). Part of these "*cesuras*" are explicable by environmental influences and points of contact (distractibility).

"One must have arisen sufficiently early and then there is usually the necessary 'appetite' present. '*L'appétit vient en mangeant*,' says the Frenchman. * With time and years the individual becomes so lazy in public life that he is not even capable of writing any more. On such a sheet of paper, one can squeeze many letters if one is careful not to transgress by one 'square shoe.' * In such fine weather one should be able to take a walk in the woods. Naturally, not alone, but with a girl. * At the end of a year one always renders the annual accounting. * The sun is now in the sky yet it is not yet 10 o'clock. In Burgholzli, too? I don't know since I have no watch with me as I used to have! *Après le manger, On va p. . . .* ! There are also plenty of entertainments for people who do not and never did belong to this hospital. In Switzerland it is not permitted to do mischief with human flesh!! * *Le foin*, hay, *L'herbe* grass, *mordre*-bite, etc. etc. etc. and so on! R. K. In any event, much 'merchandise' comes to Burgholzli from Zurich. Otherwise we would not have to stay in 'bed' until it may please this or that person to 'tell' who is to blame that one is no longer permitted to go about freely. O . . . * 1000 hundredweights. * Appendage to acorns!!!

"A. *Les Eschelles d'un homme qui ne peut plus aller au piège* XII. *Vous connaissez ça?* In 'Germany.' The acorns, and that means in French '*Au Maltraitage*.' * Tobacco (I saw you looking so pretty).* When something is written on each line then it is correct. Now it is exactly 10:30. The other. * Hu, hu, umme no ha? * Prisoners' Club. Burgholzli. * Is there nothing après le manger!? My wife was rich."

In the usual speech and writing, this peculiar disconnecting of associative threads is often combined with other disturbances, so that it is quite difficult to find a pure sample. In acute states, this anomaly can go so far that it becomes an exception if a sequence of thoughts can be traced along its many links. This has been termed "dissociated thinking" (Ziehen, 842) or "incoherence"; the external disease picture can be labeled "confusion." Sometimes, however, only the patient's manner of expression is obscure so that logical transitions may still be assumed to exist. In the presence of abnormal connections one cannot say with certainty that a total break in the thought-process has occurred; as, for example, in the following which was transcribed stenographically:

"Swiss pride must be deserved. Salu K. . . ., I am the nun. If that's enough, you are still his. That is a brave cavalier, take him as your husband. Karoline, you well know, though you are my Lord, you were just a dream. If you are the dove-cote, Mrs. K. is still beset by fear. * Otherwise I am not so exact in eating. Handle the gravy carefully. * Where is the paint-brush? Where are you, Herman? Herman, Altdorf, Anna, Walder, or Z. H. engine-stoker, give, in your arms I sleep sweetly. * This here is Burgholzli. * Ida, have you become a Mexican?; you seem to me very well-read. Now it is one side, a Knight of Burgholzli, then they have a Sea festival or bring a torch-light procession. The poor lost child has a brick-head. Where are the Lords of the Holy Feast? That is the source of life."

All the indicated disturbances may range from a maximum which corresponds to complete confusion, to a minimum which may be hardly noticeable. Not every thought-association in a schizophrenic is of this kind. Whereas in the severe cases, false associations are actually dominant, in cases of "cured" or latent dementia praecox only patient and persistent observations reveal even a single such error in thinking.

The emergence of new ideas becomes most apparent in question and answer interviews and in association experiments in which the patient must respond to a stimulus-word with the first word or idea which comes to his mind. Thus, a patient stares at a candle and replies to the question what he sees: "There is a candle; eternal light: * Barbara v. R. in S. * Something right behind. Barbels (a kind of viol), yes, they are found in the Rhine." On ordering the patient to go to work, one might receive the following answer: "Why do you let it drop? * The sun is in the sky. * Why do you let it drop?" (No one had dropped anything.) Aside from breaks in thought, marked with the symbol (*), it is apparent that even the first sentence has no connection with the order given the patient. This is quite usual; often a reply to a question is only a formal retort, but its content has nothing to do with the question posed.

A female patient, supposed to help in the household work, is asked why she is not working. The answer, "But I don't understand any French", is logically related neither to the question nor to the situation. Or, in an experiment the word, "ink", brings the association "ink-spot; * that is what we may want to inherit."

At times the gap may be bridged by the grammatical forms so that a connection is simulated. Different ideas that do not belong together are combined into one sentence, analogously to the above example, "But I don't understand any French", which gives only a form, not the content of an answer.

"That is the little Jew's clock in regard to Daniel" is given in response instead of a greeting. In the above-mentioned "Autobiography" we find: "In any event, much merchandise is sent to Burgholzli from Zurich. Otherwise we would not have to stay in bed." The new idea of "staying in bed" is introduced formally as proof of the preceding idea.

At this point, we can sum up the discussion as follows:
In the normal thinking process, the numerous actual and latent images combine to determine each association. In schizophrenia, however, single images or whole combinations may be rendered ineffective, in an apparently haphazard fashion. Instead, thinking operates with ideas and concepts which have no, or a completely insufficient, connection with the main idea and should therefore be excluded from the thought-process. The result is that thinking becomes confused, bizarre, incorrect, abrupt. Sometimes, all the associative threads fail and the thought chain is totally interrupted; after such "blocking," ideas may emerge which have no recognizable connection with preceding ones.

It is only in stuporous conditions, however, that we may find a complete cessation of thinking. *It is more usual for new ideas to emerge at once or after only a short interval even if the associative threads have been broken.*

The emergence of an idea without any connection with a previous train of thought, or without any external stimulus, is (in spite of Swoboda) so foreign to normal psychology that one is obliged to look even in the patient's seemingly most far-fetched ideas, for the associative path originating in a previous concept or in an external stimulus. In this way, it may be possible in some, though not in all cases, to demonstrate the connecting links. Still, in a sufficient number of cases, we will succeed in pointing out several of the main directions along which the derailment of thoughts took place.

Even where only a part of the associative threads is interrupted, other influences, which under normal circumstances are not noticeable, become operative in the place of logical directives. As far as we know, they are for the most part the very same directives which determine the emergence of new connections after the total break in thought: connections with accidentally aroused ideas, condensations, clang-associations intermediate associations, and perseveration of ideas (stereotypy). All these thought-connections are not foreign to the normal psyche either. But they occur only exceptionally and incidentally, whereas in schizophrenia they are exaggerated to the point of caricature and often actually dominate the thought-processes.

Most frequently, we can observe how *two ideas without any intrinsic relation with each other, preoccupying the patient simultaneously, are simply being connected.* The logical form of the connection will depend on the accompanying circumstances. If one asks the patient a question, he responds with any idea which he may have at the moment. If he looks for a reason, such ideas are simply causally connected. If he has a pathologically exaggerated self-consciousness, or if he feels slighted, he will refer the new ideas directly to himself in accordance with the affective valence of these complexes.

Thus a patient calls a drawing of a comb, "a wash-tub," because a wash-tub happens to be in the drawing next to the comb; a beetle is called "a beetle-bird" because a bird has been shown to him just previously.

"Why have you not said anything for so long?"—"Because I am angry."—"Why?"—"I want to go to the toilet and look for toilet paper, and there is none." (Abraham) Here the first haphazard thought is being offered as a reason. Or: The wife of a schizophrenic school-teacher lost a key. On the very same day, a certain Dr. N. had visited the school; hence Dr. N. must be having illicit relations with the teacher's wife.

It is quite the usual thing to have the patients give us answers which merely seize haphazardly on any thought of the moment. Consequently, it is only natural that the patients should contradict themselves at every turn when they are presented with the same question several times.

Dawson's hebephrenic patient, who had thrown himself into the water, gave the following motives for his act at various times: he did not believe in the future and did not expect to get any better; he was one of the lower classes of society and must make place for those of the higher class; he was poisoned; he did it because of a religious depression.

Occasionally the two thoughts originate in the external circumstances or in the train of thought itself:

"How are you?" "Bad," (with a smiling face). "You look very well; everything going all right?" (patting the patient on the back). "No, I have a pain in my back," (pointing out the place where she was patted). "Why are you laughing?" "Because you are clearing out the chest of drawers." "But you already laughed before that." "Because the things were still in it."

Most commonly, thought-connections are made with things which are of emotional concern to the patient.

It is an everyday occurrence to see the patients soiling themselves or tearing their clothes, "because they won't let me go home." A patient associates to "ship," "the Lord is the Ship of the Desert." Before the key word he places the Lord who is in the foreground of his pathological religious interests and often emerges in his thoughts in other ways; at the end, the key word is supplemented by an idea belonging to an entirely different chain of thought. To "wood" a young girl associates, "that my cousin Max would come to life again." The patient employs the partial idea of "wood-coffin," which had played a role in her unhappy love-affair, to connect the stimulus-word with her complex.—The socially ambitious *BO*sshard of *OERL*ikon is *BO*naparte of *ORL*eans, as his name suggests to him. As these examples illustrate, this sort of association of an accidental impression with an underlying complex [2] plays a large role in the origin of delusional ideas.

Furthermore, clang associations are very frequent. Head-bed; frog-bog; sad-mad-bad; beaten-betrayed-beloved-bedecked. Such associative connections are certainly comparable to the clang associations of the "flight of ideas." Yet such associations as head-bed would be quite peculiar for a manic; while betrayed-beloved or diamond-dynamo, would be quite rare. The sound similarity would be much too thin. We find many far more unusual associations like: woman-room-boom; sea-sow; read-violin; needle-nose. In read-violin, the healthy would find hardly any common sound. The "ī" in read has quite another sound from the "ĭ" in violin which is shorter. Such associative connections as "buy a pair of shoes," immediately followed by "beat the war drums" would hardly be sought by anyone acquainted only with the associations of the normal and the manic, in the mere assonance between buy and beat. Yet hundreds of such associative combinations have shown beyond doubt that the

2. Complex: a shortened term for a complex of ideas which are strongly affectively charged so that it permanently influences the content of the psychic processes. The normal influence of the affects on the associations results in the complex having a certain tendency to become fixed and delimited even in the healthy. It strives to obtain a kind of independence. It becomes a resistant structure within the changing mass of concepts.

identity or even the similarity of one single sound, suffices to give the direction of the association. Thus, the clang association very often has the schizophrenic mark of the bizarre.

In the hearing of a catatonic, something was said about a fish-market. She begins to repeat, "Yes, I am also a shark-fish." Thus she employs an entirely peculiar and impossible clang association; impossible, that is, for every other waking human being except a schizophrenic. The association "fish-market—shark-fish" is used in order to express the idea that she is someone very bad; yet she ignores the complete impossibility of the reality of her identification.

Other examples of clang association in the freely-flowing thought-processes of the patients are: A hebephrenic patient who is capable of work and gets along fairly well even outside the institution was reproached by her physician for the poor order of her room. She answers, "I don't want any Italian money." Asked what she meant, she says, "A sou is either an Italian or French coin. I am not Surberli (a hospital employee who can hardly be considered in connection with the idea of "keeping order") and besides Madame Suter has died."

Either consciously or unconsciously the patient assumed that the doctor's reproach included the (among uneducated people not unusual) expression "sow-disorder" [3] (a word which, actually, he had not used however). Now, this word is pronounced *sou* — or *su;* thus the words and ideas *sou—Surberli—Suter* are partially determined. The negative form of her sentence expresses the idea that the patient does not wish to be considered as disorderly. (Riklin) A patient varied the stereotyped phrase, "I don't feel good," used by her over a span of thirty years, by way of substituting various dialect expressions for "good," also using the English word "well." One day she took the word "well" and changed it to say, "I don't feel velo (velo—bicycle).

Of course, assonance by itself is never sufficient to determine a given association. When to the word "buy" there is an association of "beat" the assonance is only one of the many determinants involved. There are certainly hundreds of other words beginning with "b"; then why precisely did "buy" and "beat" appear?

In the example, "read-violin," we know at least one other co-determinant: the patient is preoccupied with sexual thoughts which are very bluntly expressed in many associations. In Swiss slang, violin is almost always used in its obscene sense and rarely used for the name of the musical instrument. This same sexual determinant can be demonstrated in many of the associations of this patient, as well as in the productions

3. German: "Sau-Ordnung."

of many another. The clang and sexual determinants are so frequent in schizophrenics, that they must often be found in combination. Very often we find misunderstanding of a spoken word, determined by the patient's prevalent complexes as delusions of persecution.

However, two determinants do not define an association unequivocally. There certainly exist a great many more words assonant in the widest sense, and having a sexual connotation. The actual choice of the association must then be determined by other relationships which, however, in most instances, escape us.

Of nearly equal significance as the clang associations are the simple continuations and completions of everyday phrases which the schizophrenic may use in an entirely inappropriate way. Thus a woman patient, who was reporting about a walk with her family, began with enumerating the members of her family, "Father, Son," then adding, "and the Holy Ghost." She then proceeded to tack on, "the Holy Virgin," her thoughts having been distracted further in the direction of the bible phrase.

The *condensations*, that is, the contractions of many ideas into one, are in principle not different from the accidental associative connections. We saw this process in operation in the previously mentioned example of thinking, "the Lord is the Ship of the Desert." There two entirely different concepts, belonging to two distinct complexes of ideas, were fused into one thought. A catatonic associates to the word, "sail," "steam-sail," combining in the two ideas, "steam-boat" and "sail-boat." In the construction of delusions and symbols, condensation is an outstanding component and the cause of a number of portemanteau words: "sadsome" for sad and lonesome, or, to use a German example, "*trauram*" for "*traurig*" and "*grausam*."

In experimental investigations of association, we find a notable frequency of "mediate associations." I suspect that only the lack of sufficient observation has been responsible for our inability to demonstrate them more frequently in the thought-processes of our patients. The above mentioned example, the association "wood (wood-coffin)—dead cousin," may be considered as a mediate association. Certainly to this group belong such examples as "sea-spirit" by way of the mediate concept of soul; cook-pole by way of "Cook-Northpole." A catatonic patient is shown a key and asked, "What is it?" Promptly she answers "That is the white keeve." An association that certainly came by way of the word, "key."

In an experiment using words inscribed on a revolving drum, Reis (p. 617) found mediate association in the sense that instead of "war"—"dispute," instead of "cattle"—"horse" was read. The primary sensory impression does not come into consciousness but nevertheless determines a new association. Gross also calls attention to the fact that patients often respond to a definite question not with the answer, but with an association to the answer. (See Stransky, 748, p. 1077.)

Not infrequently the tendency toward stereotypy is a further cause for the derailment of the patient's associational activity. The patients are caught in and remain fixed to the same circle of ideas, the same words, the same sentence structures, or, at any rate, return to them again and again without any logical need. In the course of experiments on comprehension, Busch found that in some cases numerous false assertions would evoke the repetition of the previous stimuli.

In association experiments, the patients take up a previous stimulus or reaction-word: "star"—"that is the greatest of blessings;" "caressing" —"that is perfection;" "wonderful"—"the will;" "child"—"of the deity;" "purple"—"heaven and earth." The word "star" evoked a religious idea which was then elaborated in the following responses regardless of, and wholly indifferent to, the subsequent stimulus-words. The first two answers reveal the formal stereotypy which can be demonstrated in most of this patient's responses, resulting in structures such as "cat"—"the cat is a mouse;" to the stimulus-word, "mouse" has been associated, but because of the previous associations it is put in the form of a predicate.

The stereotypies can remain fixed for long periods. In a few cases, we noted that after four weeks the same answer was given to 40 per cent of the stimulus-words as was given on the first occasion. A patient reacted to the word, "so," with the incomprehensible "that is a canal;" it then was found that on a previous day she had given the very same sentence in response to "sea." The same patient associated: to "count" —"that is to eat," and later, "country"—"that is to eat a great deal." There again we have the same fixation on the assonance of the words.

In the pseudo-flight of ideas of the acute confused schizophrenic the consistent return to what was said before, is a common occurrence. The tendency toward stereotypy, combined with a lack of purposeful goal in their thinking, leads on the one hand to "*Klebedenken*" (adhesive, sticky type of thinking), to a kind of *perseveration*, and on the other hand to a general impoverishment of thought. The patients then always talk about the same topic (monoideismus) and are incapable of interesting themselves in anything else.[4]

It may be due to purposelessness and stereotypy of ideas, that the patient is really unable to pursue a thought to its conclusion; a senseless compulsion to associate may replace thinking proper. Thus, a hebephren-

4. Cf. the experimental associations at the end of this section.

ic was unable to tear himself away from the concepts "love" and "have;" and for a long time kept spontaneously associating such chains as the following: "love, theft, gift, lady, have, love, theft, gift, lady, love, theft, taken back, taken back, taken back, taken back, have . . ."

In this manner patients get entangled in long enumerations which clearly betray the schizophrenic character of their associative disturbances.

A patient wrote, "The Heavens not only stand over the parish house in Wil, but also over America, South Africa, Mexico, McKinley, Australia." Occasionally, a certain idea will be elaborated on by associating to it from all possible angles. "I wish you, therefore, a very happy, pleasant, healthy, blessed and fruit-crop-rich year; and also many good wine-harvest years thereafter, as well as good potato-crop years; as well as fine potato years, and sauerkraut years, and sprouts years, and cucumber years, and nut years; a good egg-year, and also a good cheese-year," etc., etc., etc. A patient, whose daughter had turned Catholic, wrote to her that the rosary was "A prayer multipler and this in turn is a prayer for multiplying and as such is nothing else but a prayer-mill, and is therefore a mill-prayer machine which is again a prayer-machine mill" and so on for many pages in the same fashion.

In association experiments it is not at all a rare occurrence that patients begin to name whatever they see, so that they respond, for example, to the different stimulus-words by enumerating all the furniture in the room. They do this even when they have understood the point of the experiment perfectly and want to get away from this idea.

This symptom has an external, and at times also an inner similarity to what Sommer has called *naming* and *touching*.[5] In many patients, and especially in those who are somewhat confused, the only recognizable association to impressions coming from the external world, consists in naming them: "mirror," "table"; or they are rendered by sentences: "This is a barometer. This is a gas-lamp. These are coats." This sort of "naming" does not only appear in response to visual impressions. For example, I take a patient by the hand; and she says, "the hand"; or asked to do something, she designates it by some catch-word: "into the garden," "to undress." In a quite analogous way hallucinating patients will often "name" their activities: "Now he is sitting down"; "Now he wants to write"; "Now he is writing." The transition from the writing of letters simply enumerating things or events around them to this "naming" is very fluid. The patient who described what was written on his steel-pen is not so very far removed from the "naming" patient. Also to this group

5. Some authors count this phenomenon among the motor anomalies. Kleist called it a "short-circuiting act."

belongs the patient who, on seeing somebody approaching carrying a lantern, remarked: "I declare that this is a lantern." Common to all is the fastening upon a sense impression because of the lack of a goal-concept. The patients link up and tack on ideas to any and all possible ones whether they come from within or without. The idea with which they link, and the direction which this process takes, is variable and, as far as the associative activity is concerned, determined by accident, exactly as in the case of our letterwriting patient.

A similar process is the "touching" of objects as described by von Leupoldt.[6] This "touching"[7] or palpation consists in the patient's feeling with his hands along the contours of objects within his reach. Here, instead of the "naming" of objects, the corresponding motor activity is associated.

If a given conception involves motor-elements, then the only recognizable association can be that the corresponding idea is acted out. The patient acts out, imitates, copies what he hears and sees: *echopraxia* and *echolalia.* In fact, I cannot separate "naming" and "echopraxia," at least not as a matter of principle. Every idea or concept has a motor element; in the actions he sees performed before his very eyes, in the words he hears spoken, this component is quite obvious in the healthy person. If there are no reasons for drawing on other associations, it is very understandable that such motor components will not be inhibited or repressed. Therefore we include here such occurrences as the following: a patient cracked the glass-panel out of a door; another patient proceeds to creep in and out of the hole thus made. He keeps it up continuously without knowing why he is doing so.

While a patient may be so caught up in the "fetters of the visual impression" that under certain conditions this sensory perception takes on a pathological predominance, still the reverse is also seen. Under other conditions the patient may completely ignore the outside world. Between these two extremes there is every intermediary stage.

The schizophrenic's "distractibility" (or what Ziehen termed, "vigility of attention") is not necessarily altered in any specific direction as far as the associations are concerned. Here we are dealing rather with the resultant of many primary processes among which one of the most important is the patient's active exclusion of the outside world. At times, the patients appear to be completely dependent upon and at the mercy

6. Just why von Leupoldt speaks of it as a compulsion I do not understand, particularly, since he himself states that it is not a compulsion "in the narrow sense of the term." Nor will his assumption that the lack of ability to comprehend complex ideas is fundamentally responsible for this phenomenon, apply to all cases. His own patient comprehended the unveiling of a monument "as a whole," as a festive parade.

7. Hypermetamorphotic movements (described by Wernicke).

of external impressions, and not to be in possession of their own directives and aims, as when naming dominates the clinical picture. At other times the patients are in no way distractible. The most powerful stimuli are incapable of influencing their train of thought or of arousing their attention.

The majority of chronic cases show very little in their usual behavior that is remarkable in this direction. These people concentrate on their work; when something special happens, they look up exactly like the healthy and occupy themselves with the new event *as far as it interests them.* When they speak, it is possible to interrupt them. Often, however, particularly in all severe cases, distractibility is lessened. Sommer (724) has demonstrated this experimentally inasmuch as he obtained the same results in calculation-tests as usual in spite of the great noise around the patient. Should the schizophrenic be aroused emotionally, particularly in anger, then we regularly see a disturbance of distractibility. Objections are disregarded entirely or only understood in the sense of their thoughts and often serve only as new ammunition for their effusions. Even a change of circumstances will hardly influence these patients, as long as they are in a passion. Indeed, it is quite the usual thing that an abusive schizophrenic whom we leave should continue to curse or abuse, not the least bit disturbed that no one is there to hear him, or at least no one to whom he can direct his abuse. The complete lack of interest of the patient may at times be mistaken for a lack of distractibility. Since they bother about nothing, nothing can influence them in their behavior. However, one can demonstrate in the self-same patients that they comprehend quite well what goes on about them, even though they do not appear to direct attention to anything.

In certain acute clinical conditions, distractibility is considerably reduced, sometimes down to zero.

In most of the productions of the severely ill, we can find the various peculiarities of schizophrenic thinking all demonstrated at the same time.

"I have never yet been in Hamburg, Lubeck or Berne; I have never seen Professor Hilty; I have never been to the University of Basel; I have never seen Luther, nor ever had the *lütter* (a vulgar expression for diarrhea). But I have already seen all the members of the legislature; I am going to see General Herzog, I will show that carrion. . . ."

Here we have the negative form maintained through seven thoughts. The enumeration of place names is not systematically arranged. The transition from Lubeck to Berne is abrupt (perhaps through the assonant Bremen?); the latter name reminds the patient of a professor at the University of Berne facilitating the transition to "University of Basel." This institution played an important role in the history of the Reformation; therefore the association, "Luther." Then follows the quite senseless clang association "*lütter*," but the change of verb indicates that the patient was thinking of what the word usually means (diarrhea). The "legislature" depends again on the earlier idea of Berne (which is the capital of Switzerland and seat of the legislature). From this it is not completely illogical, although rather strange under the circumstances, to think of the long deceased General Herzog. To this there ties on the unreasonable notion that the patient should wish to go to him. The idea, "General," is bound up with the conception of "power" or something like it. That may very well be the reason why the completely senseless, "I will show that carrion. . . ." follows, as the concept of power is associated in the usual way with the patient himself and he therefore suddenly feels stronger than the General.

In the following letter, the chain of ideas does not seem to permit any further analysis. All of it appears to us as a disconnected, confused babble. But precise knowledge of the affectively accentuated complexes of the patient would certainly permit us to elucidate much of it.

"Burgholzli, 20 November 1905

Dear Family Fridori and Family Graf or Schmidli!

Here in this smith-house it doesn't go very well. This is indeed no parish-house or even a poor-house but in this place there is noise, anger, grumbling—sunny—heavenly-knells all year round. Many a small and large landowner, wind-bag or poor drunk from Thalweil, Addisweil, from Albis, from Salz, from Seen, from Rorbach, from Rorbas have never again returned to their own homes, etc., etc., etc.

Greetings to all who are still alive

My own relatives no longer exist.

Anna"

Thus we see that the more intense schizophrenic disturbances of association lead to utter confusion. Confusion itself must not be considered as a symptom, sui generis. It is the result of the various elementary mental disturbances which have finally reached such a degree of intensity that the connections and relationships have been completely lost for the patient or for the observer or for both. We must insist emphatically on separating the manic flight of ideas from the schizophrenic disturbance of the flow of ideas. The manic's flight of ideas may also lead to confusion if it is sufficiently intense, as does the melancholic inhibition when the slowness of the ideational flow and the incapacity to link ideas together make the orientation and the conceptual elaboration of complicated ideas impossible. Hallucinations can also lead to a condition which we may term confusion, when they become mixed up with reality perceptions and thus bring confusion into the picture of the world.[8]

Thus in schizophrenia, the confusion is at times the consequence of a sort of dissolution of ideas, at other times the result of a "blocking" by newly emerging ideas, and at still other times the suppression of single associative determinants with inroads by secondary associations; or again it may be the result of a pressure of thoughts (see below), of a real flight of ideas, of hallucinations, or even several of these factors acting together.

The Course of the Associations

We know almost nothing relative to the time-relations of schizophrenic associative processes. It is possible that there is nothing characteristic about them. Naturally, we have in intercurrent manic conditions an "accelerated" flow in the sense of a flight of ideas and in depressive conditions, a slowing-up. We must further assume that in certain stuporous states which may be considered a manifestation of an exacerbation of the schizophrenic brain-processes, the associations are slowed. In all such cases it is not a question of permanent conditions but of episodes or complications.

Pure "pressure of thoughts" can continue for years, although in completely burnt-out cases it can hardly be observed. Many patients complain that they must think too much, that their ideas chase each other in their heads. They themselves speak of "thought-overflow" (because they cannot hold anything in their minds), of "pressure of thoughts," of "collecting of thoughts," because too much seems to come to mind at one time. Many times, the information about this "too much thinking" is such as to give the observer the impression that, in contrast to the subjective feeling as described by the patient, the patient is thinking less, rather than more. However, it is certain that in many a patient there is a pathological pressure of ideas. The patients then have the feeling of being compelled to think. Often enough, they will say that someone is making them think in this fashion. They complain of a consequent feeling of exhaustion. When the feelings of compulsion are absent, the patient believes that he is accomplishing a great piece of work. Superficially, this pressure of thinking appears to stand in direct contrast to "blocking"[9] or the arrest of thought. Frequently, we can observe that both these phenomena appear together. One of our well-educated patients drew a line on one side of which there was "compulsive pressure" of many ideas, and on the other side there was "simply nothing."

8. I leave aside those conditions in which the very hallucinations and illusions themselves produce a general mix-up which is then of course nothing other than a manifestation of the confused associations on which the hallucinations are based.

9. We will discuss blocking a little farther on.

The content of such pressure of thoughts is essentially the same as in any other type of schizophrenic thinking. A theologian spent a whole night laughing quietly to himself because etymological witticisms constantly occurred to him as he lay there thinking: "I am quite a wits—a nix—a Nietzsche." We owe one of the best descriptions of this phenomenon to an intelligent patient of Forel's (229). One can also note in this same patient's production how the constant return to the same or previous ideas even impressed the patient himself. "In my mind there ran like an endless clockwork a compulsive, torturing, uninterrupted chain of ideas. Naturally, they were not too sharply defined or clearly developed. There were joined idea upon idea in the most remarkable and bizarre series of associations although there was always a certain definite or inherent connection from link to link. There was sufficient coherence or system to the whole so that I could always differentiate the light and shadowy side of things, people, actions, or spoken words which struck my interest. What ideas, what images have not tumbled around in my head! What amusing associations of ideas have cropped up! I always seemed to come back again and again to certain conceptions, to certain images which, now, however, I can hardly remember, e.g. France's Divine Right! Barbera! Rohan! They did seem to constitute steps in that racing train of thoughts; and I would speak out loud rapidly, like a pass word, the idea which my restless thoughts had just reached. I also used this means in order not to lose the threads and to maintain a certain control over the overwhelming, maddening, rushing train of thoughts. This was particularly necessary at certain periods of my daily life—such as coming into a room, or when the door was opened, or on going to eat, when someone met me in the hall, etc."

The most extraordinary formal element of schizophrenic thought processes is that termed "blocking." The associative activity often seems to come to an abrupt and complete stand-still. When it is again resumed, ideas emerge which have no or at least very insufficient connection with what went on before.

While conversing with a patient, one does not note anything abnormal in the temporal aspect of his chain of ideas. Statement and counter-statement, question and answer follow one another as in any normal conversation. But all of a sudden, in the middle of a sentence or in passing to a new idea, the patient stops and cannot continue any further. Often he is able to overcome the obstacle by repeating the attempt. Another time, he succeeds only in thinking in a new direction. Frequently, the blocking cannot be overcome for quite a long interval; in such cases it can spread over the entire psyche, the patient remaining silent and motionless and also more or less without thoughts.

This concept of blocking we owe to Kraepelin. It is of fundamental significance in the symptomatology and diagnosis of schizophrenia. We meet it again in the motor sphere—in actions, in remembering, and even in the field of perception. Blocking is essentially different from inhibition, which is a usual concomitant symptom of the more marked affective depressions of all kinds. Inhibited thinking and acting proceeds slowly and with difficulty under abnormal expenditure of psychic energy. This psychic energy seems to behave like a viscous fluid in a system of tubes which however are everywhere patent. But in "blocking" the free-flowing fluid is suddenly stopped because somewhere a stop-cock was abruptly turned off. We could also compare the psychic mechanism to a watch. Then inhibition corresponds to a greatly increased amount of friction in the works, while "blocking" corresponds to a sudden stoppage of the entire mechanism of the watch. This difference can often be demonstrated easily in the motor sphere. A patient who until now has made few movements and those only very slowly and weakly, and who has hardly spoken a spontaneous word, is ordered to revolve his hands around one another as fast as possible or to count rapidly from one to ten. The inhibited patient will turn his hands or count slowly in spite of the greatest effort; the "blocked" patient will of a sudden begin to count as well as a normal person and move his hands when once the blocking is overcome.

The "blocking" of the train of thought is perceived by the patients themselves who usually describe it under various names. Mostly, but not always, they find it a condition that is quite unpleasant. An intelligent catatonic woman had to sit still for hours at a time, "in order to find her thoughts again." Another patient could find nothing to say about it than, "I can sometimes speak and sometimes not." Another patient feels as if "he died away" (Abraham). Still another complains of "obstacles to thinking," or "a tightness in his head as if my head were drawn together." Yet another describes it "as if someone drew a rubber sack over him." A peasant woman expresses it as "if something was being pressed against her face and chest, it is just as if my mouth was being held closed, as if someone said 'keep your mouth shut!' " In this last example, there is also blocking of the motor functions of speaking which a patient of Rust described with the words "that his powers of speech were being withheld from him." It is something quite common to find that the blocking is attributed to foreign influence. Thus, while one of our patients was asked to sing songs, he was suddenly unable to continue. The "voices" told him, "See, you have again forgotten." But these "voices" were those very agents who, according to the patient, provoked his lapse of memory.

Jung heard from one of his patients the best term for designating the phenomenon; subjectively she experienced it as "thought-deprivation." The term is so apt that many schizophrenics know instantly what is meant by it. If a patient immediately answers with a "Yes" to the question, "Do you experience thought-deprivation?" and then goes on to describe what he understands by this expression, one can very well make the diagnosis of schizophrenia with a considerable degree of certainty. At least, we have not found any exception to this conclusion as yet. Even patients who have used different descriptive words for the concept of "blocking" know what is meant by "thought-deprivation." A patient promptly responded to Jung's question as to whether he suffered from deprivation of his thoughts with: "So you call it thought-deprivation, up to now I have always called it 'thought-obstruction.'" Kraepelin's patient expressed it similarly as "withdrawal of the thoughts."

"Blocking" apparently has something capricious about it objectively for the observer, and subjectively for the patient. At times the patient is able to speak easily and readily, move quite freely, and then again thinking or movements will halt, freeze, coagulate. However, on closer scrutiny one finds that the basis of the blocking generally lies in the significance the blocked chain of thought has for the patient. Conversely, in a patient about whom we do not know very much, one can conclude from the appearance of blocking that we have struck upon one of his important complexes.

We question a young girl about her previous life. She gives a good chronological account of her past. Of a sudden she cannot continue. We inquire what has happened, but nothing more can be obtained. Only much later, by use of all sorts of circuitous means, she reveals that at that particular time in her life she had become acquainted with her sweetheart.—A teacher, who threw all his efforts into trying to improve his position and earnings, answers to the question whether he got his promotion: "What is a promotion?" He cannot understand this phrase because the whole "promotion-complex" has been blocked off. Many patients insistently demand to see the doctor because they have important things to discuss, yet when he does come they do not know what to say.

A very intelligent and well-educated patient sings a love-song, but claims afterwards that the song was merely a description of a beautiful countryside. He cannot reproduce it any more, even when parts of the song are sung to him. He maintains quite firmly and with conviction that he never sang such a song.

In our patients the affectively charged complexes are generally connected with delusions and hallucinations. Therefore we get very little information about these processes from the schizophrenic, even though they generally dominate the entire thinking and feeling of the patient. A patient knows "that certain people are possessed" because she cannot speak to them. The "possessed" were those who were involved in her delusions.

The "blocking" is not absolute and invincible in each case. By persistent questioning, by using various stimuli[10] and especially by distraction, one can often break through or circumvent it. The patients, however, have an unpleasant feeling about such manoeuvres. A patient became quite frightened after she had managed to answer, as if she had done something improper.

Thus also, the will or, at least, the desire of the patients has some share in the appearance of the blocking. A hebephrenic calls the symptom-complex of "blocking" (bound up with delusions and other pathological conditions) the "post-marker." This he often conjures up when someone wants to give him some undesired work. He was then "blocked" for everything and there was nothing more to be done with him. It is evident that there is every shade and degree of transition from such behavior to conscious unwillingness and simulation. In the same fashion, the limits defining "blocking" from negativism are neither theoretically nor symptomatically sharp. Both phenomena pass almost imperceptibly into each other; and passive negativism may perhaps be explained as a combination of blockings.

Almost entirely like negativism were the effects of blocking in a patient who gave slow, hesitating, whispered answers. At times her voice failed completely, especially if she was questioned insistently. It was possible to circumvent the blocking if one did not attempt to question her directly.

In some cases it is simply impossible to differentiate blocking from negativism, particularly when the patient gets around the resistance by employing "approximate answers." During the examination a patient revealed neither blocking, negativism nor "approximate answers" except when she was asked when she had first come to the hospital. To this oft-repeated question she gave such responses as: "In an ambulance," "Nurse H. brought me here," "I have been here three days and long nights." (Actually the patient had been admitted to the hospital on the previous day).

Partial blocking such as we have just described can manifest itself in other ways too. It is not at all rare that speech is blocked while the thought process continues to be expressed in the form of a brief series

10. Even alcohol can often assist in overcoming a block, and may be utilized during examination.

of gestures which serve to complete the sentence already begun. In my experience, the train of thought usually ceases with the completion of the mimicked gestures of the same sentence. There is a type of partial blocking which one of Jung's patients called "fixation" (*Bannung*). The thoughts seemed to be completely stopped or fastened to some one sense impression and only this one sense impression remains in consciousness to the exclusion of everything else. What Sommers designated as "visual fixation," probably partially covered this same symptom.

As far as our present knowledge goes, the experimental associations often do not appear to be disturbed in the chronic states of the milder cases. However, generally we do pick up peculiarities which are, to be sure, in themselves not sufficient to establish a diagnosis with any degree of certainty. Nevertheless, they suggest the probability of the presence of the disease.

1. Great irregularity in association time, which cannot be completely explained by the dominance of emotionally toned complexes. The time variations are much greater than in complexes of the healthy. Frequently striking changes occur, at times the associations go very slowly; then suddenly one sees the patient can think very rapidly (in the same experiment, of course). Naturally, in the face of such irregularity, one is inclined to ascribe it to vacillations in the good will or at least in the patient's attention. In acute cases, the reactions have a tendency to become progressively slower during each individual experiment.

2. Notable also is the reverting to previous stimulus words or previous answers. This after-effect of an earlier thought does not have to be continuous. A patient may drop one train of thought only to come back to it again in later associations, as did the patient (mentioned above) who joined "Berne," "legislature," etc., after three entirely different ideas had diverted him far from his original idea. Frequently, we find that the perseverating ideas seem to link themselves with each other.

3. The after-effect of previous thoughts shows itself also in the tendency to stereotypy of answers both in form and content. Some particularly acute cases respond quite senselessly at the end of the experiment with a few answers which were previously used during the experiment quite correctly: "for thinking," "to write with," "to eat with," etc. (Naturally, poverty of ideas facilitates such behavior.)

4. Sometimes the patients stick to the stimulus word and repeat it without adding any further thought. This sort of echolalia appears more often in acute conditions (clouded states) than in the chronic.

5. Even when the repetition of the same word does not occur very often, we still see a striking poverty of ideas in many patients. It is true

that they do not stick to the same word but they do fix on similar ones or on very closely related ideas.

6. Schizophrenics show far more individual types of reactions which do not show up in others. (Kent and Rosanoff.) If after a long interval one offers them the same stimulus words one finds much more variety than we get in the healthy. (Pfenninger.)

7. Most noteworthy, however, are the bizarre associations, examples of which were given previously; as well as those associations which apparently or actually are disconnected and in which the stimulus word merely served as a signal for the uttering of any word whatsoever (the naming of a piece of furniture which happened to be in the field of vision, etc.).

8. Frequently one is unable to discover any connection between the associations even with the help of the patient. In most of these cases, one may assume an emotionally toned complex of ideas to be operative. When I say "operative," I do not mean "operative in the patient's conscious," since the patient himself can not really give us any information about it. Thus a patient, who was apparently completely oriented and rather intelligent, associated to concepts which touched on his emotions with the word, "short," without knowing himself just why he did so. The solution to the puzzle lay in the fact that he himself was a "shorty," a short man, and this was involved in his complexes.

9. Marked tendency to mediate associations is not at all rare.

10. The signs of emotionally accentuated complexes manifest themselves often in very exaggerated fashion. The reaction time to complex-touching stimulus words increases immeasurably; or the reaction may fail to appear altogether. All the complex-indicators, as described by Jung, are in many cases especially obvious: superficiality if reaction-times are long; quotations, response in a foreign language; rapid forgetting; intellectual and affective after-effect is reflected in the subsquent associations. In some cases, the complexes are so predominant that associations can only be made to the complexes. All these signs, however, are very variable not only from one case to the next, but they may vary from a maximum to a minimum in the same patient within a very short period of time.

The need to appear intelligent (intelligence complex) manifests itself here, as it also does in mental defectives, in inclinations to definitions; their bizarreness often betrays the specifically schizophrenic origin: eye—viewpoint, grandmother—sex participation, oven—article for warmth, and so on.

In spite of much investigation, no direct traces of *negativism* are found in the association experiments. Only in two patients did we see a tendency to negation and contrast associations, but it was precisely these patients who were not negativistic.

Ziehen (847) also tested the reversal of association. In clinical conditions which we consider to be schizophrenic, he found some difficulty in the reproduction of series in reverse. However, it is so difficult to separate the disturbances of association from those of attention, good will etc., that I do not dare to draw any definite conclusions from the author's short paper.

The disturbances of association, as described, are characteristic for schizophrenia. *Besides these disturbances there are also other types of anomalies of thinking which appear intercurrently.*

In manic phases of schizophrenia, flight of ideas is added to the typically schizophrenic association disturbances. In depressive episodes, we find inhibition of thinking and disturbances of association brought about by abnormal affective reactions. Above all, however, hysteriform isolation mechanisms may often dominate the clinical picture. Compulsive thoughts are frequent.

The description given here of the association disturbances is inadequate inasmuch as little attention has been paid to the acute clinical conditions of this disease. However, we have not as yet found any new qualitative peculiarities in such syndromes, but rather only exaggerations of those already described. (Of course, we are leaving aside any discussion of the signs of manic, melancholic or organically inhibited clinical conditions.)

I consider it to be a serious defect that we are forced to deduce most of the anomalies from the oral and written productions of the patients. However, even the more complicated actions are no doubt the result of thought-processes similar to those brought out in discussions. It is our custom to question our patients about the motives of their activity. It is different with the associations which rule our minor activities or behavior and which we do not consciously direct, while in our consciousness we see emerging only the purpose of this or that act or behavior. If I write something, I consciously think about my theme, but I do not know exactly how I got the paper from my desk, what sort of specific motions and coordinations I employed, etc., etc. There are indications that in schizophrenics even these very well practiced mechanisms are altered, as, for example, the appearance of apraxic-like phenomena demonstrates. However, as yet we do not know whether these disturbances can also be traced back to an incompleteness of the required sum of individual associations related to these special activities. It is possible that the awkwardness is due to negativistic counter-currents or perplexity.

(b) *Affectivity*

In the outspoken forms of schizophrenia, the "emotional deterioration" stands in the forefront of the clinical picture. It has been known since the early years of modern psychiatry that an "acute curable" psychosis became "chronic" when the affects began to disappear. Many schizophrenics in the later stages cease to show any affect for years and even decades at a time. They sit about the institutions to which they are confined with expressionless faces, hunched-up, the image of indifference. They permit themselves to be dressed and undressed like automatons, to be led from their customary place of inactivity to the mess-hall, and back again without expressing any sign of satisfaction or dissatisfaction. They do not even seem to react to injuries inflicted on them by other patients.

Even in the less severe forms of the illness, indifference seems to be the external sign of their state; an indifference to everything—to friends and relations, to vocation or enjoyment, to duties or rights, to good fortune or to bad. "I don't care the least, one way or another," is what a patient of Binswanger said. Generally the defect shows itself most strikingly in relation to the most vital of the patient's interests and it does not make any difference whether or not their comprehension requires complicated thinking. A mother may show right at the beginning of her illness that she is indifferent to the weal and woes of her children; yet she may employ not only the words of a normally feeling mother but really understand everything that is good or bad for a child. She may, as the occasion requires (e.g., when she uses it for an excuse to try and obtain her release from the hospital), discuss the matter quite competently. It is a matter of indifference for such a patient whether her family or herself are going to wreck and ruin. The sense of self-preservation is often reduced to zero. The patients do not bother any more about whether they starve or not, whether they lie on a snowbank or on a red-hot oven. During a fire in the hospital, a number of patients had to be led out of the threatened ward; they themselves would never have moved from their places; they would have allowed themselves to be suffocated or burnt without showing an affective response. Illnesses, threats of every possible evil will not disturb the peace of many a schizophrenic. What happens to others is of course of no concern at all to them. In a ward one patient kills another; his ward-mates do not find it necessary to call the attendant. A student almost choked the life out of his mother; he cannot understand why such a fuss is made over "a few harsh words!" A patient writes home for the first time after a month-and-a-half in the institution; but aside from a few irrelevant and insignificant phrases, he can only ask how the cat is getting along.

Schizophrenics can write whole autobiographies without manifesting the least bit of emotion. They will describe their suffering and their actions as if it were a theme in physics. A Croatian woman, who could speak only her native tongue, manages to wander off to Zurich; remains in the hospital for months without being able to make herself understood since she pays no attention to gestures, although she is of lively temperament. Finally a country-woman of hers speaks to her. The patient answers the questions but does not show the least affect. A hebephrenic talks about his father's death: "Since I was at home at that time, I went to the funeral and was happy, however, that it was not I who was being buried; I am buried alive now." Generally, it is very striking how many patients, particularly the older ones, reveal the same indifference to their own delusions, with which, however, they are constantly preoccupied.

During a lengthy clinical presentation a paranoid complains constantly about his persecutions but sits very calmly and nonchalantly as he tells his story. Asked if he thought his hallucinations were real, he answers with a shrug of his shoulders: "Perhaps they are pathological, perhaps they are real." The question very obviously does not interest him. It is common knowledge that older paranoids relate with the greatest calmness how they were flayed and burnt during the night; how their bowels were torn out. A hebephrenic comes to the doctor to ask him, please, not to kill her. Although she really believes that it is a matter of life and death, she remains completely affectless.

In milder cases, this indifference can be absent or disguised. At the beginning of the disease, we often see an over-sensitivity, so that the patients consciously and deliberately isolate themselves in order to avoid everything that may arouse affects, even though they may still have some interest in life. Latent schizophrenics may appear almost too labile in their affect, almost sanguine. But there is a lack of depth to the affect. Also, one finds on closer observation of such cases that there is generally a partial indifference to this or the other interest which once was a matter of concern to the patient. However, I would not maintain that this description also applies to those numerous schizophrenics who are never seen by a psychiatrist. Furthermore, there are many schizophrenics who display lively affect at least in certain directions. Among them are the active writers, the world improvers, the health fanatics, the founders of new religions. These people are one-sided in their thinking and inconsiderate in their behavior. It is very difficult to say whether their affects as such are also pathologically onesided.

Often we do note significant "basic moods," so that one cannot really speak of an all-pervading indifference in these patients. The mood may be euphoric, sad, or anxious. We see the transitions from a euphoric mood to indifference or a mixture of both in the very frequent emotional states of hebephrenics who show what is called a "callous indifference," or what the French call "*je-m'en-fichisme*," and the English, "I don't give a damn!" The patients are then, if not happy, at least quite pleased with themselves and the world. Unpleasant occurrences are not felt as disagreeable. On such occasions their answers become quite insolent. This reaction is facilitated because their inaccurate associations supply them with very appropriate material. Also, other moods express themselves in a similar way. For twenty years one of our patients was known as "the good-natured mad-woman" because she presented her senseless complaints with so much laughter and bonhomie.

In those acute episodes of this disease that were formerly called mania and melancholia, the affect is of course not lacking but it takes on a special coloring or tone which often in itself permits the diagnosis of the disease. In place of the clear, deeply felt affect of the manic-depressive psychosis, we have the impression of emotionality which does not go very deep at all. Above all, however, consistency of affective manifestation is absent. The words which are supposed to express pain or pleasure, the tone of voice, the gestures do not seem consistent or appropriate to the patient's total attitude. The mimic lacks unity—the wrinkled forehead, for example, expresses something like surprise; the eyes with their little crows feet give the impression of laughter and the corners of the mouth may be drooping as if in sorrow. Often the facial expression seems exaggerated and highly melodramatic. The stiffness or awkwardness of movements are very striking in these cases. Both complaints and jubilation become monotonous.

It is easier to sense these phenomena than to describe them. What can best be emphasized in the presentation is the lack of adaptability to changing thought content, the deficiency in the capacity for modulation. The affective mood of the manic schizophrenic hardly follows or does not follow at all the changing content of thought. The true manic, just like the normal individual, accompanies the emotional nuances of his thoughts with the appropriate qualitative and quantitative modifications of affective manifestations; the definitely schizophrenic patient shows little or none of such modulations, whether he is making a witticism or complaining about his incarceration, or telling us his life-story.[11] A catatonic patient complained that her husband was in prison. I as-

11. If we hear a schizophrenic speaking in a language foreign to us he offers us no indication of what he is talking about. There may be an important change of theme (food—to mother's death) yet the change remains completely symptomless.

sured her that he was free upon which she answered, "Is he, that's fine." Yet she made this answer in as unchanged, complaining a tone as if I had confirmed her husband's imprisonment.

Such an attitude is only apparently different from indifference. Whatever affect there is, it certainly is not a reaction to a thought, but rather some abnormal basic state of affectivity, a different adjustment of the affective zero-point.[12] Patients with other types of psychosis will react according to their concepts with vacillations either upward or downward from this affective zero-point; not so the schizophrenic.

In some cases, we clearly see vacillations of affect which almost approach the normal. Nevertheless, an underlying affective rigidity may invest the expressions of the most varied moods with a sort of common denominator which is difficult to describe. In comparison one may say, it seems as if the whole mimicry were dipped into the same color. These people seem to laugh and to cry with the same tone of voice. Even when they pull the corners of their mouths upward in one emotion and downward in another, there remains an element of obvious similarity in both expressions.

Often the affect will show its inadequate depth inasmuch as the patient will be unable to maintain a mood. A catatonic patient was in great fear of a hallucinated Judas Iscariot who was threatening her with a sword. She cried out that the Judas be driven away, but in between she begged for a piece of chocolate. Next day she complained about these hallucinations, apologized for her acts of violence; but in the middle of her complaints she expressed pleasure in a pretty belt. She managed to weave this belt into her delusions sufficiently to need reassurance that it was not a "Judas kiss." Another catatonic spends her days and nights in desperate self-accusations and attempts at self-injury. However, when she is able to evade the attendants, she laughs very heartily about it.

In acute stages, rapid alteration of affective expression may occur even without any basic, continuing mood, within a brief space of time, e.g. during a clinical presentation. Because of some haphazard, accidental association, the patient will switch in one second from exaggerated, intense, angry agitation with cursing, screaming, jumping about, to an exaggeratedly erotic, happy mood, only to become tearful and sad a few minutes later. In these cases the entire personality seems to change with the affect. In contrast to the above discussed fixation of certain compon-

12. Author's Note: The independence of such schizophrenic moods from the thought content shows itself particularly clearly in the not unusual cases when a patient who has elaborated certain appropriate delusions during a depression will cling to them despite the rapid change of mood (to euphoria) but express it with the completely inappropriate cheerful tone which contradicts the content.

ents of a previous affective expression, we find here that previous affects do not seem to operate as far as they normally would. Quite suddenly, there will appear a completely new emotional register. This kind of quick reversal and emotional rigidity differentiates these cases easily from the organic types.

Thus it is understandable that Masselon (p. 83) counts among the emotional peculiarities of schizophrenia not only nonchalance, indifference, irritability, but also an enormous "lability of affect" (mobility of mood, versatility, etc.). Even their irritability appears to stand in a certain contrast to their indifference, and even more so does their lability which presupposes an abnormally heightened responsiveness.

In mild cases, such as are rarely seen in hospitals, the lability often appears to dominate, but on closer observation one can note the affective defects. A hebephrenic was under impending sentence for some violation of the law. He was slightly euphoric, considered himself lucky to have come to the hospital for medical care. He praised the paintings (bad ones) on the wall, did not want to be transferred to a better ward because the patients in his ward were so nice. After being transferred to the new ward, he berated and cursed his old ward endlessly. During a slight fever (and occasionally without any discernible cause) he became depressed, cried like a child that he was going to die. This same reaction showed itself for the most insignificant reasons; for example, when he related how reluctant his father had been to pay the small semi-annual tuition fee for him. If someone said anything which displeased him, he would become excited, threatening, shattered objects nearby, threw money away in his rage, beat up his wife. In spite of this lability of affect with a mild manic mood, the schizophrenic affect disturbance was quite clear. He did not seek any contact with his environment as does the true euphoric. He remained quite indifferent to the most important events in his life (confinement, business, divorce, etc.). In this well-educated and polite man there was complete loss of his sense of social tact. His facial expressions were stiff, fixed, completely incongruent with his bombastic speech. Ideas of different affective value were presented with the same mien. He could state how frightfully excited he was in a tone of utmost indifference.

To some extent it would appear that this lability of affect is certainly related to the patient's inability to comprehend many important events as such. Even the healthy person will not bother much with unimportant ideas. Therefore, it is quite understandable that the schizophrenic, for whom nothing is of importance, often jumps from one affect to another. On the other hand, the lability of affect corresponds to his dissociated thinking. A hebephrenic patient struggles desperately, yells that he has ruined everything; suddenly he will say in a calm tone, "Now I am laughing," and then laughs dryly. Soon after, he states, "I am going to yell," and again screams and struggles. Another patient would break out into wild rage at each visit from the doctor, grinding his teeth and threatening to assault so that he had to be restrained. Yet, shortly after he would jump into his bed and with an elegant gesture send the physician "a kiss of forgiveness." Occasionally we see in the oriented hebephrenic that he sincerely regrets his actions committed during periods of agitation. One of our paranoids would sob after mistreating his wife. However, I have never again seen such stark, outspoken repentance.

Even when the affects change, they usually do so more slowly than in the healthy. The affects seem often to lag behind the ideas. During an interview, a female patient was repeatedly shown the picture of a child. It took one-quarter of an hour for the corresponding sorrowful affect to appear. Also, during celebrations one can observe how much longer it takes the schizophrenic to get into the party mood than it does the healthy person. Although anger and fury tend to linger on, they may set in as abruptly in the normal as in the schizophrenic. One cannot regard this as special lability of the patients. However, there undoubtedly is a pathological lingering of affect in the usual tendency of schizophrenics to persist in their anger or even increase it for long periods, even though the reason for this emotion no longer exists.

From all of this we must draw the conclusion (in opposition to Masselon) that the lability of the schizophrenic represents an unessential phenomenon.

Far more striking than the quick changes of affect (externally at least) are the unprovoked mood swings and variations; the "moodiness" associated with the setting in of affects. Today a patient may appear quite indifferent, tomorrow he may be irritable or accessible to quite different feelings. Pfersdorff (562, p. 18) remarked about his patients: "Their basic affective state was manifest only when the patients talked, which they seldom did spontaneously." As is so often the case, the affects begin to reveal themselves when the patients are compelled to deal with and react to their environment. But most often the patients are emotionally aroused only when they are forced to think certain definite ideas which before the onset, or during the early stages, of their illness preoccupied them most (complexes). Thus a hebephrenic patient would sit around in dumb-erotic euphoria, only to show a quite normal affect when her relations to her husband were being discussed. Even decades later it is possible to evoke in these patients the pain or joy of a long-past love affair in all its vividness when we succeed in overcoming the blocking never absent with regard to these topics. The affects appear as if they had been preserved. All the nuances of sexual pleasure, embarrassment, pain or jealousy, may emerge in all their vividness which we never find in the healthy when it is a question of recollecting the past. Frequently these memories are expressed so as to convey the character of the experiences of former times, in conspicuous contrast to the patient's present ripe old age.

A hebephrenic patient is brought to the hospital for a mild depression at the age of seventy-one. She had had her first transitory attack of illness soon after puberty. She spoke with the greatest indifference of the events and experiences of her life, particularly of her husband. When we succeeded, however, in reminding her of a lover from the period immediately preceding her first illness, she exhibited the bashful mien of a young girl who is being questioned about such matters. She showed all the characteristic reactions; she not only blushed and lowered her eyes, but also giggled with embarrassed gratification, twisted the hem of her apron around her fingers, prettied her hair and showed all the other little gestures that have to be seen but can hardly be described. Thus, the girlish emotion could be evoked, almost one might say, excavated, in all its freshness even after half a century; and all of it stood in most moving contrast to the sunken figure and wrinkled face of an old woman.

In this case, as in many another, it was possible to repeat the experiment many times.

Analogous observations, although perhaps not as striking, can be made in most schizophrenic cases who have been thoroughly analysed. When, in a clinical demonstration, one has revealed the affectively accentuated complexes for the first time, it is often very difficult to convince the audience of the actual lack of affect in the patient, so normally does he appear to react although for years he has not only displayed but experienced complete indifference.

With some patience, one can demonstrate the presence of affects in relation to the delusions in an individual who is apparently a mere vegetative organism. Often it requires months to establish any intellectual rapport with such completely apathetic and mute patients. But if one succeeds, one finds quite regularly a delusional system which has not only originated in wishes and fears but is still accompanied by wholly appropriate emotions.

Even when cerebral atrophy sets in, the affects often still make their appearance, with the result that some of these disturbed individuals differ little from the usual cases of senility, "who can cry and laugh whenever they so desire." I observed a catatonic for ten years who, except for the very earliest period of her illness, had only hurled insults at me and had sat with her tongue protruding from the corner of her mouth, in a demonstratively negativistic attitude. When I visited the hospital ten years after having left I saw her again and she rushed to greet me and threw her arms around me as if I were an old friend. A paranoid patient, whom I had known to be emotionally indifferent for thirty years, had an apoplectic attack. As she was attracting flies with sweets, I asked her once jokingly whether the flies would not eat her up too. She fell in with the joke: "There are big, big ones which want to eat me." She laughed at the first half of the sentence, but with the second half she was so overcome that she burst out crying (as do true senile cases) being overwhelmed by the idea of being eaten.

Thus there can be no doubt at all that the psyche's capacity to produce affects has not disappeared in schizophrenia. Therefore, it should be no cause for surprise to find one or the other affect still well preserved even in the severe cases. But the specific nature of the affect we find is largely determined by "accident." Still, there are certain emotions which have a better chance of being encountered than others.

As we saw above, we were often able to reveal erotic strivings (in the subtle sense). Quite frequently, when we are able to follow up the patient's day-dreams, we find most delicate feelings in the very patient who displayed nothing but violence and filth to the world.

Even in advanced cases, instead of interest we meet its equivalent —curiosity. Patients who apparently were not the least concerned with anything around them, always seemed to be able to manage things in such a way that, should a door open, they would be able to look through it or overhear a conversation, or get a glance at a book lying open. They will do this even at a time when they appear too torpid even to touch what they consider peculiar. In cases institutionalized for a long time we observe a certain growing attachment to the hospital. Schizophrenics who have worked in a hospital for many years develop a kind of affection for the institution. They show an interest in the management of the farm, and occasionally even spontaneously contribute something to it. They might show homesickness for the institution after they have been discharged. Just as often, however, we find that these hard-working patients perform their daily stint like veritable automatons unperturbed by rain or snow, heat or frost.

It is in the range of irritability, anger, and even fury, that we find most frequently preservation of the affects. Many institutionalized patients show reaction only in this way. The attendant personnel is always in danger of being insulted or attacked while carrying out the ordinary, daily routine care, even when bringing the patients their food. Between such extreme and nowadays rare cases, and just the ordinary irritability, there is every degree of gradation.

In hospitals and institutions, this irritability in connection with the delusional system and negativism of the patients is particularly difficult to manage. The "persecuted" are dissatisfied with their environment, considering it the source of the persecution. Other patients, who believe that all their desires have been fulfilled, are disturbed by their environment in their happy dreams—reason enough for anger and fury. Thus, anger is the usual reaction of many patients to their hallucinations, and, what is very significant, even when their "voices" do not have anything especially unpleasant to say.

Not quite on the same level is the indignation, frequently met with in institutions, over lack of freedom, or other discomfort which the treatment inevitably brings in its wake. Many patients complain of feelings of homesickness, but it is relatively rare that one can detect any objective signs indicating the presence of a genuine homesickness, or even of any real longing to return home. In fact, it happens frequently that a schizophrenic who has been pestering continually for his release, on receiving permission, refuses to use it, or aimlessly leaves the hospital without ever going back to his home.

Quite frequently one finds that parental love is the only affective element that is preserved apart from the patient's irritability. Mothers, in particular, often remain truly concerned about the well-being of their children; whereas they may not care about anything else, not even about their own physical health. Such patients will show real joy when their children visit them or when they receive good news of their children. A woman patient, who had been ill for some thirty years and who for a long time had been in an advanced hallucinatory condition, tried to convince her physician, whom she had singled out for her son-in-law, that her disease had not been inherited by her daughter.

Also, the feeling of sympathy for others is not always extinguished. Often patients can very well sympathize with another's situation or condition, especially in institutions where the majority know each other quite well. A hebephrenic, whose very speech was confusion, held the cigar-holder to the mouth of another patient suffering from muscular atrophy who could no longer hold the cigar between his own lips. He did this with a patience and indefatigability of which no normal person would ever be capable. It sometimes happens that such schizophrenic Samaritans succeed in feeding an abstentious patient who could not be fed by anyone else.

Even artistic empathy is not so rare. Mildly schizophrenic poets and musicians may show this ability. While in an apparently deep stupor, an acutely catatonic woman would dance to music with self-improvised steps and movements which gave a delicately aesthetic, as well as astonishingly accurate, interpretation of the feeling expressed by the music. One of our female catatonics, continuously irascible and inclined to violence, quite indifferent to her environment, dirty and indecent in the highest degree, could yet not only dance but could very accurately adjust herself to every nuance of the music and of her partner's motions.

Few patients show a humorous inclination; perhaps one might say they are more inclined to produce something humorous themselves than to appreciate the humorous efforts of others, yet coarse jokes often find a certain appreciation.

It is indeed striking how early those feelings that regulate social intercourse among people are blunted. It hardly makes any difference to the patient whether he is addressing a person in authority or someone more humbly-placed, whether a man or a woman. Often there is not a trace of modesty left, even in patients who are otherwise relatively not too deteriorated. They will confess or relate all sorts of misdeeds which they themselves recognize as such. They will expound on their sexual experiences in the vilest terms. They will masturbate openly. A patient, an intelligent high school student, writes to his mother as follows: "Dear Mother, come to see me as soon as possible. I must know how old you were the night my father made me."

Yet the strong emotionality exhibited in petty matters can be in marked contrast to the severe defects described above. A hebephrenic who worked for a time in our office, strutted around carefully togged out, manicured and pomaded and did not in the least seem to mind the teasing which he was subjected to by another uncouth employee. Yet when his mother wrote, asking him to come home to see his dying father, he sent her a few words of "consolation" but did not go home. Two female patients eat their own excrement. One of them, an old maid, is still very reluctant and coy about revealing her age; the other, a painter, took the greatest delight in the pretty colors of her "odd food."

On the occasion of various festivities held at the hospital, the patients react in different ways. In general, they are somewhat rigid and the lack of initiative in their games is conspicuous. The quickening of the patients to the mood of the occasion seems often delayed for an abnormally long time; yet on the other hand, it is often quantitatively increased inasmuch as many will become so increasingly thrilled by the festive mood that they cannot stop when the time comes. During a ball attended by some more or less selected patients, a layman would hardly observe anything particularly striking or abnormal.

The ethical qualities of the schizophrenics are of great variety. By and large, the patients appear as much blunted in this direction as in others. Since most of them are not very active, few of them become criminals. Occasionally one does become a thief or a swindler subsequent to the outbreak of his illness. It is then impossible to say whether a previously inhibited tendency has made its appearance or whether the disease itself produced the criminal behavior. Thus, as far as morality is concerned, one can trust schizophrenics just as little or as much as one can normal persons. The situation is far worse with regard to their unpredictability. But on the whole it can be said that there is less lying, stealing, swindling and slandering among the patients than among the healthy. In milder cases there appears quite often a very painstaking conscientiousness and scrupulousness. Of course, the assaults committed as results of delusions have nothing to do with the question of ethics, since from the patients' point of view they are merely justifiable acts of self-defense.

Thus the character of the schizophrenic is as manifold as that of the normal. Nevertheless, the indifference, the tendency to withdraw, the inaccessibility to influence, the moodiness and the irritability—all these peculiarities are recurring characteristics which doubtlessly invest all the advanced cases with a certain common external appearance. In spite of all difficulties some are able to maintain a likeable, even loveable, character until quite late in the course of the disease. Others become monsters of the most vengeful, cruel, deceitful type, given to every sort of excesses. The disease can transform a congenitally bad person into a harmless one by the very loss of energy and activity, but apparently it cannot make him better.

The lower drives and related to these, the emotional emphasis on bodily processes seem to suffer less than the "higher" affects, but the difference is not sufficient to permit one to demonstrate regularly such a relationship in any given case. Kraepelin describes how frequently patients will receive the visits of their relatives without a word of greeting or any sign of emotional participation, but instead will grab their bags and baskets and search for food which they will devour immediately, greedily and down to the last crumb.

In contrast, there are many who seem totally impervious to hunger, thirst, loss of sleep or mistreatment of every type. Often extreme accumulations in rectum or bladder or uncomfortable positions are not accompanied by any feelings of discomfort. Not even the loudest and shrillest acoustic stimulations, nor the pain of blinding light seem to disturb them. I have seen many patients who gazed continually into the blinding sun with apparent pleasure. Why they did not destroy their retinas, I do not know. I have not observed especially small pupils in any of these patients; however, I could not examine them in critical moments.

Patients with schizophrenia react differently to their affective disturbances. The majority are not aware of them and consider their reaction as normal. The more intelligent, however, may reason about it quite acutely. At the beginning they sense the emotional emptiness as rather painful, so that they may easily be mistaken for melancholics. One of our catatonics considered himself as "insensibilized;" one of Jung's patients could not pray any more because of "hardening of her feelings." Later, they tend to displace the changes in themselves to the outer world which itself becomes hollow, empty, strange, because of these affective changes. Often the element of strangeness has a touch of the uncanny and hostile.

Others, as for example Aschaffenburg's patient, express it in a very characteristic way. After a mild attack of the illness she felt herself subjectively decidedly better than she had been before her illness. Previously whenever it was necessary to lend a hand with family matters, concerns and chores, she felt compelled by her moral feelings to sacrifice her rest and her health; after her illness she was able to live for herself without twinges of conscience. Some hebephrenics exhibit their indifference quite consciously.

Occasionally, a patient will maintain that he has a marked and powerful affect, whereas the observer can note none or another type of affect than that which the patient professes to feel. (Schott, 666, p. 262.) Whether the patient means something other than we do in his use of terms or whether the phenomenon can be explained by the psychic splitting, I must leave to future research.

On the whole, but not always, the physical manifestations of the affects correspond to the psychic process. Often one single manifestation, such as a change in respiration, will express or betray an affective change or variation.

Special mention can be made here of the psycho-galvanic phenomenon (Veraguth, Jung) which can serve as an index of the course of the affective wave. Further studies of this problem would be most desirable. At this point, all we can say is that indifference and stupor express themselves in a completely straight curve of the resting type, but that there are also to be found quite labile curves, usually in hallucinating patients. The responses to psychic and physical stimuli are on the whole reduced, in severe cases down to zero. Ricksher and Jung found a slow-down in the vacillations in their paranoids.

The lack of the volume-changes of the limbs, the pulse and respiration variations under stimuli of pain and cold (compare also the pupil reflexes) which were noted by Bumke and Kehrer[13] have a similar significance.

Especially conspicuous in schizophrenics is the frequently encountered parathymia. The patients are able to react to sad news with cheerfulness or even with laughter. These patients will often become sad or, even more frequently, irritated by events to which others would react with indifference or with pleasure. A mere "how-do-you-do" can upset them. Many times they will attach erotic feelings to someone or something which does not at all appear to be suitable. A patient states that her bath water was poisoned, that it had a very bitter taste, and she accompanies her words with a coy erotic giggle. Other patients are in love with a ward-mate with complete disregard of sex, ugliness, or even repulsiveness. They will relate laughingly their torturing hallucinations, or portray themselves with a cheerful mien as unfortunate creatures (Foersterling, p. 288). A particularly frequent form of parathymia is represented by unprovoked or inappropriate bursts of laughter. The dysfunction of affect may manifest itself in the quantitative relation of the feelings to each other. Thus a patient of Masselon's broke out into loud laughter at the news of her brother's death, because she was so pleased at receiving letters with black borders; but the loss of the brother did not seem to arouse any feeling.

In the fields of taste and smell, the parathymic disturbance can often be very prominent. Many patients will swallow with ease objects which would give a normal person a decidedly uncomfortable feeling: bugs, saw-dust, wire, spoons, dirt, gasoline and, of course, frequently their own excretions, both solid and liquid. A catatonic whom I asked why he drank his own urine, answered with a blissfully entranced expression, "*Herr Direktor*, if you should taste it but once, you would never want to drink anything else."

Parathymia can never really be differentiated from paramimia. One of our catatonics appeared melancholic on admission, yet soon after said that she had enjoyed the admission-formalities and that the physician's handshake, for instance, appeared to her as something holy. Another female catatonic patient approached one of the women attendants whom she liked and told her in the friendliest manner and in her sweetest tone of voice: "I really would like to slap your face, people like you are usually called s. o. b.'s." A third patient danced about and hummed a popular song but maintained throughout an expression of distress and a heart-breaking tone of voice.

13. Archiv für Psychologie, Vol. XLVII, p.945.

The above-mentioned lack of essential unity in expression can lead to a sort of paramimia. A woman patient complained bitterly about her "voices" and body-hallucinations; her mouth and her forehead manifested disgust, but her eyes expressed happy eroticism. After a few minutes the mouth also assumed the expression of happiness while her forehead continued to appear gloomy and wrinkled. She herself stated that the feelings which she described as uncomfortable, in certain respect were also pleasant. Thus each and every component of an expressive attitude (including voice, posture, movement of hands, feet, etc.) may be dissociated and react in contradiction to the others.

(c) *Ambivalence*

The tendency of the schizophrenic psyche to endow the most diverse psychisms with both a positive and negative indicator at one and the same time is not always quite explicit. Yet, after sufficiently long observation, one will find it to be present even in the mild cases. It is such an immediate consequence of the schizophrenic association disturbance that its complete absence appears highly improbable. It is for this reason that we include it among the fundamental symptoms.

The very same concept can be accompanied simultaneously by pleasant and unpleasant feelings (*affective ambivalence*): the husband both loves and hates his wife. The patient's hallucinations reveal to the mother the "longed-for" death of the child by the unloved husband. She breaks out in endless sobbing and moaning. She suffers the most intense anxiety that they are going to shoot her and yet she constantly begs the attendant to shoot her. She claims there is a black man outside her room. Then she breaks into a startling confusion of tearful demands, complaints and violence, demanding that she be kept in the hospital and permitted to join the black man. She verbigerates, "You devil, you angel, you devil, you angel." (She is referring here to her lover.)

In *ambivalence of will* ("*Ambi-Tendenz*"), the patient wishes to eat and does not wish to eat. He starts to bring the spoon to his mouth dozens of times but never completes the act, or makes some other useless movement. He clamors for his release and then resists with much cursing when he is informed that he will be discharged from the institution. He demands work, only to become furious when something is given him to do, and cannot decide to do the work. One patient, during one of his first attacks of illness, was bitterly conscience-stricken because once, in his youth, he had committed fellatio on a young boy. Yet in later years he persistently, and with crude violence attempts to commit fellatio on other patients. The "voices" advise him to drown himself and in the very same sentence, much to his surprise they scornfully berate him for wishing to drown himself.

It is *intellectual ambivalence* when a patient says in the same breath: "I am Dr. H.; I am not Dr. H.;" or "I am a human being like yourself, even though I am not a human being" (Foersterling). Quite frequently we hear such statements, and often indeed without the same words used in the second sentence being given another meaning than they had in the first. (Possibly, this kind of obscurity of thought obtained in Foersterling's patient.)

A philosophically educated catatonic made the following observation himself: "When one expresses a thought, one always sees the counter-thought. This intensifies itself and becomes so rapid that one doesn't really know which was the first." A less sophisticated patient, whom I had made aware of the fact that in reply to a very friendly letter from his wife he had written her a farewell letter stated: "I could have just as well written another letter; to say good-day or to say good-bye; it is all the same."

One can easily demonstrate that the patients do not note contradictions when we take their negative answers for positive ones. I asked a patient: "Do you hear 'voices'?" He definitely denied it. I continued: "What do they say to you?" "Oh, all sorts of things." He may even offer an example of what they say. More often it is obvious from the speech and behavior of the patients that they think a thought and its converse simultaneously, though it may not always be as conspicuous as in the following sentence: "She had no handkerchief; she choked it with the handkerchief." The expression of an idea by its opposite falls into the same category: a patient complains that the master-key to the wards was taken away from him, whereas he really wants that the key be given to him. In Schreber's "special language," "reward" means "punishment," and "poison" means "food," etc.

The three forms of ambivalence are not easily distinguished from one another as these examples illustrate. Affectivity and will are merely different facets of the same function; even the intellectual contradictions often cannot be separated from the affective. A mixture of megalomania with delusions of persecution and inferiority may result from wishes and fears, or from assertion and denial of one's own stature. The patient is especially powerful and at the same time powerless; the beloved or the protector becomes just as easily the persecutor without surrendering his previous role. It is more exceptional for the enemy to become the friend and ally. A Catholic paranoid patient had joined the Old-Catholic sect. He claimed to be persecuted by the Pope who nevertheless wanted to shower the patient with millions of dollars. Similarly, many patients complain about persecution but really believe that the persecution serves for their education, improvement, and as a preliminary step to their elevation to some higher rank or station.

Mixed ambivalence in somewhat different form is shown to be present in the following examples. A patient praises and berates her husband, her possessions and wealth, as well as stating many more things in her negative and positive fashion. It is entirely impossible to say in which sense she really means it. A hebephrenic explains in angry tones, and with marked affect, that the time passed in the hospital was never too long but rather too brief. In this he had not made a mistake either, since shortly before he had associated "time" to the word "long." It is quite well known that patients who believe the doctor is poisoning them still cling to him, and those who are very bitter against both doctors and attendants, suddenly, almost as a sequel to their berating, pour out their grateful hearts effusively.

Ambivalence shows every gradation down to negativism, particularly in the form of "Ambitendenz." We will see later that this is of significance in the structure of delusions.

2. The Intact Simple Functions

In contrast to the organic psychoses, we find in schizophrenia, at least with our present methods of examination, that sensation, memory, consciousness and motility are not directly disturbed. A very far advanced disease process may perhaps alter even these functions; but in those patients in whom such disturbances do appear we cannot differentiate these changes from the secondary alterations which are seen at times. The anomalies we know in those areas are all secondary, and thus merely accidental phenomena. Although at times they may dominate the whole clinical picture (as for example, the hallucinations), they are to be classified as "accessory" symptoms.

In the literature we find much discussion of alterations in these functions. They are based for the most part on the misconception of the patients' negativism, indifference, and reluctance to think, and above all on their random responses. These and similar sources of error led Masselon (457, p. 115) to say that the patients are rarely able to give the year, month or day, and often do not even know the season of the year. The physician must always use indirect methods to obtain correct information concerning the actual knowledge that a patient may possess. Never must one conclude from merely negative answers that a patient does not know what is asked of him. The simple question concerning the year is very often answered incorrectly; whereas the same patient, when he has occasion to write a letter, shows himself fully oriented as to the date. A patient coming to us from prison does not "know" the year is 1899 but immediately afterwards admits that it was in 1897 that she went to prison and "remained there for two years."

Disturbances and defects are very often falsely diagnosed because the examiner and the patient do not really speak the same language. The patient takes symbolically what the physician understands in its literal sense. Thus a patient insisted that he could not see, that he was blind, while it was more than obvious that his eyesight was unimpaired. What he meant was that he did not perceive things "as reality." A female patient insisted with the greatest firmness, in answer to the question as to how long she had been in the hospital, that she had been there only three days, although she had given many proofs of her normal temporal orientation and had been in the institution for many weeks. This time-period of "three days" was for her identical with "my whole life." She herself was able to give the explanation: that the "first day" corresponded to the one in her earliest youth when she had been morally delinquent; the "second day" corresponded to that on which she had done the same thing as a grown-up young woman; the "third day" had not yet been brought to completion. This last idea was in unmistakable reference to the fact that she had transferred her love onto the resident physician. Just as often, we encounter the reverse phenomenon: a figurative phrase is taken in its literal sense by the patient.

It is especially important to know that these patients carry on a kind of "double-entry bookkeeping" in many of their relationships. They know the real state of affairs as well as the falsified one and will answer according to the circumstances with one kind or the other type of orientation—or both together. This last is especially frequent in misrecognizing people: the physician "is now here as Dr. N.," at other times he becomes the former lover.

(a) Sensation and Perception

Sensory response to external stimulus is quite normal. To be sure, the patients will complain that everything appears to be different, and frequently we can observe the absence of the "feeling of familiarity" with known things. However, this strangeness is usually attributable to a deficit in customary associations [14] and particularly to an alteration of emotional emphasis (see above), not to disturbances of sensation. Even the normal person may, under special circumstances, feel that all of a sudden certain percepts are different from the usual. We know the feel-

14. Cf. chapter on illusions.

ing of the "world having turned grey" from the melancholics. Very often it is assumed that the sensations derived from the body organs are altered in these patients and any number of complicated symptoms have been explained by this alteration. It is impossible to distinguish the patient's sensations from his hallucinations and illusions to which certainly many, if not all, of these paresthesias properly belong. In any event, one is able to show quite frequently that such sensations are a consequence of affectively charged concepts while a true primary disturbance of sensation has not yet been demonstrated with certainty.

Rosenfeld (626-7) maintained that in catatonics there is a frequent disturbance in the stereognostic sense. In spite of thorough research, I have not been able to corroborate this, and I cannot help suspecting that this author was misled by the negativism, blocking or poor cooperation of the patients. Wiersma observed prolonged after-effects of stimuli in three cases of "paranoia." But these observations were not consistent enough to warrant any definite conclusions.

Even in well oriented patients one may often observe the presence of a complete *analgesia* which includes the deeper parts of the body as well as the skin. The patients intentionally or unintentionally incur quite serious injuries, pluck out an eye, sit down on a hot stove and receive severe gluteal burns, etc. According to Alter (11, p. 252), the sensation of pain can be cancelled out by lack of attention.

We can also add that up to the present time we do not know of any primary disturbance of the capacity for perception which in our observations cannot always be sharply separated from sensation. Of course, we are not including the hallucinations and illusions. No more can we include among disturbances of perception the patient's fixation and resulting inability to tear himself loose from some one sense impression, or blocking which prevents sensations or perceptions from entering his consciousness. This latter phenomenon is fairly frequent. A hebephrenic student complained that often he could hear nothing of the lecture to which he was listening; he felt as if he had suddenly gone deaf. Another patient was suddenly unable to see, which he explained as the workings of some mysterious "influence." A catatonic woman felt "as if something struck her;" and suddenly it was as if her ears were plugged. She could hear sound only but could not make out any of the words.

Busch and Kraepelin have found in perception experiments (using the shutter and revolving drum apparatus) that schizophrenics show many more errors and particularly omissions than do the healthy. The patients' number of correct readings was decreased, although it fell within the range of normal individuals. Naturally, the acute and especially the stuporous cases show the poorest results. However, the experiments showed definitely that one was not dealing with disturbances of perception but rather with disturbances of attention and higher interest. Other factors involved are the tendency to stereotypy as well as the difficulty of differentiating concept from percept. The patients seem to have a greater feeling of certainty from their erroneous readings of the inaccurately perceived than do the healthy. Characteristically, the authors found the same disturbances in a case which they considered to be hysteric as they did in the schizophrenics.

In another book (388, II, p. 177), Kraepelin reports that very short-acting stimuli are, as a rule, perceived quite incompletely. Using accurate apparatus, we were unable to substantiate this finding. The observations of the patients' reactions to external stimuli during play, during fights, and in experiments using the shortest possible exposure of pictures, have not revealed any evidence of anomalies of conception provided the patients co-operated with good will and attention and if we could exclude such factors as negativism, lack of interest, affective splitting, clouded states, etc. Even in explicitly delirious conditions patients are able to identify the presence of certain persons from the sound of footsteps, distant coughing, etc., almost as well as the healthy.

We therefore prefer to leave the question open as to whether or not Kraepelin's results do not concern disturbances of attention, association of ideas or of other central processes. Kraepelin himself adds in his paper, "That the patients always make an unusually large number of completely false statements besides a few correct ones (in the experiments), a sign that there is an increased tendency toward arbitrary choice of random concepts."

(b) Orientation

The integration of perceptions concerning spatial and temporal orientation is quite good; even delirious schizophrenics are for the most part well oriented as to place and even to time. Nevertheless, there are often considerable secondary disturbances to be noted in these patients. Numerous hallucinations can deliver to the mind, instead of real perceptions, so many false images of the environment that a correct and proper concept is made impossible. Whoever sees a royal chamber and not the hospital ward is naturally, during such times, incapable of orienting himself correctly. Whoever, because of his complexes, wants to be eight days ahead of himself will in most connections give a date much later than the real one. Whoever wants to be with Jesus when He was on this earth can give his correct age and birthdate only if he can disregard this delusion. Therefore, he will at times answer correctly and at other times incorrectly, according to the constellation present in his mind at the moment. Nowhere does the "double-entry bookkeeping" stand out more prominently than in orientation. A patient, who for years speaks almost nothing but word-salad and acts accordingly, may nevertheless be perfectly capable of registering everything that goes on around him, even to the very day and hour.

The orientation as to the general situation, the recognition of one's own relations to one's neighbors and their strivings and doings results from rather complex reasoning processes which our patients often cannot perform, partly as a result of disturbance of association and partly as a consequence of their delusions. Whoever cannot draw on his associations in order to carry on his logical operations so as to be able to know his exact relations to his superiors certainly cannot attain a clear picture of his personal position. Whoever believes that he was incarcerated in the hospital through the intrigues of hidden enemies cannot estimate that it is best for him that he should remain in the institution. Thus we find that orientation as to his own situation is so often disturbed in the schizophrenic; in hospital patients it is almost always so. *However, there is no primary disturbance of orientation in time and space.*

(c) *Memory*

Memory as such does not suffer in this disease. The patients are able to recall, as well as any healthy person, their experiences and the events of the time before and during their illness—in many instances the latter much better than the healthy since they can register things almost like a camera which fixes the unessential equally as well as the important. Thus they often are able to give many more details than a normal person would be able to relate, a fact which is of decided advantage in giving testimony (as a witness) as to events occurring in the hospital. Even dates, and similar facts are retained by the patients with astonishing tenacity. Especially, many paranoids are able to give exact dates for the events reported in their long-winded petitions. "I know cases of paranoia in whom the peculiar alteration of memory is most striking. It is almost a kind of hyperfunction (hypermnesia). These paranoiacs can remember the most insignificant details of long past events." [15]

The gradual waning of memories, of course, also affects our patients. Many a thing learned in school is gradually lost with time. When one compares this, however, with what the normal person forgets, for example, of his high school learning, it is really often astonishing how much is still preserved in the memory of our patients. Even bodily skills which, according to the customary view, require some exercise of muscle and

15. Berze (58, p. 443) who classifies our paranoids under paranoia.

joints, can suddenly be employed again after a period of many years as if they had been kept in continuous practice. A catatonic who, one might say, had hardly made a normal movement for thirty years, and for many a year had not touched the piano, can suddenly play some technically difficult piece of music correctly and expressively.

Yet we read almost daily in case-histories that "forgetfulness" was the first or one of the first of the important symptoms of the illness; and the patients themselves often complain about their memory. Even such observers as Masselon (457, p. 105) find that "memory" is weakened in dementia praecox. This author even goes so far as to say he has found that memory is poor for complicated things and good for the simple (p. 117). Also, Ziehen finds in all his cases of "defects" a weakness of memory to be present, although not as significant in the "secondary dementias" as in the paretic cases.[16]

The apparent contradiction is very easily explained. The registration of experience-material and the preservation of the memory-pictures is precisely what is very good in the schizophrenic. However, the reproduction of past experience may be disturbed at any given moment. This is quite obvious considering the fact that this reproductive effort must pass along the path of the associations which are themselves influenced by the affectivity. Precisely these two functions are so badly disturbed in schizophrenia.

The blocking of the recall of memories is a common occurrence during the examination of patients, and above all hinders the recall of those memories which are connected with emotionally accentuated complexes. This "derailment" of association accounts for the great number of false answers; the lack of interest and particularly the negativistic tendencies prevent proper consideration of the questions, and thus favor haphazard or "approximate" answers.

Thus it is quite understandable that in questioning schizophrenics we so very often get no answers at all or only false ones. Whether the response demands memory or reflection, the result is as a rule nearly the same. The patients respond as incorrectly, even when they are supposed to discuss a topical matter. From all this we see that we would be quite wrong to identify memory as the source of the disturbance. Naturally,

---

16. It would seem self-evident that an idiot can retain in his memory as little of a conversation that he does not understand, as I would of a Chinese opera. Nevertheless, there are many mental defectives who can retain in memory more non-comprehended details (the multiplication table, entire sermons, etc.) than can most normal people. They even have the capacity of reproducing events they understood with the greatest accuracy after many decades, despite the fact that they are barely able to speak. I consider an examination to be a proper memory-test only if it is as independent as possible of all other disturbances, such as the ability to understand in a mental defective, blocking, lack of interest or sluggishness of thinking in schizophrenics.

the more complex and less practiced functions will be more easily disturbed than the simple and commonly used ones. Thus, Masselon is right in certain respects. However, when we consider the numerical relation between the failure of simple and more complex operations, we must conclude that both, the simple and complex psychic activities, are equally affected by the pathological process. The influence of the disease on the higher functions is merely more apparent, exactly as the normal waning of memory has less effect on recollections of the place where we went to school than on remembering what we learned in school, for instance about the events in the life of Alexander the Great.

As far as our present knowledge goes, we can say that memory as such is not disturbed in simple schizophrenia. However, the capacity for associative recall of memory images is certainly altered. But in general this is secondary to the disturbances of all associative and affective processes and holds only for specific constellations.

Thus it may come about that patients appear forgetful, that they often cannot recall the simplest things, that something which they were just going to do "slips their mind," or even that like senile patients, they will repeatedly ask the selfsame question in the same company. Above all, however, it is important to note that at times these patients "forget," and at other times they "know" the same fact according to the circumstances involved. Of course, memory disturbances may also be caused by other psychic factors. Frequently a patient may give excellent and accurate information about the period preceding his illness, whereas the description of the period of his illness is obscure and long-winded so that it becomes impossible to comprehend what he says. The reason for this may be that the psychic experiences of the disease can hardly be expressed in the language of everyday speech. A further contributing factor may be the circumstance that the experiences during the disease appear to be devoid of ordinary logical connections so that both, patient and observer, even when the experiences are accurately reproduced, believe to be faced with a confused train of thought. The frequent amnesias and paramnesias belong to the accessory symptoms of this disease.

Busch conducted reading experiments with schizophrenics using a shutter-apparatus. He noted the striking fact that an interval of ten seconds between perception and reproduction, which improved the results in the normal person, only serves to make the results far worse in schizophrenics—and the poor results are still present even if the interval is lengthened to thirty seconds. Apparently this phenomenon is more closely related to the defective integration of impressions in the schizophrenic than to what we call memory.

(d) Consciousness

The expression, "disturbance of consciousness" which up to a certain point coincides with the old term, "clouding of the sensorium," does not really correspond to any clear-cut concept. Orientation and memory make up an essential part of consciousness in this sense.[17] "Consciousness of time" and "consciousness of place" are nothing but orientation in time and in space. Usually anomalies of consciousness ("clouding of sensorium") coincide with a primary disturbance in the integration of sense-impressions into a consistent concept of time and place, as well as with an alteration of feeling and perception. The sensory stimuli are for the most part (never all of them) hardly grasped at all or transformed in an illusionary manner. That is why the psyche creates from within an entirely personal world which is then projected outwards. We speak then of "*Dämmerzustände*" (twilight states).

Therefore, consciousness (in the sense that the patient has lost all sensory connections and relations with the environment) is not altered in the chronic conditions of schizophrenia. In this respect the schizophrenics behave as do the healthy. On the other hand, there are a great many acute syndromes which are analogous to hysterical twilight states and marked confusional conditions of varied etiology. Furthermore, the permanent symptom of autism (see following chapter) can, in a certain sense, also be termed a disturbance of consciousness.

---

17. Consciousness primarily refers to the (not easily describable) mental property which differentiates "the feeling" creature from the automaton. This consciousness may be present or absent; the latter condition does not appear in psychotic states but is present in coma or deeper syncopes. There is no disturbance of consciousness in the sense of a "para-function" (dysfunction). One can consider consciousness to be markedly altered as far as quantitative relations are concerned since at any given moment many or few mental processes may become consciously known and since these processes, in order to become conscious to us, must acquire a more or less sufficient degree of intensity. Such concepts do not seem to carry us very far, however. The "consciousness" of a dreamer or that of an intelligent epileptic in a "twilight state" is certainly far richer in content than that of a mental defective. Yet we call the first, "clouded," and the second normal. As far as the question of the necessary intensity of the stimulus is concerned, a very minimal stimulus, which would hardly be noticed in a normal state, may very easily become conscious in a twilight state. (Hysterical twilight states!) Also, the internal stimuli during the twilight states are generally very conscious to the patient, without giving us any reason to assume that they are of special intensity. Indeed, we really know very little about the dynamics of psychic processes. The word "consciousness" assumes a very different meaning when we speak of "disturbed consciousness" in cases showing incomplete orientation and insufficient rapport with the outside world. There are even people who speak of disturbed consciousness when delusions appear on the scene. Often also the subsequent memory serves as an indicator of the presence of consciousness at a certain moment. It is quite clear that such concepts are not very fruitful. Equally unfortunate is the concept of "self-consciousness," which generates much confusion. Whoever is conscious never confuses himself with the external world; he must possess "consciousness of self or self-consciousness" in the psychologist's sense. Therefore the self-consciousness cannot very well be altered. If we understand by this term the concept of our own personality, then we would much prefer to employ this latter and clearer term for the phenomenon.

(e) Motility

As far as our present-day researches have taken us, motility appears to be altered only in an accessory way (catalepsy, etc.). According to the circumstances, the patients are quite nimble; the psycho-motor aspect of speech reveals nothing abnormal; handwriting appears just as little affected as speech.[18] Even such delicate and refined movements as violin-playing do not appear to be disturbed. Certainly a completely satisfactory performance is rare but this is due to musical and emotional complications.

B. The Compound Functions

The complex functions which result from the coordinated operations of the functions previously discussed, such as attention, intelligence, will, and action, are, of course, disturbed to the extent that the elementary (simple) functions on which they depend are altered. Only association and affectivity have to be considered here. However, schizophrenia is characterized by a very peculiar alteration of the relation between the patient's inner life and the external world. The inner life assumes pathological predominance (autism).

(a) Relation to Reality: Autism

The most severe schizophrenics, who have no more contact with the outside world, live in a world of their own. They have encased themselves with their desires and wishes (which they consider fulfilled) or occupy themselves with the trials and tribulations of their persecutory ideas; they have cut themselves off as much as possible from any contact with the external world.

This detachment from reality, together with the relative and absolute predominance of the inner life, we term autism.[19]

---

18. Cf. accessory anomalies of writing, p. 147.

19. Autism nearly coincides with what Freud has termed auto-erotism. Since, however, for this author the concepts of libido and erotism are so much broader than for other schools of thought, his term cannot very well be used here without giving rise to many misunderstandings. In essence the term, autism, designates in a positive way the same concept that P. Janet (321) formulated negatively as "the loss of the sense of reality." However, we cannot accept Janet's term without discussion because he understands this symptom in a far too general sense. The sense of reality is not entirely lacking in the schizophrenic. It fails only in relation to matters threatening to contradict his complexes. Our relatively advanced hospital cases can very correctly comprehend and retain such experiences and events which are irrelevant to their complexes. These patients can give detailed anamneses which turn out to be quite correct. In short, they show daily that they have not lost their sense of reality, but that this capacity is inhibited or falsified in certain connections. The very same patient who for years never seemed to bother about his family can, when he is anxious to escape from his persecutors in the hospital, suddenly come up with a number of perfectly correct and valid reasons why he is so badly needed at home. However, this does not prevent him from *not* drawing the other consequences of his deliberations. If he were really discharged from the hospital, or if easy conditions for release were offered to him, it would never occur to him to do anything to realize his "longing" for his family.

In less severe cases, the affective and logical significance of reality is only somewhat damaged. The patients are still able to move about in the external world but neither evidence nor logic have any influence on their hopes and delusions. Everything which is in contradiction to their complexes simply does not exist for their thinking or feeling.

An intelligent lady who for many years was mistaken for a neurasthenic "had built a wall around herself so closely confining that she often felt as if she actually were in a chimney." An otherwise socially acceptable woman patient sings at a concert, but unfortunately once started she cannot stop. The audience begins to whistle and hoot and create a disturbance; she does not bother a bit, but continues singing and feels quite satisfied when she finally ends. A well-educated young woman, whose illness is hardly noticeable suddenly moves her bowels before a whole social gathering and cannot comprehend the embarrassment which she causes among her friends. During the course of about ten years, a patient gave me from time to time a note on which the same four words were always written and which signified that he had been unjustly incarcerated. It did not make any difference to him if he handed me a half-dozen of these notes at the same time. He did not understand the senselessness of his action when one discussed it with him. Withal, this patient showed good judgment about other patients and worked independently in his ward. Very frequently schizophrenics will give us numerous letters without expecting any answer; or they will ask us a dozen questions one after the other without even giving us time to answer. They predict an event for a certain day, but are so little bothered when the prophecy does not come to pass that they do not even seek to find explanations. Even where reality has apparently become identical with the patient's pathological creations, it will often be ignored.

The wishes and desires of many patients revolve around their release from the hospital. Yet they remain indifferent to the actual discharge. One of our patients who has a marked complex about children made an attempt to murder his wife because she only bore him four children in ten years. Yet he is quite indifferent to the children themselves. Other patients are in love with someone. If this person is actually present, he makes no impression on them at all; if he dies, they do not care. One patient constantly begs to be given the key to the door of his ward. When it is finally given to him, he does not know what to do with it and returns it almost at once. He tries a thousand times each day to open the door. If it is left unlocked, he becomes embarrassed and does not know what to do. He continuously pursues the doctor at each of his visits with the words: "Please, Doctor." Asked what he desires, he appears surprised and has nothing further to say. A woman patient asked to see her doctor. When she was summoned to the interview, she at least was able after a few minutes of perplexity to make her wishes known by pointing to his wedding ring. For weeks on end, a mother exerts every means at her command to see her child. When permission is granted her, she prefers to have a glass of wine. For years a woman longs for a divorce from her husband. When at long last she gets her divorce, she refuses to believe in it at all, and becomes furious if she is not addressed by her husband's name. Many a patient consumes himself with anxiety over his imminent death but will not take the least precaution for his self-preservation and remains totally unmoved in the face of real danger to his life.

Autism is not always to be detected at the very first glance. Initially the behavior of many patients betrays nothing remarkable. It is only on prolonged observation that one sees how much they always seek their own way, and how very little they permit their environment to influence them. Even severe chronic patients show quite good contact with their environment with regard to indifferent, everyday affairs. They chatter, participate in games, seek out stimulation—but they are always selective. They keep their complexes to themselves, never saying a word about them and not wishing to have them touched upon in any way from the outside.

Thus the indifference of patients toward what would be considered their nearest and dearest interest becomes understandable. Other things are of far greater importance to them. They do not react any more to influences from the outside. They appear "stuporous" even where no other disturbance inhibits their will or actions. The external world must often appear to them as rather hostile since it tends to disturb them in their fantasies. However, there are also cases where the shutting off from the outside world is caused by contrary reasons. Particularly in the beginning of their illness, these patients quite consciously shun any contact with reality because their affects are so powerful that they must avoid everything which might arouse their emotions. The apathy toward the outer world is then a secondary one springing from a hypertrophied sensitivity.

Autism is also manifested by many patients externally. (Naturally, this is, as a rule, unintentional.) Not only do they not concern themselves with anything around them, but they sit around with faces constantly averted, looking at a blank wall; or they shut off their sensory portals by drawing a skirt or bed clothes over their heads. Indeed, formerly, when the patients were mostly abandoned to their own devices, they could often be found in bent-over, squatting positions, an indication that they were trying to restrict as much as possible of the sensory surface area of their skin.

Misunderstandings stemming from the autistic thought processes can hardly ever, or only with great difficulty, be corrected by the patients.

A hebephrenic lies on a bench in a thoroughly vile mood. As she catches sight of me, she attempts to sit up. I beg her not to disturb herself. She answers in an irritated tone that if she could sit up she would not be lying down, apparently imagining that I was reproaching her for lying on the bench. Several times, using different words, I repeat the suggestion that she remain lying quietly as she was. She merely becomes more and more irritated. Everything I say is interpreted falsely by her in the sense and direction of her autistic train of thought.

The autistic world has as much reality for the patient as the true one, but his is a different kind of reality. Frequently, they cannot keep the two kinds of reality separated from each other even though they can make the distinction in principle. A patient heard us speaking of a certain Dr. N. Immediately afterwards he asks whether it was a hallucination or whether we had spoken of a Dr. N.—Busch (doing reading experiments) has demonstrated the very poor ability of patients to differentiate between idea and perception.

The reality of the autistic world may also seem more valid than that of reality itself; the patients then hold their fantasy world for the real, reality for an illusion. They no longer believe in the evidence of their own senses. Schreber described his attendants as "miracled up, changeable individuals." The patient may be very aware that other people judge the environment differently. He also knows that he himself sees it in that form but it is not *real* to him. "They say, that you are the doctor, but I don't know it," or even, "But you are really Minister N." To a considerable extent, reality is transformed through illusions and largely replaced by hallucinations (twilight states, *Dämmerzustände*).

In the usual hallucinatory conditions, more validity is, as a rule, ascribed to the illusions; yet the patients continue to act and orient themselves in accordance with reality. Many of them, however, no longer act at all, not even in accordance with their autistic thinking. This may occur in stuporous conditions, or the autism itself may reach such a high degree of intensity, that the patients' actions lose all relation to the blocked-off reality. The sick person deals with the real world as little as the normal person deals with his dreams. Frequently both disturbances, the stuporous immobility and the exclusion of reality, occur simultaneously.

Patients who show no clouding of consciousness often appear much less autistic than they really are because they are able to suppress their autistic thoughts or, like certain hysterics, seem to be occupied with them only in a theoretical way, and ordinarily allow them only very little influence upon their actions. These patients rarely remain under our observation for very long because we are inclined to discharge them as improved or cured.[20]

A complete and constant exclusion of the external world appears, if at all, only in the most severe degree of stupor. In milder cases the real and the autistic worlds exist not only side by side, but often become entangled with one another in the most illogical manner. The doctor is at one moment not only the hospital-physician and at another the shoemaker S., but he is both in the same thought-content of the patient. A patient who was still fairly well-mannered and capable of work, made herself a rag-doll which she considered to be the child of her imaginary lover. When this "lover" of hers made a trip to Berlin, she wanted to send "the child" after him, as a precautionary measure. But she first went to the police, to ask whether it would be considered as illegal to send "the child" as luggage instead of on a passenger ticket.

Wishes and fears constitute the contents of autistic thinking. In those rare cases where the contradictions to reality are not felt at all, it is the wishes alone which are involved; fears appear when the patient senses the obstacles to the fulfillment of his wishes. Even where no true delusions arise autism is demonstrable in the patients' inability to cope with reality, in their inappropriate reactions to outside influences (irritability), and in their lack of resistance to every and any idea and urge

In the same way as autistic feeling is detached from reality, autistic thinking obeys its own special laws. To be sure, autistic thinking makes use of the customary logical connections insofar as they are suitable but it is in no way bound to such logical laws. Autistic thinking is directed by affective needs; the patient thinks in symbols, in analogies, in fragmentary concepts, in accidental connections. Should the same patient turn back to reality he may be able to think sharply and logically.

Thus we have to distinguish between realistic and autistic thinking which exist side by side in the same patient. In realistic thinking the patient orients himself quite well in time and space. He adjusts his actions to reality insofar as they appear normal. The autistic thinking is the source of the delusions, of the crude offenses against logic and propriety, and all the other pathological symptoms. The two forms of thought are often fairly well separated so that the patient is able at times to think completely autistically and at other times completely normally.

20. The very common preoccupation of young hebephrenics with the "deepest questions" is nothing but an autistic manifestation. The "questions" about which they are so concerned are those that cannot be decided because reality has no part in them. Freud considers doubt and uncertainty as a preliminary stage of what he calls auto-erotism. (cf. *Jahrbuch für Psychoanalyse,* Vol. 1, p. 410.)

In other cases the two forms mix, going on to complete fusion, as we saw in the cases cited above.

The patient need not become conscious of the peculiarity, of the deviation of his autistic thinking from his previous realistic type of thinking. However, the more intelligent patients may for years gauge the difference. They experience the autistic state as painful; only rarely as pleasurable. They complain that reality seems different from what it was before. Things and people are no longer what they are supposed to be. They are changed, strange, no longer have any relationship to the patient. A released patient described it, "as if she were running around in an open grave, so strange did the world appear." Another "had started to think herself into an entirely different life. By comparison, everything was quite different; even her sweetheart was not the way she had imagined him." A still very intelligent woman patient considered it a change for the better that, at will, she could transpose herself into a state of the greatest (sexual and religious) bliss. She even wanted to give us instructions to enable us to do likewise.

Autism must not be confused with "the unconscious." Both autistic, and realistic thinking can be conscious as well as unconscious.

(*b*) *Attention*

As a partial phenomenon of affectivity (74) attention is affected with it by deterioration. Insofar as interests are extant—in milder cases this means for the majority of events, in severe cases at least for the emotionally charged activity (such as the working out of plans for escape)—attention appears to be normal at least according to our present methods of observation. However, where affect is lacking, there will also be lacking the drive to pursue the external and internal processes, to direct the path of the senses and the thoughts; i.e. active attention will be lacking.

Passive attention is altered in an entirely different manner. On the one hand it is evident that the uninterested or autistically encapsulated patients pay very little attention to the outer world. On the other hand, however, it is remarkable how many of the events which the patients seem to ignore are registered nevertheless. The selectivity which normal attention ordinarily exercises among the sensory impressions can be reduced to zero so that almost everything is recorded that reaches the senses. Thus, the facilitating as well as the inhibiting properties of attention are equally disturbed.

Events on the ward which did in no way refer to the patients, newspaper reports which they heard only in passing, can be reproduced after years in every detail by patients who appeared completely absorbed in themselves, who always sat gazing into some corner, so that one can hardly understand how these people managed to learn of these matters. One of our catatonics, who for months on end had been constantly occupied with pantomiming toward the wall, showed after some improvement that she was fully familiar with what had happened in the Boer War during the period of her illness. She must have snatched single remarks from her demented environment and preserved them in an orderly fashion. Another patient, who for many years had not uttered one reasonable word, had never carried out a sensible action (not even fed herself), knew the name of the new Pope a number of years after his investiture, although she herself had always lived in a Protestant environment where no reference was ever made to Rome.

The tenacity and vigility of attention can be altered independently of each other in both a positive as well as a negative sense, but there is nothing characteristically schizophrenic about the disturbances. (A part of the concept of vigility coincides with that of distractability.) Indeed, there are specific inner disturbances which give rise to a condition of hypovigility, as for example when "thoughts are withdrawn." On the other hand, if the train of thought loses itself in deviations tenacity is no longer extant.

The extent of the span of attention is variable; it may be quite normal. On the other hand, the intensity of attention can be so disturbed that the patient can hardly concentrate, even though he makes a very special effort to do so. In that event, the extensity of attention suffers as well. The patient is then incapable of drawing on all the associations necessary for proper reflection. Such disturbances may be conditioned by primary obstacles in the psychic processes which are as yet unknown to us. However, apart from the affects the success of attention is mostly dependent on association disturbances. If the train of thought has disintegrated entirely, correct thinking becomes impossible without abnormally intensive efforts.

The general tendency to fatigue in some cases also causes the rapid dwindling of attention. Most chronic patients, however, show a normal or even hypernormal capacity to maintain the span of attention whenever it is possible to engage their active attention.

Preoccupation due to complexes, blockings, inhibitions, often prevents the patients continuously or momentarily from following a definite chain of thought or from thinking in a desired direction. Thus, many can only follow in a very fragmented way the story they are reading or the dramatic performance they are watching. Others can relate to perfection what was heard or seen, even though throughout the entire time of their listening, they were constantly in conversation with their "voices." *Even attention can be "split."* Very often the attention, like the other functions, is blocked: the patients, in the midst of a conversation or while working, appear to be following another train of thought or not to be thinking at all. Peculiarly, in either case, they can continue to think with full knowledge of what went on during the period of inattention; and for example, later answer a question which seemed not to have been comprehended at the time.

Many catatonics demonstrate a compulsion to direct their attention to specific external or preferably internal activities. The hallucinations, in particular, often seem to compel continuous attention against the patient's will.

The state of attention in cloudy states, in dream-like and hallucinatory conditions, is not considered here because on the one hand it is difficult to describe, and on the other it is not under discussion.

(c) Will

The will, a resultant of all the various affective and associative processes, is of course disturbed in a number of ways, but above all by the breakdown of the emotions. Even mild cases frequently come into conflict with their environment because of their abulia. The patients appear lazy and negligent because they no longer have the urge to do anything either of their own initiative or at the bidding of another. They can spend years in bed. In mild cases, where wishes and desires still exist, they will nevertheless do nothing toward the realization of these wishes. However, we also see the opposite form of weakness of will which consists in the patient's inability to withstand impulses coming from within or from without. Whatever desire, whatever notion strikes their fancy, many of them proceed to carry out at once. Some do this because they do not consider the possible consequences; others have full insight into these same consequences but totally lack resistance, or are indifferent to the consequences. In a state of affect they are thus capable of anything, even of committing serious crimes.

However, under certain conditions, one may even see what can well be termed hyperbulia. There are patients who carry out with the greatest energy whatever they may have taken into their heads to do, whether it be something reasonable or something senseless. They can be utterly ruthless even towards themselves, exert themselves to the utmost, bear pain and hardships of every kind, and will allow nothing to distract them from their purpose. In such instances they can show a perseverance which can be maintained for years under certain conditions.

On the other hand, we often see the combination, found frequently in normal people, of weakness of will with stubbornness in which one or the other prevails, depending on the circumstances.[21] In general, most of the patients evidence peevishness, capriciousness and vacillation. They will make all sorts of promises without keeping any. Hospital patients, for example, may ask for work but on being assigned a task prove unable to cope with it. Likewise their threats usually remain unfulfilled.

In the sphere of will, blocking is particularly striking. Frequently a patient really wants to do something but is unable to carry it out because his psychomotor apparatus fails him. Persistent blockings of will then constitute a form of catatonic stupor. Under different circumstances, compulsive or automatic acts and the various forms of command-automatism may occur. These matters will be discussed in the chapter on catatonic symptoms.

(d) *The Person*

The auto-psychic orientation is usually quite normal. The patients know who they are in so far as delusions do not falsify the person. But the ego is never entirely intact. Certain modifications reveal themselves regularly, especially the tendency to "splitting." However, these disturbances are not sufficiently explicit in the simpler cases to lend themselves well to description. Therefore, they will be described in more detail under the accessory symptom complexes.

(e) *Schizophrenic "Dementia"*

The schizophrenic disorder of intelligence is really most clearly characterized by the state of the associations and of the affectivity. No description of the resultants of these functions could ever do adequate justice to their endless variety. Therefore, we can only hope to illustrate the most important trends that this disturbance takes by means of random examples. Here we propose to discuss only the true schizophrenic dementia, not the special coloring it takes on through the accessory symptoms.

In no other disease is the disturbance of intelligence more inadequately designated by the terms "dementia" and "imbecility" than in schizophrenia. We see absolutely nothing in this disease of "definitive loss of memory images" or other memory disturbances which properly belong to the concept of dementia. Thus some psychiatrists are able to maintain that even the severest schizophrenics are not demented; others, mostly French authorities, feel the need to separate this disorder of in-

---

21. We use "weakness of will" here in the sense of a lack of strength of drive (= apathy) as well as of a lack of tenacity and unity of will (= flightiness, capriciousness), and of a defect of inhibition.

tellect under the term of "pseudo-dementia" from the other types.

Dementia, in the sense of the organic psychoses, is something fundamentally different. Equally different are the manifold forms of congenital idiocy even though the defective intellectual attainments in these various kinds of disorder may ultimately give an externally similar result, leading to inadequate reactions to the external world. In other words, the concept "dementia" is nearly as broad as that of mental disease in general, and contains nearly as many subdivisions as does the latter.[22]

It is of prime importance to establish that even in a very severe degree of schizophrenia all the fundamental functions that are accessible to present tests are preserved. In mental deficiency complicated connections of ideas and associations are never formed; in organic cases much has been lost, if not by actual brain-damage at least by the very poor utilization of the psyches. In contrast, even the most demented schizophrenic can under proper conditions suddenly demonstrate productions of a rather highly integrated type (cunning attempts at escape, etc.) Aside from the pronounced lack of interest and activity, the severe schizophrenic dementia is characterized by the fact that in all thinking and acting there occurs a large number of mistakes ("Fehlleistungen"); the relative difficulty of the task is of secondary importance. Conversely, in the mildest cases the dementia is characterized by the fact that, though these people are usually quite sensible, they are also capable of every possible stupidity and foolishness. The mild paretic or mental defective demonstrates his ineptitude when reflections are necessitated which, for him, are too complicated. In simpler situations he behaves normally. In such patients, the degree of dementia can be gauged by the extent of the possible accomplishments, and even then only by careful testing which takes into consideration the total constellation, mood, fatigue, individual peculiarities, etc. Patients who are incapable of doing multiplication are even less apt to do division; those who cannot get the point of a fable will not understand a novel; on the other hand, whoever can understand the whole context of a novel should find no difficulties in grasping a simple story. It is quite different in schizophrenia. A patient who at a certain moment cannot add 17 and 14, even when he earnestly tries, will suddenly be able to solve a difficult arithmetical problem or to give a well-composed and successful speech. A schizophrenic can estimate with excellent judgment the behavior, the pathology and the

22. How obscure the concept of dementia really is, is best illustrated by the discussion and controversy concerning the presence of dementia in paranoia. Some consider the paranoiacs to be demented because they think and act in such an illogical fashion; others insist they are not demented because they can still very ably exercise such professions as judges, architects, and teachers.

expediency of the therapeutic measures applied to his ward-mates. But at the same time he is unable to understand that he cannot possibly maintain himself outside the hospital since he causes a row each night and beats up his neighbors.

A patient may have sat around for years in a demented euphoria, uttering nothing but the most banal phrases; then all of a sudden he may take part in every kind of work and appear recovered in every respect. Therefore, the external picture of schizophrenic dementia is characterized much more by the state of affectivity and, in particular, by interest and spontaneity, than by the intellectual disturbance in the narrower sense. The latter is essentially a numerical concept and cannot be graded in accordance with the degree of possible attainments but only according to the ratio of correct to incorrect performances.

Thus, it is wrong in every respect to compare the dementia of schizophrenics with the intelligence of a child of a certain age. (Rizor, p. 1027.) It shows a complete misunderstanding of the peculiarities of schizophrenia if one believes that schizophrenic dementia can be proved or excluded by means of an "intelligence test," whether it be one which takes but a few minutes or several days to perform. The actual amount of knowledge remains preserved on the whole but it is not always available or it is employed in the wrong way. What may be inaccessible in one constellation of the psyche, may be freely utilized in another. That is why the Ebbinghaus completion experiments, as well as the Heilbronner (293a) picture-tests frequently fail and are not at all applicable in this disease precisely when we desire to estimate the degree of intelligence.[23] The habits of life, the lack of adaptation to the environment only can show in the milder cases how far the dementia has progressed. In the hospital the quickest way is to use a brief test consisting of questioning the patient about his present situation, the reasons for his confinement, his relations to his superiors and those in charge, and about his future plans. Even then there may be complete understanding and comprehension present, although very severe defects are to be noted in other spheres.

Therefore, if one wishes to speak of intellectual dementia in our patients, one must express oneself approximately as follows: the schizophrenic is *not* generally demented but he is demented with regard to certain periods, to certain constellations, and to certain complexes. In mild cases, the defective functions are the exception. In most severe

23. Indeed, many of these patients need abnormally long periods of time for correct solutions, while many of the more severe cases are not capable of solving such problems at all. They fill the gaps with inappropriate or even completely false words disregarding meaning, as well as grammatical structure.

cases, those who sit around in our mental institutions taking no part in anything, the defective functions are the rule. And in between we find every transitional form. The difference between moderate and severe dementia is an extensive, not an intensive one. The mildest case of schizophrenia can commit as great a piece of folly as the most severe, but he commits it far more rarely.

Nevertheless, the intellectual defect does occur not entirely haphazardly. The particularly poor intellectual performances are, for example, tied up with emotionally toned complexes. Furthermore, it is self-evident that in each stage of the disease alterations of intellectual functions will increase with the complexity of the specific function. When on an average one out of one hundred associations is pathological, then the function which involves merely a few associations will only rarely be disturbed, while the one which involves several hundreds of individual functions is almost always disturbed. In addition, in schizophrenics the capacity for condensation of many ideas under one unified logical viewpoint is evidently rendered more difficult, which in turn impairs the complex functions more than the simple functions. Thus, on the whole, the higher mental functions are more severely disturbed.

The anomaly called schizophrenic dementia consists of the effects of association disturbance, indifference and irritability in the affective sphere and the autistic seclusion from the influences of the outside world. The disintegration of the associations effects the concept formation. To be sure, the majority of concepts does not seem to be much less clear cut in the permanent clinical conditions of this disease than in the healthy. For example, one sees very little of the vagueness which is so striking in the concepts of the demented epileptics, even though now and then there is a tendency to apply general ideas where specific ones would be indicated. Thus our patients call an instrument made of iron, "iron," or call a dust-pan, "a domestic utensil." Although the use of such terminology is rare except in response to explicit questions yet it reveals an anomaly of concepts and not simply of expression. I have not met with an actual schizophrenic reduction in concepts in the sense of some having been lost entirely. On the other hand, the concepts frequently lack some of their component parts. All these disturbances may fluctuate from one moment to the next. More or less consistent and constant defects are displayed only in concepts which are woven into delusions or else are composed of emotionally accentuated complexes.

Wernicke's method of asking the patient to differentiate between related ideas is therefore entirely inadequate for investigation of this disturbance, even though it is evident that, under certain circumstances, comparison and differentiation of incompletely conceived ideas must be impaired. It is highly probable that the hebephrenic (quoted on p. 41 of his clinical reports) knew quite well the difference between city and village in spite of her very bizarre answers which incidentally did not at all indicate her ignorance but were primarily a "para-functioning" of her actual associations. Just as little can I believe that Wernicke's patient, who mistook the attendant for his sister, Laura,[24] had forgotten the memory picture of male and female clothing. As a rule, lucid schizophrenics have a fairly good grasp of such ideas and memory pictures. Exceptions are noted only in definite psychic constellations, e.g., when complexes are activated, in states of distraction, and in all probability in states of organic disturbance. Thus a hebephrenic associates "wheel" to "barrel" and indicates that the ideas, "wheel" and "hoop," were really almost identical for him at the time. The same patient can later differentiate these two ideas quite well without the disease having shown any change whatsoever. Often objects are mistaken because only a part of their properties is noted (the other properties are not entirely "forgotten"), and then freely associated to form another object. A picture on a wall with a deep frame is therefore a spittoon. The fire-ladder in front of the ward becomes "our barn-ladder." The director of the psychiatric service is Reverend F., because he administers here as does Reverend F. in the hospital. The cotton mill where the patient worked is called a "clothing-factory."

By means of condensation several concepts are compressed into one. Particularly often, several persons are conceived of as one. A patient is his father and mother, and his children. During an acute, although mildly cloudy episode of his illness, another patient does not distinguish between his children as they are now and as they were as infants. When the conversation turns to sexual matters and the education of children, his wife and his own ego seem to run together into an indivisible concept; likewise he confuses the institution with his home. On questioning or other stimulation it does not make any difference of which part of this conceptual pair he or the observer are talking since he says the same things about either part and it is quite impossible to force a separation. A female patient identifies the story of Moses' childhood with that of Herodes' slaughter of the Bethlehem infants.

Often enough the emotionally toned complexes determine the transformation of concepts. Thus a patient, who expects something extraordinary to happen to her in the future, speaks of her "future parents" as if it were something entirely self-evident. An ambitious paranoid patient has seen himself portrayed as a "general in a French and Swiss uniform."

---

24. Quoted from Sandberg, p. 627.

The confusion of both armies does not seem to disturb him in the least. To the objection that Switzerland has no general, he replies that a colonel is also a general.[25] In such cases it is easy to demonstrate that not only the terms but the concepts themselves are altered. A hebephrenic signs a letter to his mother with "your hopeful nephew." How he arrived at this conclusion could not be discovered. The patient defends this nonsense with the argument that his mother did have a sister and that he was her (the sister's) nephew. However, it is certain that at least for a few moments his ideas about family relations had become obscured. A female catatonic had received a watch as a present, which gave her much pleasure. But she also found pleasure in all of her other possessions as well as in her sweetheart. All this had merged into one single concept which she designated mainly with the term "gift." The inappropriate expressions of hallucinating patients frequently conceal grossly extended concepts. A hebephrenic "had pain twice, and that is murder by poisoning."

The identification of two concepts on the basis of one common component, in many instances, leads to symbolism which plays such an outstanding role in delusions. A patient signs himself as "The Beginning and End of the World." His delusion is expressed in this phrase. For our patients the symbol is readily transposed into reality. They may come to believe in real people burning them with real fire when their secret love "burns" within them. The following ideas are somewhat similar: a catatonic makes a certain movement of his eyebrows in exact imitation of a Miss N.; then he insists that he had sexual relations with her. Miss N.'s gesture executed by his own body is equated with Miss N. herself.

The alteration of concepts in schizophrenia has the peculiarity that simple ideas can just, or almost as easily be disturbed and distorted as complex ones. The decisive element is, above all, the relation to an emotionally toned complex which, at times, facilitates and, at others, impedes conceptualizations. But aside from this, the disturbance varies with the oscillations of the disease, which at times may involve the major part of the thought processes and at other times again recede to involve only a few isolated functions.

Of course, no clear and accurate thinking operations can be carried out with fragmentary concepts.

A rather lazy patient had finally been induced to do some work for a half-hour. He then believed that he had a right to obtain all sorts of rewards. When these were not forthcoming he again stopped working. He was still correct in his thinking that he should be compensated for his work but he did not distinguish between half-an-hour of work and

---

25. Colonel is the highest rank in the peace-time Swiss army.

persistent work; and just as little did he distinguish between small and large compensation. A short bit of work was to him *work* in general. By the idea of compensation he understood anything which his heart desired. His concepts of accomplishment and recompense were unclear, therefore a correct quantitative correlation between the two ideas was impossible.

The inaccurate delimitation of concepts favors quite senseless generalizations of some ideas. A paranoid patient suddenly no longer hears the hallucinated noise of a machine; therefore the whole hospital ceases to exist for him. Another paranoid had solemnly made peace with an enemy of his; he then wanted to act as peacemaker everywhere. A hebephrenic had given his father a rude answer. He then believed that he had to purify himself for that sin. Finally, he extended this purification to everything around him. He not only washed himself and the furniture but also laid his clothes out on the roof so that the rain could clean them. Delusions proper frequently extend into such generalizations.[26]

The disturbances of affect influence the intelligence in a multiplicity of ways. When interest is lacking there is little thinking or the thinking is not carried through to its proper end. Whenever the patient has an earnest aspiration, he shows himself capable of making exceptionally sharp-witted and complex deductions to achieve his desired ends. Conversely, many paranoids think incorrectly only when their complexes are involved. Schreber could criticize the expert opinions on his tutelage most pertinently at the very time when he was defending his most preposterous delusions.

In general, the intellectual accomplishments vary with the emotionally charged complexes, which at times suppress reflection and at others make use of and favor reflection. (These functional variations are not to be mistaken for oscillations of the disease itself. A patient often appears to be much more demented at certain periods because the disease process has become more intense.)

The disturbances of affect are the most important cause of "the loss of the psychic value system" (Schuele). Mental defectives and organic cases also may lack the feeling for the difference between the essential and the unessential; the defectives because they are unable to grasp complex ideas in their totality; the organics for the same reasons and also because their chains of ideas are limited to those which correspond to the dominant affect.

The process is far more complicated in schizophrenia. Ideas are

---

26. Here the extension of the concept is at the same time a displacement; the feeling of moral uncleanliness leads, as it so frequently does in neurotics, to exaggerated physical cleanliness.

thought of in entirely haphazard fragments which frequently retain far-fetched connections and miss the closer related ones. The affects inhibit and facilitate the associations to a far larger degree than in organics, and moreover are themselves changed both qualitatively and quantitatively. If it does not make any difference to the patient whether he and his family go to rack and ruin, whether or not he remains institutionalized forever, or whether he lies in filth or not, then these ideas, so vitally important for most other people, can have no influence on the patient's reflections. If such a patient is given the choice of renouncing a whim or losing his job, he will decide for the latter course without thinking twice because only the whim is affectively charged. This is one of the most important aspects of schizophrenic dementia.

Suggestibility is also altered in conjunction with the affectivity. It is generally lowered. This impedes psychological influence from the outside but facilitates the utilization of judgment where such is still possible. In this respect, the more intelligent schizophrenics have an advantage in the carrying through of new ideas. Due to flexibility of their associations, they can more easily than the normal person conceive and comprehend ideas which deviate from the normal. But they are also more independent of the opinions of others and therefore have the mettle to carry through ideas and plans which would appear unthinkable to a healthy person. I was once consulted about a schizophrenic who at the present time is executing some highly important economic plans with governmental aid in many different foreign countries—plans (of his own invention) which a normal person might have thought up but which he would not have considered as feasible. Every new movement, good or bad, usually draws its quota of schizophrenics into its orbit.

In other cases there is a combination of superficiality of affect with the associative disturbance of thinking resulting in an exaggerated gullibility. An externally entirely lucid hebephrenic, who worked as a compositor in between attacks of illness, permitted himself to be taken to the hospital on four different occasions under the same pretense of having to go to see a doctor about some physical ailment. In complicated business transactions, the patients easily become the dupes of those who know how to take advantage of them. Hypochondriacally disposed patients can have an illness easily suggested to them merely by an injudicious question. Naturally, the tenor of the complexes determines the direction of this partial suggestibility. The condition of an intellectually well preserved patient with hypochondriacal ideas was considerably improved by us in the course of a two months treatment by means of various suggestions. But close association with a melancholic patient for only a few days was sufficient to reduce her to her former state. Paranoids can be talked by any dumbbell into believing that this or that one is their friend or enemy, yet will remain inaccessible to logical influence.

It is also amazing how easily schizophrenics react to neutral influences. I once answered a paranoid with "noi" instead of "no", using a word from the Swabian dialect which had absolutely no connection with our conversation. The patient began to imitate me immediately, using the Swabian idiom, although she herself had no closer connection with this dialect than would any other native of Zurich. She kept this up till the end of our conversation, though I gave her no further reason for it.

Both recent or old cases of schizophrenia can be hypnotized. However, the power of hypnotic suggestion does not go very far in combating this disease. Many schizophrenics can resist mass-suggestibility far better than the healthy. Still, here, too, the influence of a suggestion increases when given to a number of people simultaneously. Peculiarly, schizophrenics are also the most delicate re-agents to the *spiritus loci.* It cannot be mere accident that the external forms of this disease should vary so markedly from institution to institution, from physician to physician, from attendant to attendant. Catalepsy, negativism, hyperkinesis, violence, suicidal tendencies, necessity for tube-feeding, and restraint, all these are quantitatively very variable, according to time and place, even when the members of the administrative staff do their utmost to make the handling of the patients as uniform as possible. Also suggestion does not only come from the hospital personnel and the hospital set-up but equally as much from the other patients. A single patient can disrupt an entire ward. If someone cleverly sets the tone on the ward, then he will quickly have any number of imitators among the active schizophrenics. In one ward, for example, a certain dish of food is disliked; in another ward, it is another type of food which is detested. This will go on till the instigator of this fad is removed.

The power of suggestion also manifests itself in the induced psychoses whereby an active schizophrenic frequently will impose his delusional system on a family member who is a latent schizophrenic. A very special increase in suggestibility appears in "command-automatism" which will be discussed later under the catatonic symptoms.

Naturally the state of schizophrenic intelligence is also in a reciprocal relationship to the autism. The latter cannot arise without concomitant weakness of intelligence and thus brings about the really demented logical errors by the exclusion of reality from the material of thought.

Thus, an erotomanic, hebephrenic, young girl believes that a certain highly placed gentleman is going to marry her, whereas in reality he does not want to have anything to do with her. A hebephrenic promotes his uncle to the rank of general so that the uncle will be in a better position to help him than he is in his present rank of colonel. The association that this promotion can have absolutely no effect is simply not made. Another patient answers to the question, "Have you been in a mental hospital before?", with "No, but unjustly."

Autism is also connected with the reduced influence of experience. A burnt schizophrenic does not always fear the fire! No matter how painful the consequences, they permit themselves again and again to be misled by their distorted ideas or by their negligence. However, this does not hold good for all experiences. Often disciplinary punishments or rewards still have some influence, even on the quite severely sick patients.

Of course, the association disturbances are responsible for most of the confusion in logical thinking. Logical thinking is a reproduction of associations which are equivalent or analogous to those which experience has taught us. Through the loosening of the customary connections between concepts, thinking becomes detached from experience and takes a turn into deviant pathways. Blocking occurs precisely at the important points so that the patient is incapable of completing his thinking on certain subjects. What is worse, instead of the blocked associations, others crop up which do not belong at all to this train of thoughts or belong to another juncture of it. Thus, the story about the donkey crossing the brook first with a load of salt and then with a load of sponges may be repeated as follows: "They overloaded the donkey so much that it was crushed . . . now it is the custom in the Catholic religion . . . , it has been said that was the last rites given to the dying."

If the inappropriate idea-connections become very numerous, the train of thought cannot reach any conclusion since the direction of thinking is constantly changing.

Therefore, many logical operations fail because any one thought is immediately linked to the dominant complex (delusions of reference), or, conversely, because the patients are unable to find any connection with their complex. Therefore most direct questions about affective occurrences determining symptomatology are answered at first or persistently in the negative, or the patients evade the question. The patient has come to the institution, "because he sprained his ankle;" or (to the question, why?) "I came in a cab." These are really cases of "misdirected thinking" and not merely of "misdirected talking."

(What do the voices say?) "I also have two children." (Repeating the question), "People say so many things here." (Repeating the question again), "Not much." (Repeating.) "I do not talk much anyway." (Repeating.) "Yes, not much." (Repeating.) "Yes, I can't say it." (Why not?) "I don't know." (What do the voices say?) "Yes, we talk with each other, but I don't talk much."

This kind of thinking can be carried over to neutral topics; indeed, it can become quite generalized. The question as to what date it is can then be answered with, "The same." (The same what?) "The same date that we have today." Such types of responses can be given by perfectly lucid patients even when they make an effort to think correctly. They never get beyond such generalized phrases.

The impression of a high degree of dementia can easily be evoked by the very frequent responses of a type which may be termed "at random replies" (*In-den-Tag-hineinantworten*): (When were you born?) "1876." (Is that correct? When?) "1871." (Which is right?) "1872." (In reality none of these answers was correct.) It is particularly in questions that can be answered by a Yes or No that one must be wary of taking the response at its face value. Often we get something like this: (Do you want to get up?), "Yes." (Do you wish to stay in bed?) "Yes."

The inadequate application of necessary associations also causes a premature termination of reflections. Often, the patient will give an answer before one has completed the question, therefore, the many incomplete, "demented" judgments.

The abrupt emergence of new ideas leads to pathological notions. Suddenly a catatonic demands in all earnestness that he wants to see Niagara Falls. On his admission to the hospital, another patient found nothing more important to ask than whether the Sahara was still in Africa.

The results are particularly senseless where there is a split between the logical directives of the thought-train and the substance and content of the associations and where each of these functions goes its own independent way.

I asked a patient what a gentleman acquaintance could do for him. The answer was, "Nothing, except if I could receive a poem from him." Thus, formally, he did give me an answer to my question. The poem is named as the desired object in a perfectly correct and logical form. In truth, however, the patient picked up this idea only because shortly before I had conversed with another patient about poetry; he had no real desire for any poem. I argue with a patient as to the fact that she claims to own a house. "Yes," she answers, "the music proves it." Actually, music could be heard in the distance, and thus she obtained the idea which is immediately used as a proof against my objections.

The thought-content is often determined by some passing notion or sudden fancy; (Why do you shake hands?, "Because I can't eat any students"), or by a wish or fear which happens to preoccupy the patient.

(The patient smears "in order to get transferred to a better ward.") Then again he gets his content from the outside world (see the examples cited above); or the notion belongs to the circle of thoughts involved in the question. Thus it is not a question of motivation by the content when Stransky's patient declares that he flies into a rage because the doctor is wearing a grey suit. According to my experience the patient really becomes furious for quite different reasons which have some relationship to his complexes. He then, purely at random, mentions the grey suit, as the reason for his fury.

Such ex post-facto pseudo-motivations in which the patient himself believes are quite common in schizophrenia. One of our patients was quite aware that he always made up the motivations subsequently, "after he himself had been startled by the stupidities which he had committed." After an attempted suicide, a woman patient was brought back to bed and then insisted that she had attempted the suicide because she had to lie in bed. We have the same sort of after-the-fact justification of behavior when a very good-for-nothing hebephrenic tells us that he got into debt only in order to show his wife that he could obtain money without her assistance; or when a dangerously aggressive patient allegedly bought his revolver only to prove to his wife that he would not hurt her even though he had a revolver. In such cases, the hindsight type of justification can appear as the real reason to a superficial observer, so that often even intelligent people allow themselves to be fooled into attributing sound judgment to the patient.

It is amazing to see the indifference of the patient to his grossest contradictions. A hebephrenic can complain in the main clause that he never gets a night's sleep, while in the subordinate clause he indicates how wonderfully well he slept. Patients complain bitterly and emphatically to their relatives that they are not allowed to do something or other. As soon as they receive permission to do what they desire, they do not wish to exercise the privilege. A patient requests in a letter to his wife that firstly, she should send him his razor so that he may commit suicide; secondly, that she should come and get him out of the institution; and finally, she should bring him a pair of shoes.

Except on rare occasions, it does not help much to draw the patient's attention to the contradictions. Generally the necessity to shape things into some logical order, to reflect on them and to bring them under a common heading, is markedly reduced. At the other extreme, we have the alcoholics who liberally invent elaborations of their stories in order to round them out, and seek a causal motivation for their actions. In contrast, the schizophrenics' thinking is composed of logical fragments. Causality frequently does not seem to exist for them. Few of them are concerned with where their "voices" come from. They may remain confined to the hospital for long periods without asking the reason. This appears to be not only an affective but also a logical defect.

In certain respects, the patients lack the capacity for discussion. They think about something, and then take it for granted. As supporting evidence, they will offer sham-proofs, and the most logical counter-evidence remains utterly ineffectual.

If confronted with complicated tasks, the patients often appear so confused, their psyche so split, that it is not easy to discover the genesis of their thinking errors. Nevertheless, with some patience, it is possible even in such cases to find cues here and there.

The thinking disturbance in its various forms reveals itself in the recognition of pictures. Certainly, many patients can recognize simple and complex pictures as well as the healthy. The paranoid B. St. (described by Jung) was superior in the comprehension of pictures to the attendant personnel subjected to the same test. On the other hand, many patients are not at all, or only partially, capable of comprehending complicated pictures; or they give wrong interpretations, particularly when the pictures are in some way associated with their complexes. However, even illustrations of simple objects are mistaken.

A mildly agitated hebephrenic calls a student a "tobacco-pipe;" she pays attention only to that one detail. She calls a hammer, "Nature sperm, the hammer;" the hammer's handle is still the hammer's handle but in connection with her sexual complexes, it is also the penis. A clock becomes for her the "electrolyzer-clock" because she connects it in some way with her sexual hallucinations. Shown the picture of a pine-cone in its natural size and colors, she calls it an "ear of corn." She takes note only of its form, and even that very inadequately. Another patient calls the ears of a zebra "a hair-bow on the head," in accordance with her tendencies toward grandeur and adornment. A part-concept is indicated in the following answers: "hung" (instead of wash hanging on the line), "a heap" (instead of potatoes). Often the blocking becomes as systematized as the abnormal linkings (of ideas): (Bride?) "I don't know what;" (What are they [musicians] doing?), "Making noise." (The bride is shown again), "a woman, wearing a hat" (the nose-gay is designated as a hat). Objects such as asparagus and snakes are readily falsely designated usually in conjunction with other indications of an aroused sexuality.

Sometimes no associations at all are given to pictures shown to otherwise attentive patients. (Just as we do with thousands of things which we see as we pass along the street without paying any attention to them.)

Sometimes the narration of things experienced or read is also very characteristic. Frequently there is a difference between experiences undergone before and after onset of the illness. In the latter case, the various disturbances of comprehension may of course affect the result. Occasionally, even cooperative patients with good comprehension evidently do not assimilate something new any more. They then relate stories read in former times, in fragments, but still in proper context; whereas recently read stories are repeated inadequately. At times they also insert new ideas into the old stories. Thus, an educated hebephrenic calls William Tell a "ship's captain." Or it is too much for them to recall memories and we then get as answer to the question: "What do you know about William Tell?", such remarks as, "There has been already a good deal of discussion about the matter."

Stories which have been read [27] can be repeated perfectly and also summarized and applied in other connections by many patients who otherwise commit the grossest stupidities or are occupied with the most senseless delusions. But for the most part, hospital patients fail completely in such tasks; or the moral is deduced in the sense of their complexes, or from purely accidental associations. Thus a patient drew the moral from the test-story that one must not get frightened if faced with a difficult task.

The comprehension of a story may be impeded by blocking even for patients whose thinking is otherwise unimpeded. A usually attentive and naturally intelligent patient was unable to get a simple little tale into his head, although he strained his attention so intensely that he got red in the face, perspired and breathed heavily. "The voices interfered too much." Sometimes repeated readings help, but not always is the result improved by this means.

Some patients will relate a story entirely different from the one read, about a donkey, salt, etc. Others bring fragments of the given ideas into a new context. Thus we will hear "that a donkey wanted to drown himself." Then again disconnected fragments are reproduced, often with schizophrenic additions. "A donkey was loaded up heavily with salt and bolted—through the desert." Occasionally the patients no-

27. For various reasons, the following story was found an appropriate test for simple achievements: "The Donkey Carrying A Load of Salt." A donkey loaded with bags of salt had to wade across a river. He slipped and fell and remained lying comfortably in the cool water for a few moments. Standing up, he noticed how much lighter his load had become because the salt had dissolved in the water. Long-ears registered this advantage and decided to use it the following day when he was carrying a load of sponges across the same river. This time, he fell deliberately but was badly disappointed. The sponges had soaked up a great deal of water and were far heavier than before. Indeed, the load was so heavy that it drowned him.

"One means does not hold good in every case."

tice the disjointedness or obscurity of their own story. (After the second reading): "A donkey was carrying a load of salt and had to go through a river; then along came a sponge—I don't know, is it a sponge, or a swan—or a goose?" (Here the patient noted that a sponge cannot very well move along, and then changed the sponge into a swan).

In more severe cases, the various ideas of the stories are mixed up and then simply linked up grammatically: "A donkey waded through a stream in which there were sponges, and then the load became too heavy." Conversely, if the causal connections are especially stressed or further elaborated by means of unnecessary additions, then we are as a rule dealing with a complicating alcoholic condition. "A donkey had a load of sponges. He was thirsty and went down to the river in order to drink water. . . ."

Actual transformations of the story usually reveal themselves as results of the influence of the complexes. A woman patient who was conscience-stricken because she had not defended herself vigorously enough against an attack, was supposed to say that the axe fell into the river. But instead of "river," she said a "hole." When it was pointed out to her that it was a river, she said, "Yes, it was a hole full of water." Aside from such cases, we see remarkably little of this kind of personal reference in the reading of the fables in schizophrenia, whereas organic depressives, as a rule, refer the story of being drowned or overloaded to themselves. Also, most alcoholics find a reference to their weakness in the mention of water.

In this disease, the majority of changes appear as accidental; nevertheless they can be maintained very persistently. A hebephrenic insisted that she had just read about a "deep river;" and as the book was shown to her she insisted that the printed words had been changed in the meantime. Real fantasies hardly seem to prevail. But if they are present, they are given free play due to the lack of a sense of reality. A hebephrenic painter described the technique of painting quite accurately. Yet his own experiences, as well as stories from the Bible and William Tell were reproduced incorrectly—"as they might have occurred."

The general impediments of thinking may become obvious in sudden interruptions of the narration, and in the slow progress of the thought process. "It was a donkey." (What was he doing?) "He went through a river."(And then?) "He fell down." (And then?) "Remained lying there." (And then?) ". . . . got up." Another patient answered to the repeated, "and then?", only with single words. "Long-ears—swims—heavily loaded—raised head—wade—He stop one's ear—shake off—street to—must be beaten. . . ."

Insight into one's illness has served as a time-honored measure of intelligence, and this insight is quite characteristic in schizophrenia. As in other mental diseases, at the height of the disease insight is lacking either completely or at least partially. However, at the onset many of the patients consider themselves not only to be "nervous" but they also recognize the anomalies of thought, the abulia and many other symptoms. If they do not think themselves insane, they fear that they will "become insane," whereas in later phases of their illness they insist that "they were made insane." Even in those cases, partial insight is not rare although the patients only exceptionally draw practical consequences from this insight. The paranoids are most remarkable in this respect. They will come to consult the physician with complaints that they suffer from delusions of persecution or from hallucinations, and describe the anomalies as objectively as possible. A normal part of their ego judges the abnormal correctly in all details without, however, being able to influence it. Of course, there are also periods when these patients are completely dominated by delusions, and even during examinations one can regularly find associations in which insight is lacking or is at least very inadequate.

Many patients notice that they see things differently from before but they believe that they formerly were in error and that now they have recognized reality. They even claim to have "a re-inforced intellect." At the height of the disease they misjudge their own actions and motivations. Thus, even so intelligent a patient as Forel's Miss L. S. believed that she had borne everything with great patience, whereas actually she had been an exceedingly difficult patient for quite some time.

In each recurring episode of illness, the patients may repeat actions which they had acknowledged as wrong during their intervals of improvement, but which they now once more defend as entirely justifiable.

During good remissions, the delusions are recognized as such; but almost without exception one can demonstrate that under certain conditions they are still operative. Also, the "cured" patient may regard his behavior during the illness as abnormal and senseless, yet even then for the most part there is a lack of complete insight. I have seen a catatonic who, while she was in the hospital, was very violent toward herself and others,—smearing, refusing food, etc.—and who, during a period of the greatest agitation, was taken home by her father. From the very first day at home she was able to take charge of the household and eventually she even edited her father's memoirs. She remembered her stay in the hospital in all its details. She could indicate this or the other symptom as abnormal but she still maintained that she had been most unjustly committed. My cautious objections that her violence and refusal of food were hardly to be considered as signs of health she believed she could refute by stating that she had acted in that way "because she had wanted to disturb the administration of the institution in which she had been so badly abused."

The severely affected patients are hardly able to learn anything new Often they are still able to adjust themselves to simple agricultural tasks. They can also be trained for some industrial activity, although they always have to have supervision. In the hospital for chronic mental disease at Rheinau, I made great effort to introduce basket-weaving. However, it was impossible to get even a single one of this group of severely ill patients to work independently.

This, of course, does not exclude the possibility that in another case a patient, who had been very severely catatonic for some years and who now suffered from paranoia hallucinatoria, could suddenly begin to study English and continue his auto-didactic activity in the hospital to the point where he was able to sell his translations.

According to Specht (733), the capacity for practice, as measured by the facility in adding, is normal. According to Reis, the progress made in practicing is somewhat reduced, as demonstrated by various psychological tests. In one case it was completely lacking. Further research on advanced cases is certainly still needed since attention and cooperation on the part of the patients naturally affect the results.

In the severe cases, the ability to calculate is easily altered, yet it can be re-established at any moment when the patient is sufficiently composed to be able to concentrate on the problem. Naturally, in hospital patients, mistakes of all sorts appear frequently, due to perplexity and poor attention. In addition they often do not have the desire to answer correctly. Even intelligent schizophrenics will be in no way embarrassed during a clinical presentation to say 3 x 4 is equal to 100. However, milder cases in the chronic stage sometimes adapt themselves very well to office work requiring calculations. They are not easily distracted, think very little except about what they are doing. They work like robots year-in and year-out with the greatest conscientiousness, or perhaps we should say with the greatest "exactitude."

In every kind of game the patients behave as they do in other mental performances; that is, extraordinarily variable. Many do not seem to have any need or desire for entertainment. Others who do have the drive to play often apply to this activity as complete attention as do the healthy. Indeed, not only can chronic cases take part in the usual games, especially card-playing, with cleverness and full understanding of the intricacies of the game, but even a seemingly confused catatonic in an acute state can surprise us with his virtuosity as a chess-player. Naturally the patients for the most part are not able to carry out those social games which require "esprit."

As a rule, the schizophrenics' imagination is markedly affected. Most of them do not have the drive to think something new, and still less the ability to do anything new. Novel thoughts often result from peculiar combinations of their old stock of concepts; however, they are reshuffled without any intellectual goal. The ideas are therefore merely bizarre and not actually creative productions. A paretic patient, in a manic state, can produce more novel ideas in one day than can an entire ward-full of schizophrenics in years.

The aesthetic capacities are almost completely destroyed, or at least markedly damaged. This is due to the lack of consistent thinking, judgment, the emotional matrix, and above all, the initiative and capacity for productiveness. The sense of appreciation for a work of art is lacking for the most part.

Now and again we are astonished that a patient, who seemed to have deteriorated completely and who for many years never expressed an appropriate emotion or a sensible word, has been able to create in musical fantasy an artistic expression for the most varied moods. But moods and means of expression change very abruptly in most of the musically inclined patients. The schizophrenic way of thinking, with its sudden transitions, oddities, blockings and perseveration, reveals itself as clearly in musical productions as it does in speech. Sometimes one can make the diagnosis almost with certainty from listening to a short piano recital.

For the most part, the plastic artist is severely handicapped by this disease. Here the bizarre idea, technique and execution strikes the eyes almost at once. Obviously, productivity suffers. Yet there are painters who always, over a long period of time, repeat the same idea an endless number of times. Often art serves as a medium of expression for the delusional system, and it can then be recognized as morbid, almost at first glance.[28]

Naturally, poetic talent suffers greatly from the schizophrenic thinking process, from looseness, from lack of feeling and taste, and from the lack of productivity and initiative. While considerable amounts of schizophrenic poetry have been printed, little of it has been of any great significance or value. At best the productions are rather unimportant; most of them are quite revolting.

The later poems of Hölderlin are good examples, among which "Patmos" is the best known. The schizophrenic train of thought has rarely been more beautifully illustrated. Christian (126, p. 27) gives us

28. In mild cases, the peculiarity of subject, conception and technique can make the schizophrenic painter quite famous.

the following pertinent example of emptiness and obscurity of ideas with preservation of a certain formal technical skill:

"Sous le chaud soleil qui rayonne
Cachée à l'ombre du Sumac,
La dormeuse mêle au tabac
Sa crinière épaisse de lionne."

The banality of thought and form is shown in the verses published by Stawitz.

"Der Chorgesang.
Stärker als die Sprache der Natur
von bekannten Sängern schallte nur,
eines Tags ein Lied mir zu.
Manch Träne, die mein Herz verbarg,
trat hervor, im Überwinden karg,
schaffte so der Seele Ruh!
Mehr noch schätzte ich das Singen
als vorher; es gab ja Schwingen
Meinem Rückblick in die Zeit.
Meinem Ohr ward es zur Weid."

The bizarre and strange is expressed in the following verses whose author I cannot recall any more:

"Wie hat die Liebe mich entzückt,
Als ich noch schwer und kugelrund!
Hier sitz ich jetzt und bin verrückt,
und wiege kaum noch hundert Pfund."

In severe cases, the result is usually a word-salad, or merely a more or less versified string of unknown words.

Even where such blunders are not made, the mental productions of the schizophrenics suffer a great deal from the lack of integration, the vacuity of thought and the banality of content, or the lack of integration renders otherwise good ideas quite insipid.

All this is valid for the more severe cases which come to the attention of the physician. However, we also know that several very well-known artists and poets (e.g. Schumann, Scheffel, Lenz, van Gogh) were schizophrenics. It cannot be ruled out that very mild forms of schizophrenia may be rather favorable to artistic production. The subordination of all thought-associations to one complex, the inclination to novel, unusual range of ideas, the indifference to tradition, the lack of restraint, must all be favorable influences if these characteristics are not overcompensated by the association disturbances proper. In fact, almost all truly artistic natures are individuals with markedly split-off, emotionally charged complexes; perhaps for this reason they have hysteriform symptoms so frequently. Schizophrenics too are "*Komplexmenschen*" (people dominated by complexes). The question deserves a good deal more study.

In acute stages we even find a kind of pathological productivity. Forel's patient had been unable to write poems; in the preliminary stage of her illness she was all but "persecuted" by verses in formation.

(f) *Activity and Behavior*

Outspoken schizophrenic behavior is marked by lack of interest, lack of initiative, lack of a definite goal, by inadequate adaptation to the environment, i.e., by disregard of many factors of reality, by confusion, and by sudden fancies and peculiarities.

The mild latent cases live essentially like other people and are considered as healthy. What is striking is mainly their sensitivity and now and then some peculiarity. They are able to work both inside and outside the hospital, some very diligently, others in a more capricious, irregular fashion. They are active in all the simpler vocations, occasionally even in artistic or academic activities. Often they do well, sometimes even very well. However, in the latter case it is only in clearly defined jobs, e.g., as farm-helpers, or maid servants. Much more often they "are different." They are prone to change jobs and occupations frequently. One will even leave his work without waiting to draw his pay. A young sculptor, who did quite well in his profession, wandered around for a whole year with a phonograph. Most of these people limit their contacts with the external world to a more or less significant degree; some do so in general, and some only in certain respects.

What is most striking in these mild cases is usually their irritability and sensitivity. Because of some small matter which at a given moment displeases them, they will sulk, curse, run away. If the fiancé does not show up, that is not right; should he come promptly then the girl will find plenty to scold him for. They develop an unpleasant stubbornness, in small matters as well as in large ones, besides which, they are moody, and occasionally they may run away in the middle of the night.

The tendency to seclusion from other people can be combined with excesses in dissolute company. The indifference to important things and their laziness often lands these people in the street or in some other unfavorable milieu. They become vagrants,[29] thieves, more rarely swindlers and other types of criminals. I have also seen two schizophrenic pyromaniacs. Yet their apathy and lack of will power generally makes them relatively harmless. Though every prison has its share of schizophrenics,

29. Cf. Willmanns

their number is in no way proportional to the number of those living in freedom, many of whom more or less lack social feelings or are prone actually to think and feel antisocially, either because of delusional ideas or because of rage about previous commitments. Nevertheless the absolute number of schizophrenic murderers is not quite inconsiderable.

Their striving is mostly ineffectual if it has not ceased entirely. Indeed, in isolated cases, it can even be overstrong, though one-sided (world-reformers, pseudo-poets, etc.). In work to which the patients are not accustomed it is the energy rather than the intelligence which seems to fail first. Many of the more severe cases will avoid any kind of work with some silly excuse, or even without one. Occasionally they work like machines. If one gives the patient a saw he will pull it back and forth till the wood is sawn through and remain standing apathetically till the attendant fixes a new piece of wood under the saw. Others make themselves very useful if one can give them some type of work which does not require much thinking or personal initiative. They can haul coal, weed, knit, keep certain rooms in order; they will fetch the mail. Now and then we find schizophrenics who seem to feel no fatigue and will work all day long, partly without thinking very much, partly even with an occasional reflection. They actually have to be protected from their own "addiction" to work.

Kraepelin's (390, Vol. 2, p. 315) observation of a case in which there was an utter inability to finish or stop what he was doing is interesting and worthy of further study. This lack was to be expected where neither fatigue nor interest was present.

The defective intelligence in the narrower sense of the term makes these people, who are more severely ill, totally or partially unfitted for complicated work. Thus one of Kraepelin's patients could still copy fairly well but he could no longer draw a curve. Another could copy with exactitude but could not correctly apply the insertion marks. Altogether, these patients show little capacity for variation in their work. Many of them must do the work the way they figure it, no matter how inappropriate the method. Their inability to reflect is very noticeable. A retired teacher demands that he be re-instated, but in his letter he insults the authorities. A physician, who had been committed to the hospital because of his violent and dangerous threats believed in all earnestness that he could obtain every kind of concession by starting a lawsuit against me. Then I would be the defendant in the lawsuit and could not employ my power as expert and hospital director to restrain him. Every day we observe ill-considered attempts at escape of apparently lucid patients which they will execute before the very eyes of the attendants, or by dashing out of their room into the corridor, from where they would still have to pass several locked doors.

The patients' goals are often in obvious contradiction, not only with their actual abilities, but also with their mental predispositions in general. World-reform, poetry and philosophy are the cherished activities of many schizophrenics. Nevertheless, in large matters and small, they point out the truth which the healthy would not notice.

Also, in smaller matters they can appear quite impertinent and precocious. Thus an uneducated patient, in a long letter gives some excellent advice to his physician as to just how the doctor should treat his own relative. In another instance, one has a demented patient giving instructions in an impressive tone of voice, regarding good manners in polite society. This is, however, no worse than a newspaper article written by a patient, discussing the educational value of the circus for the Zurich public. At times, even in externals there is revealed an exaggerated vanity which may go on to the point of the wildest caricature. Yet it is far more usual to find the patients ultimately becoming dirty and slovenly in every respect.

However, sometimes even severely sick individuals can impress their fellowmen precisely because they leave all difficulties out of consideration. A schizophrenic woman succeeded in marrying almost against his consent a man of good standing who otherwise displayed quite a strong will of his own, and who had made a reputation for himself in a very prominent position. In public speeches such individuals can convince an entire auditorium of their health and many another equally fictitious matter. The poet-author of the song "Freut euch das Lebens" chose a schizophrenic bride precisely because of her "*naive étourderie*" which distinguished her from their stiff social circle.

In the moderate and severe cases it is the desultoriness in the intellectual sphere which often is most noticeable.

An educated lady writes a number of letters, marks them "registered mail," and then does not mail them. A teacher suddenly applies for a position paying 2,000 Swiss francs salary, and quits his present teaching position. An uneducated person wishes to study the theory of music. A sales clerk rides back and forth on the train between Romanshorn and Geneva because he had heard that some people had become engaged to nice young women while riding on the night trains. A man takes off all his clothes outdoors in winter, walks naked through the village in order to take a dip in a river which lies a half-hour's distance away. A young girl sews stockings upon a rug.

The pathological fancies make it impossible for some patients to earn their own living. Otherwise quite diligent individuals will one day not come to work without any obvious reason; and they consider it quite self-evident that they should later return to their job without even offering an excuse.

A hebephrenic who for years had spread the fertilizer over the spacious horticultural area of the hospital with never-failing industry was one fine day found cutting the roots of the dwarf trees in order "to raise" them, as he thought. In his vague idea of doing something useful he had ruined several hundred trees. There is no absurdity so great that our patients will not commit it regardless of consequences. One patient will merely hit the table a few times, or crow like a cock. Another, however, will set fire to a house or throw his mother down the well.

Often the patients depart more and more from the norm in their behavior and become progressively more "whimsical." This can go so far that three of our patients from good families while they were considered normal took to wrapping up their feces in pieces of paper and hiding them away in closets. One of our patients who did good work in the hospital would go home each Sunday for a visit and sit there from 1:45 p.m. to 5:30 p.m. on a certain chair always staring in the same corner, without having a single word to say to anyone in the house. More advanced cases show the habit of collecting all sorts of objects, useful as well as useless, with which they would fill their apartments so that there was hardly room to move around. Ultimately this collecting mania becomes so utterly senseless that their pockets are always crammed full of pebbles, pieces of wood, rags and all kinds of other trash. The tendency to buffoonery can also become so overwhelming as to lead to the external picture of monotonous, chronic "clowning."

At times patients exhibiting the most incomprehensible behavior will again appear more or less normal. They can once again take up their jobs or often go through their periods of military training very satisfactorily.[30] Conversely, a sudden outbreak of excitement with or without provocation may disrupt a hitherto composed clinical picture. An "improved" patient wanted to kill a cat but was scolded by his father. Thereupon, the patient got very excited, exclaimed, "Now everything is over," jumped into the river, swam back to the bank and resumed working as he had before.

Intercourse with other people is not disturbed merely by the schizophrenics' irritability and their peculiarities. In their autism they can comport themselves in a crowded work-room as if they were alone; everything which concerns the others does not exist for them. On the ward, many patients will not change their position in any way whatsoever during the coming and going of the doctor, except to make their rejection

---

30. It is indeed much more frequent that the latent schizophrenic does not succeed in adjusting to military life.

more marked by mimic or attitude. They have turned their backs on the world, and seek to protect themselves from all influences coming from the outside. This may develop into a sort of stereotypy in which the patients feel comfortable only in some corner where they can hug the walls. Where they are left to themselves, one can even find them lying in the angle between wall and floor, their face to the wall, and often even covering it with a cloth or with their hands. In milder degrees of the illness, it can happen that a hebephrenic will return from America without any warning, make his nightly quarters in his parents' barn, where he is discovered only after some time since he gets up early to go to his distant place of work. A desire for entertainment is usually absent even in those schizophrenics perfectly capable of work. The patient's life is then a monotonous cycle of working, eating, and sleeping.

Should schizophrenics have to have relations with others, they assume quite a peculiar form. Sometimes patients are obtrusive, continue endlessly to repeat the same thing over and over again, and are completely deaf to all objections. At other times, they comport themselves very disdainfully, curtly, rudely. A hebephrenic pharmacist reproached his customers when they brought prescriptions which involved much work.

* * *

Such are cases that are still capable of acting and having relations with people. However, when autism gets the upper hand, it creates a complete isolation around the sick psyche. The most severe schizophrenics live in their own rooms as if in a dream, at times moving about like automatons, without any external goal; at other times, they remain silent and motionless, their contact with the external world is reduced to an intangible minimum. Should accessory symptoms come to the fore at any stage of the illness, it is they which determine actions and behavior.

CHAPTER II

THE ACCESSORY SYMPTOMS

It is not often that the fundamental symptoms are so markedly exhibited as to cause the patient to be hospitalized in a mental institution. It is primarily the accessory phenomena which make his retention at home impossible, or it is they which make the psychosis manifest and give occasion to require psychiatric help. These accessory symptoms may be present throughout the whole course of the disease, or only in entirely arbitrary periods of the illness. It is they which give the external stamp to the disease picture so that prior to Kraepelin's work, it was believed that separate diseases could be defined and delimited exclusively according to these symptoms and their grouping.

The best known among them are the hallucinations and delusions. Apart from these, the disturbances of memory function and the changes in personality have received relatively much less consideration. Speech, script, and a number of physical functions are often changed in an irregular but typical way. Following Kahlbaum, a special group of phenomena has been gathered together under the name of catatonic symptoms. All of these disturbances can be either transitory or of long duration. Besides all this, however, there are definite acute symptom complexes which consist of the above mentioned symptoms, as well as of other phenomena, and which have led to the impression that they are independent acute psychoses. For us they are only episodes or exacerbations in the long drawn-out course of the disease.

(*a*) *Hallucinations, Delusions, and Illusions*

In hospitalized schizophrenics it is mainly the delusions and particularly the hallucinations which stand in the forefront of the picture.[1] The complaints of the patients, the peculiarities of their behavior, agitation and seclusion, ecstasies, despairs, and outbreaks of anger—all these phenomena are usually related to, if not direct consequences of, the delusions and hallucinations.

Characteristic of schizophrenic hallucinations is the preference for the auditory sphere and for the sphere of the body sensations. Almost every schizophrenic who is hospitalized hears "voices," occasionally or continually. Almost equally as frequent are the delusions and illusions which are related to the different body organs. Tactile hallucinations are relatively rare, although occasionally the patients do complain of a sensation of animals, particularly, of snakes on or in their skin. Hallucinations of being abused, beaten, burnt, or of having electrical currents passed through their bodies may have a tactile component. If we take into account the number of patients who complain about them, it would seem that hallucinations of smell and taste fall into a third important class. Visual hallucinations and illusions are not frequent in lucid patients but they do appear in acute hallucinatory excitements and in clouded states. As far as the other senses are concerned, illusions take a decidedly secondary place to the hallucinations. As far as taste goes, it

1. Concerning the paresthesias, see under physical symptoms.

is very difficult to decide whether they are illusions or hallucinations in view of the fact that they occur mostly while eating. In the present state of our knowledge it is equally irrelevant whether the common misinterpretations of the kinesthetic senses are to be considered as illusions or hallucinations.

The content of schizophrenic hallucinations can be furnished by anything which the normal person perceives and to this can be added all the sensations which the diseased psyche is able to invent.

The patients hear blowing, rustling, humming, rattling, shooting, thundering, music, crying, laughing, whispering, talking. They can see individual objects, landscapes, animals, human beings, and every other possible figure. They smell and taste pleasant and unpleasant things, whatever may affect these senses. They feel things, animals, and people, and are struck by rain-drops, fire, sticks. They experience all tortures, as well as every pleasurable sensation which the sense organs can transmit.

In reality, however, the major bulk of the hallucinations which we can observe restricts itself to a far smaller selection. It is most exceptional that a schizophrenic hallucinates an entire sermon or drama, or that he finds a piece of hallucinated bread in his coffee, or that he sees common, everyday landscapes. Music is rarely heard. [2] Neither are very common nor very complicated events and experiences easily hallucinated by our patients. Complicated ones do not occur because very few of these people are capable of high attainments since the peculiar condition of their associative processes restricts their abilities. Simple everyday events are not hallucinated obviously because those have no great significance for the hallucinating psyche which hypostatizes primarily affectively charged thoughts in hallucinations.

The usual occurrence is that the "voices" threaten, curse, criticize and console in short sentences or abrupt words; that the persecutor or heavenly figures, certain kinds of animals, fire or water and also some desired or hoped for situation are hallucinated: paradise, hell, a castle, a robber's cave is seen; that ambrosia or some frequently mentioned poison or a vile substance is tasted in food; that a poisonous vapor or a wonderfully glorious perfume surrounds the patient. They feel the passion of love or all kinds of torture that can be affected by physical means on their abused bodies.

It is in this way that they express ever the same wishes, hopes and fears. The ambitious hear that power and money are going to be

2. Not so long ago one of our female patients heard singing. Her paranoid husband had predicted great things for her and himself. They would then be escorted by a crowd of people to the accompaniment of solemn songs.

offered them, but certain signs also disclose the maneuvers of their opponents. The confined patient hears voices that promise him impending freedom, and others describing his "imprisonment" as eternal.

The hallucinations of the individual senses reveal many interesting peculiarities. The elementary auditory hallucinations are relatively rare. However, they too have a reference to the patient: rustling sounds mean danger; shooting is done either for their salvation or to their detriment. Yet there are a few cases in which such akoasmata have no more significance than would a ringing in the ears to the healthy person. However, it is questionable whether these phenomena really merit the name of "hallucinations."

The most common auditory hallucination is that of speech. The "voices" of our patients embody all their strivings and fears, and their entire transformed relationship to the external world. The "voices" are the means by which the megalomaniac realizes his wishes, the religiously preoccupied achieves his communication with God and the Angels; the depressed are threatened with every kind of castastrophe; the persecuted cursed night and day. For the patient as for his attendant the "voices" become, above all, the representatives of the pathological or hostile powers. The voices not only speak to the patient, but they pass electricity through his body, beat him, paralyze him, take his thoughts away. They are often hypostatized, either as people, or in other very bizarre ways. For example, a patient claims that a "voice" is perched above each of his ears. One voice is a little larger than the other but both are about the size of a walnut, and they consist of nothing else but a large, ugly mouth.

Threats and curses form the main and most common content of these "voices." Day and night they come from everywhere—from the walls, from above and below, from the cellar and the roof, from heaven and from hell, from near and far. The patients can also hear their relatives and liberators arriving, and the doctors refusing them admission, imprisoning and torturing them. While the patient is eating, he hears a voice saying, "Each mouthful is stolen." If he drops something, he hears, "If only your foot had been chopped off."

The voices are very often contradictory. At one time, they may be against the patient (when he is thinking of God, they deny His existence); then they may contradict themselves. (A patient had an abscess; she hears the voices say, "Blood-poisoning," and then "A good recovery." During menstruation an elderly spinster heard, "Period, but it should be a change!"; and then she heard, "Spring change.") The roles of pro and con are often taken over by voices of different people. The voice of his daughter tells a patient: "He is going to be burned alive"; while his mother's voice says, "He will not be burned." Besides their persecutors, the patients often hear the voice of some protector. At other times the same voice will amuse itself by driving the patient to utter despair in that they approve of his intentions, or order him to make a certain purchase and then berate him for doing so. The voices command him to go bathing and then jeer at him for obeying. The attendants, the doctors, policemen, "the voices," in general, like to criticize his thoughts, behavior and actions. While getting ready in the morning a patient hears, "Now she is combing her hair," "Now she is getting dressed;" sometimes in a nagging tone, sometimes scornfully, sometimes with critical comments.

Also, the voice may forbid the patient to do what he was just thinking of doing. At times, the hallucinatory voices represent sound criticism of his delusional thoughts and pathological drives. For this type of voices, the patients find special terms, such as "voices of conscience," or "nagging devil," to indicate the negative aspect. The voices of conscience may criticize an intention even before it has come into the patient's awareness. An intelligent paranoid who came from the Swiss canton of Thurgau harbored hostile feelings toward his personal attendant. As the latter stepped into his room the voice said in a most reproachful tone, "There you have it, a Thurgauer beats up a perfectly decent private attendant!"

Perceptions can also be transposed into voices without the patient being at all aware of it. In that event the voices become prophetic; a patient hears, "Now someone is coming down the hall with a bucket of water"; then the door opens and the prophecy is fulfilled. Other prophecies are nothing but the patient's own desires and fears: God's voice tells him that tomorrow the hospital and all the doctors will be destroyed by a great catastrophe, and that he himself will be elevated to high rank.

Sometimes the voices merely state what the patient does and thinks, clearly analogous to the symptom called "naming." In the usual symptom of "naming," the idea of a perceived object is converted into "action" words; here into acoustic representations. We also find that a patient will look at a picture and hear the voice say, "This is a marriage ceremony." The voices literally "name" the object seen.

Frequently we find in dementia praecox the phenomenon of the patient's thoughts becoming audible. (It is sometimes misleadingly called "double-thinking"). The patients hear their own thoughts expressed in gentle whisperings or in unbearably loud tones. "The telephone lines take up all my thoughts." Illusions may also sometimes embody the momentary thought. "Whatever I think, the bells ring it out, the wheels creak it, the dogs bark it, the birds sing it; such a thing has never happened before in this whole world." Then again, when a patient speaks, his thoughts can be hallucinatorily echoed: "When I say something, it seems as if I hear it being repeated in the distance" (666, p. 260). "When I stop speaking, then the voices repeat what I have just said." This phenomenon appears especially frequently, although not exclusively, in reading and in writing.

As a rule, other hallucinations mix with this "thought-echoing." A hebephrenic patient complains that everything that he says is repeated as he says it; an old woman comments on all he says; a man reads aloud what the patient writes; another man is discussing him with a woman.

The voices may also reveal information about themselves. They tell who they are, what they look like, where they are, etc., but this is an infrequent occurrence. The patients usually know all this already or do not seem to be very interested in it. One of our patients first heard the voice and then was told from whom the voice was coming.

The patient's own confusion often finds its expression in the voices. Often several voices talk at once so that the patient cannot follow them. Often enough what the voices say, is such a mix-up that the patient is unable to grasp it. Frequently he hears confused or incomprehensible utterances.

As a rule, however, the patients hear short sentences or single words which in themselves need not always make sense. It is the patient who usually imputes some meaning to the words or sentences. Except as a complication of alcoholism, the patients rarely hear consistent or long speeches. Much more frequent are thought-dialogues, be it with God, a protector or a persecutor. Often enough, the voices take on some special peculiarity. They speak extraordinarily slowly, scanning, riming or in rhythms; or they speak in foreign tongues, etc.

Besides being localized in the near or far surroundings, the voices are often localized within the body, mostly for obvious reasons. The mother speaks in the heart or in the ears of the patient; familiar voices are preferably localized in the heart or the chest. Many times, however, the whole body will be intoning, "You rascal," "You whore." A polyp may be the occasion for localizing the voices in the nose. An intestinal disturbance brings them into connection with the abdomen; heavy breathing or belching establish a connection with the corresponding organs. In cases of sexual complexes, the penis, the urine in the bladder, or the nose utter obscene words. A really or imaginarily gravid patient will hear her child or children speaking inside her womb. One of our patients has a girl in his left hand (with which he masturbates) who speaks to him when he places his hand on his ear.

The basis for localization is not always discoverable. As when a patient hears only his leg talking or when the voices come from various places under the skin, and constantly call out: "Don't let me out," "Don't cut it open." It must be an extraordinary sensation that moves a patient to this description: "Particularly the last word was wound around my head, as it were, for several minutes." (Kraepelin), or "The heart-voices have grown to my body in ring-shaped form," or "I receive many voices and in such a fashion that it seems they rain down on me." A patient describes a definite category of her voices "as if you were colliding with a sound, like a blow on your nerves." Another, reprimanding kind of "voice" is described "as peculiarly crooked, but not as if it were bellowing, and it makes a black linear drawing appear on one's face; that is black lines like decorations."

Occasionally, the voices are not localized in the body but in the clothing. One of our hebephrenics was constantly shaking "little talking-imps" out of her skirts. In another patient the voices seem to meet crosswise over her shoulders. Also inanimate objects may speak. The lemonade speaks; the patient's name is heard coming from a glass of milk. The furniture speaks to him. How little hallucinations differ from illusions is illustrated by the fact that, when it is quiet, the patients hear voices coming from any odd corner, but when real noises come up, they are at once localized at their source.

Magnan found that, when good or bad voices are differently localized, the "good" voices come from above, the "bad" ones from below. This constellation is not at all rare and corresponds to our religious concepts. However, we can hardly establish it as a rule because there are far too many exceptions. The same significance can be attached to what a patient tells us: that on the quiet wards he hears the voices as from above; while on the disturbed wards he hears the voices coming from below. He particularly fears the voices coming from below.

Frequently the two parties concerned with the patient may be divided between the two sides of the patient's body. In particular, the auditory hallucinations are usually pleasant "in one ear," and unpleasant in the other. However, I could not always find a definite preference of the good voices for the right side which some authors report. Nevertheless, one of our patients spoke symbolically of the Holy Ghost in his right ear and the snake in his left one.

Sometimes, the voices are localized in one side only. Often, but not always, this phenomenon may be caused by a diseased condition of the ear so that an illusionary interpretation of ear buzzing or ringing may be involved.

The hallucinations of bodily sensations present such kaleidoscopic multiplicity that no description could possibly do justice to them.

Any organ can be the seat of the most severe pain. The scalp can become so sensitive that the slightest touch of the hair may produce terrible pain.[3] Every bone in the body may ache. The patients are beaten and burnt; they are pierced by red-hot needles, daggers or spears; their arms are being wrenched out; their heads are being bent backwards; their legs are being made smaller; their eyes are being pulled out so that in the mirror it looks like they are entirely out of their sockets; their head is being squeezed together; their bodies have become like accordions, being pulled out and then again pressed together. They have ice inside their heads; they have been put in a refrigerator. Boiling oil is felt inside their bodies; their skin is full of stones. Their eyes flicker, as do their brains. They are being plucked as one pulls horsehair out of a mattress. A cartridge ball rolls around in a spiral inside their skull from base to vertex. There is a feeling in their stomach as if their food was not retained; they feel bloated. Their lungs are stretched as if a stout man were being drawn through the body from the genitals through the abdomen into the chest. They feel heart-beats in their navels. The heart-beat is at times slow; sometimes it is speeded up. Their respiration is hampered, their urine drawn off or blocked. Any and every organ has been removed, cut-up, torn to pieces, inverted. One testicle is swollen. The nerves, the muscles, various organs are being tightened.

Also bodily sensations unknown to the normal person appear in great numbers. When someone is nice to one of our paranoids, then he feels "touched delicately." If someone is mean to him, "he is struck a blow." He feels it not on his skin, but rather more in his head; it then spreads through the entire body, changing the patient's posture.

Illusions and hallucinations of the kinesthetic senses or the vestibular organs are usually in the background of the clinical picture. Yet the patients may firmly believe that they are carrying out certain actions, whereas in reality they are lying still in bed or standing motionless against a wal'. Obviously then these organs must be participating in the hallucinatory activity. In dream-like states we note the patients making uncoordinated movements, almost like epileptics while they themselves believe that they are fighting for their lives or participating in some love-scene. Under certain conditions, they believe that they are being carried from one place to another; that they are being tossed in the air or stood on their heads. It may also happen that patients believe that one of their limbs is in motion, whereas objectively nothing is to be noted. A paranoid feels his head and shoulders moving but he believes

3. Probably analogous to the exacerbation of "voices" while some noise is going on.

they belong to a hallucinated person. Similarly, a patient says (526), "When the voices wag their tongues, I feel it in my own mouth." More rarely the patients feel the words as motor writing in or on their hands (38, p. 153).

The kinesthetic delusions of the organs of speech are the most common. The patients believe they are speaking, whereas objectively they are not.[4] Of course, one cannot offhand connect the auditory hallucinations with hallucinations of the muscle-senses of the organs of speech. However, kinesthetic hallucinations do deserve more thorough study.[5]

Among schizophrenic body hallucinations, the sexual ones are by far the most frequent and the most important. All the raptures and joys of normal and abnormal sexual satisfaction are experienced by these patients, but even more frequently every obscene and disgusting practice which the most extravagant fantasy can conjure up. Male patients have their semen drawn off; painful erections are stimulated. Then again, they are made impotent. Their internal and external genital organs are burned, cut, twisted. The women patients are raped and injured in the most devilish ways; they are forced to have intercourse with animals, etc., etc. Often the sexual sensations are concealed not only from the observer, but also from the patient himself. Stabbing, cramp-like pains or similar sensations of female patients are very frequently displaced, primarily to the chest, whereas it can be established by judicious questioning or, even better, by allowing the patient to speak freely, that these phenomena really are located in the genitalia. It is not rare to find that this is not merely an euphemism but that there really is a displacement of genital sensations to other parts of the body, especially to the heart; in men, at times, to the nose; in women, to the mouth. Indeed, even the genital "voices" later undergo such migrations. A hebephrenic with a powerful masturbation complex for a long time heard his penis say, "Bird-song, bird-song." Later the voice was heard innocuously in his right ear. Very often sexual hallucinations are disguised with regard to their content. Being electrolyzed or burned usually has a sexual significance. One of our patients complained about rocking-horses in her bed whose thrusts she could feel. Careful examination revealed that those were really sensations of coition which, however, had most certainly been metamorphosized, even for the patient herself, into rocking-horses. Actually, in spite of the symbolic meaning of many such hallucinations, the majority of them correspond to real sensations and are not only

---

4. Dumont de Monteux (Ballet 38, p. 148) termed this *chique nerveuse;* that is, a patient feels the muscularly hallucinated words as foreign bodies in his own mouth.

5. Cramer (135) overrated the importance and frequency of kinesthetic hallucinations.

simulated by the metaphoric expressions of the patients. Certainly the figurative meaning of some words is applied much more frequently in connection with body hallucinations than in the descriptions of delusions of any other sense. In a few cases, being burned does not have any sensual significance. When a patient states that she is "choked" until she utters certain words, it can be established by closer scrutiny that "being choked" is the figurative expression for the compulsion to say those very words.

The body hallucinations have a special tendency to appear as *reflex-hallucinations.* They often appear in the form of definite attacks. Then they give the impression of abortive catatonic attacks. "It begins in the feet like a cramp, passes up the body to the arms and itches; passes into the belly and rumbles; then it gets to the heart—tears, pulls, and then goes into the throat till one almost chokes. Then it stops. Often it goes up into the head and then I am completely lost."[6] Such attacks often enough are of a clearly sexual nature. A few patients spontaneously admit that they are accompanied by sexual feelings which may have a pleasant or unpleasant character at different times. In others we can conclude that such is the case from disguised hints in their statements or from other indications.

Visual hallucinations in a state of lucid consciousness are comparatively rare. When they occur in such a state, they may assume the character of pseudo-hallucinations proper, inasmuch as they are recognized as hallucinations. Far more frequently they appear to the patient as real "pictures" or "images" but not as real objects.

The following examples came from patients chronically ill but lucid. Phenomena such as light, fog, darkness, etc., are among the most frequent hallucinations. A patient sees before her eyes fog and clouds, "that darken her face and her thoughts." Geometric figures are also seen. A patient constantly sees before him a pair of white eyes, another sees heads all around him. People float around him in the air, some of whom appear joyful, while others are crying. "Angels no bigger than wasps," fly around the patient. A hebephrenic sees hands appear whose bearers remain invisible. Ghosts of different colors float around the patient, slip into her through her arms or legs. Another, sees elephants and other animals, even people, passing in and out of her chest. One patient sees two-storied, multi-colored wagons drawn by two horses pass under her abdominal skin from left to right, then out from under her right arm, continuing their way on the street.

Visions of animals are not very frequent where alcoholism is not

6. Transition to the catatonic attack.

a co-determinant of the symptoms. However, animals such as snakes, elephants, horses, dogs, appear quite frequently with sexual connotations, although they are more often *felt* rather than seen. A patient saw how her bones were turned into a dog.

Outside of acute twilight states, whole scenes are rarely hallucinated. But in such states they are quite common, vivified by hallucinations of the other senses. A depressed hebephrenic saw, in broad daylight, a flock of sheep unaccompanied by a shepherd against an unknown landscape. Three corpses lie there in specific positions, and at the same time the patient's mother is present in the scene to protect him. Blankets are seen lying on a neighbor's roof; the neighbor's house is on fire; a snake is winding around the nightlight; a man is being decapitated continuously; people—men and women—sit around the light. The cousins of a young catatonic girl are beating each other, much to the enjoyment of the patient; then they stand on their heads. Above the woman-doctor's head a group of people are standing; in the front row are the good ones, in the back row the evil ones, among them her parents (whom the patient fears for good reasons). The heavens stand open; the angels and the saints and God Himself communicate with the patient. The appearance of frightful figures from Hell are very common. Robbers threaten the patient. Words in all sorts of lettering occur quite often, even whole sentences. Sometimes the writing appears very suddenly, as the embodiment of any odd notion. Thus a paranoid suddenly saw the word, "poison" in the air at the very moment when the attendant made him take his medicine. Also, perfectly conscious thoughts or the very sermon that is being listened to can be seen written in various letters and signs: "Thoughts-becoming-visible." (Halbey)

The relation of the visual hallucinations to the actual environment is very variable. Often the hallucinations are simply fitted into the surroundings. People are seen standing above the doctor's head; others are seen walking through the room like real people. Sometimes the patient is struck by the deviation of his experiences from the common course of events. Visions are seen in which people become transparent while the real surroundings remain visible behind them. Objects may appear in particularly sharp or very vague contours. At night a patient sees a man and a woman against the distant wood "as sharply and as clearly as if they were cut out." Figures are "radiated" toward the patient; they disappear when he opens his eyes. At other times, visions are only seen with his eyes open. In contrast to the "voices," the visions are only exceptionally conceived of as representatives of the "whole ghostly host." Visual images are then seen as not only moving about, but they also produce noises and actions.

The schizophrenic hallucinations of taste and smell have no special characteristics. The patients taste sperm, blood, feces, and all sorts of poison in their food. Soap is tasted in the noodles; grease in the coffee. Something dusty and something bitter in taste is blown toward them. Bad smells and poisons are forced into their mouths so that they have no other recourse than to stuff their mouths full of wool or rags, till they turn blue. "The meat stinks as if a golden egg had been squashed on it." The room smells of corpses, of chloroform, of tar, of "snake-sweat." The bed smells bad; it has been soiled by onion skins and tobacco. One patient smells his own masturbation. In ecstatic conditions, all sorts of pleasant odors appear. A female patient smells a heavenly taste in her mouth and nose when she attends the service of a certain minister.

Tactile hallucinations are rare and when they do make their appearance are rather vague, especially when one compares them with those accompanying delirium tremens.

Occasionally little animals are felt crawling all over the patients' bodies, particularly snakes, but also other small animals. A female patient lies "in a bed of ants or snakes." Hallucinated objects are also grasped, pushed away, etc.

Illusions of the lower senses are not easily separated with any degree of certainty from hallucinations, and we will not discuss them at this point. Of far greater importance are the auditory illusions. Everything which can be perceived hallucinatorily can also appear as an illusion. In general, every noise, every sound which is able to stimulate the acoustic nerve can give rise to illusions. It is especially important to note that the spoken word can also very often be illusionally misinterpreted. The patient can interpret the most casual remarks, greetings, or conversations with other patients in the sense of his delusions. Occasionally, it is only the localization of a perception which is altered. Thus a patient heard the actual conversation of a neighbor as coming from her own chest.

Visual illusions assume the greatest significance. One can hope to manipulate oneself properly in one's environment only if the latter is comprehended visually to a certain extent. A completely delirious patient who hallucinates away his entire surroundings and substitutes his own imaginings for the real is relatively rare in schizophrenia. In the long run a patient who is still capable of acting cannot maintain visual hallucinations, but only illusions, and of these only those which can come to some compromise with reality. The patient by means of his illusions may see palaces or prisons instead of a hospital ward. He may even be able to stick to this kind of illusion without serious consequences. However, if he should see a door instead of a window, he runs the risk of breaking his neck in a fall.

One patient sees everything as colored red; another sees everything as white. The attendant looks like a Negro; the street lights look like the eye of a ghost. The coffee cups begin to jump. One individual sees two heads on everybody; another sees all small objects, such as keys, fingers, and the like as double, and on every page of the Bible she finds the name of the doctor to whom she has transferred her love. A patient thrashes another because the latter stood in front of the window so that the patient was prevented from reading the very important words formed by the iron bars. The doctors appear as devils. Everyone around appears to be white and dancing about. Each night different figures are substituted. Two men in long shirts appear; the patient beckons to one of them. It turns out to be the woman patient H. Wardmates change their faces the very moment that one looks at them. Men and objects may change their size mainly in the sense that they appear larger than normal or that they become larger and larger before the very eyes of the patient in a terrifying manner. Objects can also become smaller but this is rarer. One catatonic saw people upside down, on their heads.

Frequently, there is simply a feeling of "strangeness." Everything seems to be different from what it used to be for the patient. The world, the trees recede. The sleeves of the coat seem much longer, the hair of a fur seem of a different color. A factory-worker sees a grass-hopper and becomes very disturbed and excited at the sight of this very strange and unknown animal. It appears to a hebephrenic as if the farmers in the fields were not really working but merely going through the gestures.[7]

Combinations of hallucinations and illusions of the various senses appear quite regularly in twilight states and in acute hallucinatory, excited states. The patients believe themselves to be in a certain place; they are in a robber's cave. The attendants are robbers and murderers who wish to torture them. The beds are torture tools. Whatever the patients perceive corresponds to these imaginings; or they are in Heaven and see, hear, feel and taste all the joys of Paradise. However, even in comparatively lucid hallucinating patients, these combinations of delusions, illusions and hallucinations are not at all rare, particularly the combinations of disturbances of the two main senses—the auditory and the body-sensations. Patients overhear discussions and plans of how they are to be tortured. They also feel the consequences of these influences on their bodies, etc. Often, even in very composed patients,

7. Cf. pp. 197-205.

all the various senses may be involved at the same time.

A paranoid who was always able to work gave the following description. He feels that his occiput is movable, as if he could swing it open like a flap. He feels his head has been moved over to the right or to the left. He sees heads everywhere—small, large, moving, motionless ones; some are black, reddish, or transparent, and some opaque. He mostly smells unpleasant odors—gasoline, ammonia, the bad odors from mouth and ears. He complains of a taste which is like "disappointment and anger (i. e. bitter)." While reading he hears comments made about the orthography. He hears that he is going to be beaten, and feels the blow. He hears words coming from a piece of wood which is being sawn; feels something hanging from his head, perhaps a watery goiter. One side of his chest is protruding. Something moves in his throat. The small of his back hurts. He feels a bone sticking out of his leg and sees it in "water-colors" as he is taking his bath. There is a foreign body in his scrotum. His penis is slimy and enlarged. Voices come out of his larynx and move toward the back of his head. They squeeze his head out of shape; twist his mouth and eyes. He detects a voice in his left nostril. He is being controlled by voices, this "is stimulating but should be over by now."

The release of hallucinations: As in other diseases, so too in schizophrenia, the hallucinations are most likely to occur when the patients are left to themselves. [8] Distraction reduces them, the loneliness and quiet of the cell favors them. Darkness multiplies the visions but the difference between night and day which we see in alcoholics, seniles, and fevers is not as pronounced in this disease. Nevertheless, the rule has numerous exceptions. Some patients are most bothered by their voices precisely when they are working. An irritating condition of any organ, inflammations, overloaded stomach, intestinal tension, bronchial secretions can release body hallucinations. Also, real noises can help produce the "voices" which in the majority of cases cannot be considered as illusions. The patients will stop up their ears, not only to be able to hear the voices *better* but also, conversely, in order *not* to hear them. Electrical stimulation of the acoustic nerve can call forth "voices." [9] Electrical stimulation of the head can also stop them. [10]

Even accidental factors can influence the hallucinations and illusions. The patients often obtain peace as long as certain preconditions which they deem essential have not come into play. A paranoid was much surprised that one could make the other patients talk about him even

---

8. This happens frequently in under-staffed hospitals.
9. Chvosteck.
10. Fischer (221).

when they kept their lips closed. If no other patient was in his neighborhood, he heard no voices. A patient best heard voices, which were localized in his heart, when she placed her hands over her heart. Many are able to stop the voices by all sorts of magical and ceremonial rites or by means of utterances such as, "Oh, yes that is so." Sometimes yelling or talking helps to stop them. Very frequently the hallucinations set in when the person who is involved in the delusion appears on the scene. Many patients hear their voices or feel themselves "electricalized," choked, etc., the very moment the doctor steps into the ward. They feel in their breasts the turning of the key in the door-lock. They feel themselves "knitted in," "spooned up," when someone near them knits or eats. The appearance of a certain woman attendant just takes their breath away. Then again, the hallucination is stimulated through another sense organ (reflex-hallucinations). A patient had hallucinations of smell when she was subjected to certain visual impressions. One of Pfister's patients, while she was being tube-fed, heard that the tube had just been used to irrigate the vagina of an unclean patient. A catatonic detected the smell of a corpse whenever he saw someone get pale. As a patient was cutting the meat on her plate, one of her neighbors sitting at the table believed she was being cut up, felt the pain, and fainted. Even hallucinatory "naming" can be conceived as a sort of reflex-hallucination. Whenever one of our patients saw a ship he also heard, "The ship, the ship."

In a certain sense, many schizophrenic hallucinations are dependent on the *will*. True, it is rather rare that the patient can arbitrarily see or hear what he desires. On the other hand, very often the voices will reveal information about definite complexes of the patient. The patients hold a sort of conversation with their voices or turn to the voices when they cannot answer a question posed by the physician. If attention is concentrated on the voices (or at least turned away from other things), then the voices are better perceived by the patient. Yet they will often overcome the patient in the midst of other thoughts. It can happen that taking notice will obliterate the hallucination. For the most part, however, the hallucinations draw attention to themselves. Or to express it differently, the pathological process consists not only in the pseudo-perception proper (the hallucination) but also in the directing of attention to this same pseudo-perception. Thus it is already a sign of improvement when patients succeed in "taking command" of the hallucinations; that is, when they are able to withdraw their attention from the hallucination. Only exceptionally can they be suppressed completely. A paranoid who had a "mummified feeling" (dry and shrinking feeling) which started in the feet and rose up to his head was at least able to stop this feeling at the level of his chest.

Also, of course, all internal and external influences which in general aggravate the disease act as *agents provocateurs* of the hallucinations: unpleasant affects, particularly excitements, alcohol, exacerbations of the disease-process, etc.

In two cases, I observed auditory hallucinations appear only when the patients were recumbent. Brierre de Boismont mentions a case in which inclining of the head provoked the voices (blood-pressure changes in the head?). Temperate or intemperate use of alcohol will often provoke hallucinations of all sorts.

In schizophrenics, the four main characteristics of hallucinations: intensity, distinctness, projection, and reality-value, are entirely independent of each other. Each one can vary within maximal limits without affecting the others.

Intensity. Almost anything can be hallucinatorily perceived and the intensity can vary from the slightest whisper to the most terrifying thunderous voice; from slightly abnormal body-sensations to the most unbearable sensation of being torn asunder, burned or electrocuted; from the most delicate haze to blinding light. The intensity does not necessarily have any relationship to the obsessive attention which the patients turn on them although, *ceteris paribus*, intense hallucinations will enforce attention more easily. Yet at times even the slightest, barely or not at all comprehensible whisper will preoccupy the patient more than the loudest (hallucinated) shouting. In any case, intensity, obsessive attentiveness, and distinctness of projection to the outside, all have the common quality of frequently increasing or decreasing with the oscillations of the disease.

Distinctness. At times all perceptions are of an obtrusive clarity and vividness. Then again, the patients will hear only a rustle or a confused murmur; or they will see only something nebulous, vague forms, which they more or less unconsciously designate as specific figures. A patient could not understand any of the words of the voices but understood from the confusing sound that she was going to be killed. Two patients of Pfersdorff (560, p. 742) heard cursing in French, although they did not understand French. "The words themselves are not clearly understood, but the meaning is" (ibid. p. 743). Thus, patients frequently do not tell us literally what they have heard but rather express themselves in general phrases. "The neighbors are full of hate and envy toward me." "There were public sneers and jeers." The patient detected "a disgusting smell of vipers." To the objection that she did not even know what a viper smelled like, she retorted: "One could also say morphine." The subjective effect of the hallucinatory experience is in no way encroached upon by such vagueness. The patients believe in their interpretations which they take for perceptions.

The situation with regard to projection is most remarkable. Many hallucinations are projected outward exactly as are real perceptions and cannot be differentiated subjectively from them. The hallucinations of organ sensations apparently occupy a very special position. For these hallucinations, the body becomes what one otherwise considers the external world. As a rule, one is able to distinguish them easily enough from mere paresthesias which appear in other diseases because they parallel the hallucinations of the other senses in every respect. The hallucinations are not conceived of as sensations indicating some abnormality of the body. The hallucinator does not have a burning or stabbing pain but he is being burned or stabbed. Thus, at least, the causal factor is completely projected to the outside. In the case of combined sensory hallucinations, these body sensations constitute an element equivalent to all other hallucinatory components.

On the other hand, many patients do differentiate between what they really see and hear and that which is "imposed" upon them. Nevertheless, even they are frequently inclined to attribute reality to the content of these hallucinations. It is quite usual that these patients although they make such distinctions, will still consider many other kinds of hallucinations as real sense perceptions.

Furthermore, there are any number of transitions from normal images to sensory hallucination of the utmost sensory distinctness.

Although auditory hallucinations are a matter of great preoccupation, even intelligent patients are not always sure that they are actually hearing the voices or whether they are only compelled to think them. There are "such vivid thoughts" which are called "voices" by the patients. At other times they are "audible thoughts," or "soundless voices." These are two expressions which may perhaps mean the same thing and certainly signify very closely related phenomena. One of our schizophrenics maintained that he did not actually hear words but that he felt as if his own voice spoke them (transition to hallucinations of muscle sensations of the organs of speech), yet the words seemed "louder" to him when he made some bodily effort. Another patient had no real voices any more but "only some peculiar goods on his lips." Another has the voices at times "in his memory," at other times "behind his ears." The independence from real sensations was very emphatically expressed by Koeppe's patient: "I could be stone deaf and still hear the voices." Sometimes it appears to the patients "as if they heard," which does not prevent them from opening the window a hundred times a day in obedience to such commands, or from making a special journey to the Rhine to jump in. The latter patient described the feeling: "It was as if someone pointed his finger at me and said, 'Go and drown yourself.' It is as if we were speaking to each other. I don't hear it in my ears, I have the feeling in my breast. Yet it seems as if I heard a sound." At times one meets with a very noteworthy expression: the voices "Seemed to me as if my ears breathed them out," or as if "Someone was talking to me from inside my ear." It would appear that these patients have a certain feeling that the voices come from inside. A patient disclosed that previously he was being spoken to from the "outside," into his ear. In order to hear this, he had to take up a "special position in relation to the ear." The same patient "also heard a twitching in his legs." During the examination it (the leg) said: "Be silent or something like that." Thus it would appear that here the twitch of the leg released the thought (or expressed it?) that it were better if he kept silent. The patient believed he heard this thought in his leg. The acoustic component is so vague, however, that the patient cannot say at all by which words this thought was expressed. Phonemes may well come closest to actual perceptions inasmuch as "They are not at all real voices but merely reproductions of the voices of dead relatives."

These examples are far from exhausting the possible nuances of the projection of auditory hallucinations. Two main classes in general are differentiated by the patients: the voices which come from the outside like ordinary ones—and those projected into their own bodies which have hardly any sensory components and are mainly designated as inner voices (Baillarger's psychic hallucinations).

Therefore, the latter are less hallucinations of perceptions than hallucinations of conceptions. The pathological process of these borderline phenomena is more closely related to conception than to perception.

There are relatively few gradations of the projections of visual hallucinations. In general, here the patients recognize the abnormal more easily than in the *phoneme*. They see whole regiments "before their eyes;" living acquaintances are made to float in the air "in semblance to the real." The visions are "like shadows," "like an illusion." All sorts of things are "produced" at night for the patient. For example, a Negro catatonic had "seen everything filled with green snakes." But she had not really seen them; it was only "as if they were there." Visions can also originate in the sense-organs, as the trousseau and children in the following account by a young woman. "Think of it, Papa, I have become a child prodigy. Many things come out of my lovely blue eyes, e.g., bed sheets, smoothly ironed pillows and quilts of soft feathers (white or colored), bedsteads, commodes, baskets, thread, stockings of all colors, clothes from the plainest to the most elegant; and finally, people fly out, fortunately not naked but completely dressed. . . ."

In the case of smell, taste, and tactile hallucinations, the differences in projection become even less distinct. Still, even in such cases we get every type of transitional form from image to perception.

Extra-campine hallucinations show a very peculiar localization which up to now have only been observed with any degree of certainty in the visual spheres, as far as schizophrenics are concerned. (These are hallucinations or visions outside the visual field.)

An intelligent hebephrenic, while we were talking to him, suddenly saw the devil standing behind him; and it was so clear and vivid that he could draw it for us. He declared, in response to our objections, that he just had the gift of seeing through the back of his head what was behind him. When he overheard us speak of "imaginings," he protested vehemently that these were no imaginings but an actual ability to see these things.[11] In this way, the patient sees whole landscapes and the like. Indeed, many patients cannot escape their frightening visions, although the latter do not change their localizations in space. The patients try to turn their backs on the visions; they crawl under the mattress, but still see the horrible sight before the window. Others do not seem to consider their unusual visual capacity as anything out of the ordinary. It must certainly be considered an extra-campine hallucination when a patient sees heads which make faces at him right through the floor which he is quite aware is opaque. It must be a transition from simple imaginings to the extra-campine hallucinations of smell when a patient "feels" (not smells) behind his head that he emanates a peculiar odor.

The localization of hallucinations to another person is a partial effect of transitivism. Many schizophrenics not only believe that everyone around them can hear the "voices" as well as they do, but they also believe that even people far away can perceive them. From this it is but a short step to transitive hallucinations in which the patient assumes that a third person can hear the voices while the patient himself receives the information in a mysterious manner. (Séglas called the phenomenon in which patients believe their thoughts are heard by others, "echo de la pensée.") Sometimes the patient "imposes them on the third party," inasmuch as he can arbitrarily think something which the third party must hear.

In the visual sphere we have the same case when the attendant *must* "see" something which the patient has in mind. This phenomenon shows

11. It is not a question here as Kreapelin (Psychiatry I, p. 225) states of vivid visual images "which do not, by any means, have the character of sensory perceptions," but of phenomena which intelligent patients who are able to discuss this problem equate with perceptions.

a gradual transition to the notion, widespread among schizophrenics, that everyone knows their thoughts.

For the most part, the reality value of hallucinations is as great as that of real perceptions, or even greater. Whenever reality and hallucinations conflict, it is usually the latter which are considered as real. If one doubts the reality of the patient's hallucinations, we usually get the following retort: "If that is not a real voice then I can just as well say that even you are not now really talking to me." When the patients do differentiate the voices from what the healthy call reality, it is usually by means of characteristics which have nothing to do with normal projection: a certain kind of content, an unusual place of origin, the invisibility of the originator of the voices and similar points indicate to the patient that he has to do with something out of the ordinary. Olfactory and taste hallucinations are also, as a rule, not recognized as such; whereas visual hallucinations, which constantly collide with real visual images, are easily appreciated as something extraordinary. This does not mean, however, that they are recognized as sensory hallucinations. A photographer seems to show the patient "pictures which are not quite properly in the here and now," like angels, God, etc. Nevertheless, she insisted that she had really looked into Heaven through a glass. This is the usual situation. The voices are conversations of other people, although they originate in one's own ears. A patient explained the origin of the phonemes as analogous to the rustle we hear when we place a shell to our ear; yet, he believed in the reality of the sounds he heard. In agitated or twilight states the crudest contradictions with reality are only rarely appreciated. Even visual hallucinations are interpretatively adapted to the illusion, or the patient lives in two worlds visually without bringing them into any relation with each other.

In the visual sphere, Kandinsky's "true" pseudo-hallucinations are among the most frequently seen. These are visions which are distinct, and completely projected to the outside, but are recognized as hallucinations by the patients. They are distinguished from the ordinary hallucinations by the patients' critical attitude towards them rather than by any special property of sensory experience. They appear to occur less frequently in schizophrenics than do other types of hallucinations.[12]

In this place we may also mention negative hallucinations (Löwenfeld's "systematic anaesthesia"). They appear to be rare unless one includes the factor mentioned under "blocking," namely, the phenomenon

12. Hagen's pseudo-hallucinations are a vague concept and include "psychic hallucinations."

in which the patient will suddenly no longer see or hear what goes on about him whether it be definite incidents or just everything around him.

One of Jörger's (p. 52) patients constantly believed himself neglected by the attendant during the dishing out of the food. He then prayed and saw his portion of meat grow larger and larger and the portions of the others got smaller and smaller till there was nothing more to be seen on their plates. Schreber relates that more than once in broad daylight he had observed his attendant "melting away," that is he saw him disappear gradually until his bed was empty. According to the description, this was a negative hallucination or possibly perhaps the disappearance of the positively hallucinated attendant.

The subjective conception of the hallucinations is very variable. As a rule the patients ascribe the voices to people talking or to apparatuses; the visions, to real people or "projected pictures"; the smell and taste hallucinations to contamination of the air or food; and the body hallucinations to physical or chemical influences. In some cases the patients recognize the pathological nature of their hallucinations; particularly, the connection with or origin from their own thoughts are more or less known to many patients.

They "do not have voices, only thoughts which other people do not have"; or "instead of thoughts, they have voices; all their thoughts suddenly become voices." The indistinctness of the acoustic component may be expressed in the following sentence: "The voices are unlike spoken voices but are as if thought." Another patient who had heard the voice of Jesus Christ expressed himself thus: "When a person is filled with the Spirit of God then he knows well enough what he has to do. It is not exactly a mere voice; it is rather—(blocking)—through the Spirit. One doesn't really notice it; and one can't describe it either. However, I feel the Spirit here in my heart. Then it goes up into the brain, and then one calls it thoughts. When it is in the heart, one calls it plans, images, ideas, which can be brought to fulfillment."

Concerning the manner in which the hallucinations arise, the patients have all kinds of notions. Where, as usual, they are ascribed to people, or apparatus in the external world, the matter is very simple. In that event, there are persons in the same room, behind doors, in secret corridors in the walls, in the attic, in an inaccessible cellar; or in these same places, the most devilish, modern, technical apparatus ever invented has been put up and is used to speak from a distance, to project pictures, to name, to electrocute. By means of an "aero-telephone, the latest invention," a patient heard people going down to the cellar and stealing things from her.

Often no resort is made to any such explanations. Patients will hear the voices of absent people without even thinking about the strangeness of the phenomenon: "After all, the voices may be here."

Another patient seemed surprised only that he had to speak so loudly in order to be heard by his (absent) relatives, whereas *he* could hear them even when they spoke quite softly. Others have such "keen ears" that they can hear people speaking all around them. Whenever a certain patient read about famous men, she would afterwards, by a special favor of God, see these same men. "Everyone has some special talent or gift. I have the gift of being able to hear things." This same patient also "heard" pictures; that is, he designated his visions with the more familiar acoustic expression. Yet another patient had the news of her husband's death "blown" into her ear. The voices were taken from the mind of a friend and forwarded to the patient in the institution. Another patient had voices which belonged to other people who spoke through him, using his throat and chest. Ziehen(840, p. 34) found a most peculiar idea in a patient. She believed that the buzzing in her ears from which she had suffered even before her illness was, now that she was sick, "contaminated by the voices."

The thoughts of one of our hebephrenics were being guessed before he even had a chance to speak. He also had a certain power of attraction by which he drew others to himself and which drew him to others. If he thought about a question, he at once "drew" an answer or he "drew" the voices. The bread told him who had baked it. This was due to a "nervous fluid" which all people had on their hands. They transfer it onto objects and so the answer comes to him. Others could hear things by means of "nervous tension;" or they "hear by perspective." Such phrases, which are original designations rather than explanations, are heard commonly enough. "The talking machine is going all the time." The patient is "wired for sound." He is at "war." The last two expressions designate hallucinations of all senses.

In spite of the fact that many schizophrenics constantly complain about the annoyance occasioned by their hallucinations, it is not always easy to obtain exact information as to the content of their hallucinations. Above all, we daily meet the answer: "You know more about it than I do." Also, it is plausible that the patients find it "too stupid" to give information about matters which, in their opinion, the questioner knows more about than they do themselves. Indeed, he may even himself have produced them. However, there are still other obstacles. Sometimes it appears as if the patients were too embarrassed to talk. Often they openly admit that they are afraid to reveal their experiences because these will be considered pathological and they themselves will be judged "crazy." One patient would quite promptly give an answer which might not be very clear. Upon the question, "What did the voices say?" he would suddenly assume a different facial expression, lower his head, and move his chair back and forth, as if he were turning and twisting under intense pressure. "I will say nothing about voices, of such things one does not talk." At times, the reluctance to talk about the voices is obviously of a sexual nature. Especially women act bashfully when they are asked about hallucinations which, for the inexperienced observer as well as for the patients themselves do not have anything sexual about them. However, it is certain that many patients can only give inadequate or no information at all about their hallucinations. In recent cases, even more than in older ones, we can daily observe generalized or partial "blockings" when the patient is asked about the content of his sensory hallucinations and delusions.

Older patients are often very well aware that the hallucinations slip away from their memory. "When the voices leave me, then I don't know anything about them any more. I can only tell about them when I am actually hearing them. The voices are so transitory." A patient excitedly curses his voices; they are saying things which he would never even dare to think. Asked what they say, he does not know what to reply. Frequently one first obtains information about the voices by using leading questions which are then verified by the details obtained. Very often the introduction to an examination concerning hallucinations goes something like this: What do the voices say? "Nothing." Do they reproach you? "Yes."

Appearance and transformations of hallucinations. In some cases the hallucinations slip into the patient's consciousness almost entirely unnoticed. Certain thoughts continue to become more vivid till they assume a sensory character; or it all starts with a very gentle, vague whisper which was at first scarcely noticed. A patient feels her thoughts dividing. "It began to talk loudly as if it were inside the brain." In rare cases, the hallucinations first appear as the ordinary dream; then they appear in the hypnagogic state; then finally in the full waking state. Often, however, the patient will be struck right at the start by single audible calls which exercise a powerful effect on his mental state. Just as they come, they may again disappear, only to reappear sooner or later. In acutely agitated states of all types hallucinations are frequent, but like delusions they may easily outlast the acute episode. Often they come and go with the variations in mood or the undulations of the disease. They may come and go in accordance with the occupations, domicile, surrounding people, etc. Many patients do not have for decades a single waking moment free of hallucinations. The special content may be accidentally determined. A paranoid, at the beginning of his illness, had a quarrel with someone. The curse words uttered during that altercation persisted for many years as hallucinations. In general, schizophrenic hallucinations are very prone to become stereotyped.[13] Complex ones become simple. Finally, they may be reduced to one word or one inarticulate sound which confirms his delusions to the patient.

The attitudes toward the hallucinations show the greatest variability. Many patients, particularly in acute phases, react to them as if they were real, and therefore appear externally as completely "crazy." On the other extreme, some patients do not seem to concern themselves about them, whether out of sly self-control or out of plain indifference. Often the patient struggles not only against the content of the hallucinations, but also against the inroads into his personality. They discover and employ defenses which may vary from apparently reasonable measures (like stuffing their ears) to those which can only be partially understood by normal people, comprising the most senseless buffooneries and cabbalistic exorcisms. Others again will indulge in their hallucinations partly as an outlet for their hostility, partly because they are obviously pleasant. ("Doctor, I have such nice dreams.") Often the partial splitting of the psyche permits the patient to enjoy, during the period of hallucinating, a normal centripetal as well as centrifugal contact with the outer world (even in Bostroem's precise psychological perception experiments).

(*b*) *Delusions*

In delusions everything which one wishes and fears may find its level of expression; and as far as can be judged by the present state of our knowledge, many other things, perhaps even everything which can be experienced or thought. Yet even here, certain types of delusions and even certain minor traits recur in all patients with a remarkable degree of regularity.

The persecutory delusion is the most frequently met of all the well-known types of delusional content. "There is no kind of human corruption by which one has not sinned against me," said one of our paranoids. These patients are driven from their jobs by calumny and, particularly, by every kind of nasty chicanery. They are assigned expecially hard work; their materials are ruined, all kinds of defamatory or otherwise injurious insinuations are made against them. Before a patient entered a village, his visit would be heralded and he would then be berated by all the people. They wanted to send him to Siberia, to enslave him. Two whores lived across the street from him; and each time that he sat down to his meal they called out such disgusting things that he could put noth-

13. Schreber, p. 56.

ing into his mouth. He has been robbed. The attendants and other patients wear his clothing. He is used as a lavatory.

Schizophrenics in a more lucid state consider themselves to be the victims of a certain "gang of murderers" with whom the patients connect every difficulty they encounter. The Freemasons, the Jesuits, the "black Jews," their fellow-employees, mind-readers, "spiritualists," enemies invented *ad hoc*, are constantly straining every effort to annihilate or at least torture and frighten the patients. Wherever the patients find themselves they are exposed to these hostile forces, be it that their enemies in person pursue the patient from place to place and hide in the walls, in the next room, in the cellar, in the very air; be it that these hostile forces observe and note his every action and thought by means of "mountain-mirrors," or by electrical instruments and influence him by means of mysterious apparatus and magic. They make the voices; they cause him every conceivable, unbearable sensation. They cause him to go stiff, deprive him of his thoughts or make him think certain thoughts. One woman patient cannot go to the lavatory any more because there she is watched, not only through the walls but from the bottom of the toilet bowl as well. Her last confinement was watched by the whole neighborhood.

A schizophrenic rarely tries to obtain clear ideas as to how his enemies accomplish all this, and he does not even have the desire to know. "It is just so", and with this he appears to be quite satisfied. Often words will satisfy the need for causal explanation. He is talked to by means of "secret-signs" or by means of "the gangster charm". He may also think in terms of magic: when his name is spoken, then his strength is drawn from him.

Rather than being concerned about the technique of the tortures, the patient seeks more often to find some reason as to why so much trouble is being taken to do all this to him. There are people who are jealous of him, who fear his commercial or sexual competition, or who out of meanness, out of pleasure in torturing, out of inquisitiveness or for some other private purposes, use him for experiments.

The bodily "influencing" constitutes an especially unbearable torture for these patients. The physician stabs their eyes with a "knife-voice". They are dissected, beaten, electrocuted; their brain is sawn to pieces, their muscles are stiffened. A constantly operating machine has been installed in their heads. Someone has injected something in their tear-ducts. Their eyes have been exchanged for those of old women. They are put to sleep. A woman patient is told that her flesh would make delicious veal chops, which are then devoured by wolves. Their sexual organs are cut off and exhibited in a neighboring city. Their intestines have been twisted. Elephants and all sorts of beasts inhabit their bodies. A patient has human beings in her fingers who want to kill her and drink her blood. The patient's health and beauty is taken away to be given to someone else.

The delusion of being poisoned is also a very common one. Poison has been put into the patient's food, the air, the water, in the wash-basin, the clothes. It is injected into them from afar, through the mouth and other body orifices. The patient was given "first rate hydrochloric acid, hair-bread, and urine to eat". Besides the poison, all sorts of utterly disgusting ingredients are mixed in his food. The soup was made with foot-bath water; liquid manure is pumped into his stomach.

The notion of being poisoned is often generalized. The patient is "cursed". "If one can speak by means of audible thoughts, then one is cursed—the curse is something that is tacked on a person, something entirely inexplicable. It has been thought to be a poison composed of human and animal carcasses, but that is, of course, a great Vatican secret. One thing is certain, a body can be terribly tortured by it. They speak the 'thought-language' without moving their lips. By means of the curse, one can listen in. It is the powerful interrogation-curse, the gangster-curse."

Delusions of persecution are easily extended to include other people, particularly the patient's relatives. The relatives are incarcerated in the hospital, tortured in every way, even murdered. If the patient remains here "more than one year and 87 weeks," his father will have a leg torn off.

The delusion of grandeur concerns itself very little with either facts, feasibility or the conceivability of the fulfillment of human desires.

Certainly, often enough things sound fairly plausible. The patient has a talent for mathematics; he will fill in the gaps of his education and become a great mathematician. His father has a fine business and he will soon be rich. A prominent lady is in love with him; she sends him a box of cigars every day. However, for the most part this thirst for grandeur of some kind transcends all bounds. The patient has "as much money as there are snow-flakes on the ground." He is going to be King of England. A palace of gold and precious stones is being built for him. The Lord is his only master. He has cured all these poor souls in the hospital. He must have "Three strokes of luck". First to go riding with Mr. Oscar. Secondly, to be Mr. Oscar's valet. Thirdly, everything in the whole world stands at the beck and call of himself and Mr. Oscar. All these ideas stem from the same patient and illustrate how each and every desire is considered as fulfilled, even though it has already been implicitly fulfilled by a preceding one. In another patient there is just the glimmer of proof by argument when he claims that "since he is the Lord, all the gold and silver in the world is at his disposal". The patients take no trouble at all about thinking these ideas through. They can be simultaneously or alternately not only the King of Britain, but Britannia herself. Another patient is the Austrian emperor, the Pope, and the Bavarian crown-prince, and at the very same time is married to a sow (really thought of as an animal, too). In some cases, the megalomania is, in a way, concealed; a patient believes her foster-daughter to be Snow White; i. e. she herself is a queen. The patient's intelligence is remarkable. The patient "didn't lead his class in school as much as he really deserved". He is also the inventor or discoverer of all the machines and inventions made in the last fifty years. (That he is only twenty years old himself, does not seem to disturb him even after the discrepancy is pointed out). He is going to invent "a perpetual motion machine", "become a soldier and conquer the world". He also possesses a remedy against spinal cord diseases. He can fly; and refuses food because he receives manna from heaven.

In the religious sphere, the patient is a prophet or even God; and as such he has brought to the earth all the carriages in which men now ride. A woman patient "is Christ and the Lord of the World." She is the "Highest Good" and at the same time speaks in the "name of the Highest Good". She is the Savior's Housekeeper, the Bride of Christ, "the five-hundredth Messiah, God's Golden Book and must be rewarded". The patient is like God at least inasmuch as everything which she even dares to think comes to pass at once. In women, these religious, grandiose ideas usually have an erotic character. Rarely is it simply a sublimation of sexual love in religious ideas. More frequently, there is a condensation of vague religious ideas in certain definite forms. The Lord or Savior to whom the patient is related or with whom she identifies is usually characterized by certain traits of a real man who had played some part in the patient's life. In men, religious ideas mainly represent the wish for spiritual power. Yet the "Queen of Heaven" or the "Lord's Angels" may also be thought of as mistresses or as a harem, respectively.[14]

Occasionally, providence merely plays the part of a friend in need: the patient's dead mother will help her escape on a certain night, from the hospital by means of a special heavenly dispensation; or the religious ideas may have, in women, an even more cosmic character. An illiterate seamstress "is in league with the comet of prophecy". There are strange powers, both evil and good, floating around in the air. An idealistically

14. Poets have been aware of these phenomena for a long time. Thus, in Gottfried Keller's "Ursula," Saint Gabriel becomes the lover and is at the same time the son, of Ursula. The venerated teacher in *Hannele's Himmelfahrt* by Gerhart Hauptmann becomes the Savior.

inclined patient is influenced by the powers of good. After his death he will become a spiritual and free-floating force, while the unclean, impure individual is destined to become merely a physical one."

Various complexes could all be satisfied simultaneously, if the patient "were given four things: God, Spirit, Devil and Exorcism, that is more than any man ever possessed"; or: "All the world's murderers wait for me; they cannot die without me." (The patient had unsuccessfully attempted suicide.) "I have more brains than any other man. All Kings pay me tribute and none can do anything to me." (The patient is committed for trial.) "I was not born but have always existed." One patient calls himself Solog Carl Napoleon I., because he is accompanied by Sociology. As such he is also infallible and every wish is fulfilled at once. If we refuse to release him then "every misfortune, like a well-functioning volcano, Venusberg, will pour itself on the hospital." The dreamed-of greatness is very often, objectively, not nearly as desirable, great, or important as it appears to the patients; or it may be expressed so queerly that it merely gives the impression of ridiculousness. A hebephrenic is "Deus" and can live for two days on bread and water and on the third day on nothing at all. For one prophet among our patients, a brilliant star arose which led him from his bed to the toilet and back again three times. Besides that, he had the power to absolve others from their sins. A mathematics professor had to build bridges with the power God^1 God^2 God^3 etc. A schizophrenic was able to save a lady from sickness by masturbating while thinking of her, and so forth.

Usually the delusions of grandeur are combined with the delusions of persecution. Often this is already demonstrated by the fact that two parties or powers are concerned with the patient—one for, and one against him. More often the great man stands alone because a certain gang uses every possible means to prevent him from obtaining the recognition and fame that is rightly his.

During sleep his most valuable inventions are stolen, right out of his head. A hospital attendant robbed an invention from his body by touching him. He is constantly being irritated or even sent away to hamper the carrying out of his ideas. The patient is of such immense importance that in retaining him in the hospital the very source of life is being extinguished; the "sparkling organisms," which he has in his eyes are being annihilated.

Erotic aspirations express themselves in innumerable delusions of being loved or defiled. The erotic delusions consist mostly of a mixture of grandiose and persecutory ideas. When a female schizophrenic establishes a delusion, the sexual component is hardly ever absent. Indeed, it is usually prominent, although it is often disguised or concealed under what appears to be religious or hypochondriacal delusional content. With women it is mainly a question of marrying into a higher social class and not only of love itself. In men frequently other strivings are in the foreground. Yet also here, as a rule, we meet erotic factors, whenever the patient's delusions can be analyzed.

A working woman would like to marry her employer. The latter is in love with her but is so "oppressed" by S. (the residence of his real fiancee) that her lover cannot get near her. A male patient believes that every woman, who strikes his fancy, is in love with him. He seeks out certain amusement places, in the firm conviction that his adored one can be found there. Women give birth to 150 children every night. A sterile woman was examined as to her pelvic organs by a doctor and a policeman, both admiring her "talents". A love-sick young woman had to hold the world all night long, and it was terribly tiring; yet, as long as there were chaste women, the world would not be lost or destroyed. A love-sick schizophrenic believes that a young girl, whom he has not seen since his schooldays or whom he perhaps saw only once from a distance, is in love with him. He climbed into a princess' carriage and kissed her. Though he is completely lucid, he expects the Queen of Holland will come into his hospital bed which he has decorated with flowers for this occasion.

Very often the beloved one becomes the persecutor. Women especially are defiled or raped by those with whom they are more or less in love. Female patients who accuse the hospital doctors of having committed all sorts of immoral attacks upon them show an erotic attachment to the self-same physicians. In one case I saw the opposite happen; the hospital doctor who was first considered an enemy became the beloved.

Another form of negatively expressed erotic delusion is that of jealousy which, however, is not too frequent in schizophrenics unless complicated by alcoholism, and which may have still other roots.

In severe chronic cases and during transitory cloudy states, the sexual wishes of the patients are more or less completely fulfilled. They *are* united with their beloved, have had so many children by him, etc.

Delusions of inferiority may assume the form of those of poverty and sinfulness. They usually belong to an intercurrent melancholic depression inasmuch as they were induced during such an episode and occasionally retained later. The delusions then have the same content as other melancholias, except that schizophrenia often tinges them with its own peculiar coloring of contradiction, incompleteness and senselessness.

The patient has robbed and murdered through negligence; has been the cause of the death of a relative; has sinned against the Holy Ghost. God has withdrawn from the patient through his belly. A republican Swiss "has committed the horrible crime of lese-majesty".

Occasionally we find false self-accusations based on what could as well be called memory distortions as delusional ideas. A hebephrenic saw an epileptic girl fall down in one of her convulsive attacks. He accused himself of trying to rape her; she fell during the struggle. Another became ill at the time that several fires broke out in his village. He was at first fearful that other fires would ensue. He then conceived the idea that he, himself, must start one. Finally, he accused himself of having set fire to a certain house (which turned out to be wholly intact).

The hypochondriacal ideas are of far greater importance in these patients. In many cases, particularly in the mild ones, they completely dominate the picture. A patient, bedridden for many years, complains of terrible pains which are caused mainly by outside influences. She has had a relapse because she had remained out of bed for twenty minutes instead of only her customary five minutes; or because the unloading of potatoes had caused such a racket. The use of a bit of iodine ointment provokes a host of long-persisting complaints. The patient gets "blood cramps". Others feel themselves weak, their spirit escapes, they will never survive the day. There is a growth in their heads. Their bones have turned liquid; their hearts have turned to stone. (Change from the originally symbolic to the literal meaning.) They cannot be drowned since only their heads are alive, and all the rest of the body is dead. The patient's wife must not use eggs in cooking, otherwise he will grow feathers. Hair is growing down his back. He has no nose anymore; he has become a rubber ball. His genitals are gone; they were destroyed by fire. His spinal marrow runs out in his sperm.

The patient's very person is also changed in the sense of the delusional complexes. A hebephrenic H. is "son of the financier G., that is Napoleon". Why he is currently called H. is very puzzling to him. The catatonic K. is not named K. any more, but M. because he wants to marry M.'s daughter. Often the patients believe themselves dead. One of them has been dead three times before which does not prevent him from prophesying his imminent death and at the same time making suicidal attempts. The living and the dead, the original and the delusional personalities can exist side by side in these people. The patient is "dead and yet living". "He is in two worlds." "He was frozen in a bathtub, yet is still here." A young woman (who in her delusion believed herself married to a minister) "can be switched around; at times, she is a virgin maid, at other times a married woman". She finds this fact rather strange.

The delusion of being possessed is very commonly seen as a specific type of "double personality." Nowadays we rarely see it in its ancient religious form or sense. Instead of the Devil, God may be the commanding spirit; or "God has hurled a spirit at the patient's head. His spirit is then possessed.". Now and then the patient's sex appears altered delusionally. The male patient may feel himself at times, or even continually, a woman, or vice-versa. Even to-day we still see transformations into animals, but this is not often maintained in states of full lucidity. A catatonic feels himself to be a frog with a cold clammy skin. Of two other catatonics, one believed for a long period that she was a dog and often barked like one; the other insisted she was a shark. In the two cases, the meaning of the delusion is obvious—a symbolic degradation of the personality.

The patients may even come to consider themselves inanimate objects. A patient is a box. He used to be a drawing in a book, but he finally got away and came to the hospital. He is a machine.

Other people may be transformed. Demented people often find in the hospital a host of old friends and schoolmates who, as far as we know, are of no importance to the patient; or they may find people who play a role in their other delusions. The doctor really is the sweetheart, Mr. So-and-So. A ward mate is King William. A woman patient is tenderly embraced as "daughter." Often, particularly in cases of inconsequential confusion of persons, the delusion may be released by some vague resemblance. Sometimes there is complete absence of any points of reference. Frequently the patient considers his entire environment as transformed, "shammed." We also find that people's characteristics and station in life are being changed. The patient's sister has become engaged. The doctor is divorced from his wife and the nurse becomes a man in disguise. The patient's late mother continues living as a bull in his stable.

If a patient says the doctor is Count N., this confusion of persons should not be understood in the sense of a normal individual confusing persons. Patients will assume the presence of real or imaginary people in accordance with the momentary situation. A woman patient wishes to strike me because I am her acquaintance, Mr. R. When I protest, she says, "Don't come here as R. Come at least as O. or P." ("No, I prefer to come as M.") "You can't possibly be that person. He is an angel, a god. . . ." A patient is very rude to a lady visitor. However, the patient claims that while she certainly cursed that woman, it was not aimed at her personally and should not be held against the patient.

Many other delusions cannot easily be classified under the usual categories. It may be closely related to a persecution delusion when a patient "belongs to an association where people are cut to pieces alive". Another paranoid, while sawing wood, saws apart marriages and double beds. Without any further reason, a patient prophesied "fire and floods". Patients also feel persecuted when it begins to rain each time they speak of weather; when a dog begins to bark whenever they do a certain thing, or when everyone else in the room begins to write whenever they do. This latter occurrence was ascribed to "sub-terranean influences".

The following notes have the appearance of megalomania: "Trees can be reconstituted from old furniture by treating the ashes with electric current." A patient "sleeps concentratedly" thirty years in a single night; he is in two places at the same time, in his own home and in a previously visited health resort. In the hospital an attendant is the transformed woman attendant of an earlier period of hospitalization. The patient intends "to dig a hole in the ground and then ride down it on the spade and come out on the other side of the globe". A confused catatonic refuses to swallow because each time that she does so, she swallows the whole world. A paranoid makes notes on all the foreign language quotations which appear in the newspapers in order to analyze and interpret them "by means of mental powers". While sewing, a religiously preoccupied hebephrenic pulls the Holy Ghost out with her needle. While drinking water, a patient swallows the other patient's devil. While cutting up beans in the kitchen, she breaks the Lord's Prayer. A paranoid believes potatoes to be evil; blackbirds are evil animals (in a religious sense). He maintains that he masters many foreign languages perfectly but knows only a few words of two of them.

The creation of a second world is expressed in the delusion of a Russian patient for whom an identical duplicate "Russian Burgholzli" had been erected. Something similar is expressed when Burgholzli is conceived as submersible, being at times above, at other times below the earth.

A patient who had just masturbated refused to shake hands with the doctor because it might cause children to be born in the women's ward. Another has to prevent his family from thinking. A third complains that the doctor pulled his intestines out of his mouth and made another human being out of them. A fourth finds it very sad that so much water runs down the toilet.

The Nature of the Delusions. The delusions of schizophrenics do not necessarily represent a logical unity. Unconnected or even mutually contradictory ideas can be maintained simultaneously or appear one after the other within a short interval of time. Even related delusions are not easily combined into a logical system. Details are not connected logically even in those instances where they contain a common denominator such as persecutions by a secret society. They constitute an amorphous mass of delusional ideas, a "delusional chaos" as Schuele phrased it. There are exceptions, however, in the rare cases of paranoids whose intelligence is relatively well preserved. Furthermore, it must not be forgotten that each delusion possesses its own logical fallacies, and that the claims of each observer vary greatly in that many assume complete systematization where others find nothing of the kind. In our opinion, one should speak of a logical system only when everything is developed into a logical construction on the basis of several erroneous premises.[15] In this sense schizophrenic delusional ideas are hardly ever systematized. Rather, they are usually characterized by contradictions and infeasibilities. A hebephrenic, for some time, considered himself to be dead and buried; a negro had cut off his head; he had seen his own head lying at his feet. A patient's woman attendant is simultaneously her brother, sister, and a third person as well.

As a matter of fact the contradictions with reality are, for the most part, hardly noted at all. An able-bodied hebephrenic is very dissatisfied with us because we do not deliver to him the many shipments which arrive for him. True, they are addressed to different names, but still they are definitely for him. Another hebephrenic patient believes himself to be Mr. S., the owner of a large factory; the only thing he lacked was the naevus (which the real owner of the factory had on his face). The patient decided he would make the naevus "in effigy" and then he would really be Mr. S.

Not only do delusion and reality exist consecutively in various states of lucidity, but they can also exist simultaneously in conditions of full consciousness where one would expect that they would be mutually exclusive. A gentleman looks at a woman patient: "Then I knew that he was the teacher, although in fact he is not." A catatonic's bed is a polar bear. "I lay on it and it seemed like a bed, but it was nevertheless a polar bear." A hebephrenic writes: "The forms are nothing but the abovementioned personalities (doctors, etc. etc.); and they must cease being in the same way in which they originated." Here we note that the "forms" must cease but not the real people identified with them. "One or two rubber dolls" (which were created by an incubus) are identified with the beloved one who completely dominates the patient.

Many of the ideas are quite vague and indefinite. A schizophrenic does not care whether he is Pope or king. A claim for $100,000 can be identical for him with one for $10. The poisoned patient had noticed that someone put a brown powder in his soup. But during the discussion about it, he says that it may have been a liquid. "The chef put it in the food." ("We don't have a chef.") "The cook, then." ("The cook doesn't know about you.") "It is done on the ward, and each gets what is meant for him." A very vague idea is concealed behind the precise words, "a brown powder". A paranoid tells us: "I have something like a doublehead in me. Inside it is as if I were Christ or the Apostles on the Mount of

15. Certainly erroneous premises are continuously produced in most cases. Thus, pathological self-references can support the further development of a delusional system for decades.

Olives. Twenty-six Apostles on the Mount of Olives are in my arms. In my head I have a tile given me by Kaiser Wilhelm." A hebephrenic goes to the railway station to meet "somebody". Another orders "12 thick law books."

Often various ideas will be combined in an entirely obscure arrangement. "Yet France is right. I was suddenly told in France that there is no Trinity, 4 men made God. It is only now that I recognize this as being correct and that is why I want to be released on April 24".

The ideas can remain quite fragmentary. A hebephrenic, who for years was capable of acting as the head of a pharmacy, believed that he had invented a moving picture camera. Yet all he knew about this invention was "that the respective motor elements were arranged in the form of a right angle." White lice were thrown into a patient's bed; and then a big black louse was tossed into her bed. She cannot describe the latter insect but includes it among the white lice. Frequently, the delusion seems senseless without being so, principally, because the patients employ inadequate symbolic or otherwise bizarre expressions. When a patient says she is the "Cranes of Ibykus", she does not always mean it in the literal sense of the normal person.What she really means is that she is "free and innocent of blame or blemish." Therefore she ought to be "free"—that is, not confined in the hospital.

Personality and Delusion. The splitting of the personality is never more strikingly expressed than in the relation of the delusions to the remainder of the psyche. Parts of that total complex which we call the ego, the "self," always remain alien to the delusions. This constellation accounts for the fact that the non-affected part of the ego may disbelieve and even criticize the delusions; on the other hand, the incorrigibility and senselessness of the delusions are precisely due to the fact that many associations contradictory to the delusional are simply not brought into any logical connection with it.

Thus under certain conditions the patients can laugh and joke about ideas in which at other occasions they firmly believe. This usually happens when megalomanic ideas are involved. But I have even witnessed a patient's hearty laughter over his own delusion of persecution without the latter being corrected. Sometimes an idea which had just been expressed emphatically, may be toned down again in the next sentence. ("It was not so bad.")

A hebephrenic made fun of himself because he, the Lord, walked between two doctors and yet did not know how to get out of the hospital. While he was a patient in another hospital, he used to make the weather, right after tea time. Here in this institution, nothing seemed to happen after coffee-time. A "King of the Whole World" himself asked the question "whether all this did not sound rather fantastic."

There are many intermediate stages between delusion and conscious fantasies, particularly in acute states. Forel's patient, Miss L. S., gave one of the best descriptions of this phenomenon. "Bordering on the true delusional idea yet definitely distinct from it, there existed another condition throughout the entire course: half-driven by an inspiration, half-aware and half-willing, I created for myself a role which I carried on playing and reciting. I became so enwrapped in, so completely absorbed by, this role that I acted in accordance with it, without precisely believing that I was identical with the persons portrayed. Sure enough in all this, there were many gradations from the borderline of the delusional idea, perhaps from the delusion itself, to the merely exuberant or excited mood; all this happened while I was completely clear as to myself and to my surroundings or, at least, so it seemed to me."

However, attempts at criticism are usually quite ineffective. Frequently, the patients are unable to escape the compelling force of the delusional ideas even when they themselves feel a need to overcome them. A catatonic notified the court that his illness had been diagnosed as paranoia and the apparitions as hallucinations. "Be that as it may," the patient asserted, "there are still sufficient reasons to proceed against this gang." It was pointed out to a hebephrenic, who had interpreted a slash in a valuable painting as an injury to herself, that this was not serious. "Naturally, it does not necessarily mean that it is serious but, I only want to know why it was done to me."

Not infrequently the delusions are split off from the personality in such a way that they appear to the patient as a product not of his own mental activity, but rather as the resultant of the workings of another psyche. The delusional ideas are "suggested," "manufactured"; yet, he believes them.

However, the associative isolation of the delusions is most obvious in its relation to the affectivity. The content may be in contradiction with the actual mood of the patient. The delusional content may correspond, in the same individual at the same time or at successive times, to positive or negative affects. Often the patient connects completely inadequate or no feelings at all with the delusion. Megalomanic ideas may be accompanied by an expression of despair. Tales about the most horrible persecutions are related with perfect indifference; indeed sometimes even with a smile. Or the affect may show marked variability. Thus a nurse deplored her golden spine. Later she sang happily, "I have a golden spine."

Since the whole personality need not be involved in the delusion, and since the affects, and with them the drives do not have to correspond to the delusion, it follows that the reaction to the delusion is frequently also inadequate. One can almost say that those actions which would follow on the basis of logic from the delusional premises are the very ones which are met with rather infrequently.

Certainly we see the persecuted patients busily cursing and complaining as they move about the hospital wards. They attack their supposed persecutors physically or with legal complaints. They seek to escape their tormentors by constant change of residence or by means of elaborate precautions or various magical practices. Occasionally, the erotomanic ones even take steps to get closer to the beloved object. A woman patient went to the theater every night for two years in order to speak to her fancied bridegroom who did not know her at all. Graphomanic authors write as much as they are able to, and often even have as much of this material printed as their circumstances will permit. However, in comparison to the number and duration of the delusions, acts which would correspond to them in terms of normal logic are rather rare.

The apathy and the lack of interest extend to the delusions not only in the "end-state," but quite often even from their onset. One of our hebephrenic patients had long felt persecuted; but at first he was not quite sure and therefore could not act accordingly; later on he "no longer paid so much attention" to the needling, "since he felt quite sure that he was being persecuted."

Kings and Emperors, Popes, and Redeemers engage, for the most part, in quite banal work, provided they still have any energy at all for activity. This is true not only of patients in institutions, but also of those who are completely free. None of our generals has ever attempted to act in accordance with his imaginary rank and station.

Some persecuted patients are subject merely to an occasional, quite unavailing bout of cursing; or they will commit some foolish prank and will then withdraw from those around them; but for decades they will omit all purposeful activity which according to common experience would bring them some peace and rest. Their reactions are thoroughly autistic, and unconcerned with reality.

Frequently, they behave in accordance with the trends of their delusions but without the least adaptation to reality, which they may otherwise still take into consideration. The persecuted patient may slap some passerby who is not at all involved in the patient's delusions. The sinner most earnestly demands that he be killed, without paying attention to the obvious objection that such an act would land the doctors in prison. A pious paranoid wanted to seat himself on a red hot stove and pass wind in order to drive out the evil spirit inside the stove.

The splitting of the pysche into several souls always leads to the greatest inconsistencies. A persecuted patient, upon release from the institution, took leave, movingly and with real emotion, of her chief tormentor who had so often wanted to kill her. The patients will confidently hand us their letters to be forwarded, in which they accuse us of the most atrocious crimes, as well as of constantly defrauding them of their mail. They curse us in the strongest terms as their poisoners, only to ask us in the very next moment to examine them for some minor ailment, or to ask for a cigarette.

Often the measures which they take as a consequence of their delusions are as illogical as the delusions themselves. They invent all sorts of magic, which does not stop at the most senseless or disgusting. The most bizarre behavior and words are used as "conjurations" to protect them against hostile influences.

At times one can partly understand the connection between reaction and delusion, even though it cannot be justified by normal reason. A young woman was in love with a coffee merchant. Therefore, she was mocked (hallucinatorily) by the word, "coffee"; and as a result she forthwith refused to drink coffee.

In many cases, particularly in the acute agitated states, we do not find any relationship between delusion and behavior. Thus, a catatonic suddenly begins to scream, "I am God, I am God," strikes blindly and wildly about him and wants to ram his head through the wall.

Origin and Fate of the Delusions. The acute states are the cradle of a great many delusions. Delusions can originate, in known ways, during melancholic and manic mood disturbances; and these delusions correspond to the affect because the latter inhibits any contradictory associations and deprives them of their value. In the schizophrenic confusional states, there arises an apparently wild chaos of false notions which the patients believe in. Both kinds of ideas can survive their nascent state. They then continue to exist as "residual delusions" (Neisser), without any affective and intellectual connections, in the "secondary" stages of the disease.

The genesis of the delusions of the confusional state can only be uncovered by thorough analysis. It is somewhat easier to trace these origins in the chronic conditions than in the acute states; and it is in these chronic conditions that we first find some logical forms which may sometimes also be demonstrated in the acute confusional states.

Some delusions arise from those already existing in the patients. The unrecognized prince can, logically, look upon his parents as merely his foster-parents. But such conclusions are certainly not always drawn by the schizophrenic.

Other elaborations are unsuccessful attempts at an explanation of delusional relationships. Thus we have the delusion of being transparent because everyone knows the patient's thoughts.

Naturally, the thousands of peculiar experiences which the patient has gone through provide innumerable occasions for similar "explanation-delusions." But the patient's lack of need for logical thought is likewise reflected by the relative rarity of ideas of such origin. Thus the "transformation" of delusions of persecution into delusions of greatness (megalomania) is not nearly as frequent as many authorities seem to think. I have never seen cases corresponding completely to such a description (Kelp agrees with me). To the healthy mind, it appears to be quite plausible or even necessary that an individual, who has been so strenuously persecuted, must also be worthy of such an effort, but this is not a necessary conclusion for the schizophrenic. In general, megalomania can be as primary as a delusion of persecution. For the most part both forms are combined in the same patient right from the start; only their quantitative relationships change.

In the severe clinical conditions of this disease, the delusions have the tendency to spread. A patient is being poisoned; the water of the lake where he lives is consequently also poisoned. A young Protestant's engagement was broken because his fiancee was a Catholic. He now believes himself to be persecuted by her and hence also by the Catholic attendants on his ward; and then by all the attendants. A worker is accused by a discharged employee of being a spy; soon after he believes that everyone in his group also takes him for a spy; finally, this includes everybody, even his brothers. A woman insists she is persecuted by a certain gentleman; then by all men, and finally even by women. Love, too, can thus be transferred to more and more people. An old maid is in love with one of her superiors. In the hospital, she is in love with the ward physician of the moment. She is sufficiently lucid about this impersonal sort of love to be able to write to one of her so-called lovers: "Thus I will remain true to you until I know another."

Sometimes this generalization takes the form of obscuring the distinction between the patient's identity and that of other persons; even the difference between people and abstract ideas is wiped out. The hebephrenic who heard the voices of "singing birds" knew that his own masturbation was thus being referred to; he himself was the "singing bird." Later he also heard the word in other connections; then the "bird-song" wanted to kill him, and was the essence of his persecution delusion. A catatonic has lightning-like thoughts which appear very strange to her. Later, she connects this idea with her feeling of being transparent: the flashes of lightning read her eyes and thus steal her thoughts.

In the above instances, the spreading of the delusion may be attributed to simple analogizing or to a generalization of the idea involved. Whoever fears a Catholic may finally fear all Catholics, and then all people. In accordance with the schizophrenic modes of association, however, all kinds of inner and outer experiences may have adhered to the delusional idea, without having either a logical or an affective connection with it. A patient hears voices through "electric wires and gas-lamps"; originally the gas-lamps had nothing to do with the voices, but seem to represent an obvious association to "electric wires." A religious patient feels persecuted and expects help. He notices a woman walking up and down the railroad station platform. Delusion: The woman has been sent by heaven to save him. A catatonic woman had known her physician's wife before she fell ill. The patient was worried about her release and the cost of her hospitalization. Delusion: The doctor's wife must pay for her; and if she had not known the doctor's wife, she would not have had to remain in the hospital.

Many times mere analogy forms the basis of the connection. A patient is bound; therefore he is Christ. He curses the police and thus considers himself the last of the Bourbons. A ward-mate in the next bed also berates the police; therefore the latter is also a Bourbon.

However, the connection may be quite incomprehensible to the healthy person. The doctor accidentally touches the patient's nose during an eye examination: the patient rises and solemnly declares that this "was a sign from God indicating that he was chosen to be His son."—A hebephrenic presented with a piece of chocolate sees some letters printed on it: they are aimed at her. . . "She does not know what the letters are or what they mean. She could certainly have found out but was so angered that she immediately scratched the words out." This disposition to delusions—the predilection for interpreting everything that happens—is constantly present. It may be attached to any accidental event. Even such pseudo-connections as the following do not invalidate this statement. "In front of my window there stands a lamp-post like the one we have home; thus once again I find something very peculiar here." When such logical constructs no longer have any real connection with the ego and its wishes, they appear more like a game than delusional ideas. They can hardly be distinguished from similar productions of the manic: the doctor is the "optician" because he wears glasses; he wears on his finger the "Ring of the Nibelungs."

Such analogies can be meant seriously, even when they are directed to the patient's own personality. One of our hebephrenics identified himself with all kinds of things ("I am elder-bush," "I am an old umbrella") yet we could not establish symbolizations or similar processes.

A paranoid had once misunderstood the proper name of the village where he had asked the parson for help. In spite of repeated proof to the contrary she persisted in the use of her own distorted name of the village. These delusions are unrelated to the patients' ego. The false conception of the village name has become delusional only because it accidentally became linked to a delusional idea. The "eccentric delusional ideas" which have no direct connection with the patient's complexes arise in the same way.

Since some authors (e.g., Specht) have denied the occurrence of such delusional ideas, a few more examples may be offered. A hebephrenic occupies herself with heraldy. (In our part of the country it is, naturally, Allemanic heraldy.) During the Russo-Japanese War he developed the notion that the noble Japanese were of Allemanic ancestry, without bringing these ideas into any recognizable connection with his own complexes. A woman patient heard a rumbling noise: the Prince of France (who otherwise played no particular role in her ideas) has been murdered. A hebephrenic who was not concerned with the Boers in his delusional ideas, maintained one day that Cronje had been murdered. A patient declares that a ward-mate had been robbed. Another insists that one of his ward-mates has some money in the bank. These statements are made without any discernible relation to the patients' own preoccupations. Now, one could say that such ideas are not delusions but rather errors. However, in that case one gives both ideas new *ad hoc* limits.

Of course, a number of delusional ideas appear to be formed like errors inasmuch as conclusions are drawn from inadequate premises. As a paranoid passes by, someone spits; hence that person wishes to show his contempt for the paranoid. A patient sometimes wakes up with a headache; therefore, she must have been beaten during the night. The far too broad conclusions reached by analogy also belong to this category.

If such false conclusions are to generate delusions, the concurrence of affective factors is of course necessary. Therefore we usually find them in the following form. The patient refers a perception, on the basis of inadequate logical reasons, to a complex which happens to be in the foreground of his interest at the time. The *delusions of reference* ("pathological self-reference") can be seen in their crassest form in schizophrenia. A child passes in front of the patient; he protests, "I am not the father of this child." Everybody is in the street because of him; each gesture of these people has some significance for him; newspaper advertisements refer to him; the storm was made especially for him; the edition of Goethe's works in the hospital library is full of hints at him and has been falsified for his sake. A still fairly lucid naturalist rejoices that the small infusoria wave to him when he looks at them through the microscope. During a meal, a catatonic is asked by his sister whether he wants some more bread; in a wild rage, he wants to stab her because she thus referred to his unemployed status (in German his "breadlessness"). In this example, it is quite clear that the releasing factor was not the entirely harmless and matter-of-fact reference to the ego, but the reference to the emotionally charged complex of the patient.

In the usual discussion of the genesis of delusions, aside from the delusions of reference, suspiciousness is considered an important source of delusional ideas. It is then regarded as a still undirected persecutory delusion which only later assumes a more definite form. One of our women patients writes: "Above all, I experience any friendliness as unpleasant. Suspicion always arises in me and I harbor it against everyone and everything." Another expresses it even more emphatically: "One cannot trust one's own shirt." The feeling of discomfort in all situations which is so often present may arouse varying degrees of mistrust. ("The very walls of my house want to devour me.") At the start of the disease, megalomaniacs usually have great hopes and great ambitions in a general, undefined and vague way. Yet in spite of all this, I would not like to establish as a principle the development of delusions from indefinite "feelings." Indefinite ideas and pathological intellectual feelings can appear any time in the later course of the disease (the above examples of suspiciousness come from older patients) and are rather common during periods of remission.

On the other hand, the sudden appearance of sharply formulated ideas may be the first perceptible symptoms of the disease. Likewise, delusions will often develop from the definite toward the indefinite and vague. A catatonic woman patient believed during the period of her puberty that she had been engaged to a physician. Later she claimed to be the daughter of two other physicians and to have wanted to study medicine; subsequently she thought of herself as the owner of the hospital and of the Polytechnic Institute. Behind these thoughts, we can still detect the idea that she desires to marry a physician.

We cannot yet formulate any laws pertaining to the development of schizophrenic delusion. Certain possibilities may lie in the direction of wish-formation. A man who had always been avid for money and honors wants to marry a rich girl and make the family very happy. Therefore, he must divorce his wife and sacrifice his child (in the literal sense). Then he becomes Jesus, then God, finally possessor of the Hapsburg and Kyburg fortresses.

During his first attack of illness, a scientist directs great battles and makes great inventions to honor his beloved. During his second episode of illness some years after, his heart tells him that his beloved one is not married (incorrect, in fact). A certain clerk has great aspirations. A lady treats him kindly, he wants to marry her; at the time the Queen of the Netherlands figured prominently in the news; the Queen also wants to marry him. He regards his wife, who refuses to divorce him, as unfaithful to him; she wants to poison and libel him. In this case, we see the simultaneous formation of the wish and the delusion of persecution developing from the obstacles to its fulfilment.

Women frequently have delusions, first of being loved, then of getting married and finally of being pregnant. Many of them even have children by their imaginary lovers. This sort of development may take only a few weeks in twilight states, but years in more lucid cases. If the adored person is a cleric, the delusion will be further elaborated in a religious direction.

The forms of expression in which the delusional idea becomes conscious are exceedingly variable. They often appear as logical conclusions and in such cases do not differ normally from the results of healthy thinking. But quite frequently, the delusions seem to emerge "primordially" from the unconscious in their complete and finished form. They are simply here, without any conscious reflection and without the patient being able to say how they got into his psyche. These ideas may have the subjective quality of newness or even strangeness, or the patient may have accepted them as a matter of course as if he had never thought in any other way. Between these two extremes we frequently see the entire scale of intermediate degrees. "Those who understand only now" are particularly often found among the paranoid patients.

Even this mechanism does not necessarily always yield sharply defined delusional ideas. The delusions can appear in the form of "hunches," "intuitions," etc., which can persist permanently in their indefinite forms.

Most delusions become conscious in the form of sensory deceptions. Third persons reveal to the patient the conclusions of his unconscious false logic to which he subsequently may also attach explanatory delusional ideas. This state of affairs is not different in principle from memory-falsifications which introduce new material, whether those be illusions or hallucinations of memory.

At times, the whole conscious personality in a more or less altered condition of consciousness participates in building the delusion. In addition to the usual delirious confusional states, there are other states in which the patients appear lucid but have "dreamings," or as one of our patients put it, "day-dreams." The patients' relation to these phenomena is objective to the extent that they are aware of something special taking place, though they generally believe in the contents of the "dreams." The patients will also complain a little about these states. Often the development of the delusion occurs in the form of the ordinary dream. A patient, whom we had observed for many years, elaborated her delusional fable only in dreams. She knew it, but believed in it nonetheless.

A well-educated, employable, and socially adaptable patient complained one morning that I had gotten her with child while she was asleep and that I had cut it out of her arm. She knew very well that she had seen this in a dream but, nevertheless, clung to the idea. I attempted to make her understand that I was not responsible for what she dreamt, and that in reality I had not been with her during the night. My persuasiveness failed, however, when she asked me in turn, "Then why do you come in the dream?"—A teacher, in financial difficulties, awoke one night quite happy. He related that he had dreamed that his salary had been increased; this delusion persisted and marked the start of a very severe illness. A catatonic patient "has dreams, and when she awakes everything remains just as she had dreamed." Many patients experience the same persecutions in their dreams as in their waking state; paranoid patients like to interpret this as a result of their having been put to sleep so that experiments might be performed on them. Not infrequently, hallucinations in dreams and in the waking state can no longer be kept apart.

The latter situation may also be observed in the analysis of dreams which should be carried out according to the same rules as with the non-psychotic patients. One of our paranoid patients had, over a prolonged period of time, quite undisguised wish-fulfilment dreams. If something unpleasant happened to her (rebuttal of her erotic aspirations, etc.), she would promptly dream the following night about the opposite, and would then maintain this as a delusion. [16]

Occasionally the dreams may carry over into twilight state. A catatonic patient dreamed for two nights that she had a fight with her husband, who was in reality a very brutal man. During the dream, she talked aloud and stared with wide-open eyes. Similar attacks then occured first when she went to bed, and finally also in daytime.

The delusion may, of course, also change under the influence of various internal and external circumstances. Needless to say, the delusions vary with the severity of the disease (by which not merely the anatomic and physiological disease process is meant). The delusions often elaborate themselves in episodic thrusts, even when no acute attacks seem to occur.

---

16. Cf. The relation of schizophrenia to dreams.

Often, but not always, the delusions vary parallelling the (primary) mood changes. The patient who is the Queen, in a manic phase, becomes the Queen of Night or Hell in a melancholic phase. The infinitely long tunnel through the earth seen in a state of anxiety becomes, during the euphoric mood, the patient's technical invention. Yet such transformations are not as frequent as one would expect. For the most part, other delusions appear in the foreground with the changes of mood: the despairing sinner not only turns into a prophet, but also into a happy lover, an inventor, etc.

Delusions connected with certain localities, and people are often abandoned for some time following a change in environment. Indeed, new surroundings may be regarded at first as protective instead of as persecutory. Sometimes the delusions are simply transferred; the new ward-physician is the same persecutor or beloved as the previous doctor. In other cases, particularly where the persecutors are completely imaginary, a change of place will hardly influence the delusional ideas.

The Duration of Delusions. As "morbid notions" delusions may last a few seconds; as "fixed ideas" they may persist for a life-time. In chronic forms with only slight disturbances of intelligence, long duration is the rule, while ideas developed during acute attacks often fade away simultaneously with the acute state. A moderately ill patient who had been able to stay out of a hospital until past her climacteric had had a revelation in her twentieth year to the effect that if she remained a virgin for another thirty years, she would receive 20,000 francs. At the end of the thirty years, she went to a bank to collect the money.

Many delusions recede into the background as a result of losing their emotional valence by being monotonously repeated. They then gradually cease to influence the patient's behavior. They recede similarly when the patients lose interest in the delusion. The patients do not correct their ideas, but simply do not think about them anymore. This process is often the beginning of the frequent "forgetting" of delusions. However, in special situations, these ideas may be brought back into consciousness by way of an appropriate association. Sometimes they may be as clear and complete as ever. At other times, they may be as vague as a blurred memory in a healthy person. Sometimes this obscurity of the old delusion constitutes the way in which the delusional ideas gradually sink into oblivion.

It is very doubtful whether schizophrenic delusions may ever be completely corrected, unlike the errors of the healthy mind or the delusions of the manic-depressive psychosis. As yet I have seen no schizophrenic who after his "cure" was completely objective about his delusions. Either the patients dismiss them lightly without real associations or they are still emotionally charged; sometimes the patients even produce thoughts which are only understandable if it is assumed that the delusions still retain some reality for these patients even though consciously they may reject them. Thus Riklin's (612) patient, Karl B., insisted that his imaginary bride had no further significance for him, but he thought it "outrageous" that she should now appear to him as an ordinary servant girl. Sometimes the manner in which the delusion is declared to be senseless shows that in a way it is still alive; e.g., this correction is often made in the manner of a lesson learned by rote.

One of our patients, who for many years had been the Lord and had corrected this idea, nevertheless continued to write "The Lord" after his name. A professor dedicated an outstanding scientific work to his delusional mistress.

The continued existence of apparently abandoned delusions is also proved by the fact that such ideas formed in an earlier attack are as a rule taken up again in subsequent exacerbations as if nothing had happened in the meantime. Not infrequently they prove immediately upon their reappearance, to be further elaborated, so that it is probable that they have not only been active, but have continued to grow in the subconscious.

There is of course, no proof that a schizophrenic delusion can never be entirely corrected. However, the above experiences make it quite probable that such an idea always continues to lead a sort of existence in some corner of the psyche. Indeed, we see in the normal also that some ideas (religious or political), which were previously charged with emotion but were fully corrected by reason, never completely lose their influence on the individual and may completely dominate the psyche again in old age and *ante mortem.*

(c) The Accessory Memory Disturbances

We already mentioned the peculiar capacity of many schizophrenics to register more details than a normal person under identical circumstances. But there is also a hyperfunction of memory in the sense that during (an acute or chronic) delirium old memories going back to the earliest childhood emerge or obtrude themselves in all their freshness. In the latter case, one may almost speak of "a compulsion to remember." These often very detailed reminiscences may seem indifferent to the patient; very often, however, they are clearly related to a complex and can then be altered in the sense of a memory-illusion. They may disappear just as suddenly as they appeared, or they may take permanent possession of the psyche. Such memories may also express themselves as hallucinations instead of as thoughts and the patient once more sees and hears his earlier experiences, at times, with great fidelity. Something similar may be observed from one attack of illness to another. In periods of remission, the contents of a past delirium may remain completely forgotten for many years, only to reappear during a later episode of the disease. During her first attack, one of our patients had given a preacher her Bible; twenty years later, in a second attack, she sent him a bill for 50 francs for it.

There is a special kind of memory operation, in which a patient is so powerfully reminded of an earlier situation by some external event that he can, at least psychically, recreate it. One of our patients had changed clinically, so that we had to consider her now as catatonic rather than, as previously, paranoid. Visited by the physician who had cared for her during her paranoid phase, she temporarily altered her behavior completely to that exhibited in the earlier paranoid phase.

In some cases, memories from childhood emerge in a more or less connected fashion. These may then induce the patient to behave accordingly. Such an infantilized patient began to deposit her feces on a piece of paper and then to take the paper to the lavatory, just as she had done as a child.

Much more important than the hypermnesias are the memory gaps or lacunae. Acute agitated episodes often leave behind them a markedly poor memory for the events of that period. However, the most frequent memory gaps or lapses arise through blockings. Just as in the healthy, only to an infinitely greater degree, events which are in contradiction to the wishes of the moment or those which for some other reason are not willingly recalled are blocked, sometimes forever, sometimes only in specific constellations. The tendency of blocks to become generalized, may delete events which are often but barely related to the original unpleasant feeling.

When the agitated state begins to subside, the patients particularly like to forget their own acts of violence, or to regard them as mere consequences of preventive measures taken against the patient. These measures, harmless and necessary as they may have been, in turn appear to the patients as gross abuse. The splitting power of the complexes has already been mentioned in relation to hallucinations. However, the entire hallucinatory excitement, together with a portion of the external events, may also be forgotten in this way. The patient may become aware of this in the following manner: "Now I am happy again and don't get excited anymore, because after a few minutes I have already forgotten what I said." Such affectively determined memory disturbances may also assume the form of anterograde amnesia.

After acute and agitated phases of the disease we frequently encounter an amnesia varying widely in intensity and extent.[17] Sometimes the patients sense these lacunae and are then disposed to ascribe them to hypnosis or some other influence. Often the period they have lived through will also seem much shorter to them; or they will believe that repeated experiences, such as doctor's visits, took place only once. Normal persons frequently cannot reproduce their dreams; in the same way, patients frequently may be incapable of recalling spontaneously their deliriums. However, the memories may emerge when they encounter something similar or when one can give them a cue. Such amnesias are not fixed, but may change. One of our catatonics, who had awakened from a twilight state, was at times unable to remember the entire episode, while at other times he could remember nothing at all. Inconsistency of memory is not rare; thus a catatonic would remember nothing about her agitated episode except an injection that had been given her; but of that she even knew the exact date. After states of "double orientation" both sets of events are remembered even though they are not always simultaneously accessible. One of our severest catatonics mistook his parents for demons and treated them accordingly. Upon improvement, however, he knew precisely when his parents had visited and what they had said.

It is not easy to test the memory during the acute attack itself. Where there is no real "confusion" present, one can often see that the memory has remained fairly good, although falsifications in the direction of the delusions frequently becloud recall. I have only once seen a clear case of anterograde amnesia which was not determined by complexes; it was observed in a hebephrenic who was also mildly alcoholic. She arrived at the hospital considerably agitated, was moderately clouded, and would forget most of the events of the immediately preceding days. She displaced to the day before an extensive examination which had taken place the day of her arrival at the hospital.

Paramnesias are especially frequent in schizophrenia; memory illusions often constitute the main material for the construction of delusions in paranoids. The entire previous life of the patient may be changed in his memory in terms of his complex.

A visitor appeared so aristocratic to the patient that he could only be a delegate from the Emperor. The patient was now being poisoned, exactly as he had been poisoned as a child. The patients constantly reproach us that we had recently promised them their release, whereas in reality we had said just the opposite. A patient insisted his long dead mother had told him certain things which in reality had been said by the

17. See below: memory for acute attacks.

preacher at her funeral. Frequently things are interchanged because they are equivalent in terms of the complexes. A patient became her daughter's imminent unhappiness. For weeks afterwards, she was inconsolable because she believed she had slandered her daughter (a complex of sexual jealousy of her daughter who had just become engaged). Another patient was very annoyed with herself over her hearty appetite; some months later, she was convinced that during that time she had been unable to eat. A patient with an otherwise excellent memory sang the psalm "The Lord Is My Shepherd." However, on the following day, she thought she had sung "On the Meadow There Ain't no Sin." Transitive memory illusions and other falsifications of personal relations are also frequent. Forel's patient, L. S., thought that she had been continually transferred from one bed to another, whereas in reality it was she who constantly changed her bed against everyone's will. The frequent false complaints of the patients that they were being agitated and attacked while they were quite peaceful are not all based on hallucinations.

Many patients find all their thoughts in print. They invented the story which they have just read, and even long ago told it to their brother. They have invented everything, and have painted certain famous pictures 600 years ago. This sort of paramnesia [18] is not at all rare in schizophrenia, and is not clearly distinguishable from the *memory falsifications based on identification.* For a long period of time, one of our hebephrenics believed that he had experienced exactly one year before everything that was happening. "The very same visitor in exactly the same clothes was here one year ago today and said the same things." Another patient maintained upon admission that he had already been in this hospital once before, only he was not sure for how long. Then he suddenly remembered that he had been here twice before, once in 1893 for 10 minutes, and in 1895, overnight. However, this is not an insane asylum but the naval barracks. He also claimed that he already knew the doctor, which shows the negligible difference between many misidentifications of persons and memory falsifications based on identification.

The frequent phenomenon of actual experiences appearing to the patient as having been foretold for a specified time constitutes only a slight deviation from the abovementioned mechanism. Whatever is experienced may appear to the patient to have been foretold, be it by others or by himself. The latter seems the more common.

Real memory hallucinations are very frequent. It suddenly comes to the patient's mind that he has experienced this or that, at this or that time. Usually, he clings as firmly to this idea as if it were a true memory;

---

18. A. Marie called this phenomenon *"déjà fait,"* and compared it with *"déjà vu"* and *"déjà voulu."*

as long as there is no essential improvement it continues even more firmly. A patient, who told us how her small son ran out of the house and was brought back, afterwards maintained that he had been run over. In response to our remonstrances, she then said that she did not know whether she meant that the boy was dead or alive. Delbrück mentions a patient with memory hallucinations who had written a veritable Odyssey of adventures all of which had taken place only in his memory: he was placed naked in a cage and exhibited in all the inns of the town; he was forced to perform acrobatics on church steeples and was then thrown off them. Finally, these adventures were extended all over the earth and into space. Delusions of reference can also express themselves as memory illusions and falsifications. The patient had read public notices in the newspaper that he was to come to our hospital. In most cases, the memory falsification, like the hallucinations and delusions, is related to an emotionally charged thought. Thus a patient, who was dissatisfied with his wife, suddenly thought that he had once told the attendant that he wanted to poison his wife and marry someone else. Another patient had once seen a young girl in a field. He then confessed to his minister that he had raped the girl, which was not true.

Sometimes it occurs to the patients that they had not previously thought of the imaginary event. They then seek an explanation for it: the patient had received a letter stating that in a certain place a million francs are deposited for her; then she was allegedly put to sleep so that afterwards she remembered nothing; when later it again comes to her mind, the letter has been stolen from her.

Kraepelin thought that such memory falsifications only occurred in conditions of clouded consciousness and in a state of impaired capacity for criticism. This contradicts my own experience. The patient who had those fantastic adventures was at the same time an excellent office worker. After ten years' duration of his severe condition, during which he was completely dominated by his memory illusions and falsifications, he could again do the relatively complicated work of a salesman. He has now been at it for about 8 years.

Negative hallucinations also can be observed quite often. They are differentiated from simple exclusion in that the patients suddenly become conscious of the fact that an event has not occurred. The patient begins abruptly to curse that he has only seen his doctor once to-day, although the latter was with the patient about seven different times during the course of the day; or the patient complains that all the ward patients except himself were offered cigarettes. In reality he has at that very moment finished smoking.

Until now, in contrast to the views of some authors, I have not observed *confabulation* as it appears in organic cases; e. g., memory hallucinations which fill in memory gaps which at first appear at a (usually externally) given moment and mostly adapt themselves to such an occasion; indeed, their content may be influenced in accordance with it. The case cited by Neisser (519a) could not be fully observed, but it was certainly not a question of confabulation, but rather of an ordinary memory hallucination.

On the other hand, we may see some *pseudologia phantastica* in the sense of a hysteriform wish-formation. If it is very pronounced and accompanied by unimpaired consciousness, it almost always indicates a complication.

(d) The Person

The ego may undergo the most manifold alterations. Loss of the feeling of activity and, particularly, the inability to direct one's thoughts robs the ego of some essential components. The process of association travels along unusual pathways. Everything may seem different; one's own person as well as the external world, and indeed usually in a completely unclear manner, so that the patient hardly knows any more how to orient himself either inwardly or outwardly. Parasthesias of bodily sensations may further complicate the auto-psychic orientation. Thus it may happen that a very intelligent patient needs hours of strenuous inner effort "to find her own ego for a few brief moments." The patients "can't catch up with themselves"; they "have lost their individual self." A certain patient had to look continually for his own body. Since any part of the ego may split off and, on the other hand, since entirely alien concepts may be attached to it, the patients become "depersonalized." The person "loses his boundaries in time and space." The patients may identify themselves with some other person, even with inanimate objects, with a chair, with Switzerland ;[19] conversely, they may lose all connection with themselves. *Single emotionally charged ideas or drives attain a certain degree of autonomy so that the personality falls to pieces. These fragments can then exist side by side and alternately dominate the main part of the personality, the conscious part of the patient.* However, the patient may also become a definitely different person from a certain moment onwards.

Thus the patient may not only permanently feel himself to be the Emperor but he may also have lost his entire past. To be sure, he usually still knows what he has formerly experienced, but he ascribes it to another person; he himself has not experienced it. His past is an entirely different one, usually not very clearly reconstructed.

---

19. Such identifications are at times thought of in the literal sense, and at other times symbolically or in some other unreal sense.

A Swiss citizen, J. H., employed in a Paris business firm E., came to the Charenton Hospital in 1877. He no longer knew who he was; once he even signed himself as Midhat Pasha. He thought he had been born in 1870 in Charenton and had not eaten in seven years. While there, he had been "pinched from his chest to his feet, and down his back to his ankles, because he was a triple organism." A certain J. H. was indeed employed by the firm E. and placed by them in the Montparnasse Almshouse. There he was thrown on a bed and sustained a head injury. Mr. E. notified J. H.'s brother; the latter had, by mistake carried off the patient instead of the real J. H., and thus it was that the patient lived under this name in the Rheinau Hospital. Such was this patient's conception. He had distributed his life experience between two personalities and to complete one of these (his present one) he invented a few facts (such as the birth in Charenton, the name of Midhat Pasha, etc.). A certain Mrs. S. who was brought in from police detention, was not Mrs. S.; the real Mrs. S. was at home, working in the vineyard according to the patient.

Naturally such patients must speak of themselves in one of their two versions or they may speak in the third person of the other two. This sort of reference is here not merely an unusual or awkward figure of speech such as we may find in mental defectives or in children, but is the expression of a real alteration in personality. But even when such a splitting cannot be demonstrated, a patient may speak of himself only in the third person. Usually he designates himself by one of his several names. I do not know yet quite how these cases are to be understood.[20] One of our chronic catatonics persistently spoke of herself in the second person singular.

In general, a complete alteration of personality is associated with severe degrees of so-called dementia.

In milder cases, the patients are at one time an imaginary person, at another the real one. The imaginary personality may always be the same one or it may assume different forms. Some of these patients are at any one time so consistently and completely the one personality or the other, that they do not even think of the other person when they assume the part of one; the person whom they represent at the moment is considered as the natural one. Other patients may become conscious of the change. A woman patient may be "switched, from a virgin to a married woman." Another woman is "a man named Bauman, and then again myself." For the most part, the different conceptions are mixed up in an irregular way, occasionally even in the very same sentence.

The delusion of sex transformation also alters the personality.

---

20. I am, of course, not including those cases where there is simply the use of a figure of speech.

The lack of a sense of reality may also extend to the personality itself. A patient "is not really herself, she is merely a reflection of herself." Another finds it quite remarkable that "Often she is not here, and yet is here."

Not infrequently, a part of the personality detaches itself and is then attached to another person (*transitivism*).[21] Whatever the patient does or hallucinates, is an experience of another person.

A patient often claimed that she had holes in her hands and was half-blind; now she maintains the attendant also has holes in her hands and is half-blind. Many patients believe their relatives are mentally ill; or, even more frequently, they believe them at last to have been committed to the mental institution; or these relatives are receiving electro-therapy like themselves. A patient strikes himself twenty times, thinking that he is striking his enemies. Another patient screams, but thinks that it is his neighbor who is screaming. A third one speaks in a confused way but accuses the doctor of being unable to express himself clearly; her eye glasses do not fit, so she says to him: "What awfully silly glasses you are wearing!" Frequently the patients will blame their surroundings or attendants for what they themselves have done. A patient hits the attendant on the head and screams, "Oh, my poor little head!" Another seeing the attendant, calls out, "There goes the maid with the lantern. I am the maid with the lantern."

There is a slight difference when the patient believes that other people have taken and are using his name. There is a transitivistic component in that very common answer to a given question: "I didn't ask you." It may be considered as a kind of semi-transitivism when a patient is not quite clear as to whether people or his hallucinations influence him, or whether he influences them; indeed, he does not care which way it works; the direction of his actions from himself or to himself, and hence the persons involved, is not clearly distinguished.

A hebephrenic thinks that whatever he does (for example, scratching his face) is being done by another person; it is always a person whom he happens to see at the moment. During such activity he feels he is that person, though he may not be quite sure.

In this instance, there was not only an act "transitively" displaced onto another person, but that person was reflexively incorporated in the patient. Such cases of *appersonation* sometimes occur without the transitivistic phenomena. The patient believes he is going through the actions or experiences of another person.

A woman was taking care of her husband who was ill with intestinal

21. A patient of L. Binswanger claimed that other people possessed certain parts of his personality. This is a preliminary stage of transitivism.

cancer, and came to believe she had the same malady. A patient's neighbor died; the patient thinks that he himself has died and covers his face with the sheet. Particularly frequently, the patient has done things which just happened or which others have done (*sentiment du déjà fait*, etc., cf. accessory memory disturbances). During a thunderstorm, the patient believes he, not God, is punishing his persecutors. Things seen may likewise be appersonated: the chief attendant holds a black-bordered letter in his hands, hence the patient's hands become completely black.

The above instance of appersonation was favored by this patient's obsessive thoughts of sin and death. In general, the splitting of the personality takes place, essentially, in accordance with its affective complexes. The hallucinated persons are indeed never anything but personified and projected fragments of his own personality; the patient's various personalities (Emperor, Mother of God) represent nothing else.

Often, however, these relationships are more complicated. A female patient adores both a music teacher (a woman) and a minister. Occasionally she identifies with both.[22] In her hallucinations the patient obtains sexual satisfaction from the minister. But occasionally, she sees the music teacher and the minister in a sexual embrace, and this arouses tremendous excitement in herself. Thus she has projected both her wishes, to be the teacher and to marry the minister, by means of her transitivistic hallucinations. Marie (p. 45) reports a case in which after an alteration of the personality, the discarded personality became the hallucinated persecutor.

Personality transformations during twilight states need no special description. Less attention has been paid to similar changes occurring during the frequent fits of rage. The patient, with whom one has just had a pleasant talk, suddenly becomes agitated, says what otherwise he does not believe, and distorts his logic entirely in terms of his anger. He is an entirely different person, only to return shortly to his former state. The affectively charged fantasy may, conversely, turn a negativistic, irritated creature at least temporarily into a social person. I address a sulking patient as a bride and woman (not as *my* bride or woman); this reminds her of her delusionally fulfilled hopes and she responds to my greeting with a friendly handshake and begins to chat with me. Similarly, autistically preoccupied patients may become accessible during a visit or by an allusion to a complex, etc. These patients may change toward the same person, from one moment to the next, and this switch of personality is entirely internal. The patient may rage

---

22. The same thing occurs very frequently in the dreams of normal people. Cf. Krafft-Ebing's patient who could only love women who limp and could not resist the impulse to imitate such women.

at his wife only to embrace her in the very next moment as his dear one and to beg her "to save his life."

In a few cases the "other" personality is marked by the use of different speech and voice. The patient converses normally with his doctor, but intermittently lapses into confused neologisms and a strange tone of voice, or whispers asides to his "voices." In such cases the changes of personality may occur every few seconds. Some patients may be constantly preoccupied with their hallucinations during conversation or reading; they may answer them softly, and yet have simultaneously as exact a perception of reality as an attentive normal person. For example, the patients may retain in detail a story read to them. Thus we have here two different personalities operating side by side, each one fully attentive. However, they probably are never completely separated from each other since one may communicate with both. Personality too has its "multiple bookkeeping." In conversation, a patient may completely ignore or misunderstand any of our arguments and yet interpret them correctly at some later time.

(e) Speech and Writing

In the mildly sick patient, linguistic expression as such is, for the most part, normal. These patients express their normal or pathological ideas, orally and in writing, in the same way as the normal person. However, in the cases in our care, more or less marked abnormalities are frequently present.

Blocking, poverty of ideas, incoherence, clouding, delusions, and emotional anomalies are expressed in the language of the patients. However, the abnormality does not lie in the language itself, but rather in its content.

The impulse to speak has frequently undergone a change. Many patients talk a great deal, often indeed continuously. For the most part, they do not thereby want to convey anything to, or communicate with their environment. Their thoughts are transformed into speech, without relation to the environment. Or such a relation may be entirely one-sided, as when a patient asks a question which is somewhat suited to his interlocutor but shows no need for an answer; he gives us no time for one, nor does he listen. The presence of a person often serves as a stimulus to mere speech activity, not as a motive for saying something. Many patients are constantly uttering chains of words; they talk but do not say anything.[23]

---

23. Speech, like any other activity, may proceed automatically or compulsively. In such cases its content is usually also pathological; coprolalia, for example, is not infrequent.

Conversely, there are other patients who will not talk at all (*mutism*). Some will not write, no matter how great the opportunity. From some we may obtain only oral answers; from others, only written ones; and from still others, no answer at all. Between oral and written mutism and constant chattering and scribbling any intermediate symptom may be encountered.

Mutism is a common accompanying symptom of stuporous states, but it also appears in other combinations. Even patients fully capable of work may long remain mute. In the severe forms of illness this is a frequent symptom, sometimes transitory, sometimes lasting for decades. The behavior of such individuals on being spoken to may vary greatly. Some do not react at all, as if they had not noticed anything. In others the facial expression, particularly, their gaze may show us, intentionally or unintentionally, that they have heard us. Blushing and other signs of affect prove their comprehension. Some patients often faintly move their lips, without uttering a sound. In acute states, we find that mute patients may answer by means of gestures or writing. Indeed, they may thus spontaneously express their wishes. Mostly, however, mute patients are at the same time negativistic. Mutism is never absolute, even though some patients do not utter a sound for years. Most patients do speak now and then; they are more likely to curse; sometimes they sing.

The motor side of speech is generally intact. True disturbances of articulation do not form part of the picture of schizophrenia. General blocking may naturally also affect the function of speech. This function, however, possesses a certain autonomy. Any disturbance of it may be more intense—or more commonly—milder than that of total motility. Speech may also be the only function which remains entirely normal or which may be inhibited or blocked.

The form of linguistic expression may show every imaginable abnormality, or be absolutely correct. We often find very convincing ways of speaking in intelligent individuals. At times, I was unable to convince all of my audience attending clinical demonstrations of the pathology of such severely schizophrenic logic. Thus a catatonic engineering student had had to be tube-fed; he justified his refusal of food in a brilliant speech, saying that he had seen a ward-mate conduct himself so stupidly while being tube-fed that his mental disease was immediately obvious. Our student's completely normal behavior during his tube-feeding was the proof of his own perfect mental health.

The intonation in the patients' speech is often peculiar. In particular, there is often an absence, exaggeration or misplacement of modulation. Speech may be abnormally loud, abnormally soft, too rapid, or too slow. Thus one patient speaks in a falsetto voice, another mumbles, a third grunts. A catatonic speaks in precisely the same fashion during inspiration as during expiration, another has no intonation at all. Sometimes, the voice will change with the set of ideas: the patient will talk to his hallucinations or to his imagined persecutors in quite a different tone than the one he employs in speaking to real people. When the patients think of themselves as different persons, they utilize a correspondingly different tone of voice. One of our patients spoke with the voice of the child who wanted to emerge through the patient's mouth.

When specific "persons" speak through the patients, in various cases of automatic speech, each "person" has his own specific voice and distinct manner of speech. The latter may also vary in accordance with the complexes involved. A catatonic woman ordinarily employs the German usually spoken in Zurich. However, when discussing her illness, she always used the St. Gall dialect; speaking of her husband, she would lapse into vulgarisms and curses; on the subject of America (which was connected with her aspirations), she would change to an educated, polite manner of speech. The constant use of diminutives, and other anomalies of speech and writing, often appear only when the patient's complexes are touched. A hebephrenic speaks and writes quite normally in neutral situations but when his complexes are involved, his expressions become vague and hard to understand; he begins to stutter, his lips tremble. A catatonic woman formed neologisms only when, for external or internal reasons, she became agitated.

Corresponding to an absence of affect on the one hand, and a tendency to exaggerated mimicry on the other, speech too will sometimes express too much or too little. Often speech will sound peculiarly inappropriate in relation to its content. The patients may say cheerful things in a sorrowful tone, and vice versa. Occasionally their speech sounds remote, similar to that of healthy people in their sleep.

Some of the anomalies of speech really belong in the category of *mannerisms*. Other abnormalities may be classed with the stereotypies, such as *verbigeration*, and the insertion of a long *hui*-sound between pairs of words (which we have seen in one case).

Often one gets the impression that the connection between concept and linguistic expression has loosened. Strikingly enough, there need not be any correlation between the degree of this disturbance and the rest of the association disturbances or the level of what we call intelligence. There are patients who are capable of expressing themselves very correctly, yet their intellectual faculties are extremely reduced and conversely, there are those who cannot utter a single intelligible sentence, but are still able to perform relatively complicated work such as distributing laundry. Thus in schizophrenia too, linguistic confusion is to be distinguished from conceptual confusion, although both may sometimes be found together. Particularly noteworthy are those instances where the patient can express himself clearly only in writing, or only orally, and his productions in the opposite form of expression are confused. For many years one of our hebephrenic patients could talk only about the simplest matters; however, he was still capable of writing good letters. In such cases the patient does not simply let himself drift, or alternately pulls himself together; rather his attitude changes according to the circumstances.

Krafft-Ebing's postulate that words lose their meaning until there remain mere chains of word-husks, is valid only for the verbigerative speech productions. The striking words and phrases used by our patients can hardly be looked upon as empty shells but rather as shells which conceal a content different from the usual. Forel's patient described the phenomenon very well:

"I used some words in order to express a concept entirely different from the usual one. Thus, I blithely employed the word *mangy* to mean gallant. If I could not immediately find an appropriate word to express the rapid flow of ideas, I would seek release in self-invented ones, as for example, *wuttas* for *doves*."

According to our present point of view, the distortions of speech in schizophrenia are not to be differentiated from those which occur in dreams. Unfortunately however, the fundamental work of Kraepelin (398) does not yet lend itself to classification, since the two sets of experiences—that of subjective dream observation and that of objective experience with schizophrenia—are still too incomplete for adequate comparative evaluation. In the following, I can contribute only a few indications arrived at by observation of schizophrenic speech disturbances.

For the most part, words are so used as to designate an idea which is similar to the desired one, or one which has some common components or determinants. Thus, *bureau* is used to mean *grandfather clock* which is relatively easy to understand from the external similarity of both pieces of furniture; *an hour* for *grandfather clock* because of the relation of the clock to the hours of the day (Masselon). We may understand likewise the use of the word *potato* for *starch*.

Sometimes the figures of speech misuse the principle of *pars pro toto*, in such a way that its least essential component is selected to represent the total concept. For example, a shoe is called "something used to dance in" (Masselon).

It is more understandable that a patient, instead of asking for his release, asks for a "change of work"; or when another patient calls all his persecutors and ideas of persecution "shapes," although both of these do not appear to him only as visions. Very striking as an indication of the extent of the schizophrenic disturbance is the phrase, "the attendant's child-system," used by a patient to say that the attendant was not at his disposal when he needed him, but would, instead, change the patient's bedding to indicate that the latter was as incontinent as a small child. Two ideas which may be subsumed under one overall concept may be used interchangeably particularly when they are abstract. Thus a patient says that he is being "subjected to rape," although his confinement in a mental hospital constitutes a different kind of violation of his person.

To a large extent, inappropriate figures of speech are employed, particularly the word, *murder* which recurs constantly for all forms of torment and in the most varied combinations. In many cases, however, it is obvious that the patients are apt to forget that they are using a figure of speech. Their concept of being *tormented is so overwhelming that* they can only express it by such a word as *murder*; in certain situations they actually believe they have been murdered. Naturally they prefer to use emphatic words in their accusations, while de-emphasis is employed defensively. However senseless such phrases as "I was the patience of Christ" may appear, they have their normal analogue e.g., in "I am the Truth and the Life!"

Frequently, the similarity of concepts which leads to the interchange of words is an extremely tenuous one and involves thought processes which have no connection with the idea being expressed. Thus, a patient "owns a branch office of God," which means that she has the right to coin money. Equally far-fetched is the analogy used by a patient who complains that she is not "selling"; she thus identifies amorous with business activity.

Where the similarity of concepts is closer, a more intelligible, if daring, imagery appears; for example, "vaccination while being mounted" used by a female, and "to perform holy vaccination" used by a male patient, both to designate coitus. Another example is "Who has hammered this deep hatred into me?" or "Mr. S. has been promenading in figures of speech" which means that Mr. S. was mentioned during a conversation. The expression, "We shall long have been guests of the crematorium," i.e., dead, is indeed quite highbrow.

Sometimes the similarity is not in the concepts but rather in the words. This can result in dull plays on words; thus when a patient is "among *burghers*," meaning that he is in the *Burg*holzli hospital.

The schizophrenic construction of new word combinations is of course well-known. They are, indeed, partly comprehensible but only rarely concur with the usual rules of the language.

"Lie-truths"—that is, lies which we present as the truth, is a pleonasm. A patient "writes the nativity Luise Muller; she was at that time Muller-like," which means that her maiden name was Muller. Another patient is "be-millioned," that is, she had received millions. A third patient is "enchambered by winter." A paranoid says "he-was-rightly" confined, that is, the person who had him committed said that he was right in doing so. The basis of these constructions may be onomatopoeic: a hebephrenic has "hurricanes" in her throat, that is, she clears her throat with a sound like that word.

A mass of neologisms must be constructed by the patients to designate new concepts for which our language is not suited. Particularly the hallucinations, the persecutions and everything connected with them must be characterized with *one* word by the constantly preoccupied patients. Thus to "snortie" means to talk through the walls. One of Jung's patients called her neologisms "power words"; she spoke of "double-polytechnic" which for her meant the very essence of all her skills as well as of the accompanying rewards. [24] A patient spits "cage-weather juice"; that is she must expectorate so much because she is full of cage-weather, i. e., she is locked up. The sister of a woman physician extends the concept of "colleague" to her family relations: She is "the doctor's colleague through her sister." The phrase, "The Prince of Wales is in today's ego of the uncle" expresses a thought impossible for a healthy mind, that the uncle has been transformed into the Prince of Wales. ("He has not become the Prince, but has actually developed the Prince's personality.")

New expressions are also coined by way of *condensation.* However, one must distinguish between concept condensation which fuses several ideas and expresses them by one single word, and verbal condensation which fuses various expressions, whether these words designate the same concept, or whether the combination of words also corresponds to a combination of ideas. The contraction of different words to designate the same idea is indeed frequently seen in the slips of the tongue of normal persons. [25]

A special confusion is introduced into speech by the fact that ideas designated by correctly chosen words are distorted by the structure of the sentence. Also, in the construction and use of neologisms patients

---

24. Many such neologisms designate a very complex idea, or even pathological experience extended over long periods of time. For this reason, they have been called ellipses, and have been considered as a sign of long-established illness. The latter notion is not quite correct; patients may construct such concepts and words even at the start of their psychosis.

25. In children's essays, condensations are a frequent error, particularly as picturesque figures of speech.

may select the correct root but vitiate the meaning by use of incorrect suffixes, conjunctions, etc. My own observations do not permit, as do Kraepelin's, the separation of acataphasic from agrammatic disturbances. Provisionally, I would designate all these distortions of grammar as paragrammatisms.

The thought "there is in my mind no presence of absent-mindedness" is abnormally but not incorrectly expressed. Distorted word construction is at the basis of the expression, "As a child I was already an apartment," (that is, "apart," different); also the phrase, "I am inheritant by three millions" (he has inherited three millions). A patient who has "Catholically insinuating pains" wishes to say that the Catholic attendants are painful to her. One patient's persecutor "suffers from delusions of persecution"; this is here interpreted as an active, instead of the usual passive meaning. The patient who says, "Until the time of resourceful vocation, I am dependent on government charity," employs the adjective "resourceful" incorrectly. The catatonic to whom belongs Lake Constance wants to say that she should drown herself in that lake.

The auxiliary verbs are similarly misused: "I am England" means "England belongs to me"; "I am the sun," is equivalent to "I am the Lord and Creator of the Sun." In all these examples, however, the basic thought is certainly not as clearly defined in the patient's mind as it would be in a healthy one.

Just as the link between ideas, so the link between idea and word may be entirely accidental, and yet be subsequently retained by the patient. A paranoid used practically any foreign word he happened to hear to designate all or part of his persecutory ideas: he is persecuted "by a dossier"; through the "cosmos, genital pains" are induced in him. In such instances, the patients actually believe that they have correctly and intelligibly expressed their ideas.

In most cases a variety of errors is concentrated in these pathological expressions.

"I don't want any part of Turkey" means: "I won't be your harem-woman, or your whore, you polygamist!" Here we have a displacement of the meaning of the word "Turkey" and simultaneously a condensation of two ideas. "Friendly relations to all who belong" at the conclusion of a letter has likewise arisen through paragrammatism and condensation of various ideas normally used at that point. The masturbator who calls himself "penis-murderer" employs the word "murderer" in the sense of "sinner" or "corruptor" and then makes a paragrammatic contraction. The patient is "blued-off" because a letter was returned to him marked "addressee unknown" in blue pencil; the neologism is entirely paragrammatic. The patient suffering from "neuralgiers" owns Asia, Africa and

Algiers. He substitutes a consonant word for the proper one and then continues to associate. New thoughts, new expressions and abbreviations were used by the patient analyzed by Riklin; he wrote and spoke as follows:

"Centraleurope andt centraleruopera No. 3258 Ernest Gisler Troth also the key to Mr. Minister Dr. Kaiser DDiv. etc., etc. Standdenbank pprr p. 96 or letter-post 3 vvia Imperially andt Royally also Imperially Royally business Titt, Rheinau. Mo work Badd goodd 3|8 Herr dr. N. C. 30|7 Bern 27|7 AD 18|7 short 30|7 3|8 Aa 1906 Datum. Tthey pay on presentation of a receipt Frcs 8 thousandd in banknotes also Titt. Bernese Central bank in Berne or BCB frcs. 8000 cash. at 10 per cent. FRCS 8,800 equally 800 FRCS times 10 at eleven: Titte. Government chancellory Aaltdorf by reason of damage sustained through Mr. Aalt missionary and hotel-guest, living with Dr. Christaller in Bellevue Andder madtim Poag Francs c 12 half-Octav Trvel-work, travel-work = process verbal qa 29|9 Ao 1889 Newspaper date the Neue Zurcher Zeitung. Shall Forel stone-healthy guggenbuel 330 FRCS b = anat FRCS half Dho coarse st 15 also added after 139 waiting years on Mr. Chief Attendant and minister Dr. hc. vegetarian Steeiger Bro. . . ."

Exactly what the frequent doubling of letters may mean we still do not know. However, even after many years, the patient is consistent in this. He is the Emperor of Central Europe and counts the era from that particular event. His hospital number is 3251. He changes the last digit to 8 because otherwise it would not fit into "his system" in which the figure 8 plays a large part (Central Europe at that time consisted of 8 countries). E. is his own name. Gisler is the name of his imaginary sweetheart to whom he has been wed in his delirium. This fact is indicated by the word "Troth." "Also the key is entrusted to him" means he wants the key. Pastor St. whom he promotes to Doctor was the hospital Chaplain. "Kaiser DDes Titt. standenbank" is another of his titles (Des= der = the). He changes the last letter of the word "Standdenbank," an imaginary bank, which the patient pretends to use to pay for his small needs in the hospital. "p prr" = per = through. "3 vvia" = triple = in 3 ways. "Mo work" = Monday, a work day. "Badd goodd" = after the pleasures of a bath. 3|8 = the date on which the patient is writing, Aug. 3. "Mr. Dr. hc. 30|7" = the day on which Mr. Doctor honoris causa (= the attendant) writes, the 30th of July. "Bern 27|7" = the date July 27 on which the people of Berne write to him. "AO 18|7" = the average date according to his own peculiar reckoning. "30|7 3|8" expresses in an abbreviated fashion the various dates in accordance with his calculating system. "BCB" = Bernese Central Bank. The patient was first apprehended in the town of Andermatt. Therefore, he claims that the Government Bureau of Altdorf was responsible for seeing that he was indemnified for his confinement in the hospital. The owner of the hotel was also to be held responsible. "C" = 3 billions that he claimed in damages. "Half-octav" is the toilet paper on which he used to write and of which he rarely got enough for this purpose. "Travel-work" is the work of getting his release so that he may travel again. "Process-verbal qa 29|9 Ao 1889" is similar to a legal document which the patient drew up concerning these objects (qa = these same objects). This very document was to be sent the day the Neue Zuricher Zeitung carried the date (Sept. 29, 1889). The head of the hospital at that time was Prof. Forel who is condensed with a former friend of the patient, a certain Guggenbuhl, and owes him 300 million (b) francs to which ("also added") 816 (haf), 480 (Dho), 730 (Geo) millions. "St" = 15 figures (thus 816, 480, 730, 000,000). "139 waiting-years," is not at all clear. He has conferred upon the chief attendant an honorary doctorate and Premiership. He is a vegetarian as are all good doctors (the patient has a sexual repulsion for meat.) Furthermore, he condenses the attendant with a man named Steiger. Bro . . . is the attendant's name.

Summing up, the piece of writing goes something like this:

"We, the Emperor of Central Europe, E. no. 3251 wed to Miss Gisler (whereby the right to be free was given), Possessor and Lord of the bank through which we satisfy our needs by using postal-notes, and owner of the factory in Rheinau, issue the following decree:

"You, or the Bernese Central Bank are to pay on demand on the presentation of a note, 8000 francs in cash plus 10 percent. This is to be drawn on the account of the Altdorf government bureau which owes me the sum for damages and injuries caused me both by the government and by hotel-keeper Christaller in Bellevue, Andermatt; each day you are to pay 3 billions and 12 pieces of toilet paper and my freedom, as we have already set forth in the *procès-verbal* and had published on the day that the Neue Zuricher Zeitung carried the dateline Sept. 29, 1889. Also Prof. Forel owes 330 million francs to which is to be added 816, 480, 730, 000, 000 francs. This is to be paid to our Prime Minister, the chief attendant of the hospital."

In many instances, the phrases and expressions used cannot be understood, as for example, when a patient is "botanized" or tormented by "elbow-people," or when instead of words, numbers are substituted (and 473 means "Do you understand?"). Some of these numbers are connected to the words for which they stand by a similarity of sound.

In advanced cases, there results a complete word-salad which is entirely unintelligible even though it may be built up, in the main, of ordinary words. The utterly inconceivable combination, both as to grammar and content creates the impression of an unknown language.

Up to the present time, I have not been able to get a shorthand transcript of a complete word-salad. In the following letter the sentence structure is, for the most part, still maintained by the patient:

"At Apell plain church-state, the people have customs and habits taken partly from glos-faith because the father wanted to enter new f. situation, since they believed the father had a Babeli comediation only with music. Therefore they went to the high Osetion and on the cabbage earth and all sorts of malice, and against everything good. On their inverted Osetion Valley will come and within thus is the father righteousness" (Hebephrenic production).

New words are often coined for the whole language, so that we may have an "artificial language," as one of our patients called it. The neologisms may still be discernibly based on words in common usage, or they may be entirely new creations, often obviously pretending to imitate a specific language. In that case, the patients may themselves designate their language as French, Chinese, etc. Sometimes, at least, it may be shown that identical words are always used to express certain concepts. For the most part, however, the "artificial language" seems to be a product of the moment, and is soon replaced by another. It cannot always be determined just how seriously the patients take these "languages"; they often seem to have the meaning of a joke or mystification. However, in a few cases the patients really believe that they have expressed themselves correctly; they believe that they are speaking their usual or another existing language; or they may be conscious of their new creation. A patient, who despite her catatonic state is still very intelligent and self-observant, wanted to say "Give me a sedative." Instead, she said "Give me 20,000," or "I give you 20,000." These two forms were identical in her mind, although she noticed the difference subsequently in a normal fashion.

The written productions of these patients correspond entirely to the oral ones, except that in the former certain peculiarities are even more obvious. Often the patients will write when they have nothing to say. Thus one may receive from educated people stories of all that goes on in the hospital—when they get up, at what time they wash, what this or that attendant does at a certain time. What is intended as a written communication may then appear like an exercise in composition, often purely stylistic and without any content. Words are formed into perfectly correct sentences whose purpose, however, is unintelligible.

It is not unusual for a piece of writing to founder in a mire of uncontrolled associations. Thus a catatonic who was delighted when we ordered her to write home concerning her eligibility for release, wrote as follows:

R. (her home address,
instead of the hospital's)
27 April 1887. (Actual date 1906)

Dear Parents:

Be so kind and come and get me my sister washed for me and we must to the kitchen

(born 66) from your sister, L. S.

The patients' lack of purpose and appropriate thought is shown in the many deviations from the starting ideas; both the content and the sound of words lead them astray. A hebephrenic lists among the sources of information about himself: "My father in N., whose judgment is worth everything to me, even my life if he asked it of me."

Inconsistencies, such as the above, where the letter starts with "dear parents" and then ends with "your sister," are frequent in schizophrenia. Letters to different persons are written on the same sheet of paper. The same person will be addressed in various ways, formally or intimately, in one letter. A hebephrenic concludes every letter, no matter to whom it is addressed, with "affectionate love and kisses from your truly loving E. F. in W." (though she does not live in W. but in the hospital).

Despite the presence of normal orientation, the use of incorrect dates and places is not unusual. An institutionalized catatonic always puts her home address on all her letters, even on those written to her mother.

Genuine anomalies of style are very common in hospitalized patients. The wording is preferably bombastic; indeed it is so not merely in the passages which are intended to convey emphasis or feeling. "The patients utter trivialities using highly affected expressions as if they were of the greatest interest to humanity." Often the expressions are badly chosen so that one might believe to be listening to a pretentious school boy. In addition, there sometimes appears a preference for certain figures of speech which are then employed in a stereotyped fashion, regardless of their appropriateness. Besides the telegraphic style, we also find an inclination toward endless sentence structure containing the most varied mixture of ideas. A peculiarity not only of style but also of thought results in written elaborations of the obvious, e. g., "The undersigned writer of these lines takes the liberty of sending you this by mail. . . ." Multilingual patients freely intermingle different languages or use the foreign tongue with which they are least familiar.[26]

Emotionally charged complexes are often expressed indirectly: a patient writes a long letter filled with church hymns and songs; all of these have some reference to the patient's relationship to her lover whom she has identified with God. In other cases, the complexes are expressed by the choice of refined, obsequious, or childish prose style, or by the liberal use of diminutives.

Yet there are anomalies of style which cannot as yet be brought into connection with the complexes, and which must therefore be regarded as pathological whimsies. Thus a patient insists on speaking almost exclusively in participles accompanied by an auxiliary verb. Frequently, the patient's style of writing or thinking is characterized by striking images. A paranoid with a wrinkled face writes: "My face is like a ceiling with heraldic and architectonic carvings." The most heterogeneous objects are associated by content as well as by modes of expression, in a most unlikely and bizarre way. "The physical examination was not only very interesting, but seemed to me to cry out to heaven," or "I not only delighted in hunting but also in being a burden to my father."

Such errors (as in the above example) have their source mainly in the writer's lack of affect. Emotionally different concepts are placed on the same level. Even such constructions as the following are based on this kind of anomaly: "I have been here ten days, they want to starve me; I want to vomit on the whole world, and there is a bed made up for sleeping," or "I feel very well and cheerful, relieved, I am tremendously hungry and homesick."

The form, in the strict sense of the word, often demonstrates this lack of affect too. A well-bred girl writes her aunt a letter intended to show her devotion. But because of this lack of affect, the letter sounds extremely cold; the patient expresses her deepest feelings in the most impersonal of sentences. ("This is to thank. . .," "It is desired. . . .")

Occasionally, "blocking" is expressed by an interruption of the sentence, after which there appears a completely new thought; in severe cases, the writing stops altogether. Occasionally a gap will indicate a suppressed thought as in the ending of the following letter:

Most affectionate and cordial greetings
J. W.

in the ....(large gap)
Address: Hospital, Zurich, Room 2

26. Translator's note: It may be noted that in Switzerland with its three official languages (German, French and Italian) it is quite common for patients to be familiar with two or three languages in varying degrees.

The very appearance of a piece of writing often permits one to recognize the presence of schizophrenia. The use of space may be quite bizarre. The varying margins betray the writer's changing mood. The letter may start at the bottom or side of the paper or very close to the top. Paranoids have the peculiar habit of leaving no margin and are inclined to fill the page completely. Conversely, a catatonic uses an entire sheet to write:

Zurich, July 28, 04

Mother:

Send sugar

A.[27]

The script itself is often quite slanted, running in different directions all over the paper. In one place there may be a shaded square design, while in another place there is a circle with words written around it. All sorts of more or less bizarre figures are formed either by the script or are added by drawing. The letter paper is folded in a most complicated way so that one wonders how the patient obtains the desired form and size, despite his apparent lack of control.

The catatonic peculiarities of script are legion. Capital letters and small letters are employed without any apparent rules, the former even in the middle of a word. After each vowel, "something like an h" is placed (Pfister); slang expressions are spelled phonetically so that they are most difficult to decipher. The spelling itself will be changed in every conceivable way. The patient will divide words without any obvious motivation; punctuation may be wholly absent; after each word a comma may be inserted. Words may be agglutinated. Completely meaningless numbers may be written first in digits, then in words.

The catatonic peculiarity of stereotypy and mannerism are strikingly expressed in writing. We frequently observe written verbigeration, in random repetition of words and sentences, and particularly of single letter and punctuation marks, either in a characteristic pattern or mixed with crosses, circles, triangles and other figures. For many years a hebephrenic always wrote the same row of numbers whose zeros were always continued to the end of each line. Mannerisms are revealed in the affected and queer shapes of the letters and the various curlicues which themselves have a tendency to become stereotyped. Some patients invent an individual script (cryptography), which may be a caricature of known scripts or an entirely new invention.

Perseveration may influence the script, especially in acute phases

---

27. This the entire signature, somewhat ornamented.

of catatonia and in clouded states. It will then affect not only the words but single letters as well; the latter may crop up at inappropriate points ("would woush" instead of "would wish"). Even more frequently, we find contamination by subsequent words and letters which the writer already has in mind.

Condensations such as "notl" instead of "not at all" are usually encountered. Incompletely written words or the omission of letters also belong in this category (such as "attent" instead of "attendant," "nt" instead of "not"). However, these distortions may also be caused by sudden "blockings."

Some graphological aspects in their narrower sense, may often—though not in all cases—be so characteristic for schizophrenia that one can make the diagnosis from them. Kraepelin had already noted that in catatonic states the entire control of the script is uneven and irregular. In stupors, also, rapid and sometimes even powerful strokes are made. Thus, we can see powerful and weak, small and large, straight and slanted, careful and careless strokes intermingled in the same piece of writing. The same patient often uses wholly different handwriting styles on the same page.

Frequently, the shift of complexes during a train of thought may be demonstrated as the cause of these changes.[28] Generally, the constellations of complexes are more strikingly apparent in schizophrenics than in the healthy (through all sorts of irregularities, deviations from the lines, etc.).

When autistic catatonics who have completely lost contact with the outer world are prevailed upon to write, they at first often have difficulty in holding the pencil correctly, and then it seems as if the pencil will not write properly. Usually they will then make a few strokes in the air and finally on the paper itself. The lines are then very often much intertwined. If one is very patient, one may see how letters gradually evolve from these lines. Ultimately, intelligible, although incorrectly spelled words and even whole sentences may appear. By subsequent study, one may recognize that elements of the words were already contained in the first unrecognizable scrawl. Thus, the handwriting also develops in quite the same way as does automatic writing only more rapidly, sometimes in "one sitting." By the same token, the results are completely lost by the time the next attempt to write is made.[29]

---

28. For this reason, the study and deciphering of Lenz's poetry to Friederike Brion was so difficult.

29. In quite an analogous way, patients will play the piano. At first, there is just a cacophony of chords and notes out of which a melody very gradually develops.

(f) The Somatic Symptoms

In schizophrenia we find a number of somatic symptoms, most of which, however, are not very pronounced and in some cases cannot be detected at all. Viewed in their totality, these symptoms suggest that the disease is based upon a more fundamental alteration of the brain, or perhaps even of the entire body.

In acute cases one encounters severe psychic symptoms reminiscent of those due to intra-cranial pressure. On the somatic side, tremulous and wavering movements may lead to the conclusion that there is some gross cerebral disturbance. According to Reichardt, there may be encountered an increase in brain weight in proportion to skull size, and even choked discs.[30] The pupillary disturbances should also be mentioned here. At times, the bodily state may resemble that seen in severe infections. In acute catatonic states, particularly, we often find a coated tongue, anorexia (even without physchogenic refusal of food), and poor assimilation of food. The patient's physical and nutritional condition deteriorates rapidly, quite independently of any motor strain; his movements become tremulous. Often such conditions are accompanied by slight rises of temperature. Reichardt found up to five per cent of albumin in the urine of stuporous patients. We have found smaller quantities, temporarily, in various catatonic states. It is as yet impossible to say whether there is any connection between this symptom and the psychosis.

In acute forms of the illness the patient's *weight* in particular is often subject to irregular and wide variations for which there is no known explanation.[31] A rapid gain in weight, without any corresponding improvement in the patient's mental condition, has always been considered as a bad prognostic sign in an acute psychosis. We have, however, frequently been able to observe a marked gain in weight during the subsidence of acute episodes, in some instances of twenty-five kilograms and more, above the patient's norm. Hence, this cannot be a matter of simply regaining the weight lost during an agitated state. Some patients maintain this abnormal gain in weight for a long period, while others return to their norm within a few months. Further investigations are needed to determine whether these cases have a less favorable prognosis than those with less marked variation in weight. Sometimes the weight varies with the mental condition; loss of weight occurs during agitated

---

30. See below, death resulting from catatonic cerebral paralysis, and also the clouded catatonic states.

31. Loss of weight "at the beginning of the illness", as far as considerable differences are involved does not occur as a rule. The acute condition for which the patient was hospitalized may have been considered as the beginning of the illness.

periods, and a gain during quiet periods. Most of our hospitalized patients, however, differ very little from the healthy in respect to weight variations, except that in chronic conditions the fluctuations appear to be wider and more frequent.

Weight is by no means parallel to food intake. Particularly in acute phases, there may be extreme loss of weight, indeed, death from inanition,[32] even with ample or at least adequate intake. Conversely, many patients remain in a remarkably good condition despite a very low food intake even during periods of marked motor agitation. In the same patient, weight may for a time vary inversely with food intake. The irregular oscillations of body weight during one or several days, which Rosenfeld has shown to be due simply to unequal water retention, are not to be confused with fluctuations due to nutritional conditions.

Anorexia is frequently accompanied in acute states by symptoms of "gastric catarrh" (coated tongue, foul breath, sometimes mild elevations of temperature). In chronic states, anorexia more often occurs without these accompanying symptoms. Alternately with the anorexia (or by itself), we may observe *bulimia*, acutely or chronically. Such insatiable eating is very rarely accompanied by the corresponding and appropriate body weight.

As yet we know very little about *gastro-intestinal secretory activity*. Undoubtedly this activity is for the most part undisturbed, though there are exceptions. Now and then we encounter ptyalism, indeed in a very marked degree. In one case I have collected up to 3 liters of saliva on several occasions; this continued for months and was repeated several years later.[33] Some patients complain about a dryness of their mouths which as a rule disappears after a few weeks or months.

According to Leubuscher and Ziehen, there is a disposition to hyperchlorhydria in catatonic and stuporous patients and a tendency to hypochlorhydria in cases of acquired mental deficiency, while acute paranoid states show a normal acidity. We have as yet no reason to conclude on the basis of these findings that these pathological phenomena are different in principle; the matter certainly needs further investigation.

In schizophrenia as in other psychoses, *food intake* as well as *general intestinal activity*, is dependent to the highest degree upon psychic factors. Delusions of poisoning, negativism, autism, agitation, etc. often prevent them or render them difficult. Furthermore, due to the extreme variability of these psychic conditions, intake may, intermittently, increase to the point of bulimia. In no other mental disease

---

32. Observed by Rosenfeld.

33. Ptyalism is not to be confused with the peculiar habit of many catatonics not to swallow their saliva but to retain it in the mouth as long as possible or let it drool out.

does complete refusal of food occur so frequently and so persistently as in schizophrenia. Particularly in the catatonic conditions of more than average severity there is, as a rule, a more or less consistent abstinence. One of our patients had to be tube-fed for sixteen years, that is until her death.

Intestinal function. Some patients seem to retain their stools deliberately for the most varied reasons. Conversely, others defecate far more frequently than is necessary, partly because they employ the material for smearing, partly as a consequence of delusions, or for as yet unknown reasons. However, there does appear a true intestinal atony, especially in catatonic states. Among the schizophrenic symptoms, Masselon (p. 81) mentions merycism, which may, however, merely be an accidental accessory symptom.

Body metabolism as reflected in the urine has been more intensively studied, but so far without tangible results. It would appear that in chronic conditions the urine, on the whole, does not show any abnormalities; whereas in acute states and during activation of the illness the composition of urine varies, of course, much more widely, if only in view of the patient's irregular food intake and expenditure of energy, etc. Therefore, it is quite understandable that many deviations from the normal are found. One must, however, be very cautious in ascribing such variations to the disease itself.

According to d'Ormea and Maggioto, the excretion of alkaline earths, especially magnesium, is somewhat decreased, most markedly in catatonics, less so in hebephrenics and paranoids; the acidity of the urine is also apparently diminished. Dide and Chenais found that the amount of urine secreted is somewhat decreased in dementia praecox; secretion of urea is markedly decreased, that of phosphates unchanged, that of chlorides greatly increased; albumin and urobilin is rarely found. However, these findings should certainly not be generalized.

Urinary sugar does not feature prominently in the findings; according to d'Ormea, though, the amount of reducing substances in the urine is less than that in the normal. In those delirious states which we would include with schizophrenia some albumin seems to appear in the urine (cf. above, albumin in stuporous cases).

In the chronic states, the *quantity of urine* excreted seems to be in normal proportion to the amount of food and liquids ingested. In activations of the illness there may be marked irregularity, from excretion of large amounts of urine to oliguria. In a catatonic girl I have even found complete anuria lasting for two days (using the catheter). The rapid changes in body weight are therefore hardly surprising. Arndt (23) found in one patient salivation and polyuria with each appearance of catalepsy. Conscious *retention of urine* is very frequent but it rarely requires special intervention.

As yet we have no *blood studies* which take into account not only the systematic classification of the cases, but also correlations with their previous condition, the present clinical picture, the patients' way of life, etc. No definite conclusions which might contribute to the knowledge of this disease can be drawn from what facts are now at our disposal.

Kahlbaum (346, p. 52) consistently found a high degree of oligemia or chlorosis in his catatonic cases. Others, however, such as Tschisch, found exceptionally good nutritional conditions, to which this blood picture corresponds. According to my own experience, which is not based on measurements, schizophrenics are much like others in this respect. Whitmore Steele claims to have found decreased hemoglobin (average 71%) and red blood corpuscles in his melancholics among whom he includes the depressed schizophrenics. However, Schultz (681) finds in his catatonics "a certain tendency to a decrease in the number of red cells in the blood of the main blood vessels," and almost normal hemoglobin content. Vorster found the specific gravity and the hemoglobin lowered in his cases of melancholia attonita, in acute delusional states, but also in other acute psychoses. Pighini and Paoli claimed to have found juvenile forms of red cells (cf. Muggia, however). Obici and Bonon, as well as Agostini also have found a decreased isotonicity of the red blood cells in other mental disorders and in dementia praecox (especially at its beginning). Pugh has stated that in chronic cases (including, above all, schizophrenia), the alkalinity of the blood remains unaltered; Schultz makes the same statement for catatonics. Bruce notes that in catatonia and "acute mania," the blood coagulates less readily. It is remarkable that this has not been observed in the frequent injuries and operations to which schizophrenic patients are subject.

Particularly noteworthy are the studies of the white blood cells; here, definite anomalies have been established. It is on this factor that Bruce, in particular, bases his theory of the infectious origin of diseases which we, for the most part, would designate as acute conditions of schizophrenia. His researches still need careful verification. It is impossible for us to summarize briefly his studies since they are based on an entirely different classification of the psychoses. The essence of his position is somewhat as follows: In acute phases of certain of these diseases, the white blood count rises to almost double the normal, and is greatest in the cases with a good prognosis; it is much smaller in the others. The polymorphonuclear cells are somewhat more numerous than the other types of white cells in the more favorable cases, while the percentage in the prognostically unfavorable cases seems to sink to about one third of the normal. After recovery, the leucocytosis persists markedly but the ratio of polymorphs to the other white cells goes back to normal; in unfavorable cases, this ratio may remain below normal for years. During exacerbations both counts are temporarily increased.

Most recently Heileman [34] found in twenty-four cases of various forms of dementia praecox marked and regular decrease in the number of polymorphs with a simultaneous increase in the number of other leucocyte forms.

Perhaps the most striking changes, independent of pyschic conditions, are found in the *cardio-vascular functions*. Even in quiet periods the pulse rate is quite variable, a fact which cannot be attributed to temperature changes (Moravcsik, Pighini) or to affective influences. In acute states, the pulse variations may be great and quite sudden. In a paranoid patient who subsequently was to develop catatonic symptoms the pulse rate changed abruptly several times during a single observation, e. g. from eighty to one-hundred and thirty, without any apparent reason. In a moderately stuporous patient, the pulse remained for some hours at one-hundred and forty, although usually it kept within normal limits. The pulse will show variability due to psychic influences, even though there may be no discernible changes in the patient. A changing pulse rate may be the sole indicator of psychic activity. A catatonic woman in complete stupor showed a pulse acceleration from 85 to 134 per minute as soon as the doctor entered her room. With all these irregularities there is far less complaint of palpitation than one would expect.

The *vasomotor system* is markedly altered. In catatonic conditions lividity and cyanosis are very common, particularly in the hands and feet but also in other skin areas. These conditions change very rapidly. One of our catatonics, for example, had very cold hands before noon; at noon, the head, hands and lower half of the forearms were very red and hot. She also developed warm hands, cold head and cold feet; or the head became warm and the hands cold, etc. All of this occurred without any change in the total body temperature. In another patient, the extremities and abdomen were often quite cold, both objectively and subjectively. Cyanosis is not merely a consequence of not moving the extremities, although in rigid patients, it is on the whole, more frequent and more marked than in others; in some cases, however, it seems to have no relation whatsoever with immobility. A patient may develop cyanotic hands only while working, and can therefore be employed only during part of the day. Not rare at all are transitory flushing or pallor, not only of the face but also of other portions of the skin surface.

---

34. Heilemann, "Bluntuntersuchungen bei Dementia praecox", *Allg. Zeitschrift fuer Psychiatrie,* 1910, vol. 67, p. 415.

As a sign of abnormal irritability of the vasomotor system, we find frequently a moderate degree of dermographia; that is, a marked reddening following a slight stimulation; this rarely progresses to the point of welt formation although even this may sometimes be observed.

We do not yet know anything fundamental about the tensions within the vascular system, in psychoses. It would be important to study them in view of the possibility that they very well give us a clue to the influence of certain complexes on the patient. According to Pighini, the sphygmographic curves are somewhat lower in dementia praecox than in healthy individuals. Variations in elasticity are expecially pronounced and the secondary elevations are reduced to a minimum. All these are indications of increased vascular tension. According to Stoddart, blood pressure increases in catatonic stupor.

The tendency to edema is usually ascribed to poor circulation, but it must also have other causes. We find edema without demonstrable passive congestion, and conversely, marked degrees of passive congestion without edema. According to our views on pathology it is easy to see that patients who stand for decades should indeed often develop edemas of the ankles and the legs. Less understandable is the fact that others in the same circumstances remain free of them. In general, the edemas, too, develop independently of passive congestion and of the patient's position. One may likewise find edemas in areas where congestive phenomena rarely occur, for example beneath the eyes. In this connection, Kraepelin speaks of a myxedematous thickening [35]; on palpitation edemas at the ankle also appear myxedematous, and are often almost entirely non-pitting. Yet we have no real basis for considering these conditions as myxedematous. They may appear and disappear far more rapidly than do true myxedemas. In a physically strong female patient with a beginning mild schizophrenia, edemas were noted in the thigh area; they varied markedly in the course of a single day in size and intensity. In such cases, analysis of the urine provides no clue. At times, more severe edemas may make movements painful, probably because of the tension which they cause.

Besides edema, other trophic disturbances which may be related to the vasomotor system are found in schizophrenia. Susceptibility to frostbite is much more marked in schizophrenics than in the healthy. One may occasionally observe cases of *pernio* among our patients during a cool late spring or early summer. We must mention the disposition to

---

35. Trépsat (771) claims to find "pseudo-edemas" as Dide has called them, in all cases where sufficiently long observation has been possible. Fahrmann does not yet regard the facial edema as defined, and calls it *pachydermia facialis*. English authorities have called the somewhat succulent, glossy and (possibly as a result of lack of motion) completely unwrinkled skin *varnished skin*.

decubitus although it is quite rare. I have, however, seen a young female catatonic, in good physical condition and clean in her habits, who developed a decubitus within 24 hours without any obvious external cause.[36]

In most cases, wounds heal remarkably well, except in acute confusional states where the opposite is true. The tendency to infections is not pronounced. Scar formation is on the whole satisfactory.

The *fragility of the blood vessels* which appears in many schizophrenics, both acute and chronic, seems to indicate a real vascular pathology. Some of these patients, particularly the catatonics, are liable to subcutaneous hemorrhages, as a result of routine traumatisms, e.g., even from careful handling such as is necessary for ordinary care. Conjunctival hemorrhages also seem to be much more frequent than in the healthy; they may occur, for instance, as the patient washes his face. I have been definitely able to establish in some cases that otohematoma is not necessarily the consequence of external trauma. In one instance it likewise occurred as the patient washed himself; another patient constantly pressed his ear because of the voices he heard, and so provoked the bleeding. The hemorrhagic tendency may be temporary or may persist for longer periods of time. But in no case did I find that it was permanent. Death by cerebral hemorrhage is not especially frequent.

Disturbances in the function of the sweat glands are not part of the usual picture, yet they are not at all rare in the various types of the disease. In view of the wide physiological variation of activity of these glands, it is very difficult to demonstrate any inhibition of function. We may, perhaps, notice that patients lie in the blazing sun without sweating. On the other hand, abnormally increased sweating is frequent, particularly in connection with some psychic excitement. Sometimes, it may occur in attacks, particularly those which express sexual excitement, but often it is without any known cause. A female catatonic masturbated quite compulsively for many weeks by compressing her thighs; during this activity she perspired so profusely that the frequently necessary linen changes became a nuisance. Another catatonic would break into heavy perspiration thirty minutes after each tube-feeding which she never resisted. Localized sweating is even more frequent than in other nervous individuals; it may appear on any part of the body or unilaterally. Some of these phenomena are probably connected with the complexes, and certainly with psychic excitation. Hoche (309, p. 231) also mentions markedly increased secretion of the *sebaceous glands*.

Osteomalacia and *bone fragility* may be mentioned among other

36. Trépsat has described two cases of catatonic dementia with a pemphigus and an ulcer respectively, in both cases on the leg; he has attributed these to trophic disturbances. It remains questionable, however, whether there is a connection with the psychosis.

trophic disturbances observed in old hospital inmates. Without reliable proof, these conditions have been linked with the mental state (Haberkant). It may perhaps be due to unfavorable hygienic conditions, though we know little about such influences. In Rheinau, osteomalacia occurred in men and women who went outdoors too little, regardless of the type of their pyschosis. Even an attendant who rarely left the hospital contracted it. The disease was cured by more outdoor living, but not by any of the usual methods of treatment. There may be similar factors at work in *bone fragility*, which must be distinguished from osteomalacia.

We might also mention Forel's (229a) case of a catatonic woman, whose hair turned grey during the depressive stage at the beginning of her illness, but with a change in her psychic state again resumed its dark color. A similar case was noted by Urstein (p. 59). Bertschinger (p. 303) mentions a patient whose hair color alternated semi-annually between dark chestnut and light blond. The hair of one of our female patients became curly during a period of agitation and straight during one of remission.

Abnormalities of respiration are very difficult to study because psychic factors cannot be excluded. Catatonics often breathe very superficially. Occasionally, definite rhythms are maintained. Thus one of our catatonics would stop breathing entirely for a few seconds, and then would suddenly sigh very deeply; then she would breathe superficially, and finally, again hold her breath for a brief time. Observation of the respiratory pattern is, nevertheless, of importance during examination because its changes are among the most delicate indices of affective changes; particularly when a remark has touched upon a complex, this may very often become apparent in the breathing.

Menstruation is disturbed in perhaps the majority of cases in an acute stage of the disease. Usually it stops or becomes quite meager. Even in chronic conditions, however, menstruation may cease for many months or years. Abnormally frequent menstruation may also be connected with the psychosis. As a rule, however, menorrhagia will be conditioned by pathology of the genital organs. Subjective menstrual disturbances are much more infrequent than in the healthy female. Obviously, the patient's indifference precludes auto-suggestibility in this direction.

Impotence and decreased sexual drive are frequent in male patients. For the most part, the *temperature* remains normal in chronic cases. Occasionally slight variations do appear. It is curious that these variations have a downward rather than upward trend, in relation to the normal. The temperature may even drop as low as 34° C. In stuporous states it remains in the lower limits of the normal. Elevations of temperature are usually explicable by some complication (gastro-intestinal disturbance, constipation, contusions, etc.).[37] The daily variations of temperature may be irregular. Particularly, typus inversus is at times noted; this is a frequent phenomenon in other mental disorders, also e.g. in melancholia.

Sleep is habitually disturbed, as in other psychoses, during acute agitated states. Yet a patient may seem very agitated, noisy and plaintive during the day, and still sleep well through the night. In chronic states sleep is, in the main, satisfactory, provided that it is not too disturbed by hallucinations. Many hospitalized schizophrenics can sleep very peacefully amid the loudest noise. Other patients continue to feel well despite months of irregular and inadequate sleep.

During acute thrusts of the disease, though rarely in the chronic conditions, we often encounter *somnolence*. Patients are asleep all night and most of the day. Indeed, they often fall asleep at their work. Frequently this somnolence is the only sign of a new thrust of the malady. Thus a female hebephrenic would, from time to time, pass through periods of such somnolence. One of our patients was affected by it at the time of his final examination in pharmacy, which he passed. He became a successful pharmacist. At the age of twenty-eight, this symptom reappeared, together with depression and withdrawal. At thirty-three, he had "neurasthenia," which led him to give up his profession. At thirty-five, there were several confused paranoid attacks, with some deterioration.

Sleep, also, is subject to direct psychic influences. Many patients do not want to sleep because they want to know what goes on during the night, or because they fear some violence to themselves while asleep.

Symptoms of *fatigue* are varied. Many schizophrenics hardly ever tire. They move about noisily, day and night, or work endlessly, with hardly any sign of fatigue. In catalepsy the feeling of fatigue often seems to be entirely lacking. Other patients have an almost normal need for rest. Still others tire very easily, both physically and mentally, especially while the disease is progressing. Many patients are continuously tired (usually without morbid sleepiness). Every movement, at times even thinking, is an effort. Hence these patients cannot work even if they want to; they consider it an enormous presumption to be asked to get up; merely to give their age is for many of these patients such an effort, that they consciously or unconsciously try to avoid by not answering at all, or by giving an irrelevant answer. Some of the patients experience as a great strain the preoccupation with their complexes which they cannot escape; they complain in all earnestness about their very hard work

37. *"Deny et E. Roy signalent enfin l'existence de poussées fébriles éphémères qui passent assez souvent inaperçues."* (Masselon, 457, p. 27).

and cannot understand why they are looked upon as idlers.

Abnormally rapid fatigue during actual work is a different matter, and appears less frequently. Yet we have noted fatigue during association tests, after about one hundred associations.

Patients who do not feel tired in advance usually are not fatigued even by examinations lasting many hours. This is a very striking difference from other psychoses, especially the organic ones.

Spasms and intensifications of idio-muscular contractions are the only two purely (not physically conditioned) *motor symptoms* which have been demonstrated with certainty. The idio-muscular contractions are rarely absent and in many cases are so obvious that upon a light percussion of the muscle of the pectoralis major, the muscle bundles under the pleximeter stand out in long bulges. Even in the most marked of these cases, examination of the spinal cord has never yielded any pathological findings, at least not with the methods used twenty years ago. Bernstein found idio-muscular contractions in 95.7 per cent of his dementia praecox cases, in 90 per cent of his paretics and 11.9 per cent of his manic depressive patients; whereas in healthy people it mostly appears in puberty only.

According to Curschmann (148), the idio-muscular contraction is a sign of intoxication which is favored by dehydration of the tissues and occurs especially in severe nutritional disturbances. An abnormal mechanical and probably also electrical irritability of the nerves is usually connected with it. Curschmann, Gatz and Rudolphson found that this was more common in men than in women.

Fibrillary contractions are particularly noticeable in the facial muscles, and "sheet-lightning" (as this phenomenon is called) has long been known as a sign of a chronically developing illness. Contractions of single muscles or of entire limbs are observed more rarely. The tremor, which may be traced even in the completely "cured" cases, may perhaps also be indicative of poisoning of the motor apparatus. In such cases, it is usually a rather regular, fine tremor which, on the whole, is independent of the psychic state. However, as in all nervous individuals, tremor may of course develop as a consequence of psychic excitement; in that case it is usually a coarse, irregular tremor which is a signal of the conscious or unconscious emotional agitation.

Indeed, for many observers the motor symptoms occupy an important place in the symptomatology. Catatonia, the group of schizophrenic disorders first recognized, got its name from what were considered to be pure motor-tension states. The Wernicke school and some French authorities still postulate disturbances of motility in the strict sense; and Schuele locates the origin of some of the motor symptoms in the deeper parts of the central nervous system. It has even been thought that individual muscle groups are affected preferably or singly. Although such views are based on routine observations, I could not convince myself of their accuracy. It is indeed possible that such phenomena occur; it is conceivable that the general tendency to dissociation may, at one time or another, be strongly felt along Wernicke's bundle; but certainly neither idea has been proven as yet. Individuals who "cannot" even sit up are capable of carrying out complicated, powerful, and correctly coordinated locomotions upon some psychic stimulus. Before excluding psychogenesis, negativism (and the effect of hyoscine?) must be eliminated, apart from other possibilities. Even apraxic symptoms may be an expression of a general psychic disturbance. The frequent uncertainty of the patient's movements may be a consequence of the aimlessness of their behavior in general, as well as of the single movement.

The *gait* is often especially striking. The coordination of arm and leg movements is often disturbed; some patients keep their arms stiff while walking. Particularly important however, is the fact that the feet are often set down quite irregularly, both in regard to time and space.

In the women's divison of the hospital in Rheinau, many patients were able to circulate freely in a rather large garden with many hedges; these have been so trimmed as to give a view of them. From certain positions one saw the patients only up to the knee. Yet in many of them, one could make the diagnosis simply from their will-o'-the-wisp-like gait; it did not lose this peculiarity even when the patients were moving toward a definite goal. Mönkemöller and Kaplan fixed the footprints of two catatonic patients and thereby obtained a graphic record of the spatial disturbances of their gait. Gross (390, II, p. 566) found a similarly disturbed rhythm in the handwriting.

Moravcsik found in all cases of catatonics tested a lowered electrical irritability with slow, inert contractions. Unfortunately, the report at my disposal, does not state what kind of current was used, nor whether muscles or nerves were stimulated. Ostermayer found the galvanic irritability of the motor nerves to be reduced but with no qualitative change.

Organic paralyses will hardly be manifested as partial symptoms of schizophrenia. On the other hand, I have now and then seen psychogenic ("hysterical") paralyses, often of the greatest stubbornness. Astasia and abasia are also observed. A female patient could not open her eyes for several hours. The general or localized paralysis due to "blocking" does not differ in principle from the above-mentioned conditions. However, hysteriform contractures are very rare.

As for the *reflexes*, those of the skin (as in other types of psychoses) are so difficult to test while excluding the psychic factors that we know nothing definite about them. Séglas[38] states that the skin and mucosal reflexes are diminished in the secondary forms of dementia. According to Maillard[39] the plantar reflexes are absent in 75 per cent of cases of dementia praecox and in 41 per cent of other psychoses; increased patellar reflexes plus lack of plantar reflexes appear in 70 per cent of dementia praecox, in 15 per cent of other psychoses. The pharyngeal and the gag reflex is frequently absent in both recent and old cases, as is well known to every practitioner. Tears and blushing can illustrate the preservation of sensitivity, while in other cases intense stimulation of the pharynx or even of the bronchial mucosa causes no unpleasant sensations. Phthisis without cough, even up to the time of death, may likewise occur. The conjunctival and even the corneal reflexes may sometimes be entirely absent, but as far as I have observed, only in severe cases of catatonia. As always in cases of diminished cerebral control, we regularly find the deep reflexes to be increased, especially those of the tendons. Sometimes one obtains a series of clonic contractions from the patellar. At times hyper-reflexia can also be recognized in the patients by the irritation of the flexors at the beginning of extensor movements, so that the leg rebounds like a tight spring. Frequently the contraction spreads to a number of other muscles; in the case of the patellar reflexes, it may extend to the other thigh. In one of our cases, there was a contraction of all muscles on one side of the head, neck, and chest when the corner of the jaw was tapped. Unilateral increase of tendon reflexes also belongs to the picture of schizophrenia (Kleist, 366, p. 76). The increased tendon reflexes are not correlated with the tonus of the musculature. I recall an early, moderate catatonic who had a marked degree of hypotonia of the musculature, yet her tendon reflexes were increased. In one single case I found a decrease of the tendon reflexes, without discovering any experimental error. Kleist (p. 43) reports decreased tendon reflexes in hypotonia.

The *pupillary reflexes* have been studied repeatedly and successfully. Pilcz's lid-closing reaction is found in about one-half the cases. Bumke and Huebner have shown that the pupillary changes, such as the widening during intensification of attention, during fright, etc. as well as during sensory stimulation (particularly if unpleasant) are very often absent in schizophrenia. Bumke assumed this to be a regular phenomenon at the height of the catatonic state, whereas the second author noted the loss of psychic and sensory reactions in 75 per cent of his schizophrenics

38. In Ballet, p. 109.
39. Société de Psychiatrie, Paris, 12-16-1909, in *Neurologisches Centralblatt,* vol. 10, p. 623.

but could definitely substantiate his findings only in 8 per cent of his cases. However, these figures are as yet of little value since such factors as the testing method, the type of instrument, the strength of the light used, and the systematic conception of the disease itself must necessarily make for wide variation in the results.[40] It is certain, however, that the psychic reflexes are nowhere else as frequently absent or diminished as in schizophrenia.[41]

Parallel to the absence of reaction one finds at times a strikingly intense reaction to psychic stimuli precisely as in the affective phenomena. In catatonic agitated states of all sorts, the pupils are very widely dilated, but still react to variations of light. In the most varied conditions, they are often found to be unequal without having lost their ability to react. This symptom often led to the unfounded diagnosis of paresis. But as distinct from paresis, this pupillary inequality is rarely persistent; it often varies within a few hours, becoming equal or reversed. I have only twice seen pin-point pupils in schizophrenia.

On occasion one may encounter such curiosities as the following: On admission a catatonic had small, equal pupils which were not quite round and did not react at all. After about 10 minutes, they were wide and reacted very normally. In a catatonic girl during a quiet period, we observed spontaneous widening and narrowing without any alteration in the light or accommodation. Now and then such anomalies appear to be connected with the psychic constellation although this can only rarely be proven by a repetition of the reactions. Thus the pupils of one of our paranoids once remained widely dilated and did not react to light for about one hour, while he eagerly talked about his delusions.[42]

The "paranoid look" is well known. It appears when the patient thinks about certain complexes. In a few patients, this phenomenon can be evoked or made to disappear again momentarily by changing the subject of conversation. I do not know on what it is based. Often it remains perfectly recognizable even if a mask leaves nothing but the eyes visible.

Headaches of long standing are very often found among the sensory disturbances which are part of the somatic symptoms. Many of

---

40. Cf. Wassermeyer.

41. Cf. Weiler's important paper in the *Zeitschrift fuer die gesamte Neurologie und Psychiatrie,* 1910, II, p. 101.

42. Leeper (Journal of Mental Diseases, 1904, p. 520) found that the pupils may be widened in the morning and narrowed at night. I am very often able to demonstrate wide pupils in patients during evening clinics. Dide and Assicot claim to have found even Argyll-Robertson pupils but more often the opposite. Frequently, light and accomodation reactions were reduced. Blin claims to have found Argyll-Robertson pupils in 13.8 per cent of the cases, which is certainly remarkable. A. Westphal described irregular and oval-shaped pupils. I have encountered them as transitory phenomena.

our patients have suffered from headaches since their youth. During the period of manifest disease this symptom is found in the greatest variety of forms: as pressure in the entire head, behind the forehead, and especially frequently in the occipital region; as pulling, splitting, burning, burrowing pains which usually spread from some one spot to the entire head. It may also take on a migraine-like character and then disappear again, so that one cannot justifiably consider it as a complication. We do not know the causal factors which release these headaches, as far as the latter are a part of the schizophrenic symptoms. The occipital headache may have some relation to sexuality. Burning, roaring, buzzing, and knocking sensations in various parts of the head very frequently accompany these headaches, but may also appear by themselves.

Every possible variety of *paresthesias* and *hyperesthesias* are also observed. They resemble, mostly, those of neurasthenia, though they may often arouse the suspicion of an organic disease of the central nervous system. Sensations in the heart, stomach, and colon are quite common; mastodynia and ovarian pain have also been reported. Sensitive *pressure points* (without hysteria) are frequently found (Ziehen 840, p. 378). At times schizophrenics complain about *vertiginous sensations*, which may be persistent or episodic. The frequent analagesias have been discussed in another connection. In a case of absolute anesthesia to pain, there was *no bleeding* after deep needle punctures. Other disturbances due to absent sensibility hardly come into consideration. The contraction of the visual field which is sometimes found naturally has psychic causes (Klien). The dissociation of sensory impressions which has been observed in isolated cases (particularly in "dazed" states) is perhaps independent of attention. The patient may take the picture of a head of cabbage for that of a rose, by ignoring the color (as do delirious alcoholic patients), or a corncob for an ear of wheat, by ignoring its size.

The various fits of paroxisms which occur in schizophrenia are also included in physical symptoms. Many of them are certainly independent of the psyche; conversely others are entirely of psychogenic origin. The accompanying phenomena which are due to affective influences on heart, vessels and possibly even on the intestines and kidney activity, must be included as psychic, although they appear as physical symptoms. In between there are many intermediate phenomena to which the permanent state of the brain constitutes a general disposition, but the fit itself is released by a psychic event; or conversely, in an organic attack, the psychic symptomatology is determined by the complexes present.[43]

43. Some paroxysms or fits are disguised sexual acts. Cf. Abraham, *Jahrbuch für psychoanalytische Forschung,* vol. II, p. 29.

Naturally, by "organic" we understand a change in the physiological activity of the brain whatever be its determinants.

At the physical end of the scale, there stand the apoplectiform attacks which are not too frequent in schizophrenia. Suddenly or gradually, with or without prodromes, the patients collapse like apoplectics. Speech becomes thick or fails completely; swallowing or ocular fixation and other functions may be distinctly disturbed; saliva may flow from the mouth; all movements of the body may become uncertain, etc.; incontinence of feces and urine is less frequent. Sometimes the symptoms have a clearly *hemiplegic character*, one half of the body slackening during the attack and seeming weaker afterwards. If the attack is accompanied by contractions, they may be unilateral or more marked on one side than on the other. Consciousness is for the most part clouded, but may also remain normal or be completely abolished; the same holds for subsequent memory. Such attacks usually last a couple of hours; occasionally they may pass more quickly or extend over some days. A patient, in whom neither the long observed course of his illness nor frequent examination indicated any diagnosis other than schizophrenia, often lapsed into a coma which lasted for several days, during which he even showed the Babinski reflex.

At times the failure of cerebral activity takes the form of *fainting spells*. These may, however, be psychically determined, as in nervous individuals. We may also observe states of irritability, such as cramps of isolated muscle groups, which are generally independent of the psyche. On the whole, the cramps may be due to either pyschic or physical influences. It is important to note that they are often typically epileptiform (tonic, then clonic phases of short duration, rarely lasting more than a minute). Therefore, many of our patients were first sent to us with the diagnosis of epilepsy, and were so labeled in the clinics. These epileptiform attacks may remain isolated phenomena or may repeat themselves over a period of years and then finally disappear. In exceptional cases, they may even lead to a kind of status epilepticus.[44] The epileptiform attacks may appear at any stage of the disease. They may be the first manifestations of schizophrenia, or complete an old deteriorated condition. But I have not definitely observed them to become a permanent part of simple schizophrenia. Whenever these attacks persisted, the psychic symptoms of epilepsy would also appear so that we may regard such cases as a combination of both diseases (Morawitz). As in simple epilepsy, the attacks may be released by psychic factors, but

44. Tetzner reports a case in which the attacks increased greatly, ultimately becoming so frequent as to cause death. It appears to have been a case of catatonia in our sense of the term.

only in exceptional cases. An older schizophrenic had her first epileptiform attack immediately after having observed, with great interest, a fit in an epileptic patient. During the next ten years the attacks were repeated at irregular intervals. They ceased when the patient was transferred to another building and never recurred again.

At the psychic end of the scale, we find the purely hysteriform attacks which are not rare in schizophrenia. They show no symptoms indicating an organic factor. The disposition alone may be organic, even though we must assume that it may vary momentarily with the intensity of the schizophrenic process, so that the attacks are now more, now less, easily provoked. For reasons to be discussed in a moment, we must, in this connection, also consider the psychically determined attacks of cursing and confusion, which constitute the transition to the simple reaction of the schizophrenic psyche. Typical hysteriform attacks as well as all the other hysteriform symptoms are frequently encountered in our patients. We find all the forms of attack which occur in hysteria, from the most severe fits to the simple shaking spasms of single limbs. They may alternate with other types of attacks or appear by themselves. In most cases, they occur singly or at least infrequently, though we often observe mild indications of such phenomena or abortive attacks. One of our patients predicted that she would die during the night. She then appeared for some time as if unconscious and breathed quietly; suddenly she began to scream and to shake. There was immediate improvement by the use of hydrotherapy.

The frequent *laughing* and *crying spells*, described by Kahlbaum as physical symptoms, may be considered as hysteriform phenomena. We regard them, of course, in most cases as an expression of unconsciously operating complexes. One might mention, as a curiosity, the patient who was sometimes seized with attacks of *singultus* while talking.

The most common attacks, which may at once be considered as the type-form of the schizophrenic fit, appear to us to be organically conditioned attacks of paralysis and irritability in which particularly the intrapsychic associations are altered. Thus they take on a close similarity to the attacks often observed in cases of gross brain disease or intoxication (such as uremia). They can be differentiated from the latter only through the accompanying symptoms. "Abortive," i. e. mild attacks of this kind tend to recur in contrast to the more severe ones.

Often the seizure opens with a tonic phase which, in distinction from true epilepsy, may last very long and does not attain the terrifying intensity of the *morbus sacer*. As a rule, there is rather a kind of generalized rigidity of the body; rarely does the patient fall down; respiration usually remains either relatively or absolutely free. A female catatonic, for example, suddenly ceased to react when spoken to and lay on her bed rigidly with eyes closed. There followed profuse sweating over the whole body. Her pulse was soft and full, at 100-110 per minute, her temperature rose to 38° C. Then she began to contract her hands spasmodically. Calls, appeals and threats elicited no reaction. Only pinching and direct illumination of the eyes caused some moderate defensive movements. The attack lasted for four hours. When the sweat and temperature had receded, the patient recovered rapidly. She cried, with little affect. Her speech "had been cut off by the machine, someone had wanted to kill her, and she had heard the thud of the executioner's axe." An old hebephrenic, who had shown some catatonic symptoms in his fifties, was in a very mild twilight state for a few days when he suddenly became quite rigid but did not fall down. A moderate tremor of the entire body appeared. On being pricked with a needle he did not react with movements but only with a plaintive sound about two seconds after each prick. Simple commands to move his limbs were obeyed automatically. There was *flexibilitas cerea*; the pulse was rapid. After a few minutes, the tension relaxed to be followed by strong perspiration. The patient was carried into his bed and sat there for several hours with outstretched arms. He remained confused and enuretic for some time. The tonic phase may also appear alone, as an abortive attack. While sitting in a chair, a catatonic suddenly became rigid. For some ten minutes she remained sitting in this fashion clenching her fists and gazing at the floor. Then she suddenly stood up and said: "Now it is over."

In other cases, the tonic phase is absent. The patients merely show a dreamlike agitation accompanied by nervous weakness. While lying in bed, a manic hebephrenic suddenly began to roll, to groan and to vomit. There were irregular contractions of the extremities; he buried his head in the pillow. He was dazed, gave vague and confused replies. His face was pale and cool, its muscles slack, especially around the mouth which remained open and profusely salivating. He tried to swallow but could not close his mouth. He verbigerated slowly with a pause between each word: "horse-carrion[45]—whore—horse-carrion—one—two—three—four—five—mother—not—die—." Tendon reflexes were increased, eyes half-open with eyeballs rolling. Pupils were dilated and reacted to light. There was marked anxiety, with the patient clinging desperately to everything and everyone around him. A few hours later he fell asleep. The next day, he knew only that he had been very anxious and

45. The word "horse-carrion" (*Translator's note*: in the Swiss-German dialect, "cheibe") is a kind of universal expletive, which still has a magic-religious significance in popular usage.

unable to speak. For several days after the attack he would suddenly change in the midst of a conversation, turn pale, roll his eyes and give irrelevant answers to questions.

Other examples: A catatonic woman, while in bed performs every possible twist, turn and change of position, groans during breathing, salivates, has a flushed face, and cold hands. Out of bed, she rotates rapidly on her toes; there is pupillary oscillation, pulse at 80 and full; duration of attack: two hours followed by a daze. She lies in bed as if asleep but can still perform some acts, e.g., go to the toilet, even though unsteady and wobbly; subsequently, full recollection of the episode. A hebephrenic had two identical attacks with shaking and twisting of his limbs, turning of the eyeballs, facial pallor, foaming at the mouth. Each attack lasted several hours, and was followed by total amnesia. A periodically catatonic patient with manic interludes suddenly developed contraction of the neck and arm muscles, while eating; his flexed arms moved clonically towards each other; the head shook and nodded. There was no loss of consciousness; duration: thirty minutes. Somewhat later, he still showed some irregular contractions and refused to return to the table to eat, because he was apt to drop his dishes. Finally, he returned to his previous state. A catatonic woman: clonic contractions of all the extremities, maintaining, however, a given position passively for some time (prior to the attack this patient was not cataleptic); violent crying and marked flushing of the face; duration: thirty minutes. A hebephrenic began with grunts and belches, followed by rapid swinging movements of his body while frantically gripping the bedstead. A paranoid woman suddenly started to laugh loudly at the table, then stamped her feet and finally fell asleep; awakening some time later, she resumed stamping with one foot holding her arm in front of her eyes so that it could not be passively moved. There was no amnesia; she was simply unable to answer questions at the time, and had to act in this manner. Later she intermittently had a flushed face, and during these periods believed herself persecuted. A hebephrenic had "fits of trembling in her legs, which made her feel agitated inside, and unable to work." Another patient suffers irregular clonic contractions of her face and limbs. A catatonic patient rolls her eyeballs, kicks with her feet, and foams at the mouth; duration: about two minutes, with total amnesia. These attacks may also appear during sleep: one of our patients was awakened by an upward jerk of her body. A hebephrenic suddenly flushed in his face, and then woke up and began to curse.

The above examples show that there is a continuous scale of transitions, from the true organic cerebral attack to the agitated states. It is certain that some of the latter are exclusively psychic in that the patient's train of thoughts or some external occurrence has touched upon a complex. However, if one considers the hallucinatory attacks which are so common among the older of our hospitalized schizophrenics, one gets the impression that the majority of these attacks are based on some organic process. One cannot influence either their origin or their course in any way; the most that one can do is to train the patients gradually to retain some hold of themselves even during the attacks; or one can bring them to the point where they will themselves ask to be isolated "when it comes," so that they will not annoy the others.

Some abortive attacks cannot be differentiated from epileptic *petit mal* attacks: the facial expression of an ordinarily cheerful female hebephrenic suddenly assumes a sullen expression, as she mutters a few incomprehensible words; duration: a few seconds. A hebephrenic stands up very abruptly, grasps his head; "everything before his eyes is black, everything shimmers"; duration: a few seconds. A periodic catatonic remains prostrate and slack with eyes closed as if dead; pulse remains normal. Here again, psychic origin is not to be excluded.

Wernicke saw *fits of rigidity* which appeared particularly when something was wanted of the patient. I have seen externally similar attacks which were certainly sexual orgasms. Huefler also recognized *fits of pain.*

To my knowledge, there do not as yet exist any useful studies on the frequency of *physical deformities* (I deliberately avoid the term "signs of degeneration") in dementia praecox. According to Laubi, with most of whose work I am familiar, far fewer deformities are found in the psychoses now considered to be schizophrenic than in idiocy or epilepsy, but some more than among the healthy. A very pronounced schizophrenic disorder need by no means express itself through such anomalies. Since among hospitalized schizophrenics, there is a relative predominance of individuals who were originally intellectually inferior, one cannot as yet say whether the non-imbecilic among them really show more deformities than the healthy.

Wintersteiner has observed congenital changes of the fundi in two thirds of his cases of "paranoia" (classified as such according to the Viennese school).

Many would also mention *struma* in this connection. There is no doubt that in the goitrous regions more large goiters are found among the schizophrenic than among the healthy population. The goiter may also enlarge and decrease, with the patients' agitation (Bertschinger). However, there may be an external cause for this. (The goiters of our patients are treated only if they threaten to cause trouble. The patients' screaming may cause the goiter to swell.) In any case, there is no proof of a connection between goiter and schizophrenia or the schizophrenic predisposition.

(g) The Catatonic Symptoms

The term catatonic symptoms covers a number of the phenomena which Kahlbaum had found in his catatonia: peculiar forms of motility, stupor, mutism, stereotypy, mannerism, negativism, command-automaticity, spontaneous automatism, and impulsivity. I would not insist that all these symptoms are intrinsically more closely related to each other than to other symptoms. Nonetheless, the idea is a convenient one, and it corresponds to the most frequent combinations of the individual symptoms in that form of schizophrenia which we call catatonic. More than half of the institutionalized schizophrenics show catatonic symptoms either transitorily or permanently.

1. Catalepsy

The patient's stiff facies often gives the impression of tense lines and features. Also, the persistently maintained forced posture suggests a state of muscular rigidity. We frequently sense a certain degree of resistance to passive motion which in the more severe cases may become absolutely insurmountable. However, in reality, we do not as yet know in schizophrenia of any condition which could be termed tonic muscular contraction in the real sense of the word. What has been described as such are complicated phenomena of primarily psychogenic origin.

Indeed it is not at all rare to meet with a patient who can assume and maintain a certain position for months at a time; he will seem quite rigid, too, when one attempts to move his limbs passively. This can go so far that one can move the patient's whole body as if it were a piece of wood by using his arm, hand, or leg as a lever without changing in the least the relative position of the part grasped to the rest of the body. But if one observes such a case more closely, then one can always see that the muscular contraction adjusts to any external force applied and that the muscles flex exactly as much as is needed to maintain the assumed position. The preciseness of muscular control and the absolute fixation of the joints are indeed quite remarkable. A healthy person would hardly ever be capable of such resistance. As yet, I cannot prove that at any given moment, in order to maintain the desired position, the muscles are more strongly contracted than is necessary to resist the force of gravity or some other external influence. Yet, on the other hand, we do note in a few cases that the tension has spread over to muscles which are not directly involved in the action, exactly as in healthy people who are making a physical effort.

Ballet (38, p. 105) termed this tendency to muscle tension, catatonism; he and others (Kleist) assumed that certain muscle groups, especially the neck flexors, are in some way predisposed to this sort of reaction. As yet, I have not been able to convince myself that this phenomenon is confined to any definite muscle groups. It appears to me as far more likely that our patients persist in maintaining definite postures which are ordinarily employed such as, for example, the bending of the head in lying on one's back. We prefer, therefore, to discuss this phenomenon under that of stereotypies of posture.

Far more common than complete rigidity is the "waxy or flexible" catalepsy: In typical cases, the patients make no, or hardly any, spontaneous movements. No matter where or how one places them, they remain motionless. Positions in which they are passively placed are maintained; apparently they are completely indifferent as to whether they are comfortable or not. It is possible to raise the leg of a standing patient, stretch out the arms horizontally, and even bend the trunk, yet the patient will remain in this position, occasionally for twenty minutes or longer. A feeling of fatigue seems to be lacking in these instances (always?). After some time, the outstretched limbs sink down or gradually, almost imperceptibly, change for another, equally bizarre position, or a sudden jerk will bring them into a more comfortable position, but in such a manner that the original position is still noticeable. The arms which were stretched forward remain raised forward a little as they hang down; the arms which were raised laterally still extend a little to the side of the body.

Often one scarcely senses any resistance to passive changes of posture; indeed, it is as if the patient wished to anticipate the intention of the examiner. The limbs seem to elevate themselves at the least touch and assume the desired direction as if they guessed what it was to be. If one proceeds rather rapidly, they often overshoot the mark.[46] In other cases, one finds a distinct resistance so that one must at least raise the weight of the arms as if they belonged to the body of a dead person. In still other cases, it is necessary to overcome a mild degree of muscular resistance. One cannot categorically separate these various pictures from one another. Therefore, I prefer, like other authors, to include them in the rubric, flexibilitas cerea.

In most cases, this symptom is present to a limited degree only. The

---

46. Wernicke called this symptom pseudo-flexibilitas and considered it a milder degree of flexibilitas cerea. Ziehen differentiated this pseudo-flexibility from flexibilitas cerea inasmuch as in the former there is no evidence of the effect of a definite idea or concept.

patients can move their limbs freely; but if one gives their limbs a certain position, they maintain it for some time, often without letting this interfere with other movements of the same limb. For example, they make gestures or stereotyped movements with a hand; if one holds the same arm up in the air, they leave it there but continue with their previous hand motions above their heads.

The manner and way in which one moves the patient's limb usually makes some difference. Often catelepsy shows itself only when one brings the limb very abruptly into a new position as if one were suggesting that it should be held in this particular way. However, suggestion in the usual sense of the term is of no avail. The patient does not have to believe that one demands the maintenance of a certain position. I often successfully test for the presence of catalepsy in the following way: I take the patient's pulse and, as if inadvertently, hold his arm high and fully extended. Then after taking the pulse rate, I release the arm. Conversely, one can examine other patients or normal individuals with the usual methods of testing for catalepsy without being able to demonstrate this phenomenon.

In rarer cases, catalepsy expresses itself in the continuation of movements which the patient is asked to perform. If the patient is requested to rotate his hands around each other, he starts and cannot stop. When asked to copy a definite number of somersaults, they do far too many, etc.

In cases showing marked catalepsy, spontaneous movements are absent. In the milder cases, the spontaneous movements are distinctly impaired; they are executed slowly and weakly. One often observes patients straining, for example, to open their lips when they wish to reply, but often only managing to utter soft low whispers after many attempts to speak, so that one thinks of inhibition. Others are still able to perform some activities; they are still able to get around, but even then, it is for the most part slowly, tremulously, feebly. The final movement in an act may become fixed, or the patient may become arrested and rigid in the very midst of performing a certain act or movement. Thus a patient wishes to bring the spoon to his mouth; half-way there he stops and for many minutes does not change this position. Then the hand may gradually sink down following the effect of gravity, or the action begun may be completed. This fixation can affect the entire body as well as a single limb.

Even the most intense degrees of catalepsy may be dissolved momentarily by internal or external psychic influences. As in every other catatonic stupor, the cataleptic who appears completely immobile can suddenly get up and knock a neighbor to the floor, bite or commit some other unpleasantness, only to resume his rigidity after a few moments. They can also suddenly begin to talk very reasonably or hold a conversation with their hallucinations. At such moments, the patient's movements do not show any evidence of disturbance; on the contrary, they may be executed with great force and skill (cf. above, the dancing catatonic woman).

Certain patients become cataleptic only under definite conditions or circumstances. Whenever a patient thinks she is alone, she begins to sing merrily, laughs contentedly, or curses obscenely, only to become cataleptic immediately when she knows she is being observed. It is of little importance whether negativism is the explanation or not. Other patients move about quite freely while at work, but become cataleptic, when one wishes to examine them. One of our convalescents, who seemed to be free of catalepsy for some time, became quite cataleptic during a game in which a somewhat greater than usual demand on his attention was made.

Catalepsy may alternate with complete rigidity. In negativistic individuals, one can even provoke the latter. Between such periods of rigidity, such a complete and total relaxation of the musculature appeared in one of our patients that he collapsed like a cadaver. In other respects, the muscle tonus is quite good in flexibilitas cerea. We observed a patient who had many attacks of only right-sided catalepsy (combined with tremor, analgesia, and auditory hallucinations of that same side.)

The combinations of catalepsy and negativism are quite strange. For example, one such patient, when one raised his right arm, very negativistically and abruptly pulled it down, but instead he would raise his left arm into the desired position. (I have already observed something quite similar without having any reason to assume the presence of negativism, with the only difference that the involved limb was brought into a normal position less abruptly.) Abraham also observed a case of flexibilitas on one side of the body, and negativistic stiffness on the other (of course, without suggestion).

In combined echopraxia and catalepsy, we may even have one side of the body imitating the other: a patient's right arm was raised high while the left was extended slightly downwards. Then as both arms began to sink, the left arm took its natural position, while the right arm pressed closer to the head and finally came to rest on the back of the head; this position was imitated by the left arm from its hanging-down position. The patient remained like this for a long period of time.

In combination with the various catatonic conditions and only very rarely as an isolated phenomenon, we can observe another symptom: a generalized and persistent, or at times a very capricious and fleeting, difficulty or impossibility of movement. The patients have to make a great effort and strain to contract their muscles; the movements become weak, slow, trembly, indeed, often utterly impossible. The patients may feel as if their muscles and limbs were paralyzed or rigid, or as if some outside power were restraining them. Frequently the patients will falsely explain their condition by some hallucination or delusion. To be sure, akinesis may be caused in this way, but then we are not dealing with a disturbance of motility in the above sense of psychic paralysis or paresis.[47] Usually the patients are extraordinarily little concerned with or frightened by this condition; however some anxiety is often associated with it, but then it seems to be independent of the akinesis. In stuporous and clouded states,[48] the markedly decreased ability to move occasionally creates the impression of generalized cerebral torpor.

2. Stupor

A good many catatonics have been called stuporous. In Ziehen's precise sense (aprosexia plus inhibition of thought plus immobility), however, we find stupor almost only in the clouded states,[49] obviously as a consequence of generally reduced psychic activity, or of total "blocking." However all akinetic catatonics present an external picture of absent or markedly diminished reaction to the environment. Moreover, stupor may be brought about by generalized blocking, by intense inhibition (melancholic) of the psychic processes; by lack of interest, affect and will; by autism, by mechanisms producing twilight states; by negativism; and by numerous hallucinations which even without any systematic exclusion of reality, transplant the patient completely into his own fantasy-world. Naturally, the many forms of stupor easily combine, inasmuch as various causal factors are operative simultaneously. The stupor need not be a complete one. Many stuporous patients sort of wander about in a daze, but they can still enter into a simple conversation or even do some work. One of our patients wanted to look for something behind a haystack. He lit a match for the purpose and soon found the haystack in flames. At that period he was still able to do some work under his wife's supervision. However, he could not judge that it would be extremely dangerous to light a match near a dry haystack, or take the proper precautions once he did so; he certainly was incapable of putting out the fire after it had started.

With the possible exception of the "clouded states" practically all

---

47. Often the "voices" commanding and forbidding the movements, and the impairment of motility are parallel consequences of a common cause.

48. *Benommenheit.*

49. Cf. following chapter on the acute syndromes.

schizophrenic types of stupor may partially or completely disappear under psychic influences. If one happens to touch upon the patient's complexes, one often sees a marked reaction, be it as a tensing of muscles, or as a change in the innervation of blood vessels. Thus it is evident that the patients still grasp and assimilate what is going on. Riklin's (612) stuporous catatonic answered and read only those ideas and words which were fully and directly connected with his morbid wishes. A completely rigid negativistic patient immediately clenched her teeth when I told her that she was far too thin to have stolen some food, as she had insisted. A motionless patient broke out into hearty laughter when another patient dropped a piece of butter which he had hidden in a paper bag. Stuporous patients can very suddenly become perfectly capable of playing chess correctly, or of writing and playing the piano rapidly, etc. A visit from the family may often induce such patients to "wake up" completely.[50]

3. Hyperkinesis

The akinetic symptoms of stupor and flexibilitas cerea stand in marked contrast to catatonic hyperkinesis. They have been described by Wernicke's school as a separate disease characterized by hyper-irritability of the psycho-motor functions. Up to now, however, there is no proof that hyperkinesis is not merely a part-phenomenon of a general catatonic psychic condition. As other movements of catatonics, the "pseudo-spontaneous" movements appear to be arbitrary, automatic, and stereotyped in the most variegated patterns. Since hyperkineses may often completely dominate the external clinical picture of a catatonic excitement, they will be described in greater detail with the other acute symptom complexes.

4. Stereotypies

One of the most striking external manifestations of schizophrenia is the inclination to stereotypies. We find them in every sphere: that of movement, action, posture, speech, writing, drawing, in musical expressions, in the thinking and in the desires of the hallucinating patients.

We find patients rubbing their right hands over their left thumbs, intently and energetically for decades. Others will tap a saliva-moistened fingertip on every conceivable place, on tables, chairs, walls; or they will run their fingers along the edges of all the furniture and walls as if taking the dust off. Others beat on their beds rhythmically, clap their hands or perform all kinds of manipulations with their teeth, etc. Then

---

50. As for the mutism which is often described as a partial symptom of catatonic stupor, see below.

again others walk about in a very special fashion, tapping a certain spot with their feet, dancing around, as if at a quadrille, nodding their heads, turning around when lying in bed or standing upright continually. Some always perform the same somersaults or other gymnastics. Often the stereotypies appear to be willed acts; some patients tear their hair out by the roots, frequently in a very definite pattern so that, for example, a fringe is left which may run down the middle of the scalp. They keep their finger stuck in their ani or smear feces in certain designs; they pull and knot their clothing, or twist the buttons off constantly.

The stereotypies of posture show somewhat less variability. Very many catatonics, while lying quietly in their beds, hold their backs and even their heads raised off the mattress or pillow in a position which a healthy person could not support for very long without tiring quickly. They curl up, sit or stand rigidly like an Egyptian mummy. They hold their legs spread apart with the hand held in a special manner on the cheek. They perch in the bath with their mouths barely held above water and their backs arched completely out of the water. For weeks they may gaze at the very same spot, often with the eyes in the most extraordinary position which a healthy person could not maintain for two minutes.

Stereotypies of position are expressed in two ways in that the patients always select the same corner of the room, the same place in the garden; and they will actually fight for these places if, accidentally or intentionally, someone else happens to claim their spot. Or, the patients always go to exactly the same place to carry on a particular activity; for example, always striking three times on the identical spot on the wall of the corridor.

Acts and behavior which per se need not be senseless are repeated incessantly, with an almost photographic sameness. The patient goes to bed always exactly in the same way, starting from exactly the same place, getting out of bed exactly in the same manner. In the garden, he will run around the same circle or square, so that before long, he has dug tracks in the earth which have to be filled in. Many years before his illness became manifest, a physician had made deep holes in the hardwood floor of his room because he always turned on his heels at exactly the same place on the floor. The walls and furniture of many a mental hospital bear the traces of such stereotypies.

Naturally, the different kinds of stereotypies very often combine to form complicated clinical pictures. A woman patient always stands in a specific place when she knits, with a particular orientation and posture. When the work is done for the day, she goes out into the corridor and places herself with her forehead against the dining room door till the food is brought up, whereupon she goes in and eats her meal also in a very special way.

The expressive movements, too, become stereotyped. One patient grins; another makes a sad face, quite independent of his real mood. Often enough stereotyped yelling, screaming, roaring, or squeaking has the same significance, equally so the pursing of the lips (*Schnauzkrampf*). At this point, one might also mention the musical stereotypes. For years a patient plays the very same trill or chord, sometimes as often as a thousand times in succession; then again the same few notes. Usually it is the same song or a fragment of a song, which is sung repeatedly and monotonously, by one patient in the self-same shrill voice, by another very softly and delicately. It may be a self-composed melody or a well-known tune to which the patient may use every possible text for words. The same rhythm may be tacked on in answers to questions, or the identical rhythm may be retained in speaking.

The majority of severe cases, when they do trouble to express themselves at all, have the tendency to employ certain expressions of speech again and again, both in appropriate and inappropriate places. The same words or sentences are repeated innumerable times in their ordinary tone of voice, in screams, whispers, or sing-song; they are repeated regardless of context and without any intention of communicating an idea. Affective expression may be entirely lacking; but if it exists it is highly artificial, exaggerated, and unrelated to the content (verbigeration). Thus one patient always repeats the sentence, "You steal the Saviour's rights;" another, "Merci bien, Monseigneur." Many women patients abuse the word, "love" in their verbigeration.

Utterly senseless combinations of sounds such as, "the crossed crux in a circumrex house" (Kraepelin) are quite common. In the main, however, the content of speech is not stereotyped in all its details. One patient calls and repeats the names of her children; another catatonic enumerates (in no definite sequence) the names of places, cities, towns, etc. A Miss Muller counts: "Twenty-one Mr. Mullers, twenty-two Mr. Mullers, twenty-three Mr. Mullers . . ." Another patient calculates aloud, "1 times 4 is 90, 2 times 3 is 72, 2 times 1 is 24, 2 times 2 is 28." Still another enunciates softly, "A, o, u, e, e, a, u, e, a, o, etc." in different variations. Another says, "I think, I will," and in between he continues to conjugate the present tense of the verb, "to love." At times the patients will get a bit further with their themes: "Baba, ba ba ba ba, s, s, s are good people, s, s, s, are nice people, nice people, nice people, baba, bababa, ba, hm hm hm, yes, I slept, yes, I slept, I have slept. . . . What is this there, what is this, this, this, this? bababa ba." One of our patients rings the changes on one of her few themes, for many hours a day. For example, she talks endlessly about the "concierge," describing in greatest detail all the janitors she had ever known, as well as their homes, etc.

Verbigeration also combines with other kinds of stereotypies. Thus Neisser's patient rocked herself back and forth as she verbigerated, "Pity us, pity us, etc."

Such stereotypies of speech as the following cannot quite accurately be considered as verbigeration: the insertion of stereotyped words as "Are you there, dear little protector, bumps, are you there, bumps?" or the insertion of mere sounds which need not even belong to the language spoken. For example, one of our paranoids tacks on to each word, as he speaks it, a sort of grunting sound. It is something else, however, when a patient answers each and every question put to him with the word, "pretty" using different tones each time. Exclamations which are not immediately repeated one after the other, are also stereotyped and dragged in independently of their proper sense. Thus every minute for thirty years, a patient says, "I don't feel well," as a sign of joy or displeasure or in an apparently completely indifferent mood; occasionally she translates some of the words into a foreign language (bene, bien, bueno, etc.).

Written verbigerations show the same characteristics as the oral. Words, sentences, and letters are repeated endlessly, whether they make sense or not, with or without variations. In addition, curlicues may be attached to the letters or written independently of them. Catatonics particularly love to play with punctuation marks. A definite number of periods are combined with dashes; figures are designed with them which are repeated, etc. A large number of pages may be written, and each page will be precisely like the other; they will match point for point, letter for letter (Antheaume).

Also their drawings show a tendency to stereotypy. They love to use the same monotonous theme over and over again, shortening it till it becomes unrecognizable. They do this regardless of whether they are scribbling a simple ornament with a few crochety lines and strokes, or drawing figures and other illustrations. Thus, one of our patients paints, quite skillfully, an endless number of overly-slim nude women in the crack of a rock, without ever varying his theme.

Stereotypies of thoughts and desires, which of course are always expressed in the same words, are to be distinguished from stereotypies of speech. To these belong the usually automatic requests for release which are repeated daily to us, in precisely the same words to which the patients hardly even expect an answer. Quite similar are those instances, when a patient will request daily that we hold a garden party, although she must know that it is entirely impossible, if for no other reason than the fact that it is winter. It is much less comprehensible when over a long period of time, a patient answers each question with the counter question: "Wouldn't it be a good idea to apply court plaster?"

Stereotypy of thoughts is often so intense that the patient is incapable of thinking anything except a very few thoughts. To this group belongs the catatonic physician who invariably and unfailingly prescribed the identical medicament for each and every disease regardless of its nature.

The stereotypies of hallucinations are most obvious in the auditory sphere; the patient always hears the same words, the same curses and threats over and over again.

The stereotypies do not always become manifest spontaneously from within, without any external stimulation. As the patient relates a story, the stereotypies very often indicate certain definite constellations of his complexes. For many years, a catatonic made a certain circular motion with her arms which meant that she had millions of dollars; she not only made this motion while her thoughts were on such things as money, but even when speaking of other things as well.

The patient's attitude toward the stereotypies is varied, indeed. The majority behave as if the stereotypies were something self-evident. Some try in vain to suppress them. Working patients interrupt their stereotyped movements while they are at work; some try to combine both together; others stop their work in order to carry out the movements.

Direct questioning rarely yields any information as to why the patients perform the movements. The patients will just give any explanation: "So as to have something to do," "To save the church," etc.; or they simply refuse to answer. However, very often all sorts of symptoms related to their complexes come to the fore in such investigations. Thus, a very torpid patient, who for months never made a single quick reaction, answered to the question as to why he constantly kept his fingers over his face: "It is my habit." He responded far more promptly than a normal person would and with visible signs of agitation. Frequently such questions provoke negativism.

The stereotypies strongly influence the entire psyche: they inhibit other actions and often force the patient to maintain the most uncomfortable positions. In addition they may enforce their hold on the patient at the expense of the very integrity of his body. Even with a relatively healthy circulation, the fact that the same position is maintained for a long time may lead to decubitus ulcers. It is often extremely difficult to protect patients from wounds and infections if they continually rub the same area of skin. Women patients who persistently hold the raised hem of their long skirts with their little finger often develop Dupuytren's contractures. At the time when it was still customary to leave the patients to their own devices, contractures of the legs with the knees held near the chin were no rarity.

As we have already pointed out in some of the examples mentioned, the stereotypies are not always completely unalterable. They can be modified by external influences; indeed, they often adapt to circumstances. A patient had the strange habit of singing repeatedly a not at all unpleasant self-composed melody whenever a male person entered her ward. The tune went, "O, what a handsome, pleasant minister." Once when I entered the ward with my shoes all dusty from the street, she sang, "O, what a handsome, filthy minister." Very frequently patients will pick up some words or snatch at fragmentary notions and incorporate them in their original stereotypes. Also word combinations which have arisen through fortuitous associations are interwoven in a very novel fashion: "Hallelujah (five times), holla, holla, holla. Oh, la, oh, la, oh la, what has happened?"

Wishes and desires which are expressed in the verbigerations, may be further elaborated, and find new forms of expression.

The gradual abbreviation of the stereotypy is one of the most common phenomena. Movements, which at first served a sensible purpose—such as the imitation of a shoe-maker sewing, the pirouetting of a dancer—become abbreviated till they are unrecognizable. The verbigerated phrase, "going home," gradually becomes, "go;" then simply "gg." An entire story relating a journey to the beloved one may ultimately shrink to a single gulping sound such as, "hm."

5. Mannerisms [51]

Many patients take on a certain pose. This one runs around with his arms crossed on his chest, like a prime-minister whom he had once seen in a photograph. That one apes Bismarck including his handwriting. The majority are usually content imitating something special in a general way: a pose, a facial mien, clothing, speech, handwriting. Some remain consistent in their mannerism for decades; others are constantly stepping out of their roles. Almost always there is something artificial, stilted, and pompous about their conduct. It remains inappropriate to the occasion and inadequately modifiable. Thus almost always mannerisms soon become caricatures.

---

51. Mannerisms are striking alterations of ordinary activities. Ziehen has termed them "modified stereotypes." But not all mannerisms have to become stereotyped.

Most mannerisms, however, have become entirely incomprehensible to us. Everything one does may be modified in the sense of schizophrenic mannerisms without the reasons being apparent.

The gait changes; a hospital patient, still intelligent and diligent, no longer walks but gallops. Washing and dressing are done differently from the way it is done by the normal person. In eating, the spoon is held by its handle tip only or reversed. Before taking a mouthful of food, the patient knocks on the plate three times. The food is taken up on the fork and dropped back again seven times before it is taken into the mouth. The patient circles the toilet bowl three times before sitting down on it. A mason makes a waving gesture with both hands above every brick he lays.

Besides eating, speech offers the best opportunity for mannerisms. The patients not only employ all kinds of pathos, they speak in telegraphic style, in infinitives and diminutives. Foreign words are used with affected pronunciation or "ism" or "io" is added to every word. They scan their speech, use peculiar rhythms, write in rimes. For many years one of our patients barely opened his lips while speaking and was completely indifferent to the fact that no one could understand what he said. The voice may be altered. Over a period of ten years, I never heard a certain catatonic woman speak except in high falsetto or in squeaking tones.

The expressive gestures are also modified. Every conceivable stilted gesture occurs. Shaking hands is done very stiffly with the hand turned or only the little finger is presented; the hand may be shot forward quickly and withdrawn just as rapidly. Grimaces of all kinds, peculiar ways of shrugging the shoulder, extraordinary movements of tongue and lips, finger play, sudden involuntary gestures—all these peculiarities are the reason why some authors have spoken of choreic or tetanic movements in catatonia, quite mistakenly, though. On the other hand, many of these movements cannot be distinguished from tics.

6. Negativism

We subsume under the term, negativism, a number of symptoms which have the common characteristic that a reaction which would be expected in a positive sense occurs in the negative sense instead. The patients cannot or will not do what is expected of them (passive negativism); or they do just the very opposite or, at least, something else than what is expected (active or contrary negativism).

When the patients should be getting up, they want to stay in bed. When they are supposed to be in bed, they want to get up. They will neither dress nor undress in accordance with the rules of the hospital. Neither will they go for their meals nor leave the table once they are there. In short, they oppose everyone and everything and, consequently, become exceedingly difficult to handle.[52] They refuse food at mealtimes but eat avidly whatever they can cage in a roundabout way; for example, what they manage to take away from others. They may eat only secretly or at unusual times. They grumble about the food but when asked what they would like to have, their only answer is: "Something else, not what we have." They do not go to the lavatory by themselves; if led there, they do not attend to their needs, but immediately after they have left the proper place for such things, they soil themselves, their bed, or their clothes. They turn away whenever anyone addresses them or close their eyes tightly. A patient did the latter so forcefully that, at times, the upper lid was partly everted without anyone ever being able to demonstrate any anomaly of the lid. To "Good day," they say, "good-bye." They do their work all wrong; sew buttons on the wrong side of the clothes. They eat their soup with a fork and their desert with a soup spoon. They continually sit down in somebody else's place, enter every bed but their own. They call our children by their surnames (which they have picked up somehow) instead of by their nicknames. A hebephrenic is asked to saw some wood; he hauls some small boards instead, then he has to bring small boards, which he puts on the wrong stack. He is supposed to go down the staircase but resists; then suddenly takes the whole flight in one great leap.

A partial phenomenon of negativism is the already discussed muscular rigidity which maintains a stereotyped (or more rarely a transitory) attitude against every and all influences.

Many patients go beyond the stage of mere passive resistance and defend themselves with might and main, frequently with vilification and blows, against all measures. Any trifling request made of them may throw them into the greatest rage. Yet there are also cases, which are not at all rare, where the patient laughingly bites, scratches, and punches; or pursues the doctor, whom he has been so vigorously opposing, with friendly mien, showing that he really does not hold anything against the doctor but that the negativism is related only to what was requested of him. With a nasty remark, they refuse to shake hands, but at the same time give the doctor the cup from which they have been drinking.

Some patients invariably do exactly the opposite of what is asked; this fact can be utilized to manage them ("command-negativism"). Thus

---

52. The English speak of "mulish resistiveness."

a patient's wife had eventually elaborated this trait in her husband into a regular system. If she wanted to take a walk in a certain direction she would propose the opposite to her husband; in this way she could be quite sure of getting where she really wanted to go. Even in hospitals, it is often possible to get patients to do something by using this method: that is, by forbidding them to do it. If one wants to get them to go to the dining room for their meals, one says, "Don't go to eat." If one wants them to move forward, one restrains them, holds them back a bit, etc., etc. A less objectionable way of utilizating negativistic tendencies is, if one has to move patients, to let them go backwards for a short distance; they will do this more readily than going forward.

Very little information can be obtained by questioning negativistic patients. They wrap themselves up in a deep silence, begin to curse or give answers to questions that have not been asked. One of our patients told us frankly that if she were aware of what we wanted to know, it would be precisely that which she would refuse to tell us. Others offer excuses; they can not answer because it involves a stupid, silly, or delicate matter. A very characteristic example of negation *à tout prix* is a patient's reply to the question as to what her name was. She answered with, "That is not my name." Although they seemingly answer everything, many are so skillful in dodging that one never attains one's purpose. To the repeated question as to how many years he had been persecuted, a patient answered first: "Since a certain law suit in which I lost a good deal of money;" then: "I had many such law suits;" finally: "I lost over 800 marks."

Negativism is one of the roots of the schizophrenic "approximate answer." Very often questions which touch on a complex are first negated almost without thinking, even when the patient has no conscious reason for not answering correctly, and even though subsequently he may give the desired information quite willingly. However, this symptom is also met with in non-negativistic schizophrenics and in a far milder way, even in normal people. In many complexes there is something that prevents any attempt at even touching on them; this often looks like negativism and also facilitates it as well.

Negativistic patients, who refuse to answer questions put to them, will at times respond to questions which are asked of others. Thus, for example, they will give the name of their own husband when one of their neighbors is supposed to answer that question.

Persuasion will overcome only the lighter cases of negativism; the more severe cases will only be made more stubborn and resistive. It is far better to ignore their behavior and to wait. Frequently, a request will be complied with as soon as the proper time for it has gone by. The patients will withdraw their hands when they are greeted only to thrust their hand forward suddenly after one has turned to shake hands with another patient. Usually, however, they finally shake hands in such a way that the contact is as superficial as possible, or they miss the proffered hand. In the same fashion, they answer or wish to speak only when one is about to leave the room. They do not work when they are asked to, but start spontaneously if one does not say anything about working. A physician who still practices could not decide to get into the trolley-car at the conductor's request but as soon as the car was in motion, he started to run after it. If one can yield to the patient the negativism often disappears. A patient refused to remain in his room when commanded; one merely had to open the door and he would stay put or return at once.

Indeed, often even in apparently mild cases of negativism, it is useless either to wait or to yield. There are cases in which the negativism seeks opportunities for its expression and degenerates into a highly unpleasant capriciousness. Such patients resist most vigorously eating their meals, getting up, going for a walk; yet they will complain, not only to strangers but to the hospital personnel as well, that they are forced to lie in bed all day, that they are forbidden to take a walk, etc. A patient, who had become deaf but who could speak very well, always wrote down everything she wished to say, but she insisted that we give her only oral answers, thereby making conversation completely impossible. She would also hide her own and other patients' handkerchiefs whenever she could, and then complain and protest that the nurse had stolen them. The patient demanded baths of unusual temperatures and when given them, she raved and ranted that we were trying to scald or freeze her. For years these activities were her only occupation. These cases become so difficult because the patients always know how to put themselves in the best light with a third party, so that they easily find credence everywhere.

I have not yet discovered to what extent negativism falsifies these patients' thinking and knowledge. Certainly they consider at least part of their complaints as justified; perhaps they lack entirely any awareness of being in the wrong.

We also have to count as negativism those processes in which not the demands of the external world but the inner strivings and feelings of the patients are denied ("inner negativism"). There is a well-known phenomenon which appears very frequently and in an exaggerated form in negativistic schizophrenics. It is the phenomenon that one always considers the things one has accomplished and done as wrong. Thus, we have a patient who eagerly promoted her engagement to a man;

but after having accomplished this, she reproached herself bitterly for being too hasty, and thereupon her illness became manifest. A hebephrenic knows that he is outdoors, but not why he went out; and when he stays inside the building, he does not know why he remained there. When the door is open, he gazes at it fixedly; when it is closed, he gets very angry that he did not take the opportunity to go out. The same phenomenon can also express itself in the form of a compulsion; after having finished a piece of knitting, a patient must unravel it again; one patient "always says what she does not want to say." Thus many patients get to a point where they deny what they have said immediately after they have said it. "I have to deblock it, not debarrel (self-constructed words which the patient employs). I must debarrel it, not deblock it." "I am Mr. Papa and not Madame Mama; I am Madame Mama, and not Mr. Papa." Or, "I have come to Burgholzli to get a certificate. No, I don't want any certificate, absolutely not." In the first of the two cases, we are dealing with spontaneous verbigeration; in the third case, the statement was intended to express a wish. In all these cases there was a great deal of such talk (intellectual negativism, or intellectual ambivalence).

Often the "inner negativism" reveals itself in the antithesis between statement and act. Thus a patient (who had already eaten her meal) sits down in another patient's chair and says to those present, "Don't worry, I won't have anything," and straight away begins to eat.

The discrepancy between various "personalities" within the patient is not to be regarded as "inner negativism," although the two phenomena obviously have much in common. A patient declares, "I am God in Heaven;" then he corrects himself and says, "Don't write that down; it is a damned lie that I am God." In this instance, the contradiction is determined by the fact that the autistic delusion is followed by the healthier insight corresponding to the still normal fragments of the patient's personality.

The inner negativism may spread to the hallucinations. The voices continuously tell the patient to do the very opposite of what he should do even according to his own opinion. Then also, when a patient does do something, the voices forbid it or at least declare it is not right. But when the patients obey the voices, it is not right either. Many patients, who are not yet in a state of complete indifference, are brought to a point of despair by these things. A patient with technical training called them, "the plus and minus voices."

Inner negativism may also manifest itself in the patients' actions so that they are incapable of doing what they want to (Kraepelin's "counter-will").

Thus of their own free will they may go to the toilet, but once there do not tend to their needs; instead they will evacuate their bowels or bladder later, when they are in bed. They would like to eat the food placed before them but they can not take it. A patient wishes to read aloud. She takes visible pains to do so, but cannot open her mouth and develops an esophageal cramp. In this way, a few negativistic individuals appear incapable of performing certain acts while they are being observed; but even healthy people cannot always perform before an audience.

At times, the negativistic speech disturbance is localized more centrally, if I may use this figure of speech. The organs of speech are controlled by the will-power of the patient, yet negativistic expressions, quite contrary to the patient's will, are uttered so that the very opposite of what the patient wants to say comes out. A certain patient is expected to mount the podium to give a lecture. She constantly protests that she will not "stand down there on the floor." However, in some cases, negative phrases and expressions are employed where positive ones should have been used, without changing the sense of what they wish to say.

For example, a catatonic woman patient says, "not ugly" instead of "beautiful." After some time, "not ugly" becomes for her a uniform positive expression; then she proceeds using "not, not ugly" when she means "ugly." This expression soon becomes a rigid formula in which she no longer senses the negation involved, and the word, "beautiful" becomes "not not not ugly." As the process continues to advance even further (not merely in this particular phrase but in others as well), the patient easily becomes confused since she may stop at the even number of negatives cancelling each other instead of the uneven one, or reverse herself, and then get lost completely. She will then complain bitterly that people are trying to confuse her.

The "counter-will" does not always produce the opposite of the desired action; action per se need not be inhibited completely. Often it merely leads to the patients' inability to carry out what they wanted and to their substituting something else instead. The result is an external picture of apraxia. Instead of combing her hair, the patient runs the comb over her coat. I cannot immediately differentiate many such acts from organic apraxia. It is equally impossible for me in some cases to evaluate the part played by negativism, "*Benommenheit*" (mental clouding), and emotional stupor. I am convinced, however, that all these various elements represent concomitant influences.

The transition from common negativism to such apractic-like symptoms can be observed in cases in which only part of the muscles are employed to carry out a desired activity while other muscles hinder the success of the desired action by counter-contractions. Meschedes' patient, when he wanted to direct his gaze to the left, turned his head only to the left, whereas the eyes were turned in the opposite direction. I have frequently seen the same kind of thing when asking patients to play the piano for us. The patients will make the necessary movements with the arms, often in a markedly exaggerated fashion and with great strength, but at the very same time they will dorsiflect the wrist and fingers so that the hands do not even touch the keyboard.

Intellectual negativism may even extend to orientation and comprehension of the environment. Thus a patient insisted that the Zurichberg (a hill) used to be West, while the Uetli (another hill) used to be in the East (in reality the hills are located in exactly the reverse positions).

There is no specific affect which causes negativism. Negativism may appear with every and any kind of manifest affect. We see negativism in manic excitements and in the indifferent euphoria of schizophrenia, but also in depressions or in affectless moods. Naturally, however, irritability and anger are very frequently both the cause as well as the consequence of negativism.

It must also be noted that reflection does not, primarily, play any role in negativistic phenomena. If delusions or fallacious concepts are the causes of the "negation," then we are not dealing with negativism but rather with normal behavior under abnormal circumstances. This does not prevent the patients from using their delusions to justify their negativistic behavior. Of course, delusions and negativisms often influence and increase reciprocally.

The instinctual quality of negativism, its independence of intelligence, also manifests itself (as Bernstein has pointed out) in the utter indifference to pleasant or unpleasant, useful or injurious events. A very thirsty, negativistic patient will get quite angry even when some one offers him a drink.

Thus for the most part, the patients cannot give any reasonable grounds for their negativistic behavior. Often enough they offer excuses made up on the spur of the moment; they easily change when one repeats the question several times. At best, they only explain some isolated activity or attitude, never the whole behavior. The argument that it is the "voices" is obviously insufficient, since we are then faced with the same question as to why the "voices" are negativistic. The argument that the negativism is due to the delusion is also plainly insufficient in very many of the cases. In the first place, here too, one may ask why the delusions are negativistic. Secondly, the allegations involving delusions and excuses do not provide a really adequate explanation, partly because normal persons would not react negatively to the same ideas, and partly because even the patients do not always act in accordance with their delusional ideas. Thus, one patient refuses to take a bath because she claims she is physically clean and has never bathed; another patient will not eat because she is unhappy, but secretly devours whatever she can get hold of. The situation is no better in those cases where the patients think they *must not* act differently. The fundamental symptom is always negativism and it is negativism that determines the form and the content of the other manifestations.

As unapproachable as our strongly negativistic patients may seem to be, even very pronounced negativism is not absolutely, invariably, and completely rigid. It is more conspicuously exhibited toward some people than towards others. Many patients are negativistic only in relation to the hospital physician; others include the attendant personnel. Patients who for years were negativistic often may have quite normal contacts with other patients, relatives, or even strangers, for a short time. Negativisms are closely related to the complexes. Many patients appear entirely uninhibited during a conversation until a complex is touched upon. Then the negativism becomes manifest, with or without "blocking;" and at least for that day, and often for longer periods of time, further contact cannot be established with them. But we can also observe exactly the opposite behavior: a patient may be negativistic until we happen to touch on one of his main ideas and then they become quite approachable although usually only for a short time.

7. Command-Automatism and Echopraxia

Command-automatism shows a striking external contrast to negativism. Many patients will more or less mechanically obey any and every suggestion and command coming from the outside. Occasionally, they are hardly capable of resisting such suggestions, even if they wish to. Short, authoritative orders are often immediately executed, even by patients who are otherwise resistive. Of course, the orders must deal with simple activities, such as getting up from the table or getting dressed, etc. A piece of continuous work, for example a composition, cannot be obtained from them in this way. Such patients will even comply with unpleasant orders: thus non-anesthetic patients will continue to stick out their tongue, although they know very well that each time it will be stuck with a pin.

Kraepelin includes flexibilitas cerea in command-automatism. We have described the former in another connection because, among other reasons, cataleptic symptoms may also appear without the patient having been given any suggestion that a certain position is to be maintained. To be sure, the command to do a certain thing does not have to be given explicitly even in command-automatism. The motor element inherent in every idea is often sufficient for its execution. Thus, one of our patients would promptly close her eyes whenever someone mentioned sleep. The clearest and most frequent aspects of command-automatism are echopraxia and echolalia; that is, the imitation of impressions which have been gained unselectively. Slightly confused, but often even completely lucid, patients imitate and echo, usually without thinking and also without any evidence of resistance, the various actions which they see in others: facial expressions, gestures, cries, words, etc. Therefore, this symptom becomes quite an unpleasant one on the wards. In a hospital with poor discipline, I frequently saw a half-dozen plates flying through the air after one patient had thrown a plate off the dinner table. Cries and shouts are quite contagious; a single restless patient can easily provoke uproar in a whole ward. The bizarre gestures and stereotypies of one patient are imitated by other patients. Von Muralt described a catatonic who for years always copied another patient. If one asks questions the patients repeat them. In other instances, they copy particular movements, which impress them because, for example, they are very briskly carried out. As a matter of experiment, one can suddenly raise an arm or rub one's hands only to be imitated by the patients standing around. Even animal calls and pictures from books will be copied.

Particularly noteworthy is Riklin's (612) case of a catatonic who from time to time answered questions concerning his complexes quite sensibly but repeated all other queries. In general, it is not at all clear why certain impressions are selected for echopraxia. In some cases delusions may be the determinants; thus for example, a patient repeats loudly each and every question asked of him, so that God may hear it and tell him what to answer. There are also transitions in the direction of compulsive behavior: whenever a hebephrenic hears talking, she has the feeling that voices come up from beneath her, and feels the impulse to repeat everything she hears. Ballet (38, p. 149) also describes a "mental echolalia" in which the patient must mentally repeat everything he hears; and an "hallucinatory echolalia" in which the patient must repeat his hallucinations.

Command-automatism appears in combination with negativism, simultaneously or alternately. One of Kraepelin's (389, p. 36) patients repeated whatever was said, but with closed lips because of negativism.

8. Automatisms

Internal stimuli may also lead to automatic behavior; but only the simpler activities are caused in this way: insignificant movements, raising of the arms, assuming the position of the crucified, pressing the feet against the wall, walking in circles, creeping on all fours, screaming, animal cries, etc. Most of the motor-stereotypies are performed automatically. Much of the ordinary behavior exhibited by institutionalized patients has frequently become automatized; e. g. boxing of ears, tearing, smashing of window-panes, smearing, etc. On the other hand, patients outside a hospital may commit murder or arson. Yet despite the impulse, such crimes and acts are rarely carried out completely. The patients behave so awkwardly that they do not achieve their purpose; and often one gets the impression that they are not really in earnest or that an inner resistance prevents them from executing their intentions.

Self-injuries usually are carried out more successfully than crimes, although the majority of suicidal attempts do not achieve their goal. It seems that some fugues (see below under acute syndromes) also belong to the automatism; the majority, however, are hysteriform.

The degree of automatism varies with the number and forms of "split-off" associations.

1. The patient rips to pieces his clothes, fully conscious of what he is doing. He himself believes that he wants to do these things but he does not know the motives. He is quite ignorant of the motivation and purpose of his activity. On the other hand, the carrying out of an idea, the entire centrifugal part of the process, runs its course in combination with the conscious ego.

2. On the second level, to be sure, the patient also knows that he has knocked out a pane of glass but he really does not want to do it. The action appears to him as something beyond his voluntary control. In this case, not only the motive, but also the very translation into action, remain unrelated to the conscious personality. However, the latter is still so influenced that it regards the action as something indifferent. The patient does something which he really does not want to do; however, he does not offer any resistance.[53] The patient does not oppose his personality to the impulse; it is still too much bound up with the drive.

3. On the third level, the patient struggles against the emerging impulse. He senses it as a compelling force. The personality with its will and insight opposes the impulse. The compelling drive becomes a compulsive act when it is stronger than the personality. There are

53. Schreber simply "allows the screaming (which he himself is doing) to pass through."

fewer compulsive acts than compulsive drives or simple involuntary actions which appear most frequently.

4. An educated catatonic woman committed a number of silly acts during a phase of acute excitement; she said that she remembered everything as if it had been a dream. She seemed to obey a commandment or moral law but had no feeling of real compulsion. It all seemed very reasonable to her. Here the impulses influenced the intellectual functions which had been weakened in the trance-like state. Yet, the impulse still appeared as something foreign ("commandment"), but it was so bound up with the ego and so influenced the conscious thinking that the patient could not reason about it.

5. In a few cases, the patients will ask for food or shake hands like normal people; their acts correspond to their intentions, but they have the feeling that the arm moves by itself without their participation. "I don't do it, the hand proffers itself." Here the entire drive to action is bound to the ego in normal fashion; however, the discharge along the centrifugal paths has no relation to the ego-complex. The patients register the behavior of their own limbs with their eyes as well as with their kinesthetic senses. In my experience, one can observe this phenomenon most easily in sub-acute states. Such cases, however, are rare.

6. Often enough, the entire automatic action is split off from the conscious personality of the patient. The limbs do something, the lips say something, of which the patient is informed by his senses as if he were an observer during his action, as if he were a third person. In particular, writing and speaking often present themselves like this. Only these split-off actions are to be considered as automatisms in the full sense of the word. They are often designated quite erroneously as compulsive acts. But there is no opposition, therefore no compulsion. The patients are under compulsion only insofar as they cannot utilize the acting organ for anything else during the course of the automatic activity.

Numerous intermediary forms may be found between these various categories of automatic activity. But it is astonishing, how accurately even quite uneducated people can describe these anomalies if one refrains from making any suggestions.

Some melancholic schizophrenics may complain about being automatons. This should not be confused with automatisms, however. What these patients wish to express is the fact that they do not have their normal affects, that they have lost all feelings.

Automatisms also may interfere with willed activities. A somewhat complicated piece of knitting always gets worse. The patient asserted that she knew very well how the pattern should really go, but "it simply all goes awry." A bicycle rider has to dismount but he cannot lead the bicycle with his hand; it simply will not go the way he wants it to. "It is as if the bicycle had gone crazy." A paranoid patient desires to write a letter—against his better judgment he must include the word, "crazy" and then afterwards cross it out.

Automatisms of speech seem to have a special character. The patients themselves are surprised by what they have said or (which is not precisely the same) what their tongues have said. They grasp it only by means of their own auditory sense. At times, "the words are placed on their tongues, so that they must speak it out;" or the "mouth speaks without the patient willing it." The words, "come to the tongue, fully pronounced."[54] In schizophrenics, it almost never involves a long, connected conversation but usually single words, sentences, or fragments of confused nonsense. Cramer (141) has observed in bilingual catatonics that the compulsive speech appeared only in the mother tongue, not in the acquired language.

Here we might also mention coprolalia; often foul words are not merely uttered but substituted for words which make perfectly good sense.

Automatism also extends to the inner psychic processes. Willingly or unwillingly the patients direct their attention to external or internal processes; or "something goes on thinking inside," "ideas are made to come to their minds." Thinking is not experienced as a spontaneous process. In addition there is often a real compulsion to think (what and when they do not want to). "I must think a thousand, a million different things." Such statements are often accompanied by a sense of working and straining, by a terrible feeling of fatigue. Frequently simple memory pictures rather than elaborate thoughts emerge compulsively ("compulsive-remembering").

The thought-content may torture the patients: a patient is forced to imagine that her relatives are dying and subsequently feels guilty (transition to delusions). Another patient must think of chickens being plucked, an idea which disgusts her. In a paranoid, "the thinking-machine works," so that it is as if a voice were calling to him: "Do that!" (Transition to hallucinations; afterwards he developed a powerful murderous impulse at the behest of his hallucinations which he was able to resist.)

Some automatic thoughts may also have pleasant contents. The patients are preoccupied with their wish complexes which may be carefully concealed. Songs which well up are related to the beloved one.

---

54. Cf. Pfersdorff (562).

The thoughts may also be simultaneously pleasant and unpleasant, (i. e. ambivalent). One paranoid woman must think persistently, "I love you and your beautiful face but if you are not willing, I must use force." She has to imagine the beloved one at the very same moment.

The compulsive thinking (obsession) is the most common of all the automatic phenomena. It has its counter-part in the compulsive cessation of thinking. Even the ordinary blockings which are due to unconscious processes cannot be distinguished clearly from automatisms. However, when the patients' thoughts "slip away" or "are snatched away," then one must assume an automatic thought interference.

Even affective processes may be experienced subjectively as automatic, compulsive, or foreign. Many patients are merry or sad and do not know why; therefore they feel the "voices" as "having been produced" on the outside. Mimetic expressions without affect can originate in this way. Laughter without reason, or the occasional cramp-like sobbing are often automatisms. Sometimes, only the mere motion of laughing, not the complete act as such, is felt. Then the laughter strikes the patient as if it were a peripherally released muscle movement ("artificial laughter"). Frequently, the laughter occurs when some allusion to the patient's complex is made. In some cases, the patients themselves recognize the connection between the complex and the schizophrenic laughter.

Centripetal functions, too, may be experienced as foreign, yes, even as forced upon the individual. This phenomenon is well-known in hallucinations. One of our catatonics "is being forced to feel sick." Indeed, even dreams may seem to the patients as being a product of foreign, outside influences; subjectively they may have the same character as obsessive or compulsive thinking.

The patients conceive of the automatic processes in different ways. The majority hardly even trouble to reflect on the abnormality; but they are keenly aware of the loss of spontaneity; therefore they look upon these processes as something alien in themselves. Some less indifferent patients believe themselves to be under the influence of electromagnetism or some other physical force. The superstitious persons naturally are bewitched or possessed, partly by good or evil spirits, partly also by men who have settled inside the patients; occasionally, even by various kinds of animals. Christ or the devil act or speak through the patients, move their limbs in certain positions, etc. Thoughts are "thrown at them" by some natural or supernatural means; thoughts "are pressed, squeezed into their heads" (Schuele).

The doctors, the parents, the lovers, the birds and all the vague concepts by which the persecutions and the persecutors are designated become the ones who, out of evilness and for purposes of experimentation and with all sorts of machines and magic, impose, repress, or distract the patient's thoughts, movements and affects. Many patients distinguish between those automatic thoughts which are made and imposed by others and those which arise spontaneously. "The minute my thoughts are accompanied by a painful knee or a pressure on the shoulder, I know that the thoughts have been fabricated" (Schuele).

In any event, the personality senses that its inner and outer activities are no longer under its control, and that it is at the mercy of a foreign power. It has become "the merest slave of the will." Conscious feelings rarely accompany the automatisms, which are psychic manifestations split off from the personality. The patients can dance and laugh without feeling happy; can commit murder without hating; do away with themselves without being disappointed with life. Usually, the automatisms do not affect the fundamental mood and, in the main, are not influenced by the mood. Nevertheless, secondary emotions may be related to the automatisms. The automatic thinking is quite unbearable, directly or because the patients realize that they are not their own masters. Compulsive drives are felt as oppressive since they are connected with anxiety and provoke internal conflicts.

The patients' reaction to their own automatisms can be very varied. Many simply allow them to take place. They rarely lack a certain resistance to criminal impulses even though they may not be conscious of this inhibiting force. If all the various destructive drives which the patients have in the course of a day, if all those drives would lead to action, then the schizophrenics would constantly keep the world in suspense. Even an individual, who had already committed a murder, may be capable of resisting the impulse to kill the district attorney and regard his homicidal tendencies as an annoying foreign element. Some individuals invent protective devices against their compulsive drives. For example, one who was merely driven to sing managed to get hold of a small block of wood, which he would cram into his mouth in order to stop himself (or rather, his organs). Frequently patients will apologize after their automatisms have caused them to commit some blunder.

In more moderate cases, it may even be that obsessive ideas and compulsive drives are felt not only as something strange and alien, but also as something pathological. The reaction to them can then be similar to what we see in simple compulsion neuroses. Nevertheless, it is very rare that the presence of other symptoms, such as the indifference to the automatisms or even completely distorted concepts of them, does not permit us to recognize the existence of schizophrenia.

The patients are completely powerless, of course, in face of their inner automatisms. However, some do react to the unpleasant feelings by occasional or continual cursing; others withdraw even more into themselves.

9. The Impulsiveness

The impulsiveness which often dominates the catatonic picture is not a homogeneous symptom. A large part of the so-called impulsive behavior is automatic in the previously discussed sense. Others are affective actions. A patient is completely at a loss as to what to do with himself; all his sensory impressions as well as his own thoughts torment and irritate him. He can no longer tolerate it; there must be a way out, something must happen—precisely how and what is irrelevant just as long as it is something else. After he has been in this sort of mood for a few days or weeks, he suddenly breaks loose, strikes out, destroys in the wildest fury and anger. Then after a few seconds to a few hours (very rarely does it last more than a few days) he calms down, sometimes quite suddenly, sometimes more gradually. The "discharge" has eased the "tension" for a time. The patient is relieved, both internally and externally. What he actually did during his outbreak is generally a matter of indifference to him. He discharges his fury on the first thing that comes to hand. In milder cases, outbursts of cursing are sufficient for their needs. Regrets after such releases are rare, of course, in schizophrenia. The patients feel their behavior is justified or they are too indifferent to desire it to be otherwise. Often they assert that it was the "voices" which drove them to fury; that is not, however, an adequate reason for the observer.

A second group of impulsive affective actions differs in degree only from normal affective actions. The patients are easily aroused; as in the process of splitting associations, the inhibiting components are not included. This factor leads to all kinds of rash behavior, physical attacks, unrestrained abuse and vilification, sudden interruption of work, alcoholism, and a variety of other pranks. In this sense a number of non-catatonic schizophrenics are impulsive. The friendly, cheerful card player suddenly turns on his neighbor and starts to beat him or smashes a bottle because the other player received better cards than he did.

In contrast to the affective actions we have actions due to pathological notions. The schizophrenic processes of associating bring into consciousness not only simple thoughts without adequate relation to the existing ideas, but they also bring into awareness thoughts with prominent motor components. "It kind of strikes the patient" to do this or that thing. Often he has no reason for or possibility of resisting the impulse. The notion is immediately translated into action, whether it be to place the chamber pot on his head, to set fire to a house, or to tear the buttons off his clothes. The patient's consciousness knows neither affective nor intellectual motives for his actions.

Naturally in actual practice the various kinds of impulsive actions are not so clearly separated from one another; there are many mixed forms. Certain bad moods preceding the release of emotional tension may have some factual basis in unpleasant experiences. The prison bedlams which are so frequent in schizophrenics are affective outbursts motivated by both factors: the treatment accorded them in prison which is considered to be unjust, and the need for release of tension operate toward the same end. Bizarre notions may also be released by a specific event; or their content may be determined by the complexes so that, for example, a person will destroy his enemy's trees, although the patient is not conscious of any motive.

(h) The Acute Syndromes

The course of the disease is frequently interrupted by acute syndromes, transitory states of various kinds which for the most part, have been considered as independent pyschoses and designated by various names. These acute syndromes are very varied both in manifestations and in genesis. The following phenomena may be involved:

1. Thrusts of the pathological processes. Here belong the many catatonic hallucinatory forms, as well as some of the stuporous, clouded conditions (stuporöse Benommenheiten).

2. Simple exacerbations of chronic states: for example, the hallucinatory excitements in chronically hallucinating patients; severe, acute catatonic states in patients who have been in chronic states with a mildly catatonic coloring. The hyperkinesis of the catatonics often seems to be merely an increase of the usual movements of the patients, while the akinetic catatonic appears as an exaggeration of the chronic lack of will power. In similar fashion, most of the acute syndromes may simply be intensifications of the chronic states.

3. Abnormal reactions of the sick psyche to emotionally charged experiences. Here we may include the hysteriform twilight states and many of the outbursts of screaming and cursing incident to external stimulations.

4. By-products of the disease processes whose connection with these processes we are not able to understand at the present time: perhaps part of the melancholic and manic moods.

5. Conditions which do not belong to the disease as such but are either released by the disease or complicate it: perhaps part of the

periodic and cyclic forms of melancholic and manic moods seen in schizophrenia.

Yet these various conditions cannot be differentiated clearly, not only because of the present state of our knowledge, but also because in reality they tend to combine rather arbitrarily. They all grow in the same soil and are all symptoms of the same pre-disposition. An exacerbation of the disease processes can change a mild chronic symptom into an "acute psychosis." However, even in such cases the visible phenomena are to a large part also psychically determined. Conversely, therefore, a powerful psychic shock, even without any intensification of the disease process itself, can provoke the same or a similar clinical picture. Thus, it is quite obvious that the various conditions treated separately for purposes of description must fuse and combine in the most manifold ways, and that we rarely find entirely pure groups of symptoms. Mixtures of the different conditions, for example, melancholic, catatonic, twilight and clouded states, confusion, etc. are indeed quite common. Thus, it is a purely arbitrary procedure what particular symptom group we single out for the designation of a particular manifestation.

Consequently as far as the general manifestations are concerned, we can only lay down rules insofar as each established clinical entity necessarily includes certain symptoms and excludes certain others. We do not designate a clinical picture as catatonic if no catatonic symptoms are present; normal orientation cannot be found in twilight states. Moreover, in each clinical condition clarity and "splitting" of the consciousness can vary to a maximal and minimal degree; the same goes for distractibility and capacity for reaction to external stimuli.

We are not yet able to select, define, and delimit all the various acute disease pictures. Hence, it is not possible to classify all cases in the categories we shall describe, but we will cover most of the existing clinical pictures.

Acute episodes occur more frequently in the first years than in the later course of the disease. They may set in with or without prodromes (mood changes and other psychic symptoms, vasomotor disturbances as well as infections of the sclera, tremors, etc.) A given attack may last a few hours or years.

The subsequent memory for acute episodes is very variable. It is in the very nature of a twilight state that the patients remember very little (or nothing at all) of what transpired during the episode. (In distinction from hysteria and epilepsy, complete amnesia for the entire period is quite rare.) After clouded states (*Benommenheit*) amnesia is usually more or less prominent. In manic and melancholic syndromes the capacity to remember is usually quite well preserved; in catatonic and paranoid episodes, ability to remember varies. In those instances where there is no amnesia, one is often amazed at the amount and accuracy of the material of inner and external events and experiences which the patients can reproduce even months after the attack. But in some of the most diverse clinical states we also find—apparently without rhyme or reason—that certain events, a few weeks or a few months, are forgotten whereas the rest of the material can be reproduced.

1. Melancholic Conditions

The melancholic symptom triad of depressive affect, inhibition of thinking and of action is one of the most frequent acute disturbances in schizophrenia.

Insight into or vague feelings of the incapacity to accomplish things, as well as the lack of satisfactory rapport with the environment often occasion ill-humor and moodiness which are normal reactions to painful perceptions. In accordance with the very nature of the matter, they are more commonly encountered at the beginning rather than in the later course of the illness. Besides such physiological depressions, we also find those which somehow must stem from the disease process itself. These are probably the usual schizophrenic "melancholias." Aside from these, there are many cases which give us cause to think that a manic-depressive psychosis is complicating the situation. As yet, we have no criteria by which to separate the latter two forms *symptomatically*.

The schizophrenic depression has all the various characteristics which we have come to know in other diseases: simple, painful feelings and emotions independent of events; anxiety mounting to panic, more rarely crying, but often loud screaming and desperate lamentations, and finally depressive inhibition up to complete immobility. Many patients insist also that they are entirely without feelings and complain bitterly about it.

The melancholic clinical picture becomes obscured and troubled not only by the schizophrenic symptoms but also because at times one part of the personality is not at all melancholic, ignores the painful anxious ideas, and goes so far as to criticize or joke about these melancholic ideas; depressed schizophrenics can laugh about their own melancholic delusions and behavior. Whereas the patient is unable to do anything useful, often even unable to eat, he is in constant motion which may often enough seem monotonous, but is not an expression of dissatisfaction and inner restlessness as it is in the agitated forms of organic melancholias. True, the patient groans, laments, repeats the same thing a thousand times: that his head ought to be knocked off, that he wants to go home, that he is the worst of men, that he is going straight to hell—but with all this, he goes on doing any number of things which cannot be explained by the depression. He tears his shirt, his bedclothes, scratches not only himself but also the wall; leaves his bed a hundred times; hinders and disturbs the attendants in their care of the other patients; smears his feces, smashes dishes, etc. He makes brutal attempts at suicide by ramming his head against a wall, jumping out of bed head-first on to the floor; inflicting all kinds of mutilations on himself. Sometimes these suicidal attempts have a playful quality: for days the patient will keep stuffing a pillow into his mouth in the presence of the attendants. A woman patient tries to throttle herself by using her long braids in an impossible fashion; she stuffs her fist into her mouth in order to choke off her wind. The refusal of food is quite common; nevertheless, the use of the feeding tube is not always necessary.

Even if the affect does seem to dominate the entire personality, its expression, as a rule, still has something of the typical schizophrenic stiffness, superficiality, and exaggeratedness; one cannot quite believe in the presence of deep feelings. Yet, we do find genuine states of melancholic depression even in schizophrenics of long standing. These patients may be painfully conscious of their sad situation, their inability to act. Many will then try to obtain some clarity about themselves and their state but do not achieve this goal.

The melancholic motor inhibitions are often mixed with the symptoms of blocking and catalepsy so that it becomes most difficult to analyze the total picture into its various components. The inhibition of ideas betrays itself not merely in the slow thinking process and marked indecision, but especially in an extreme form of monoideism which, in contrast to that seen in simple melancholias, may here be almost absolute. Often for long periods there seems to be no trace of any other thought except the constantly repeated wishes, complaints or maledictions. Every attempt to change the theme or even to elaborate the monoideic one usually fails utterly.

Delusions and especially hallucinations are rarely absent. Threatening and accusing voices, poisonous vapors, electrical currents, and fire are often perceived. The patients believe they are tortured in every conceivable way. They are being killed; their children's eyes pierced; they are forced to spend the night in subterranean torture chambers. They are handed over to the other patients to be torn to pieces; they have committed every earthly sin; they have ruined and rendered their dearest ones miserable and unhappy.

Frequently, the delusions are purely hypochondriacal. The "hypochondriacal melancholia" of other authors is usually a schizophrenic melancholia when it is not an organic one. Particularly Cotard's symptom-complex, when it is non-organic, is nearly always schizophrenic. In this condition, ideas of grandeur unhampered by logical contradictions, may exist side by side with the most appalling fears and terrors. The greatest of sinners is simultaneously Queen of Night; she fills the universe and is eternal, but even these ideas are charged with negative feelings.

2. Manic Conditions

In contrast to the various kinds of melancholic conditions are the manic conditions which are characterized by euphoria, flight of ideas, pressure of activity. They may appear alone or, more rarely, in cyclic form alternating with melancholic conditions, but they also combine readily with mild catatonic features.

Ordinarily the schizophrenic manic is capricious rather than euphoric. The patients delight in all kinds of silly tricks, stupid and bad jokes. These pranks are quite typical of hebephrenics. They make silly puns and jokes; tease, laugh at everything and everyone in their family, ridicule the most cherished human values, etc. These patients curse, fume, label everything with a nickname, stick out their tongues, roll their eyes, speak loudly and in bizarre tones, gesticulate a great deal, exaggerate, caricature. Their speech becomes inappropriate, snappy. They turn somersaults, stand on their heads, twist themselves like snakes, declaim, sing, pray. Day and night, every and all unpleasant little habits are practiced; they are destructive, scream and smear. Outbursts of wild rage are even more common in these people than in the usual type of manic; much rarer are the transient shifts to tearful sadness. The frenzies may set in without any apparent cause or occasion. In many of these cases one sees very little of euphoria. In his cheerful moods the patient remains mechanical as if he were ordered to be gay. The behavior, but not the facial expression or the speech, is that of a cheerful child. Manic schizophrenics may also be incommunicative, almost mute. In general, they do little to enter into relationships with their environment; they close their eyes, in some cases continuously for weeks or months at a time. Distractibilitiy may be absent for short periods or at all times. These patients go through their tricks, speeches, gyrations, quite oblivious to their surroundings. Often the flight of ideas is mixed with confused schizophrenic associations; indeed, the former may be completely concealed by these schizophrenic associations.

Often the manic pressure of activity becomes a mere compulsion to move. In our examples the activities still seemed to serve a certain purposefulness, yet to an observer they may appear to be wholly senseless, mere motions and movements. The patient twists and turns, throws his legs in the air, then his arms. He starts to sing, swings his towel, bangs on the chair, picks it up and throws it. He wraps himself up in his clothing, sits down; then throws himself to the floor crying and shouting. Such cases form the transitional states to a full-blown catatonic excitement which itself need have nothing manic about it. This process shows itself as the many movements begin to be constantly repeated and finally become moderately or completely stereotypied. In some instances the schizophrenic diminution of the need for activity becomes manifest in a particularly striking way. Although these people show the flight of ideas and euphoric-like moods, make plans and shower us with letters, one never succeeds in getting them to undertake any task or work. Equally striking is the tendency to withdrawal. Whereas the manic of the manic-depressive illness absorbs the world around him passionately and is most avid and eager to busy himself with the whole world, the schizophrenic manic more or less ignores the world.

Here also we frequently see the appearance of hallucinations; but it is usually very difficult to obtain information as to their content. When delusions are present, they are usually transitory, and of a persecutory or grandiose character. They appear for a moment, only to disappear in the next. Yet, particularly, ideas of persecutions are often continually maintained; the same can be said for erotic ideas.

In schizophrenia I have not as yet seen manic-depressive mixed states, in Weygandt's sense, but it is very possible that they also exist.

3. Catatonic Conditions

As a rule, catatonic symptoms mix with the manic and the melancholic conditions, in some instances to such a marked degree that the catatonic symptoms dominate the clinical picture and one can speak of a manic or a melancholic catatonia. The old "melancholia attonita," insofar as it deserves this name, belongs here. However, the following discussion will deal only with those acute groups of catatonic symptoms which cannot be considered as part of the affective psychoses, in the old sense of the term. We are dealing here with a variety of clinical pictures which are diverse, not only in their external manifestations, but also in their psychological mechanisms. They are only held together by the catatonic manifestations which may appear in different groupings.

The external clinical picture of these forms can best be described by two extreme types which correspond to Wernicke's akinetic and hyperkinetic motor psychoses. The akinetic conditions of stupor, of "attonita," and flexibilitas cerea have been known of old. The patients lie, perch or sit all curled up in some peculiar position. Flexor action of the musculature usually predominates. In severe cases, movement is reduced to almost zero. These patients do not even swallow the saliva but let it run down from the corner of the mouth, or let it accumulate in the mouth for long periods of time. The many other psychically affected reflexes function only in exceptional cases. It is here that we find the most frequent and the most stubborn types of the various irregularities of evacuation of bladder and rectum. Food is often not swallowed or must be administered by tube usually with marked resistance from the patient. It is hard to determine the frequency of true alimentary tract disturbances; a coated tongue, even fulgio, is often seen in confused catatonics. Otherwise the physical findings are usually not greatly altered; but most of the patients have a rather bloated appearance, even when they have lost weight. The skin color is often significantly or suggestively livid. Sleep is ordinarily disturbed if not entirely lacking.

We may find numerous intermediary phases on the continuous scale from reduced to hyperkinetic reactions. Complete akinesis as described above is quite rare; a few isolated movements or even certain routine performances are usually still present. The patients may change their posture somewhat, albeit slowly, unsteadily, hesitatingly, moving on their toes in some bent-over, cramped fashion. Many slowly chew the food if it has been pushed into their mouths. Sometimes they even answer, softly and haltingly. Often more active catatonic symptoms inject a little more life into the picture. The patient may verbigerate loudly or softly; he may make stereotyped movements or defend himself vigorously against any change of his position (whereas he may remain unresponsive to needle-punctures or other far more unpleasant sensations). The spontaneous movements or actions of patients with generally decreased motility have a typically catatonic stamp. The patient's entire activity for many weeks consists of merely leaving his bed to go to the toilet and back again, all of which takes a half-hour or at times, an hour to perform. He moves slowly, raises the toilet seat and closes it again without taking care of his needs; he returns to his bed and then repeats the whole thing over and over again many times, until he finally uses the toilet. If he be disturbed during this activity (or even spontaneously), he draws up his toes in a cramped, claw-like fashion and walks back and forth with his head sunk, his eye-lids squeezed together but only half-closed. He reminds one of a bored crane in an aviary, a drop of secretion dangling from the tip of his nose. If someone disturbs him, he very angrily evades. But if one should attempt to hinder him or merely follow him, he retreats to a specific place near his bed, utters a piercing cry and begins to sob as if he were deeply unhappy.

At times, the peace and quiet is broken by the appearance of a catatonic raptus. Suddenly the patient springs up, smashes something, seizes someone with extraordinary power and dexterity, or moves some object in the room so that it is placed otherwise than it had been. A catatonic arouses himself from his rigidity, runs around the streets in his night shirt for three solid hours, and finally falls down and remains lying in a cataleptic state in the gutter. Even external stimuli may suddenly evoke prompt and even reasonable reactions; a sudden answer or unexpected bit of conversation may astonish the persons present. A highly stuporous innkeeper suddenly picks up a cork which had accidentally fallen to the floor. Some mute patients will answer in writing or they may even spontaneously fill whole pages with writing.

The hyperkinetic cases (as the term suggests) are constantly in motion without really doing anything (pressure of activity, "flight of activity" as Fuhrman called it). They clamber about, move around, shake the branches of the trees in the garden, hop over the beds, bang on the table twenty times, and then on the wall; they bend the knees, jump, strike, break, twist their arms into impossible positions between the radiator and the wall, totally unconcerned about the burns which they receive. They cry, sing, verbigerate, laugh, curse, scream and spit all over the room. They grimace, showing sadness, happiness or horror. They pick up some object, move it, turn it over and put it down some place else. They make a thousand and one other movements which are usually limited to a definite number as far as each single patient is concerned. The motions always have something abnormal about them. If a patient picks up an object, he always does so in a peculiar way, in a way that is not ordinarily done. When they get into bed, they always do so from the head-side of the bed with an unusual twist and turn, etc. The movements are often executed with great strength, and nearly always involve unnecessary muscle groups. They may show as much disregard of themselves as of other living and lifeless things around them. They seem to have lost control of measure and power of their movements. In stuporous cataleptic individuals, vague lifeless movements predominate. Then again, all actions may be executed with far too much power and energy for the purpose. A simple gesture accompanying speech is readily repeated always more extensively and more energetically. Some phrase, some meaningless figure of speech the patient may have uttered, easily becomes a loud scream in the course of catatonic repetitions. But even isolated, non-repeated movements are often executed with maximal strength. The other signs of catatonia—verbigeration, sterotyped repetitions, caricaturing of facial expressions, empty pathos, etc.—are never absent. These patients talk less than do other excited or agitated manics, often they are even mute. Parts of their actions and behavior apparently make some sense; for example, imitations of the preacher, of a soldier or of a bad girl, etc. But one rarely sees complete imitations. Even when such an idea seems to recur again and again, it is constantly interrupted or broken into by other extraneous behavior or actions. We can rarely deduce the purpose of their behavior: the patients barricade themselves in very special ways behind the bed; they make themselves a cave out of their bedding; they arrange whatever comes to hand in very odd but very definite ways. Such actions tend to be repeated, usually in the same way.

Aside from the constant repetition, we find a common denominator in the admittedly weak schizophrenic affect which seems to permeate everything. A number of these patients are manifestly manic (with demonstrable flight of ideas); others are melancholic; still others are irritable, anxious, or feel themselves persecuted. However, many catatonics roam about like automatons showing no definite or proper affect; or they may constantly change their caricatured affective expressions. Hallucinations frequently accompany these episodes but they need not be present. Delusions too may be absent.

The hyperkinetic form may also be interrupted suddenly by periods of calm which are usually of short duration and complicate the clinical picture.

In the akinetic catatonics especially, but in others also, we often note vascular disturbances (livor, edema, etc.). Of course, the constant movement and activity usually tends to wear down the patients' strength. Others are able to support this activity remarkably well, so that one is forced to assume some abnormality of the metabolism as in many cases of hysterical agitations and excitements. Naturally, the nutritional intake is very irregular; often there is abstinence from all food. Sleep is always poor and frequently entirely absent for a period of time.

Analgesias are quite common. They may be simulated by the simple lack of reaction on the part of the patients. I have never observed the presence of anaesthesia; and I suspect that the catatonic anaesthesias of which many authors speak are merely analgesias.

For the most part, the patients are rather unconcerned about their peculiar condition. Certainly many of them think very little about anything, a few perhaps do not think at all, as Brosius believes. Nevertheless, much of what goes on around the patients is passively registered. There is no doubt, however, that vigility of attention is for the most part markedly reduced, particularly so in the hyperkinetic forms.

A rather large proportion of acute catatonic patients simultaneously find themselves in a more or less marked twilight state and in some other hallucinatory or delusional world. They attempt to explain their immobility by falling back on notions about being surrounded by moats, holes, threatening voices which invoke horrible punishments if they dare so much as to move, or promise them every paradisical joy if they do not move; they dare not swallow, must not tend to their physical needs, etc. Often they subjectively sense their inability to move as a kind of stiffness, rigidity, or paralysis.

Often, but not invariably, massive hallucinations seem to determine the behavior of the hyperkinetic forms. Frequently it is a matter of movements of defense, flight, and aggression; however these movements appear to be purposeless, even apraxic and uncoordinated. The patients will explain their peculiar activities as well as their inactivity, in terms of hallucinations. However, from the viewpoint of normal logic these explanations are not very satisfactory or adequate; take for example, the patient who hammers on his bed because somebody poisoned him.

The "faxen[55]-psychosis" is a special form of hyperkinetic catatonia. The patient constantly makes disconnected, caricatured grimaces and gestures. One has the impression that these patients want to play the buffoon, though they do this in a most awkward and inept fashion.[56] They contrive any number of stupidities and sillinesses, such as beating their own knees, interchanging pillows for blankets when they go to bed, pouring water out on the floor instead of into a cup, lifting doors off their hinges. The patients will do all this while they are seemingly well oriented. As a rule they speak very little or not at all and what they have to say is, in the main, completely illogical cursing or other nonsense. Undoubtedly the "faxen-psychosis" has an origin similar to that of the Ganserian twilight state. It usually involves individuals who for some unconscious reason pretend to be mentally deranged.

4. Delusion

Hallucinations and delusions often dominate the picture. Manic, depressive, or catatonic elements may also be present but in many cases they may be entirely lacking. We term these conditions, delusional forms. Most of the manic and melancholic delusions of earlier writers belong here since manic-depressive delusions are rare.

Such "acute paranoias" are rarely characterized exclusively by the

---

55. Buffooneries.

56. The buffooneries of spiteful hebephrenics are something entirely different and only a few isolated symptoms are at all comparable to what we see in the "faxen-psychosis" of the catatonics.

delusional ideas since hallucinations are absent only in exceptional cases. Usually they predominate, crowding in on the patient, persistently and massively, making him appear confused, particularly when they are changing rapidly. "Now I am being pierced; here it squeezes me; now it is gone again; now someone is calling me; now the cloud is drawn over me. . . ." The hallucinations are less stereotyped in very acute cases then they are in the chronic conditions. In the former the visual hallucinations are usually more prominent. The patient hears numerous voices in a most confusing and persistent fashion; there is a band of men under his window who want to catch him, burn him, behead him. They lie in wait for him, threaten to enter through the walls, climb up and hide under his bed. Then there are others who want to help him; at times God is a protector, at other times, even He is part of the plot. His nearest relatives are being murdered, the patient himself is being electrocuted, sexually assaulted and abused. In these states the reaction is usually a very lively one. It is difficult to keep the patients in bed; they wander about, climb up the windows, crawl into odd corners, engage in fights, etc. In sharp contrast to the catatonics the behavior of these patients is quite comprehensible in terms of their delirious ideas because we are confronted with actions and not with buffooneries (faxen). The patients flee, defend themselves, or attack. The pleasantly toned hallucinations, on the other hand, enable the patient to enjoy some festivity, to ride to heaven, or to participate in other entertaining activities.

In the very same patient the delusional forms may pass over into other acute disturbance or develop from these. Other intermediary forms develop in the direction of the chronic conditions. In chronic hallucinators, these acute delusional forms may give the impression of being merely an exacerbation of hallucinatory state. But in other cases, they differ sharply from the usual deteriorated (demented) states which may be interrupted by limited episodes.

The Viennese school would designate these cases as amentia. However, I do not employ this term because its meaning varies from school to school in terms of the particular frame of conceptual reference which is not compatible with our theories.

5. Twilight State

The twilight states, like those in hysteria, are waking dreams which portray desires, wishes, or fears in a direct or symbolic way as already fulfilled. The typical instance is that of the maiden disappointed and unhappy in her love affair who now in her pathological state sees all her desires and hopes attained. She is now in hallucinatory communication with her sweetheart, becomes engaged, marries, gets pregnant and finally delivers a child. The entire environment is then interpreted in accordance with these delusions. The hospital inmates are turned into members of the family or guests at the wedding; at other times they are considered as obstacles and enemies of the dearest wishes and hopes. The ward, too, is misinterpreted in the same sense. A woman patient with marked religious aspirations regarded the hospital ward was a church.

Still, the basc idea of the delusion only gives us the leitmotif of the whole dream which is further elaborated in all its vivid details: the patient must eat a good deal in order to be able to breast-feed her children properly. She must pick some flowers to decorate herself. By other remarkable maneuvers, she prevents her enemies and those of her husband from injuring the children. Thus the kernel of the delusion is concealed under a mass of incidental and superfluous details. Altogether, the wishes are not always clearly expressed. The patient may dream of a battle or a war instead of a love scene. The many inconsistencies and impossibilities which are ordinarily present even in the dreams of healthy people are woven into the twilight delirium and perhaps many more things as well.

The ecstatic twilight states have received particular attention at all times. They often obscure the schizophrenic character of the clinical picture, more or less concealing it behind the common peculiarities of the religious complexes: the marked tendencies to visions, to rigid posturing in ceremony and worship, to ecstatic, trance-like states leading to the exclusion of the outer world to the point of complete analgesia. However, not all twilight states with religious content lead to ecstasy; often enough the patients, who are in communication with the holy saints, are still in part on earth; therefore they experience the evil of this world more keenly and constantly struggle with it.

The patient's experience of his actual environment may be fused with his religious notions. He recognizes people around him for what they are but still has the idea that they will prove to be other persons (God, Judas, the Apostle), who merely chose to appear in the guise of doctors and nurses.

In a certain case of abortive ecstasy, the patient, after taking communion, felt, "Bathed for two whole days in an infinite, heavenly happiness so that all he could do was cry with sheer joy." The schizophrenic ecstatic mood can also be transferred to quite insignificant things. Thus a catatonic with ecstatic expression verbigerates, "I have knitted, I have knitted, I have knitted, yes, indeed, I have knitted (she had never as yet done any work in the hospital); it was beautiful, wonderful! These beautiful embroidered curtains! (there were no curtains at all). When the curtains were parted, how they did sing! ("Who was there?") Mother was there, everyone was there, etc., etc. I follow the Lord God!"

The behavior of patients in twilight states varies considerably. Many of them go through all sorts of experiences while actually lying quietly under the blankets in their beds. Others act in full accordance with their ideas which brings them into continual conflict with their environment. They climb around, talk loudly or softly to their hallucinations, make all kinds of incomprehensible gestures and motions the meaning of which can be understood only after a more thorough analysis. They want to leave the hospital, tear open the doors, repeat making the same demands which are impossible to grant, or in pleading tones they call out sentences which to our ears do not contain any pleas or any demand at all. A woman patient believed she was wandering in a meadow guarding the horses. She refused to leave her bed because then the horses would be left unwatched and would wander away.

"Double registration" of external events (that is she registered the events of her dream world and those of reality) is commonly seen even in severe cases. Thoughts from both series of events often fuse; the patients plead for their release from the hospital giving evidence that they have correctly understood the hospital situation, but their reasons for wanting to leave are derived from their dream life.

The schizophrenic twilight states may persist longer than others. Six months' duration of such states is quite common. Many patients, during the remainder of their lives, appear as if they had never completely come out of their twilight state. But then we are dealing with severe catatonic-like conditions which we have not yet been able to analyze sufficiently in order to form a definite opinion concerning the inner processes operating in these people. With time, the patients tend to become calmer; if negativism does not feature too prominently they adjust themselves to the environment so that they get into little or no conflicts with their surroundings. In the main, however, they live in another world and care only for their most immediate needs; they eat when food is placed before them; go to the toilet when necessary. Although they are able to dress and undress themselves, even such simple routines represent an accomplishment and cannot always be expected of them.

Fragments of delusions originating in twilight states may persist into the chronic conditions. Thus, for one such patient the hospital became permanently the "house with the black shutters;" she had first referred to a prison in this way and then carried the same idea over to the hospital.

Occasionally, these twilight states may last only a few minutes. Thus a patient suddenly became very agitated about his surroundings and just as quickly calmed down again. He was able to relate that he had believed himself to be in a forest where he had had to defend himself against wild animals, especially against an orangutan. These episodes differ in degree only from the hallucinatory excitements of our patients on the chronic, "disturbed" wards.

Conversely, the twilight states may be interrupted by periods of lucidity which, in turn, may last anywhere from a few minutes to several days. If these clear periods last for as long as several weeks, then it is preferable to consider them as an improvement in the patient's condition. It may also happen that clear periods and twilight states are almost equally balanced, so that the patient is clear one day and in a twilight state the next day.

Schizophrenic twilight states may also take on some characteristics of the Ganser syndrome, whereby complete, although negative, rapport with the environment is maintained in accordance with the delusions preoccupying the patient. The Ganser syndrome in schizophrenics is released by the same causes as in the hysterics. Prisoners being detained for judicial or medical examination are particularly afflicted with this syndrome. Although they seem to be making every effort to meet our requests, these patients answer even the simplest questions incorrectly. Usually they proceed rather systematically, so that one recognizes at once the (unconscious) intention. Two times two usually becomes 5, or 3; 4 o'clock is read as 8 o'clock; 12 o'clock is 6 o'clock, etc. Ordered to open a lock, the patient attempts to push the wrong end of the key into the lock, or holds the key wrong side up. He attempts to find the lock above the door knob. Should the key be in the lock already, then he is sure to turn it the wrong way. Given a package of cigarettes, he attempts to open the side instead of the top. Asked to strike a match, he uses the wood end of the match stick on the sand paper; or he uses the proper end on the paper side of the box and not on the sand-papered side. However, only very mild schizophrenic patients behave as consistently as this. The majority of our cases, in marked contrast to the hysterics, often fall quickly out of their role. While many things are done quite correctly or at least not essentially wrong, they appear "confused" only during examinations; but in dealing with other persons they immediately behave quite normally. Frequently a sharp dividing line between the twilight state and ordinary behavior is absent altogether. The patients are incapable of discussing their abnormal condition after the episode has passed, although they do remember something about it. For the most part, other schizophrenic symptoms are present too.[57]

A very special sort of unconscious disease simulation was shown by a patient who was accused by her supervisor of being crazy. From that moment on, she behaved as if she were "crazy;" while still living at home, she insisted that the house janitor was an attendant of an insane asylum; refused to take food, etc. After one tube-feeding, there was a sudden cure.

The twilight states can show a good deal of variability. In some cases we find a consistently carried out dream-activity. The twilight state is then essentially the reaction of a mildly schizophrenic personality to a psychic trauma; an external event appears to be the main determinant. The schizophrenic symptoms hardly obscure the hysteriform picture. In other instances, the essential element is the advance of the disease itself with its splitting and fragmenting of associations; some perhaps ever present desire suddenly gains dominance over the non-logical thought processes. There are a whole series of transitional forms leading, on the one hand, to the previously mentioned hysteriform twilight state and, on the other hand, to diverse confusional conditions which because of the lack of uniformity can no longer be termed twilight states.

Besides the real twilight states, there are an infinite number of various pyschic conditions manifesting the same pattern, but they only strike us when they are markedly pronounced or when they change very rapidly. They have their intermediary forms in every direction.

A latent hebephrenic, who had vagabonded about for many years, was admitted to the hospital with the following condition which had already been present for a long time: on the whole he was negativistic, mistook his surroundings for the Devil, conversed with his "voices," continually crossed himself, and executed other unusual acts. At times he showed some insight, except that the illness was due to "being touched by evil spirits." Recollection of his previous condition was scanty. At other times he could be approached quite easily. Then again we find various misconceptions: the hospital became a naval barracks; the doctor was the God of war. The patient held long conversations with the stars partly in his own native Italian, and partly in a self-invented jargon which was supposed to be Italian.

---

57. Of course, we must bear in mind, that the Ganser syndrome is something entirely different from the approximate answers given by negativistic or indifferent patients.

6. Benommenheit [58]

I propose to consider "Benommenheit" as a special form of the symptom-complex of the stuporous conditions, at least until we know more about these states. Not all stuporous patients are "benommen" and the great majority of the "benommen" patients hardly appear stuporous. In most forms of stupor, the patients can still think and act insofar as they have the desire to do so, and only very few sense any defect at all. However, there is a condition characterized by a slowing up of all psychic processes. It usually occurs in conjunction with an incapacity for dealing with any relatively complicated or unusual situation. Since will power seems to be relatively well, or completely, preserved, we are not dealing with the ordinary cases of stupor. Because of the absence of depression and evidences of a very mild degree of confusion, this condition cannot be considered an instance of melancholic inhibition. It is this condition that I wish to designate tentatively by the term, "Benommenheit."

The external behavior of such patients is rather diverse. Many of them idle about, others scratch themselves or keep themselves amused with equally non-strenuous tasks. Still others are somewhat agitated and indulge in various catatonic stupidities. Some may still be capable of helping a little around the house; usually they are able to do a bit of sewing or knitting although with many errors. Generally, the difference from other catatonics usually becomes clearly manifest in experiments or tests. The patients answer questions very slowly, if they answer at all, although they try to understand what is being demanded. These patients will often repeat the first sound of a word many times before they succeed in uttering the rest of the word's sounds, yet there are no other signs which give us reason to assume the presence of either inhibition or blocking, in the usual sense of the words. They follow only simple directions, and even then make many mistakes. If they are asked to stick out their tongue, they first gaze at the doctor blankly. After repetitions of the command, they attempt to do what is asked, but still do not get the tongues out. They merely move their lips, or even their eyes which they prefer to close. Asked to place a spoon in the dish, they take the spoon, turn it around or put it in their mouth or elsewhere; they may confuse it with a fork. In short, they demonstrate what appears as marked apraxia. A patient required five hours to dress herself; she substituted the blouse for the skirt or the slip. She picked up the shoe

---

58. Translator's Note: There does not appear to be an adequately appropriate term for this in English. Terms such as "clouded," "doped" or "mental inertia" do not quite convey its full meaning. I have retained the German term in some instances or used "clouded" or "abstracted" state as its equivalent, albeit they are hardly satisfactory.

brush to brush her teeth, but brushed her clothes instead and spread tooth paste on the shoes. Only after years of vain trials, I finally succeeded in getting her to close a door on command. Spontaneously she could do such little things very well, but on command she usually failed and became more and more confused. Instead of closing the door as asked, she would pass through it or open it even wider. When she finally had succeeded in closing it, she would usually find herself on the outside of the room instead of within. Thus, all their acts seem to be disturbed by cross-purposes or cross-impulses (Trommer).

At first one is inclined to think of negativism: and perhaps negativism is involved in some cases of this kind of schizophrenic apraxia, but it is certainly not the essential cause of the symptom. We are dealing with a similar type of confusion as in emotional stupors. The patients cannot combine the necessary ideas. They do things contrarily like a very frightened person at a fire who throws clocks and porcelains out the window but very carefully carries down some old rags. Thus they are also not to be considered parabulic in Kraepelin's sense of the term.

Echopraxia appears most frequently in these clouded states, but can also be observed in other conditions.

The comprehension of external impressions is very inadequate. Complex phenomena are not grasped at all; only a few details of a picture are understood. Orientation becomes considerably impaired; patients cannot find their own room when minute changes have been made. They do not understand even the very simplest of stories when reading. The patients will proceed to read another story in the same tone, or begin another paragraph without noting that something new has appeared. They make many mistakes in reading: "feet" instead of "fleet," "suckle" instead of "sucked;" they remain fixed in the middle of a simple word, read the commas, etc. One patient could not reproduce any part of the tale entitled, "A Donkey Loaded with Salt." Asked what the story was about, she finally said, "About a shepherd;" (And about an elephant?) "Yes." (Or about a horse?) "Yes." (About a donkey?) "Yes, yes, yes." Thus she finally did remember when at last the donkey was mentioned. Even those things which she knew very well prior to the illness could be recalled and reproduced only fragmentarily and gradually.

A hebephrenic met an acquaintance (in the hospital) who had recently killed another of the patient's old friends. The patient recalled that he had also known the murdered man. (What happened to him?) "He also had an accident." (Then after a long pause and much thinking, it came to his mind,) "He shot someone." Then, "I knew the man he killed, K. He was a neighbor." Not once did this important story come to the patient as a whole; only little by little was he able to recall it.

Benommenheit can most easily be observed in the patients' writings. Words and sentences remain incomplete; some words are omitted; false corrections are made which are noted, and new efforts made to correct them which in turn do not succeed. Words are crossed out, rewritten and the last effort is usually the best. Sentences such as the following appear: I lie almost constantly in bed, where I can wo home (that is, whereas I can work so well at home). Frequently found are hints of perseveration and anticipation of letters of words which are to come later in the same sentence.

In the only case that I was able to analyze up to a certain point, affectivity was preserved, in fact it was quite strong and labile. The patient insisted she was getting better, did her own housework correctly and well. Yet she was unable to repeat correctly, "round the rugged rock, etc." or "the third artillery brigade" without making many (psychic) slips.

Clouded states do not appear only in acute states, or as an acute condition. Benommenheit as such has the tendency to linger, and can even persist for decades in the way we have described it above, or in more attenuated forms. The underlying cause of this condition may be a uniform impairment of all the psychic processes.[59] Apparently however, it is again a question of various causal determinants. In acute clouded states with catatonic symptoms, one gets the impression of a gross disturbance of the central organ with a uniform impediment of all the psychic processes, including those of motility. Complex functions or rapid performances are very rarely seen. In other instances, particularly in chronic cases, it is difficult to differentiate this condition from severe, long persisting cases of perplexity. However, in the latter case some activities are performed promptly.[60]

In any event, there are all sorts of transitional and mixed forms involving pyschic and organic factors, in the sense that organic disturbances may very well increase or evoke the disposition to psychic perplexity. It is possible, however, that there are also other disturbances which lead to the same picture.

7. Confusion, Incoherence

Most disturbances of association, if sufficiently pronounced, lead to confusion. Special attention has to be given to these confusional states

59. Increased intra-cranial pressure, toxic injury, or something similar.

60. Thus we observed a catatonic woman painter who was perfectly capable of executing many difficult tasks, but once she was simply incapable of drawing a chair in perspective. The converse is indeed more frequent; that is, it is the common, ordinary, and simple tasks which can be performed, whereas anything unusual, even though simple, cannot be carried out.

which are a direct consequence of the fragmentation of the associations. This type of incoherence represents an acute syndrome in almost all cases. The patients speak completely disconnectedly, often in half-broken sentences. They are quite restless and constantly busy doing something, but their activities lack purpose and are not carried through to the end, even such simple actions as leaving a room. We see merely fragments of their behavior, as we do of their thinking, even though certain emotionally charged ideas, such as fear of misfortune or the joy of some dreamed happiness may to some extent become intelligible in terms of their total behavior. Physical symptoms, such as a coated tongue or a coarse tremor, are often present in these cases.

One such patient felt much better the day after being examined and seemed better able to manipulate her fund of information. She remembered only fragments of the examination itself which she subsequently could reconstruct in part. She knew she had been in a room with a number of gentlemen; that there had been a sofa in the room; that one of the men sat on the same sofa with her. She could later identify who it had been and partly describe the doctors who were present at the time, but she was entirely unaware of the fact that one of those doctors was her own ward surgeon. This sort of fragmentation differs strikingly from the usual catatonic excitement in which, even during the wildest outbreaks, the patient is able within a few minutes to identify the names of a whole room of patients, attendants, doctors, etc.

All forms of confusional states may combine with melancholic, manic, and particularly catatonic symptoms, but they need not do so.

8. Fits of Anger

We also have to mention the fits of anger, cursing and vilification which are released usually by some external event or experience. These patients may begin to curse, not only if one has said something unpleasant to them, but also after a friendly greeting or even in the very midst of what appears to be a congenial conversation. At that moment, it is absolutely useless to attempt to correct any misunderstandings. No matter what one says, they still feel insulted, and only become more angry. The picture is frequently complicated by the emergence of hallucinations and delusions of which there may have been no indications during the quiet periods. After the patient is left to himself, the attack usually persists for a while, often for hours, sometimes for a few days. Such episodes rarely result in permanent aggravation of the patient's condition.

The fits of anger just described differ strikingly from the endogenous, mainly hallucinatory, excesses of fury which appear frequently in many chronic conditions. Under the influence of hallucinations, very rarely without it, the patients may suddenly begin to curse profusely or even become violent at times. These episodes may last anywhere from a few minutes to several weeks and show characteristic patterns for each individual patient.

9. "Anniversary" Excitements

We are concerned here with an etiological group. Many episodes of agitation appear only on definite calendar days. The patients celebrate special days on which something happened that had some connection with their complexes. On these particular days they become agitated, irritable, hallucinating, stuporous, etc. On the seventeenth day of each month a still employable hebephrenic always had olfactory hallucinations, many delusions, and masturbated compulsively; he was born on the seventeenth. The patients themselves are ignorant of the reasons for their moodiness before one has analyzed the situation with them. Days on which the patient lost or won a husband or sweetheart, the marriage anniversary of a sister, or even days on which the patient may have celebrated certain sinful "orgies" in the past can give occasion for these outbursts of excitement. These episodes may disappear with the passing of the special day or persist for longer periods once they have been provoked. Generally these attacks of excitement disappear after a few repetitions. We observed only two cases in which the periods of excitement lasted longer.

10. Stupor

Acute stupors occupy a very prominent and important place in the descriptions of mental disturbances of many a psychiatric authority. However, since stupor is not a uniform symptom, but rather the external manifestation of many very different disturbances of will, thinking, and rapport with environment, it can not properly be given any special place at this point. A summary of the anomalies which may appear as stuporous manifestations has already been given earlier in the volume.

11. Deliria

How many of the hallucinatory conditions of schizophrenia should be designated by the term delirium is purely an arbitrary matter in view of the fact that it is not a clearly defined term. However, it should be remembered in this connection that states resembling the fever deliria also occur in the terminal stages of fatal catatonic states. Since the patients do not react to the environment at all at that time, a characterization or investigation of this condition is not possible.

12. Fugue States

Intercurrent episodes of agitation and excitement can also assume the form of fugues. Some patients may have been quite dependable in many respects, led a life devoid of desires and interests, yet suddenly they may run off, often getting quite far away. Some return spontaneously but the majority have to be sought for and brought back. Many different conditions are at the basis of this symptom. It may be no more than a sudden feeling of discontent appearing with or without occasion. They run off, giving no thought to the consequences or to their destination, intent only on getting away. Often the patients are driven on by genuine feelings of unhappiness or even fear. From this situation it is only a small step to the hallucinatory excitement in which the patients suddenly receive the command to clear out of the hospital. Occasionally, the symptom is obviously motivated by some pathological notion. Other fugues may be based on a twilight state. A final category of these running away episodes may be formed by compulsions or some other automatic type of action.

The patients' behavior varies as much on their travels as it does otherwise. Some may give the impression of being normal, although in the hospital they may have been rather asocial or bizarre. Others run off without any suitable clothing or even entirely nude, create disturbances, attack people, etc. The subsequent explanations and memories are, of course, variable: they differ for each patient in accordance with the various causal factors involved. Schizophrenic fugue (or wandering) states often give occasion for desertions from military units.

13. Dipsomania

Some, though not many, schizophrenics suffer attacks of dipsomania. As far as their drinking is concerned, they do have a certain degree of insight into their difficulties. If they are not too severely ill, they will even make fine resolutions not to drink anymore. But from time to time, they are subject to tense, anxious moods which drive them to obtain alcohol, by any and all means, until after a few days of heavy drinking, they are found lying somewhere completely exhausted.

SECTION II

THE SUBGROUPS

INTRODUCTION

At the present time, we cannot solve the problem of dissecting schizophrenia into its natural subdivisions. Nonetheless, we do have the practical need of characterizing the various clinical pictures that present themselves to us in this disease by terms corresponding, at least, to rather broad and crude subdivisions. This much is possible, but not much more.

Yet, others have gone a good deal farther than this. Charpentier recognized eleven subgroups. We prefer to adhere to the already quite current labels used by Kraepelin, in view of the fact that nothing better has as yet been established to take their place.[1]

Even then, however, it is not a question of defining and delimiting different disease entities, but of grouping symptoms. This sort of classification corresponds in a way to the division of pulmonary tuberculosis into cases with or without fever, with or without hemoptysis, with or without intestinal tuberculosis, amyloidosis, etc. A case which begins as a hebephrenic may be a paranoid several years later.

The symptom combinations are endless, but since many syndromes repeat themselves so frequently and in so similar a manner, one can select a few of these forms as examples. They are most easily arranged in four main categories.[2]

The Kraepelinian groups, catatonia and hebephrenia, are about equally represented in our hospital population. The paranoid group is somewhat less numerous. The simple type is hardly ever seen in hospitals, but outside the institutions it is perhaps the most frequent type.

---

1. Cf. below for characterization of the four groups.

2. When we observe one catatonic symptom, we can also expect others with a certain degree of probability. However, a more definite or a more accurate correlation of symptoms, in the sense that from the presence of one phenomenon, one can reckon on the absence or presence of others, is not as yet possible at this time.

A. The Paranoid Group[3]

The majority of cases, which were called "paranoia" by the older authorities, comprise the first part of this group. The patients do not feel as they used to anymore; at times, everything seems different than it was before. Then come "suspicions," notions that they are destined or dedicated to this or that. They refer completely indifferent events to themselves. In the beginning this is done quite uncertainly, they themselves ask, "Is it really so?" Gradually, but also quite suddenly, the delusions of reference attain full credibility and certainty. School children run after them; the children chase after the street car whenever the patient is riding in one. It is clear enough that they despise and insult him. Someone "calls out" after him that he has done nasty things with small children, that he masturbates, that he steals. Always more and more people give him to understand, by all kinds of signs and allusions, etc., that they know all about these misdeeds of his. Even the newspaper reports contain more or less concealed allusions to him. The minister's sermon is directed at him. The patient changes his dwellings, his jobs, but everywhere there is whispering about him. Wherever he turns, signs and signals point at him. People begin to vex him, play tricks on him; they want to drive him away. He is given only the worst, the hardest work. They spoil and sabotage whatever he makes. He is constantly being discredited. There is a conspiracy; they take a great deal of trouble to persecute and hound him. One day he hears how they are talking about him; then they actually speak to him, call him nasty names, curse, reproach, scorn him. Other hallucinations come along, particularly those of body-sensations. Finally, the patient becomes violent, turns on his tormentors. He clouts somebody on the ear or shoots, or creates a disturbance, especially at night. He does not dare to leave his quarters and lives there in peculiar disorder, filth, and hunger. He is then seized and brought to the hospital. After some time, he becomes more sociable; he begins to do a certain amount of work. Ultimately he can be released, quiet, but without any essential improvement in his delusional ideas. For a time he maintains himself outside the institution, but not for long. He again begins to change jobs, or he is dismissed from his work because he cannot get along, makes too many mistakes,

3. It is impossible to keep using the cumbersome expression "paranoid form of schizophrenia." Therefore, partly for this reason, and partly because many authors misunderstandingly employ the term, "dementia paranoides" which was employed, however, by Kraepelin in a much more restricted sense and which he created at a time when he did not as yet include the other paranoid forms as part of dementia praecox, I prefer to use the term "paranoid."

shows up far too irregularly. Then the previous excitements and outbursts are again repeated; he is again hospitalized. Here, he finally remains be it either after this or another admission. For a long time, he continues to be very unpleasant and difficult; he curses, shouts, is aggressive. Gradually, he begins to quiet down. He can be given work once more, but has lost his powers of initiative in pursuing his persecutory ideas as well as in other things. He works at whatever is assigned to him, when it is laid out, like a machine. He may wander about the hospital; or under favorable circumstances, he may even maintain himself outside the hospital by working, but generally he lives from day to day, indifferent and idle.

Things do not always follow this pattern; generally the course is far more irregular. The delusions may appear suddenly like a bolt of lightning in a clear sky—fixed and complete while the patient is still fully competent at his work. They may disturb and excite him for several days only to fade away and reappear again later. Often the real paranoid state begins very acutely after a more or less lengthy period of marked "prodromes" which in themselves need not have any paranoid character at all. During the night an angel, Christ, or God appears to show the patient a New Way. In the persecuted, there is often a period of hallucinatory excitement lasting several hours or even several days, frequently combined with marked confusion and disorientation. On some occasion, mostly when the patient finds himself alone, he experiences a kind of revelation and his whole attitude to God and humanity is changed; he has become convinced of his own greatness, or of the evilness of his persecutors. Such revelations are found in the case histories of most delusional schizophrenics. They are of little significance in the non-paranoid schizophrenics because in these cases the persistent delusions are absent.

In the majority of paranoids, the disease does not develop along a steadily rising curve but rather in prominent swings and oscillations which at times may approach normality, and at other times are far removed from the base-line. The hallucinatory confusional states are about as frequent as the melancholic depressions. The manic excitements are quite rare; but catatonic symptoms of every kind appear as transitory phenomena in the wake of acute thrusts or as permanent behavior manifestations. Thus a patient had assumed a certain position against a wall with outspread legs which he maintained for several years, verbigerated, and was negativistic (more or less independently of his delusions). At other times, he was able to do some work.

There are also paranoids without hallucinations; these people have merely false self-reference which can be elaborated in delusional ideas;

or they link a delusion to some event which they then pursue for years without ever being able to discuss it.

The many litigious schizophrenics belong in this group. A young woman had charge of a physician's household. Perhaps he really did make some erotic advances to her. In any event, she imagined that he had promised to marry her. She demanded that he fulfill his promise and marry her; she made all sorts of scenes, difficulties, and unpleasantnesses, and he finally had to dismiss her. She carried her complaints to the courts, always of the opinion that she had and could prove all her allegations. Then she lodged a complaint against the judge himself because he had not found in her favor. She became more and more confused, could not work. Lawyers got most of her possessions in the course of the many lawsuits. She was judged to be mentally ill by a board of experts; she filed a complaint against the expert testimony, etc. From time to time, she managed to spend a year outside the hospital although never without difficulty.

The delusions may remain stationary in their quasi-embryonal stage. Such patients refer many a thing to themselves which even a normal person might regard as referring to himself, but we would not pay much attention to it. However, these patients see insult and injury to themselves in everything that does not precisely meet with their complete approval; they cannot be satisfied, never get along with anyone. Even in the hospital, they do not remain too long, to the great satisfaction of the other inmates. They do manage to get along in occupations which do not require contact with other people.

Conversely, we see patients who have no real delusional ideas; there may be only hallucinations which in many cases are almost completely limited to the auditory sphere. At first, the patients react only by an altered behavior; and the persons of their environment are quite in the dark, often for years, about the real inner processes of the patient. But sooner or later, they break out into vilification. In accordance with the character of the individual involved, the illness may be expressed in the form of hallucinations, persistent or episodic attacks of sobbing, suicidal attempts or senseless destruction of objects. These patients, when they are severely ill, are unemployable for long periods even in the hospital. In the mildest cases, they learn to get along with their voices; they withdraw into a corner when they are driven to curse, or more or less repress their reactions. In between these two ends of the scale, we find every type and degree of intermediary form. In the hospitals, particularly, we find numerous patients who are able to work in an orderly way but who because of "voices" suddenly suffer spells of excitement and agitation which may last from a few minutes to a few days. As soon as the voices stop, the patients are again quiet and externally often appear normal. At times, it is extraordinary to see the degree of self-understanding and comprehension of their difficult situation.

The delusions both of grandeur and eroticism show essentially the same variations as do the delusions of persecution. The patients believe that they are loved by persons of a higher social standing than themselves. In the main, the patients wish to give these persons an opportunity to communicate with them. They heap curses and vilification on their lovers and occasionally transfer their affections to still other persons who are then treated in the same way. The megalomanic patients have made marvelous inventions; they are prophets, philosophers, world-reformers, who, only in relatively exceptional instances, are able to collect followers because they are, after all, often too confused, behave far too badly, far too awkwardly to really impress others.

Aside from the paranoid symptoms already described, there appears almost always, of course, a greater or lesser degree of "dementia" (deterioration). These same patients do not really act and behave even in accordance with their own distorted notions: the prince or king assists in all the farm work; the Bride of Christ hardly bothers about the heavenly sphere but does the laundry of her dirty wardmates quite mechanically and is very happy if presented with a few candies. Only some of them possess the consistency and the energy to attempt to bring their delusions into some relation with reality and to desire to realize their wishes. Only those with persecutory delusions remain indefatigable in demanding the cessations of their tortures and vexations and even the stern punishment of those responsible.

In the more moderate cases, it is not possible to demonstrate any defect of intelligence in matters which do not concern the patients' complexes; yet, even here the patients are rash, show poor judgment, and are often distraught. For the rest, the affective deterioration is expressed in the way described earlier, but it is precisely in the true paranoids, that this is least obvious.

As far as our present diagnostic skills and competence are concerned, the very same disturbances as those described above can also appear as "sequelae" of initially melancholic, manic, or catatonic excitements. It is particularly erroneous to assume that the "deterioration" must appear as well marked or even severe in the so-called "secondary" cases. Occasionally we find even in these patients excellent intellectual achievement existing side by side with the all too often, constant hallucinations and senseless delusions.

Kraepelin's "dementia paranoides" merits special mention. "In these cases, after an initial depression, there immediately begin completely quixotic, constantly changing and florid delusional structures which are at first influenced by rationalizations and memory falsifications. Aside from the occasional outbursts of rage, the delusions very quickly lose every power of influencing the patient's behavior and actions. A true advance or progress in the disease does not take place after the initially rapid development. Rather, the condition may remain almost unchanged for a decade and even longer. Clarity of consciousness and external deportment remain quite undisturbed in spite of completely confusing and confused delusional ideas, accompanied by massive neologisms." All there is left to add to this description is that a period of depression is not always to be found, and that there are symptomatically similar cases but with chronic onsets. Furthermore, it must be particularly emphasized that catatonic symptoms are completely lacking in the long run.

The "pre-senile delusions of being wronged" (Kraepelin) often take this form. In other cases, it can be differentiated from dementia paranoides only by its subtle and insidious beginning and by the somewhat lesser degree of elaboration of the symptoms.

B. Catatonia

With or without a preliminary or prodromal period, the most striking instances of catatonia begin with an acute outbreak which shows the characteristics of the usual schizophrenic excitements. For the most part, although not always, these agitations reveal right from the start an admixture of catatonic symptoms. Especially stuporous forms, in combination with cataleptic symptoms and hyperkinesis, very often dominate the clinical picture. The nature of the agitation may alter many times, in an irregular way, betwixt manic and melancholic conditions, confusional and stuporous states. Then, quite arbitrarily, after one of these phases there sets in a period of quiet which is at the same time an improvement of the patient's condition in more than one-half the cases. The patients begin to be able to do some work, hallucinate much less, or not at all, correct some of their delusional ideas and show "healing with defect or scarring." Some symptoms, particularly the catatonic, remain more or less distinct. In the cases with favorable outcomes as well as those with poorer ones, there again often appears, sooner or later, another acute thrust which is frequently, although not always, similar to the first. But after each of them, the deterioration usually becomes more and more pronounced.

Catatonia can also begin with chronic paranoid symptoms. Delusions or hallucinations, or both, bring the patient to the mental institution with the diagnosis of "paranoia" where, sooner or later, peculiar behavior and negligence, not directly related to or motivated by the delusions, become very prominent and to which suddenly or gradually catatonic symptoms associate themselves.

As exceptions the chronic forms which, for the most part, are considered to be end-stages, have right from the very start a marked catatonic character. This was the case in a patient who had ceased to talk about a year prior to admission to the hospital but who could still do her housework relatively well. In the course of the next two years, there were added negativism, catalepsy, and all sorts of bizarre acts, violence, uncleanliness and complete refusal to work—symptoms which have now been maintained for many years. In many cases, the initial symptoms of chronic catatonia are the peculiarities of behavior and, particularly, actions which the patients committed while they were still apparently healthy, with steadily increasing frequency.

The chronic catatonic states show little variations regardless of the fact that they began with or without excitement and agitation. Many patients sit around in a kind of continuous stupor, with or without negativism, and permit themselves to be completely cared for. Others are excited, agitated or violent as a consequence of active negativism. They form some of the most unpleasant and difficult hospital inmates. Very many of them, who are ordinarily totally indifferent to the external world, have spontaneous, transitory excitements in which they rage, insult, vilify, become violent, smear themselves, etc.

C. Hebephrenia

One is inclined to characterize this group by emphasizing "dementia." In that case, however, all the numerous and practically important mild cases to which the term, "dementia" cannot be applied, even though one does not believe in a complete *restitutio ad integrum* for such cases, would have to be excluded.

Thus hebephrenia comprises:

a. The acutely beginning, non-catatonic forms (melancholic, manic, amented, twilight states) insofar as they do not pass over into chronic paranoid or catatonic conditions.

b. All chronic cases with accessory symptoms which themselves do not completely dominate the picture.

Unfortunately, the name chosen for this group is suitable only insofar as the majority of the patients who are victims of this form of the disease are between fifteen and twenty-five years of age, but there are also (rarely, it is true) hebephrenics, in the above sense of the term, whose anamneses for the period of their lives before the fifth or sixth decades do not indicate the presence of any of the symptoms of this disease.

The hebephrenia of Kahlbaum-Hecker was a deterioration (or a dementia) which appeared relatively quickly in early puberty, usually developed with various affective disturbances and was, moreover, characterized by immaturity and callowness. For us, the question of age is irrelevant; and the symptoms of affectation and studied mannerisms, of the pathetic, and the veritable joy in pranks and clowning on the one side, the precocity and the drive to concern themselves with the most abstruse problems on the other—all these symptoms can be found in other types of schizophrenics whose complexes signify a self-elevation, a desire to be great.[4]

Moreover, Hecker's own case histories reveal that the excitements in his sense were not so prominent as to assume the character of acute psychoses. We find in them simply that the deterioration is in the forefront. However, even Kraepelin had already spoken of an onset with acute mental disturbance, although he found it much more rarely. But since the acute initial disturbances cannot very well be designated as catatonia because they do not display marked catatonic symptoms or are followed by such, we must conclude that all the acute "psychoses" with subsequent deterioration and without catatonic or paranoid characteristics are to be reckoned as belonging to hebephrenia if we wish to avoid setting up still another totally unnecessary new group.

There are no specific symptoms for this group. I am not even certain that the teenagers' symptoms are any more frequent here than in catatonia. Perhaps, they are more prominently in the foreground only because there are no catatonic symptoms to conceal them.

Yet there are theoretical considerations which lead us to expect such phenomena precisely in the hebephrenics. It is perfectly true that these manifestations are not at all as frequent in paranoids as in the hebephrenics, and if they do appear at all, it is much later. Furthermore, we know that complexes and habits, present at the time of the disease's onset, easily become fixed so that for years afterwards they are still recognizable. Thus, we may readily assume that the attitudes and habits of puberty are being caricatured and at the same time leave a strong imprint on the psychic organization. On the other hand, there are many people who have first become sick long after they have passed the stage of puberty and who nevertheless exhibit "hebephrenic" manifestations.[5] Supposing it were correct that catatonic symptoms do have their roots in sexuality, then it would be precisely those individuals with predomi-

4. Cf. the theory of mannerisms.

5. Jahrmärker (316) also mentions cases who reveal boyish, foolish, skittish behavior and who fall victims to the illness in their fifth and sixth decades.

nantly sexual complexes who would become catatonic, while those in whom they were less dominant would become paranoid or hebephrenic according to the age at which they fell ill.

Under the term, hebephrenic, then are to be understood, first of all, the simple forms of what used to be called secondary dementia with acute onset of the psychoses. To these we must also add the not too rare cases in which excitements and agitations first make their appearance after the onset of deterioration. These cases are far more frequent than one would assume from what other authorities have written about them. Melancholic and manic excitements, twilight states, etc., can appear at any time in the course of the disease just as well as at the beginning. It is precisely the hebephrenics with their not very striking symptoms who are first brought to the hospital because of some acute episode, although very commonly the disease has already been of many years' standing.

The excitement may be quite mild or completely lacking. In the latter case, the patients simply deteriorate; lose their efficiency; become careless, negligent, dirty; commit all sorts of blunders and stupidities, etc. There are many among them who, for years, were considered to be neurasthenics, or if women, to be hysterics. A distinct hypochondriacal coloring often constitutes the transition to the paranoid forms. In view of the great practical importance of timely diagnosis, Kraepelin was correct in emphasizing these "hypochondriacal deteriorations" as he termed them. "The picture is always dominated by the ever more pronounced feelings of mental and physical incapacity, the various pathological sensations which gradually induce the patients to renounce all activities. At the same time, their emotions become dull, their affect blunted, their attention slackens, without hallucinating or having formed clear-cut delusional systems."

Thus hebephrenia manifests itself in some form of schizophrenic deterioration. It may take a permanently chronic course, or it may show acute syndromes at its onset or even later. Hallucinations and senseless delusions, occasionally even catatonic symptoms, can complicate the clinical picture but they do not dominate it.

D. Schizophrenia Simplex[6]

"The patients simply become affectively and intellectually weaker; the will seems to lose its power; the capacity for work, for caring for themselves diminishes. They appear stupid and finally show the picture of severe dementia." (Clouston)

We do not follow Kraepelin in including these patients in the hebe-

---

6. Cf. Weygandt (813) and Diem (180).

phrenic group, for practical rather than theoretical reasons. In spite of serious attempts of some very competent investigators, the concept of "primary dementia" is still not generally accepted. In fact, many authorities do not recognize it at all. It is these patients who make our world uncertain under the banner of psychopathy, of degeneration, of moral insanity, alcoholism and perhaps, most commonly, under that of health. The only possibility of acquainting physicians with this type of individual rests in giving it a distinct name. This distinction also possesses a minor theoretical value inasmuch as it demonstrates the difference between the essential and accessory symptoms: the latter are absent in simple schizophrenia.

This group is rarely found in hospitals but outside it is as common as any of the other forms. In private practice, we often see it, indeed as frequently in the relatives who bring the patients as in the patients themselves. On the lower levels of society, the simple schizophrenics vegetate as day laborers, peddlers, even as servants. They are also vagabonds and hoboes as are other types of schizophrenics of mild grade. On the higher levels of society, the most common type is the wife (in a very unhappy role, we can say), who is unbearable, constantly scolding, nagging, always making demands but never recognizing duties. Her family never considers the possibility of illness, suffers for many years a veritable hell of annoyances, difficulties, unpleasantnesses from the "mean" woman. They usually employ every possible means to conceal the true state of affairs in the home from the prying eyes of the outside world. The possibility of keeping the anomaly secret is facilitated by the fact that many of these patients still manage to conduct themselves in an entirely unobtrusive way. Frequently one is veritably forced to keep the situation secret from the world at large because there are many people who readily step in and defend these women who themselves know how to play the role of injured and persecuted innocence.

Kahlbaum (348) coined the term "heboidophrenia" or "heboid" for those cases which show only disturbances of social feeling, tact and behavior. However, he also knew that formal thinking disturbances (such as, approximate thinking and answering) were not absent and he quite correctly incorporated them into his class of hebephrenia. He was inclined to consider that their prognoses were relatively fair. Cases, such as he described, take a course, however, which is not at all different from those of other mild cases of schizophrenia. Therefore, the attempt to establish a class of "heboids" has not met with much response.

A far more important and very common type is the schizophrenic alcoholic. For the most part, he is misjudged or not recognized as such and is, therefore, always improperly dealt with. Many schizophrenics surrender to drink; usually the basic disease is overlooked (cf. Graeter).

It is purely a matter of arbitrary selection to include the schizophrenic litigants in this group. We find numerous transitions from simply unbearable people to the paranoid litigants with marked delusions. The best solution perhaps is to draw a line somewhere in the middle of the scale and place the half that do not have real delusions there, and count the others as paranoid.

Furthermore, there are many simple schizophrenics among eccentric people of every sort who stand out as world saviors and world reformers, philosophers, writers and artists, beside the "degenerated" and deteriorated.

A young Swiss, who had successfully completed his studies in the commercial field, chose to become a naturalized German citizen in order to take up a subordinate officer's position in the German army. As such he took part in the wars of 1866 and 1870, after which he became a photographer and wandered about from job to job as an assistant photographer and travelling salesman. Two attempts to become independent failed miserably; he lost all his money in those deals. His marriage at the age of forty did not alter the situation. He became increasingly more incapable and more indifferent, and finally stopped working altogether. He did not concern himself much with the fate of his children after his wife's death. He stayed at home or sat around in bars, without, however, any real alcoholic indulgence. It was only at the age of fifty-two that he was admitted to a hospital for the first time. In this case, the presence of schizophrenia was revealed only by the fact that, without good reason, he gave up his vocation and changed his nationality. But it was only very gradually that he became more incapable of working or achieving anything, and more and more indifferent and apathetic. Only towards the end of his fourth decade did the disease process seem to progress more rapidly before it finally led to total deterioration.

A teacher, who had done very well in school, goes to Roumania as a tutor because he was unable to find a teaching position immediately after graduation. He remains there some eight years but in the end permits himself to be cheated out of his salary by his employers. He returns home penniless. He seeks employment as a teacher, substitutes in various places, but for years is unable to find a permanent position. Finally a tiny village appoints him to a permanent teaching job only to dismiss him after six months because of inefficiency. He tries another canton with no better success. Given one position which he might have been able to retain permanently, he suddenly leaves without reason and without notice or consideration for others. Naturally, he was always in very poor financial straits; got into debt and mortgaged his pension under rather unfavorable conditions for himself; pawned most of his belongings. All this he did with the idea that circumstances would somehow change since up to now it was only this or that which was merely accidentally lacking. If someone would only advance him some money, he was quite certain that he would then be able to find a position and then everything would easily be straightened out once more. That he himself was to blame for his bad luck and difficulties, he did not suspect at all, despite many efforts to give him insight. Finally he bombards the government officials with demands for his "rights" in which demands he mixes a good bit of cursing and insults, etc. He proceeds to insult and injure those who had given him financial credit. At the age of forty-five, he is admitted to the hospital where he is completely indifferent to everything, cannot work and only insists that he must be given a teaching position which he can fill perfectly because of his diligence and ability.

Another type with marked irritability: A normal, intelligent girl marries at twenty and lives happily for more than five years. Very gradually she becomes irritable, gesticulates while talking, her peculiarities continue to increase; she cannot keep a servant anymore; she is constantly quarrelling with her neighbors. Within her own family group, she has developed into an unbearable domestic tyrant who knows no duties, only rights. She is unable to manage the household or do the housework any more because she makes all kinds of silly, stupid, and useless purchases and is proving herself utterly impractical. During the many years in which she is in the hospital, she exhibits the same behavior only in increasing measure, so that it is only possible to keep her either in her own room or outdoors where there are very few people. However, after some ten years of hospitalization, she can be released although she still causes trouble by her gossiping and disagreeableness. She complains continually of some vague nervous troubles because, as she says, she was not properly treated in the hospital. Yet she is entirely indifferent to important things such as her relations to her family, etc. She has no love for her children. She is incapable of pulling herself together although she knows quite well that she could have a very decent life if she were less of a nag and a scold. There were no traces of paranoid or catatonic symptoms.

If we examine some individuals more closely, we often tend to suspect the presence of simple schizophrenia without, however, being able to make a definite diagnosis at the given time; but very often, after days or years, our suspicions can be confirmed. Thus, there is no doubt that many simple schizophrenics are at large whose symptoms are not sufficiently pronounced to permit the recognition of mental disorder. If one observes the relatives of our patients, one often finds in them peculiarities which are qualitatively identical with those of the patients themselves, so that the disease appears to be only a quantitative increase of the anomalies seen in the parents and siblings.

Such mild cases are often considered to be "nervous" or "degenerated" individuals, etc. But if we follow the anamnesis of those who are admitted to the hospital in later years because of an exacerbation of their difficulties, a criminal charge, a pathological drinking bout or some such episode, we can usually find throughout the entire past history of the individual mildly pathological symptoms which in the light of their recent illness unquestionably have to be considered as schizophrenic.

There is also a latent schizophrenia, and I am convinced that this is the most frequent form, although admittedly these people hardly ever come for treatment. It is not necessary to give a detailed description of the various manifestations of latent schizophrenia. In this form, we can see in *nuce* all the symptoms and all the combinations of symptoms which are present in the manifest types of the disease. Irritable, odd, moody, withdrawn or exaggeratedly punctual people arouse, among other things, the suspicion of being schizophrenic. Often one discovers a concealed catatonic or paranoid symptom and exacerbations occurring in later life demonstrate that every form of this disease may take a latent course.

E. Special Types of Groups

1. Periodic Forms

It may be of value to select a few groups and to discuss them from several other points of view.

First, there are the "periodic" cases. The concept of periodicity is a very indefinite one in psychiatry. In the main, this name should be applicable to those psychoses whose acute phases follow the repetitious pattern of the manic-depressive psychosis. Soon after puberty, rarely later, the first manic or melancholic episodes appear and tend to recur after longer or shorter intervals. Also cyclic forms are not so rare. In the majority of these cases, we find initially only slight traces of residual deterioration after each attack. However, the schizophrenic symptoms are usually quite pronounced and leave no doubt whatever about the diagnosis and the final outcome.

In a few cases, the periods may be very short and recur with an astonishing regularity such as I have not even seen in the manic-depressive psychosis. I have observed a patient who for more than thirty years was always manic on one day and depressed on the next; further, this state of affairs did not change as the cerebral atrophy of senility added its symptoms to those of the schizophrenia. In another instance, the phases lasted for twenty-five hours and this regularity was maintained for many years; the shift of mood occurred at all hours of the day and only took a moment. Over a long period of time, a certain catatonic woman was on one day able to work, ate a great deal, but spoke little, on the whole she was relatively well-behaved; but on the next day she was stuporous, negativistic, immobile, abstinent. A chronic catatonic patient was excited and agitated, screaming and verbigerating every second day; on the other day, she was stuporous, docile. If she received a sedative on her agitated day, the cycle would be delayed. On that day she remained quiet, but on the following day she would be excited.

Thus we are not always dealing with manic-depressive symptoms in the short periods any more than in the longer ones. Every kind of agitation may alternate with every type of diminution of psychic activity. Näcke (505, p. 645) termed such cases, *catatonia alternans.* In one of his patients agitation lasting for about twenty-five hours alternated with stupor lasting about twenty-nine hours.

Most remarkable are those alterations of the clinical picture in which, usually under some psychic influence, the patients oscillate between their delusional world and reality. Generally the changeover from one phase to the other is so brief that one should regard it as a homogeneous clinical picture with different aspects. Thus a catatonic of long standing would show two alternating conditions during a single conversation with her. Her first condition was characterized by good orientation to her environment and a certain degree of insight; in her second state, she considered the doctor to be the devil, misinterpreted her environment in the same sense, and hid under the covers with tremendous anxiety.

Of course, one ought to draw a sharp dividing line between those cases whose periodically recurring behavior seems to be internally determined, and the other cases whose periods of excitement and calm change in accordance with psychic influences. But as can easily be gathered from the previous discussion, such clear separations are not at all easily achieved, not only because we rarely know the releasing factors for each single phase, but particularly because both causes may be operative in releasing or ending the phase.

2. Age Groups

Schizophrenia is not a puberty psychosis in the strict sense of the word, although in the majority of patients the sickness becomes manifest soon after puberty. With relatively accurate case histories, one can trace back the illness to childhood, or even to the first years of life, in at least five per cent of the cases. In this process, we completely disregard the anomalies which do not have a distinctly schizophrenic character, although we know that the disease includes many symptoms of general significance.

At the present time, we know of no differences between the infantile and other forms of the disease. If we observe patients during childhood, they present the same symptoms as those seen in adults. We did note, however, that the analyses of such youthful patients are more difficult. In contrast to adults, children are not less clear in their desires and wishes, but the content is less distinctly defined. The difficulty may also be due to our inadequate experience with the technique of handling youthful psychotics.

The prognosis of those cases in which the onset of the illness occurs before puberty does not appear to be too poor for the next few years. What happens to them later, I do not know. I can recall only two who had to remain in the hospital. However, the case histories of the adults admitted to the hospital show that at least part of these early cases relapse and then usually become markedly deteriorated.

Those who succumb during the second and third decades of life are, for the greatest part, the hebephrenics and catatonics; whereas, those in the fourth decade, and even a little before this time, seem to show a preference for the paranoid form of the disease. This latter type continues to increase for some years after the fourth decade, so that Kraepelin was able to define a form of "delusion of being wronged and injured" as being "pre-senile" although we include it in schizophrenia.

Lugaro (428) has given an interesting explanation of these facts which still need further confirmation, however. He claims that the immature psyche is far more damaged by the disease process than is the more mature psyche of the adult. We also know that old memory pictures are much less disturbed by brain disorders than the more recently acquired memories. The personality of an individual as well as his relationships to the environment continue to grow and remold itself up till about the third decade of life. Thus, before this period, it must be especially vulnerable while the more firmly set and mature personality of the older individual may be changed, to be sure, but cannot be so completely annihilated. However, it may also be that the milder "predispositions" tend to postpone the onset to a later age and to show less severe personality changes.

In any event these relationships must be expected to vary in each individual case in accordance with the severity of the disease process and, in some cases, also with the intensity of the psychic factors. For we see adolescents becoming paranoid; and we know of catatonia developing at a much later age. Kraepelin was the first to draw attention to the high incidence of cases who develop an apparently common melancholia during the involutional period, but then present catatonic symptoms, and ultimately proceed to a condition of catatonic deterioration. We also have to add that the same forms which we usually see in earlier age periods may make their appearance in a later age period. We cannot as yet decide whether those are relapses or exacerbations of an earlier illness. However, we have never seen a case in which the possibility of an earlier onset of the illness could be excluded with absolute certainty.

3. Etiological Groupings

The present state of our knowledge does not permit us to establish valid etiological groups of schizophrenia. We must assume that head trauma can produce or release a schizophrenic disease picture. It is certain that fever states and normal puerperal conditions lead to outbreaks or thrusts of schizophrenia. Indeed, the first episodes of the disease often follow directly after such events. However, we do not know the specific forms or symptoms corresponding to such an etiology. On the other hand, prison psychoses show signs which correspond to the occasioning factor. But then it is not a question of characterizing the entire disease, but merely that of the symptoms. The "prison complex" expresses itself in the wish to be free, in the need to be innocent, or at least to be thought innocent. Consequently the patients hear the director, an angel, or some other equally competent person, say that he has been promised his freedom or that he is going to be released. He becomes euphoric, but of course is not released. Thereupon some enemies wish to hold him prisoner; they will not let him go despite the decision of competent authorities. They intercept the messages coming to him. They begin to torture him, blow poison gas into his cell, mistreat him during the night, show him horrible pictures. At first he becomes irritable then tearful and violent. He has to be transferred for psychiatric care to the hospital where the psychically released episode subsides relatively rapidly, that is within a few weeks. What is left behind is chronic schizophrenia in some form or other. Of course, the attack does not always take this course. Instead of contenting himself with being thought innocent, the prisoner may become a world reformer, a second Savior. This enables him to tolerate the persecutions for a longer time. It also happens that an individual being held merely for investigation by the courts, suddenly develops an acute psychosis, especially if he is an alcoholic. As if in a continuous delirium, he then imagines that every possible attempt is made to save him. His being saved is identified with saving the whole mankind. After going through experiences which surpass the Apocalypse, he is solemnly received in the seventh heaven. Furthermore, the imprisonment may release a Ganser syndrome or the "faxen" syndrome. Naturally the "prison complex" may remain without effect even in schizophrenic prisoners; in that case, the original schizophrenia presents a picture pretty much like any other.

We also see, as we do in other psychopaths, that the intense hatred of society and the utter failure of any means of escape from the prison leads to outbursts of destructive fury. After a few hours these individuals return to their earlier more peaceful state which usually occurs after a sleep of exhaustion.

The so-called "menstruation psychosis" also deserves some mention. It is certain that a considerably larger proportion of the severe cases becomes more intensely agitated during periods of menstruation. For years, even completely mild cases appear ill only during the menstrual periods. Such conditions may occur as residuals after acute episodes, as prodromes of a severe illness, but also without further complications. In the latter case, such patients may recover, particularly, at the climacterium.

I knew a woman who was quite efficient both in her household work and her business. For more than ten years each menstrual period was accompanied by ill-humor, delusions with suicidal drives, schizophrenic thinking, and schizophrenic reactions to her illness. For some years now, she has been free of all manifest symptoms. In this particular case, there was obviously a great possibility of confusing her ill-humor and depressions with that of the depression of a manic-depressive psychosis.

4. Classification in Terms of the Intensity of the Pathological Manifestations

There are many intermediary types from latent schizophrenia to the most severe form of the disease. At this point, we only wish to mention the fatal cases. As far as I know, these have all had a catatonic character. Naturally, we are not including in this discussion all those cases who die because of poor nutrition, exhaustion from incessant activity, infections, or innumerable epileptiform attacks. But aside from such causes as just enumerated, the health and resistance of some patients can be so reduced that food is generally very poorly assimilated. In spite of special feeding methods, special diets, and every possible nursing care, the patients die from generalized atrophy, often within a few weeks or months.

However, there is another group who appear to die from a kind of catatonic cerebral paralysis. At first, the patients impress us as very much the usual schizophrenics but they soon attract our attention because of a certain debility and weakness. In spite of their agitation, their movements do not seem very free, lack strength. Their reactions and relations to the outer world seem more inadequate than usual; one can establish no rapport of any kind with them, not even a negative one, as we do in many other catatonics. If they react, they do so slowly and only to external stimuli. Their mouths are not kept clean anymore; blinking becomes rare or ceases completely. Despite all measures taken to combat this condition, which in itself is very difficult because of their resistiveness, the cornea shows necrotic areas; decubitus ulcers appear under some conditions. The patients continue to get worse and die within a few weeks. That we are dealing with schizophrenia, very much like others, is proved not only by the symptomatology of these fatal cases but above all by the fact that such manifestations may appear in patients in whom a definite diagnosis was established long before these events. Also rather calm and stationary cases may suddenly develop this kind of cerebral paralysis which leads to death in a few days.

SECTION III

THE COURSE OF THE DISEASE

A. The Temporal Course

It is impossible to describe all the variations which the course of schizophrenia may take. Our textbooks do not deal with the most frequent variations, but only with those which are easiest to describe. One comes closest to reality if one makes it clear that merely the general direction of the course of this disease is toward a schizophrenic deterioration (dementia), but that in each individual case the disease may take a course which is both qualitatively and temporally rather irregular. Constant advances, halts, recrudescences, or remissions are possible at any time.[1]

Earlier writers believed to be nearer the goal of knowing the exact course of this disease. Kahlbaum and Hecker had assumed that hebephrenia always ended in dementia. Kahlbaum's catatonia was supposed to pass through a very definite cycle of various phases.[2] These and many other proposed rules or laws proved to be incorrect.

Yet, there are a number of cases which, to some extent, fit into certain categories. Many schizophrenias become manifest with an acute excitement. During this period of excitement, the level of intelligence often sinks so low that even after the very first attack of the disease one can already speak of the presence of dementia (deterioration); this is the "secondary dementia" of many authors. Or the acute syndrome may leave behind chronic hallucinations and delusions ("secondary paranoia"). The acute attacks may be repeated and with each attack the intelligence is still further reduced; or the deterioration of the mental

1. There are many reports about "unusual courses" of this disease. But none of these cases with which I am acquainted reveal anything which, in general, a practising psychiatrist has not seen often enough. The author of these "unusual cases" has somehow or other constructed a picture of what he wishes to consider as being the "usual course," a construct which hardly does justice to reality. The unusual lies only in the fact that the author has noted a particularly striking case deviating from his own schema.

2. It is reasonable to assume that he himself, no more than I, ever saw a case which developed along the lines of his schema, because he did not publish a single case history which would be typical in his sense.

powers may become noticeable only after one particular attack. However, the concept of "secondary" states does not correspond to facts, not even in the cases with acute "onset," in view of the fact that the deterioration continues to progress even after the acute syndrome has passed; or the deterioration does not begin until some time after the acute phase has subsided. Nevertheless, as far as we know, there are no acute forms of this illness which inevitably lead to permanent deterioration of the patients' psychic status.[3] As a rule, the cases showing twilight states seem to run a course which is benign.

The acute episodes may last from a few hours up to some years. In institutionalized patients the episodes usually subside after a few months. They may never recur, or repeat themselves numerous times.

The forms marked by acute syndromes of every kind have to be contrasted with simple schizophrenia because it evolves relatively insidiously and may require decades until it fully develops without showing striking advances or remissions. However, there are also simple deteriorations which may reach such degrees of intensity from one day to the next that the patients are rendered completely incapable of working and maintaining themselves in society. (I do not know, however, whether the few cases which I have seen taking such a course did not later on develop accessory symptoms.) But the process of deterioration may take a wholly irregular course; acute syndromes may appear and then we can no longer speak of simple schizophrenias.

The paranoids tend to take a rather chronic course. Since we do not separate the uncomplicated cases we may have to consider the frequent occurrence of thrusts, outbursts, intercurrent agitations and remissions, entirely apart from the so-called "secondary" cases. Yet, we do see textbook cases taking a course of development along a regular, flat curve. The dementia paranoides usually has a subacute onset and then for many years takes the course of a stable type of paranoid.

The irregularly progressing cases are most common. It is quite impossible to describe them. A few random examples will have to suffice to characterize them.

A young farm girl, age seventeen, has been catatonic for a period of two years. Then she became a nursing attendant. Two years later, she was released. She then became a midwife. She married, her husband had a very difficult time with her. For example, she would not permit him to sing while he worked. She formed strong unfounded sympathies and antipathies. At the age of thirty-eight, she was again mildly catatonic

3. Since I have been differentiating the syndromes showing *Benommenheit* (clouding, haziness) from the others, I have seen only in a few instances such cases with very poor prognosis.

for some six months. Since then she has been working for eight years outside the hospital, but not as a midwife.

Merchant: Suffered from headaches for twenty years. At the age of twenty-one, had attacks of anxiety and believed he might become insane. He was abulic but able to work effectively. Then at the age of twenty-two, after having improved slightly, he developed the same symptoms as before, but more severely; now he was unable to do any work.

Castings-polisher: He suffered a serious leg injury in his youth. While he was taking various electrical treatments for the injury, he thought they were affecting his heart. At the age of twenty-eight, at the time when he was getting married, an attack of depression and anxiety. "Mentally always in good health." Since his thirty-fifth year after an attack of influenza, he always had headaches. At the age of forty-six, he developed precordial anginal attacks, insomnia, absent-mindedness, irritability, acute startle reaction, moodiness and brooding, delusions of persecution and inferiority. After suicidal attempt he was hospitalized and improved.

Silk weaver: Intelligent. At the age of fifteen: religious ideas of grandeur. At twenty: catatonic frenzy, improvement. At age of twenty-seven: diagnosis of dementia. From ages twenty-nine to thirty-one, catatonic. Until the age of fifty-five, he continued as a diligent, quiet weaver who supported his parents and himself. At the age of fifty-five, auto-castration; since then he has been in the hospital with some catatonic symptoms.

Merchant's wife: liver disease at the age of twenty-nine; moody, depressed, hysterical cramps. Since then during each menses, very irritable, mean and gloomy. At times dipsomanic. At age of thirty-five, persecutory delusions. "Cured" after a few months of hospitalization. She remained quite irritable and touchy, however. Between ages of thirty-seven and forty, she developed a gradually and continuously progressing hallucinatory paranoid state.

Housekeeper: markedly religious. Was melancholic for many months during puberty. A voice whispered to her what she was to write in a letter. Then for the next ten years, "the very model of young maidenhood," very devoted, tractable and conscientious. Then a manic condition which lasted for many years with foolish, silly, erotic, and religious delusions. Later she was again able to resume work.

A female factory worker: Was manic for several weeks shortly after her first menses. Then well, but irritable, seclusive, withdrawn; she felt she was being mocked, laughed incessantly. At age twenty-one, silly manic delusions; was released as "cured." She remained well until age twenty-three. Then, confused religious delusions, but again improved. However, she was no longer able to hold her job. After about five years, gradual elaboration of a hallucinatory, confusional state; agitated, even in the hospital; she is no longer able to do any work.

Farmer: Insomniac since age twenty-five. At age twenty-eight, a twilight state lasting several months. "Cured" overnight. Was "well" till age thirty; but at the funeral of a neighbor who had committed suicide, he became very excited and agitated. After he met an old sweetheart of his, he became dull, mute, refused food for several days. At age thirty-one, his sweetheart wrote him a letter which he read. Thereupon a sudden, severe, depressed catatonic state, improved after a year; released as able to work. One year later, suicide.

Outstanding student: Since sixteenth year, he seems to get worse with each passing year. Yet, he manages to graduate from high school, with good grades at nineteen. After a gonorrheal infection, an agitated depression. Then he improves but insists on taking up a vocation requiring purely physical labor. Shortly thereafter a severe catatonia, definite deterioration.

Woman: Was in a mental hospital at age ten. At age twenty, following a rape, she is "crazy." Then recovers and is apparently well. At age seventy-one, she is again a patient in a mental institution (Bertschinger, 295).

Woman: depressive catatonia after puberty. Then considered as well. Marries and has children. Then in her 70th year, melancholic schizophrenic episode.

Physician: Neurasthenia at twenty-nine. Then at thirty-one after typhoid fever, catatonic. At forty-seven, apparently "cured." He then resumes his practice, marries. Has been well for the past two years (Schäfer, 651).

Exacerbations may occur in all the various courses of development; be it that the chronic condition gets worse, or be it that accessory symptoms appear, or even that acute episodes of some sort set in. Such exacerbations may be internally determined, or by physical influences such as an alcoholic intoxication. But above all, they may be released by insidious, slowly operating, or sudden shock-like psychic causes.

If the deterioration of the condition takes the form of recurring, intermittent acute episodes, or if it begins after prolonged remissions, we speak of recidives. These frequently imitate the previous attacks but may also present new characteristics.

Once a relatively stable condition has been reached, the thrusts of the disease are not so frequent anymore. Among some two hundred patients of the Rheinau hospital, the majority had been ill for many years prior to their admission to the hospital. After ten years, I found that only about a dozen had become essentially worse in any way.

It appears to me, however, that in the material of our own hospitals, complete halts in the disease course were really not as frequent. For the most part, although one may not notice any advance in the deterioration as long as one is in constant daily contact with the patients, I am usually struck by the increased decline when I have occasion to see the patients again after an interval of many years. Even outside the hospital, these advances of the illness can be noted. The majority of our hospital cases are first admitted to the institution in their fourth or fifth decades—long after their illness had begun. The reason for this may lie in the gradually increasing asocial peculiarities and not only in the external circumstances (e.g., the environment becomes more distasteful to the patients; their parents and relatives die one by one). The outcome of any single attack or any given hospital stay is therefore in no way equivalent to the outcome of the disease itself. On the other hand, it is certain that a large proportion of the milder cases who manage to maintain and support themselves outside the hospital, also do not get very much worse over periods lasting for decades.

True arrests in the progress of the disease may appear at any time; of course they are not as prominent in chronic conditions as in the acute ones. If a number of symptoms disappear during an arrest of the disease, then we count the cases as remissions.[4] Special attention should be given to the frequently occurring sudden remissions in the very midst of an acute episode, particularly, in such as have the characteristics of marked delusional ideas or catatonia; such patients may then appear quite normal to a layman. However, on closer observation, one finds a remarkable indifference, at least, toward the events which took place during the attack.

While performing her morning toilet, a servant girl suddenly begins to rave, smashing everything in sight, creating a terrible uproar in the house. Finally, as help comes, the patient is seen to be very quiet, lucid, and busy with doing the cleaning. But she cannot understand why everyone is making such a fuss. Half a day later, the fury begins anew and then persists for many weeks. One of our confused agitated catatonics often had such periods of calm which were then utilized to feed him.

Short remissions may also occur in the later course of the disease. They may even last a few hours or long enough to result in real im-

4. Others term this an intermission or cure.

provement; but relapses can be expected to occur sooner after such sudden improvements than in cases where the process of amelioration was a gradual one.

Definitive or transitory improvements occur spontaneously, or in connection with psychic influences or factors such as a transfer to another place, a release, a visitor, a curl paper, even after a chloroform-narcosis (Näcke and Steinitz).[5] These improvements occur significantly less frequently in the chronic conditions than in the acute, but are not completely absent from the former.

It is almost a rule that chronically agitated cases become calmer as the years pass. This process can come about in various ways. Many become truly better inasmuch as they have fewer hallucinations and delusions. In others, the quieting down really equals deterioration since the patients are no longer capable of acting consistently with their delusional ideas. The affects which are connected with these morbid manifestations lose their intensity in different ways: partly, as in the healthy because one eventually gets used to unpleasantness and discomfort, but partly also because they are simply split off and dissociated. Thus after many years, some patients may again be able to adapt to reality in some fashion. Occasionally, they can even become employable outside the hospital without having undergone any perceptible intellectual improvement.

Concerning the qualitative course of the schizophrenic symptomatology, at the present time only the following can be said: although the addition or disappearance of symptoms cannot be excluded in any case, the majority of patients maintain patterns which are fairly consistent and typical during the entire course of the disease. The catatonics exhibit catatonic symptoms in the acute as well as in the chronic stages of the disease. The hallucinations and delusions are constantly in the foreground of the paranoid picture. Acute phases of the disease tend to facilitate the development of the affective disturbances and twilight states.

However, changes in any directions are not at all rare. Catatonic or paranoid symptoms can disappear so that an initially catatonic or paranoid patient may later on exhibit symptoms of simple hebephrenia. In the course of relapses, hebephrenic excitements of various kinds are combined with catatonic symptoms.[6]

5. I, myself have performed many chloroform-narcoses without ever seeing such effects.

6. For example, one of our patients has been in Burgholzli for five years. He was admitted as a hebephrenic, listed as a paranoid, and transferred to a sanitarium as a catatonic. All three "diagnoses" were entirely justified.

Marked deterioration is usually indicated by chronic catatonic symptoms. Unfortunately, we are far from being able to recognize and predict the outcome in all these cases.

In such transformations from one group to another, we are often merely dealing with variations of intensity. The cases of all three groups appear very similar to each other during periods of remission because then only the most general symptoms are to be observed. Naturally, the "cured" catatonic does not have any more manifest catatonic symptoms than does the hebephrenic. Conversely, there are numerous mild catatonics whose symptoms are so inconspicuous that we reckon them as paranoids until an aggravation of their situation teaches us better. Nonetheless, the majority of such cases have right from the start something peculiarly rigid, physically and psychically less flexible than the true paranoid so that one can suspect at least what the future development will be.

B. The Onset of the Disease

The onset of schizophrenia is usually an insidious one, though the relatives of the patients generally insist that it first started acutely. To be sure, an hallucinatory or catatonic state may break out at any time or at any moment for that matter. Kahlbaum's patient suddenly became cataleptic while making a purchase in a bakery. However, whenever we have a thorough case history, it is an exception if we are not able to detect the previous, earlier signs of disease whether it be nervous symptoms, character changes, or even direct overt schizophrenic manifestations. It is certainly difficult to evaluate personality changes when they do not point directly to the disease, or when the later manifest illness did not evolve from this character. For example, throughout her entire school career a young girl exhibited only average scholarship with the exception of brilliant work in music. Suddenly, immediately after the onset of puberty, she developed a passionate interest in her studies, an energy and drive which was totally unknown to her before, until an abruptly starting catatonic delirium ushered in the subsequent deterioration. Yet, it is impossible to say whether the personality changes had already belonged to the disease picture itself or not.

Far more frequently, the differentiation of schizophrenic characteristics from what might be called "original" peculiarities makes for unsurmountable difficulties. Yet there are early character anomalies which can be demonstrated by careful case histories in more than half the individuals who later become schizophrenic: the tendency to seclusion, withdrawal, together with moderate or severe degrees of irritability. They already stood out as children because they were unable to play with others and followed their own ways instead. It is certain that many a schizophrenia can be traced back into the early years of the patient's life, and many manifest illnesses are simply intensifications of an already existing character. It seems probable to me that these autistic character anomalies constitute the first symptoms of the disease and are not merely expressions of a disposition to the disease. The peculiar intellectual characteristics often induce the comrades of these candidates for schizophrenia to regard them as "crazy" at a rather early stage. All ten of my own school comrades who later became schizophrenics, were quite different from the other boys.

If we disregarded the peculiar personality characteristics, the onset of the disease is easily recognized when real schizophrenic, or at least psychotic, phenomena appear. Often, however, not even the most searching examination by an expert succeeds in demonstrating the presence of any specific symptoms in those early years. As a rule, the relatives do not see or do not want to see the first and early signs of mental illness; and they often prevent us from making a correct diagnosis during a consultation.

Thus when we speak of the initial symptoms of schizophrenia, we must limit ourselves to the first symptoms which come to notice. All too often we do not know the first real manifestations.[7]

As far as we know, any symptom may initiate the disease. Adhering to older concepts, Kahlbaum thought that catatonia usually began with a melancholia. But in his twenty-two case histories, we can only find one which suggests a melancholia. To be sure, he does say: "While it is obvious in these cycles of three main phases that melancholia represents the first developmental stage and that mania constitutes the acme, it can be debated where *attonita* should be placed."[8] That very word, "obviously" reveals in the most glaring manner how a preconceived construct can distort the clarity of thought of even this pioneer of psychiatry.

Relatives rarely note the real intellectual disturbance although it is often far advanced by the time the patient is brought to the hospital. Entirely "crazy" acts in the midst of normal behavior are much more striking but also more easily forgotten if the patient does not become more severely ill soon after. A young soldier on border patrol had to present his rifle to his Major for inspection. The soldier assumed a very hostile and threatening attitude saying: "As long as I'm alive, I will not

---

7. We do not speak of "prodromes." If one wishes one can generally isolate or separate the prodromals of an acute attack and the intercurrent manifestations from the full-blown picture. However, for myself, I cannot conceive of prodromes of any disease. What is meant are the first symptoms which one is able to interpret correctly.

8. Kahlbaum, 345, p. 29.

give up my rifle." It was only six years later that a litigious schizophrenia first became manifest in this soldier (Yennacopoulos).

The character anomalies which introduce the disease soon after puberty can throw into relief the most varied aspects of the schizophrenic personality. The inconstancy and irritability often precede by many years the more definite and more significant symptoms. Then also such manifestations may be entirely transitory, e.g., come and go with the menstrual periods.

Aside from the character abnormalities, hysterical and neurasthenic symptoms are by far the most common precursors of overt mental illness. Many schizophrenics, particularly young women, wander for years from one doctor to another with these diagnoses. The not unusual periods of improvement in such cases also seem to confirm the diagnosis of a neurosis.

Schott (666) described such a case to which Neisser[9] remarked: "By means of case histories it is very interesting to follow the genesis of the symptoms which initially are rather mild and inconspicuous but gradually take on increasingly odd, bizarre, and psychotic qualities, transforming the patient's behavior until it is ever more rigid, stubborn, and negativistic." In such cases we cannot assume that the "neurasthenia" developed into schizophrenia, but rather that in the beginning stages of schizophrenia, neurasthenic symptoms dominated the picture.

These people often struggle against their disease for years before they finally succumb to the affective paralysis or hallucinatory conditions. To take one example, students may feel incapable of doing mental work. Night after night they will drive themselves to do such work, trying all sorts of methods, such as taking evening walks, tea, coffee, gymnastics, and whatever else may come to their mind. As a result their peculiarities are thought to be youthful foolishness while the patients themselves suffer deeply from the difficulties of their situation.

Among the most common neurasthenic symptoms are headaches. Although these headaches come and go, they are far less affected by psychic influences than those of the hysteric. In any case, there is no neurasthenic symptom which cannot appear in schizophrenia; among others, we find fatigue during physical or mental effort and severe thinking disturbances which are experienced as particularly unpleasant.

Before the actual onset of the disease, the patients frequently complain about disturbing dreams which keep haunting them during their waking hours. Obsessive and compulsive ideas frequently precede all other manifestations by many years. However, they should not be in-

---

9. In Mendel's Jahresbericht 1905, p. 1041.

cluded here since they may be of neurasthenic as well as of schizophrenic origin.

The fundamental affective symptoms often dominate the picture from the very start, in that the patients become increasingly indifferent and apathetic. The essentially different manic and melancholic moodiness is not seen as often at the onset of this disease as the theories of "secondary" psychoses would lead us to expect. Nevertheless, chronic as well as acute depressions are found more frequently in the beginning of an outspoken illness than any other syndromes.

The most conspicuous symptoms are the catatonic manifestations of chronic, and even more frequently, of acute catatonic states, whereas paranoid symptoms may often remain concealed for years until they accidentally become manifest.

When the physical complaints constitute the first symptoms they can be related to the psychosis only after the psychosis has become overt. All kinds of episodes (fainting, cramps, etc.) occur while the patients are apparently in good health. However, the latter symptoms probably occur more frequently in the course of the manifest psychosis than in its latent phases.

C. The Termination of the Disease

1. Death

Schizophrenia as such leads to death in hardly more than one per cent of all institutionalized patients. The immediate causes may be cerebral pressure due to cerebral edema or increased cerebro-spinal fluid; metabolic disturbances (including auto-intoxications) and cerebral paralysis as seen in catatonic or epileptiform attacks. All these are more frequent in the acute states than in the chronic.

Lethal terminations as indirect consequences of the psychosis are much more common: refusal of food, intentional or unintentional injuries,[10] suicide, tuberculosis[11] and other diseases resulting from unhygienic ways of life. Thus, the mortality rate of schizophrenics is somewhat higher than that of the general population. Among the patients at Rheinau we find a ratio of about 6.8 : 5.0[12]

---

10. It is noteworthy that the tendency toward infection is quite low in chronic cases, while it may be increased in the acute confusional states.

11. The number of hospitalized schizophrenics who die from tuberculosis is not greater than that in the general population. According to many authorities, tuberculosis appears to be an especially frequent complication of dementia praecox.

12. Kerner, Mortalität der Dementia praecox. Psych.-neur. Wochenschrift, 1910/11.

2. Degree of Deterioration and Possibilities of Cure

In order to arrive at a clear conception of what finally happens to those cases which survive the acute stages, it is necessary to examine the concept of "cure." Kraepelin released many of his patients as cured since a clear concept of cure demands a *restitutio ad integrum* be demonstrated. None of these cases were considered as cured by Aschaffenburg, who saw the same patients.

To begin with, practical[13] and theoretical cures should not be equated. An individual who can again support himself outside an institution can be considered cured in a certain sense. However, such individuals may retain a number of peculiarities and sensitivities resulting from the disease. From a scientific standpoint, one cannot call them cured since a clear concept of cure demands a *restitutio ad integrum* or at least the *status quo ante*.[14]

As soon as we no longer define cure exclusively in terms of restitution to the previous condition, it becomes a purely arbitrary procedure at what point and number of residual symptoms we may choose to speak of "cure." If social restitution constitutes our criterion, we have to consider some factors which lie beyond the patient's control.

A farm laborer with evidences of considerable defect may still be capable of working and supporting himself whereas even a tiny psychic scar may prevent a great merchant or banker from resuming his business. Furthermore, the degree of sensitivity of the patient's relatives will often determine whether he is cured or not. Such a conception of cure cannot be applied in pathology. Apart from the real cures, if there are such, social cures include the majority of improved cases.

But we also encounter difficulties with the theoretically accurate concept of cure, as a restitution to the previous condition. The episode which led to the patients' admission to the hospital is rarely the real beginning of the disease which had already begun to develop furtively a long time before; but the first indications were mistaken for character peculiarities. Not all schizophrenic twilight states inevitably entail worsening of the patient's status; restitution to the condition preceding the episode occurs quite frequently. But this process does not affect the malady which originally caused the patient's shyness, seclusiveness and irritable instability. It is often impossible to take as point of comparison

---

13. According to E. Meyer: "social cure."

14. I know very well that even the healing of a wound leaves a scar behind, and that one speaks of a "healed amputation." But a scar which interferes with the function of the organ is considered a defect; and the "healed amputation" assumes a concept of cure which must be distinguished clearly from what the psychopathologists call "healing with defect."

the individual's condition before the onset of the disease because schizophrenia begins surreptitiously at the time of the most rapid psychic transformation or even in early childhood. Once again we are confronted with that difficult question: "What is a peculiarity of character and what is a schizophrenic symptom?"

In individual cases the substantiation of cure is dependent on the psychiatrist's psychological skill and, above all, on the amount of time at his disposal to examine and observe the patient before his release. Good mental health cannot be directly diagnosed; we assume it when we find no signs of disease inspite of thorough examinations. The physician who has no time to examine his patients carefully finds many who are cured who would be considered as merely improved by another physician.

In view of my own experience, I agree completely with Aschaffenburg and Ilberg. *As yet I have never released a schizophrenic in whom I could not still see distinct signs of the disease; indeed there are very few in whom one would have to search for such signs.* Also, when these released patients were seen in the course of subsequent examinations, which of necessity were brief, we never found complete restitution. Indeed, I must add that reports of clergymen and relatives, from whom we always try to obtain information after a certain period of time has elapsed, speak only occasionally of a true cure although the majority of the released individuals are employed or employable. I have never yet seen really cured patients who had been released as "cured" from other institutions.

In this respect one must never rely on the judgment of the laity who may have observed no symptoms. I cannot understand how Strohmayer ever arrived at the erroneous conclusion that affective deterioration is usually detected by ordinary lay people. Some time ago, I failed to make the diagnosis of schizophrenia in two educated and intelligent families because I believed the relatives who claimed that the patients (women) were still very sensitive and perceptive. A few days later, one of these two patients very calmly wanted to shoot her husband; she had no, or only negative feelings for her children. In the light of this we can understand when an ordinary man considers his wife as perfectly well although she does not speak, will not eat spontaneously, and wallows in her own filth in her bed. This experience of Aschaffenburg, I can easily match by similar ones from my own.

I know schizophrenics who, after their illness, have conducted and developed complicated business. I know one who, after two catatonic twilight states about seven years apart, is still able to teach, to do independent scientific work, and to maintain an international reputation in his specialty. One of our catatonics was later able to make an important name for himself as a poet. Schreber became a presiding judge after his first attack. One of Hess' (301) heboidophrenic patients was a university professor. The composer Schumann and the poet Scheffel were schizophrenics. In the thirteen years during which I acted as an examiner on the State Board of Medical Examiners, I have had to pass many a schizophrenic medical school graduate, some of them with excellent grades. These few examples may serve to illustrate that we do not ignore the favorable cases.

There are even patients who seem to be better after an acute exacerbation than they were before. The narrowing down of interests can make a schizophrenic a smoothly working automaton. Persons with few emotional needs may find such quiet companions ideal marriage partners. Two of these "cured" patients seemed to be even livelier and more alert than they had been before their illness. A young, rather withdrawn girl of good family who had lived in complete dependence on her mother, became more independent, self-reliant, and happy after having suffered from catatonia. An educated man spoke willingly about his previous illness; it seemed that he had abreacted his complexes which had formerly made of him an autistic oddity; and now he was invigorated, friendly, and approachable.[15] Another patient had always been seclusive, moody and ill-humored. After a severe, melancholic, catatonic attack when he was about thirty years old, he could at least laugh occasionally.[16]

An often discussed criterion of cure is that of the patients' insight into the nature of their illness. People who speak of their delusions and their weird behavior during the attack as being pathological phenomena, who understand that they had to be handled the way they were, and are even grateful to the doctor or hospital—these people are not without reason easily considered as cured; whereas the opposite is thought of as being a rather certain sign of continuing disease. But one must recall, that many schizophrenics have keen feelings of illness even during slight exacerbations but they do not always locate the illness where the observer sees it to be. They realize, for example, the poor state of their "nerves," the senselessness of their behavior, but they insist that both are quite understandable reactions to stimuli and irritations of their environment. Occasionally, a schizophrenic physician will make the correct diagnosis on himself. Naturally, these people

15. Although he had regained his official and social positions, he still insisted that a snake had been placed in his room by the doctor for experimental purposes.

16. Wille describes six cases in whom the disease seems to have had a favorable influence.

have their "insight" also during periods of remission, but it is often completely worthless. Even true insight may be distinctly pathological, because one gets the impression that only one part of the patient's psyche understands what is going on. Often the patients talk about rectified delusions as if they had happened, not to them, but to somebody else; the connection between their pathological experiences and their present ego is lacking. This situation can become particularly clear when one is able to contrast such cases with, for example, a recovered melancholic patient. In the latter instance we have a free discussion and description with reproduction of the feelings and emotions of those moments of their illness; in schizophrenics, on the other hand, we get a labored, strained presentation of events and experiences which are termed delusional with a few scanty words or phrases and accompanied by an affect which hardly corresponds to the situation of a human being saved from a delusional world. The previously mentioned man, "improved by disease," spoke of his acute attack as if it had been an especially successful experience or adventure. It is a question then of a "cold intellectual" insight (Jung) which does not influence the emotional life of the patient, or at least very little. We also saw above that we have rarely, if ever, been able to substantiate the evidence of a full, complete rectification of schizophrenic delusional ideas.

Therefore, we do not speak of *cure but of far-reaching improvements* and differentiate them from the severe deteriorations (in which the patient is wholly incapable of social relations) and from the mild deteriorations which include all the rest of the cases between the two extremes.

If we give actual figures for these various categories, we must first warn against attributing to them any great importance or value; not merely because the subjective nature of the criteria lowers their objective significance, but even more because of the circumstance that the varying conditions of admission and release for each institution determine the average prognosis of the disease in that institution. Thus, for example, one hospital has a long waiting list; therefore far fewer of the milder cases are apt to be admitted; that is, there will be fewer favorable cases admitted than in those hospitals where there may be a bed available for everyone for whom admission is desired. Any figures then will serve to estimate not schizophrenia, as such, but the schizophrenics admitted to any given hospital. The innumerable patients, who never get inside a hospital and who would, of course, very markedly improve the over-all prognosis, escape completely from these figures.

As a criterion of the severity of the deterioration, I take the individual's capacity for carrying on his vocation, or his ability to support himself outside a hospital. Those capable of earning a living, I call cases of "mild deterioration"; those completely incapable of social living are called "severe deterioration"; the intermediary types who do not fit into either of these two categories are placed as "medium deterioration." This criterion depends of course on the patient's vocation and on other external circumstances, yet it makes for a certain degree of understanding. Thus, we find the following figures in our group of 515 cases in the Burgholzli Hospital (between 1898—1905):

After the First Episode

Mild Deterioration	Medium Deterioration	Severe Deterioration
307 (60%)	92 (18%)	116 (22%)

Naturally, these results get considerably worse with time. Yet few of those with a good remission, have had to be returned to the hospital for permanent commitment because of a later exacerbation of the disease.

The over-all prognoses of the individual groups vary in the following way: Kraepelin claims an extensive improvement in 8% of his hebephrenics of whom he says, "One is perhaps justified in speaking of a cure"; while about 17% remain at the level of moderate dementia. He estimates that of the catatonics, 13% show apparent cures, with another 20% that show "remissions" persisting for so long that they are comparable to cures. Of the paranoids, he merely indicates that only "in a very small number of cases" could one speak of extensive improvement.

Zablocka, using our material, found:

Group	Deterioration		
	Mild	Medium	Severe
Paranoid	65*	16	19
Catatonic	57	13	30
Hebephrenic	58	22	20

*Figures are in percentages.

In terms of our criterion, it is apparent that the paranoid, whose ability to work is least affected, has the best prognosis. That the hebephrenic does not have any better prospects is partly due to the definition which lays particular emphasis on the deterioration, and partly because hebephrenia breaks out far more commonly in an age group in which the individual has not yet fully developed his social capacities. The latter factor also holds true for the catatonic. But catatonia is also the expression of a most intensive disease process of the brain which must do the greatest damage to these same social capacities. Yet, it is noteworthy how small the differences really are.

However, other more important factors than those already mentioned above may determine the relationship between the form of the disease and its outcome; the difference between the sexes is particularly striking.

	Mild Deterioration		Moderate Deterioration		Severe Deterioration	
	Male	Female	Male	Female	Male	Female
Paranoid	78*	51	6	27	16	22
Catatonic	54	59	9	18	38	23
Hebephrenic	56	61	22	20	21	19

*Figures are in percentages.

Perhaps the differences in working conditions and nutritional needs between the sexes is of some significance.

The sex difference in the outcome of catatonia must recall to us that women are more inclined to develop catatonic symptoms than are men; it seems that in women the catatonic symptoms are present in milder cases of the disease. The ratio between the sexes remains rather constant even if one places in one group all the cases with catatonic symptoms, and in another group all cases without such symptoms, disregarding the particular form of disease involved:

	Mild Deterioration		Medium Deterioration		Severe Deterioration	
	With Catatonic Symptoms	Without Catatonic Symptoms	With Catatonic Symptoms	Without Catatonic Symptoms	With Catatonic Symptoms	Without Catatonic Symptoms
Men	56*	67	12	17	32	16
Women	58	57	20	22	22	21
Total	57	63	17	19	18	26

*Figures are in percentages.

There remains one group of paranoids who, as far as their delusions and hallucinations go, would not offer a very good prognosis, but they must be considered as milder cases of the disease because they do not lose their grip on things nor do they really deteriorate. They do not become confused in speech, nor autistic in their behavior; they maintain contact with their environment; in short, they are very similar to the paranoiacs. Even their delusions do not become very senseless. They do not exhibit any catatonic symptoms; manic and depressive attacks are almost wholly lacking. Yet, on the other hand, hallucinatory confusional states do make their appearance. Except during acute thrusts, many of these patients are perfectly capable of working although it is true, they are rarely able to remain for long in any one place. Unfortunately, in the first years of their disease, they appear so much like those forms which later become quite deteriorated that we are unable to separate them at this time from these other forms either theoretically or practically. For the most part, they are individuals who become ill after their thirtieth year. I also prefer to include in this group, Kraepelin's pre-senile delusions of prejudice and injury. Yet some psychoses of the period of puberty may take the same course.

Dementia paranoides is one other form with a rather special prognosis; but this form, also, has no clear-cut boundaries which could be used to separate it from the other types of schizophrenic manifestations.

As yet we have not discovered any correlation between the initial disease symptoms and the severity of the outcome of the illness (Zablocka, Bleuler).

On the other hand, the kind of attack which brings the patient to the hospital has some bearing on the average estimate of the severity of the eventual outcome. It lies in the very nature of the disease that patients with quite acute attacks have a very good possibility of coming out of them with only a mild degree of deterioration. But if in such cases the disease continues to advance, there is then a tendency for it to go rather far. We include here those patients with manic-depressive syndromes who either have relatively good intervals between episodes, or who may belong to some of the worse cases of deterioration in our mental institutions.

For the rest, the evident connections between the admission status and the severity of the outcome are based on reasons lying outside the disease itself. It is the acute syndrome which makes for the earliest hospitalization whether the condition reached by the patient be mild or severe. The chronic cases, particularly the simple deteriorated patients, only come to the hospital when the degree of deterioration makes it necessary. Thus right off, these cases are a selection of the severely ill. Therefore of the patients admitted in manic-like attacks, we release 83%; of the deteriorated (on admission) only 33%, in a working capacity.

We cannot check with the rather one-sided hospital material whether the acuteness of the disease attack has any relation to the severity of the end-state, entirely aside from the fact that an acute syndrome and a real advance of the illness are two different things, although it is not always easy to differentiate them.

The influence of age can only be demonstrated insofar as those forms which, despite powerful delusions, do not lose control of their behavior, are somewhat more frequently manifest after the age of thirty.[17]

The physical condition of the patient at the time of first falling ill appears to be irrelevant for our question in spite of the fact that other schools include the cases of amentia. At the present time, not much more can be said for the other physical symptoms of the disease. Only the pupillary differences have given us any indication of a somewhat, although only slightly, poorer average prognosis, but we used our own far too meager material.

In regard to the intelligence, we can merely say that, naturally, those patients in whom a schizophrenia is added to their already existent, congenital, mental defect, remain more readily confined to hospitals than those individuals with originally good intelligence. There is no proof of greater resistance to schizophrenia either in the mentally defective or in the intelligent.

On the other hand, as far as our own material goes, the abnormal characters have a far poorer outcome than do others. This observation, however, does not mean very much so long as under the term, "abnormal characters," various deviations from a type and even latent schizophrenia are included.

We would have expected that the causes of the disease would have some bearing on the prognosis; one could assume that patients whose illness was apparently released by psychic shock would find it less difficult to regain their equilibrium; for example, a patient in a twilight state almost always returns to his previous condition. Our statistics, however, show no connection between the disease outcome and our present concepts of either physical or psychic causes.

The fact that the not at all rare schizophrenics who are brought to the hospital because of alcoholism do not have a particularly poor prognosis, deserves special mention. Their tendency to keep to themselves protects them somewhat from temptation to indulge; their autism makes them much less sensitive to the temptations as well as the raillery of society.

The tendency to recidives is recognizable when one has been able to establish that one is dealing with the manic-depressive type of this disease. As for the rest, investigation of every possible factor which could be considered to be of significance in the recidivistic patients gives quite the same figures as for the non-recidivists.

---

17. According to Herzer, the sickness of older people has a better prognosis (cf. Lugaro).

D. The End States of the Disease

In view of the fact that severe schizophrenics almost never show complete cessation of the process, and that in the milder cases one can never be certain that an aggravation may not come about, the usual term, "end-state," must be taken with a grain of salt. The majority of the terminal conditions escape our observation. The individuals live outside the hospitals; they are often considered as healthy, although perhaps as rather peevish, stubborn, whimsical, sad or stupid, etc. Many of these people have merely lowered the level of aspirations with regard to their accomplishments and claims on the world. The high-school teacher may vegetate quietly in a grade school. The technically educated student does manual labor. The college graduate who once had such brilliant prospects manages to get along as a gardner. The excellent mechanic is satisfied to help his wife in her sewing. Many hold jobs which do not require any responsibility although they are steady, careful, and precise workers. On a still lower social level, these people become migrant workers, odd job men, vagrants, hoboes, habitual criminals (usually involving minor offenses).

Those who remain in our hospitals exhibit the same characteristics but more prominently. What usually makes it impossible for these patients to live in freedom outside a hospital are the accessory symptoms: the catatonic manifestations, among which negativism in particular is as frequent as it is unpleasant; the delusions and hallucinations with their frequent agitations and secondary conflicts with the environment.

Even the severe end-states show an infinite number of variations which cannot be separated from each other, as far as we now know. Kraepelin has given the best description of these end-conditions of the disease in which he emphasizes nine main types:

1. "Cure."

2. "Cure with defect" (healing with scarring); that is improvement (which is probably the most frequent outcome).

3. Simple deterioration (simple dementia).

4. "Imbecility" with confusion of speech. This picture develops rather rapidly after an initial depression and then remains stationary for a long time. Delusions never fail to appear. Hallucinations are present at least in the beginning.[18] After a long time, even this form can still go on to simple dementia. It is not a very frequent form of the disease.

5. Far more frequently, the disease terminates in hallucinatory de-

18. The course of the disease does not always follow the Kraepelinian outline of depression, rapid development of speech confusion, then a long stationary period.

terioration. The delusions and hallucinations persist in a rather uniform, stable fashion, often with periodic aggravations, but they do not gain any further influence over thought and actions. The patients remain consistently lucid and orderly in behavior.

6. In a smaller number of cases, the delusions advance and develop continually without, however, attaining the severe forms of dementia (deterioration). The delusional ideas are elaborated slowly, and gradually become more and more fragmented. Without exception they are delusions of physical influence and control, etc., often accompanied by ideas of grandeur. Kraepelin's term, "hallucinatory insanity," seems the most appropriate.

7. Dementia paranoides.

8. Flighty, silly deterioration (or dementia). "It is dominated, aside from the manifestations of a deep-seated psychic weakness, by residues of the disease which correspond somewhat to those of a catatonic excitement." In the manneristic types, the eccentricities in the form of mannerisms, and the stereotyped movements occupy the foreground of the picture; in the agitated types, there is also a special impulsivity besides the monotonous, more or less uniform, compulsion to move. Common to both types are the confusion and fragmentation of speech and the confused behavior and actions.

9. The most extensive form is that of the dull, apathetic deterioration (or dementia). Alongside of extreme apathy and dullness, we also meet here with the remains of negativism and of command-automatism. "On the one hand these factors produce the rigid inaccessibility, and on the other hand the dull, indifferent willessness which give the large mental institutions of the custodial type their particular stamp. Many of these patients can still be quite useful as mechanical workers."

"Both last mentioned forms of deterioration seem to constitute distinct and terminal states, and not merely stages of development of the same disease process. It seems to me that they do not pass over into one another, but, when once established, continue in this path unchanged to the end of the patient's life" (Kraepelin). I believe that I also have been able to demonstrate that these two forms do not alternate in one and the same patient. Yet there are so many intermediary forms in the manifestations of the severest degrees of deterioration (dementia) that I am not yet absolutely convinced of the correctness of Kraepelin's view.

The Question of Heredity

Up till the present no attempt has been made to study the course of the disease or the predisposition to this disease beyond the individual patient himself. Investigations in heredity always start from the individual patient and work backwards to his antecedents. It would be interesting, for once, to pursue the task by investigating the fate of the descendents of the patients, instead of their antecedents. The 647 patients studied by Wolfsohn had at the time of their hospital admissions, 404 children of whom 10% were suffering from mental or nervous diseases: 11 were mental defectives, 11 were "mentally ill," 14 were considered nervous, 2 were epileptic, 1 was a deaf-mute, 1 committed suicide. Of course, most of the children were not yet beyond the age when schizophrenia appears. Should these figures be substantiated on far larger material they would need to be given further attention.

SECTION IV

SCHIZOPHRENIA IN CONJUNCTION WITH OTHER PSYCHOSES

A. Schizophrenia may develop in individuals who are congenital mental defectives (propfhebephrenia). In such cases the symptoms of both diseases add up and it requires a great deal of patience on the part of both physician and patient to determine to which disease the various manifestations actually belong. With some of the symptoms this is often utterly impossible. Thus cases of severe (congenital) dementia may show a marked obscurity of concepts which, at least at present, cannot be differentiated from the schizophrenic obscurity of ideas. Otherwise, these cases do not present any unexpected symptoms; mild and severe forms can be observed side by side.

As with other types of mental deficiency, schizophrenia may also appear in conjunction with cretinism, regardless of whether the cretinism is a total one or merely restricted to the physical aspects. In such an event, also, the disease does not show any extraordinary features.

B. With respect to organic brain diseases, the different forms of cerebral atrophy due to advancing age very often complicate the clinical picture of schizophrenia; it is certainly not the rule that senile dementia occurs to any marked degree in our old schizophrenic patients. In this particular complication, too, the symptoms of both diseases add up in a very distinctive fashion. Disturbances of recent memories, of orientation, and poor perception are added to the schizophrenic deterioration already present. If it is still present, the energy invested in delusions and actions seems to decrease. The hallucinations do not necessarily disappear; sometimes, however, senile hallucinatory deliria occur. The only remarkable feature is the manifestation of affects. In some of these cases hardly any response can be obtained from the patients; they vegetate, indifferent to their surroundings. Sometimes, however, the organic psychosis releases some of the affects; then the patients become again somewhat more approachable.

Besides these cases there are others of slowly progressing senile dementia that show uniform catatonic symptoms up to the very end, mostly coupled with some form of agitation. Thus we have a woman patient who verbigerates constantly like a schizophrenic, who is noisy and filthy and rather unconcerned about her environment. Another patient is at first "melancholic" but in a strikingly rigid way as far as feelings are concerned; all her responses are monotonous and meager. She continues to have automatic suicidal impulses, even after the affect seems to have exhausted itself; she makes violent attempts to escape every time a door opens; she constantly whispers to herself stereotyped fragments of her former complaints. A third patient who is mildly depressed shows, besides the superficial affect, completely unmotivated changes in mood and exaggerated hysteriform symptoms. A fourth patient struggles continually to get by the doors, is in constant motion and exhibits a peculiar negativism which may be compared to nihilism in that the patient expresses everything in the negative. It is utterly impossible to establish any affective rapport with her. In all these cases, the faculty of orientation has been preserved. There are no obvious disturbances of memory through many years. A diagnosis of senile dementia is usually made at the onset, although one may not be aware of the exact reason for it. Autopsy results, however, confirm this impression. The combined disease is usually observed in the fifth or sixth decade. Even prior to their recent illness, these people were not quite like all the others, but in many cases it is not possible to ascertain the presence of schizophrenia by questioning. It may well be that here, too, we are always dealing with latent schizophrenia which only becomes manifest with the onset of cerebral atrophy. As yet, we have been unsuccessful in our efforts to obtain more precise analyses, which would throw light on this question, from these very resistant patients.

In conjunction with senile dementia, or without it, focal phenomena may naturally appear as consequences of apoplexies or cerebral softenings. Of these phenomena, we are interested only in the aphasic disturbances, inasmuch as they may cause simulated mutism and since particularly paraphasia may complicate schizophrenic speech disorders. However, closer observation enables us to differentiate the two symptoms.

The complications in cerebral tumors (and other localized brain diseases) demand special study for which we do not as yet have sufficient material. Cerebral tumors are occasionally accompanied by catatonic symptoms. If a clinical catatonic should subsequently develop symptoms of brain tumor, we are as yet unable to determine whether the catatonia was complicated by the tumor, or whether the tumor primarily induced the catatonic symptoms. However, in cases where the course of the psychosis does not correspond to that of the tumor as, for example, in the case of a schizophrenia of many years' duration accompanied by a rapidly growing glioma one knows very well what the real state of affairs is.

Many attempts have been made to find combinations of psychoses (which we now consider to be schizophrenia) with general paresis, and a number of such instances were discovered, although they are great rarities (Joffroy and Gombault). So far, the rarity of this particular combination can be explained only by suppositions, e. g., paresis is "the disease of the healthy brain." I can only add to this that in our patients, perhaps, syphilis is not very common either. In any event I cannot recall a single case of syphilitic schizophrenia in all my twenty-seven years of psychiatric practice (auto-erotism!), although I am aware that such instances have been found elsewhere in recent years.

Regarding the symptomatology in the combination of schizophrenia and paresis, nothing can be learned from the literature on the subject. I myself have observed closely only one single case[1] and it was striking how rapidly the patient deteriorated although it was still possible to establish some fairly good rapport with her. It was impossible to get her to do any work; she kept her hands constantly in her mouth and she became unclean, although there was no evidence of paralysis or catatonic conditions which could satisfactorily explain this manifestation. The nursing personnel favored a diagnosis of paresis because of the patient's lack of orientation and poor memory. The medical examinations during which she pulled herself together revealed no defect of memory, or orientation; the physical signs of paresis were not sufficiently marked to justify the diagnosis. On the other hand, the complexes were as predominantly in the foreground as in a schizophrenic. Death through marasmus followed after three years of hospitalization. Autopsy revealed an early, but definite paresis and the case history to which subsequently more details were added established, with certainty, a schizophrenia dating back more than ten years.

The unstable schizophrenic can easily turn into an alcoholic. Nearly ten per cent of our alcoholics are also schizophrenics. The characteristics of this combination are described in the following chapter.

In such cases, alcoholism can probably be considered as a symptom of schizophrenia. I have not yet seen a case where the schizophrenia appeared subsequent to alcoholism.

Combinations of schizophrenia with melancholia and mania or with manic-depressive psychosis have not yet been demonstrated with any certainty. Manic and melancholic symptoms are so common in our patients that we must assume that they are usually released by the disease process itself, and thus are part of the schizophrenia. However, real

1. I have rarely been able to make the diagnosis of this combination.

melancholic depressions are not common in patients who are paranoid from the start and mania is so infrequent that it is considered a rarity. One would rather be inclined to regard such an instance as a complication. Those cases, which follow the pattern of cyclic psychoses or which show a certain periodicity, are probably for the most part mixed forms of manic-depressive psychosis and schizophrenia. In individuals who are accordingly disposed, we may also be dealing with manic-depressive attacks released by schizophrenia. We will especially tend to this assumption in cases where the deterioration, even after a number of severe episodes, remains rather slight, which is, however, seldom the case. The verification of a manic-depressive heredity increases this probability in some instances. Since, however, all manic-depressive symptoms can also occur in schizophrenia, the disease picture is not markedly altered by such complications, as far as our present knowledge goes.

The question as to whether there exists a combination of schizophrenia with epilepsy is even more difficult to answer.

Since epileptic attacks are rather frequent in schizophrenia, we must not consider them from the start as complications of both diseases, even though earlier literature emphasized the complications of "paranoia with epilepsy." Ever since we have had at our command more thoroughgoing methods of diagnosis, I have not seen a single case in which such a complication seemed likely. I must, therefore, leave it to further studies to investigate the existence and perhaps the symptomatology of such cases. The situation is made diagnostically more difficult by the fact that the schizophrenic blocking of affects and the epileptic excess of emotion may compensate each other up to a certain degree (Morawitz).

The question as to whether schizophrenia can appear in conjunction with hysteria cannot be answered as long as we are familiar only with the secondary symptoms and not the fundamental processes of both diseases. Schizophrenic cerebral changes are, indeed, some of the most frequent predisposing causes of hysterical symptoms; hence, the many hysterical paranoias and hysterio-degenerative diseases, which were classified in a purely arbitrary manner by various authors. Currently, we need only remember that every hysterical symptom may also originate on a schizophrenic basis.

This also applies to all those manifestations which used to be characterized by the term, "neurasthenia" (including obsessive-compulsive ideas, etc.)

In this sense we also cannot speak of a combination of paranoia and schizophrenia because positive symptoms of paranoia can also appear in schizophrenia. At present, therefore, we call delusional systems without schizophrenic symptoms, paranoia, whereas all others must be termed schizophrenic.

We still have to mention fever deliria. Every psychiatrist has seen schizophrenic patients in whom fever deliria were altered by the addition of schizophrenic, particularly, catatonic symptoms. At times, however, one can also detect catatonic signs, particularly catalepsy and verbigeration, in fever deliriants in whom neither prior nor later the presence of schizophrenia could be established. One always feels that these symptoms are part of the delirium. However, it must be remembered that illnesses accompanied by high fevers often make manifest or even cause schizophrenia. Should it then not also be conceivable that a latent catatonia becomes manifest for once, during a fever delirium?

SECTION V

THE CONCEPT OF DISEASE

Dementia praecox comprises the majority of psychoses heretofore designated as functional. This very idea implies a special systematic conception of mental diseases. Therefore, it is not possible to discuss this conception without a careful consideration of other ideas as to the nature of diseases.

Prior to Kraepelin, only clinical pictures or syndromes were differentiated in this great group of psychoses. Dementia praecox should be considered a disease in Kahlbaum's sense of the term. Dementia praecox basically differs from "acute hallucinatory insanity," "mania," and a "melancholia" (in the pre-Kraepelinian sense); from an "acute paranoia," or an "amentia" of the Viennese school. One cannot ask whether a specific case is an acute paranoia or a schizophrenia (the one does not exclude the other), any more than there can be any question as to whether a disease exhibiting edema is anasarca or nephritis. Not only the names but the entire concepts of anasarca (of the old medical authorities), of acute paranoia, of states of confusion were arbitrarily constructed by this or that observer, depending on which symptom he considered the most striking one. On this basis an actual delineation of such clinical pictures of disease is impossible. Aside from symptoms such as confusion or paranoid disturbance of intelligence, we find in every case still other manifestations of varying frequency and intensity. If such "secondary" symptoms are especially pronounced or if the "cardinal" symptoms recede into the background, then the designation becomes uncertain and the very concept vanishes, or it must be arbitrarily limited in every case. Such changes in the clinical picture may occur in the very patient who has just been considered a typical case; even more frequently, however, in many cases of similar diseases which can be arranged in a continuous series. The first link in the series may be, for example, the melancholia simplex, then follows hallucinatory melancholia, and the final links are constituted by acute hallucinatory paranoias; yet there is no evidence of any line of separation between the various forms. In the days when an anasarca was considered a disease entity, it was easy to find a way out when the clinical picture changed. To the original illness there was then simply added an abdominal anasarca, a thoracic anasarca, and a cardiac anasarca. In the psychoses, however, the clinical picture seemed too homogeneous to attempt such elementary additions frequently. Instead each disease was permitted to transform itself into another one. Wernicke was the most extreme representative of this notion of[1] transformation. Whenever a new symptom-complex developed, he was confronted with another disease: the motility psychosis of today was the paranoia of tomorrow.

The situation is quite different when it comes to the concepts of nephritis, general paresis or dementia ex atrophia cerebri. No matter how the clinical picture may change, whether there is a uremic attack, heart failure, or retinitis; the manic triad, "insanity," paralysis or remission — we do not change either our terminology or our concept of the disease. The possible appearance of such symptoms was already implied in the diagnosis.

Not many symptomatological concepts of diseases have survived in other fields of medicine. Where no substitutes could be found for them, they are being employed in full awareness of the fact that they are merely temporary formulations, not diagnoses. Yet in psychiatry, such obvious conceptions must still be fought for. Of course, paresis is always proudly cited as the model of a clear-cut concept; it is, however, in direct contrast to the symptomatological conceptions of disease.

We have to try to prove then: 1. That the various other diagnoses under which the Kraepelinian dementia praecox is usually classified do not represent any real concepts of disease. 2. That the concept of dementia praecox substitutes something far better, a genuine concept of disease for the clinical picture and we must prove at the same time that this concept corresponds to what we can actually observe.

That such terms as confusion, acute paranoia, acute hallucinatory insanity, confusion mentale, as well as mania and melancholia in their ancient sense (in which they are still being employed in England and France) do not designate "diseases" should be clear to anyone who has observed mental patients. I can, therefore, restrict myself to just a few points. It would take me far too long if I were to say all the unpleasant things which I really ought to say about these notions; and I am hardly equal to the task since I simply cannot understand those who believe that these terms connote actual concepts of disease.

First as to form: a concept built upon the basis of a single striking characteristic is always somewhat vague and arbitrary. What one ob-

1. This very doubtful concept of transformation could hardly be avoided. Nasse even described how one psychosis was transformed into another one in the course of a few hours.

server considers as important, another may hardly notice. Until a few years ago, the psychiatrists were about equally divided over the question as to whether the dementia, or the delusions and hallucinations were the dominant feature in elderly schizophrenics. Indeed, it happens frequently that one physician does not note a symptom which another finds immediately striking; one may see a stupor where the other wants to hear nothing of it because he has a much narrower concept of this term. One doctor may be certain that he can directly observe hallucinations, whereas another doubts their existence because the patient does not supply any information and because what has been interpreted as hallucinations can also be explained on the basis of other fundamental phenomena.

Secondly as to content: a symptom, regardless of whether it is psychic or physical (pain, anasarca) is never a disease; neither is a symptom-complex. It would certainly be a great coincidence if, at any time, any psychic or other syndrome should correspond to a true disease, that is, necessarily, if it should be dominant in each and every case of that disease without being present in other illnesses. If a sympton or a symptom-complex has been found in any patient, it is not the end of the systematics, the end of the formation of a concept of a disease, but it is merely the beginning. Only now we must ask ourselves the questions: in what connection with other symptoms and anatomical findings, in what sort of course, as the result of which causes does the symptom appear? Perhaps we must also ask what fundamental disturbance is the basis for this symptom? Only the answers to these questions can provide us with the concept of the disease. Most of the symptoms employed for the definition of the old pseudo-psychoses were as such entirely unsuited for this role. Hallucinations, for example, can be seen in all mental diseases, and even in the healthy persons. Thus they are in no way useful criteria for the distinction between healthy and sick; and even less so for the purpose of separating the various psychoses from each other. Even the quantitative relationship of these symptoms to other manifestations of disease cannot mean anything to us. Indeed, we can observe, for example, that cases of paresis, epilepsy, or senile dementia are at times accompanied by many hallucinations whereas at other times there is no evidence of such phenomena in these diseases. Yet this would never cause us to change our interpretation of them in any way. Even in the various attacks of the same manic-depressive patient which, for good reasons, we regard as equivalent, hallucinations are at times prominent, at other times absent. If, as in schizophrenia, there are disease-complexes which are fairly identical regarding symptomatology, course, etc., the only difference being the presence of hallucinations, we are still not justified in considering these varying clinical pictures as anything special.

The nature of hallucinations would be of greater importance for the diagnosis. We can recognize a delirium tremens with some degree of probability when a combination of specific types of visual and tactile hallucinations is present, and we can make the diagnosis with certainty if certain peculiarities of the patient's pattern of reactions are added. In the same way, the described combination of auditory and body-sensation hallucinations permits the diagnosis of schizophrenia — the diagnosis, but not the delimitation of the concept of schizophrenia, since in many otherwise similar cases hallucinations may be completely absent or may completely dominate the picture. Thus, they may only appear for the brief period of eight days in a case with a disease of fifty years' standing; in another case, of equal duration, they may be absent only for brief periods. In short, in order that we may conclude anything from hallucinations, they must be present; and the diagnosis is then based simply upon the correlation of certain kinds of hallucinations with the other symptoms of schizophrenia, which our experience has taught us. Thus, for good reasons, no one has dared to base the concept of a disease upon the kind of hallucinations exhibited.

The situation is far worse regarding the concept of confusion which is basic to the entire idea of amentia. Confusion is an end-symptom which can be caused by a variety of disturbances if they are sufficiently intense. The manic, epileptic, hysterical, delirious, and catatonic patients may occasionally show confusion. However, closer analysis reveals that in spite of this common feature, we are dealing with many entirely different, and clinically distinguishable conditions. The founder of the concept of amentia logically comprised these various conditions under one heading, and thereby discovered his theory; that is, he, himself showed that his assumptions were false because they necessarily led to false conclusions. Even the purified "amentia concept" of the more recent Viennese school[2] still suffers from the basic defects of the original definition. Stransky's attempt to improve matters by considering as amentia only those cases of confusion which do not fit into any other disease-concepts could only be of practical value if we already knew these other diseases and had defined them. But the Kraepelinian school unquestioningly considers most of his cases as dementia praecox. Thus, even if we recognized Stransky's definition, we would not make a diagnosis of amentia any more frequently than we do now.

---

2. Stransky, Pilcz.

Stupor, too, which is often used in making a differential diagnosis, is entirely unsuited for such a purpose. All kinds of inhibitions and blockings may manifest themselves as stupor when they are sufficiently intense. For knowledge of the disease, only the primary symptom underlying the stupor is of any importance, not its external picture. Manic, epileptic, schizophrenic stupor due to sudden fright — all these are entirely different things.

For many it is of the greatest significance whether the disturbance in a mental disease affects primarily the intelligence or the affectivity. Aside from other difficulties, there are, however, two circumstances which make such a criterion wholly useless: we do not know whether there exist primary disturbances of one sphere which leave the other entirely unaffected; and in any given case we know even less about what is secondary. Thus in the affective psychosis "mania," even flight of ideas and euphoria reveal themselves not as dependent upon each other, but as correlates (proof: the mixed types); thus, there is much lively discussion as to whether in the "intelligence-psychosis par excellence," i. e., paranoia, the disturbance of feelings is not after all the primary disorder. Thus we may be dealing with a criterion which perhaps does not even exist, and which in any event no one has as yet proven.

Some authorities attach particular importance to the temporal sequence in which symptoms appear. Ziehen, for example, assumes the presence of mania in certain cases where the affective disturbance has appeared first; on the other hand, he regards as acute hallucinatory paranoia those cases where the hallucinations were the first to make their appearance. Who will undertake to prove this difference? Ziehen's recommendation that we question the patient himself appears to me as a far too uncertain method in many cases.

It is obvious that no sharp definitions can be made when such criteria are used; thus we find always a great number of transitional and atypical cases when symptomatic diagnoses are employed. The need for the postulation of atypical diseases is always an indication of some weakness in the theory. In nature there is nothing typical or atypical. The "*forme fruste*" has as much justification for existence as the "typical." When we describe a malady as being atypical, we mean that it deviates from a norm which we have established. The occurrence of such a deviation proves that our norm does not include all the cases which it should include, or it proves that, for the purpose of description we have selected a certain group of cases as "typical," in order to then describe others as deviation of variations. The latter method offers great advantages. However, one must not confuse delimitations of description set up for didactic purposes with the definition of a concept. If there is such a thing as scarlatina sine exanthemata, then the very concept of scarlatina includes this form too. What is typical can be determined only arbitrarily. Compare Kahlbaum's or Arndt's concept of versania typica with reality, and with Clouston's statement: the typical form of insanity is hebephrenia, which passes over into secondary dementia.

Transitional forms[3] appear in some places in nature. No sharp line can be drawn between mountain-climate and the climate of lowlands; between honest and bad; healthy and abnormal; and none between the various kinds of "psychopathic personalities" of Kraepelin's theory. In these instances a natural unity has been artificially dissected by us. We admit theoretically the possibility that such a relationship may also exist in the psychoses or at least in those of its forms which we are considering here. It may be that there really is only one kind of mental disease; in that case, the clinical conditions which we delineate would be artificial creations and there would be no corresponding boundaries in nature. This hypothesis was, indeed, advanced some decades ago and consistent supporters of the old diagnoses, such as Ziehen, still stoutly defend the idea of transitions, at least for those forms which are involved in the diagnosis of dementia praecox. Furthermore, the psychoses may be simple deviations from a norm in varying directions and degrees. In this way, everything which Magnan includes in his concept of degeneration can be regarded as a unity. According to this concept, there are no more boundaries between the various clinical conditions falling into this group than there are between Kraepelin's criminals and his pseudologues. However, we have no evidence that any of these hypotheses fits schizophrenia. On the contrary, all authorities tend to consider schizophrenias as poisoning or some similar novum of the body. In that case, the disease should be placed alongside the paresis group and it ought not to show any transitions to other diseases.

There are also excellent reasons for excluding such intermediary forms; and if Pilcz finds more atypical than typical forms in his material I cannot understand why this fact should not be considered the end of his system of classification. We wish to add that the Viennese school, too, has increasingly delimitated its idea of amentia and that Pilcz, himself, cannot differentiate his secondary dementia from dementia praecox. What the author means is that different processes can leave identical psychic scars; this cannot be disputed. But if the terminal

3. We cannot consider Ziehen's converging forms.

states cannot be delineated by anyone and if the initial states can be defined only by members of a single school, and even then not very sharply and not even in half the number of their cases, then there is little reason indeed for considering such "diseases" as different from each other.

These remarks lead us to a discussion of the actual psychiatric practice which shows up the old principles of disease classification with bitter irony. Our literature is replete with complaints about the chaotic state of the systematics of pyschoses and every psychiatrist knows that it is impossible to come to any common understanding on the basis of the old diagnostic labels. No discussion among clinicians, even those with closely allied views, is possible unless each one outlines his special point of view as to classification.[4] Fürstner's concept of hallucinatory insanity is utterly different from Meynert's; Schuele pleads for continued recognition of Kahlbaum's catatonia but includes in it primary dementia;[5] Fürstner insists that the amentia was never included in paranoia;[6] whereas Wernicke claims that acute paranoia is included "in the masterly description of the amentias given by Meynert."[7] Thus, not even the masters of science can make themselves understood on the basis of the old concepts and with many patients the number of diagnoses made equals the number of institutions they have been to. It is obvious that every author of a textbook was obliged, above all, to construct his own system of classification since the systems established by his predecessors were useless to his way of thinking and to his method of observation. Even within the very same school, one physician defined as paranoia what another termed a melancholia. The in-between forms, the atypical cases, had to be fitted in somewhere, if need be forcibly. Situations as the following are rather common: In a certain hospital there would be a big pot, labelled "dementia." Now along comes a new physician who enlarges the pot standing alongside the other one, and labels the second pot, "paranoia." He then carefully proceeds to seize the old inmates of the institution by some vestige of a delusion and puts them, one by one, in his new pot — and in doing this believes that he is correcting the errors of his predecessors.

An even better illustration of the incomprehensibility of the former concepts of disease is provided by the following incident: discussing the differential diagnosis of "degenerative dementia," Cramer was forced

4. Compare, e.g., the discussion about paranoia in the Psychiatric Association in Berlin, March 17, 1894. Allgem. Zeitschr. f. Psych., 1895, p. 178.

5. Allgem. Zeitschr. f. Psych., 1901, p. 705.

6. Allgem. Zeitschr. f. Psych., 1894, p. 1081.

7. Allgem. Zeitschr. f. Psych., 1899, p. 642. Of what use was the "masterly description" to the two authors?

to offer the following advice: "Cases in which stuporous manifestations appear rapidly followed by mental deterioration can best be considered as catatonic paranoia or catatonia in the Kraepelinian sense." "Can best be" — those few words express more than the entire treatise.[8]

In the attempt to do justice to the actual clinical picture, the co-existence of various diseases in the same patient has often been assumed. By that method, the cases were certainly more fully described — but they were just as certainly not more correctly classified. In the hands of some originators of systems of classification, the number of combinations of psychoses grew to extraordinary proportions since one incomplete diagnosis could always be supplemented by a second and third.

In recent times, many German as well as foreign authors have been unable to escape the influence of the dementia praecox concept. They acknowledge the presence of a hebephrenia, a catatonia, or a dementia praecox, yet they limit the scope of the concept so that acute and chronic hallucinatory paranoia, amentia, and *confusion mentale* continue to appear alongside the other diseases. Naturally, nothing is gained thereby except another symptomatological picture, which is then called a disease and which, moreover, is misleadingly defined by the same term as the qualitatively and quantitatively quite different Kraepelinian concept. It will suffice to quote just one more foreign author. As far as the differential diagnosis between *confusion mentale* and dementia praecox is concerned, Anglade is able to state merely the following: The schizophrenic makes no attempt at all to answer; the confused patient shows more cooperation; but the answers of both are inexact, disconnected, and absurd. The confused patient is usually physically rundown, not so the demented. The differences are "sensed" more often than they could be described. Now in order to find these really non-existent, and if existent, hardly demonstrable criteria, Anglade had to call upon two other authorities, Hannion and Chaslin. What sense does this sort of classification make?

The establishment of the dementia praecox concept has brought clarity and order into this confusion. The Kraepelinian dementia praecox[9] is an actual disease concept. The concept includes symptoms which

---

8. In the sense of the Kraepelinian diagnoses there is no "best" but only "true" or "false," just as a certain fever illness cannot "best" be considered a case of typhoid, or a miliary tuberculosis.

9. Since this was written, Kraepelin has somewhat narrowed down his concept. I cannot follow him in that direction and maintain my position on the basis of the sixth and seventh editions of this textbook of psychiatry.

occur only and always in dementia praecox. Thereby the disease group is provided with concrete delimitations.

Those of the symptoms which are designated as accessory are unessential in that they may appear or disappear without altering the essence of the disease.

Further proof that the various clinical conditions included in this concept constitute an entity is the following fact: according to our present knowledge, these clinical states can pass over into one another or can alternate with each other in the same patient; no one group of conditions can be singled out which would not show definite connections with all the others.

The concept also corresponds with reality since its criteria can actually be discovered very easily; and as far as I know, no one has as yet proven the presence of any contradictions in the facts of this concept.

It is not yet clear just what sort of entity the concept of dementia praecox actually represents. It probably includes one or very few diseases, in the narrower sense, which constitute the major portion of cases, in the same way as general paresis embraces the majority of all cases of the *dementia paralytica* of the previous century. Furthermore, some rare disease processes probably cause symptoms which appear to be of the same kind, at least, as far as our present knowledge can take us. It is true, we have been able to establish the diagnosis in schizophrenic-like cases of organic brain disorder; at least, we were able to see that there was something "atypical" about the patients. Yet we cannot exclude the possibility that certain mild organic disturbances bring forth symptom complexes which we now designate as dementia praecox. It is possible, furthermore, that some kind of intoxication, for instance, by alcohol, may bring about similar clinical pictures(cf. below). As long as the real disease process is unknown to us, we cannot exclude the possibility that various types of auto-intoxication or infections may lead to the same symptomatic picture.

For the time being, then, dementia praecox must be regarded not as a species of disease but as a genus, in the same sense as the "organic psychoses," or perhaps in a narrower sense, like the dementia paralytica of previous decades.

We have not yet developed the concept of dementia praecox as thoroughly as, for example, that of infectious nephritis. Our tentative idea has approximately the same significance which was formerly attached to the chronic *Morbus Brightii*. Chronic Bright's disease included many different renal processes all of which, however, agreed as far as the most important and, at that time, only recognizable signs were concerned. A similar situation still exists today regarding the concept of rheumatic arthritis which includes, in all likelihood, many different infectious processes; but these cannot as yet be separated and still represent for us a single entity; thus, it does not occur to us, for example, to consider rheumatic arthritis as a distinct disease from rheumatic arthritis without "complication;" nor do we attempt to subdivide the disease on the basis of its localization in the various joints.

So far, we have been unable to discover any natural lines of division within the described clinical picture of the disease. The various symptom combinations are of such transitory nature in the individual patient as well as in different patients, that all distinctions appear vague. Our sub-groups, such as hebephrenia, catatonia, paranoia, are, therefore, probably "accidental" manifestations of the same disease; in any event, they correspond to mere clinical pictures which are being designated *a potiori*, and in which the *potius* refers only to unessential symptoms.

For a long time I have refused to include in dementia praecox all the paranoid forms; especially dementia paranoides, with its easily described and peculiar symptoms and course, has been a constant objective of my particularistic desires. On the one hand, however, a thorough study of the psychopathology revealed everywhere the same fundamental phenomena; on the other hand, a closer study of our cases showed so much that was identical, so many transitional forms, and such a complete absence of any distinguishable boundaries (at least, with our present methods of investigation) that I could only side with Kraepelin. He, again, has recently expressed my previous assumption that there exists an in-between group between paranoia and schizophrenia. In this respect, I cannot agree with him any more because I am unable to narrow down my concept of paranoia until it corresponds with Kraepelin's.

Thus, the subdivision of the group of schizophrenias is a task for the future. However, of even greater importance than the definition of the disease, is, in my opinion, that we clearly state once and for all: as yet we know of no natural lines of demarkation within this group; what, up to now, has been considered as such boundaries are boundaries of clinical states, not of diseases. Errors are the greatest obstacles to the progress of science; to correct such errors is of more practical value than to achieve new knowledge. We have here eliminated chaos of terms[10] behind which useful concepts of disease were

10. Chaslin (118) counted thirty-one terms alone for acute hallucinatory states, conditions which occur most frequently in dementia praecox.

mistakenly sought; we have eliminated a veritable forest of boundary posts, not one of which indicated any natural line of demarkation.

However, the concept is as yet not well defined in two directions: one is that of paranoia, the other that of alcoholic psychoses.

In the Kraepelinian paranoia, there is an absence of emotional and associational disturbances outside the delusional system; furthermore, all gross anomalies, such as catatonic symptoms, are missing. Thus we cannot demonstrate any evidence of disease in a paranoiac outside his delusions. At the same time, the prognosis also changes: the paranoiac does not deteriorate (unless, for example, senile dementia complicates the picture) even though he may occasionally become somewhat "simple," like all people with a one-track mind.

However, our present methods of investigation show that in paranoia the mechanism of the construction of the delusions is identical with that of schizophrenia; thus it may be possible that paranoia is an entirely chronic schizophrenia which is so mild that it could just about lead to delusional ideas; its less striking symptoms, however, are so lacking in prominence that we cannot demonstrate them. I would consider this extremely probable if it were more common that an originally pure paranoia at a later stage also develops schizophrenic symptoms. Only in very few cases have we been forced to change our diagnosis from paranoia to schizophrenia and among these there were none that were not right from the start suspected of being schizophrenic. Unfortunately, such experiences are not sufficient proof for the basic difference between the two diseases since paranoia is very rare among hospital patients.

Equally obscure is the relationship of schizophrenia to the various paranoid forms of alcoholism, whether they take an acute or a chronic course. Naturally the two most frequent psychoses, alcoholism and schizophrenia, have a number of external features in common. Thus we frequently observe that the hallucinations of schizophrenics who drink during acute attacks, have an alcoholic coloring; this may be in the nature of the vivid, multiple, moving visual and tactile hallucinations of the delirium tremens, or it may be the type of dramatically connected auditory hallucinations of alcoholic hallucinosis[11] during which the patient is addressed in the third person. I have never seen this kind of coloration

11. An accompanying alcoholism can generally lend a logical coherence to the acute symptoms of schizophrenia, whereas, conversely, the fleeting hallucinations of delirium tremens are arranged into a more unified picture both as to content and course under the schizophrenic influence of the complexes. The patients remember such hallucinations far better than less coherent details of the ordinary delirium tremens. Through this and on account of the predominance of auditory hallucinations, there may develop on the basis of a schizophrenic substratum forms of delirium tremens which constitute transition to alcoholic hallucinosis.

unless alcoholism was complicating the schizophrenia.

However, schizophrenia, itself, also predisposes to delirium tremens. I have seen delirium tremens in young people (up to the age of about twenty-five) only in schizophrenics after merely a few years of alcoholic overindulgence.

I have also seen alcoholic hallucinosis develop on the basis of schizophrenia. According to various authorities, alcoholic hallucinosis shows a tendency to develop into paranoid forms which we cannot anymore differentiate from the schizophrenic ones. On the basis of my own material, we cannot exclude the possibility that acute alcoholic hallucinosis may represent an alcoholically-induced and specifically colored intermezzo in the course of schizophrenia. This interpretation also clarifies why the other signs of alcoholism are so often absent in alcoholic hallucinosis, and why von Speyer and Schuele find the briefest misuse of alcohol in their cases of acute alcoholic paranoia.

Chronic alcohol-paranoia has frequently been diagnosed by others; I, however, have not yet seen such a patient, who gave me even the slightest reason to see in him anything other than an ordinary schizophrenic who also drank. Not even genuine signs of alcoholism were present in all cases, yet the anamneses were usually schizophrenic. For me, therefore, there can be no doubt that the greatest portion of the chronic alcohol-paranoias of other writers are only schizophrenias.[12] In agreement with this are the observations of E. Meyer and Bonhoeffer, who state that the prognosis of chronic alcohol-paranoia becomes worse with the appearance of ideas of grandeur and hallucinations, that is, of schizophrenic symptoms. The "paranoid disposition" which E. Meyer places at the root of the alcohol paranoia would, then, actually be a latent schizophrenia and we would not be dealing with paranoia which has developed on the basis of alcoholism, but with alcoholism on a schizophrenic foundation. In any event, up to the present, there exists no proof for the existence of non-schizophrenic alcohol-paranoia.[13] Even so, of course, I cannot exclude the possibility that material from others may still demonstrate it. I have not yet observed the alcoholic stupor[14] which is supposed to be common in the Orient, but we sometimes see stupor in schizophrenics who drink too much. Neither am I familiar, from my

12. The simple alcoholic delusion of jealousy disappears when the patient becomes abstinent, as far as I can judge.

13. Pilcz's textbook offers for purposes of differential diagnosis between an alcoholic hallucinosis and his true paranoia (i.e., schizophrenia) only the anamnestic proof of an acute onset in a habitual drunkard. Thus, according to him, there is really no difference at all since many schizophrenias become acutely manifest in habitual drunkards. Neither can Schroeder answer the question as to the existence of chronic alcoholic psychoses "with any certainty in the affirmative." Also compare Chotzen.

14. As a disease, not as the emotional stupor of alcoholics.

own experience, with Kraepelin's hallucinatory dementia of the drunkard. Unfortunately, I also have not had the opportunity to see such cases which were diagnosed by others. Therefore, I ought not doubt its existence and I have also another reason for reserving judgment. Ultimately, abuse of alcohol leads to brain atrophy, that is, to a form of mental deterioration. During abstinency the brain process becomes stationary and the functional disturbances are more or less compensated for. The result is that often it may not be possible anymore to demonstrate the organic origin of the deterioration. Hallucinations may appear in all cases; then why not in some brain-atrophied alcoholics? Yet, Kraepelin's and Schroeder's descriptions still do not prove the necessity of separating alcoholic hallucinatory dementia from schizophrenia.

Only further observation can determine whether a severe Korsakoff can lead to a chronic schizophrenic-like picture, or whether a Korsakoff which seems to pass over into schizophrenia, was not originally a schizophrenia complicated by a Korsakoff. This latter situation probably applied to two cases which I have observed. I believe this particularly because, from a certain point on, the patients led such a senseless life that it is better explained by dementia praecox than by simple alcoholisms.

Difficulties such as the above are bound to occur in every conception of a disease. For that matter, the concept of dementia praecox is a very well defined one. It has the advantage over symptomatological disease pictures that with it there is no "more or less."

Once the schizophrenic affective disturbance or the schizophrenic anomalies of association have been proven, the diagnosis is assured. Then it only remains to ask whether an only slightly marked affective disturbance is not already a schizophrenic one. These are difficulties which are inherent, not in the disease concept, but in our diagnostic shortcomings, and which apply to any disease. Whether a certain irregularity of breathing can already be considered as pneumonic bronchial breathing is a technical question, not one involving the disease concept. The concept of schizophrenia, therefore, is superior to any symptomatic one because we are dealing with absolute, not relative criteria—absolute in the sense that once the criteria are demonstrated, the diagnosis is under all circumstances assured. Particularly the course of the disease will reveal this. Once the diagnosis is made, it does not have to be changed any more; in the course of the disease no more symptoms will appear which do not belong to it. It cannot happen that a correctly diagnosed dementia praecox changes suddenly into a general paralysis or epilepsy. The disease always remains within the same groups of symptoms.

Of course, not all symptoms must appear in each and every case, no more than intestinal hemorrhages occur in every case of typhoid. In mild cases of schizophrenia as in all other diseases we may, of course, at a given moment, be unable to demonstrate the presence of a symptom with the means at our disposal at the present time.

Schizophrenia may come to a halt at any time, just as, for example, a pulmonary tuberculosis. If, at such a point, the acute symptoms regress and if the disease is not in any advanced stage, we may, at present, under certain conditions hardly be able to observe anything of a pathological nature anymore. In the same way, the residuals of an apical infiltration cannot be recognized unless they have attained a certain size. However, if symptoms are present at all, it is a matter of indifference as far as the disease-concept is concerned, whether they are barely noticeable or markedly severe: in every case they remain within the framework of schizophrenic symptoms. Therefore, schizophrenia must not, of necessity, lead to definite deterioration—a strange argument used by some opponents; however, if the disease continues to advance, it leads to deterioration, and this deterioration has a specific character. However, the disease does not have to advance.

A few of the most frequent objections made to the concept of dementia praecox will be mentioned in the following.

To begin with, the variability of the external clinical picture of this disease has been the greatest obstacle to the acceptance of the idea. However, since it was proven that there exist certain constant symptoms and that the changing ones are of no systematic significance, it is no more difficult to recognize the unity in the multitude of forms than it is in general paralysis. In any event, we are dealing with a group of diseases which is differentiated on principle from all other Kraepelinian groups.

One of the most common objections which is still being voiced, especially in foreign countries, is strangely enough that we are not always dealing with either *dementia* praecox or *precocious* dementia. Considering Kraepelin's clear definition of the concept and his emphatic mention of cures and of the incidence in older age groups, an objection such as this must be termed a gross misunderstanding on the part of those who do not want to recognize the concept and who instead continue to cling to names.

An objection which deserves more consideration is the one which states that when some cases of a disease recover whereas others deteriorate, they cannot belong to the same group. Yet this reproach is far more appropriate when directed against the old concepts of disease than against the concept of dementia praecox, with its *semper aliquid haeret*. It could only be directed against dementia praecox if it had been proven that the progress of the deterioration constituted an essential part of the disease concept. The contrary happens to be the case, however. To go along with this objection would be equal to attacking the concept of pulmonary tuberculosis because, although most of the cases are cured, many others become chronic or suffer relapses, and a number of others die from it.

Many find a certain difficulty in their own conception of dementia. Schäfer, for example, thinks that a disease which for fourteen years gave the impression of dementia and was then cured could not possibly be a genuine dementia. In accordance with our ideas, we consider such a case a rather striking example of late recovery in schizophrenia, but Schäfer had to regard it as a disease distinct from the one identified with the hopelessly deteriorated patients in the mental hospitals. Those who clearly realize what a small portion of the organ of thinking has actually been destroyed in schizophrenia, and those who have grasped that precisely the main symptoms of the specific "dementia," i.e., the submersion into a private universe of thought and the absence of affect, are secondary, potentially changeable manifestations, will see no difficulties in occurrences such as those mentioned.

However, there are also psychiatrists who, conversely, refuse to classify in accordance with the outcome of the disease and who, for exactly this reason are opposed to our concept of disease. Bruce believes that if we were to differentiate according to outcome all diseases would become identical since all ultimately end in death. As for dementia praecox, it is not the outcome that is important but the direction of the course toward the outcome. When Pilcz states that different processes may lead to the same end, it must be pointed out that careful examination will reveal the elements of the later, specific dementia in every stage of schizophrenia, but not in other diseases. Thus, it is a matter of investigation and experience whether one can agree with that author or not. Our experience proves him completely incorrect.

Wernicke has also mentioned that the etiological concept of "hebephrenia" must not be paralleled with the symptomatological one of "catatonia." Had he read Kraepelin correctly, he would have realized that for Kraepelin these terms did not define only etiological or symptomatological ideas, but that they designated the ways of manifestation of an entire disease as well as all its partial concepts.

Others have spoken of a "catatonic psychosis" as an entity,[15] thereby reproaching us for extending our conception too widely. I must stop to discuss this objection because even Kraepelin himself and

15. Sommer, Zeitschr. f. Psych., 1899, p. 260.

Aschaffenburg[16] have found it regrettable that our disease concept has such a wide scope. For science, however, the point is whether or not the concept has been correctly formulated and I cannot see that it would be less regrettable if coryza and typhoid or elephants and horses were found to be equally common. It would not occur to anyone to consider the concept of paresis too wide only because thirty per cent of male admissions to the hospitals happened to be composed of such patients. Certainly there can be no argument whatever against the assumption that one type of psychosis is relatively much more common than another. On the contrary, with respect to the disease under discussion, wherever such patients gathered there has always been the need, rooted in the very nature of the subject, for the "big pot," which changes its label only in the course of time.

THE SCOPE OF THE CONCEPT

According to our experience, Kraepelin's presenile delusions of being wronged cannot be separated from schizophrenia. They show exactly the same symptomatology as dementia paranoides or other paranoid forms; sometimes the disturbance can be traced to a rather early age; now and then isolated catatonic symptoms appear. In our opinion, this is a late paranoid condition.

Most recently, the manic-depressive psychosis has again gained ground at the expense of dementia praecox. In contrast to Dreifuss, I cannot recall a single case where we were obliged to change our diagnosis from schizophrenia to manic-depressive psychosis. On the contrary, the very reverse has been necessary from time to time as the years passed. Our own experience directly contradicts Wilmann's statement: "Catatonic symptom complexes, which follow definite manic-depressive cyclothymic episodes, must be considered as peculiar and curable manifestations of this disease." Whenever we were able to analyze catatonic-like syndromes in manic-depressive psychosis, they always proved themselves as really not at all catatonic. Thus, we are not yet convinced that catatonic symptoms occur in manic-depressive psychoses. However, we find manic-depressive symptoms in schizophrenia as well as in paresis or senile dementia. At present, therefore, we cannot understand how Wilmann came to his conclusion, that "the manic-depressive symptom complexes have a far greater significance for differential diagnosis than the catatonic ones." For us, it is a matter

16. Allgem. Zeitschr. f. Psych., 1899.

of course that where there are combinations of manic-depressive symptoms with schizophrenic symptoms, we do not designate the disease as a manic-depressive psychosis but as dementia praecox in the manner of Kraepelin. There is, for us, no more "catatonic form of periodic insanity" (Geist) than there is a paretic form of that disease. Instead we recognize catatonias which run a periodic course and general paralyses. Probably, there are also mixed cases of manic-depressive psychosis and schizophrenia.

Aside from this widening of the scope of the concept, we are in complete agreement with Kraepelin. On the other hand, we must come to terms with the ideas regarding classification set forth by other important schools. Since epilepsy, paresis, and senile dementia are diseases with generally well recognized limits, we are not including them in our discussion.

However, idiocy already causes some difficulties. Attempts have been made to designate the psychoses which develop during puberty as late idiocies. However, in idiocy, a number of other diseases and developmental defects are involved which must not be confused with schizophrenia.[17]

In England and France, particularly, the concept of melancholia and mania is still of a very wide scope; the majority of the illnesses included in it must be regarded by us as belonging to the group of schizophrenias. The German concept of melancholia and mania was considerably narrower even before Kraepelin. Yet, many of these cases, especially those with hallucinatory mania or melancholia, or with manic and melancholic delusions respectively,[18] belong to schizophrenia. Therefore, we must define the limits of schizophrenia in relation to the manic-depressive psychosis and to involutional melancholia, if the latter is actually a disease in itself. After what has been said above, this presents no theoretical difficulties.

Schizophrenia, moreover, embraces the greater part of those cases whose designations emphasize hallucinatory excitements or confusions, which include amentia and the hallucinatory paranoia. In this direction the limits are difficult to define because as yet we do not

17. Kraepelin and Weygandt are inclined to include schizophrenia itself in those diseases which may cause idiocy. Since the term idiocy merely designates a type of mental deficiency which occurs intra-uterinally or in very early childhood, and inasmuch as schizophrenia may also develop during the first years of life, we have, in principle, no objection to this interpretation. I must merely add that I have not seen any such idiots as yet. None of the cases of infantile schizophrenia which I have observed were idiots. The stereotyped behavior of idiots is basically different from catatonia.

18. A very small percentage of acute delusions (melancholic and manic) belong to the manic-depressive psychosis according to our ideas.

know the rather manifold though not very common diseases which must be considered in addition to schizophrenia. However, acute hallucinatory and confusional states occur in fever diseases and renal insufficiency — in short, under circumstances which cause us to suspect some kind of intoxication. The only attempt to describe these conditions comprehensively resulted in Kraepelin's amentia. But among the last 4,000 admissions to this hospital I have not been able to discover any such amentia and I am beginning to doubt if it really has the significance which its author attributes to it. Unfortunately, the other toxic deliria — toxic, in the widest sense — have disappeared among the general concepts of the diseases included here, so that as yet they do not have any specific symptomatology. In these cases it should be possible to trace the "confusion" to elementary symptoms other than those of dementia praecox.

Schizophrenia has little in common with the all-inclusive concept of delirium acutum, but it may happen that a particularly acute and fatal case of schizophrenia is regarded as an acute delirium. We would include in our disease most cases of Ziehen's "ecnoia."

Obviously almost all of Wernicke's "motility psychoses" are also schizophrenias.

Of the chronic diseases, all[19] those designated as dementing types, primary and secondary dementias, etc., belong to our disease, as well as the greater portion of the paranoias of other writers.

Of the minor clinical pictures, we might mention hypochondria which even now has a great significance for many psychiatrists. Most incurable hypochondriacs are schizophrenics whose delusions are primarily concerned with their own bodies. After close study, and especially since I was able to observe some clear-cut, entirely analogous cases, I must now also consider as schizophrenic the woman whom I described in my book *Affectivity* (page 133). Many physicians would also label as hypochondriacs those whom we would designate as neurasthenic, hysterical, etc. Some genuine paranoiacs may perhaps also be hypochondriacs with delusions concerning their health.

Some cases which fitted Kraepelin's description of "expectation-neurosis" exactly were schizophrenics.

A large number of women whom I considered schizophrenics passed for hysterically insane in other places whereby it was implied that the insanity was somehow or other a further development of

19. It is probable that there are also other brain diseases which leave psychic scars. These, however, have not yet been described (not even in the form of the concept of amentia, which has prevailed up to now) and it is hardly worthwhile to enumerate them.

the hysteria. I have never yet had any reason for making a diagnosis of "hysterical psychosis." All cases so diagnosed by others differed in no wise from other schizophrenics. When a supposed hysteric becomes psychotic or deteriorates, he is, in my experience, not a hysteric at all, but a schizophrenic. I am holding this opinion in spite of Charcot's authority and in spite of work done recently by Rancke and Kaiser; the latter has diagnostic difficulties in flagrant instances of schizophrenia and interprets them partly as hysterics. By the same token, the "hysterical" melancholias and manias of other authors are also mostly schizophrenias although, occasionally, real combinations of mania and melancholia with hysteria do occur.

"Nervous" persons, too, whose conversations are often confused, who refuse nourishment and exhibit delusions of jealousy, are, as far as our experience goes, neither neurasthenics nor narcoleptics,[20] but catatonics.

Many, although not all, of the very severe forms of compulsive conditions, of *folie du doute* (*Grübelsucht*), and of impulsive behavior undoubtedly belong to schizophrenia. In most instances, definite signs of basic disease make their appearance sooner or later. These clinical pictures termed pyromania, kleptomania, etc., are sometimes schizophrenias.

Our attitude in respect of the problem of juvenile psychoses is obvious from what has already been said. Schizophrenia begins most frequently between the ages of fifteen and twenty-five; it is at the same time the most common of the psychoses; thus it follows that it is also the most common of juvenile psychoses. Aside from schizophrenia, however, all other psychoses also occur in this age group. Excepted are the involutional types of psychoses (in case they exist) and the senile dementias. For us, therefore, there exists no characteristic juvenile psychosis or a psychosis that is typical for the age of puberty.

The masturbation insanity described by various authors must obviously be included in schizophrenia.

We still have to come to some understanding regarding the concept of degeneration. In Morel's sense, the term denotes a type of mental insufficiency which increases from generation to generation in any given family. Since this kind of degeneration is seen only rarely nowadays, the word is hardly ever understood in that sense. Instead, there was introduced a broader concept, which is about the equivalent of "hereditary predisposition." Magnan's term *dégenérés* designates indi-

20. *Schott* (666).

viduals who come from degenerated, i.e., mentally abnormal families. It was believed that certain clinical symptoms appear only in the degenerated persons (in Magnan's sense of the term). The concept is valid for most deviations from the normal, such as, for example, genuine moral idiocy, pseudologia, and a multitude of eccentricities of intelligence and character. However, it will hardly apply to all of them since there are also acquired cerebral diseases which produce apparently similar clinical pictures. To date, however, the true psychoses have resisted any such interpretation. It has never been proven that any particular clinical picture appears only in those who are hereditarily predisposed. If one is looking for "*The* heredity," one can nearly always find it in mentally ill patients; there is far less eagerness to seek the hereditary factor in diseases which are considered non-degenerative and consequently it is less often found. Since Magnan's large scale attempt has failed, there is no more reason for us to consider this idea at any length. If a man with Magnan's experience and clinical knowledge failed so completely, it is proof that with our present knowledge of symptomatology there is nothing we can do with that idea. We will not be able to do anything about it even later on, unless the single factor of heredity can be broken down into many hereditary factors along specific lines. Thus it may suffice to indicate that at Saint Anne's Hospital the big pigeon-hole is labelled "*dégenérés*" and that we could find in it many of our schizophrenics. This is all the more likely since many mild schizophrenics have not been recognized as such and are consequently regarded as inherently psychopathic characters.[21] In addition, Wolfsohn[22] has shown that heredity which, by the way, can be proven in ninety per cent of schizophrenic cases, has no appreciable influence on either the course or the symptomatology of schizophrenia.

A third, more clearly defined idea, which stands out among present-day concepts of degeneration, is that of a congenital or very early acquired brain deficiency on the basis of which various other diseases develop. Since many schizophrenias can be traced to early childhood and since its incidence among poorly endowed people is as common as it is among normal ones, it is obvious that this type of degeneration will frequently be found in schizophrenia. So far, we have discovered no evidence that would distinguish the schizophrenia of such degenerated individuals from that in persons with normal brains. All criteria,

---

21. Morel (Brain, 1889) considers schizophrenic symptoms as signs of degeneration. Bonhoeffer also describes in his degeneration psychoses many degenerative symptoms which might just as well be schizophrenic.
22. Allgem. Zeitschrift f. Psych., 1907.

even Schuele's, have failed in my attempts to establish any such difference.

A similar concept is that of the constitutional types, which even form an important class by themselves in Swiss official statistics. As far as moral idiots are concerned and intellectually or emotionally defective individuals, schizophrenia has absolutely nothing to do with that concept. However it is being used in some places as a sort of waste basket for all otherwise unclassifiable diseases: whatever would not fit into the classification of psychoses, was ascribed to "*Anlage*" (constitution). Obviously, under such circumstances, the previously poorly understood schizophrenia yielded many of these cases of constitutional disease. It even happened, for instance, that a mania was diagnosed after the first attack and that the patient was released as cured. When he returned as a chronic schizophrenic and appeared sick, although it was not possible to establish the presence of a "secondary dementia," it was assumed that he suffered from constitutional insanity.

The fourth type of degeneration is the "degeneration of the individual disease." According to this concept, the appearance of "degenerative symptoms" in the course of a disease, means that the disease tends toward dementia, toward a bad termination. Some connect this concept more or less clearly with the idea that it is this degenerative *Anlage* (in its earlier meaning) which is responsible for the aggravation of the patient's condition.

Concerning these various ideas, we must state that the first three types of degeneration include schizophrenias in our sense of the term. Individuals with a direct hereditary predisposition to mental disorders acquire schizophrenia more frequently than others; however, the predisposition is not a prerequisite for the development of the disease. We do not know of any significant differences in symptoms or in the course of a schizophrenia between individuals who are hereditarily predisposed and those who are not. At this time, we know only little about the specific type of hereditary predisposition favorable to schizophrenia.

Magnan's mentally ill *dégénérés* are for the most part schizophrenics. The patients with "degenerative symptoms" in the sense of the fourth type are all schizophrenics, with only very rare exceptions.

I am of course, well aware that acute syndromes occur in psychopaths of every type. On the basis of our theory of the secondary origin of most symptoms, it is understood that, under certain circumstances, such syndromes can resemble schizophrenic deliria. Such cases, however, which seem to occur often in big cities, come to us so rarely,[23] that I am in no position to draw the line of demarkation between them and schizophrenics. However, those authors who describe the degenerative psychoses understand the concept of dementia praecox far too narrowly, and for this reason miss the lines of demarkation or ignore them completely. Our knowledge at this point, therefore, has a regrettable gap.

It is also apparent from the symptomatology that many disorders regarded as "moral insanity" must be included in our concept. Levinstein-Schlegel even recognizes only a moral insanity stemming from schizophrenia. Kahlbaum's heboid and parethosia, as well as Wernicke's moral autopsychosis, come close to this idea.[24] However, it is certain that, apart from schizophrenia, there are various kinds of moral deficiency. Among these, moral idiocy, showing a complete absence of moral feelings, is the best defined.

In our experience, furthermore, many acute prison psychoses represent the thrust of schizophrenia which in most cases was present already before imprisonment, and which was the very cause of the antisocial behavior.

We cannot entirely pass over Wernicke's peculiar classification although it is quite impossible to come to terms with it in any brief discussion. His symptomatological ideas, no matter how cleverly they are constructed and how much they are supported by observations, are of no use to us. Thus his concept, "sejunction," includes not only blocking, but also other forms of dissociation which have an entirely different significance both psychologically and nosographically. Thus, in order not to cause any misunderstanding, we are forced to avoid the use of many of his terms. To construct disease pictures on the basis of his concepts would be an impossible undertaking. Many of his most diverse diseases occur in the same patient. He then helps himself with his hypothesis of compound psychoses. Usually, however, a psychosis can be diagnosed as a compound one only *expost*. He has so many compound, mixed, and combined cases that, for this reason alone, the probability hardly exists that his conceptions of symptom complexes represent distinct diseases. What would we think of pulmonary diagnostics which interposed different diseases such as emphysema, tuberculosis, and pneumonia in the course of a compound pulmonary disease, and

23. All our cases with an apparently psychic etiology taken together, have the same prognosis as the rest. Therefore, there cannot be an appreciable number of degeneratives with psychogenic conditions among them.

24. Schäfer (653) describes the (moral) mental defectives in such a way that, among others, mild hebephrenics also fit into his picture. Keirn recognizes a "moral deterioration" which later develops into insanity

even this in a completely irregular manner? The best proof for the incorrectness of Wernicke's definitions of diseases is provided by the fact that they did not even permit an ingenious observer to exclude paresis in a case as simple as No. 28 of his case histories (Volume 1); I would not easily forgive a medical student during examination if he mentioned paresis in such a case. Things are also rather bad with Wernicke's prognostics, unless his knowledge is superior to his systematics. He claims on page 105 that the initial attacks of an acute hallucinosis can always be cured; however the acute hallucinoses (in his sense) are almost identical with our schizophrenic deliria, where the prognosis is not a good one. If he is mistaken, he must change his diagnosis as in case No. 10 of the same volume of case histories. The situation is analogous to what the author has to say about case No. 28 (p. 113): "Our error teaches us, as does many another case, that there are acute diseases in which it is impossible to make a diagnosis without knowledge of the anamnesis." Another evaluation of the symptom would have easily prevented this error.

SECTION VI

DIAGNOSIS

A. General Remarks

In fully developed cases of schizophrenia the diagnosis is very easy to make; however, in less advanced forms of the disease, it runs into more practical difficulties than in most other psychoses.

As in every other disease, the symptoms must have reached a certain degree of intensity if they are to be of any diagnostic value. Yet in milder cases of schizophrenia we find a number of prominent manifestations, which strongly fluctuate within the limits of what is regarded, if not as healthy, at least as "not mentally ill." Character anomalies, indifference, lack of energy, unsociability, stubbornness, moodiness, the characteristic for which Goethe could only find the English word, "whimsical," hypochondriacal complaints, etc., are not necessarily symptoms of an actual mental disease; they are, however, often the only perceptible signs of schizophrenia. It is for this reason that the diagnostic threshold of schizophrenia is higher than that of any other disease; and it is because of this that latent cases are such a common occurrence.

Once the presence of a mental disease has been established, the specific diagnosis of schizophrenia offers further difficulties. Only a few isolated psychotic symptoms can be utilized in recognizing the disease, and these too, have a very high diagnostic threshold value. Manic and depressive moods may occur in all psychoses; flight of ideas, inhibition and — as far as they have not assumed specific characteristics — hallucinations and delusions, are partial phenomena of the most varied diseases. Their presence is often helpful in making the diagnosis of a psychosis, but not in diagnosing the presence of schizophrenia.

As far as the true schizophrenic symptoms have been described up to the present, they are not *nova*, as, for example, a hallucination or a paretic speech disturbance. They are distortions and exaggerations of normal processes.[1]

1. I certainly hope, however, that some day we may learn to differentiate the schizophrenic splitting of ideas, and also the more general splitting of associations from similar phenomena which take place outside the field of normal attention.

Thus, the individual symptom in itself is less important than its intensity and extensiveness, and above all, its relation to the psychological setting. In the multitude of psychological paths there are many that lead to the same goal. It is of no pathological significance if someone draws stereotype "doodles" on the paper in front of him during a boring lecture; but when the same "doodles" are included in a serious letter, they may assure for themselves a diagnosis of schizophrenia.

Many people appear indifferent because they are preoccupied with something and because the affect of the preoccupying complexes is present even when they are thinking of other things; however, if one succeeds in arousing their interest in other subjects, it is often possible to receive an emotional response from them. A reserved attitude or the exaggerated control over affective expressions acquired through training (Americans, Japanese, etc.) can also impress misleadingly as lack of feeling.

In the following discussion, then, we shall always presume that the reader is capable of taking into consideration the accompanying circumstances as well as the total psychic constellation, so that it will not be necessary for us to enumerate the infinite possibilities of the situation every time.

It is especially important to take into account that an affect may normally release some schizophrenic-appearing phenomena and that much takes place on the periphery of our attention or in our night- and day-dreams, which is identical with schizophrenic disturbances of association and with stereotypies. In states of excitement, therefore, symptoms such as blocking, confusion of symbols with reality, transitivism, and neologisms, only have specific diagnostic value when they are very pronounced. However, if they should appear in a state of full clarity of consciousness, an observer who has carefully evaluated all the circumstances can often establish the diagnosis with certainty from a single such symptom. The clearer the patient's state of consciousness and the fewer reasons there are for the presence of affects, the milder may the symptoms be which permit a diagnosis of schizophrenia. The same applies to the differential diagnosis: epileptics may create symbols; they may confuse concepts such as man and woman, or coin neologisms, but only when their consciousness is clouded. Hysterics may show rigidity of affect, but only when they are dominated by a complex. Sick people as well as healthy people of all kinds may ignore the subject of conversation in their talk if they happen to have reason for adopting a negative attitude. But only schizophrenics exhibit such traits outside these general psychic conditions.

The generalization of symptoms is often decisive for the diagnosis.

Unless we can demonstrate an emotional stupor, the affective blocks of healthy individuals only apply to matters which are emotionally charged. The schizophrenic, however, often extends this blocking to all possible ideas — in very severe cases, the patient's entire psyche may be persistently blocked. At times, everyone may obscure concepts and ideas or make logical errors, especially when he happens to be in an unusual state, such as that of an affect, or that of exhaustion. In such cases these symptoms will appear and disappear with the releasing cause, whereas in schizophrenia they exist independently of all surrounding conditions.

Schizophrenic symptoms are not necessarily present all the time. In no other mental disease is it so uncertain whether or not a specific symptom will be present at any given moment. Even in advanced cases which usually appear wholly deteriorated, the affective disturbance and the characteristic pathological changes in associations may not be demonstrable at certain times. Even after examining the patient for several hours, one may be unable to establish the diagnosis with certainty in all cases.

It is, therefore, a matter of course that cases where the disease has come to a halt in its early stages are generally not recognized by laymen and psychiatrists. People spend a lifetime arguing with a schizophrenic housewife; "bad" children are punished in every possible way; attempts to use force with them fail miserably because the attending physician cannot testify to the presence of mental disease, or because even if he has testified to it, the director of the mental hospital will occasionally release the patient as well or cured to the dismay of the desperate parents; since they are considered hysterics, or, preferably, neurasthenics, such individuals are subjected to all sorts of therapies which often enough exhaust the entire savings of the worried family. These patients are admitted to hospitals with a diagnosis of "floating kidneys" when they are actually having hallucinatory birthpains; some gynecological deviation from the norm set forth in textbooks is considered a disease and consequently the patient's abdomen is being treated; they are turned over to the police and the courts, i.e., the agencies least suited for psychiatric treatment; they may even be taken seriously and be permitted to form clubs and organizations for the purpose of combatting some social malady which they claim to have discovered; and many other things are done with them that were better left undone.

Perhaps we will never succeed entirely in eliminating such situations. However, their incidence can be reduced considerably if we think more frequently of the possibility that we may be dealing with a case of mild schizophrenia and if we learn to recognize the signs of the disease.

In certain cases, emotional excitement will serve to activate the disease, in that it may make a latent symptom manifest. There are patients who reveal their pathological chain of ideas, their affective disorder, neologisms and other symptoms only under such conditions. Alcohol may sometimes serve as such an activating factor; it may provoke a typical schizophrenic excitement which, under certain circumstances, may outlast the alcoholic intoxication. However, neither one of these activating factors works in all cases and they cannot be recommended for experimental purposes for various reasons.

Yet we are not as badly off as Kraepelin's dictum would have it. He states that there is no single sign of this disease which is decisive for the differential diagnosis. The previously described disturbance of associations and also probably the type of hallucinations are characteristic and sufficient for a positive diagnosis; in addition, a general flattening of affect may serve this purpose.

It must be emphasized that the experience of one or two decades and of relatively few observers does not suffice to enable us to voice definite opinions on every aspect of this disease. One or the other symptom which at present we consider as belonging to schizophrenia exclusively, may possibly appear some day as a rare, accompanying phenomenon of other diseases.[2] Furthermore, we do not as yet know all psychoses, so that a delimination of schizophrenia in the direction of unknown symptom complexes can only have a one-sided tentative character. The general reservations will limit our discussions as to diagnosis, which must be based on the present state of knowledge.

If one is not reluctant to deal with simple probabilities, it can be considered a rule that the majority of doubtful cases reveal themselves as schizophrenics if one has the opportunity to observe them through a number of years.

In many instances, the patient's history provides such a good basis for a diagnosis that it is possible to recognize with certainty the existence of schizophrenia from the reports of relatives. In fact the behavior of many of our patients is so characteristic that it can be adequately described for us also by laymen.

2. Ths will apply especially to some symptoms which, at present, are not necessarily included in the concept of schizophrenia but which, nonetheless, are commonly seen in this disease and not in other psychoses. Indeed, we cannot exclude the possibility that we may sometime find a non-schizophrenic with predominantly auditory and body hallucinations and a schizophrenic in a state of clear consciousness with predominantly visual and tactile hallucinations. Heretofore, however, we have made only the reverse experience.

Alterations of character are important. A young man who has become "different" is in most cases mentally ill and most frequently hebephrenic.[3]

Just how prominent the various symptoms have to be in order to permit a diagnosis of schizophrenia can hardly be described. Indeed, we have no objective standards by which to measure the gradations of complicated psychic processes. In these cases only experience and, above all, a precise evaluation of the accompanying circumstances can decide. If the severity of a symptom permits the diagnosis of mental disease in general, it also can in most cases be utilized for the definition of the special psychosis involved, if it has specific significance.

B. The Significance of Individual Symptoms for the Differential Diagnosis

With respect to intellectual symptoms, disturbances of perception, orientation, and memory, in the sense that they were previously defined, never belong to schizophrenia; whereas they prove the existence of some other psychosis, they do not exclude the possibility of schizophrenia. On the other hand, definite schizophrenic disturbances of association alone are sufficient for the diagnosis.

In healthy persons and other non-schizophrenics blockings are transitory phenomena for which there are always some definite reasons that can be discovered. In schizophrenics, the blocks mostly prove themselves insurmountable; their psychological roots are often not easily discerned, and they have a tendency to generalize themselves, i.e., they are also found outside their connection with the complexes. However, it is sometimes impossible to differentiate a hysterical blocking from a schizophrenic one at a given moment. Furthermore, one must not confuse the emotional stupor, which in imbeciles, particularly, may last for weeks, with the pathological symptom.

The systematic splitting, with reference to personality, for example, may be found in many other psychotic conditions; in hysteria they are even more marked than in schizophrenia (multiple personalities). Definite splitting, however, in the sense that various personality fragments

3. However, a weakling has not become "different" if he lets himself go when transplanted to a new environment, although, under parental supervision he had behaved in a model fashion; the same is true when the opposite takes place. It is also not a change in character when an individual shows a conversion or striking modification of his previous good behavior as result of a conflict between two drives within himself, in which, at one time or other, each drive gains the upper hand, because of inner or external circumstances. If we learn how to avoid such misunderstandings, character changes can be very important sign posts.

exist side by side in a state of clear orientation as to environment, will only be found in our disease.

Autism in itself cannot be utilized for the diagnosis since it occurs in hysterical dream states, especially, and since it dominates also in some way the delusional ideas of the paretic. In the non-schizophrenic cases, the symptom has a somewhat different appearance, but it is difficult to describe that difference. Epileptics and organic cases simply withdraw into themselves when they assume attitudes which resemble autism, whereas the schizophrenics place themselves in conflict with and opposition to reality. Moreover, in non-schizophrenics, the isolation from the outside world is not as complete as in our patients; under certain circumstances, non-schizophrenics may not take an active interest in reality, but they immediately establish rapport with it when they are addressed, for example.

Obscurity of concepts is also a partial phenomenon of other diseases; however, if it has progressed so far that different persons or things are identified with each other in a state of clear consciousness, we must assume schizophrenia with certainty. Transitivism may also be observed in non-schizophrenics, but only when they are in a state of clouded consciousness. Isolated neologisms are of no significance from the standpoint of diagnosis (epilepsy), but if someone expresses an essential part of his thoughts in new words, he is schizophrenic. As a joke, a manic person may speak in a selfmade language, with no thought of making himself understood. The schizophrenic speaks his "artificial language" in the same way as we use our habitual idiom, but it does not matter to him whether or not he is understood.

The absence of ability for discussion is nowhere as conspicuous as in schizophrenics. Even when our patients agree to discuss their false notions, we regularly find alongside of correct and cleverly defended ideas others which are simply "so," as the patients like to say, and where entirely senseless deductions are made. The schizophrenic can split off facts which do not suit his affects; the obstinate person will just ignore them.

The expression of sudden ideas, especially when they are at the same time senseless or in contradiction to the rest of the personality, is a fairly reliable sign of schizophrenia.

The schizophrenic type of attention is often unmistakable; despite a complete lack of interest, the passive registration of external events functions perfectly. I have observed this phenomenon only in schizophrenia.

As for hallucination, it is important to note their preference for the auditory sphere and for body-sensations (cave: neuritic phenomena which can stimulate body hallucinations.)[4] Where delusions of physical persecutions, and auditory hallucinations continually dominate the clinical picture, one can practically always conclude that one is dealing with schizophrenia. The phenomenon of thoughts being heard (*Gedankenlautwerden*) occurs only very rarely in other psychoses. The isolation of the hallucinations from the realistic content of consciousness is also characteristic.

Schizophrenic hallucinations surely have still other characteristic peculiarities. But I do not venture to elaborate on them here because we know too little about the other hallucinatory psychoses.

Delusions often characterize themselves as schizophrenic merely by their content. Their senseless, poorly thought out, and fragmentary quality cannot be mistaken. Yet similar delusional ideas often occur in organic diseases (e.g. the hypochondriacal delusions of a depressed paretic) but the differences are not easily described. It is most indicative of schizophrenia when the delusions are not at all developed, when they are in strongest contrast to the simplest reality, and yet are expressed during periods of apparently clear consciousness. When a person continually produces entirely illogical ideas of persecution in a state of full clarity of consciousness he is nearly always a schizophrenic; if the characteristic hallucinations are also present, the diagnosis is certain.

The delusion that everyone already knows what the patient is thinking is almost pathognomonic.

The schizophrenic para-functioning and a-functioning of affectivity are decisive signs of our psychosis if we succeed in differentiating them from other forms of indifference. Persistent indifference toward vital interests is schizophrenic, even though with respect to less important issues we may find a normal emotional response. Since there are different average levels of affectivity, it is important to be alert not so much for minor deviations of mood in the direction of indifference as for the lack of capacity to modulate these moods. If the patient remains quantitatively and qualitatively rigid with regard to the same feelings, even though he responds to ideas of varying values, it would indicate schizophrenia. In mild cases, however, this symptom may be absent, or it may acquire similarity to the indifference of hysterics.

---

4. In organic mental diseases there appear at times similar false sensations which can usually be recognized as erroneously interpreted parathesias. In any event, they have an entirely different character than those of schizophrenic. Compare Sérieux, Ann. med.-psych., 1902, Sept., Oct.; also the body hallucinations of the epileptic aura.

An especially important and often very early sign is the unmotivated affect-less laughter. It is not easily mistaken for the laughter-spasms of nervous people.

As is well known, catatonic symptoms do not solely occur in schizophrenia. At least, it is still impossible to differentiate them always from similar conditions in organic psychoses. However, if they are very pronounced, and in the majority, schizophrenia is to be assumed.

Flexibilitas cerea (waxy catalepsy) is seen outside of catatonia in organic diseases. In addition, it occurs in epilepsy usually at the conclusion of attacks, occasionally in hysterics and perhaps in fever psychoses, certainly in the fever conditions of children. The rigid form of catalepsy is found more often in organic brain diseases of all kinds and in epilepsy. In such cases, however, the rigidity is generally independent of attempts at passive movements, whereas in the schizophrenic such attempts usually provoke or add to the muscle tone.

The other forms of command-automatism can probably occur in various states of non-schizophrenics, characterized by lack of will power; perhaps we can also find echopraxia, although in our cases it is extremely rare outside of schizophrenia. We encounter it occasionally in the form of echolalia in focal brain diseases, however, on a different psychological basis.

In practice, negativism cannot yet be separated from other forms of rejection. All kinds of healthy as well as sick persons become negativistic when they happen to be in a bad mood. If this mood is combined with obscure ideas concerning the environment as is so often the case with epileptics and organic patients, it can easily be mistaken for negativism. On the other hand, the simple resistance of anxious patients has rather the character of a gesture of flight and defense; it can be influenced by the physician's attitude and sometimes simply by friendly reassurance. These characteristics are absent in the schizophrenic who strikes us by contrast with his extraordinary indifference towards actual attacks made on his person. It is more difficult to distinguish negativism from a simple hostile attitude regarding the external world since hostile opposition towards the environment is one of the main roots of negativism. Negativism may also exist alongside, as well as independently, of such attitudes on the part of the patient; it is then often difficult to separate the two elements. Adamant and unreasonable negativism however, occurs very seldom in patients other than schizophrenics. Nevertheless, we must remember that even genuine negativism is not necessarily generalized and that it may manifest or conceal itself only under specific conditions or with respect to certain persons. Obstinacy, which also rests on a kind of exaggerated autism, differs from negativism in that the latter is a general symptom and that it remains entirely alien to normal feelings in most of its expressions.

Stereotypies are most common in schizophrenics, but they are not wholly absent in other types of patients and even in normal people. However, most catatonic stereotypies differ from the others in their senselessness and in their lack of correspondence with the patients' feelings and thoughts. Verbigeration is generally easily differentiated from poverty of ideas and perseveration (in organics), both of which may cause word repetition, if one only considers the possibility of these different symptoms. The stereotyped attitude of paretics is most commonly confused with catatonic symptoms.

When dealing with "mannerisms," one must also be alert for the exaggerated, the inappropriate, etc. To some degree, mannerisms are frequently present in healthy individuals as well as in the mentally ill. Once our attention is brought to bear on them, tics are usually easily differentiated. If the mannerisms are very pronounced, they constitute an important point of differentiation from other diseases.

Stupor which also occurs in organic brain diseases, in manic-depressive psychosis, epilepsy, and hysteria can as such only be utilized for the diagnosis, if the schizophrenic genesis of the stupor (blocking, autism, etc.) can either be proven or excluded. Furthermore, a stupor is probably always schizophrenic if the patient appears to be in a state of clear consciousness and carefully observes his environment. It is also important to keep in mind that Gross was unable to detect in his cases of catatonic stupor disturbances of comprehension or evidence of motor inhibitions.

As for motor symptoms, the deep reflexes which are always exaggerated in our patients help support the diagnosis and the facial nerve phenomenon, particularly, is rare both in other psychoses or in healthy persons.[5] Also, the idio-muscular irritability should be tested.

According to Ziehen (840), there is in melancholia attonita a general tension which contrasts to the debility of melancholia passiva. Gaupp (255) also finds that tension is more likely to be present in the muscles of a patient with catatonic stupor than in other diseases.

Paresthesias: Kahlbaum states that occipital headaches are common

5. Dunton W. Rush states that when a patient is struck lightly with the percussion hammer on the cheek just anterior to the ear, certain movements of the *orbicularis palpebrum* result, particularly in early cases. I do not know whether this skin reflex really has any diagnostic significance.

in catatonia but rare in other mental diseases; other types of headache show the reverse relationship. So far, I have been unable to see anything definitely characteristic in the paresthesias. For the most part, of course, they are mostly schizophrenic in those cases where the patients believe that they were "caused" by other people.

We might also mention here the reduced muscular and psychic fatigability observed in many schizophrenics (compare also catalepsy!). It might be of some significance on comparison with organic psychoses, for example (Ziehen, 846).

Of other physical symptoms, we must mention the disturbances of the pupillary reaction. Pupils which are abnormally dilated without detectable cause, such as a state of agitation, are nearly always indicative of catatonia. Such wide pupils are rare in simple mania.[6]

Naturally, edemas can only be considered as signs of schizophrenia if all other causes are excluded; perhaps their inelasticity on pressure is of some significance for the diagnosis.

Metabolic findings (urine, etc.) are as yet of no diagnostic importance. It may only be of some value to know that there is frequently great variability of body weight without apparent cause in our patients. In addition, improvement in the general nutritional status without a corresponding psychic improvement during the period of an acute attack indicates with great probability the presence of schizophrenia.

The abnormalities of gastric secretion (Pilcz) still require a great deal more investigation and a greater quantity of material before one can impute to them any value as diagnostic criteria.

In acute attacks of any kind the diagnosis is made on the basis of the presence of the specific schizophrenic symptoms. The experienced specialist can often make the diagnosis by evaluating solely the overall impression he receives from the patient; indeed, the disease is so common that he runs a very small risk if he uses some caution. However, by using such methods of diagnosis one deprives oneself of the opportunity to detect in time the more unusual states of agitation which do not yet fit into the framework of the diseases. Furthermore, complete certainty as to the diagnosis can only be gained by establishing proof of the existence of decisive symptoms. Up to now, I have observed exclusively in schizophrenia sudden remissions in the midst of an acute episode. During these remissions the patient behaves as if nothing unusual had happened in spite of the fact that his memory

6. For the significance of other pupillary anomalies, see below: the differential diagnosis of paresis.

is intact. The clouded, mentally inert states (*Benommenheit*) are naturally difficult to investigate. They are schizophrenic if we can prove that the degree of what we call "the clouded state" is out of any proportion to the actual obstruction of thinking, in so far as the patients still observe and register everything going on around them.

There are no negative pathognomic signs that would exclude the existence of schizophrenia. The fact that a disease responds to psychic influences has by some been interpreted as such a sign (Specht, and Gaupp). However, we frequently see that even what we call schizophrenic deterioration can, to a considerable degree, be improved or aggravated by psychic influences.

If signs of another psychosis are present, e.g., a paresis, the diagnosis of schizophrenia should in most cases be dropped for practical reasons. On the other hand, this is never proof that one is not dealing with a dementia praecox, in addition to the organic cerebral disease. So far, we cannot exclude the possibility of latent schizophrenia in anyone, no more than we can exclude a latent pulmonary tuberculosis.

C. Differential Diagnosis

At this point, we will deal only with the special difficulties and differential signs of schizophrenia as compared to other diseases. If the previously mentioned general indications of schizophrenia are present and sufficiently prominent, the diagnosis is self-evident.

Unfortunately, at this time, it is not yet possible to discuss the differential diagnosis of schizophrenia without considering the symptomatology of other psychoses, in whose description insufficient attention is often paid to precisely those points which are important for our present discussion.

1. The symptomatological differentiation of schizophrenia from manic-depressive psychosis can only be based on the presence of the specific schizophrenic symptoms. All the phenomena of manic-depressive psychosis may also appear in our disease; the only decisive factor is the presence or absence of schizophrenic symptoms. Therefore, neither a state of manic exaltation nor a melancholic depression, nor the alternation of both states has any significance for the diagnosis. Only after careful observation has revealed no schizophrenic features, may we conclude that we are dealing with a manic-depressive psychosis.

The disturbance of affect has at all times been considered the most important sign of deterioration ("dementia").

In manic-depressive psychosis the affects are strong and entirely distinct; but they are indistinct and often almost indefinable or absent in clear-cut cases of schizophrenia. Their absence is especially striking when, simultaneously, the content of the patients' speech expresses ideas of grandeur or despair. One must be particularly careful to note whether or not there is evidence of a capacity for modulation of the affects. The manic and in a certain sense also the melancholic individual is fixed to an abnormal level of affectivity without having lost the capacity to suit his moods to all the nuances of his thought content. However, in the schizophrenic even a marked basic affect is somewhat rigid and if there are changes of mood they often appear unmotivated, not paralleling the content of ideas.

The manic outbreaks of rage can usually be traced to normal motives; the patient is angry about restrictions, about a denied request, etc. The manic schizophrenic often has outbursts of rage which appear hardly motivated at all, or, at least, qualitatively inappropriate.

The lack of homogeneity of mood is an especially important sign. Unity is lacking, not in a temporal sense, but insofar as the various psychic expressions do not seem to belong together. We are definitely not dealing with manic-depressive psychosis when content and expression of speech contradict each other; when in the very same sentence words and thoughts appear which correspond to different moods or to different nuances, and indifferent expressions stand side by side with exaggeratedly euphoric or despairing ones; when even the facial expression is dissociated so that, for example, the upper part of the face expresses an affect different from that of the lower part. The schizophrenic can be cheerful, anxious, elated, or depressed, not only in rapid succession, but practically simultaneously. In spite of marked euphoric excitement, the schizophrenic can enjoy normally long and deep sleep. All this differentiates him from the manic.

The indifferent euphoria of many schizophrenics must not be confused with the elated mood of the manic.

In addition to the above-mentioned signs the schizophrenic lack of activity may serve as a diagnostic aid. This lack of activity is also seen in cases where the basic disease is complicated by an actually manic mood. A manic state which is not accompanied by a corresponding pressure of activity is, as a rule, a symptomatic and most commonly a schizophrenic one.

Generally, the pressure of activity is rarely absent in mania (except in the "mixed forms" described by Weygandt) whereas we see very little of it in the agitated states of dementia praecox. Brosius has drawn attention to the striking behavior of demented individuals who idly survey the remnants of objects they have ruined during a preceding destructive outburst. The manic, on the other hand, zealously tries to utilize such remnants in one way or another. Only in the schizophrenic does the continuous climbing and moving about, and his destructiveness appear completely senseless. When the manic indulges in this type of activity we know, as a rule, what he is thinking.

Wernicke (1904) directs attention to the lack of proportion between the urge to talk and the need for activity in his "hyperkinetic motility psychosis." He reports that in the manic the urge to talk is predominant; in the "motility psychosis" on the other hand, a strong need for activity is often coupled with little desire for speech, and even the latter observation is correct; but there are also types of mania in which the patients spontaneously do not talk very much. In accordance with Kraepelin, the difference is much better expressed by stating that agitated schizophrenics have too little contact with their surroundings; in general, they are remarkably independent of environmental conditions and influences; "the need for activity bears the characteristic features of monotony and compulsion; it is absolutely aimless and cannot be influenced from the outside. We are frequently struck by the stilted manner in which certain types of activity are carried out."[7]

The patients converse only rarely with those around them even when they are talking a great deal. The incitement to speech as well as its content originates for the most part autistically from inner sources. Manic schizophrenics may even continuously keep their eyes closed, not only in the ward but also, for example, during the greater part of a clinical presentation. Thus I cannot understand how Wernicke comes to present definite hypermetamorphosis as a significant factor in the differential diagnosis between the hyperkinetic motility psychosis and mania. Exaggerated distractibility may be present in catatonic excitement; however, it is rarely as marked as in mania and usually milder. More often we meet with the opposite, i. e., a state of pathological hypo-vigility.

The manic flight of ideas must not be confused with schizophrenic incoherence. In manic episodes of schizophrenia, naturally both types of disturbances occur. It is important to know that the flight of ideas cannot lead to a loosening of habitual concepts or to actual falsification of logical functions. The manic does not consider a person simultaneously as man and woman and he does not seriously

---

7. Kraepelin, Ztschr. f. Psych., 99, p. 225.

attribute to entirely accidental associations causal or logical connections which are not at all warranted.

The flight of ideas cannot always at first glance be distinguished from the incoherence of schizophrenia, since a sort of aimlessness is characteristic of both. We must note that the flight of ideas is not really lacking in direction, but that the direction changes with every movement. Since in the schizophrenic leaps of thought not all connections must necessarily be disrupted, we often find in this disturbance associations which resemble, and occasionally are identical with, the superficial auditory and motor associations of the flight of ideas. In most instances, however, the diagnosis has to be made on the basis of a relatively small amount of material since in the schizophrenic the associations are more disconnected than in the manic. Therefore, we find in schizophrenic associations the bizarre, the unscrupulously senseless. On the other hand, the genuine flight of ideas brings into the open associations which are not only understandable for a normal person but which normal individuals often have themselves and which they suppress, such as rimes, elaborations on words, etc. Thus associations, as for instance, obscene — not seen at night; pleased — policed; gymnasium — gypsy would occur in manics only under very special conditions.

Even associations which are normal in themselves or which show only slight traces of flight of ideas, become bizarre when used in sentences which appear to be devoid of sense and which show lack of homogeneity of mood in their expression as well as in feeling.

"Help me light a Christmas tree of the world on the twenty-fifth current; I may light it and decorate it with your aid by means of a small bell through my mother, I must blow a toy-horn, my modern testament without money."

In this specimen all associations are still comprehensible; however, the fact that they are thrown together in a sentence is distinctly indicative of schizophrenia. The indication is not only the absurdity of the fact that the patient should want to light the tree with a bell but also, among other things, the fact that in spite of the generally solemn mood of the sentence, he includes the business-like expression, "the twenty-fifth current."

Whereas the manic is unable to hide his agitation in either his speech or his handwriting, the schizophrenic is confused also in the absence of any excitement. Only the schizophrenic is capable of writing externally perfect thirty-page letters full of disconnected nonsense; only in this disease is it possible for patients to knit a stocking without making a single mistake although otherwise their actions are entirely irrational.

In addition, the difference between schizophrenia and mania is revealed in the explanations offered by the patients for their behavior. Manic individuals often make their actions appear quite plausible to themselves and others: the attendants were too rude to them so they proceeded to demolish the furniture, etc. The schizophrenics use their previously described absurd excuses: they smashed a window pane because they are not permitted to go home, or because the nurse wears an apron. Sometimes they do not feel the need at all to find explanations for their behavior.

In manic-depressive mixed states the patients repeat themselves sometimes in a tiresome way despite obvious signs of flight of ideas; they may also construct endless chains of similar ideas (names, places, etc.). With some attention, this phenomenon will not be confused with verbigeration in which the patient has no intention whatever of saying anything. As a rule, we are not dealing with mania if the patient constantly repeats ideas which he had expressed earlier, unless special interest motivates this behavior.

Truly indirect associations hardly ever play a particularly striking role in the mania of manic-depressives whereas they are quite common in schizophrenia.

Another important sign of schizophrenia is the meaning which the abnormal associations come to have for the patients. Whereas the individual suffering from flight of ideas with his rimes and assonances, the content of the bizarre schizophrenic associations is being utilized and often has the value of truth for the patient: thus the initials F.L. on the tablecloth in connection with the oval table itself remind the hebephrenic woman not only of the word *folle* (crazy) but they tell her that she is *folle*. There is no manic to whom the phrase, "joyful greeting" would occur and who would have the very peculiar association, "void" to the word "joy" which he utilizes in concluding a letter in the form of, "joyful greetings to the void yours Ad." In this manner, only schizophrenics employ accidental, external connections in a logically false way. It is true that the manic includes all kinds of fortuitous events into his chain of ideas. He is particularly prone to permit this chain to be completely diverted by external perceptions; his superficiality may go so far as to border on senselessness but it never leads to utter absurdity.

On the other hand, the fascination by external impressions, the "naming," the "fixation" (*Bannung*) are anomalies which are part of schizophrenia but never of the flight of ideas.

If the schizophrenic and manic disturbances of association have developed into complete confusion it may, for a short time, be impossible to differentiate between them.

We have already discussed the experimental associations in schizophrenia in the section on symptomatology. At this point, I wish to note only that in contrast to the prompt reactions of manics, the reaction-times of schizophrenics are frequently irregular and long.

Isserlin (342) states the following concerning the association experiments: "In cases where we can regularly note an attempt to do justice to the meaning of the stimulus word, despite a long reaction-time and even though there may be but a limited variety of ideas and a rather slight affect, we shall not hesitate to make a diagnosis of a depression of manic-depressive psychosis." In most cases he will be right. Pfersdorff's criterion is less reliable. According to him manic-depressive psychosis is indicated when every new stimulus-word brings out a new attitude. There are, after all, many mild schizophrenics who are able to follow every new stimulus even though their behavior may be somewhat stuporous.

Aside from the specific peculiarities of schizophrenic agitations, the affectations, the theatrical mode of behavior, and, especially, the monotony of movements which are incomprehensible for the observer, are characteristically in contrast to mania. The manic acts; some of the agitated schizophrenics merely move their limbs.

The differentiation between inhibition and blocking enables us to distinguish schizophrenic states from the stuporous and depressive states of manic-depressive psychosis, with which they used to be confused. In manic-depressive psychosis, blocking takes no part. In inhibition, we find a general heaviness and slowing up of movements and thinking, together with evidence of sad affect; in blocking, there are variations in strength and rapidity of movements and thinking. The inhibited individual carries out an order (as, for example, to rotate his hands around each other, to count, etc.) slowly, weakly, unproductively, and gives up quickly. The severely blocked patient does not obey at all to start with; but once his resistance is broken he proceeds with usually normal strength and speed. However, in rare cases differentiation may become almost impossible on account of the total absence of reaction in the severely stuporous forms of both diseases. In that event, Wernicke's (804) suggestion may be of some help. He noted that "melancholics" usually look at the questioner, even when they do not answer; schizophrenics, on the other hand, give no sign of understanding and may even turn away. Sometimes blocking distinctly differentiates itself from inhibition by the fact that it disappears at once if the patient's attention can be directed to a subject which is unrelated to his complexes; except in mild cases, however, inhibition continues in evidence, even when the patient is distracted. Although it is easy to avoid the error, inhibition is occasionally mistaken for negativism.

The apparent "dullness" of manic-depressives, which occurs sometimes as an aftereffect of the manic state, sometimes as a mild form of the depressive phase, has rather frequently simulated "deterioration." However, since the entire syndrome can be completely explained on basis of the presence of a mild form of inhibition, the diagnosis can be made with more certainty.

As yet, it is often difficult to distinguish the delusional states of manic-depressive psychosis from schizophrenia. Only after lengthy and thorough observation will the absence of schizophrenic symptoms prove that a diagnosis of manic-depressive psychosis is indicated. These cases are, however, very rare; in all likelihood, therefore, one is dealing with schizophrenia. The presence of schizophrenia must always be assumed unless a distinct depression or euphoria can be demonstrated.

According to Schuele (675a) we are no longer dealing with melancholia but with paranoia (i.e., schizophrenia in our sense) if the patient's delusions appear alien to him and as having greater importance than their logical value would merit. Although this criterion will not always be easy to apply, the statement is correct; it is precisely the split-off part of the patient's personality which forces upon the other the hallucinations and their interpretation.

After an acute attack has been "cured," the attitude regarding the delusions differs in the majority of schizophrenics from that of manic-depressives. Even if schizophrenics recognize their delusions as false, they do not really take a stand with regard to them; they block them off, they refuse to acknowledge them.

Kölpin claims that the memory of a melancholic stupor is more defective than that of a catatonic stupor. I cannot admit the validity of this. Even in the stuporous states of schizophrenia there are twilight states which are followed by total or partial amnesia and a melancholic stupor may later be quite well remembered.

I am unable to judge the merits of Pfersdorff's (560) statement that in manic-depressive delusions entire regions of the body (chest, abdomen, etc.) figure prominently, instead of an individual organ.

The differences in the course of both diseases are obvious inasmuch as schizophrenia may lead to a specific deterioration whereas between the attacks of manic-depressive psychosis the patient is in a normal state, except, perhaps for an increased emotionality, but without any actual disturbance of associative capacity and intelligence.

If manic-depressive psychosis takes a turn for the worse, it means that the healthy intervals either become increasingly shorter or that they disappear altogether. It must be noted that, on the one hand, the periodic or cyclic course may be absent in manic-depressive psychosis whereas, on the other hand, it may occur in schizophrenia. It is highly probable that the case is one of manic-depressive psychosis if there have been many previous attacks and if it is nevertheless impossible to find distinct signs of schizophrenia.

As yet we can hardly hope to find any clues to the diagnosis in heredity since the factor of heredity in psychoses has not been adequately investigated and because of the complicated nature of our origin.

Kraepelin's involutional melancholia probably belongs in the same category as manic-depressive psychosis. In this connection it must be pointed out that many late catatonias begin with melancholic symptoms to which distinctively catatonic symptoms are added only subsequently. In such cases it is always well to obtain a detailed history with special reference to earlier attacks of schizophrenia, particularly during puberty; attention must also be paid to the possibility of the presence of a schizophrenic character since it is not at all common that the initial attack of schizophrenia occurs in the involutional period. Furthermore, it must be remembered that mild flattening of affect and indications for the presence of catatonic symptoms may also signify the beginnings of senile dementia.

Ziehen also finds thought-hearing in his cases of melancholia. However, I believe that this symptom indicates schizophrenia with a good deal of certainty. Contrary opinions notwithstanding, it must also be maintained that sudden improvements or aggravations in the patient's condition under the influence of psychic factors in no way speak against a diagnosis of schizophrenia. On the contrary, I do not believe that a melancholia can be substantially improved through psychic influences, such as transfer to another institution (Stelzner), whereas improvement due to a change of environment is common in schizophrenia (Riklin, 611).

2. The two principal organic psychoses, dementia paralytica and senile dementia, can easily be differentiated from schizophrenia inasmuch as they have certain positive symptoms which assure the diagnosis. Characteristic disturbances of memory which consist in the rapid forgetting of recent events; quicker and more pronounced slackening

of habitual attention as compared with maximal attention; fatigability, slowness and uncertainty of perception; disturbances of orientation; the ease with which the qualitatively well-preserved but pathologically labile emotions can be evoked — all these are well-known as distinct symptoms of an extensive and gross cortical disturbance. They are not found in uncomplicated schizophrenia.

Less well-known and not easily described is the organic type of disturbances of association and of intelligence, which is actually the same thing. In the discussion of this subject we must limit ourselves to mere suggestions which are necessary for the differential diagnosis.

The disturbance of associations in organic cases manifests itself in the fact that their number has been reduced; the psychic horizon has been narrowed.[8] The limitations that take place are most striking with respect to the instinctive drives or the affects, which are essentially the same. The paretic who would like to make some big business deal is only aware of its favorable aspects; the bad ones simply do not exist for him. At a later stage, he will want to appropriate some object in his ward; he will steal it with a sly expression on his face and hide it carefully under his clothes—all this before the very eyes of the attendants and of the other patients who, at the moment, have ceased to exist for him. The old man wants to satisfy his sexual drives. He sees in a little girl only the woman. He does not stop to consider the moral reasons which forbid sexual intercourse with children; he abuses the first child he happens to meet. Thus the registration of events to which the patient's immediate attention is not directed suffers badly, and with it the orientation.

The schizophrenic is entirely different. His associations are also limited but in respect to his complexes which may not be acute at a given moment. Many thoughts are split off and absolutely incapable of establishing any associative contact with certain others. However, the associations remain free outside the blocked pathways; several association-complexes may develop simultaneously. Thus the patient's capacity for unconscious registration is excellent.[9]

The paretic peeps at the world through a small hole. It is possible to show him, successively, almost all the details, however, he never gets a complete view. The schizophrenic sees fragments which are as large or as small as he choses and which are connected with each other. He is potentially capable of establishing the connection between these fragments, but actually he often does not do so. In organic

8. I cannot as yet characterize in a positive manner the incoherence of paretic states of confusion and of the aimless paretic harangues.

9. The exceptions to this are secondarily determined.

delusions there exists at the given moment exclusively the complex (the wish, the fear, etc.); in the delusional ideas of schizophrenics there exists also the contradiction to the delusion; but the two are not brought into logical connection with each other. Thus the patient with a senile dementia as well as the schizophrenic, may become engaged to some woman, unconcerned over the fact that he is already married. However, if one succeeds in reminding the senile individual of this obstacle to his engagement, he will comprehend the situation, even if not entirely. For the schizophrenic, on the other hand, this obstacle simply would not exist at such a moment, although in another connection he could evaluate the situation much better than the senile.

The split also reveals itself in the manner of speech. When the paretic says, "Tomorrow my wife will come to take me home," he knows what he is saying and is pleased about it; contradiction can only come from the outside. In most cases, the hebephrenic would say the very same words in an unpleasantly assertive tone; he would noticeably struggle against some inner contradiction which he does not express in words.

The "apathy" noted in organic cases, which is found particularly in senile patients, less often in the paretics, is a secondary phenomenon. These patients are no longer able to comprehend their environment sufficiently well to take part in it. Neither can they understand their own situation in such a way that it can have any affective value for them. However, if the patients are supplied with the necessary ideas, they will respond with the corresponding affect, in contrast to schizophrenics.

In general, patients with organic disturbances are pleasant people with whom one is in continuous rapport, be it positive or negative. Thus, in sharp contrast to schizophrenics, they also show an exaggerated tendency to let themselves be influenced by those who know how to handle them.

The hallucinations can also be utilized in the differential diagnosis. Great frequency of hallucinations probably excludes a diagnosis of paresis and also of senile dementia, unless the hallucinations are, in the main, limited to night time. Besides these signs of organic disease, there are a number of physical symptoms which can only be observed in paresis.[10]

Huebner (314) sums up the differentiation of the psychic pupillary

10. It is often difficult to distinguish the awkward handwriting of the clouded schizophrenic with its many omitted letters and its multiple condensations from that of the paretic.

reactions in the following words: "Absence of pupillary instability and sensory reaction with a preserved light reflex and prompt convergence reaction favors the diagnosis of dementia praecox. If the light reflex and other sensory reactions are intact and the only abnormality is the absence of pupillary instability, the presence of organic brain disease must be suspected." The frequent differences in pupillary reactions seen in schizophrenics are, in contrast to those seen in paretics, not associated with any rigidity of the pupils, but rather at most with some weakening of the light reflex. The schizophrenic pupillary differences vary rapidly, often several times in the course of a day with the result that at times first one, then the other pupil becomes wider. Persistent pupillary inequalities are usually due to complications.

It is most important to establish proof of the presence of leucocytosis or of a positive Wassermann reaction of the spinal fluid, which are indicative of an organic lesion of the central nervous system.

Cases where paresis and schizophrenia are combined, are regarded as so exceptional (this is probably not quite justified) that they are hardly taken into consideration. On the other hand, combinations of dementia senilis with schizophrenia are quite common. Late catatonics, especially, may represent such mixed cases.

Korsakoff's psychosis also belongs with the organic psychoses. When fully developed, this syndrome can never be mistaken for schizophrenia. Schizophrenic symptoms may develop subsequently, but—as previously mentioned — we do not as yet know whether such symptoms are the outcome of arrested cerebral alterations or whether they are manifestations of a simultaneously existing schizophrenia. Therefore, the discussion on differential diagnosis cannot as yet deal with this problem.

The problem of differentiating schizophrenia from certain psychotic conditions which accompany severe focal lesions of the brain (trauma, tumors, etc.) and produce similar symptoms remains as yet unsolved. In all cases which I have observed closely, it was possible to make the diagnosis on the basis of the organic symptoms, or it was at least striking that none of the supposedly schizophrenic symptoms were particularly clear. A case of cerebral tuberculosis which we erroneously designated as schizophrenia, after much hesitation and because of the lack of any possible diagnosis, was characterized by the patient's marked clouded state of consciousness and greatly delayed reactions. Unfortunately, these cases are too rare to enable us to say anything more definite about them. Yet, it should be remembered that schizophrenia can be complicated by focal cerebral lesions.

3. In most instances, the differentiation of schizophrenia from idiocy is very easy. There are, of course, people who are of a different opinion. Masoin (454) expresses their views in the most drastic manner when he states that he considers catatonia as a late idiocy and when he asserts that without an anamnesis it is often impossible to distinguish hebephrenia in its final stages from idiocy. The entire similarity of the two diseases merely rests on the fact that in both conditions the capacity of thinking proves itself defective. Real problems arise when the schizophrenia is not very marked or when it is combined with imbecility, as happens so often. Idiots are unable to form associations which demand somewhat complicated thinking or which are unusual. An imbecile who cannot add figures, will also be unable to do subtraction or even division; anyone, who cannot construct the concept parents out of two components, father and mother, is certainly also incapable of clearly comprehending the concept "fatherland." The schizophrenic, on the other hand, can fail just as easily in a simple mental task as in a complicated one. Blocking interrupts the associative pathways according to entirely different laws. Thus, if the schizophrenic expresses himself at all in words or acts, he can always demonstrate that he has learned to understand a great deal that would be beyond the capacities of an idiot. Neither have his movements, his speech, etc., anything at all in common with those of the idiot.

The emotional life of idiots and imbeciles (I mention the latter in this connection in full awareness of the contrast to Sollier's incorrect classification) does not resemble that of schizophrenics. The emotional life of such mental defectives may vary within wide limits, but it is uninhibited. The physician's relations to the idiots in his institution resemble those of a father toward his children; but the schizophrenics remain to him as strange as the birds which he feeds.

The agitations of idiots are either outbursts of rage or hysteriform excitements caused by situations they are unable to understand or sometimes, they are, twilight states similar to epilepsy, accompanied by headaches, vasomotor disturbances, etc., all of which are unrelated to schizophrenia. The emotional stupor to which imbeciles are easily subjected may lead to confusion with schizophrenia. The stupor occurs easily when an unfamiliar situation arises, such as an interrogation, a transfer to the complicated environment of a mental hospital, etc. Sometimes the stupor appears only as a result of isolated questions which are beyond the patient's capacity of comprehension. It may then give the impression of a sudden blocking. Furthermore, in imbeciles as in little children there is a tendency to answer with anything that happens to come to mind at the moment. With a little patience, one will easily find one is dealing with guesses and not with negativism, an inadequate differentiation between knowledge and supposition, and not lack of interest in the examination.

The stereotypes of imbeciles correspond in part to the swinging of the legs, the swaying motions, the twisting of a strand of hair, and similar expressions of a need for activity which we observe in healthy persons; in that event, they have, almost without exception, an entirely elementary character. Others resemble tics; although their essential features are hard to describe, it is not difficult to note that the motions are not split off from the psyche: the entire person of the patient is "making" these movements; definite kinds of movements belong to certain poses and certain moods with their expressions. The repetition of the same exclamation, of the same words, is different from schizophrenic verbigerations. Such repetitions are generally expressions of poverty of ideas and words which can only repeat the same again and again (compare also Weygandt, 816). Mannerisms in behavior as well as in expression can be observed in many imbeciles. These people assume certain poses, employ unusual words, phrases, etc. The reason for this is that they often have what may be called the "intelligence complex;" they want to appear better than they actually are. This particular symptom is, therefore, identical with certain forms of schizophrenic mannerisms.

In moral idiocy the only feelings constantly lacking are those of ethics. The fact that the character has remained unchanged since earliest childhood proves that there is some congenital disturbance. Obviously, genuine schizophrenic signs cannot be found in this disease.

4. The differential diagnosis regarding the Kraepelinian paranoia can be inferred from the description of the malady. There is an absence of all specifically schizophrenic and catatonic symptoms. The delusions arise on false premises and are essentially incorrigible, that is, they are blocked off from any logical associations which might contradict them but otherwise they are built up with logical consistency. Thus a paranoiac is able to argue about his delusional system, whereas the paranoid cannot even comprehend the objections to his ideas, least of all, evaluate them. In paranoia I have never encountered the delusion that an inner influence is exerted by external forces. Of course, the presence of a few hallucinations is no indication against a paranoia, since they may even appear in healthy persons. However, if delusions dominate the picture not only during a rare and quickly passing excitement, other signs of schizophrenia will always be found

too. It is well-known that the paranoiac does not lose contact with his environment, but that he rather maintains an external attitude identical with that of healthy persons who have been subjected to powerful affective experiences.

There is no point in discussing the differential diagnosis in relation to the other psychoses which are still being designated as paranoia since all the known paranoid forms belong with our concept of schizophrenia.

5. The differentiation from epilepsy is of greater importance. Fuhrmann (248) finds a similarity between acute juvenile deterioration, epilepsy and delirium tremens. This similarity, however, is a very superficial one.

Let us first consider the epileptic delirium. It has in common with many schizophrenic states the hallucinations, the disorientation, and the utter lack of consideration for the environment. However, there is a great difference in the nature of the affectivity. In epilepsy we find a definite, usually entirely elementary mood, which is uniformly expressed in every single word, in the tone of every sentence and in every action. In schizophrenia, the expressions of affect are obscure or at least inconsistent, and are always somewhat rigid and artificial even in moments of real anxiety or ecstasy.

With respect to the intellect, the epileptic is slow in comprehending and has difficulty in understanding a subject matter; in the schizophrenic, the blocks in the comprehensive faculty may momentarily be replaced by very rapid reactions to complex perceptions. The chain of thoughts which is characteristic for either one disease can usually be detected. In this connection we might mention that the thinking processes of epileptics do progress, in spite of the patient's difficulty in abandoning any particular thought, once they have grasped it and in spite of their tendency to repetition. Moreover, the epileptic acts in accordance with his delirious imagination,[11] whereas the behavior of schizophrenics in a clouded state of consciousness often appears purposeless and nearly always inconsistent with his ideas.

Differentiation becomes difficult only when the patient refuses to submit to examination; for instance, in the state of post-epileptic irritability, during which the patients lie idely in bed, withdrawn from their environment, and react to any approach only with insults or with acts of violence. Occasionally, such a picture cannot at once be

11. In markedly cloudy states, e.g., during or directly after an epileptic attack, motor coordination may be so severely disturbed that it may be difficult to determine the purpose of the movements.

distinguished from schizophrenia negativism. Attacks of flexibilitas cerea as such are also common to both diseases. However, it is important to know that in epilepsy this state of waxy flexibility generally lasts only a short time, from a quarter of an hour to a few days[12] at most whereas in schizophrenia it usually lasts for weeks and months.

Superficially, the epileptic deterioration may at times resemble schizophrenia by way of its epileptic irritability, the seemingly exaggerated manifestations of emotion and the spontaneous development of ill-humor. The resemblance becomes especially pronounced when hallucinations are also added to the epileptic picture.

Often, the epileptic also withdraws increasingly into himself. However, the epileptic egocentricity of thinking differs considerably from the autism of the schizophrenic. Distortion of reality is rarely seen in epileptics, and then only under very special circumstances and only in a specific instance — as is also the case with normal people who are overwhelmed by their emotions. (We are not discussing clouded states.) The withdrawn epileptic pays little attention to reality, but no logical conflict develops between him and reality. The epileptic stubbornness is, of course, far from being autism.

The epileptic associations with their critical evaluations, their egocentricity, their perseveration, which is expressed in repetitions and in the fixation to a single theme, with consequent precise attention to details, have nothing whatever in common with schizophrenic thinking. Hesitancy in the course of ideas is easily distinguished from blocking. The obscurity of comprehension, the vagueness of more complicated concepts, and the disturbances of memory in advanced cases also differentiate epilepsy from schizophrenia.

The nature of the affectivity is entirely different in the two diseases. Whereas in the schizophrenic the affects are blocked, the emotions of epileptics are easily aroused, remarkably persistent, and deep-seated. We find indifference only with respect to situations which the patients cannot understand, but never with respect to their personal interests, which, on the contrary, are emotionally charged to a far greater degree than is the case with normal individuals. We must also note the exaggerated object-love of the epileptic in contrast to the schizophrenic who, as a rule, exhibits often extreme indifference concerning his property, regardless of its size.

According to Aschaffenburg, it may be assumed that identical variations of mood occur in epilepsy and in dementia praecox, inasmuch as epileptic attacks can also be observed in the latter disease. However,

12. At least, I have never seen an epileptic flexibilitas of longer duration.

this conclusion is not convincing since epileptiform attacks, corresponding to innate mechanisms, can occur under the most varied pathological conditions. Nonetheless, depressed moods based on inner difficulties are very common in schizophrenia — with or without epileptiform attacks. There are also conditions which are characterized by a combination of the symptoms of both diseases.

At times epileptics may suffer from hallucinations, particularly of the visual type, even outside of twilight states. This state may occasionally lead to confusion with schizophrenia. Automatic movements also occur in epilepsy as well as even the patients' peculiar feeling that their thoughts are being made for them on the outside.

According to my findings, the odd drawing-out of syllables ("singing") and the hesitating type of speech which if present, is so characteristic of epileptics, is never imitated in the mannerisms of schizophrenics; neither do schizophrenics show the pathological attention to detail observed in epileptics.

6. In practice, chronic alcoholism and schizophrenia are still very often confused since in a schizophrenic drunkard only the drinking, and not the fundamental disease, seems to attract attention. However, in simple alcoholism we find superficial, easily aroused emotions, euphoria, the need to let oneself go, talkativeness, inaccurate reports of personal experience or of something read, with a need to insert casual trimmings while telling the story — all symptoms alien to schizophrenia.

Where alcoholism has developed on the basis of schizophrenia, we find combinations of the symptoms of both diseases. However, the alcoholic symptoms gradually improve on hospitalization. A seclusive alcoholic with whom no conversation is possible, who sits around on the ward without seizing every opportunity to explain how improved he is, and how important it is for him to be released, will turn out to be a hebephrenic, unless he has very special, logical reasons for such an attitude.

The differentiation between delirium tremens and the agitated state of schizophrenia is so simple that it is hard to understand how it is possible that so many schizophrenics are referred to institutions with a diagnosis of delirium tremens. The peculiar state of consciousness, which Bonhoeffer has so well described, the well-known nature of hallucinations with the visual and tactile type predominating, the anxiously euphoric emotional state, the occupational deliria, the agility and uncertainty of movements, in contrast to the large, clumsy motor activity of the excited schizophrenic — these are characteristic signs of delirium tremens. Tremor, as such, can also occur in schizophrenia; however, if it is severe, it indicates the presence of delirium tremens. In a definite case of delirium tremens, there is no detailed recollection of the episode.

In our cases, the predominance of auditory hallucinations in genuine delirium tremens usually proved to be a combination with schizophrenia. (Only in a single case were we unable to prove this with complete certainty.) This also applies to cases where pronounced body-hallucinations or stereotypies occur.

As has been explained previously, the alcoholic insanity described by other authors develops mostly or perhaps always, on the basis of a schizophrenia. Therefore, such alcoholic delusions easily combine with the symptoms of schizophrenia. If careful observation does not reveal these signs as particularly pronounced, a relatively good prognosis can be offered for the case and it may be considered as one of simple alcoholic delusions. Conversely, if we find in a clear-cut case of schizophrenia, the coherent auditory hallucinations with good orientation which are characteristic of alcoholic delusions, we must conclude that the schizophrenia is accompanied by alcoholism.

I cannot define the characteristics of chronic alcoholic paranoia because I have not as yet seen such a case; furthermore, the authors who claim to have observed this disease did not sufficiently consider the possibility of dementia praecox, or at least did not describe any symptoms which cannot also occur in schizophrenia.

7. It is most difficult to differentiate between schizophrenia and those forms of disease best designated as "acute confusional states." A diagnostically useful description of these states does not as yet exist.[13] I do not know of any symptom occurring in these forms of disease which also include the fever psychoses, that could not also be found in schizophrenia. The main symptom is confusion, often accompanied by hallucinations. Both are very ambiguous symptoms and nobody has as yet described any characteristic features of the type of confusion and hallucinations observed in "acute confusional states." Therefore, we can only make a diagnosis of schizophrenia in those cases of confusion which show schizophrenic symptoms; however, where careful study fails to reveal schizophrenic symptoms we must assume the presence of one of these other confusional states. I might also add that marked catatonic symptoms, with the exception of flexibilitas cerea and command-automatism, are indications against the presence of a confusional

---

13. I have no personal knowledge of either Kraepelin's amentia or the exhaustion psychoses described by Räcke (587). Räcke mentions a "primary incoherence," without defining it.

state of this type, such as Kraepelin's amentia. Pronounced negativism, stereotypies of posture,[14] and instinctive verbigeration always signify the presence of schizophrenia in such conditions, even if it should be impossible at the moment to detect schizophrenic disturbances of affect or association.

I can add that we have employed this method of diagnosis successfully over many years and that we were never compelled to change our diagnosis where examination of the patient justified making it. Nonetheless, we cannot be satisfied with such a negative differentiation. If we are unable to discover any schizophrenic signs in a given case today, we may indeed see them develop tomorrow.

Stransky (753) states that the deterioration following amentia is distinguished from schizophrenic deterioration by the difference in the natural affective facial expression. However, since the schizophrenic changes of the facial expression cannot always be recognized in mild cases it is not possible to base a differential diagnosis on this one point.

Etiological factors offer very little help in the diagnosis. In many such confusional states there is no weakness or fever. In two cases we were able to prove the existence of the chronic renal disease which we had suspected, only by autopsy. On the other hand, schizophrenia becomes so frequently manifest in the course of various fever diseases, that this criterion is completely useless for differential diagnosis. The anamnesis can be far more helpful as a guide, but only in the direction of schizophrenia, which already has valuable sign-posts in its symptomatology.

8. The differential diagnosis with respect to hysteria and neurasthenia is also only one-sided. There is no hysterical or neurasthenic symptom which cannot also be found in schizophrenia. We assume the presence of schizophrenia when we can demonstrate certain specific symptoms of that disease. Hysteria or neurasthenia are diagnosed only when careful examination reveals hysterical or neurasthenic symptoms but no evidence of schizophrenic symptoms. Proof of the presence of hysterical symptoms does not exclude the possibility of schizophrenia, just as it does not exclude the possible presence of any other disease.

If deterioration, auditory hallucinations in a state of clear consciousness, definite delusions, or other signs of a genuine psychosis can be

---

14. Aschaffenburg, at least, has observed stereotypies in the initial deliria of typhoid fever. He also mentions the sensation of receiving an electric shock, a phenomenon that I once observed in a case of influenza psychosis (neuritis!). Schuele (675a) states that in a case of "asthenic delirium" hallucinations occurred without any alteration of the ego. As far as my own experience goes he is correct. Yet, I have reason to doubt that this applies to all instances of "acute confusion."

demonstrated, it is of course easy to make the diagnosis. However, in cases that are not so clear-cut hysteria and neurasthenia may create the greatest difficulties in diagnosis, since a mild schizophrenia may remain hidden beneath nervous symptoms for a long time or even permanently. Despite all precautions, we must continue to diagnose and treat many schizophrenics as nervous patients as long as we are unable to detect any specific schizophrenic symptoms in them.

Our primary consideration will be the type of affectivity which the patient presents. Generally, the schizophrenic indifference is in distinct contrast to the labile, irritable, anxious, or demanding nature of the neurotic.[15] What is particularly striking in schizophrenics is their relative or absolute indifference with respect to their illness and symptoms, their own situation, their families, etc. This indifference is often the first symptom that the observer notes: only after the patient has been urged on to some activity does he begin to complain and find excuses. Yet hysterics may also appear indifferent regarding their paralyses and other difficulties which they bear with some heroism — but which they nevertheless display prominently. For a long time, events which ought to arouse their complexes may leave hysterics quite indifferent; but then the storm usually follows the quiet in the form of agitation or of an attack. Occasionally, inappropriate reactions may also occur inasmuch as hysterics may attempt to cover up some painful association by bursting into compulsive laughter or by singing. Special attention must be paid to the schizophrenic lack of homogeneity in affective expressions, which is rare in neurotics.

The affective autism of schizophrenia can also be recognized by the fact that patients have no need to talk about themselves. The patient who has nothing to say to his doctor is not merely a simple neurotic.

In general, the defect in emotional rapport can often be best observed in the patient's relationship to his physician. After spending an hour with a neurotic talking about his illness, some sort of personal relationship has been established, be it friendly or hostile. This rapport is never absent, regardless of the patient's sex. Usually, however, it is impossible to establish any closer contact with schizophrenics (Jung).

In addition to the emotional rapport, the schizophrenic also lacks the suggestibility which the neurotic shows in relation to his physician; however, this difference is not always valid. In many respects, schizophrenia can be modified by outside psychic influences. Absence of

15. This term is used here to include all those commonly designated as hysterical, neurasthenic, and nervous.

suggestibility is found in neurotics only very rarely and then only temporarily. A twilight state that cannot be influenced is, as a rule, not of a hysterical nature. If someone risks thrusting his face close to that of a patient who is wildly flailing his arms and if the patient consistently misses hitting the face, one is most certainly dealing with a hysteric. Marked improvement in an apparently severe case through psychoanalysis indicates with a good deal of certainty that the patient was not a schizophrenic, since only mildly schizophrenic cases are amenable to such methods of treatment.

However, in order to be able to utilize these and many other symptoms for the purpose of differential diagnosis between schizophrenia and the neuroses, it is absolutely essential that one carefully evaluates the total psychic constellation. There are times when a hysteric may somehow simulate a lack of affectivity or an inapproachability which are based upon the normal effects of some complex. Occasionally every healthy person and, even more so, every neurotic shows marked blocking; at times, anyone may be vague in defining a concept or may construct bizarre associations. A symptom like this can only be used for the purpose of diagnosis if it constantly recurs under varied conditions, or if it cannot be traced to the effects of a complex. In some cases, therefore, it will only be possible to make a diagnosis when one is acquainted with the patient's complexes.

Hysterical blockings clearly reveal their affective origin. They occur in connection with certain ideas, they are absent in connection with others but they are never generalized; there is a clear-cut division between the healthy and the pathological, i.e., between the autistic and the realistic psyche.

We can best observe in the intellectual sphere how the hysteriform symptoms of schizophrenia develop on the basis of a dissociated psyche, and why they are, therefore, disturbed. Only in schizophrenic patients do we find lack of unity in the process of thinking; only in schizophrenics, can the most diverse notions exist side by side without influencing each other, and without forming a unified picture. If, as is generally assumed, hysterical desire for a child may lead to an imaginary pregnancy with cessation of the menses, the patient will never imagine that she actually has a child, unless she is in a twilight state.

The external inconsistencies are also absent in simple neuroses. The hysteric woman for whom the outside world has been transformed in accordance with some wish of hers is nevertheless not capable of regarding her doctor simultaneously as a former lover and as the ward physician. Thus hysterics show much more method in their actions and fewer deviations from the general laws of acceptable behavior. The hysteric commits serious errors only on the basis of very definite assumptions. Unless he wants to be seriously ill, he will not injure himself; he will not strike a strange doctor, even in an apparently wild delirium; he will not seek to kill his wife except in a furious attack of jealousy; he will not readily set fire to a house or soil himself, etc. Patients who show complete lack of interest for long periods of time, who completely disregard their environment, outside of a twilight state, are not hysterics. I am not yet convinced that Janet's "psychasthenics," who spend years in inactivity, are not hebephrenics. However, it would be erroneous to conclude that patients whose behavior under observation differs from the one they show when they consider themselves unobserved, could not be schizophrenics (Kaiser, 351).

Behavior, which to us appears bizarre and which, therefore, becomes decisive for the diagnosis, may be the outcome of ethnic peculiarities or of a specific attitude towards life. For example, the actions of hysterics who come from Far Eastern countries sometimes appear as bizarre to us as the schizophrenics of our own country.

The characteristic schizophrenic mixture of autistic ideas and reality also manifests itself in the twilight states. The hysteric is more or less able to register reality in addition to his delusional notions during a twilight state. However, with him this is an unconscious process, whereas in the schizophrenic we find that awareness of reality and delusions are combined in the conscious and unconscious, even in very clouded states of consciousness.[16] On the other hand, the delirium-fable is presented by schizophrenics as far more distorted and often as practically absurd. Twilight states which continue for months are probably never hysterical phenomena; neither are those which gradually develop in the course of weeks or months and disappear just as gradually.

Dissociation of concepts does not occur in neurotics. When it is present, it is a certain sign of schizophrenia. Symbolism, also, reaches proportions of actual materialization only under very special conditions without a disturbance of consciousness. In a hysteric it is impossible to "tear out the divine love and remove the seed of resurrection" in a physical sense.

In hysterics and neurasthenics we may also observe notions and sensations which can be designated as delusions and illusions of body-sensations. However, they are never absurd to the degree we often noted in schizophrenia. For the most part, they are such that even

16. It also seems that dreams, which can easily be interpreted by the patient, or dreams in which wishes are directly expressed in spite of their repression and are related by the patient in a matter-of-fact manner, can be utilized for purposes of differential diagnosis in favor of dementia praecox.

normal persons can imagine their nature. Furthermore, hysterics recognize the incorrectness of their illusions. A neurasthenic may experience the sensation that his neck is growing infinitely long and may consequently run into the woods in a state of panic. However, unless he is in a twilight state, the patient will have full insight into the morbidness of his notions and never go so far as to project his parasthesias onto the outside world. A neurasthenic may have the peculiar feeling that two buttons are growing out of his forehead; but unlike the schizophrenic he cannot feel how the buttons drop into a net placed somewhere outside his body. By the same token, detailed descriptions of drops, gnomes, and of machines located in the ear or in some other part of the body signify the presence of schizophrenia. I do not know whether nowadays it is still possible for a hysteric to have "an animal in the belly." As yet, I have not seen such patients. Moreover we will never observe that a neurotic imagines that the "alien" thoughts arising in his head were "made" by some other person.

Ambivalence may also be of a hysterical nature; in this illness, too, the "boogey man" is a familiar figure. However, hysteria can be excluded when ambivalence is very extensive in a patient with full clarity of consciousness.

Illusory or even hallucinatory misinterpretations of surroundings occur in hysterics only during twilight states or other states of clouded consciousness. Only in schizophrenics do we find meaningless akoasma ("Miss V., knit"; "Miss V., come into the garden") and combinations of auditory and body-hallucinations. Hysterics prefer visions.

The physical "stigmata" of hysteria are relatively rare in schizophrenia. I have seen hemianesthesia only a few times in schizophrenia although I must admit that I did not often look for it. Much more frequently, however, we find in schizophrenics absence of pharyngial reflex leading at times to complete anesthesia of pharynx, larynx, and trachea. When present, analgesia is more consistent in schizophrenics than in hysterics. The schizophrenic patients injure themselves both intentionally and unintentionally far more frequently than do hysterics and for no apparent reason. Concentric constriction of the visual field cannot be evaluated diagnostically in our schizophrenic patients with their poorly sustained attention. Typical hysteriform paralyses occur sometimes; to my knowledge, contractures are much rarer.

Attempts have been made to utilize for the purpose of differential diagnosis the characteristic, evasive answers common to both diseases. I believe that an experienced observer will be able to sense in most cases of hysteria the systematic effort which consistently avoids the correct answer. The hebephrenic, on the other hand, gives the first answer that comes to his mind, partly because he is too lazy to think about it and does not care whether it is right or wrong. Sometimes his negativism may resemble hysteria, but in that event this negativism will be expressed in his entire attitude. However, it must be remembered that the typical Ganser syndrome may also occur on the basis of a schizophrenia. It has also been attempted to establish a point of differentiation by stating that only schizophrenics respond rapidly with evasive answers; however, it has been demonstrated that this is not actually the case (Westphal).

Regarding neurasthenic symptoms in schizophrenia, we find that the fatigue which is commonly, but not always, mentioned in this connection is usually a subjective rather than an objective phenomenon. Observation rarely reveals distinct signs of fatigue. Schizophrenic patients have difficulty in thinking and ascribe this to fatigue. In addition, fatigue is often advanced as an excuse when there is actually merely a lack of interest. Masselon, therefore, recommends that the patient be asked to perform some small task. If his interest slackens abnormally quickly, one is usually dealing with a schizophrenic; if genuine fatigue occurs prematurely, neurasthenia is to be presumed. Headaches and irritability occur in both diseases.

Neurasthenia is often accompanied by sleep disturbances whereas schizophrenics enjoy fairly normal sleep except during acute and hallucinatory states.

9. It is impossible to make a sharp distinction between schizophrenia and the degenerative psychoses described by certain writers. In the first place, it is impossible because the latter concept includes many of our schizophrenics.

However, the discrepancy in the concept of degeneration as such is the result of a difficulty which at present cannot be eliminated: there are no symptoms at all which are characteristic of degenerations only. Bonhoeffer's "pathological notion," for example, is a very common occurrence in schizophrenia. I am willing to assume that it is also found in other diseases, but this has not yet been proven. The same applies to Birnbaum's "degenerative delusions" which are identical with the schizophrenic ones to the last detail.[17] With respect to dementia praecox, the difficulties consist in the fact that its primary specific symptoms can rarely be demonstrated in the milder cases usually involved in this situation, and that only the intensity of secondary symptoms can indicate dementia praecox. As far as other psychoses are concerned, we

17. This is, by the way, effective proof for the secondary nature of these symptoms of schizophrenia.

manage very well with these means of differentiation. The only exception is degeneration because at present nobody knows to what degree psychic processes can be distorted, even when there are no schizophrenic changes. Indeed, if schizophrenia were only a functional disease, as some prefer to believe, it would merely exist as a syndrome in degenerated patients.

Thus every diagnostician may consider latent schizophrenia a phenomenon of degeneration as long as the symptoms have not reached the degree of intensity which according to his experience is usually only seen in schizophrenia. However, schizophrenia can never be excluded with absolute certainty. Thus, this situation is different only in degree from the one described in connection with the differential diagnoses of neuroses.

10. The question as to whether the psychoses described in Basedow's disease belong with schizophrenia or not, must remain unanswered. In most cases mentioned in the literature as well as in two cases of my own observation, the prominence of affective symptoms was particularly striking. The patients were constantly either sad or euphoric.

11. Schizophrenia cannot easily be distinguished from malingering since a definite boundary between conscious and unconscious symptoms does not exist in this disease anymore than in hysteria. Negativism and indifference cause the patients to give false answers which may be deliberately or unintentionally so, or both. A patient may want to malinger and still be schizophrenic. We once had a paranoid patient here who was convinced that everything we or his relatives did was done with the purpose of making a fool of him. Therefore, he persistently simulated mental disease in order to get into a real mental institution where he would be recognized as sane. Where no real mental disease is present, close observation of behavior, the absence of blocking, the irrepressible emotionality, in addition to general inconsistencies with a truly psychotic picture, will reveal the malingering. When catalepsy is simulated, evidence of mounting fatigue facilitates the diagnosis.

SECTION VII

PROGNOSIS[1]

Since schizophrenia may become stationary at any stage, continue to progress or develop acute symptoms, it is impossible to establish any definite, systematic outline of prognosis. Improvements even in chronic states are always theoretically possible. They can be expected inasmuch as even chronic excited states abate with time, but these abatements are usually accompanied by increased deterioration. Otherwise essential improvements of chronic states are rare and cannot be counted on. Acute states, of course, pass off but they often lower the mental level considerably. Concerning rules which would permit us to estimate with any certainty the subsequent degree of deterioration in any given case, we know only the following which is applicable to relatively few cases:

When the chronic catatonic symptoms are prominent and manifest themselves while the patient is completely lucid they lead us to expect definitive and severe deterioration. In cases which have had one or several good remissions, severe deterioration is rare. The very acute syndromes with periodic recurrences are an exception to this rule; these cases for the most part end ultimately in very marked deterioration. In my observation, cases with clouding of consciousness (*Benommenheit*) have all taken a rather bad course.

The slight prognostic differences of the various subdivisions of schizophrenia are discussed in the section on the course of the disease.

Heredity (in its present broad sense of the term), age, sex, intelligence,[2] number of degenerative stigmata, state of health, individual type of disease, individual symptoms and their various groupings — all these have so little bearing on how far the disease will go toward deterioration that they scarcely can be considered in establishing the prognosis. Instead of a prognosis of the extent of the future deterioration, we have to be content, therefore, with a diagnosis of the

1. Zablocka, Bleuler (73), Räcke (591).

2. Imbeciles who also have a propfhebephrenia are, of course, much more handicapped socially than others. In Rheinau at least one fifth of all schizophrenics are rather imbecile.

extent of the deterioration that has already taken place; that is, we have to determine how far the "incurable" deterioration has already gone and how many of the acute symptoms may be expected to disappear. In this way, we determine the minimum deterioration present which cannot be expected to improve to any considerable extent. However, further advance of deterioration can never be excluded.

In deciding whether a symptom might be expected to recede, we first of all have to keep in mind that identical symptoms may be of different significance depending on the state of the disease. The prognosis will be poorer if the symptom is a partial manifestation of a chronic condition, if the development of the symptom itself took a chronic course, and if it appears in states of consciousness. These three conditions do not coincide exactly with each other. In chronic conditions individual or several symptoms may become acute at times and then disappear again. During an acute state, symptoms from a previous episode may persist, or they may only become manifest in a very surreptitious way. It is extremely difficult to define the state which for the lack of a better term I call "clarity of consciousness" (*Besonnenheit*), and which Kraepelin also used. Patients in twilight, confused, manic or melancholic states are naturally not in possession of full clarity of consciousness (are not "*besonnen*"). Chronic hallucinatory patients, even when continually agitated, are essentially different from the patients who are not "clear;" in certain respects the hallucinating patients preserve normal contact with the environment and correctly grasp and utilize connected series of events. In these latter patients only a part of their personality is not "clear" (*besonnen*), whereas in other patients the entire personality is affected. For years an autistic, negativistic patient may communicate with his environment only to the extent of taking the proffered food, clothing, etc.; he may remain completely mute throughout this period. However, his picture of the outer world is falsified only in so far as it corresponds to his delusions; the same is true of his thinking processes which, except where the complexes are involved, are only occasionally incorrect — due to the general schizophrenic association disturbances — but are not systematically falsified. A patient with rather confused speech may behave quite normally on the wards and clearly demonstrate that he is perfectly oriented in the situation. A patient is considered to be "not clear" (not *besonnen*) only when his total personality or the greatest part of it is involved affectively or intellectually in the pathological condition. Even in an otherwise "clear" patient, this clarity of consciousness may be lost transitorily due to the effects of powerful excitements, whether these are internally or externally conditioned, whether they are caused by alcohol or similar factors.

The cardinal symptoms of schizophrenia show the least tendency to disappear, particularly, the association disturbances, while autism is overcome relatively more frequently. On the other hand, the manic and the melancholic oscillations of affect are nearly always transient phenomena. Hallucinations and delusions with complete absence of clarity of consciousness during an acute episode do not have an unfavorable significance at all. It is possible, but certainly far from proven, that the pronounced schizophrenic character of these symptoms may be interpreted in the sense of a bad prognosis. Conversely, chronic delusions and hallucinations offer a poor, yet not an absolutely bad, outlook. We frequently see patients who, in complete clarity of consciousness, hallucinate for years, and finally rid themselves of this symptom.

As for the various catatonic symptoms during an acute phase, we can say that the presence of flexibilitas cerea is not at all ominous; far more doubtful are the senseless stereotypies. The other acute catatonic symptoms stand about halfway between those two. Among others, the catatonic symptoms always indicate a poorer prognosis. If these are absent and the fundamental schizophrenic symptoms are so mild that they could be overlooked, then the prognosis for the attack is a very good one.[3]

Evaluating the prognosis of the acute phases merely requires the application of what has already been said. Whatever is acute, passes off. Hence, the good prognosis of the twilight states, the deliria, and, above all, of the individual affect-psychoses as long as they are not combined with very many true schizophrenic symptoms. We cannot say whether the deterioration will progress during the course of the acute phase or directly afterwards. We only know that twilight states and certain agitated states do not necessarily signify any advance in the disease and therefore usually leave behind them the *status quo ante;* whereas the other acute syndromes are generally signs which indicate a more or less distinct worsening.

During acute states, it is not always easy to determine the actual degree of deterioration because the permanent symptoms are usually covered up by the acute manifestations. Yet one will be able to assay to some extent the flatness of affect, and often even the association disturbance. However, the degree of chronic autism cannot be ascer-

3. Hence the frequency with which the "acute paranoias" and amentias of so many other writers are "cured."

tained, for example, in a twilight state since such conditions are after all nothing else than peaks in an otherwise permanently operating tendency to autism. For the rest, it is a question of the ratio between the deleterious symptoms and the degree of the clarity of consciousness: the fewer and the milder the deleterious symptoms on the one hand, and the more severe the disturbance of the patient's clarity of consciousness on the other, the more favorable the average outcome. A cluster of catatonic symptoms or the highest degree of confusion in speech are still not so very unfavorable as to prognosis as long as the patient does not show clarity of consciousness in any spheres. Moderate catatonic symptoms, mild confusion, single impulsive acts in patients with otherwise fairly normal relations to the environment are not unfavorable signs.

In a negative sense, the amnesias can give us some important indications. One can almost be sure that a patient will not be better after the acute attack than he was before it. For the most part, he will appear more "deteriorated" or "crazier" after the attack. If his permanent condition was poor before the attack, the possibility of a favorable outcome can be excluded with certainty.

If the various other symptoms recede without the schizophrenic ones showing any particular improvement at the same time, this must naturally be considered a bad omen. The same can be said if the loss of mental agility becomes more prominent, and if such catatonic symptoms as negativism disappear without any evidence of improvement in the patient's emotional responsiveness.

The following behavior also constitutes a bad sign: the absence of tact in persons whom one could have expected to be capable of uninhibited social intercourse with normal people. Uncleanliness, abrupt negligence in patients of decent upbringing, or even obscenities of the coarsest kind in a previously respectable woman, are certain indices of far-reaching alterations. If the termination of an acute thrust of the disease is indicated by an increase in body-weight, then in favorable cases it should be accompanied by a parallel improvement in the mental status.

In chronic conditions of the disease, the diagnosis of the degree of deterioration is much simpler because it is then not obscured by adventitious symptoms. Of course, conscious withdrawal from the surroundings may easily be mistaken for lack of interest;[4] hostile attitudes toward the environment consequent upon delusional ideas often give the impression of a generally false conception of the environment.

We certainly can exclude the possibility of improvement if a deteriorated patient's condition remains completely uniform and unaltered for some years, exhibiting no acute symptoms and not reacting to changes of treatment and/or environment. As long as the condition changes, extensive improvement cannot be excluded. But we cannot consider it an alteration of the condition when a periodic patient changes from one phase of his periodic swings to another.

Pure delusions of grandeur in an easily verifiable sphere (such as that of power, love, wealth) is generally a sign of pronounced withdrawal and seclusion from the environment. However, such delusions do not have to be viewed as ominous under all and every circumstance, particularly not when the delusional system is built on complexes which are not, or only partly, accessible to logic (religion, politics, philosophy, etc.)

The appearance of unprovoked and unmotivated short outbursts of peevishness and agitation, be they regular or not, seem to have a bad prognostic significance.

Young individuals who chronically do not work, who are without drive and initiative, who show poor vasomotor control and who cannot be moved or interested by reproaches concerning their behavior—these youths must all be considered hopeless cases, even if in later years they may still be capable of doing some small menial tasks within the confines of the hospital. In general, when we see schizophrenics who are brought to us years after the onset of the disease, we often receive the impression that cases which began surreptitiously have a particularly unfavorable prognosis. However, when we study the anamneses of the mild, late cases who come to the hospital or the doctor's office because of some accidental trauma (alcohol, shock, etc.), then we find among them many whose disease obviously had such imperceptible beginnings. The result is that one comes to the conviction that even this disease course is not invariably deleterious.

---

4. Loss of mental agility and emotional blunting are, of course, not homogeneous symptoms. This may account for the fact that now and then a patient, who was given up as hopeless because of such manifestations, eventually shows extensive improvement. I know of one woman patient who sat around a hospital for many years; she could not be used for even the smallest services. Some time later she was placed in a sanitarium. Under the influence of an erotic transference to her physician, she began to be quite lively in a rather foolish way but then she started to work and eventually became well enough to be released. After her release, she organized a women's fashions business and conducted it with success.

The degree to which deterioration will advance after a given attack can be predicted with some probability if similar attacks have already occurred previously. The later attacks often maintain about the same ratio in this respect as did the earlier ones. Relatively few patients are found in hospitals who have not had one or more extensive remissions; usually of a periodic manic type.

As for the rate of deterioration, we can only say that, even in chronic cases, acute thrusts occur, but often there is a certain uniformity in the tempo of the deterioration which is maintained and persists up to the time the disease comes to a halt.

Many writers have felt the need to be able to estimate the interval of time which must elapse beyond which improvement could no longer be expected. This problem pertains to legal matters, for instance questions of divorce. Various codes of law designate three years as the period of time beyond which a poorly developing case can be considered as practically incurable. However, improvements which may be considered as cures cannot be excluded from the realm of the possible even after several decades, even though it is quite rare. In Switzerland where divorce for mental disease is rather frequent, I have acted as an expert witness in such matters. I have never had any unfortunate experience in using this time limit of three years. But I must admit that I have always had a very uncomfortable feeling with each case I declared to be incurable.

Schuele (675a and 679) draws attention to the point that the physical symptoms (among which he includes many motor symptoms) are an index to the profundity of the cerebral disturbance. There is perhaps some element of truth in this concept as far as it concerns the vasomotor anomalies (cf. Weber, 797). Nonetheless, there are certain cases which show physical symptoms proper to a considerable extent and still terminate quite well.

Moravcsick suggests that sudden unexpected psychic insights facilitate the probability of remissions. Salerini reports that good remissions can be anticipated in cases with amenorrhea, if the menstrual variations of pulse, temperature, and respirations are maintained and are recognizable. Schuele asserts that patients who masturbate extensively are especially endangered. However, I have seen extensive improvement in cases with almost continuous masturbatory activity. Bruce and others have tried to utilize hematological findings for prognostic purposes. But our knowledge in this field is far too limited.

Kraepelin (discussion of 73) has noted that speech-confused patients often do not develop any further. I can only say that there are also exceptions to this rule.

As yet we have no criteria which would enable us to evaluate the tendency to recidives. Stransky believes that, if there have been no recidives for five years following the ending of the first attack, recidives no longer will occur. Such a time limit can of course only be used in those cases in which one assumes that there was an acute onset. However, even then there are too many exceptions preventing us from considering the rule as valid. The best and most accurate estimate in the light of our present knowledge consists in saying that new thrusts of the illness appear more rarely the longer the stationary period has lasted. The danger of relapses is enhanced in women during the climacterium, gravidity and the puerperal period. Cases which show a regular periodicity naturally permit a rather definite prognosis as to the probability of a new attack.

The possibility of offering relatively certain prognostications as to the course that any given case will pursue is no better in this disease than in others. It is hardly ever possible to state in advance just how a pulmonary tuberculosis or articular rheumatism will develop; how many recidives will appear; when they are likely to occur. In schizophrenia, we have the additional difficulty that the course of the external, clinical, disease picture, which alone is of any practical value, is hardly dependent upon the course of the disease processes themselves. Indeed we are almost always dealing exclusively with secondary symptoms which may get worse or improve, within maximal limits, under fortuitous psychic influences. The effects of such influences could be predicted only if we were able either to induce or to prevent them.

SECTION VIII

FREQUENCY AND DISTRIBUTION OF THE DISEASE

Except for the great group of mental defectives, dementia praecox is the most common mental disease.

Albrecht found it present in 29 per cent of 693 mentally diseased patients. Wolfsohn found it in 30 per cent of 2215 admissions to the Burgholzli Hospital (23 per cent of the male, 39 per cent of the female admissions). In recent years the incidence rate of schizophrenia has even risen a few per cent following some slight changes in the conditions at this hospital (new additions to the custodial wing). The ratio of the absolute number of male schizophrenic admissions to that of the female is 47:53. The great sex differences in the incidence rate of this disease as compared with that of other psychoses rests not so much on a smaller number of male schizophrenics as on the large number of paretics and alcoholics among the males.

Since, for the most part, the schizophrenics remain incurable, fall sick early, and die late, their number among the permanent hospital inmates is larger than their number among general hospital admissions. Schizophrenic patients comprise 71 per cent of the men and 79 per cent of the women patients, or 75 per cent of all the patients of our mental hospitals. In the custodial institutions these percentages are lowered to 50 per cent by the presence of the mental defectives in those institutions.

Thus the social importance of schizophrenia is a tremendous one, but it is less striking and apparent than that of paresis, for example, because it affects most patients before they have had the opportunity to establish themselves in life and work. A schizophrenic who must be cared for from early youth till death often exhausts the entire possessions of his family. The disease appears in an even more pernicious light when we take into account that a vast multitude of psychopaths, who are not considered as mentally ill and who keep their families and society as a whole on edge all the time, as well as the neuropaths who keep the doctors busy without their being able to effect any cures, are latent schizophrenics. I have reason for the assumption that these latent unrecognized schizophrenics are far more numerous than the overtly diseased.

We do not know as yet of any racial differences in susceptibility to this disease. Of course, those races or communities which have a free and wide choice of mates show much less incidence of mentally diseased. Among the Malays (Kraepelin), the Japanese (Miyake) and Central Asiatics (Urstein) schizophrenia occurs as prominently, as it does with us.

We do not know in what ways race and external circumstances influence the form of the disease. If our conception of the genesis of the symptoms is correct, differences due to these factors should be found. Ziehen has noted that his dementia hebephrenica is more common in Holland than in Thuringia. Kraepelin (in an oral communication) has found marked catatonic forms of the disease to be more exceptional in Malays, and that silly dementia is more frequent among those people than among our patients. It is furthermore certain that racial characteristics have some bearing on the manifestations of this disease. The English are calmer than the Irish, Upper Bavarians are more violent than the Saxons. Indeed in our hospital, it is easy to note the difference between the reactions of the Bernese as compared with the Zurichois who are quite closely related racially.

SECTION IX

THE CAUSES OF THE DISEASE

A. The pathology of schizophrenia gives us no indications as to where we should look for the causes of the disease. Direct investigation for specific causal factors has also left us stranded. Certainly we know that "mental diseases" are more common in the families of schizophrenics than in those of the healthy; also we often see that in large families the majority of the members is afflicted with the disease. However, if an adherent of an "infectious theory" of this disease should choose to say that there is no hereditary factor in schizophrenia but merely an infection from some common source, or if some one else cares to assume that the modifications of the psychic or physical factors produced by communal living produces such accumulations of disease in a given family group, we would be unable to produce any proof to the contrary. Such skeptics could observe that in many cases, even after the most thorough study, no evidence of any hereditary *Anlage* and no individual predisposition (such as a seclusive, withdrawn character structure) has ever been proven.

And yet heredity does play its role in the etiology of schizophrenia, but the extent and kind of its influence cannot as yet be stated. In order to be able to accomplish something more than what has already been done on this question of heredity, we first of all would need a workable concept of heredity. We should know which diseases, particularly which psychoses, in a family have any connection with the schizophrenia of one of its members, and what degree of family blood relationships come into consideration. At the present time, the only useful road to the solution of such problems is the statistical one. But unfortunately there does not exist even the very first effort of such a statistical analysis.[1]

---

1. The very interesting publications of Voster and Siolis cannot be considered as such preparatory statistical efforts.

Up to now we do know that the total hereditary tainting of the schizophrenics is somewhat different from that of the healthy.[2] For the schizophrenics, 90 per cent show hereditary tainting[3] as compared with 67 per cent in the non-mentally ill, and 65 per cent in the healthy.[4] But when we consider only those who show tainting by mental diseases, enormous differences are revealed: mental disease can be shown to exist in 65 per cent of the families of schizophrenics; whereas Diem estimated the hereditary tainting by mental disorders to be only 7.1 per cent in the non-mentally ill. Unfortunately, these figures cannot be strictly compared with each other. Diem, in estimating the hereditary taint of the various members of the family, took into consideration only those factors which were present in the carriers or carrier immediately related to the test-person. But since in his figures of all the hereditary factors involved those of psychoses represent barely a sixth, and since in the mentally diseased the predisposition or tainting through the parents is numerically the most important, the comparative error cannot be too great. Therefore, the tainting by mental disorders is many times greater in the schizophrenic than in the healthy.

It is even more difficult to compare the figures of Diem and Wolfsohn in respect to the significance of the degree of relationship of those tainted by hereditary mental disease. I can only say that 35 per cent of our schizophrenics (in Burgholzli) had mentally sick parents or grandparents, or both,[5] whereas Diem found that in the non-mentally diseased only 2.2 per cent of the parents, and in the healthy only 1.6 per cent of the parents had suffered from mental disease. The corresponding figures for the indirect or atavistic psychotic tainting were 4 per cent in the non-mentally ill, and 4.3 per cent in the healthy.

Thus this high degree of tainting by mental disease can be considered to constitute an almost exclusively schizophrenic one. We well know that the organic mental diseases do not come in for consideration here, and that the manic-depressive psychosis is not so common that it could affect these figures very materially.

The differences in the figures of Wolfsohn and Diem are of

---

2. The data we discuss are always based on the parents, siblings, grandparents and on the siblings of the parents. The figures for schizophrenia have been taken from Wolfsohn's work, partly recalculated for our purposes.

3. Hereditary tainting implies a background of nervous or mental diseases, abnormal mental characteristics or predisposition, and alcoholism in the parents.

4. Diem considers as "healthy" all persons who are not mentally ill minus psycho paths and nervous people.

5. Kraepelin (388, p. 270) found only 18-19 per cent.

importance in estimating the element of tainting due to other factors. Wolfsohn found a neurotic taint amounting to 29 per cent in his schizophrenics of which about half were also combined with mental disease of a more serious type. (Diem's estimates appear too low to us.) Diem finds neurotic taint in 8.2 per cent of his non-mentally diseased and 7 per cent in the healthy. But in spite of the difference between his findings and those of Wolfsohn in this respect, it is certain that the neurotic taint in our patients is significantly greater than in the healthy.

We do not know whether these figures indicate the existence of heterogeneous heredity; that is for a family predisposition which can express itself in the form of neurosis or in schizophrenia. However, it is probable that a good share of those considered to be mentally abnormal were latent schizophrenics.

Alcoholism in the parents (Wolfsohn did not consider alcoholism of other relatives) is found in 26 per cent of the cases; in somewhat over two-thirds it was found in combination with other predisposing factors (in all members of the family). In Diem's study, 12 per cent and 10 per cent, respectively, of the non-mentally ill and the healthy had alcoholic parents. The figures in this respect are comparable in the two studies since they both involved only the parents. Ordinarily the father is the drinker; and Diem has given the predominant role to the father in the accumulated heredity rather than to the mother. Diem's figures are certainly not too low.[6] Alcoholic parents, therefore, are far more commonly found in schizophrenics than in the healthy.[7] However, is alcoholism a symptom of the schizophrenic family disposition or is it the cause of the schizophrenia in the offspring?

Persons with abnormal character structure were found among the relatives of schizophrenics in 22 per cent of the cases and in 7 per cent it was the only predisposing factor. This was the case in Diem's findings in 10.4 per cent of the non-mentally ill and 10.1 per cent of the healthy. Persons with abnormal character structure may also be latent schizophrenics.

Apoplexy and dementia senilis cannot be considered as signs of schizophrenic predisposition since such anomalies occur less frequently in all mentally diseased than in the healthy and since schizophrenia itself forms a significant part of all mental diseases.

---

6. Bertschinger (p. 270) found alcoholism in 249 relatives of 151 patients of whom 25 also showed hereditary taints of mental disease.

7. Fuhrmann (p. 817) suggests that offspring of alcoholic parents show disturbances which are similar to the alcoholic psychoses but afterwards lead rapidly to deterioration.

The hereditary predisposition certainly plays an important role among the causes of schizophrenia. However, we do not know in what this predisposition consists and how it manifests itself in other ways. It appears to be specific for schizophrenia.

Is there schizophrenia without any hereditary *Anlage?* Probably. In any event, in at least 10 per cent of the cases we cannot prove the existence of predisposition in spite of apparently precise knowledge of the family history back to the third generation or even further. To these we can add, of course, a considerable part of those judged to be "tainted" but who are not at all afflicted with a schizophrenic predisposition.

In France, particularly, the attempt was made to relate mental disease and with it, schizophrenia, to other familiar predispositions such as rheumatism and scrofula. It should be sufficient to call attention to the fact that such views are still completely unfounded. Lormer (p. 390) assumes that the greater number of specific psychopathological traits in the father will result in the catatonic syndrome, the mother's in the hebephrenic symptom complex. According to Lormer (p. 389) the combination of mental disease and alcoholism in the parents also predisposes to catatonia (cf. Fuhrmann), while the combination of mental disease and neurasthenia predisposes to hebephrenia. I have no opinion regarding the extent to which specific psychopathological traits are transmitted. On the other hand, our observations have revealed that heredity, in accordance with its contemporary principles, has no recognizable relation to the form or manifestation of the disease.

It is noteworthy that Magnan, in describing his *délire chronique* which we must consider as schizophrenia, did not find any degenerative signs; what he considers degenerative signs cannot be distinguished from psychotic heredity.

There is perhaps also a predisposition which is unfavorable to the development of schizophrenia. In certain compilations of data, "nervous diseases" appear less frequently in schizophrenic families than in the relatives of the healthy people (e.g. frenzy; cf. Wagner von Jauregg). As long as the concept of "nervous" disease, and the statistics themselves are so variable, one does well to exercise the greatest caution in such assumptions.

B. The adolescent age period[8] seems to offer a particular predisposition to this disease. Kraepelin offers the following data con-

8. The disease rarely becomes manifest in childhood. Yet there are cases in which a "primary" schizophrenia can be traced back to the earliest years of life.

cerning the age at which the disease began, derived from a study of 296 cases:

Onset Before the Age of	*Percentage*
15	6.0
20	32.5
25	24.5
30	19.0
35	11.0
40	5.0
45	1.5
50	0.7
55	0.4

Wolfsohn obtained the following figures from 618 patients at Burgholzli:

Age of Onset of Illness	*Men*	*Women*	*Total*
1-15	6*	3	4
15-20	21	16	18
20-25	25	20	22
25-30	22	18	20
30-35	10	14	12
35-40	10	11	11
40-45	5	5	5
45-50	4	6	4
50-55	0	5	3
55-60	0	2	1
60-65	0	0	0

* Figures in percentages.

According to Kraepelin over 60 per cent became ill before the twenty-fifth year; in our patients, only 44 per cent. However, I do not attach any significance at all to this difference since such figures are a function (among others) of the conditions of admission and the reliability of the anamneses. Therefore, I will not quote any other data on this question.

It seems noteworthy though, that in Wolfsohn's material the curve of the male patients drops in fairly regular fashion from a maximum in the fifth quinquennium; while that of the female patients shows a small elevation between the ages of 40 and 45 years; this rise becomes even more striking in the two following pentads in which we find more female cases than male. It may very well be due to the influence of the climacterium which leaves a much stronger imprint on the female psyche than on the male who after all does not need to resign yet at this particular age period.

The individual sub-groups of this disease differ inasmuch as (according to Kraepelin) simple hebephrenics form 72 per cent; the catatonics, 68 per cent; and the paranoids only 40 per cent of those who fall ill before the twenty-fifth year.

C. Whether there exists an individual disposition to this disease is questionable. Undoubtedly, many of the later schizophrenics were peculiar, withdrawn, and autistic already in youth. But at this time, we cannot decide whether such behavior is the expression of a disposition to the disease or the surreptitious beginnings of the disease itself.

In any event, intelligence is not related to this predisposition. Elminger and Lugaro have observed many cases of strikingly superior intelligence among their patients, whereas we ourselves could at least exclude the predominance of individuals with inferior intelligence.

Bertschinger was struck by the fact that many patients were small and slender individuals. For a long time, I had had a similar impression. But one can easily be mistaken in these energyless, hunched-up figures; and furthermore, there has been no real investigation of this point.

Schizophrenia appears to be independent of external conditions and circumstances. It is seen among the poor as well as among the rich, in all walks of life, and in the most varied conditions whether orderly or disorderly, fortunate or unfortunate. City and country harbor them equally (Gaupp, 258). There are schizophrenics in every clime (as for the factor of race, see p. 336.)

Soukhanoff finds a "constitution idéo-obsessive" among the "degenerated." There is little to be done with this concept at present.

For decades, the idea has been preserved that governesses were especially prone to develop schizophrenia. Some authors even spoke of a "governess-psychosis;" and it has even been maintained that governesses suffer a particularly severe (and unpleasant) form of the disease. There may be something in this, inasmuch as young women become governesses who have ambitions of raising their social standing beyond their capacities and among whom there must be many with schizophrenic predisposition. The treatment they often receive at the hands of their employers gives occasion for determining a schizophrenia. However, it must certainly first be established whether or not governesses really do suffer in greater numbers than members of other vocations.

Of yore, masturbation was mentioned as one of the most common causes of "juvenile psychoses." Some would even like to bring certain specific forms of our disease into direct connection with that activity. It is certainly true enough that most of our patients masturbate or have masturbated. However, if one looks at the matter a little more closely, one can find no relationship with the course of the disease. Very excessive masturbators who masturbate almost continually, can and do recover from their acute episodes or may remain on the same level of deterioration for years. Castration has no direct effect on the disease. Thus we must conceive of masturbation, in so far as it may have any connection with the malady, as a symptom and not a cause of the disease. To begin with, we have to emphasize that persistent masturbation, if practiced without any shame and modesty is much more conspicuous and more readily noticed. In addition, the lack of all inhibitions favors masturbatory activity directly. Above all, it is autism which compels the patient to satisfying himself on himself. It is only in the sexual sphere that it is still possible for him to fulfill autistically some of his desires. To the patient, the imaginary mistress is more than a real one. For this reason normal sexual intercourse is sought so little.[9] Therefore the sexual life of even those patients who are not very far advanced in their illness centers almost completely about masturbatory satisfaction.

Gravidity and the puerperium seem to have some connection with schizophrenia. There are too many women who develop a further advance or thrust of their schizophrenia during several or in each and everyone of their puerperal periods. For this reason we cannot agree with Reichardt, who believes it to be mere coincidence.[10] However, it is quite possible that there is a psychic connection which does not itself determine the disease, but makes it overt.

The connection of the disease to infectious processes equally needs further study. Schizophrenia often occurs in the wake of fever diseases; and frequently in those very cases which previously had exhibited no abnormalities. This may be a coincidence; yet we often see that mentally ill patients improve extensively after having had fever.

---

9. It seems that fewer schizophrenics suffer from venereal disease than mentally healthy individuals. This fact is particularly noteworthy in view of the schizophrenic's lack of inhibition and his general indifference.

10. As far as the puerperium comes into consideration, it can be easily proved that Reichardt is wrong. The puerperium lasts about one-tenth of the total time of the gravidity. But there are about ten times as many puerperal psychoses in mental institutions as gravidity pyschoses; yet, there are no more puerperal women than gravid ones.

If fever does influence a psychosis then we are not entitled to dismiss the possibility of some connection between fever and aggravation without any further consideration. It may be a question of some physical or psychic effect on the disease. Furthermore, it must be recalled that many cases, which are classed by others as amentia, belong to our schizophrenia, and that many writers assume that schizophrenia is caused by some physical weakness or possibly even by some infectious disease.

The thought is now being advanced by various people that syphilis has some relationship to schizophrenia. It should be sufficient to say that this view does not merit any support whatsoever.[11]

Organic cerebral disturbances have to receive special attention. We know that chronic meningitis, cerebral gliosis, and cerebral trauma can produce clinical pictures similar to schizophrenia. In these cases, the element of coincidence can be excluded. Unfortunately we have been unable to study any such cases from this new viewpoint. Therefore we can only raise the question: are these psychoses caused by cerebral (organic) disease which have the same symptomatology as schizophrenia? If the answer is in the affirmative, then what are the differences as compared to other cases of schizophrenia? If we could answer these questions, we would also know how to differentiate the true organic catatonics from those purely accidental complications which must, of course, appear in such cases (Muralt, Köttgen, Crocq).

"Overwork" or "strain" are also very often mentioned even by prudent psychiatrists as causes of schizophrenia. I have never yet seen any indications which would suggest this relationship. The idle fall sick with this disease as well as the hard-working. But it often happens that a schizophrenic in the first phases of his illness develops a veritable passion for work, completely disregarding circumstances or capacities. Indeed, his weakened efficiency often necessitates a greater effort. This "overwork," this "strain," is therefore a symptom, not a cause of the disease. Much more commonly, however, it is used as an apology for the patient's illness or his hereditary background on the part of the family, or as an apology for the ignorance of the causes on the part of the doctor.

In a similar way, we find the causes ascribed to certain of the patient's tendencies, the kind of life he may have led, or certain passions. One patient became ill because he chose the strenuous and exacting life of an actor; another, because he lived so irregularly; a

11. Roubinowitch and Levaditi recently found 3 cases with positive Wassermanns among 15 schizophrenics.

third, because he traveled too much. Closer scrutiny soon reveals that there are not even the slightest grounds for such assumptions. Schizophrenics take less heed of reality, in a good or bad sense. The autism makes their thoughts and actions more independent. They are much more prone to carry out an idea than other people who are restrained by weighing the good and bad arguments, by the spirit of the crowd, by greater suggestibility in respect of the thinking of the majority, and above all, by greater adaptability to their milieu as it actually is. All new movements, causes, fads inevitably attract, first of all, the latent schizophrenics who promote and encourage as well as endanger such movements. Thus is it explicable that several prominent leaders of the romantic German *Sturm und Drang* "became" ill with this disease, not however, because of their participation in the movement.

The etiological significance of an individual's dissatisfaction with his life is not to be rejected summarily under all circumstances. Indeed, it is probable that such psychic irritations can help make the disease manifest. But usually the conditions are such that these people are never satisfied with their lives, occupations, and positions just because they are sick.

As yet we cannot answer the question whether there are psychic causes for schizophrenia. However, it is probably to be answered in the negative. In cases of which we have excellent anamneses, one regularly notes that signs of disease existed before the suspected psychic trauma so that it becomes difficult to impute to such trauma any causal significance. In the majority of cases, it is also quite evident without much searching that the unfortunate love affair, demotion from office, etc., were consequences and not causes of the disease if there was any connection between them at all.

Yet the concept of psychic etiology of schizophrenia always crops up again and again; on the one hand, because the disease is all too often associated with unpleasant events and experiences, and on the other, because, even after the manifest outbreak of the malady, aggravation and improvement are undoubtedly dependent on psychic factors and influences. We may also add because the symptoms suggest a connection with those events; e.g., the deserted lover manifests her desires and wishes in her deliria and produces stereotypies which testify to, at least, a symbolic preoccupation and concern with the object of her desires.

We must conclude from all this that psychic experiences—usually of an unpleasant nature—can undoubtedly affect the schizophrenic symptoms. However, it is highly improbable that the disease itself is really produced by such factors. Psychic events and experiences may release the symptoms but not the disease; somewhat in the same fashion that physical strain can release a pulmonary hemorrhage when a disease-process has already eroded the tissues and vessels. To be sure, this analogy is not entirely accurate inasmuch as the symptoms of schizophrenia are not merely simple injuries, but rather a reaction of an individual under altered circumstances, a reaction which does not differ in essence from a normal one.

Thus, we do not assume that falling into the water caused the ensuing schizophrenia. Rather, we believe that, if the symptoms were not manifest, the shock led to an abnormal reaction of the already altered psyche. The same interpretation applies to those cases in whom the disease becomes manifest after an accidental encounter with the former betrothed and, later after years of remission, the disease reappears under the same circumstances. The majority, if not all the schizophrenic prison-psychoses can be explained in a similar fashion; however real advances of the disease are often co-determinant factors.

The following cases will illustrate the manner in which psychic events or experiences operate. A medical student had a mild catatonic attack with delusions each time that he had to go up for his preliminary examinations and also before his final examinations. A man who was considered quite normal became ill on each of the four occasions when he had to serve his period of military training.[12] An engineer developed hallucinatory attacks when he had to go to prison for political reasons, and also when his wife divorced him. A woman, who could still be kept at home, became agitated each time she was refused something, e.g. to go to a party, to attend a social engagement, etc. The last example illustrates the transition to those fleeting agitations due to some unpleasantness which are so common in hospital patients.

Induced schizophrenia deserves special mention. At one time we had in Burgholzli four siblings (two brothers and two sisters) who all had the same persecutory and religious delusions. It turned out that one sister, the most intelligent of the four, was the first to become ill; she imposed her delusions on the others. She deteriorated severely and later developed catatonic symptoms. The second sister could eventually be released, but had to be readmitted later. The two brothers managed to maintain themselves outside the hospital. There was no doubt that the two sisters were really schizophrenic; and we had excellent reasons for believing that the two brothers were also schizo-

12. Translator's note: In Switzerland, one month's military training is required each year for able-bodied male citizens until the age of fifty.

phrenic, not only because they never recovered completely afterwards, but also because of their peculiar modes of life already before the acute attack. In another family, the mother managed to transmit her ideas of grandeur to two daughters, one of whom was clearly schizophrenic, while the other could be convinced of the inaccuracy and falsity of her notions and then showed no further evidence of disease.

Therefore, we must assume that an energetic patient can suggest his delusions to other members of his family if and when they articulate with the complexes (wishes and desires) of these same members. However, schizophrenia will only develop if the disease is already latent in those individuals. In induced insanity, not the disease as such is determined by induction but only its delusional content, and perhaps also the manifest outbreak.

Of course, every conceivable human experience has been described, at one time or another, as the cause of psychoses which we now consider to be schizophrenia. A "religious mania" was sent to us which was supposed to have resulted from uterine infection. It should suffice to remark that we do not have any evidence whatsoever for bringing schizophrenia in direct relation with organic genital disease. Out of consideration for the reader, we shall not discuss such ideas as, for instance, the notion: schizophrenia is caused by the fact that young people no longer obey their parents.[13]

13. Journal ment. sc., 1904, p. 272.

SECTION X

THE THEORY

CHAPTER I

THE THEORY OF SYMPTOMS

The psychopathology of schizophrenia is one of the most interesting and intriguing since it permits a many sided insight into the workings of the diseased as well as the healthy psyche. In the attempt to explain this disease, we admittedly have to resort to hypotheses as we do in the theory of other psychoses. In order to avoid prolixity in the following rather long discussion it is left to the reader to make the necessary reservations at each point. I hope I have not made this task too difficult. Furthermore, we should not forget that, even in the event that all our hypotheses should eventually prove correct, we would still be acquainted with only a very small part of all the mechanisms which are probably involved in the symptomatology of this disease. Conversely, it is obvious that at this time no one can claim to be already able to explain all or even the greater part of the symptoms.

PRIMARY AND SECONDARY SYMPTOMS

We can only understand a psychically determined psychosis if we distinguish the symptoms stemming directly from the disease process itself from those secondary symptoms which only begin to operate when the sick psyche reacts to some internal or external processes. In a disease such as osteomalacia, the chemical and physiological processes, including the decalcification of the bones, constitute the disease process. The fragility of the bones is a direct consequence of those bone changes. However, a fracture or bending of the bone will only occur after the direct action of external forces. Such subsequent manifestations of the malady are not the consequences of the disease process itself but rather consequences of the altered response of the bones toward accessory influences. A lesion of the abducens muscle is a disease; the paralysis of the lateral eye movements is the direct and necessary consequence of the disease (primary or direct symptom). The contracture of the internus and the wrong localization of visual images are secondary (indirect) symptoms due to the physiological reactions of the organism to the altered conditions.

The primary symptoms are the necessary partial phenomena of a disease; the secondary symptoms may be absent, at least potentially, or they may change without the disease process having to change at the same time.

Almost the totality of the heretofore described symptomatology of dementia praecox is a secondary, in a certain sense, an accidental one. Therefore, the disease may remain symptomless for a long time. Whether a particular chronic schizophrenic is able to work peacefully today or wanders about and quarrels with everyone, whether he is neat and clean or smears himself—that is the nature of the symptom—depends mainly on past or present events, and not directly on the disease. Some affectively charged experience releases a hallucinatory agitated state. A transfer to another hospital may bring about the disappearance of the same hallucinations. Affects, which may have been entirely absent for years at a time, may suddenly begin to function normally again on certain occasions. Furthermore, it must be noted that no schizophrenic can entertain the delusion that a certain Miss N. wants to marry him if he knows nothing about a Miss N., and (I may add) if still other events had not determined this special direction of his wishes and fears. No one would hallucinate that Jesuits were persecuting him if he had never heard anything of the significance of Jesuits. The content of delusions and hallucinations can only be understood and conceived of in terms of definite external events. However, there can be no symptoms without content. Thus hallucinations and delusions (entirely aside from the releasing factor) need not stem directly from the disease process itself. The latter provides only the predisposition, on the basis of which psychic processes develop the symptoms.[1]

A. The Primary Symptoms

We do not as yet know with certainty the primary symptoms of the schizophrenic cerebral disease. In all probability we also ought to include in these same primary symptoms a number of other simpler manifestations, above all, a part of the disturbances of association. It appears as if those pathways of association and inhibition, established

1. To be sure, they are people who imagine that some central stimulus can set into motion the operations of those precise systems or cells in which the notion, Jesuits or a Jesuit threat, "has been stored." This idea has as much probability as the hypothesis which states that mechanical stimulation of the acoustic nerve could produce the sounds which compose the hearing of a poem.

by experience, had lost their meaning and significance. Associations seem to take new pathways more easily, and thus no longer follow the old preferred ways, that is the logical pathways indicated by past experience. Jung has drawn attention to the fact that even in the healthy similar unusual pathways of association are opened up during moments of confusion, distraction, and unconscious thinking. But in such people, it never goes quite so far as it does in schizophrenics. (In the healthy psyche, only the dream forms a sufficient analogy to what goes on in schizophrenia.) Especially in acute conditions of schizophrenia, one often finds so complete a fragmentation of the thinking processes that they cannot result in a complete idea or action, but merely in vague movements. In this way, even concepts such as "father" and "mother" become vague and obscure. Such confusional states usually occur without pyschic occasion, they frequently represent the peak of a subacute phase of the illness. Sometimes they are accompanied by a syndrome which we ordinarily associate with signs of infection or auto-intoxication: coated tongue, fuligo, gastro-intestinal disturbances, weakness and loss of weight, coarse tremor and even occasionally some fever and leucocytosis. From all this, it would seem probable that these forms of confusional states are a direct discharge of an increased intensification of the disease; consequently even the milder degrees of the same schizophrenic association-splitting (such as we see everywhere) represent a primary symptom. *We consider then, the disturbance of association as primary insofar as it involves a diminution or leveling of the number of affinities; blocking and systematic splitting are secondary manifestations.*

The clouded states (*Benommenheitszustände*) also give the impression of being primary symptoms inasmuch as the patients seem to try very hard to direct their thoughts and movements toward some definite goal without being able to do so. In these patients we usually also find a rather coarse tremor, weakness, and a certain awkwardness of movements. As far as I know, one cannot rouse these patients; they remain in the same state till the attack has run its course, without reacting with any essential change to psychic influences exerted to alter their state. In this condition, there appears to be a general interference with the workings of the central processes; some sort of torpor is in evidence (of course not in the sense of manic-depressive inhibition). Often one even gets the impression that the patient may be suffering from increased intra-cranial pressure, and when the patients come to autopsy, one usually (or always) finds what appears to be cerebral edema or a very taut edematous pia. I believe therefore that in certain clouded states we are presented with a syndrome which, in its essential components, is not produced by way of the psyche. However, we do not know for certain whether the underlying cerebral alteration is part of the schizophrenic process itself, or whether it is a secondary complication of that process. The pial edema could be, for example, the consequence of a schizophrenic vasomotor disturbance in the same fashion that it has been assumed for the other edemas associated with this disease. In any event, such phenomena are not seen in every case.

Manic and melancholic episodes occupy a special position among the acute clinical conditions. We know that the state of the body, its digestive system, chemical influences (alcohol) can provoke oscillations of the affects in the sense of mania or depression. In addition, we must assume that cerebral changes can produce similar conditions (paresis). It is probable that in schizophrenia too, oscillations of the affects occur which are somehow determined by organic changes. Whereas in a few individual cases we may get the impression that we are dealing with a complication of schizophrenia with manic-depressive psychosis, most of the manic episodes appear to belong to the disease process itself. In the melancholic conditions of schizophrenia, besides those which are related in some way to the disease process itself, we find many manifestations due to secondary (psychic) genesis: depressions subsequent upon the realization of being ill, anxiety, etc.

Jahrmärker also includes the disposition to hallucinations among the primary manifestations. He is probably correct; yet we encounter hallucinations and delusions in the most varied cerebral processes, in intoxications, and in the dreams of healthy people. We see them in individuals of artistic temperament where the distinction between imagination and perception is often markedly blurred. Thus we cannnot ignore the fact that a hallucinatory predisposition is, to some extent, present in every psyche, and that schizophrenia, as well as other conditions, merely makes it manifest.[2] With even greater probability, we can assume, as does Jahrmärker, that the tendency to stereotypy originates directly from the disease process. (See below, theory of sterotypies.)

Perhaps future investigations will uncover, behind part of the other catatonic symptoms, a general tendency which will have to be considered as a primary symptom. As we shall see later, however, even the catatonic symptoms are not wholly independent of accidental influences. But the chronic catatonic symptoms undoubtedly have such a bad prognostic significance that it is tempting to believe that they are the expression of some severe brain processes.

2. In schizophrenics the distinction between imagination and reality is certainly reduced altogether—often to zero—by the splitting of the psyche.

As for the physical symptoms, the first that have to be mentioned are those fatal cases with manifestations of paralyses and disturbances of metabolism which may be so severe as to lead to death from marasmus. The pupillary disturbances giving rise to marked difference between the two pupils are to be considered as organic, that is, as primary (while the symmetrical anomalies of the size of the pupils may also have a psychic basis). Besides the usual explanation of these symptoms,[3] our interpretation (the organic) is further assisted by the circumstances that we find—to be sure, on the basis of very few cases (Zablocka)—these pupillary inequalities in those cases which show a poorer termination than those with other kinds of pupillary disturbances. Thus, these symptoms also give the impression of an intense cerebral affection of some kind.

The tremors, which in acute conditions often are quite similar to the coarse shivering of the feverish, and which in the chronic arise quite independently of agitations, excitements or strains, can also be interpreted as organic; the same can be said for the fibrillary twitchings. Perhaps the increased idiomuscular irritability should also belong here; so do the many stubborn headaches and vertigo which frequently accompany the disease, and even more often precede the disease.

The vasomotor anomalies could be secondarily released. But often they do not seem to have any relationship to the affect-disturbance; or they are limited to a single part of the body, substantiating the impression that some of these vasomotor anomalies are direct symptoms of disturbances in the central nervous system. The edemas have to be conceived of in the same way. A part of these edemas appear to be directly conditioned by the disease process itself. Then also many catatonic attacks appear to be organically determined, particularly, when they are followed by paresis of some muscle groups. Psychogenic origin of such catatonic attacks can certainly be excluded, if for no other reason than the fact that such attacks aften cannot be distinguished from those of epilepsy and apoplexy.

With this discussion of probable occurrences, we have said nearly all that we know about the primary symptoms of schizophrenia.

B. The Secondary Symptoms

1. The Individual Symptoms

Let us begin by saying that the secondary symptoms are a direct consequence of the loosening of the associations: the utilization of mere

3. It is true that in migraine we find pupillary inequalities for which we do not need to assume an organic basis.

fragments of ideas in the thinking with its false conclusions, the displacements, the symbolization, the condensations, the aimless erratic thinking.

Furthermore, the appearance and disappearance of the blockings are dependent on pyschic influences and interests; thus they cannot be part of the permanent disease condition.[4]

The mode of the associative splitting can be directly attributed to the disease process only inasmuch as the more complex and less exercised functions disintegrate earlier than the others. Although this relationship is demonstrable in many acute cases and in chronic states only after precise and careful observation, nevertheless, there is quite another kind of splitting which much more frequently strikes our attention: simple as well as complex psychic structures disintegrate in what appears to be a completely irregular fashion; under certain circumstances, the immediate and most obvious associations are repressed, whereas other functions as, for example, the comprehension of scientific problems remain entirely intact. This type of splitting is subject to purely psychological laws: Those functions are disturbed which come into conflict with certain affective needs of the patients.

Thus this tendency to disconnect association and to link unusual associations is probably a primary one. However, the choice of associations which are actually disturbed, is secondarily determined by the affectively charged complexes.[5]

Currently, I consider the disturbances of affect as secondary symptoms but in doing so I am well aware that I am in disagreement with the usual conception of schizophrenic deterioration. My reasons are the following: real destruction of affectivity cannot be proved even in the most severe cases; in the course of a very thorough examination, the absent function can again be made manifest by touching on the patient's complexes or by a complicating cerebral atrophy. In moderately severe cases, the affectivity is disturbed in a way that does not at all correspond to a general weakening of that particular function: some affects may be present, and others not; indeed the choice is such that it can only be ex-

4. The dependence of a symptom on psychic factors is not in all circumstances a proof of the secondary genesis of the symptom: sedatives work poorly or not at all in agitations and excitements; the efficacy of a general anesthetic is affected by the patients' psychic state. The intoxicated individual may suddenly become sober when he realizes the terrible accident he has just caused.

5. In an analogous fashion, we see in senile memory defects that the memory fails first and most frequently in those areas where unpleasant feelings are involved. The same thing is seen in many paretics who are still fairly well oriented, but who view the ominous mental hospital only as a hotel, despite all proofs to the contrary. A mildly irritated larynx does not necessarily provoke a cough; the latter may be first provoked by the inhalation of dusty air or by an unpleasant psychic situation.

plained on the basis of psychic causes. Furthermore, the individual affects as well as the total affectivity change with time in accordance with the psychic constellation and stimulation. In the milder cases, we often see hyperfunction of the affectivity not only as irritability, but as a general sensitivity. The detailed and precise study of the affectivity, especially in man and animals, in the healthy and in the sick, definitely seems to exclude the possibility of isolated destruction of so primary a function.

It is obvious that we have to consider as secondary phenomena the well-known disturbances of memory and orientation, especially, when they appear to be related exclusively to certain of the patient's complexes; the same holds true for the automatisms (including obsessive thoughts, etc.) which can only arise on the basis of a certain independent activity of definite complexes.

It should also need no proof that the disturbances of the complex functions of intelligence (deterioration and delusions), the impaired synthesis of the total personality, the disordered strivings and efforts of the patient (irresponsibility, abulia), the altered relations to reality (autism) are comprehensible only in connection with the already named secondary symptoms; therefore they themselves are secondary manifestations for the most part. Also negativism is certainly a complex secondary phenomenon.

As we indicated previously, there are still a number of symptoms which require the operation of certain secondary mechanisms; at the present time, however, we must assume the existence of an additional cause which can only be termed a primary predisposition: here belong the hallucinations, the stereotypies, the catalepsies.

2. The Origin of the Secondary Symptoms

Outline: On the one hand, the loosening of the associations results in the opening up of wrong pathways of thought, pathways deviating from experience; and on the other hand, the patient is forced to operate with fragments of ideas. The latter abnormality leads to displacements, condensations, confusion, generalizations, clang-associations, illogical thinking, and incoherence.

The weakening of the logical functions results in relative predominance of the affects. Unpleasantly-toned associations are repressed at their very inception (blocking); whatever conflicts with the affects is split off. This mechanism leads to the logical blunders which determine (among other things) the delusions; but the most significant effect is the splitting of the psyche in accordance with the emotionally charged complexes. Any unpleasant reality is split off by the operation of autism or transformed in the various delusional states. The turning away from the outer world can assume the form of negativism. The association-splitting can also lead to pathological ambivalence in which contradictory feelings or thoughts exist side by side without influencing each other.

The contents of delusions constitute desires, wishes, and fears which, because of the disturbances of associations, are often distorted to the point of being unrecognizable.[6] The same (conscious or unconscious) activity of the split off complexes also conditions the memory falsifications and the contents of hallucinations, the mannerisms, and most, if not all, the stereotypies.

The affect-blocking has its origin in the repression of the affects (usually already at their inception), but also in the inhibition of other affects. The indifference exhibited by the patients is further increased by many other conditions, especially by the autism and the splitting off of emotionally charged complexes.

(a) The Train of Thought-Splitting

The association disturbances were conceived of as being primary; from these we can derive the majority of secondary symptoms. Although this cannot be done with absolute certainty, they can still be understood in terms of this uniform viewpoint.

In schizophrenia, the habitual well-worn pathways of association have lost their cohesiveness. Associations which used to be made regularly are omitted, while material is associated which is normally not connected with the initial idea. Obvious connections such as those existing between the essential parts of an idea may remain unused; but in turn, entirely new pathways may (but need not) be laid down. In a certain context, the father believes that he is the mother of his children, by ignoring existing attributes of his own person and substituting attributes that belong to his wife. Nonetheless, this distinction is never completely abolished in the associational links. Even in the most severe cases, the majority of associations takes the usual pathways; because innumerable, nearly correct ideas and thought fragments are still produced. We know only in part under what conditions and in accordance with what rules the deviations occur. Many schizophrenic associations strike us as being "accidental." What we see in this process is the systematic influence of the affects interrupting many associations and linking others. Often enough, instead of by ideas and concepts, the train of thought is determined

6. They can also be distorted by the patient's affective needs in the sense of Freud's dream censor.

by mere fragments of such ideas, or by incorrectly combined fragments. For this reason, the train of thought deviates in many respects.

In this way, we can explain the extreme clang-associations which are based on the similarity of a single sound (shoe-shimmer).[7] Words having many similar sounds in common are more easily and more frequently substituted for each other.[8] In some way, concepts which have only a very minor component in common are mistaken or exchanged for each other: Thus a patient is reminded of "throwing kisses" whenever she wets a thread (while sewing) with her tongue.

"Displacements," which arise because in a chain of thoughts one idea is suddenly substituted for another, are a similar consequence of the incompleteness of an association complex. The defective logic prevents the correction of the error. The very common use of symbols is a special case of this anomaly.

In this way, several concepts with common components can be condensed into a single one in which only the common element comes to have any value,[9] e.g., various loved ones, various places that were visited by the patient.

Concepts and ideas, which are only partially thought through, remain vague altogether. This may be one of the causes of the schizophrenic tendency to generalization and elaboration of symptoms. Other causes may be the lack of the inhibition which one psychic function should exercise on other inadequate psychic functions, as well as the facilitation of the use of uncommon pathways.

If the goal of a thought is not kept constantly in mind while thinking, every sort of looseness may appear. The patient soon loses himself in secondary associations; he is more easily distracted by external things than is ordinarily the case. Conversely, he pays no attention to external circumstances which rightfully ought to be considered.

If the associations no longer take the accustomed paths, then accidental links gain logical value. The patient quite arbitrarily links whatever he happens to be experiencing at the moment and gives logical form to the momentary circumstances surrounding the situation.

---

7. Lobsien has demonstrated that in children alliterations, such as "feather-flask," give rise to the formation of firm associations. Nevertheless, it makes a great difference whether such senseless associations are formed under experimental conditions (where they have no other kind of connections) or are formed in ordinary thinking. Old German poetic alliteration must have had powers similar to that of modern rhyme.

8. This occurs more frequently in children and in dreams than in schizophrenics. A child may confuse "Italian" and "lantern." I once dreamed this thought: *"Mach nur nicht zu viel"* (Don't do too much) which was expressed in the dream by the words, *"Marandon de Montyel."* Of course, there were many more determinants for the choice of these particular names in the dream.

9. This is also rather common in dreams.

(He smashed a window pane "because" the doctor wore eyeglasses.)[10]

Aside from the frequent lack of a goal-idea, there are still many other sources of association disturbances. A kind of "free" association, for example, will be facilitated, among other things, by the "*sentiment d'incomplétude*" which easily installs itself wherever there is defective incomplete thinking. Under certain conditions, the tendency to naming objects and the poverty of ideas may be explained by the fact that the patient's thinking does not seem to make any progress, which itself may have various causes, e.g., lack of affect or clouding of consciousness.[11] Intermediate, or indirect associations may also come about in various ways. What is also important here, besides the lack of a goal-idea, is the disturbance of attention, analogous to what occurs in the normal.

The logical operations naturally suffer most. Ideas and concepts which ought to come into consideration are simply disregarded, many others are not fully thought out. If the concept, "father," denotes only the partial concept, "begetter," it may easily be confused with that of "mother." Thus many logical operations end in false conclusions.

The anomalies, considered up to this point, represent direct consequences of primary disturbances of associations to such an extent that one could almost consider them as primary disturbances of association. However, there are also indirect consequences of the distorted relations between associations and affectivity. Although these indirect consequences appear only in certain specific situations, they may dominate the clinical picture of the disease. Logical and affective needs often oppose each other. The influence of the affects is more pronounced in every disease which weakens the patient's logical operations.

Whereas the intellectual thought processes take pathways which are facilitated by past experience,[12] the affects direct the associations in the direction of corresponding drives and strivings (gratification of

---

10. These symptoms are not in themselves pathological. The child must first learn which associational connections are "accidental" as far as simultaneousness and succession are concerned. A two year old child spills a good deal of water while I am questioning him about some other matter. He answers quite inappropriately, "because of the water." Mythology with its many personifications, condensations, and fusions offers a rich field of analogies with schizophrenic thought processes. The fabulous Easter rabbit lays eggs because both rabbits and eggs are ancient symbols of fertility. After the triumph of monotheism, the Trinity was conceived to contain all three of the persons who had to be honored.

11. When I pass by a poster, deep in thought, it may happen that I read the inscription, unconsciously and inaudibly, yet moving my lips.

12. It is obvious that, since the forms of our logic repeat themselves or constitute analogies only on the basis of experience-given associations, the acquired logical associations will suffer badly and much earlier from a general brain disturbance than the innate affective processes. If there exists a schizophrenic *Anlage* of the psyche, one might be inclined to consider that individuals whose ability to reproduce reality is poorly developed would be the ones predisposed to autism.

pleasure, warding off pain); they facilitate the appropriate connections and hinder the appearance of all those which do not correspond to their needs. Furthermore, the affectivity gives other valences to ideas so that, for example, the dangers of a desired undertaking are underestimated while the dangers of an undesired one are exaggerated. It is as if one displaces the decimal point in a numerical operation. In the normal, the affectivity determines essentially only the direction of the person's behavior; only during great excitement or in questions where subjective judgments are permissible (as in questions of taste) are the logical operations normally falsified in any real sense of the word. If the logical functions are pathologically weakened, the influence of the affects spreads even to those part-associations which are otherwise distinct, correct, and solidly established. They, too, are falsified in the sense of the wishes and fears of the patient. What one desires and fears becomes reality (see the theory of delusional ideas).

Blocking is the most striking consequence of schizophrenic activity. It is not a pathological symptom per se since it is seen in the healthy when they are overwhelmed by some emotional disturbance such as fright, and sometimes even in sudden pleasant surprises. Children, imbeciles, hysterics, each for a different reason, are also very easily dominated by their affects and are therefore prone to blocking.[13] Whenever we have been able to trace the development of blocking in our schizophrenics, we also found that a complex had been touched upon or some unpleasant emotion had been provoked. The conclusion seems almost inevitable that generalized and persistent blocking in catatonic conditions is an exaggeration of the same phenomena. We can in no way distinguish such blocking from the transitory, rapidly disappearing forms. Occasionally we could actually observe the development of transitory blocking from the more general type. The schizophrenic tendency to the persistence of arbitrary phenomena (stereotypies) may perhaps be involved in the origin of the massive blocking. It is certain that the tendency to generalization is involved. The following is a common observation: blocking which was limited at first to a specific thought or idea, began to spread so rapidly that it quickly became impossible to talk to the patient about anything. Kraepelin lays great emphasis on the fact that counter-drives may also produce blocking, more so in the sphere of conation than that of abstract thinking. This is obviously quite true. But the denial of any impulse is so very often associated with a counter-impulse that, in stressing the counter-impulse, we only emphasize a

13. The emotional stupor, which occurs when a person feels incapable of meeting a certain demand (Risch) and which is also seen in the cataplexy of animals (at least in the higher animals), is rather analogous to blocking.

different aspect of the same process, but we do not gain a new perspective.

Often we receive the impression that the lack of interest also contributes to blocking since, at the first obstacle, the thought process simply comes to a complete halt. Moreover, in severe catatonics with clouded states, other resistances to the train of thought seem to produce a generalized inhibition. It is obvious that in such a situation, the influence of the affects in the form of blocking, becomes much more potent; in other words, the obstacles and resistances to thinking summate. Conversely, if the psychic processes are being persistently inhibited in some way (intoxication? cerebral edema?), the patient can by an effort of will behave normally for a time. In that case, what we have is not a sudden dissolution of the massive blocking, but the very opposite: the overcoming of the obstacles by an affect.

Everything which opposes the affect is more deeply suppressed than normally, and whatever falls in line with the affect is abnormally facilitated. The result is that an emotionally charged idea cannot even be opposed in thought any more: the ambitious schizophrenic dreams only of his desires; obstacles simply do not exist for him. In this way, complexes which are joined together by a common affect rather than any logical connections are not only formed, but are also more firmly fixed in the patient. Due to the fact that the associational pathways which join such a complex to other ideas are not used, these associational pathways lose their effectiveness in respect of the more adequate associations. In other words, the affectively charged complex of ideas continues to become isolated and obtains an ever increasing independence (splitting of the psychic functions).

All (normal and abnormal) psychic processes, the affective as well as the intellectual ones, have not only a positive tendency to facilitate allied material but also the negative tendency to inhibit non-allied material. The best-known result of these tendencies is the "constriction of the field of conscious awareness"; that is the inability of healthy people to think of several different things simultaneously. But if the associations are interrupted, primarily, by the original association disturbance and secondarily by the isolating effect of the complexes, then not only the facilitating but also the inhibiting influences of various ideas on each other are decreased or entirely suppressed. In this way we can comprehend the fact that several complexes can function simultaneously in the same patient and that incompatible ideas can exist side by side. (While a patient is thinking of some specific thing, he may also hear voices, have obsessive ideas, and perform activities which belong to an entirely different constellation of ideas; the examining attorney is simultaneously regarded as the hospital physician, N. N., and as his mortal enemy, X.Y.)[14]

Of course, even in schizophrenia, there is usually only *one* complex present in consciousness at any given moment. Yet, the autistic and realistic trains of thought run side by side at the same time,[15] quite often we see in the conscious trains of thought an intimate mixture of ideas which belong to different complexes. We can see from the following facts that the complexes function in the unconscious: they appear suddenly with additional elaborations, for example, fully developed delusional systems suddenly emerge in consciousness; the complexes are always ready to assimilate every sort of experience and event (delusions of reference). The complexes also express themselves directly by way of the hallucinations, mimicry, the unconscious or compulsive behavior, and the stereotypies. Thus it is almost a matter of indifference whether a complex is conscious at any given moment, or not.

The theory need not take any consideration of the presence or absence of the conscious qualities of the individual complexes. We have reason to assume that a conscious psychic function differs from an unconscious one only in that the conscious function is associatively linked with the conscious personality. We cannot understand schizophrenic symptoms, any more than other complicated psychic manifestations, without taking into consideration the fact that there are unconscious processes which, aside from the absence of qualities of consciousness, are identical with conscious psychic processes (73 a).

It is probable that in the normal psyche there are also inhibitions which prevent the use of disparate associational material and hinder the transition to another theme, except under the influence of special forces (affects, distraction from the outside). If these inhibitions can be overcome in the normal psyche, it is obvious that they can fail completely in schizophrenics. In any event, schizophrenics not only exclude normal associations, but also make completely incorrect links. This in itself may be one of the reasons why the schizophrenic's thoughts are so easily lost in irrelevancies and why such strange associations crop up in his train of thoughts.[16] This lack of inhibition explains the various

14. The prevalent explanation of the process of inhibition loses its value in a dynamic conception of psychic processes which assumes that definite quantities of "psychic energy" are available to take the pathways offering the least resistance to a given constellation of ideas. In that case our "explanation" must limit itself to combining two pieces of observational data; that psychic energy can take unusual pathways in schizophrenia, and that this energy can split itself up into several parts each of which goes its own independent way.

15. Cf. splitting of attention.

16. The poorly thought out goal ideas and the absence of a homogeneous, unified drive naturally also have their share in the production of this symptom.

combinations of different ideas which may go so far that even the emotionally charged complexes (although they do possess greater independence than in the healthy) are often fused; or fragments of such complexes get mixed up with each other.

In view of what has been previously said about schizophrenic associations, it is obvious that the associations of the ideas of one complex with those of others do not necessarily obey the laws of logic; hence the utter senselessness of many such combinations and linkings.[17]

The isolation of the complex, even without the lack of that inhibition of which we have spoken, can never be an absolute one. The complexes are all more or less bound to the same ego, and they can therefore influence each other at least via the personality. Yet, the isolation of the complexes is most apparent in their relation to this same personality. The complexes do not fuse and combine to form a unified effort and drive; instead the schizophrenic ego is linked first with one, then with another of these individual complexes of ideas. The patient may be having an interesting conversation with his doctor; yet suddenly, in a totally illogical way, he may begin to berate the doctor for persecuting him. The patient may be worrying about his relatives; at the same time he breaks out into violent expressions of hatred toward them; or he may show, externally, the most extraordinary indifference to their fate. At one moment, he may be striving to attain the highest aims, and in another moment—he is ready to sacrifice his very existence for some utterly silly notion.

Thus the patient appears to be split into as many different persons or personalities as they have complexes.[18]

Still, the ego itself is fragmented only in the very severest cases. Ordinarily, the patient still knows who he is; he knows his past; he is oriented in time and space. He knows everything he should know insofar as he has not changed into something else in accordance with the demands of some interposed complex. All these essential parts of the personality stand in certain relationships to the various complexes. If one considers the intellectual elements as the most essential segment of the personality, then, for the most part, one cannot say that it has been split; but rather one would say it has become the football, the plaything, of the complexes. However, if one considers that the strivings are the

---

17. The latter is an important difference from hysteria. In hysteria, we also have an exaggerated dominating influence of affects on the associations, but since there is no primary fragmentation of associations, the complexes are much more sharply separated from each other and from reality.

18. "The patient so-to-speak consists, simultaneously, of a number of different personalities." (Wernicke, 804, p. 113.)

essence of the ego, then the schizophrenic certainly has as many personalities as he has complexes—personalities which are more or less independent of each other.

Even the more solid intellectual element of the personality is changed in accordance with the splitting. As long as the patient curses the physician, the latter is for the patient his hated rival, the shoemaker, N., although the patient is otherwise perfectly oriented as to this situation. If a patient maintains that he is the Emperor, it may well be that an essential segment of his past life was excluded and substituted for by the delusional ideas, during the period when his complex of grandeur was linked with his ego.

Certain circumstances, real and delusional concepts may combine to form a delusional explanation.

However, even during the period of delusional thinking, the correct and real orientation usually functions undisturbed; but it is more or less split off from the ego. As soon as the patient has stopped berating the doctor, whom he mistook for the hated shoemaker, the patient knows perfectly well what the doctor was doing during the whole time that the patient was busy cursing him. During prolonged cloudy states, the presence of correct orientation may often still be demonstrated, running parallel with the systematic mis-recognition of the whole environment. Afterwards, the patient may be able to give an excellent account of the real events that went on around him without having to ponder or explain the things to himself. In contrast, epileptic or alcoholic deliriants, whose total personality is involved in the mis-recognition, can only orient themselves by conscious, deliberate reflection, or have to be torn out of their pathological condition by stimulation of one kind or another. After the delirium, the true events can only be reconstructed with the greatest effort, if at all.

The splitting is the prerequisite condition of most of the complicated phenomena of the disease. It is the splitting which gives the peculiar stamp to the entire symptomatology. However, behind this systematic splitting into definite idea-complexes, we have found a previous primary loosening of the associational structure which can lead to an irregular fragmentation of such solidly established elements as concrete ideas. The term, schizophrenia, refers to both kinds of splitting which often fuse in their effects.

Schizophrenic splitting is again only another example of exaggerated physiological processess. Even the healthy person can harbor various complexes, all more or less unconnected with each other; and he may even continue to elaborate and develop them in his unconscious or in dreams. His personality also changes as regards content when the affects change. During a conversation, a friend passes a remark which is very unpleasant for us; only a few of us are capable of simply adding this remark to the picture we have had of this friend up to that moment. Most of us are aroused, think only of our friend's bad characteristics and forget his good ones either completely or partially. We are spurred to actions which we ordinarily would not do. The person so aroused has become like a "different person."

From this level of change, there is every intermediate stage through hysterical manifestations to autism, clouded states, and on to the paranoid syndromes; none of these manifestations differ as far as the basic psychological operations are concerned. We must imagine that in such variations of response of a normal person thousands of associations (we use this figure so as not to have to employ unwieldy large figures which obviously would be a good deal nearer the truth) are inhibited or abnormally facilitated; whereas, in an aroused schizophrenic, perhaps, hundreds of thousands; and in a clouded patient, millions would be involved.

What Gross understands by his term, "fragmentation (or disintegration) of consciousness"[19] corresponds to what we call "splitting." The consciousness, however, cannot fragment itself, but only its contents. Furthermore, we find this splitting in the unconscious as well as in the conscious; and the terms, "fragmentation" or "disintegration" cannot include those especially firm connections of certain association complexes. The term, "dissociation" has already been in use for a long time to designate similar observations and findings. But dissociation also designates more: for example, the constriction of the content of consciousness in paretics. It may thus give rise to misunderstandings. For the most part, our concept of splitting corresponds to Wernicke's "sejunction." We cannot adopt this latter term either, not only because the concept of sejunction is broader than ours, but also because it has been conceived of in anatomico-physiological terms. Sejunction leads, for example, to a stagnation of the psychokyme which then has to seek other pathways and ends up in inappropriate parts of the brain and so induces the delusions and hallucinations. All this we prefer to exclude from our concept of splitting.

Foersterling views the "splitting of consciousness" as an increase in the psychomotor disturbances. I do not find myself very much in accord with such ideas.

(b) *Affectivity*

All manifestations that we observe in affective deterioration can be

19. German: Bewusstseinszerfall.

traced back to exaggerations of normal psychic processes. Yet, we do not mean to suggest that all the factors of that enormously complex maze of psychic functions which determine the schizophrenic affect disturbance have already been discovered.

It was an old observation that the affects were not completely absent. Therefore, it was believed that there was some sort of general weakening, rather than complete annihilation of this function. This conception contradicts observation. It is obvious that the higher functions are somewhat more strongly affected than the simpler ones; but this cannot be postulated as a rule in the sense that the more complicated affects invariably suffer before the more primitive or phylogenetically older ones. The concept of a reduction of the affectivity also has to be rejected for the following reason, namely that the preserved affects often express themselves with even greater energy than before. One only has to think of the expressions of passion and anger, of the occasional cheerfulness, and the powerful energy of the instinctual life. What is more, the affective sway over the associations is far stronger than in the healthy (Jung).

Stransky (748) assumes the existence of partial dissociation, an "ataxia" of the *thymopsyche* and the *noopsyche* from which results an "uncertainty in the thymo-noopsychic relationship;" that is to say, there arises an athymia and parathymia. This is an easily understood description of the factual relations but it is not an explanation.[20]

Another attempt which was bound to fail was that which attributed the disturbance of affects exclusively to the disturbance of thinking. Foerster suggests that the higher functions are lost because the higher concepts are not constructed.[21] Such an explanation may be sufficient with respect of the affective disorders of the organic psychoses, but it does not even approach the essence of schizophrenic affectivity since we often see affectivity well preserved in patients with severe thinking disturbance; e.g., in acute attacks which are considered by some schools as manias and melancholias; and conversely, complete emotional defect in people who think so well, so logically, that they can convince not only judges, but even many psychiatrists of their mental health.

Obviously, we will also find secondary affect disturbances provoked by the thinking disturbance as well as primary ones. When concepts

---

20. This terminology misleads us into thinking that we have an explanation, and so satisfies us. The disadvantages of Stransky's terminology are that the intellect and affectivity, which are different aspects of the same psychic process, are made two very independent functions.

21. Pfersdorff (561) held a similar opinion regarding a certain class.

and ideas are only thought of in fragments,[22] when thinking always loses itself in side issues and irrelevances, when entirely incorrect associational pathways are utilized, then certainly the emotional expressions (taking the normal as standard) cannot be adequate. If thoughts jump capriciously from one idea to another, no homogeneous mood can posssibly result from such thinking. If the sick personality be divided into various relatively loosely connected fragments in accordance with its drives to each of which there is attached a corresponding affect or emotion, then none of these various feelings or emotions can possibly take possession of the whole personality and give it a homogeneous affective life. The suitable emotional tone of the delusions is further disturbed by the fact that in the patient there are not only delusions, but also constellations which differentiate between reality and irreality; that is they are able to appraise and evaluate the delusions, as such. Patients, who have observed themselves very carefully, will often offer this explanation during their periods of remission. Autistic patients do not react to reality with affects because they block them off. They do not react to their delusions because something in themselves recognizes the delusions as fantasies. However, the fundamental nature of the schizophrenic affect disturbance is independent of the thinking disturbance, it reveals a distinctive character which cannot be explained by any such thinking disturbance. It is also to be noted that many disturbances of thinking are consequencess of the affect-anomalies; therefore, they cannot at the same time be the causes.

Deeper understanding can be gained by an examination of the following properties of normal affectivity:

1. The affects have an upper limit of intensity which should not be over-stepped if they are to maintain the ordinary, subjective and objective characteristics. This limit varies markedly with the individual and the circumstances; whether every individual is capable of attaining these limits, is unknown. Our poets have been very well acquainted, of old, with these limits. I mention the fascinating observations that Baelz made on himself during an earthquake. Other examples, taken not from poetry but from scientific literature, are Livingstone's de-

22. If one takes the trouble to observe oneself, one sees that constellations of ideas which are not well thought out are easily accompanied by only a moderate or only a very small amount of feeling-tone. Obviously, in most cases, it is not the events themselves which condition the affects but the connection of such events with others. When a sum of money is stolen, it may appear to be an event which is indifferent, comic or tragic; or it may simply arouse one's sense of justice. Only if one first imagines, for example, that the stolen money was the sole wealth of a sick mother who intended to use it for the education of her child, does it appear tragic to us. Whoever is unable to think of this particular connection with the basic event as a whole will find it impossible to have an affect appropriate to this whole.

scription of being attacked by a lion. Qualitatively similar observations can be found in Bremer's objective account of the reactions of a large group of people after a cyclone.[23] Perhaps we also ought to include here the phenomenon of the sudden development of complete analgesia which appears in victims undergoing the tortures of the rack. However, it is certain that the intensity of the affects may rob them of a great part of their influence and efficacy, particularly their becoming conscious.

2. An affect which already has become conscious may be split off, if it is too difficult to bear. At the same time, the complex of ideas, which appears to be the carrier of the affect, does not remain accessible to the ego at all, or is accessible only with the greatest difficulty. Many people keep their unpleasant memories well out of reach by "forgetting" them. When they become unavoidable and when these painful thoughts must be brought into consciousness, they then appear to that person as somewhat strange, theoretical, and not well developed in just precisely those components which most intensively mediate contact with the ego. Very often it is perfectly possible to talk about a lost love without experiencing any of the feeling which would correspond to the entire complex, although it would be almost unbearable to have to remember the incident in all its painful details. Thus many connections between the lost person and our own ego are thereby carefully excluded from reproduction.

The unconscious avoidance of pain, when we have a wound or are suffering from a rheumatic joint, forms an analogy to or is perhaps identical with this mechanism. We "instinctively" avoid the critical movement, even before we actually feel the pain or even before we have any conscious idea of that pain. Because of previously felt pain, our psyche remains so "set" for some time that it will not carry out certain movements of our limbs. The result of this "set" may go far beyond its intended purpose; in many cases, movements are not made which could not possibly produce any pain; in nervous people under these circumstances, all movements may be rendered more difficult.

Even a new affect, because of its unpleasant or painful quality, may be inhibited *in statu nascendi.* Even before such an affect can begin to develop, it disposes the intra-psychic "set" in such a way that it is forced to leave the conscious personality totally unaware of its existence.

3. Such affects, blocked off from the conscious ego, are by no means always abolished; they remain distinctly recognizable by their

---

23. See also d'Abundo.

effects. Whoever is preoccupied by some emotional experience may dispense subjectively and objectively with the direct signs of the affect. Nevertheless, he is still preoccupied, still incapable of producing other affects. And one can appear indifferent, not only to earlier misfortunes, but also to all new experiences. A more powerful affect may continuously transform the personality without anyone being able to detect in the new peculiarity the presence of the affect; even the person, himself, seems to have forgotten the affect and experience which released it. It takes very special events to cause "the old wound to bleed again." Yet, the individual now has changed goals, changed ways of life, changed his basic attitude. In the hysteric, the original causal event or experience may become totally inaccessible to consciousness.

During association experiments, we note the presence of the Jungian indicators of a complex not only in the ideas which happen to concern the test-individual at the moment, but also in connection with ideas which were neither intellectually nor affectively present in the patient's consciousness during the experiment and which had not even been consciously thought of for many years. Also, psychogalvanic phenomena reveal the influence of affects which are not in the patient's consciousness.

In the dreams of healthy people and in hysteriform deliria, we can see how an unbearable experience (let us say a mistress' unfaithfulness) is excluded from consciousness not only because of its emotional tone, but also with it. Nonetheless, it still manages to exercise its influence, inasmuch as the affect so inhibits and facilitates associations that the fulfillment of the wish is simulated although no affect seems to dominate consciousness, or the very opposite affect may even be present (Freud, Jung).

4. This introduces the concept of the unconscious affects or, if one dislikes that word, latent affects. They may find their expression in many ways: in blushing, certain gestures, certain modulations and nuances of the voice, and similar manifestations corresponding to the latent affects.

The tendency to splitting, which certain intensities and qualities of affects possess, is opposed in healthy people by a tendency to include associatively whatever is important to the personality, if the occasion requires it. But since in schizophrenia the associative linkings are weakened and loosened, the result is that those very affects, which have the tendency to split off, very often become latent (unconscious) either after a very brief time or *in statu nascendi*. Since they still partly retain their influence and in many ways are developed with less restraint, they exercise a repressive influence on the rise of other affects: on the whole, the patient seems without affect, indifferent.[24] Naturally, the degree of inhibition depends on thousands of momentary influences, therefore, the inhibited affects may become manifest again in seemingly irregular fashion. Obviously the affective *Anlage* will also determine the rather large individual differences. All this is seen in the healthy, in hysterics, and—in exactly the same way, but enormously magnified quantitatively—in schizophrenics.[25]

A healthy person who is preoccupied often gives the impression of a catatonic. The absorption in his "complexes" makes him appear emotionally rigid, or even inconsiderate, indifferent, careless and weak of will. A very intelligent and emotionally perfectly normal colleague, who was in a very difficult situation for several years, had during that period not only flattened, rigid affects but also a strikingly rigid facies. One of my employees, an intelligent and otherwise sensitive girl, had a love affair which for her sake I could not approve. From then on, she was not only more indifferent to her duties, as most girls in love would be, but also indifferent to everything else, and often quite insensitive. She gave me occasion to have some serious talks with her, but she would let it all pass her by with a rigid face and an entirely stereotyped attitude without any signs of affect and consequently also without any effect. I would never have been able to differentiate her from a catatonic on those occasions. In this connection, Jung draws attention to the *belle indifférence des hystériques* which is, indeed, only a reaction to overwhelming affects but ordinarily quickly gives way to some lively outbursts of affects.

Of course, even in the splitting-off of affects, we are dealing with relative conditions. If the affects are strong, the dissociative tendencies need not be too pronounced in order to produce emotional devastation. Thus, in many cases of severe disease, we find that only quite ordinary everyday conflicts of life have caused the marked deterioration; but in milder cases, the acute episodes[26] may have been released by powerful affects. And quite often, after a detailed analysis, we had to pose the question whether we are not merely dealing with the effect of a particularly powerful psychic trauma on a very sensitive person rather than with a disease in the narrow sense of the word.

The lack of affect arising in this way is magnified by the thinking

---

24. The "purpose" of the whole arrangement, the erection of defenses against unpleasant affects, is attained in this way. The patient suffers no more; he has established a kind of *nirvana*.

25. Our view coincides with Risch's assumption of psychogenic states. His work appeared after the above was written.

26. Cf. Stadelmann.

disturbance which itself is partly conditioned by the affective disturbance, so that a vicious cycle is established.

Furthermore, autism contributes its share to reinforce the affective anomalies. The patients block off not only the painful affects but also the concomitant events. Therefore, they live in a kind of dream world which becomes reality for them. If a patient does not believe the news of the death of a loved one, he will naturally remain indifferent. Often such events are considered as only half-real; real in only certain respects —to the extent, of course, that they are not unpleasant. But where patients have encapsuled themselves completely in their autism, the outer world has reality value for them only insofar as it disturbs them in their thoughts. In that case, if an affect does attach itself to external events, it can only be that of "rejection." The apparent parathymic self-satisfaction of many schizophrenics is not at all abnormal from their standpoint since their wishes are fulfilled in the autistic thinking.

In severe cases, it is the autism which has the greatest share in the molding of the affect disturbance. In milder cases, the autism is so much less prominent (at least in the present state of our art of observation); therefore autism can hardly be used as an explanation, consequently the other mechanisms occupy the foreground.

One of the most striking phenomena is the indifference of patients toward their own delusional ideas and strivings. The dulling of all affective expression by habit and the diminished affective efficacy of the fantasy images in relation to reality must be of some significance in this indifference. Also the delusional idea is often merely a most inappropriate expression of some definite strivings. In peculiar tones, a patient complains that his children are being killed: his affect is not adequate, on the one hand, because something within him knows that this is only a fantasy and, on the other hand, because a wish, not a fear, that the children should be killed is at the root of his delusion. Probably, too, the delusions like the dreams often express precisely the opposite of what the patient really wants. A catatonic has homosexual tendencies; he builds a delusion that a woman of high society (whom he does not really know) is in love with him, and he insists that he is in love with her. Under such conditions, it is understandable that there is no affect bound up with the delusion. He does not love the woman at all; the idea is obviously only the reaction to the unpleasant consciousness of his homosexuality.

It is apparent that non-schizophrenic forms of associative weakness lead much more rarely to flattening of affect. The associative linkings are not weakened in idiots (oligophrenics); there are no other disturbances except the inability to make complicated associations. To be sure, in organic psychoses, the affects do gain abnormal dominance over the associations but it is expressed in an entirely different way because the relative strength of the associative linkings is much less diminished. Ideas which belong together ordinarily, viewed in simple terms, are still brought together. Thus, the drives and the affects remain bound to the personality; splitting off from reality and autism do not occur.

Of course, these reflections are hardly sufficient to explain all the differences between schizophrenic affectivity and the affectivity of the other psychoses. On the other hand, the Freudian theory of autoerotism and of the failure of investing libido in the object could do justice to this difference. But the theory is as yet insufficiently developed, and to go into it here would require our taking up a number of problems lying far afield from our immediate theme.

There still remain a few details that we must discuss. Often the lack of affect appears to be much more marked than usual in some of the patient's expressions because the expressions lack a specific goal or purpose. If the patient sits down to write a long letter merely because the notion of writing "something" came to him, it is quite comprehensible that the piece of writing is not likely to incorporate much, or at least no homogeneous, affect because in reality there is none that truly belongs to the situation (cf. school essays).

It is self-evident from our conception that specific affects, such as maternal love, may remain isolatedly efficacious.

The irritability, expressed in the more severe cases as an inclination to rage and outbursts of fury, requires separate explanation. We find the same tendencies in human beings and in animals when the situation in which they are placed is not understood at all or only inadequately. (The neurasthenics' irritability due to highly developed sensitivity is something else again.) The caged animal that rages blindly with utter disregard of its total situation or of its own physical integrity illustrates the active side of affectivity. The frightened shying horse, that just as senselessly runs blindly and wildly away, reveals the passive side. The same thing is seen in children and idiots, and also in individuals whose rapport with their surroundings is obstructed by disease of the auditory sense (Helen Keller).

Without exception we see disturbances of intellectual rapport with their environment in agitated furious schizophrenics. They comprehend the environment quite differently than we do, or are incapable of understanding us in everything. Therefore, adequate defense against imagined or real threats is impossible; and in severe cases, the only recourse is that of blind rage in deeds or words.

Nonetheless, other factors are also involved in the genesis of such affects although in lesser measure perhaps. These patients envelop themselves completely in their fantasy world; reality becomes not only strange, but hostile insofar as it threatens to tear them out of their autism. Thus the causes of the affect of rage partly combine with those of negativism.

Jung has emphasized the utter uncontrollability of affects, once they appear; this is a self-evident consequence of the weakness of reflection and deliberation; and it is re-enforced by the isolation of the individual drives and strivings. However, it does not appear satisfactory to me to deduce it simply from the disorder of ego-synthesis as Jung tries to do. It is precissely the entire associative synthesis which is deranged and with it the delicate balance between affectivity and logic.

The schizophrenic's behavior as regards the function of attention can be explained, for the most part, by the affectivity of which attention forms only one aspect. Where interest and aim is lacking, attention is bound to be weak. But in this connection, we must remember that thinking disturbances of all kinds may affect attention itself, as well as its consequences. The possibility of splitting of attention is naturally a consequence of the personality split.

The parathymia can be explained in various ways. On closer scrutiny, it usually can be demonstrated to constitute an apparent one, inasmuch as the patients are reacting to different thoughts and not to those which the environment expects. Masselon believes that it is not a question of tenacity, but rather of automatism or stereotypy when the patients attach themselves to a chosen person in so striking a fashion that this person can do whatever he wishes with the patients. In such cases as I have seen, the chosen person was regularly the representative of some emotionally charged complex. One can easily be mistaken in one's interpretation since the patients can have, in accordance with the context a delusional as well as correct understanding of the person to whom they have attached themselves. A similar displacement is involved when a patient believes he is homesick but does not rejoice or even becomes angry when he is supposed to go home. In reality, he is not homesick at all but suffers from some other uneasiness which he refers to his confinement in the hospital. If news of the death of a loved one puts him in good humor, he probably just does not believe the truth of the news; nevertheless, the pleasant aspects of the situation are utilized (e.g., he is happy that now he will be getting letters prettily decorated with black borders). A woman patient has a crying spell everytime fire is mentioned; for her fire is the symbol of her unhappy love affair. It may also come about that the affect (as expressed) corresponds very clearly to the opposite of the actual thoughts. This phenomenon rests mainly on the fact that the schizophrenic can easily think of the contrary of any one of his thoughts (cf. ambivalence and the theory of negativism). In other cases, the parathymia is a consequence of the perseveration of affects: the patient has been vexed; he curses his confinement to a hospital, and then he stumbles upon quite another theme which is handled by him in the same tone and with precisely the same affects as the first theme. Then again, affects, which together with their corresponding ideas may be latent or have no relation to the events of the present moment, can become manifest as a parathymic reaction on the occasion of later events which are similar in certain respects but quite different qualitatively and quantitatively from the emotional tone of the first events. Also when something troubles a healthy person, the latent effects may easily attach themselves to any minor unpleasantness which he meets (but have nothing to do with the thing with which he is really concerned) without his intellectual processes becoming conscious of it.

At times it becomes quite clear that a more pleasant affect is substituted in the place of a repressed one. Indeed we all know the "superficial gaiety," the acid wit, the inclination to act the comedian. These manifestations suggest a repressed negative affective mood. Even more common are analogous para-functions operating in the hysteric (319).

Much more rarely were we able to analyze paramimia. Sometimes its origin can be traced to the perseveration of expressive gestures despite the changing content of consciousness. On the other hand, when a patient seizes a proffered delicacy and eagerly consumes it, while bitterly wailing at the same time, some conscious or unconscious sadness is always associated with the pleasant gift in the patient's mind. But it is only in few cases that we can prove this.

The mixture of various facial expressions (as sometimes happens in the healthy) also arises from this simultaneous presence of two affects, e.g., the patient whose eyes express his happiness of being in love, while his mouth reveals sorrow. But, we do not understand as yet why, in any case, the eyes express the pleasant and the mouth the unpleasant affect. We must also add that we are far from being able to trace this sort of paramimia back to a mixed affect in every case. In particular, we are hardly able to explain the raised eyebrows which seem to be associated with all kinds of affective expressions.[27]

We might also mention here the analgesias which often have the characteristic of a psychic symptom (isolation) but as yet we cannot trace back their origin any more precisely.

(c) *Autism*

The autism is a direct consequence of the schizophrenic splitting of the psyche. Healthy people have a tendency, in logical operations, to draw upon all appropriate material without consideration of its affective value. On the other hand, the schizophrenic loosening of logical processes leads to the exclusion of all associations conflicting with emotionally charged complexes. The need which is present in all human beings, to seek a substitute in fantasy for the unsatisfactory reality can be satisfied in this way without meeting any resistance. No matter how much the products of fantasy are in contradiction to reality, they certainly do not come into any conflict with reality in the patient's brain. Indeed, they are brought into as much harmony as possible with the patient's affective needs. In severe cases, the whole of reality with its never ceasing perceptive-sensory stimulations is blocked off; at the very most, reality exists only in its most banal relationships: in eating, in drinking, in getting dressed.

Thus the autistic thought content remains incorrigible and assumes complete reality-value for the patients, while the subjective reality-value of actuality is reduced to zero. The patient is convinced that we believe him to be mentally healthy although daily he hears the very opposite from us. He does comprehend the sense of our words, can reproduce them but immediately afterwards he substitutes his own meaning for that of ours because what we, in reality, have been telling him could not be brought into logical contact with his ideas. Should the external world offer him motives for his particular views, he utilizes them quite willingly. Depending on the circumstances he will displace or falsify reality. A patient asks when he is going to be released, and receives the answer, when he is well. He responds with: "But I can go on foot!" Instead of the established conditions of his release, he assumes another set of conditions which can be met: the expenses of his journey home.

Of old, autism attracted attention, particularly among the French. The latter have described and stressed one aspect of it under such terms as autophilia, egocentricity, ego-hypertrophy, or *augmentation du sens de la personalité;* whereas the negative side was designated as *perte du sens de la réalité*, or *perte de la fonction du réel.* Pelletier says that

27. It is possible that it expresses the striving to re-establish the lost relationship with the outer world. Peritz maintains that the tic-like raised brows is a response to a sensation of frontal pressure.

above all, the patient does not differentiate anymore between reality and fantasy: "To suppose that these patients believe in their reality would be to endow their states of consciousness with an energy or force which they do not possess." While all these concepts are true in a certain sense, still they do not get at the essence of the phenomenon according to our view of the matter.

Autism, too, is an exaggeration of a physiological phenomenon. There is normal autistic thinking[28] which need not consider reality and which proceeds in the direction of the affects. The child plays with a piece of wood which for him may be a baby, and at another time, a house. But even without any physical substrate, most people indulge in fantasies which fulfill their wishes or their fears. In hysterics, this sort of fantasy can be pathologically exaggerated (cf. Pick, 570 a). A large part of poetry, our tales and myths, have their source in this kind of thinking. If anyone attempts to actualize such unfulfilled wishes in real life, he experiences disappointments which may bring him to the brink of disease. Thus, many women are bitterly disappointed in marriage, not only because their husband is not as they dreamed he would be, but because the whole of married life is something other than they had expected. If they are too completely dominated by their dream, they will not find any joy in marriage because it is not the anticipated joy; they remain frigid, just as the schizophrenic remains indifferent when his wishes are fulfilled externally. Furthermore, we find evidences of inadequate or absent distinction between fantasy and reality in dreams, in states of absent-mindedness, in children who tell lies without knowingly lying, and in the "savage." (The primitive cannot understand why it should cause any comment if today he denies with all certainty a bit of thievery which he confessed to have committed yesterday.)

(d) Ambivalence

Even for the healthy everything has its two sides. The rose has its thorns. But in ninty-nine out of a hundred instances, the normal person compares the two aspects, subtracts the negative from the positive values. He appreciates the rose despite its thorns. The schizophrenic, with his weakened associative linkings does not necessarily bring the different aspects of a problem together. He loves the rose because of its beauty and hates it because of its thorns. Thus many simple as well as complicated concepts and, above all, many complexes have for him both affective signs, the plus and the minus, which appear side by side, or alter-

28. For example, we find normal autistic thinking in the form of exercising the capacity of combining ideas. In the same way, ordinary play activities (of animals and children) constitute an exercise of physical skills.

natingly, one after the other. Certainly even under normal conditions, synthesis may be omitted. The healthy, too, feels something like "two souls in his breast"; and he, too, would be less inclined to speak so much of sin if it did not also have some pleasant connotations. The double evaluation rests not so much in the experience itself as in the double attitude toward that experience; under certain conditions, however, logic demands that both signs (the plus and minus) be left standing as they are: the same weather is beautiful or useful for one purpose, and bad for another; today's weather, compared to yesterday's is nice but bad as compared to the day before yesterday. Yet, in these instances, the normal person establishes the necessary sign in full accordance with the situation, while the schizophrenic arrives at completely inadequate and unsuitable evaluations.

Affective ambivalence has a second and equally important root in the circumstance that opposites are closer to each other than heterogeneous characteristics. Hate and love are infinitely closer to each other than to indifference. ("Where a woman hates, there she loves, has loved or will love.") In the normals hate and love often transform themselves into each other; in the schizophrenics they usually appear as merely two aspects of the same affect.

Some traces of the ambivalence of will can also be found in the healthy: precisely what one does not want to think is just what crops up in our thought. The man learning to ride a bicycle always bumps into the very obstacles which he wishes to avoid.[29] Standing in a large store, I wish to get something at a particular counter; I carefully determine the one I do not want to go to, but then it is that very one to which I go. Thus, it is often psychologically of more importance that a plan be thought about than that it be thought of positively or negatively. A patient tells me (I have perfectly good reasons to believe in his sincerity) that he will not try to escape anymore because it only gets him into trouble and results in disadvantages to himself. Thereupon, I warn the attendant that the patient is going to try to escape which promptly occurs as I predicted.

It is only a small step from volitional to intellectual ambivalence. The concept "black" is closer to the concept "white" than any others which have nothing to do with color. The thought, "The snow is white," already contains in itself the rejection of the opinion, "The snow is black"; but precisely for this reason, the second judgment is closer to the first opinion than any statement containing neither "snow" nor "black."

29. Cf. the Theory of Negativism.

Children often present us with very clear examples of this attitude. Many of them use the phrase, "Close the door," when they actually want the door to be opened. After all, the common factor is the movement of the door; in comparison, the antithesis of opening and closing becomes so unimportant that the child does not hesitate to use the expression with which it is more famililar, for both. At a slightly later age, children have the need to express some sort of opinion while playing; however, they do not care whether they express their opinions in a positive or in a negative fashion; and they do this even when they are not joking.[30]

In the dreams of healthy persons, affective as well as intellectual ambivalence is a common phenomenon. In such dreams, therefore, many ideas are almost always expressed by their opposites; thus, a "secret" may be represented by the appearance of a crowd of people.

In addition to normal ambivalence, particularly ambitendency is of great importance in psychic mechanisms. Ambitendency creates a counter-tendency along with every tendency, thereby compelling the individual to make a choice, or at least to deliberate on it. Like the physical organism, the psyche regulates the more delicate adjustments by virtue of the fact that it creates a balance between opposing forces; as Ris (1910) put it, we are dealing with the principle of the "muted" magnetic needle.

(e) Memory and Orientation

Disturbances of the other simpler functions, such as memory and orientation, can be explained by what has already been said.

Perception[31] and retention of the perceived material function well. However, the material perceived is only put to proper use if it does not contradict the complexes. No evidence of disturbance will be noted as long as the patient works, travels, or talks about matters which have no bearing on his complexes. It will be observed, however, that within the realm of his autistic thinking-process logical reproduction is replaced by reproduction corresponding to his affects; consequently, the various types of deception develop in the sphere of memory.[32] As in healthy persons and in other diseases, the gaps in the patients' memory are of various origins. The gaps may correspond to affective needs (one forgets what one does not want to know). Some delirious states differ so greatly from the patient's customary state, in their content as well as in the function of association, that the patient is unable to recall

30. Cf. Freud, *Gegensinn der Urworte,* Jahrbuch für Psychoanal. Forschung, II. p. 179.
31. I am employing this term here regardless of whether the perception is of a conscious or unconscious nature.
32. Cf. below, section on analogous misconceptions of reality.

these associative trends once he has returned to his usual state. In common with normal individuals schizophrenics, moreover, completely forget the confused mixture of certain inner experiences.

We can also understand why the schizophrenic frequently has more memory material at his disposal than the healthy person. The normal individual sifts the impressions brought to him by his senses; he much more frequently (perhaps also more intensively) associates with other ideas material important to himself, so that it can be reactivated in many ways. Other facts (e. g., the memory of all the people passed in the street) are being removed from associative ties as far as possible and, therefore, can only be recalled under exceptional circumstances. On the other hand, the aimless schizophrenic omits this sifting process. He takes equal notice of important and unimportant matters; he does not restrict the associative ties of indifferent material. Thus he will be able to reproduce everything equally under certain conditions. Of course it must not be assumed that the above explains all the sources of abnormalities of memory. However, the circumstances mentioned must exert some influence upon the function of memory; in addition, they provide an explanation for everything we know about schizophrenic memory.

In accordance with analogous Freudian ideas, Jung considers the possibility that memory-pictures of schizophrenics do not suffer any disintegration because no abreaction takes place. To me it appears probable that memory-pictures continue to exist unaltered throughout life also in the healthy persons. Therefore, I could only accept this theory if the expression "memory-pathways" were used in place of "memory-pictures."[33] If we were acquainted with the nature of the primary tendency to stereotypies, we could discuss the question as to the manner in which the apparently abnormally tenacious memory of schizophrenics may be connected with that tendency and may be identified with it.

Orientation, like memory, remains undisturbed within the scope of realistic thinking. However, under different conditions, it is altered in accordance with the needs of the complexes. Of course, the patients' orientation with respect to their own situation is most rarely completely normal, because the manifestations of the disease belong to the complex and can only infrequently be recognized as abnormal by the patient. He believes that he has been unjustly imprisoned; that the doctors are his enemies. But also in this instance we find all nuances from almost complete insight to complete misinterpretation of all situations—not only in different patients, but sometimes in the very same patient, occasionally changing from one moment to the next.

---

33. I do not claim that memory-pathways are different from other engrams.

"Double registration" and "double orientation" are self-explanatory after what has been said. The material of experience is correctly deposited and the realistic thinking process utilizes it properly; the autistic thinking process, however, distorts it. Yet the two processes run parallel without interfering with each other. The situation becomes complicated only when the falsifications are due to actual illusions and hallucinations; in that event, the patients are sometimes unable to orient themselves properly. Anyway, it is significant for the secondary character of illusions that the correct perception continues to exist alongside with the distorted one, even in cases where we must assume that the patient actually sees the devil with fiery eyes, flaming hair, and a long tail instead of his father.

(f) Schizophrenic Deterioration (Dementia)

Since we have designated as secondary the most important elements of schizophrenic dementia, it is evident that the disease as such must also be regarded as secondary in its essentials. It is likely that some primary symptoms are present in the picture of this dementia but usually we do not notice them. Future methods of observation will possibly reveal, in severe cases, evidence of primary dementia beneath the secondary one. At present, we can find only that the patients split their thoughts, that they block their affects, and withdraw from reality. We further note that no mental faculty is annihilated; indeed, observation of many individual cases shows that in all chronic states of this disease the capacity for evaluation of complicated matters has not been completely lost, but that essentially it was repressed only secondarily, that it is prevented from proper function by the splitting. Therefore, we cannot exclude the possibility of temporary or permanent improvement at any stage. The fact that perhaps one-third of hospitalized cases never, or only temporarily, recover from dementia, is, of course, no indication against the secondary nature of this phenomenon. Often even healthy persons are permanently obsessed by some idea; how much stronger, therefore, must this tendency be in schizophrenics who methodically split off the corrective influences of reality and judgment and who are generally inclined to perpetuate psychic functions.

Some of the most striking symptoms of dementia are but partial phenomena of emotional deterioration. No strivings can develop where the affects are absent or blocked. Other factors contribute to this end: when all wishes are autistically satisfied or when it seems impossible that they can ever be fulfilled, there is no reason left for strivings. When relations with the outer world are broken off or greatly distorted, there can be no desire to participate in it. The patient is handicapped in his strivings also by intellectual defects: the synthesis of individual thoughts into an idea which would motivate actions is disturbed; the incapacity for logical thinking prevents the creation of a purpose for action.

In its narrower sense, the schizophrenic disturbance of intelligence is mainly composed of the following elements: the actual disturbance in association leads to many false conclusions; blocking prevents the function of many thinking processes. Even without blocking, certain trains of thought cannot be followed for affective reasons. The patients speak and think evasively, not only because of inner and outer negativism, indifference, and as a consequence of incomplete ideas, but also because the train of thought, leading in the direction of the given goal, has been excluded.

Direct distortions of logic are due to the fact that affectively charged associations are substituted for logical operations; furthermore, distortion is caused by the splitting-off of the complexes which form a world of their own, without taking into consideration other ideas and, especially, not reality. In these splittings, the affects resist the association of corrective thoughts, often with unassailable strength. Thus the paretic makes his insane plans because he "does not think" of certain things; he can be reminded of his mistakes from the outside so that, at least, he must compensate for them with a new erroneous conclusion. A truly schizophrenic "split," however, is only rarely amenable to logical correction. The paretic fails to enter upon a certain road by mistake; the schizophrenic cannot enter it because the road is physically blocked, because he is fearful of taking it. Thus in many cases, the critical faculty is diminished by errors in thinking, but certain criticism is also made practically impossible by the fact that the criticizing ideas cannot be brought into line with the one that has to be corrected. The lack of a goal for the thoughts, due to the previously mentioned affective and intellectual defects, contributes to the desultoriness produced by the associative aberrations.

The third aspect of schizophrenic dementia, the behavior, is revealed as a resultant of all these deficient processes. In consequence of the strivings, the patients sometimes do not act at all, at other times their actions are aimless or inconsistent. The inconsistency of behavior is due to the fact that constantly changing aims present themselves to the patient, depending upon the contents of the complex involved. As the result of the patients' faulty logic, their actions are frequently purposeless or even contrary to what they actually intended. "Accidental" associations determine the unreasonable actions corresponding to impulses; compulsive ideas cause inappropriate activities against the patient's will.

Many other theories have attempted to explain schizophrenic dementia. Most of them are based on the assumption that "a weakening of mental functions" is present—a deduction that can easily be made from the very word "dementia." Many consider this weakening as dynamic. P. Janet speaks of "*abaissement du niveau mental*"[34] in patients we would consider schizophrenic. Lehmann (409) writes of a lowered energy of consciousness. However we have no standard of measurement with respect to psychic energy and are therefore unable to discuss dynamic theories. In any event, it should be noted that many schizophrenics demonstrate internal and external accomplishments which are very difficult to reconcile with the idea of a generalized decrease in psychic energy.

Other proceed from the observation that "the superior psychic function" or the psychic synthesis which has a similar meaning has been weakened. I do not believe that this type of approach can lead anywhere. As long as "the superior function" is an entirely indefinable concept or, at least, definable at will, such explanations seem to be merely playing with words. From a methodological viewpoint, it is also very risky to start out with the most complicated and, therefore, least comprehensible functions when trying to explain anything.

The concept of "weakening of the psychic synthesis" is somewhat more acceptable. We can, indeed, demonstrate that synthesis of associational material is often lacking—but not always. Since we already find beneath this complicated function disturbances of association this explanation is at best insufficient.

Another, more plausible type of dynamic explanation, proceeds from the study of attention or of affects. Even normal persons show a number of schizophrenic symptoms when they are emotionally preoccupied, particularly inattentive, or when their attention is concentrated on a single subject. Among these symptoms are peculiar associations, incomplete concepts and ideas, displacements, logical blunders, and stereotypies. However, in comparison with these affective disturbances, schizophrenic dissociation goes much further. Even in hysteria, where the results of the affects are magnified to the extreme, splitting of concepts never occurs during states of clear consciousness. In other disorders, marked by disturbances of attention and by an intensified influence of affects, such as the organic psychoses and epilepsy, we cannot observe any schizophrenic pictures. Even in schizophrenia, itself, affective and primary anomalies of association do not run parallel to each other; whereas the former are dependent on accidental events, the latter strike us as direct expressions of the cerebral disorder. However, even severely ill

34. Translator's Note: Lowering of the mental level.

patients can be very attentive under certain conditions. Moreover, these patients may commit the same errors during periods of concentrated attention as in periods when they are distracted. Perhaps we may also add in this connection that in dreams we frequently concentrate our attention on its contents, yet nevertheless produce schizophrenic-like thoughts. For most psychologists, the concept of attention as such is still very flexible and poorly delimited; in this respect, the situation resembles that existing with regard to the concept of apperception. However, if attention only includes what we actually observed, i.e., inhibition and formation of certain groups of associations under affective influence, a "disturbance of attention" cannot be a primary matter and again requires an explanation as to its derivation. This is not difficult to find from our point of view.

Claus regards the "*altération des facultés actives*" as the most important feature of the disturbance: "Dementia praecox is a disease which primarily affects the active faculties of the mind. Apathy, abulia, and loss of intellectual activity are three symptoms characteristic of dementia praecox." The large number of schizophrenics who show considerable activity (pseudo-authors, world reformers, workers in hospitals) contradicts this generalizing description of certain symptoms.

Others have mentioned the possibility of a regression to sub-cortical functions, mainly in connection with the decrease of psychic energy. At present, however, we have no means of localizing psychic functions beneath the cortex; neither can we recognize the signs which indicate the difference between sub-cortical and cortical psychological material. Therefore, we are unable to deal with such theories at this time. With his ideas of localization, Wernicke has attempted to give the most far-reaching explanation. However, the symptomatology of schizophrenia (including disturbances of motility) provides no definite indications of localization (compare the theory of motility).

(g) *Distortions of Reality*

We do not comprehend the external world directly with our sense organs. We must create its image within ourselves by synthesis of and logical conclusions drawn from the material provided by our senses. Therefore, disturbances in the thinking process lead to distortions in the conception of reality. These distortions are most clearly expressed in the delusions, but also in deceptions of senses and memory. We cannot deduce the origin of delusional ideas secondarily from the hallucinations and illusions of the senses and of memory. We are dealing with coordinated symptoms, all of which are expressions of the same distortion of reality. Forel's patient, Miss L. S., expressed this very clearly from the subjective viewpoint: "It is often impossible to make an exact distinction between delusions, illusions and hallucinations." By the same token, it is also incorrect to state that a patient does not move because he is afraid of falling into a hallucinatory chasm. Immobility and the image of the chasm are parallel phenomena which can be demonstrated in such a case, for instance by the fact that the patient also refuses to swallow his saliva, a movement which would certainly not be dangerous. The commanding "voices" give no order which, for some reason, the patient does not wish to obey.

1. The Delusions

In order to investigate the genesis of delusions, we must, of course, realize that we are including in this term a number of different phenomena of various origin. Specht (731) was the first to draw attention to this fact without, however, providing a classification which would fit our special needs. I consider the formulation of differences attempted here as entirely preliminary; I would not vouch for its validity beyond the realm of schizophrenia.

First, we must isolate the basic delusion from the various kinds of delusional ideas: the patient may be persecuted, all-powerful, a prophet, beloved, etc. The basic delusion contains the direction of the delusion, usually in terms of concrete application: the patient is being persecuted by certain people or under certain circumstances; he is the ruler of a certain land; he has a religious mission in a very definite sense; he is being loved by a certain person. Sometimes the delusion requires rather detailed elaboration. The basic delusion, as will be immediately discussed, develops only under affective influences and is very egocentric.

However, many of the delusional details are accidental delusional applications; in a logical sense they are more closely related to errors than to the basic delusion. A patient who suffers from delusion that he is going to be poisoned gets an attack of diarrhea; proceeding from the given assumption that the doctors want to take his life, the conclusion is obvious even to the healthy person, that the patient's food was poisoned. A letter sent by a patient with delusions of persecution remains unanswered. He does not consider the possibility of delay in the mails. The patient regards the addressee as a reliable friend, he cannot be at fault. On the other hand, the doctor must have great interest in the fact that the letter does not reach its destination; therefore, it was he who intercepted it. Genetically, we are dealing with a logical error which almost of necessity follows in the wake of the false premises of the basic delusion, and which is, therefore, in principle, entirely different from the basic delusion itself. Whereas the basic delusion is unalterable, such errors can sometimes be corrected; with patients in a state of clear consciousness it is often possible to discuss the matter in the same way as with healthy persons. These patients also do not consistently emphasize their error with the affectivity appropriate to the basic delusion. We actually owe the following type, the "explanatory delusion," to the residues of healthy logic which the patients sometimes retain. The manual laborer who deludes himself as to his aristocratic lineage must consider his own parents as foster parents, if he is still capable of drawing such conclusions.

A third type of secondary delusional elaboration, which may also be regarded as an explanatory delusion, originates in the need to explain causalties: Why do the doctors persecute the patient? Proceeding from the false premise of an existing persecution, the patient must give himself more or less sound explanations which also a healthy individual would have to find under identical circumstances. In another case, the patient hears voices although no one is present. Should he still feel the need to explain the causality, the only possibility for him is to think up machines which produce these voices for him by means of which someone talks to him from afar, or he must assume the existence of some supernatural powers. In that instance, of course, the schizophrenics with their detachment from reality can go much further than normal persons under the same circumstances. Often, schizophrenics not merely imagine some machine which is a mystery to themselves, but a definite apparatus which they see as clearly as any extracampine hallucination.

Frequently the need for causal explanations is determined by the outside world: a woman patient steals a watch, as the result of some incomprehensible "notion"; when questioned about it, she declared that the watch belonged to her husband.[35] A patient cannot or will not eat for some reason; to justify himself, he creates the delusion that eating is forbidden to him. Such elaborations of delusions are not at all unusual; they originate partly in logical, partly in affective needs, and partly in "notions" which are often based on vague analogies.

Because of the deficiencies of schizophrenic thinking, inadequate analogies and other kinds of logical blunder can result in the formation of false ideas which have no apparent connection with the basic delusion; or the nature of the ideas may be such that they are incorrectly brought into logical connection with others which are simultaneously provoked by external events. For the time being we must designate such phenomena as delusions since they differ from the errors of healthy persons in the

35. Such subsequent explanations are also given after the posthypnotic execution of some absurd suggestion.

pathological nature of their logical development.

These various delusions are not sharply separated from each other since several causes may contribute to the production of the same false idea. Since our patients' logic is usually also defective beyond the sphere of affective influence, logical errors occur easily anywhere in their thinking, even in the "explanations." The affect which has produced the basic delusion naturally participates in the elaboration of its various details. When an affect is present, the patients will be much more inclined to commit logical errors under all conditions; thus the affect also favors the development of other forms of delusion: by way of an inadequate analogy, a hebephrenic arrived at the conclusion that his uncle was very unhappy. The patient simply concluded that since he himself was poor but happy, his uncle who was rich must be unhappy. Probably the patient would not have made this error had it not been favored by his jealousy of that uncle. Often, however, the affect is so insignificant that it appears irrelevant to us; and often we are unable to detect any affect at all in relation with such ideas, either in connection with their origin or later. In marked contrast to the basic delusion, therefore, delusional ideas precipitated by purely logical errors must not necessarily be egocentric in their notion.

In certain instances of delusional ideas, the concept, "pseudo," is not inherent in the idea as such, but rather in an inner experience. As the result of the splitting-off of independently operating complexes, the patient often feels as if another second will existed within himself. When the patient is ignorant of or instinctively rejects the pathological nature of such experiences, he is compelled to conclude that he is "possessed" or hypnotically influenced or some such thing. The feeling of having a second soul and, in some cases, of compulsion is primary; its explanation is a necessity for the patient.

Primordial delusional ideas which enter consciousness already complete without having been precipitated by hallucinations and which the patients cannot trace to their origin, must, of course, be considered results of unconscious thinking processes which are greatly facilitated by the independent activity of split-off functions. If they originate in an emotionally charged complex, they must be egocentric in character; if their origin is different in nature, their quality may also change.

The most important type of delusion and often the one taken into consideration is, of course, the basic delusion with its elaborations and its utilization of details. Its genesis is evident after what has been said in the previous section:

To a certain degree, the affects inhibit in everyone contradictory associations and facilitate those that serve their purpose. Thus even the healthy person is often deceived when he is under affective influences. This happens despite the fact that ordinarily he automatically thinks of an unattainable wish in connection with its unattainability and that he considers the possibility that his fears may be unfounded. When we are angry at someone, we see only his faults, or at least magnify them; when we want something very badly, we minimize the obstacles that are in our way; when we are afraid we magnify the obstacles. When someone considers the external world as hostile, for some reason, he will find causes for suspicion everywhere. In healthy persons whose affectivity is persistent and comparatively very strong in relation to their powers of thinking, dogmatism and incapacity to engage in reasonable discussion lead to errors and can without transition pass over into paranoia.

When the faculty of logical reasoning is weakened,[36] the influence of the affects increases in strength; obstacles to wish fulfillment are no longer even considered in connection with the wish which, consequently, is given reality value. The distortion can eventually reach the proportions of delusional ideas which, therefore, are only quantitatively different from the deceptions of healthy individuals. Because of the far-reaching split in the psychic functions, the affect becomes all-powerful in the realm of a certain complex of ideas; criticism and correction become impossible. Thus, within the split-off complexes, the affects create fantastic worlds for themselves ignoring reality, from which they select only material suitable for their purposes. The latter process is facilitated in schizophrenia by the disintegration of the association-pathways. This enables the affects to connect any selected material with the complex which is always in a state of functional preparedness, and to utilize the material accordingly. Logic, to the extent it is being used, now serves the affective needs and the elaborations of the delusion.

In every case, these autistic worlds developed under the dominance of one or several of the most important human drives: love, power, and wealth are the desired goals; fear of lack of, or inadequate, sexual activity, of personal inferiority, and of persecution is linked to these drives.

This concept of the genesis of the schizophrenic basic delusion completely explains the innumerable observations which have been made in this field. All its individual elements are observational facts. The conclusion that these facts lead to delusional ideas is inevitable; however, it would be hypothetical to assume that no other mechanisms are involved. We realize that at present we are not acquainted with all the psychic

36. Of course, the result is essentially the same when the affects are abnormally powerful as in melancholia, or when the two anomalies occur in conjunction with each other as in manic and in melancholic paresis.

functions and that many as yet unknown factors may be operating here. This, however, should not prevent us from studying the effects of these functions as far as we know of them.[37]

It has been attempted to explain delusional ideas as the patients' logical deductions from altered body-sensations, altered perception, etc. (Schuele, Berze, Neisser, 518). We must object to this theory on the basis that in many patients we cannot find any of these alterations[38]—and certainly not at the roots of delusional ideas. According to our experience, truths, suspicions, and errors are deduced by means of logic, but they are not delusional ideas in the sense of the basic delusion.

Some derive the delusion from an "affect of mistrust" (Specht). However, this concept could only apply to the persecutory delusion and to no other forms. But is there such a thing as an "affect of mistrust?" And if so, how would it originate in our disease?

We are closest to Friedmann's conception according to which the reality value of an idea is dependent upon its intensity. However, the author also states that the intensity of the idea depends on the intensity of the accompanying affect. Thus we could accept most of his statements as long as he does not substitute the incomprehensible, vague concept of "intense idea," for "affectively charged idea."

The ideas of reference which play such a prominent role in the origin of delusional ideas are at least for us a natural part of the symptoms which contribute to the formation of the delusion. Inasmuch as in the schizophrenics the affectively charged complex continues to function even during other thought processes, it is always prepared to assimilate any and all material. There is no need for us to fall back on Neisser's "intensification of sensations" which is present only in very exceptional cases. Since the complex represents an important part of the ego, these

---

37. The origin of these delusional ideas is discussed in greater detail in Bleuler's *Affectivity* which also contains a brief criticism of the most important differing theories.

38. For this reason alone we must reject all theories which base the delusion and, with it, the entire disease on alterations of body sensations. Marandon de Montyel terms the abnormal cenesthesias the primary symptoms. Wherry goes so far as to suggest that the pathological process does not take place inside the brain and that its functions are disturbed merely as the result of altered body sensations. Schuele, also with respect to localization, speaks of "cerebro-spinal insanity" and interprets some forms of schizophrenia as "neuralgic psychoses." They are "delusional dream-blossoms of the spinal nerve tree on which they grow; the individual delusional idea is the product by an abnormally functioning sensory nerve." Schuele has also found the roots of the disease in sexuality. He was a better observer than others, but has sought to interpret his observations physiologically rather than psychologically. It has also been stated that in dreams the hallucinations originate in abnormal bodily sensations. In that case, however, we are merely dealing with specific material which is being utilized by an already existing delusional tendency in the same manner as the specific delusion of poisoning occurs during diarrhea when a general poisoning-delusion is present. Even in dreams, the direction of the delusion can originate only in psychic causes and our experience has proven that these causes are exclusively affective ones.

remarks also refute the theory according to which the delusion is based on "hypertrophy of the ego." It is not the ego that has assumed special significance but a part of it, namely, the complex.

2. Sensory Deceptions

We do not know in what way distortions of reality express themselves in sensory deceptions. We have observed that the illusions may occur along with a correct observation of the same event. This fact is an indication that the core of the disturbance should be placed as centrally as possible. The analogy between normal reactions and sensory deceptions is not merely of a quantitative nature in delusional ideas, but it is well not to overlook this possibility. Everyone has illusions, everyone may have hallucinations in dreams or on various other occasions. Therefore, disposition to deceptions is certainly present. We constantly deceive ourselves with respect to the reality value of our sensory perceptions. We believe, for example, that we perceive a gas lamp, whereas actually we only perceive differences of light and form which we interpret as a gas lamp with the aid of previously gathered memory pictures. Thus perception involves an important intra-central process which may easily become affected in schizophrenia and which may lead to illusions. The step leading from illusions to hallucinations must be a very small one because even in normal persons we find not only illusions; it is well-known that individuals with a vivid auditory and visual imagination can produce fantasies which are so "real" that they equal sensory perceptions. This is even more likely to happen in schizophrenia where the differences between reality and fantasy are noticeably obscured. Reflex hallucinations which are a specific type, may originate by way of exaggeration of a normal process: the sight of a handwriting or the hearing of footsteps may often arouse very vivid feelings and even definite ideas. These refer to the originator of the perceptions, although this is not recognized consciously.

Schizophrenic hallucinations are usually precipitated by psychic occurrences. Moreover, sensory deceptions prove themselves to be psychic, and not sensory, anomalies inasmuch as they express thoughts not only in their content; they are dependent on illusions also for minor details. We have demonstrated that their localization often corresponds to the direction of attention. When pleasant "voices" are being heard from the right or from above whereas only unpleasant ones are being heard from the left or from below, the phenomenon is usually not based on any alteration in the peripheral or central auditory apparatus of either side but on the meaning that these particular directions have acquired in conscious ideas. Ziehen's statement regarding illusions can also be applied to hallucinations: "At times they correspond to actual images, at other times they correspond to latent ones." If they are also rooted in the unconscious, hallucinations often compel the patient's attention even against his will. This is due to the affective significance of the originating complexes. It is obvious that sensory deceptions may represent not only the various individual complexes but also that part of the personality which has remained normal with regard to its critical faculties and possibly its partial insight.

We are unable to say precisely why, in our patients, deceptions of hearing and body sensations should predominate. However, it is certainly significant that in schizophrenia the alteration of the ego and its attitude toward the world, of thinking and feeling, is more pronounced than in any other psychoses. Thoughts and emotions and their expression in words are so closely related that it has been stated that one thinks only in words. Moreover, the idea that alterations of the ego are connected with body hallucinations is readily accepted, since the sensations of one's own body must constitute the foundation of the ego complex.[39] This concept may be correct but it is not proven. On the other hand, it is certain that many hallucinations of body sensations originate in displaced and transformed sexual feelings; after all, pains in the hepatic region which simulate the presence of gall-stones, may prove to be expressions of displaced labor-pains of an imaginary delivery. As in other diseases, visual hallucinations in schizophrenia are prominent only in delirious states. I do not maintain that this is *exclusively* due to the fact that, in states of clearer consciousness, correction of visual hallucinations is made too easy by the other senses and because of their contrast with actual visual images.

However, for the purpose of demonstrating clearly that the essence of the hallucinatory process lies in the psyche organ, no other disease is as well suited as schizophrenia. For, aside from the many other reasons, hallucinations do not express sensory material but thoughts, feelings, and drives. We also know, however, that hallucinations may be released by sense organs as well as by other stimuli.

Konrad, on the other hand, found greater irritability of the auditory and optic nerves in hallucinating patients. However, this observation still requires confirmation by a larger quantity of material.

Wernicke's sejunction-hypothesis is also based on observations of schizophrenics but the theory is too mechanical for the purpose of ex-

---

39. "I found in 56 percent of my cases somatic delusions of reference as expressions of loss of awareness of the self." (Albrecht)

plaining such complicated phenomena as sensory deceptions.

Kraepelin's theory of "perception hallucinations" which are supposedly precipitated by an excitation of sensory centers, does not do sufficient justice to the fact that hallucinations express entire strivings.

3. Deceptions of Memory

Anyone who keeps a diary and re-reads it after a long period of time will find that his notes on certain events differ from his memory of these occurrences. The diary version is always less pleasant than the remembered one. This indicates that the memory of this event has been altered in accordance with wishes or self-love. Such transformations are given free reign in schizophrenics as the result of the patient's weakness of logical thinking and the exaggerated influence of affects to which they are subjected. Very important experiences are changed or excluded from memory and are replaced by other material: memory illusions.

Neither are memory hallucinations specific features of schizophrenia; we even find their prototype in the healthy persons, though almost exclusively in dreams. In schizophrenia, however, they are a common occurrence. They share with other schizophrenic hallucinations and delusions the tendency to emerge suddenly from the unconscious: the complexes which are split off from consciousness create memory material which links itself to the conscious ego at some occasion.

4. Genesis of the Content of Distortions of Reality

Although of old, in isolated cases, some insight was gained into the mechanism of distortion of reality, we still owe it only to Freud that it has become possible to explain the special symptomatology of schizophrenia. In our illustrations of the relationships involved we have employed simple examples only and have ignored complications. However, it must be emphasized that the analyses can be carried very much further than was done here and that, of course, the development of the individual symptoms is not only dependent upon the factors mentioned but also on many other constellations.

We cannot enter into a discussion of the actual technique of psychoanalysis. On the other hand, it is unfortunately necessary to defend the entire theory. Freud's investigations have been attacked on ethical grounds; this objection is perhaps open to discussion when it comes to therapy. However, even then, present-day sexual practices must not be confused with ethics. There can be no ethical objections to the extention of knowledge as such; neither can the validity of results of research be opposed on this basis. Up to the present, no valid objections to our concept have been advanced. It proves, of course, nothing at all when certain "interpretations" are designated as fantastic, regardless of whether or not such a statement is justified. The entire deluge of attacks, without exception, is based upon ignorance with respect to the nature of the matter that is being opposed. This ignorance is understandable since it is impossible to form an opinion on this subject without years of personal investigation. It is, indeed, impossible to include in our descriptions even a small part of the essential analytic material involved. With respect to our cases, even the most detailed psychoanalytic records are of no consequence. Our patients convey to us the nature of the relationships by facial expression, tone of voice, changes in the rate of respiration, blushing, gestures, movements of legs or arms, trembling, and inhibitions, in short, by affective manifestations, rather than by the use of words. Unconsciously everybody reacts strongly to these expressions. The illiterate manual laborer, the young child, even a dog shows definite reactions to some manifestations of our mood. For the time being, psychiatry considers it taboo to acknowledge conscious recognition of these facts. On the other hand, no opposition is encountered when entire ideas are confined to restricted areas.

The interpretation of schizophrenic symptoms in accordance with Freudian symbolism claims validity for the following reasons:

It explains without contradictions an unlimited number of facts which would otherwise remain completely isolated and incomprehensible. That this should be merely accidental is as inconceivable as that a manuscript could constitute a coherent and logical dissertation when the meaning of various letters has been changed.

In spite of the numerous factors involved, interpretations will not result in contradictions; on the other hand, an incorrect interpretation is often contradictory and can also usually be disproved by the patients. The correctness of the interpretations is usually confirmed by the patient as soon as his resistance has been overcome. Anyway, most of the interpretations are given by the patient himself and not by the physician.

If the interpretations were purely arbitrary, they could be applied in the same manner to other conditions. However, they fail completely in delirium tremens, for example, and in all other instances which do not show an identical symptomatology. Furthermore, they can be verified from many angles: the study of experimental associations and the symbolism of dreams, of poetry, and of mythology yields exactly the same results. In some cases, also, the correctness of the results can be demonstrated by the fact that repeated experiments under identical conditions lead to identical results.

The not at all uncommon cases where interpretations permit conclusions as to the occurrence of actual events which are subsequently confirmed, prove the validity of these interpretations with the accuracy of an experiment in physics.

Thus, a novel of a well-known author enabled me to predict many years in advance that he would separate from his wife. I recognized this although there were no other indications whatever that such an event would take place and although it was long before the husband himself, to the best of my knowledge, could have been aware of any feelings of estrangement from his wife. In other cases of nervous and insane patients, certain symptoms made it possible to diagnose marital conflicts. The correctness of our diagnosis was established only later on. A certain type of facial expression can lead us to conclude that the patient practices fellatio; a delusion may reveal the bad conscience of a pederast. Our findings are confirmed by the patients without any attempt at suggestion. Many experiences uncovered by analysis can be objectively verified in other ways. Therefore, they are not, as Reichardt claims, "obviously products of paranoid imagination."[40]

Many schizophrenic symptoms originate from emotionally charged complexes. It is generally very difficult to determine the specific complexes that dominate the individual patient. Undoubtedly, certain events which must be considered accidental in respect to the patient and the disease, exert some influence. A person who happens to fall in love around the time his illness becomes acute will most likely transfer this erotic complex to his illness. Someone who is involved in an economic struggle for his existence at the time of the outbreak of his illness will easily develop ideas of richness and possessions. Religiously inclined individuals will naturally have a stronger tendency to "religious delusions" than others; this form of the disease is ascribed to intensive religious influences from the outside. It is possible that this kind of influence may determine the direction of the delusions even in persons who originally were not religiously inclined. As yet, this has not been proven to me. In cases where it was possible to trace the origin of religious delusions to some extent, everything indicated that marked preoccupation with such matters had existed previously. Where the religious tendency had not only been particularly strong but also qualitatively abnormal in the past, it was certainly reasonable to conclude that the religious activity as such was due to the presence of the unrecognized disease. Since it is impossible to make a definite distinction between

40. Detailed criticism of the attacks on Freud and also a partial criticism of the Freudian theory is contained in Bleuler, "Freud's Psychoanalysis," Vienna, Deuticke, 1911, and *Jahrbuch für Psychoanalytische Forschung, II,* 1910.

what is unusually pronounced and what is pathologically abnormal, especially with respect to religious tendencies, we again cannot answer the question as to causes. In women it has often been found that love for a priest was the root of the "religious delusion."[41]

We conclude, therefore, that the disease does not grow out of the individual's character, as the popular notion would have it; neither are its symptoms determined by the individual's character, as Tilling suggests. The symptomatology is determined by the emotionally charged complex which, in turn, is often dependent upon the *Anlage*. Only those whose drives demand that they play a certain role in the world, be it politics, religion, or science can determine the symptoms of the disease by means of a corresponding complex. One drive, however, is common to all humans: the sexual drive which, with all its implications, constitutes a large part of our ego.[42] In every case, therefore, we encounter the sexual complex, partly alone, partly in conjunction with other complexes.

Thus we find behind many of the individual symptoms wishes and fears, strivings and their obstacles.

This theory of genesis hardly requires proof in those common cases where, for example, hospitalized patients suddenly declare, without motivation but with conviction: "Today my son is coming to take me home." In the case of one patient, the idea has suddenly occurred to him; another has received the information from his "voices"; a third patient has arrived at this conclusion by way of referring certain indications to himself and interpreting them in accordance with his wish. The validity of this concept is equally obvious in many other simple cases: Two women who do not know each other believe that the men they love are close to them, sometimes because they hear their voices, at other times without any such clue, although actually both men are abroad. A schizophrenic woman who, in the hospital, gave birth but did not produce any milk is told by the voices that the infant drank from her breast throughout the night. An officer who had never been able to get along with his mother-in-law is convinced that she will be beheaded, or, when objections were raised, at least that she will be condemned to life imprisonment. In fact, he had actually accused her in a complaint to the district attorney of poisoning a woman many years

41. The love for the priest need not be primary. We may find, for example, that at first ungratified sexuality is sublimated in religiosity; and on the basis of this religious attitude, the women come to admire the priest more than any other man. In this way, their emotions are partially re-sexualized.

42. It forms *more* than half of our ego; for the other half which consists of the drives serving self-preservation is stunted in civilized people.

ago. He never presented the least proof for this accusation but he is convinced that it was justified.

In these cases, contradictions to reality are displaced into the future or the past. However, the patients really do not care whether or not they come into conflict with the present. An aging hebephrenic whose teeth are in very bad condition appears childishly happy one morning because he is certain that he has grown a new set of teeth, and proudly shows his mouth to the doctors and nurses. In order to be able to maintain this claim, even to himself, he must hallucinate the sensation of new teeth in his mouth. A latent schizophrenic whose menstruation was interrupted for the first time (menopause) awakes one night with the sensation that her limbs are shrinking, that she is getting to be as tiny as a newborn baby; she kicks and flings her arms about and her husband must carry her in his arms as if she were a small child (regeneration instead of involution, Jung). A physically miserable woman (in childhood, a hydrocephalic) thinks of herself as beautifully proportioned, like a statue. She believes that she has only lost weight because of the bath which she was given on admission to the hospital. Moreover, she has been given access to heaven and keeps company with the Saints; in this way, she has doubly overcome the miseries of this world (Norman, 526).

A very intelligent man who despite his first catatonic attack continues to occupy a prominent position and has to do a good deal of public speaking, stutters and stammers slightly. In his second twilight state, he claimed that his speech was perfect: "As clear as never before; every syllable was pronounced exactly as it ought to be." Later, this idea caused him to sing terribly loudly, even when he went to visit acquaintances. A sexually aroused hospitalized patient thinks that he is in a convent and uses his mattress as a sexual object.

The wish not to be confined to a hospital precipitated distortion of reality with regard to local orientation in the case of a rather alert woman patient who was still capable of working. She wrote to her husband as follows: "In the brief note, I must tell you that for some reasons not clear to me I have been in this convalescent home since two weeks. It adjoins the Burgholzli insane asylum." Actually she was *in* Burgholzli, not near it; she recognized the other patients as mentally ill. However, this did not prevent the distortion of local orientation which, by the way, occurs rather frequently in this form.

One of the catatonic patients also revealed a complete break with reality. For a long time he felt remorse for the fact that he killed his mother; during this phase, he earnestly believed that the deed could be undone, as he, himself, expressed it.

The wishes are not always as well-founded and persistent. Even sudden impulses which are generally held in check by stronger opposing emotions may be transformed into delusional ideas. A young girl who behaved badly at the beginning of a catatonia, was severely reprimanded and slapped by her mother. She ran out of the apartment, shouting to the neighbors. "Did you hear, Papa just shot Mother." Immediately afterwards, she begged her mother's forgiveness. The patient B. S. who was analyzed by Jung, saw persons who annoyed her, who did something she disliked, being taken away in a hearse. This applied to nurses and to other patients as well as to her doctors. At one time she saw my predecessor felled suddenly, as if by a bullet.

In general, the individuals who die in a patient's delusions were in his way if only through their relationship to hated persons. A catatonic woman patient resented the people for whom she had worked before her illness. Consequently, her former employer's innocent child had died, in her delusions.

Hated persons are not always simply thought of as dead. A catatonic patient had had quarrels with his brother. Twice during his illness, he saw Death appear between himself and his brother. The patients frequently express the idea of killing the hated person themselves. A woman patient accused herself of having murdered her brother. To the question as to whether she liked him, she answered in the affirmative, but in a tone of voice and with a smile that would have convinced anyone that the opposite was actually the case. A miserly man whose financial situation was handicapped by his mother because he had to support her, was convinced that he had inherited his mental disease from her. He told her: "I can easily imagine you stretched out on the ground, with a hole through your forehead."

Moreover, the delusion of murder may occur as a sexual symptom, as we shall see later. Up to the present, we have observed only a single case where neither the desire to get rid of someone nor sexual love could be demonstrated as the root of such a delusional idea of murder.

A quarrelsome paranoid who, by the way, is typical for many schizophrenics, fulfilled his wishes in a very complicated fashion. He accused certain people whom he disliked of various crimes utilizing as proofs his hallucinations and deceptions of memory. In addition, he had claims against these persons. He insisted that he had won a libel suit against them although actually he, himself, had lost the case, paid the fine and costs, and had been imprisoned on account of it. He persisted in this belief, even after the document containing the court's decision was again shown to him. When we examined him, we repeatedly emphasized the fact that we considered him mentally ill and that his claims were based only on delusions. However, he nevertheless insisted that we had declared him sane in our testimony and that we had declared his claims and complaints to be justified. A young man who suffered from the results of an attack of poliomyelitis, general weakness, and headaches was tired of life. He gained the firm conviction that he and all his relatives were to die on a certain day. However, when he survived that specified day, he sought to fulfill his wish by an uncontrollable suicidal drive.

Desires for greatness, wealth, power, and rank are fulfilled in delusions of grandeur. They are usually considered signs of deterioration (dementia) but, for that matter, so are the other autistic wish-fulfillments. For instance, the delusion that by his death the unloved husband has made it possible for the patient to enter a relationship she desires, has the same significance. Actually, the situation is as follows: at the beginning of the delusion we find a wish. The schizophrenic may think of this wish without connecting with it the idea that it is impossible to fulfill it; or—after the next step—he may think of his wish as already fulfilled. Only by complete exclusion of his intellectual powers can the common laborer consider himself as the *Kaiser*. The woman who lives at the side of her husband night and day and yet believes that he is dead, can do so only when she is completely isolated from reality or when there has been a complete breakdown in her logical thinking. In patients whose state of consciousness is relatively clear, continuous conflict between wish and reality must prevent the full development of the delusion and, even more important, prevent the delusion from dominating the entire personality by means of the complex; the wish is then not carried out; it remains essentially in the unconscious or is displaced and covered up by symbols. Proportionally, however, the obstacles opposing wish fulfilment or the delusion of an already fulfilled wish increase in strength. Consequently, therefore, the idea of persecution is generally the first to be elaborated. This idea is present and ready for action even in normal persons when their aspirations are frustrated. (It happens only rarely that a student who fails an examination does not place at least part of the blame on the examiner.)

There are also cases where the illusion of the already fulfilled wish does not encounter such great obstacles: the theories of the pathological world reformer, of the prophet, the philosopher, the poet, often also of the inventor, and of other individuals with similar strivings cannot immediately be demonstrated as absurd; indeed they often find followers. These people can elaborate their ideas of grandeur without losing the logical connection with reality and the delusion of persecution may develop never or only very late.

In all other forms the aspirations must conceal themselves behind delusions of persecution. Nonetheless, the wish is the primary element: a woman patient could not be fighting against the idea that she has had a child by Dr. N., unless the idea had not somehow occurred to her that she would like to have a child by him or that she has one.

Thus, we are dealing with a far-reaching separation from reality or a severe disturbance in the process of thinking, or both, when forms of delusions occur undistinguished and fully elaborated which are in extreme contrast to reality, regardless of whether or not they are delusions of grandeur. When either one of the two conditions exists in a chronic state of the disease, the patient is usually incurable and at the same time may be considered as severely deteriorated even though he may be able to evaluate correctly other situations.

However, the break with reality and the serious disturbance of logical thinking which precipitate delusions of grandeur, as well as other wish-fulfillments, may also constitute partial manifestations of any acute episode and, as such, they are transitory symptoms. Therefore, the concept that the delusion of grandeur represents an important sign of deterioration is a practical rule with many exceptions; it is a rule which does not contain the whole truth and, consequently, much that is incorrect. Aspirations of any kind are easily linked to sexual needs. A laborer who had always been very thrifty and who had always seen to it that proper respect was paid to him had been, apparently happily, married since he was twenty-three years old. At the age of thirty-one, he tearfully explained to his wife that he wanted to make her happy; he was planning to marry a certain rich young lady. In answer to the objection that this was impossible, he replied that he would simply get a divorce. He received signs which indicated to him that he should marry the young lady, and take steps in that direction. The same interpretation of simultaneous fulfillment of sexual and financial wishes applies to the case of a miserly woman whose "voices" telephone to inform her that some men are coming to bring her a sum of money. An intelligent, working-class woman had married a man who seemed to her inferior mentally, in spite of the fact that she had always put great store in intelligence and education. She does not have a lover but she takes revenge on her husband by having her "voices" ridicule and scorn him; at the same time, they console her by telling her that she has deserved a better fate and that she will inherit 20,000 francs.

In the following case, the need for love and social standing is expressed in a more complicated way. A hebephrenic peasant woman maintains contact by "telephone" with certain gentlemen who are staying at a resort; one of them, a Baron (who, in reality, does not even exist), wants to marry her. Her husband has left her (this was actually the case). However, already before this event, the patient has felt compelled to go "to another man" in a neighboring village and to ask him to marry her. Later, she has many hallucinations: many people are threatening her; a snake, a huge dragon, etc.—all of which are closely connected with sexuality, as our experience with other patients indicates. At the same time, her desire for wealth is being satisfied: she sees herself in a large garden with many beautiful flowers and a fairy-like castle decorated with garlands. As the disease becomes progressively severe, she sees, while in a state of clear consciousness, the Austrian emperor walking in her fields. Her nephew is the crown-prince of Austria. She is in contact with other great aristocrats. Compulsively she must daily go to a restaurant and order some cutlets. However, as happens often, the conflict with reality was also manifested in the disease symptoms of this patient; e.g., when she put on her grand act in the restaurant, the voices told her that she was a hussy, a vicious woman. Furthermore, she believed that her husband had tied her to himself by means of some secret power or magic. (In this way, she cannot be blamed for her undesirable marriage.)

Resentment against the marriage partner or the wish to have another one is registered by our patients in many different ways. Not uncommonly, woman patients insist that they are not married or, at least, they refuse to acknowledge that the man in question is actually their husband. Like other hated persons, husbands are frequently declared dead by their wives, with or without expressions of grief. A certain paranoid woman who had been married for a long time, was very discrete in expressing her dislike of her husband. She signed a letter with her maiden name, then quickly corrected the error by adding her married name. (In addition to this, she showed an increasing number of hallucinations and delusions, mostly directed against her husband.) This slip is a fine example of Freud's psychology of everyday life carried over into pathology.

An advanced catatonic patient, Mrs. K., does not love her husband. She is in love with one of her childhood friends. For some time she insists that there are "two K's, a white one and black one, a good one and a bad one." In this case, the patient herself recognized and explained the simple symbolism used. Somewhat later, she believes that she is married to her former lover and that her husband has also married one of his old girl friends. To make her happiness complete, she believes that all the people she has loved and who have died are again alive and in touch with her.

A vigorous peasant woman had married a man who was neither physically nor mentally her equal. She was in love with a priest. After the outbreak of her catatonia she frees herself from her husband by believing that he is unfaithful and engaged to another woman (a very common delusion under such circumstances; compare this with the previous case.) One day she goes to the Hall of Records to find out her husband had applied for the license to marry the other woman. In the hospital, she verbigerates that her genitals are being prepared for the priest. However, even this patient does some justice to reality inasmuch as she often complains that her husband gets into her bed at night (not an unusual idea in such cases) but she does not want him; she wants only the priest. Another indication that the patient attempts some adjustment to reality is the fact that after she had been in the hospital for some time, she identifies the doctor with her priest. However, the physician is a married man; and one day when he comes to visit her she receives him with the question, "Has your wife died?" When he denies this, she continues her train of thought as if the question had been answered in the affirmative: "You will easily find another wife; for example, I would marry you." Since her rival, nevertheless, remains alive she uses a distortion of memory to assist her; she claims that the doctor had assured her that he was unable to have sexual relations with his wife.

In every one of the many cases where a wife mistakenly considers her husband dead, where she believed that she was not married, that she did not have the same family name as her husband, etc., we always find, not merely resentment against some specific characteristic or action of her husband, but a deeper-seated dissatisfaction of which, however, the patient is not necessarily fully aware. One of the many causes for dissatisfaction enumerated by the patients is the husband's inability to satisfy them sexually. Only rarely is it a question of impotence. As usual, the reason for this type of dissatisfaction lies, therefore, in the absence of the wife's love for her husband or in a partial dislike for him. It is not necessary for the genesis of the delusion that the husband be hated in the usual sense of the term. The wife may have deep respect for her husband; in a way, she may even love him, but somehow he appears to her inadequate or unpleasant (ambivalence). It seems that the patients suffer particularly when they consider the husband intellectually or emotionally inadequate—in relation to their demands. By the same token, the patient's lover does not have to conform with every one of her wishes either; his image is often transformed by delusions. But he must have some important advantage over the patient's husband.

What has been said of women also applies to men though, in general, to a lesser degree. The husband is not as dependent upon a specific woman as vice versa. The idea of divorce occurs to him more readily in his delusions as well as actually. The matter seems to be less deep-seated in men than in women. In his delusions (and also in reality) a man can very well have one or more mistresses while living with his wife. He may even want to marry one of his mistresses in order to bring happiness to his wife with whom he expects to share his newly-gained wealth.

Perhaps more frequently than women, men seek to escape from their obligations by developing the delusion that the marriage partner is unfaithful to them. The nature of this particular source of delusions of jealousy[43] does, of course, not prevent the husband from accusing his wife of infidelity, and from hating and mistreating her because of it since it is the "purpose" of the delusion to give him the right to such feelings and actions. Impotence often precipitates the development of delusional ideas.

One husband is ashamed before his wife and therefore must depreciate her; another throws the blame on her; a third surrenders his masculinity and becomes a woman.[44] For the most part, the delusion is a combined one in which all three forms appear in the same patient, but one usually occupies the foreground.

An impotent husband of the first type accuses his wife of being a whore and of being pregnant; then it occurs to him that he must kill her. He obtains, thereby, the reasons for a further extension of his delusional idea—that she tried to strangle him, that she wanted to pierce him with a hat-pin, to poison him. Immediately after their marriage he had forced her to go to a doctor and confess (falsely) to him that she was eight weeks pregnant. Later, the patient himself believes in this pregnancy.

A workingman felt his childlessness very keenly. However, he had never been very active sexually; and of late he was almost entirely impotent or suffered from ejaculatio praecox. Because of his hebephrenia, he has been incapable of working at his trade for many years.

43. There are other roots as well.

44. Schreber's desire to have children was not satisfied. In the process of becoming a woman he is made pregnant by God and will renew humanity.

Therefore, he does all the womanly tasks at home while his wife conducts a business.

Metamorphosis sexualis paranoica may have other sources than that of impotence, particularly a complicating homosexuality. In one such case, which unfortunately I was unable to analyze, I had reason to suspect that the patient considered herself to be a man because only as a man she could hope to realize her scholastic aspirations. Occasionally, such a delusion is an accidental by-product of further elaborated and displaced delusional ideas: one patient had been in love with a minister some fifty years previously; gradually, the woman patient (like many another under the same conditions) became Christ, proving this transformation by demonstrating a femoral hernia as a scrotum.

The desire to have children, especially in women, plays as great a role as the erotic complex, in its narrower sense. In the beginning stages of a catatonia a very well educated girl wrote a letter, telling her sister that she had never been in love with a man, but now she was going to have a child and was very happy at the idea. (She was markedly erotic throughout her illness.)

The imaginary children are, as a rule, fathered by the man whom the patient really loves. A married woman, who had had two children by her unloved husband, claimed that she carried in her womb at least three more children by her "fiancé," and demanded that they be cut out of her at once. As for the real children, who hardly fit into the circumstances, the patients know how to solve that problem, often in very original ways. Thus one patient, who had an illegitimate child before her marriage, declared her children "supra-legitimate;" for this reason she had to marry although she was the Queen of the World.

The very lack of clear concepts permits the common identification of the beloved one with the children. Both have the same name, are addressed by the same terms of endearment, and are not differentiated in any way. Another means of uniting all the various wishes is for the patient to be, simultaneously, daughter, fiancée, and wife of the beloved.

Just as reality can be endowed with everything pleasant and desired, so can the unpleasant be removed from it. Often the patients cannot be convinced of the simplest thing if it does not suit them. We have already seen an example of this in the previously cited case of the litiginous paranoid. Often this kind of denial passes through several stages. When one of our hebephrenics learned that her husband wanted to divorce her, she took the news quite seriously and cursed him heartily. But after she had been actually divorced, it was in no way possible to convince her of that fact, and no one could even dare to address her by her maiden name as would have been proper. One of our catatonics was told of her father's death. She declared the report to be false, and immediately began to hear her father's voice. Then as she gradually began to be convinced of the truth, she displaced the unpleasant fact into the past, as so many persons do, and insisted that her father had been dead for some years. A few minutes afterwards, she was completely overcome by the entire reality of the news, shed some tears, and then was again as she had been before.

As soon as our wishes are thought of as fulfilled or as capable of being fulfilled, negative feeling tones become attached to them. They not only come into conflict with the reality which has not fulfilled our wish, but the very fulfillment of our desires brings with it unpleasantness.

In a few of the previously cited cases, we have already seen how the delusions are influenced by the circumstance that our wishes can be fulfilled. More commonly, however, we find that the obstacles provoke the persecutory delusion.[45] We see the same process in mythology: the favorable powers of nature and chance are personified by the good spirits and the kindly gods; the undesired are personified by the evil spirits, the malignant demons. Or, the individual gods are endowed with good and evil properties at one and the same time; the Sun-god not only disperses fertility but also sends out his deadly arrows. Indeed, the personifications often receive different names according to the momentary interpretations of their influence, so that the one personification may be divided into two or three or even more creatures. This splitting of a single concept remains as obscure in mythology as it does in the analogous schizophrenic phenomenon.[46]

The proofs for the similar origins of the schizophrenic persecutory delusion lie in the following facts: the delusion is not developed when the obstacles are not sensed by the patient; the obstacles are always to be found at the root of the delusion; and after an obstacle has been experienced the persecutions are seized upon as the "explanation" of an infinite number of details. Thus, if a patient does not get an answer to his letter, he accuses the doctor of having intercepted the mail; or the beloved one may be transformed, under our very eyes, into the persecutor.[47]

45. Not the content, but the intensity of the persecutory delusions can be increased by the fact that the patient, as does the healthy, often revels in the feeling of being mistreated.

46. Cf. Abraham.

47. We assume, although we cannot prove it, that the anxiety aroused by the repression of sexual wishes also plays a part in the development of persecutory ideas from such unfulfilled wishes. Even in normal people, we see that momentary feelings of mistrust to vague persecutory ideas may arise on the basis of these affects.

The origin of contrary delusional ideas can be especially clearly demonstrated in cases of prison psychosis which is, for the most part, a symptom of schizophrenia, but which can also develop in quite the same way apart from this particular disease.

In poetry and in reality, in sleep and in waking, the prisoner dreams of freedom. But this freedom is usually impossible to attain if reality is conceived of as it actually is. So the prisoner is declared blameless, or his sentence has long since been served, or similar things. Under these circumstances, it is not the walls and bars which are really the things which prevent him from leaving his prison, but certain people who "have it in for him." Naturally, they are the very people who had him imprisoned in the first place, and who keep him there—the warden, the guards, or the district attorney who already at the trial showed himself to be the prisoner's enemy. These are, then, the persecutors who play their role in the further hallucinatory elaboration of the delusion. In two patients, both Italians, the ideas of freedom were replaced by the patients' claims that other people looked upon them as God's messengers, whereas the patients considered themselves as simply pious.[48]

In accordance with the peculiarities of schizophrenic associations, the patient's enemies are not selected in terms of logic; rather the affects and the accidental constellation determine which persons are included in the delusion. Thus, quite often those very persons are thought of as enemies who least justify such a notion: those who in reality were the patients' protectors and well-wishers. One of our schizophrenics had been supported by her friends for many years although at one time she had been quite wealthy. She considered herself persecuted by those same friends who continued to help pay her hospital bills. She herself does not wish to be helped by anyone. The only persons she could link to the negatively toned thoughts of aid were those very same friends who filled the causal gap; the persecutors were to blame for her lack of help and subsequently also for her misfortune.

Even when the patient's wishes are fulfilled by his delusions, he rarely obtains any benefit from them. What good is his great wealth, the fame which he dreams that he possesses, when he is confined to the hospital? Indeed, the majority do not even enjoy the pleasures of their hallucinated love any more than their hunger can be satisfied by hallucinated food. Anxiety, shame, and other unpleasant affects which are so easily aroused by sexual activity can hardly be absent. Thus, here also a negative note enters. However, sexual activity with negative affects is

48. Many schizophrenic Italians are quite willing to remain in the hospital and be fed, clothed and cared for.

nearly equal to rape; no wonder then that the latter plays such a prominent role in our patients. Furthermore, the beloved one does not do anything to help the patient. Therefore, he is to blame, more or less, for all the patient's unhappiness and misfortune; at least, he is associatively linked with all the unpleasantnesses. It is precisely when he, the loved one, is thought of that most of the blocking and other pathological states appear. Simple experience thus proves that the beloved one is also an enemy. The patients are tortured and persecuted, electrocuted and poisoned by the beloved; under certain conditions, he even becomes the initiator of their incarceration. Usually the negative and positive notions exist side by side: a woman permits her voices to call her delusional lover, the Chief of the Devil; occasionally he appears to her visually as an eagle "which she could just as well term, an angel." (In reality, he has a marked eagle-beak nose.)

The hallucinated tortures, which are caused chiefly by the sexual complex, occasion the patients to complain about them even when they quite consciously and constantly desire these same tortures. One of our catatonics very categorically demands, at nearly every visit by the doctor, that a certain girl or girls be sent to his bed; but this does not prevent him in the least from complaining at the same time that he does not care to be used as a stud-horse. Another patient is very erotic, but demands that he be changed to another "bedroom" because of the immoral dreams which he has been having.[49]

Frequently, the unpleasant quality stems from the further logical development of the wish idea. A woman patient suddenly begins to scold and curse, stating that no one had the right to say that she was a child-murderess because she had never hurt any child, had never had a child, that after all she was not engaged to the ward-physician. Here the wish was negatively expressed to us for the first time since she entered the hospital. We see in this negation not only the reality which opposes the wish but also the fear which is produced by this very mixture of wish and reality. If the patient did have a child by the doctor, it would be a great shame and scandal; she would have to do away with it at once since "she is not engaged to him." Insofar as she thinks her wish has been fulfilled, she is also, at the same time, a child-murderess which is precisely what the "voices" reproached her with. The idea of child-murderess then goes even further. Once, many years before, a girl from her home-town killed her illegitimate child. The patient thinks that she

49. Analogous to dreams, it is not improbable that only those complexes which are ambivalent give occasion to true delusions. The ambivalence attached to the delusion is based not only on this factor, but also on a special tendency of the delusion-forming complex.

is like that girl. The voices insist that she is that girl and the patient, in great anger, tries to prove that she is not. Here, the persecutors are the representatives of the inner conflict.

We observed something very similar in a paranoid patient. His wife does not satisfy him any more. The voices tell him that he could easily marry another woman, a younger woman, in particular, his niece who is only sixteen years old and has made a great impression on him. Legally, of course, he cannot have anything to do with her sexually, but the wish to do so illegally is present. The voices make a compromise between wish and reality; they tell him that he had raped her. Of course, this idea angers him greatly. When he is transferred to a different shop in the factory, the delusion begins to spread; he hallucinates that his new fellow-workers do not want to work alongside such a vicious rascal. He becomes further enraged and, of course, even more unpleasant to his wife whose existence prevents the fulfillment of his wish.

The affective ambivalence manifests itself not only in the patient's propensities and aversions but also in his hopes and fears. When this above-mentioned paranoid factory worker was in the hospital, the voices soon began to tell him that in six weeks he would be released; at other times they told him he was going to be kept in the hospital forever. In contrast to the later nasty remarks made by his fellow-workers, the voices had previously told him that he was going to be made foreman at the factory. The same patient, at the start of his psychosis, had heard much more simple hypostatizations of his wishes and anxieties. Thus it was whispered to him that the daughter of a certain person wanted to marry him, that he was going to receive a large sum of money before nightfall. At his rifle club, all the members had whispered that he had better be careful not to shoot accidentally the referee.

A real lover may also have his bad points; he may, for example, be morally inferior to the unloved husband. A patient developed the delusion that the dolt on whom she had hung her heart was insane. Therefore, he was more to be pitied than blamed since it was quite contrary to all her feelings to assume that, out of revenge, she might desire his becoming mentally ill.

Conflicts arise primarily from the usual struggles of our various drives, regardless of whether they be called good or bad. Corresponding to those drives, the patients develop "voices" and impulses to act; the "bad" drives are exposed by the twinges of conscience in those patients who have one. The "good" drives are endowed with negative feeling tones because of the sacrifices which they demand of us. And so the patients are frequently driven to do the very things which they would like to leave undone. The voices often bring the patients to the point of despair when they first command that something be done and then make the ugliest reproaches after the command is carried out and the action completed.

In many instances the persecutor is nothing else than the personification of the patient's conscience. After the reading of his father's will, a paranoid, who had been a great profligate in his day developed voices which were those of his uncle who had been a great friend of his father. These voices reproached the patient for his scandalous behavior; they told him that he was utterly incapable of doing anything useful; that he allowed himself to be fed and cared for in Burgholzli. Subsequently new voices appeared which persecuted him in many other ways.

Perhaps, under certain conditions, the whole persecutory delusion may originate in a bad conscience.[50] However, as yet I have never seen a delusion in schizophrenics which did not also contain elements of disappointed aspirations. Some patients, though, claim that others knew about their masturbation by looking at them, and then proceed to develop the idea that they are being stared at *because* of their onanism.

The ambivalence of feelings is often revealed in the contradictory voices: there are voices which console the patient, take his part; and there are others which complain about him, annoy and torture him. They may even divide themselves as to which of the two ears they appear to speak into: the "good" voices using the right ear, and the "bad" ones using the left ear.

According to Freud, the anxiety dreams are also wishes which are being thought of negatively only because of the obstacles opposing them. I am not convinced that this interpretation is correct. At the moment, at least, I cannot see why a negative affect could not directly produce its corresponding thoughts just as the positive affect does. When a patient, who is very jealous of his brother, fears in his dreams that his brother is going to die, one could just as well interpret this as a wish to which a negative element has been added. When a hebephrenic, who had failed to pass her final teacher's examination, develops (while in the hospital) the delusion that her notebooks and textbooks are being distributed to others purely out of scorn, it suggests the interpretation that she was ashamed, and that this unpleasant feeling is expressed in her delusion.

The child-complex is a particularly frequent cause of inner conflict. It is just as common for a schizophrenic mother to believe in her

50. Cf. Case 3 in Bleuler (71).

delusional idea that she has killed her children as it is rare for her to really destroy them; in this respect, the children are often completely identified with the husband. Thus, the previously mentioned woman believed not only in the insanity of her husband, but also in that of their son. An unmarried gravid woman was referred to us by the courts for observation and examination. She was in love with the father of her child and was always happy when she received any news of him, or when anyone mentioned him. But as the lover hesitated to visit her in the hospital and, above all, gave indications of being unfaithful to her, she began to cry and sob: she said the child was disappearing from her womb and finally insisted that it was dead. A few days later when her child continued to be very much alive, she cried that she would be unable to support the child, that it would meet as miserable a fate as her own, that it were better if it were dead. Here, very characteristically, we note the distinct equivalence of the delusional idea of death and the wish that the child should die. Subsequently, this wish will even receive logical justifications. Schizophrenic women who do not love their husbands are particularly hostile to them during pregnancies (real or imaginary).

The identification of the husband with the child was also revealed in the case of a delirious woman who insisted that her husband had two wives and that she saw him trying to drown himself in such a fashion that it was exceedingly difficult for anyone to rescue him. She said that her son also wanted to drown himself to expiate his father's sins (all this during a schizophrenic delirium). I remember four other cases of psychotic mothers really wanting to kill the children of their detested husbands.[51] In one case the husband was finally killed in the delusion. One of the women who had poured gasoline over her baby and was caught in the process of sharpening a knife, gave as reason for the attempted murder: "It is not my child; I wanted to sacrifice the dear child to God." It is also very characteristic of schizophrenia that the two reasons for the attempted murder stand side by side: in one connection, it is not her child (but that of her husband); and in another connection which is juxtaposed to the first it still is her child since it is her dearest possession. Another woman gave as reason for her murderous intent that her husband had no right to any happiness from his children. A husband wanted to marry another woman in order to make his present wife and her siblings happy; but he also thought that someone wanted to kill him, that his own children would have to be sacrificed so that his life would be spared because of their innocence.

---

51. Möbius relates a story of a female stork throwing the almost fully hatched eggs from the nest and filling it with grass after she had been left by her mate.

The same feeling may be expressed in externally very different forms. A patient, whose children had actually died of natural causes, expressed her hatred of her husband by the falsification of memory that she herself had murdered her children. Another form which is quite frequent was observed in the delusions of a catatonic woman who believed that her husband had shot himself. She was able to give quite a good case history of herself except for the question as to how many children she had; she could never answer this question because of insurmountable blocking.

The identification of the husband with the child may also be reversed, attributing the characteristics of the child to the husband: a woman who was not at all satisfied with her husband, transferred all her pride to her son. "He is a doctor, and a teacher; he is only twenty years old but far older in mind." And the husband? "He's a good-for-nothing; I don't know what he's doing." With a sigh: "He is a teacher too; he is something of everything."[52]

In schizophrenic women who believe themselves to be pregnant, we can nearly always demonstrate the desire to have children. In instances they are married but childless; generally they have a lover whom they cannot meet (whether they are married or not), but who is the father of their (imaginary) child. In some cases and, especially, at the onset of the illness, the patient is not conscious of the imaginary pregnancy. They suffer labor pains which are repeated or continue over a long period. Often they are diagnosed as having some pelvic disease. In one such case, after a feverless "peritonitis" the woman cleared the matter up herself by declaring that she had become pregnant because she had to stay in her father's bed during her illness! Another patient contracted "hypochondriasis" in the same way. She had been in love with a certain officer but in deference to her father's desire she had married someone else. In spite of the fact that she was apparently suffering from schizophrenia long before her marriage, the marriage was fairly successful for many years, at least outwardly, till she learned that her husband was having an affair with another woman. Now the thought occurred to her that she could get a divorce and marry her first sweetheart. This idea, however, was none too clearly thought out (that is, it was suppressed). Then the patient became pregnant (in her imagination only), had labor pains which had been displaced to the upper abdomen in a vague way by the time she came to see us. Finally, a friend suggested that she must have gallstones in which she now firmly believed in spite of

52. A certain lady of my acquaintance clearly regulates the degree of her tenderness toward her husband by the good or bad behavior of her children.

our denial that she had such a condition. She was unable to work, had consulted any number of physicians for these pains which showed every characteristic of the nervous type of pain.

In one instance, the delusion of being pregnant was, perhaps, a product of simple fear. A girl was surprised one night by an unknown man who had managed to get into her room. In spite of many medical examinations, as well as the continuance of her menses, she still believed that she was pregnant. In a second case, a widow had once permitted herself to be seduced. She became terribly afraid of a possible pregnancy which under our observation gradually transformed itself into hallucinations of severe pain in the genital area with "hypochondriacal ideas." More than a year later, after a few prodromal signs, the menses recurred for the first time since that last coitus; and the patient was able to resume work and in a few days felt completely well.

I have never yet seen an instance where the physical symptoms were the primary factors in producing the delusion of pregnancy; what Schuele called "the allegory of the specific sensations of a diseased uterus." Still, it is possible that such physical sensations may give occasion for the delusion, but they certainly do not cause it. Thus a patient, who is already suffering from the delusion of being poisoned, may take a coincidental diarrhea as an occasion to conclude that his food was poisoned; or a patient, who believed she was the Queen of Württemberg, interpreted as evidence that she was going to give birth to a prince, the perineal abscess that developed from the patient's continually beating herself in that region. Such false conclusions from false premises are something altogether different from tracing the genesis of a delusion to physical disorders. In that case, the patients usually react less intensely to the simple application of their delusion to other things than they did to their original delusional idea: the patient, who is always very angry with his doctor when complaining about his hallucinated symptoms of poisoning, ascribes his pseudo-toxic diarrhea to his other poisonings with a simple fatalistic shrug of the shoulders.

In many cases, the cessation of the menses is clearly related to the wish to have children; and probably this phenomenon is far more common than we are able to prove. Conversely, part of the usual menstrual irritabilities are to be ascribed to the fact that the very evidence of the lack of pregnancy angers the patients.

With the previously cited allusions to love and marriage we have by no means exhausted the entire role of sexuality in the symptomatology of schizophrenia.[53] There is hardly any schizophrenic—or even

---

53. Lomer gives us some figures as to the frequency of the occurrence of sexual ideas and sexual hallucinations, but I think he has under-estimated it by a good deal.

healthy person, for that matter—in whom the sexual complex does not play an important role. Generally, it dominates the foreground of the picture; in many patients, we are able to find only the sexual complexes. Struggle as we will against it, the more experience we obtain, the more "sexual" we become in our interpretations. Concerning the objections which are often made to such interpretations, I must emphasize that in our method of questioning, we have been more than careful not to suggest sexual matters to our patients. Nevertheless, in some men, less commonly in women, we can observe other important complexes which are not related to sexuality any more than other ideas which also have their associations and connections to this vast ideational and emotional complex which we call sexual. In some men, the sexual complex has been pushed into the background by other complexes.

The most frequent objection to the sexual interpretation of hysteriform phenomena is that not everyone can be so versed in such matters and develop the kind of feeling-tones which the theory postulates. This is in direct contradiction to reality. In nervous diseases, one might offer the excuse that only such girls become hysteric whose sexual life is sufficiently developed to guarantee the necessary knowledge and appropriate feelings. But schizophrenia, which must have an organic basis, cannot be understood in such exclusive terms. We simply must acknowledge the fact that there is no schizophrenic, man or woman, old or young, from a good or bad environment, who does not know and feel more than enough of sexuality to produce sexual symptoms. How often do we hear from astonished parents: "Where could my daughter have heard all that?" These parents, like the psychiatrists who pose the same questions, have observed themselves very badly. Who has not heard of sexual matters, of the really significant problems of procreation? The answer is: no one; everyone has heard very much about such things throughout his whole life. It is impossible to protect anyone from learning these things, unless he be brought up like Kaspar Hauser. I will not mention the newspapers and literature; or servants; or what everyone hears on the streets; or, for that matter, the sparrows, pidgeons and dogs in the city, and domestic animals in the country. But history and, above all, religion, as it is so assiduously crammed into our children, teems with things which can only be grasped if one has some understanding of the most intimate facts of sexuality. And Protestant children are even given the Bible which speaks of such matters as candidly as Freud. Catholics carefully preserve the legend of the Holy Virgin Mary and have holidays glorifying sexual life processes—and the children are not to know anything of all this? They would certainly have to be the most complete idiots not to know. But there are very few idiots in the sexual sphere; for in this sphere we have phylogenetically a very ancient natural understanding, as does the suckling for the breast and the year-old child for food. And if all the nicely brought-up children did not have an adequate knowledge of sexual matters, it would soon enough be clear to them that they did not understand many things and that they would have to ask questions. However, children know what they must not ask about, or what they can only ask of their servants and comrades, proving how much they already know. We saw the same process in the patient who gave approximate answers; he responded to the question: "How much is three plus two?" with every figure from one to ten except with the correct one. The children also know quite early—long before starting to school—what, on the whole, they must not do for sexual reasons. We have recently made an observation which will vividly illustrate this point. A nineteen-year-old girl of a highly educated and extremely religious family became catatonic. In this instance, whatever was at all humanly possible to do had been done to keep her "pure." It had not been very difficult, easier than in most cases, because the girl had been somewhat sickly, and had little incentive to read or educate herself in any way, but at the same time was extaordinarily obedient. One can be fairly certain that she never read anything that had not been approved by her parents. From the beginning of her school years which had been brief, her education had been completely in the hands of her mother. Altogether, the girl led a very secluded existence, disliked company, and occupied herself only with housework, religion and a little music. During her catatonic state, she enjoyed her Savior's visits to her bed no less than a more knowing woman. She was in no way disturbed that her Savior appeared in the guise of a certain preacher who had greatly impressed her. Another girl, who had also been protected as much as possible, refused to eat eggs because she feared to destroy the "little ovaries"; while eating, she bore children from out of her mouth.

Now, I do not want to assert that all women, who insist that prior to marriage they knew nothing of these things, are liars and hypocrites. On the contrary, I am well aware of the process by which these things are isolated and blocked off; and I trust no girl in whom this blocking does not become complete when someone asks her about sexual matters, the very knowledge of which is believed to constitute a degradation of her person.[54] Perversions, alongside the manifestations of normal drives,

54. One can call this type of not-knowing a partial emotional stupor and compare the phenomenon with the generalized stupor which, for instance, army recruits show: when they are asked questions in a certain way, they do not seem to know even the simplest things.

are much more pronounced in schizophrenics than in neurotics. The homosexual components, especially, play an unsuspectedly large role. But we will not go into further details at this point.

In the schizophrenic, sexuality expresses itself, first of all in the sexual character of most deliria which are particularly prominent at the onset of the illness. Thus, we have a girl who became ill soon after she had found her ideal man in a certain policeman. In the hospital, she hallucinates of scenes with her lover. She telephones him that the family is away and that he can come to visit her. She demands that we open the window so that she can talk to him. When this is not done, she quickly finds another solution. She talks to him through the steam-pipes which for her represent the window. She does not present us with a well thought through performance: the execution of her ideas appears rather artificial and caricatured; the temporal sequence is not too well maintained; she often goes back on some of her notions, repeats requests with which her lover already complied. Her spatial ideas, too, are rather vague and free. It does not worry her in the least to lie on the floor and to maintain that thereby she is telephoning or talking through the window. Her sentences are not always completed or grammatically correct. But the trend of her thoughts can be followed without any difficulty, once one has recognized the main idea; and one was bound to recognize it without asking any questions by simple, patient observation of her apparently senseless behavior.

As her second attack of illness is nearing, a well-educated woman enters the study of a music teacher and declares that she intends to work there from now on. It takes a good deal of effort to get her out of there. Then the delirium breaks out during which she enacts an amorous fantasy she had elaborated for several months. She is in love with a music teacher, though not the man into whose home she had forced her way; that incident represented merely a symptomatic act. Now in her delirium, she is engaged to her music teacher, marries him and becomes pregnant with twins. One child looks like her and the other resembles the father. She finally delivers her twins and a remission sets in. She had done all kinds of incomprehensible things during her delirium. She must have considered her immediate environment as an obstacle and reacted to it with corresponding hostility; but she had done so inconsistently because, outside of the dream, she had fully registered the reality around her. When she was particularly pleased with her doctor, he was incorporated in her erotic system in some, not entirely explicable, way—usually, in such cases the doctor is partially or completely identified with the lover. Although we did not understand all the details, her behavior was very symbolic; she gave him poems which she had composed, wrapped up in many pieces of paper, the inner one of which contained a few strands of her pubic hair, some menstrual blood, or occasionally a little feces. Such little gifts were still being made at a time when she was sufficiently clear to converse with me about art, and similar subjects; her discrimination of judgment was decidedly superior to mine.

Such deliria may be elaborated throughout an entire lifetime. I know of a catatonic who became ill in 1874; from then on she lived with the imaginary child of her lover, for the most time identifying the child with the lover. Even now, in 1911, she has not yet come out of this dream.

In some cases, the sexuality manifests itself in less pleasant forms. It is frequently mixed with anxiety-producing ideas which, in turn, will modify the deliria. A patient hallucinated that her mother had complained about her to the patient's father; then her father "looked at her in a very strange way." He thrust a spear into her lower abdomen, at the same time dancing about in a very peculiar fashion. He was all black and completely nude. He often came to her bed like that, all black; and occasionally he also appeared to her in the form of a bull. The patient related that her father had often beaten her—and wanted to abuse her sexually. He often played with her genitalia and must have gone even further. Thus the fear of the father was quite understandable. That the attack with the spear was a sexual one is proved by the completely erotic expression of the patient as she related the hallucination which, in its contents, gave no such direct evidence apart from the frequent occurrence of such things in sexual context. While the patient related her tale, she hid her face with a guilty embarrassed laugh. When she spoke about the real attacks on her by her father she showed the same attitude that a healthy person would have; her tone of voice was objective, somewhat embarrassed, but not with active erotism.

A young man had the following delirium: he saw his sister dressed in "the costume of a ballet-dancer;" she was like Diana. Near her stood a marvelously handsome youth whom the patient, himself, had created by virtue of the connection of his grey matter to the world; "that is the arsenia which I have in my brain, it is the same thing as ambrosia." The youth is called Pseudo-N. (N. is the patient's own name.) He looked very much like the patient; he also was like Apollo. He wanted to rape Diana. The patient feared that she would finally surrender and then he would be banished from the world for 7000 years. He also related another version of the same tale, seeing himself and his sister in heaven.

In truth, he had had a (one-sided) relationship to his older sister which dated back to his fourth year, at a time when the girl herself was just blossoming out physically and sexually. Now he is constantly preoccupied with his delusional constructions. He resents the slightest interruption from the outside world because it tends to tear him away from his thoughts. Therefore he believes his environment to be hostile to him and becomes very unpleasant if one merely enters his room.

During an attack of fury, another patient saw Judas Iscariot threatening her with a sword. This is very similar to the previous case, where the patient's love for his sister was symbolically expressed by the myth of Apollo and Diana. Here Judas represents the faithless lover, a comparison which is frequently made. The meaning of the sword is less obvious. However, for this patient, as for all others, the sword has the same symbolic meaning as the spear wielded by the father in the previous case and the knife in the hands of the "black men" who appear to the hysterics and schizophrenics: they are symbols of the aggressive, male, sexual organ.[55] In mythology, Apollo's arrow has the same significance: as a sun ray or as a sexual organ, the arrow fertilizes, or kills.

I have heard two healthy women employ the words, sword and spear, in the same sense (irrespective of the idea of defloration). These weapons are always named in connection with other sexual images. "I have avoided the doctor because his eyes seemed to bore daggers into me so that I often have a burning pain in my side" (pointing to her genital region and only after a few repetitions to the lumbar region). She continued with marked sexual excitement: "I had thought I could not love him at all."[56] Very frequently the patients employ the various symbols interchangeably. One of our paranoids spontaneously changed the "fiery lance" in her body to "many fiery needles" while she was being questioned about her body hallucinations. Then the "lance" became a "thick thing" that was thrust into her chest and lower abdomen, whereby she exhibited a great deal of affect in relation to her lower abdomen but none to that of the chest. The "needle," too, is frequently used in the same sense. The symbolic significance of the needle was particularly apparent in the case of a young catatonic woman who blushed whenever she saw a needle. Occasionally, the revolver has the same meaning: one of our hebephrenics was persecuted by a man with a revolver who demanded that she do the most shameful things. Another

---

55. Kraepelin's (388, p. 198) "stiletto attached to the marriage certificate" can be understood in the same way.

56. A certain hebephrenic with marked homosexual tendencies ejaculates when his eyes and his anus are hallucinatorily penetrated by knives.

is shot in the leg by a revolver. Men, too, will think of the revolver in the same sense.

It is very characteristic that generally the commonly used symbols for the male sex organ are nearly always objects which arouse emotions, especially fright[57]. Sausages, candles, staves and similarly innocent objects, which are frequently employed in the common obscenities of both the young and the old, can appear in schizophrenia, and in dreams, as representatives of the genitalia only in very definite constellations. Thus Jung's patient B. S., speaks of pork sausages, which attain their symbolic significance by virtue of the symbolic substitution of "mouth" for the vagina, and "eating" for intercourse. The stick appears as the magic wand or as the "red staff of life." These examples illustrate the tremendous importance the affects play in the process of symbolization. Objective similarity is often merely incidental; far more important is the affective one.

Certainly, this factor also accounts for the significance of the most common sexual symbol, the snake. We constantly find it in hallucinations; and we have never yet analyzed this symbol without clearly establishing its sexual connotation. A young hebephrenic girl of blameless conduct, had "not at all unpleasant appearances of a black man or a snake coming toward her." A presenile woman saw an angel, then, "A snake came and wound itself around the angel; then the snake protruded in front, quite stiffly (the patient demonstrated with her finger the position of the erect penis) but the snake did nothing evil." In another patient, "The snake entered her vulva to drink."[58] Occasionally the snake is referred to as "fiery," but far more rarely than the sword or lance.

A hebephrenic complained that a snake had wrapped itself around him with its head in front of the patient's mouth into which the snake injected some poison. By means of his anamnesis, our suspicions were confirmed: he was a pederast and was reproaching himself for it.

Other animals, as well, often become sexual symbols. Besides the snake, we find the horse, which is feared by many a young girl and often appears in their nightmares.[59] The bull also appears as a sexual symbol; it was mentioned in one of the previous examples. The horse may also appear in the form of "two rocking-horses in the bed; they cannot be seen but only felt by the rhythmical rocking of the bedclothes; they are N. N. and X. X." (the patient's friends to whom she

57. Even here the ambivalence of sexuality becomes manifest.

58. Mörike's *First Song of Love to a Girl.* In dreams of the healthy, in myths, in Swedenborg, wherever we look, the snake is a sexual symbol.

59. The horse also symbolizes desires and aspirations to climb up on the social scale.

has attached her sexual delusions). Dogs and cats, whose sexual activities are known to every child, are also common symbols. The patients can feel these animals inside and on their bodies; they see dogs pursuing them, etc. The mouse is used similarly to the snake. We have more than once seen that the same hallucination was called a mouse, a rat, or a snake. Occasionally the mouse will begin to swell under the very eyes of the patient and turn into a large rat. Of the more exotic animals, the elephant also proves to be a sexual animal (on the occasion of perception tests, when pictures of animals are shown the patients). Probably it is the animal's size and trunk which invoke the symbolism. I recall only two instances of the elephant appearing as a distinctly sexual symbol in delusions. In one case, it represented a great physician to whom the patient had linked her sexual hallucinations; the other time it appeared in the hallucinations of a very young hebephrenic at the onset of her illness, which was distinguished by marked sexual preoccupations. A woman patient complained about our "hay-snout-beds" (hay is vulgarly used for "pubic"); there were a number of men who left "their hay-snouts in her bed" (the expression on her face showed unmistakable sexual excitement). One patient spontaneously characterized all the animals which served as sexual symbols as "animal beauties."

The idea of intercourse is often expressed by that of murder[60] —in an active sense by the males, in a passive sense by the women.[61] A catatonic woman is sexually excited by her priest. He looks at her in church with "a deadly glance;" and she feels this glance through her whole body. Furthermore, she has nightmares about dead people. As she relates her dreams, she has an ecstatic, erotic expression on her face which cannot possibly be misunderstood. Another catatonic woman, also in love with a preacher, writes in a letter: "The preacher of the Reformed Church must annihilate me." At times the nurse—*faute de mieux*—serves as the patient's love object. In this sense she once said she would love to squeeze the nurse against her own body till the nurse got so thin that she could kindle her. A third catatonic constantly verbigerates: "Murder me, dog; murder me." At the same time, however, she passionately kisses her own hands, makes other sexual gestures and interjects many sexual expressions. Another patient awakens from sleep with a scream and cries out: "The murderer is coming, he has been whoring with the women patients."

60. This use of the word, murder, is not to be confused with its use as a designation for all sorts of abuse and mistreatment.

61. In Hauptmann's *Der Arme Heinrich,* we find the passage: "Sweet death will take me away." Another poet writes: "Do not let your heart love, oh child, for loving means dying, love is death."

War and duels are also symbols of cohabitation. One of our hebephrenics displayed distinct, sexual interest in the events of the Russo-Japanese War which for her had also some other connotations that were not at all clear to me. (See below, Religious Wars.)

The delusion of being killed can also express the wish to die. Although the delusional idea of being murdered is usually meant in a sexual sense, this is not invariably so, but as yet we cannot prove with any degree of certainty any other origin of this delusion. Perhaps the following would be a case in point: A girl was abandoned by her lover after she had become pregnant; she engaged in stealing and was particularly grieved by the thought of having estranged her own parents. She "belonged to no one; she must be killed." She was unable to write a letter to her parents because of the complete thought deprivation which set in whenever she attempted to write them; but she was able to write to her lover.

The idea of being burned or having been burnt is very clearly related to and often completely identical with the delusion of being murdered. In this way the heat and fire of love is expressed, as in the symbols of flaming swords, lances, and needles. Occasionally we also find the lover making his visits in the form of a fiery man, or he appears in the patient's bed, "his entire genital area glowing red like an oven."

In this way we can also understand the girl who had been brought up asexually without success, when she tells us in her soft, gentle voice how much she feared the "murderous looking knife which continues to burn and scorch her." During an examination, a catatonic responds only with rare, fragmented, hesitating sentences. To the question, "What has happened to Konrad?" (her lover), she answers promptly with a lively facial expression and in an entirely altered tone of voice: "Must I be burned? Must I be killed?" Women patients often complain that people consider them to be prostitutes, and add: "Yes, yes, I know; I won't allow them to burn me" or something similar. Fire is also linked with anxiety: "It is almost as if I had a fire burning inside of me, thus I am afraid night and day." In the latter patient, as in many others, the idea of fire led to the notion of being in Hell or of going to be condemned to Hell (two ideas which are not always differentiated). A male patient generalizes the sensations that his genitalia are being burned into the notion that his whole body is in flames. Later on, he dampens the fire and, by virtue of displacement, he merely has a feeling of heat in his head. The original hallucination stemmed from the sexual stimulation aroused in him by his housekeeper's daughter. Thus, in his hallucinations the girl threatened him with burning, while the harmless mother of the girl consoled him by saying that he would not be condemned to burn.

A paranoid has the delusion that his wife is faithless and dead; he himself is being accused of having had intercourse with his sister-in-law. Once he heard a cry which meant that at this very moment his wife had died. At the same time, he felt as if a flame had been torn out of his heart. Another patient complained that there was a woman lying under him who wanted to seduce him in order to kill him by fire. For this patient the idea of fire has also another meaning: he believes that after his having been seduced, stinging, burning salves were rubbed all over him.

The identification of fire with intercourse is also used by the patients in relation to other persons: a jealous husband maintains that his wife has employed a man to set fire to her bed under her behind.

A woman has the delusion that someone wants to set fire to her house; she actually suspects one of her boarders. In the very same tone, as if she were talking about the same matter, she states that she is afraid that one day this boarder may go so far as to make her pregnant.

In this instance, the fire which is consuming the house does not have the usual meaning of "setting fire to a house." It also signifies the abolishment of the family, an idea which is mainly produced by unsatisfied sexuality. A woman, unhappy with her husband, becomes mentally ill during the course of her second pregnancy; she becomes jealous and suspicious. The voices command her to set fire to the house as a sacrifice to God. (Later she also wanted to sacrifice her son.) Another woman in love with her priest fears at first that her house will go up in flames. One day she believes that it has actually been set on fire; she runs out of the house and wants to see God. Afterwards, she claims that she is married to her beloved. Another woman, whose husband was a scoundrel, saw and heard the persons who were setting fire to her home; in her hallucinations also her child died. The woman who had three imaginary children in her body had attempted to set fire to her home, "the house of misfortune and unhappiness."

We saw one case in which we could not with certainty link the notion of fire to sexuality: this was a catatonic who had shot and killed his mother and injured his father in order to keep them from poverty. The following night he dreamed that his parents' home was on fire; he was sitting on the roof of the house, motionless and dumbfounded. (Nonetheless, there were some indications that there was a one-sided sexual attachment to his mother.)

Anxiety is closely related to the previously discussed symbols of intercourse. After all, for decades, psychiatrists have known that there was some connection between anxiety and sexuality in view of the fact that sexuality arouses anxiety; and that, conversely, masturbation is often compulsively practiced in anxiety states.[62] Freud recently explained all pathological anxiety as a transformation of repressed sexual libido. I cannot understand why there may not also be anxiety in the face of a threat to the very existence of an individual as well as sexual anxiety. On the other hand, I certainly must confirm that in pathological cases, as well as in the dreams which we have been able to analyze, only the sexual anxiety has been demonstrated with any certainty. Precisely what the relationship between sexuality and anxiety is, still remains unclear to me; but this much is certain, it does exist.[63]

One can assume that suppression of sexual drives—being harmful to the species—may produce anxiety, as would great danger to an individual's existence, but this is merely analogy. Furthermore, we know that, particularly in women but also in men, sexual excitement is bound up with anxiety symptoms, with fear, and tremors. We also know that, not only among human beings but also in many of the lower and higher animals, the female often offers lively resistance to courtship which is all the more striking since the female frequently takes the initiative as soon as the male seems inclined to withdraw. We could assume that a certain regulation takes place of the two tendencies opposing each other—a phenomenon we can frequently find in physiology and psychology—and that the inhibition is exactly that which we call anxiety. But we cannot neglect the question why it should appear precisely when the act is suppressed.

Thus, when it has been possible to analyze it, we always find anxiety in connection with sexual symptoms. However, if one considers the "black man with his knife" as the primary factor, then in such cases the anxiety would be an individual's anxiety. However, we know the sexual significance of the "black man"; and every day we see manifestations of the same sort of anxiety at a time when the individual is not being threatened. Furthermore, we can easily explain why the sexual symbol appears, but we do not know the significance of the physical threat in such cases.

For the most part, anxiety manifests itself under the cloak of such a threat. Sometimes this threat is not found at all. A catatonic displayed anxiety attacks devoid of content; in one such attack he demanded to

62. Cf. Cullerre (145), Oppenheim (529a), Muthmann (502a) and Bernhard.

63. Stekel offers some elucidations which help in the understanding of these relationships, but unfortunately they still do not constitute an explanation. Anxiety states due to poor cerebral circulation do not belong to the clinical picture of dementia praecox.

have a girl; in another, he masturbated. A female catatonic with rather marked negativism masturbated regularly when she was compelled to do something such as eat, sit, get dressed, etc.[64]

Many authors have long been aware of the transformation of sexual drives (Freud's "sublimation") into religious ideas and feelings. Many sick individuals, as well as healthy ones, consciously seek in religion a substitute for the love-affairs which they did not have. However, as soon as the disease process begins to disrupt the thinking, the repressed erotic complex emerges again and becomes fused with the religious ideas. Thus the Savior or God or whoever else represents the focus of the religious interests frequently takes on the distinct traits of the loved object. A woman patient who was in love with a minister draws a picture of God wearing the minister's bands and pince-nez. Even Christ was drawn dressed in the attire of a Protestant minister. One patient once drew a picture of Christ hanging on the cross with an erect penis. According to the patient's own explanation, this drawing represented the good man; she drew another picture of a man on the cross with a detumescent penis; he personified the bad man. Another drawing of a crucified figure, resembling the first, had two erect male organs. Later the patient claimed she was married to the Holy Ghost.

A latent hebephrenic was no longer in love with her husband and obtained a divorce. On the day the final decree in the action was handed down, she saw a vision of God who promised her a million; but her husband stole the million from her. God also told her, "Do not abandon your first love since it will keep whatever it promised." God spoke the Bavarian dialect, had blond hair, checkered trousers—in brief, he resembled in every detail a certain Mr. H. who was the man she had been in love with prior to her marriage. At the same time, "The whole power of God, the Suns and the Stars glowed brilliantly. But he who is mentioned in the hymn-books as the consoler—I know him in life. He is dressed in coat and trousers like the Lord God and speaks in the Bavarian dialect." Christ and the Virgin Mary were also represented by her family; she herself was Jehovah. She was not God but God's disciple; she sat at His right. The King of Glory was Mr. H. When she talked about the latter (and often quite profanely) she always mixed in a deluge of biblical phrases. Since she had ceased loving him, her husband

64. There are also healthy individuals who have ejaculations during states of anxiety. A certain young man is subject to such pollutions whenever he has to hurry, e.g., to catch a train. Children also betray sexual stimulation when they are anxious or fear a teacher (Cf. Krafft-Ebing and Moll). According to Freud, anxiety dreams have a sexual basis. Decades ago, Savage was aware of the connection between the melancholic anxieties and sexuality.

had appeared to her in the most varied forms, but he always had black hair (as he actually did). She spoke of him usually as "the black *ones*" and had divorced the black *ones*.

Among the male patients, a female saint generally represents the loved object. Yet schizophrenic men are not in the least embarrassed to be married even to God or Christ. Thus in the patient mentioned above whose first erotic feelings were directed to his sister, Christ appeared to him as a very pretty girl who looked just like his sister.

More frequently, however, the men become very active in religion. They are prophets, Christ, or even God to whom naturally all the delights of Paradise are available. In their god-like attributes and in accordance with well-known models, they can also love a terrestrial woman.

Very commonly the Devil plays the same role which in the above-mentioned examples has been assigned to benign persons. A sexually abstinent woman has been "led into temptation" by God's spirit, partaking of every conceivable joy. She saw and heard the Devil whom she identified without being aware of it, with the spirit of God. More commonly, the Devil alone appears. A girl saw the Devil with the face of her employer; the Devil did all sorts of things with his magic wand which she felt in her genitalia. Often, the Devil has very distinct features of the lover or of another man who had aroused the patients sexually.

Apart from such relatively simple and easily understood ideas, there remain many obscure ones which are distorted to the point of incomprehensibility and often combined with various different elements. Each night a patient receives a beautiful child from her pastor. "Quite obviously she is the means of the religious war." Knowing that a battle is often the symbol for intercourse, we can understand what she is referring to. A childless woman who hated her husband—especially during her menopause—constantly moaned that in religious wars a great many children were killed. The schizophrenic mixture of different ideas which are held together merely by external connections is very evident in a patient's statements who said, with every sign of sexual excitement: "The nurses are also Jesus-blood; they have also sinned." Jesus and sin are certainly connected but not in this way.

It is very likely that religious associations also determine the frequent associative linking of flesh and genitals. A very intelligent catatonic with delusions of having sinned greatly said point-blank that he did not eat meat because it reminded him of carnal lust. During an experiment, a hebephrenic associated to the word, "love"—"that is a carnal sacrifice."

Sin and sexuality are linked as frequently in schizophrenia as in normal life. Sexual sins play an important role in the patients' self-reproaches even when, at first, other things are admitted and confessed which are easier said and thought.

The need for cleanliness and purity, and the feeling of being impure and unclean have a similar origin. Earlier writers had already noted that such obsessive ideas readily appear in onanists. Freud has shown that feeling of moral uncleanliness is displaced to that of physical uncleanliness. Observations on schizophrenics prove him to be quite correct. A patient stated bluntly: "I cannot give you my hand because I have masturbated." A woman patient who has been aroused, among other things, by holding a cat against her genitalia, suffered very markedly from obsessive ideas of cleanliness. Particularly when she saw a cat, she felt compelled to wash her hands, "in order to prevent absorbing anything harmful or poisonous."[65] In a similar context, a lady wanted to have her window kept open at all times because of the impure air. In a very sensitive woman this connection could be demonstrated experimentally. She would often refuse to shake hands in a very negativistic fashion, although she was otherwise very friendly and pleasant during the conversation. She could not give any reason for her behavior or, if she did, it was that her hands perspired too freely, which in fact, was not true. It then came out that this fear of shaking hands always appeared whenever anything in the conversation touched on her masturbation complex.

A catatonic had jumped out of the attic window of his house in an utterly senseless fashion; before jumping he had taken his bed apart and put it together again. He claimed that he only wanted to look out of the window (actually he had jumped out). He had no idea why he had taken the bed apart, but "he knew that he was a sinner." This connection of the taking apart of a bed and sin permits us to suspect that it, too, was an onanistic cleanliness complex. Other associations and the direct information supplied by the patient corroborated this interpretation beyond any doubt.

Not sin, but shame about masturbation and the feeling that others can detect the vice from the patient's appearance, is at times expressed by a refusal to show one's face. This symptom is a fairly common catatonic peculiarity which certainly has also other causes. For a long time this was the only prominent symptom in a young girl during the early stages of the manifest illness. She was unable to speak to anyone without keeping her face turned away or covered. She, herself, gave the reason.

---

65. Although as yet I have not found any but a sexual compulsion to wash, one should still be cautious in explaining the symptom. I have seen two children, one and two years of age, who made the following gestures when they refused to comply with a demand: one would wring his hands in the same way as adults wash their hands; the other would wipe off his hands on his clothes.

However, even long after she had been in remission and was working, she could not free herself from this "obsessive idea." Another patient invariably found herself unable to answer the questions as to why she always kept her face covered and why she always placed her left index finger in her ear at every sexual allusion.[66]

Self-reproach may also be an expression of the desire to have intercourse, e. g., when a patient accuses himself of having raped someone, which he never did. The ideas of having sinned usually center around masturbation. I have seen only two cases where different vices constituted the content of these ideas. One case was that of a hebephrenic who was inconsolable because in his youth he had stolen some apples from a tree. The tree was later included in all his other delusional ideas. The other case was that of a young catatonic who had at one time actually stolen some candy and a few cans of sardines. In his delirium, they became diamonds of great value for which theft he was condemned to hell forever. In both these patients, however, we have some reasons to suspect that behind these self-accusations was a masturbation-complex, after all.

Another form of negating sexual thoughts is that of psychogenic vomiting and disgust which, as Freud has found, mainly signifies sexual disgust.[67] A patient left her husband who was distasteful to her. When he suddenly appeared to take her home, she began to vomit and her vomiting persisted for three weeks. Over a long period of time, another patient talked of nothing but the pains in her genital region; this notion was somehow related to raising skirts and something rather nauseating. Once she heard voices which talked of raising skirts and immediately began to vomit although her physical health was excellent. We have often seen persistent or episodic attacks of vomiting after rapes. A patient was sexually abused at the age of fourteen; since then she had had anxiety dreams of lances and bulls. She fell in love when she was nineteen, but the lovers had to separate. After this event she developed a catatonic depression which lasted one year, during this period her hallucinations had the same content as her dreams and were accompanied by sexual excitement. Since then, she frequently has had such dreams and hallucinations which are now accompanied by nausea, vomiting,

---

66. Just why the masturbation-complex is so frequent and dominates the picture with such elementary force in neurotics and schizophrenics cannot as yet be stated with any degree of certainty. After all, there are other sins which are far worse. In our patients, perhaps, "sin" is not to be understood in its religious sense at all. I would rather say that the "pangs of conscience" are the primary expression of the perverse practice of the most powerful natural drive.

67. See also H. Müller (499a).

feelings of disgust, and a sensation of constriction in the parts of her body where the man had grasped her (Jung).

Freud has drawn our attention to the fact that there is an unconscious sexual attachment between father and daughter and between mother and son which manifests itself particularly strongly in children. We have found this "Oedipus complex" more and more frequently since our attention was drawn to it. It is also an important force in the choice of love objects in both the healthy and the sick. A patient claimed that his mother had poisoned his father. Once he woke up at night believing his mother had forced her way into his room; he was lying uncovered and had an erection; therefore his mother must have carried on all sorts of misdeeds with him.

Parents may also have their Oedipus complexes. A catatonic pushed her son away when he came to visit her. She felt a burning in her heart, right under the skin and nerves, as if one had touched them with the fingers. She once had similar sensations with distinct erotic coloring in relation to her ward-physician when he had to bend over her during an examination. She was jealous of her daughter (during her delusions, but not, in the intact part of her personality) because the latter had become engaged to a young man. Very likely, this engagement had precipitated the outbreak of the mother's disease. She insisted that the daughter had been kicked out of the house by her husband, was pregnant, a whore, and had drowned herself.

Sometimes the Oedipus complex is produced secondarily by identification of the child with the lover. Two women were jealous of their husbands because they had the children at home with them; a third one was jealous of God who had taken her child. All three husbands and God were accused of perpetrating unnatural acts on their children. (Transitivistic transference of their own sexual love.)

We have often spoken here of sexuality even where the uninitiated could not have easily detected any such connections. This is due to the fact that sexual feelings and ideas are often concealed, particularly by displacement of genital concepts upward. To begin with, the areas around the genital region, the rectum, and especially the anus often have sexual significance. Psychogenic pruritis which affects the vulva easily passes over to the anus even when originally it was a purely sexual symptom. A woman patient who, at first, put her finger constantly into her vagina, later, in spite of all counter-measures, put her finger into the anus. Occasionally, defecation can become a symbol of birth.[68] A cata-

68. Kaiser reports: "Last night she smeared feces and stated the next morning that she had delivered a baby."

tonic woman constantly touched her genital area with her hand; then she put her hand under her armpit; later into or on her mouth; finally sticking her finger into her ear.

In two female patients we could follow how certain swaying movements of the pelvic were displaced upwards, inasmuch as the original movements were changed directly into swaying movements of the head in one patient; and in another, these movements first affected the abdomen, then the chest, and finally the head.

The mouth is the most common symbol of the vagina; it is used either alone or in connection with other displacements.[69] The illusionary children are usually born from the mouth. A woman patient, for whom the doctor wanted to pour some milk, said to him: "Yes, but you can't marry me." Another patient saw an angel, who represented her husband, "putting the red stalk of life into the mouth" of her dead cousin. (Other expressions of the patient clearly established that this act was supposed to be intercourse.) Another patient called her sexual feelings, "baskets," at the same time she felt a pain in her lower abdomen and received something white on her finger which she described as sperma. She also has to stick her finger into her mouth. She now has "many baskets, double baskets both above and below"—the upper and lower orifices were thereby identified. A catatonic onanist rubs his finger back and forth in his mouth, and then in his anus. A very mild hebephrenic, over fifty years of age, who still maintained fairly good social relationships, would not let the doctor examine her mouth and showed all signs of sexual embarrassment on these occasions. She behaved in exactly the same way when he had to examine her for cystitis, an examination which she provoked far more often than was necessary.

The eye also serves as a symbol of the female genitalia; whereas the nose can be both the male and female organ, even in the same patient. Women who have to be tube-fed through the nasal passage often complain that they are being sexually abused. Whenever someone touches his nose, a patient proclaims this to mean that he himself is masturbating; he sticks cigarettes up his nose which for him is a conscious symbolic act representing intercourse.[70]

Both men and women, often consider tube-feeding and injections as sexual attacks—occasionally though with slight re-interpretations. A

---

69. Cf. Jung's patient, B. S.

70. Jung studied a mentally normal man who associated in an experiment the word, "nose," to everything which could possibly be related to sexuality. He, himself, could not, at first, explain this although he stated that he was still suffering from the consequences of a venereal infection. Only during the night it occurred to him that at school the nose was often compared to the genital.

catatonic related with unequivocal expressions of sexual stimulation: "The doctor slipped a hose into my tube which went straight to my heart." After an injection a patient dreamed that the doctor had stuck a pencil into her right arm (where the needle had actually been inserted). The pencil immediately emerged from her vagina. She was not quite sure whether he had not also pushed it in there. In accordance with these ideas, the injected fluid is often called "snake-poison."

Genital sensations are often displaced to other parts of the abdomen and pelvis. When the healthy person, instead of saying genitals, speaks of abdomen and lower abdomen, the expression is for him merely a metaphor; he still thinks only of what is really meant. But, the schizophrenics transform, so to speak, the metaphor into reality. They truly feel their hallucinations in the part of the body designated by the word; and the scope of the displacement is actually much broader than the normal's expressions of expedience. Snakes and mice climb up "from the belly to the head"; the gastric region is often the starting point. Only after one has listened to the patients longer or even asked a few more questions they will also mention the genital region—with distinctly increased signs of emotionality. The displacement upward can be so complete that in the hallucinations any connection with the genitals is entirely severed—though the genitals originally gave rise to the hallucinations. A remarkable combination was found in a patient who "felt in the organ of hearing and in mental activity the sensations of love." Apparently she was not referring to auditory hallucinations. A paranoid patient complained that he was being shampooed (imaginarily), that is, his head was being rubbed, which meant masturbation. Another spoke of the parts of the body with which one sinned, pointing to the lateral parts of the body.

Many hallucinatory states are of sexual origin. One of our patients related that, sometimes before the hallucinations (mostly visual) set in at night, "I felt the most delightful sensations throughout my body." Visions which persistently take on increasingly larger dimensions and are accompanied by anxiety are nearly always sexual. Most hallucinations of body sensations certainly have the same source.

We have already mentioned burning and it seems superfluous to go into all the sexual horrors of which both male and female patients complain; horrors in which "nature is drawn off," in which a woman is abused, etc. They are all quite obviously sexual. In this category also belong the common "electricity" sensations,[71] i. e., in both senses of

71. More recently electricity has been replaced by X-rays. Thus, a woman patient was abused with X-rays; her description of their size and appearance exactly fitted the penis.

the term. In the one sense, the electricity is linked up with a "sweet delicious feeling" which a poet described as the electrical shock one received on touching the beloved one for the first time after having admired her only from a distance. A sexually aroused hebephrenic hallucinates an officer who sucks on his penis and sends electricity through him. But patients also call, electrical, some other sensations of a tickling or a pricking nature, which perhaps have no analogy in the normal. At any rate, I have very often heard patients complaining about such feelings in a sexual connection; quite often this sensation seems to start at the back of the head. Many far more crude sexual sensations occur: thus one patient is "electrically connected with a woman; this is a torture worse than crucifixion." Many of the feelings of muscular tension and constriction, which the normal person can understand more easily, also belong here. The sensations may turn into actual disturbances of motility. Many cramps may be caused in this way. The similarity of an epileptic attack to an orgasm had already been noted by the ancients. I mention it at this point without attempting to draw any definite conclusions from the resemblance. One of our patients often had orgastic attacks during the night accompanied by groaning, sensations of paralysis, loss of urine, and vomiting. Another patient "was overcome by such intensely voluptuous feelings that he had to grip the bed post." During this process she became cold and rigid. These "voluptuous feelings also climb into her head"; then she cannot think any more. It is as if a stop-clock had been suddenly turned in her head (general blocking). The hysteriform arching of the back is also a sexual symptom. In one instance this was evident only by the fact that the patient raised her abdomen and pelvis whenever a man passed by her. Another patient told us that the cramp always started when she was thinking of her lover who seemed to draw her up by her labia.

We have already learned that rhythmical movements[72] can have a sexual meaning. We observed two women who, after the death of their husbands, made such rhythmical pelvic movements; later these movements spread to the legs. But only one of the two women was definitely schizophrenic.

Sometimes the masturbatory movements become stereotyped. We have already mentioned the catatonic who constantly kept her finger in her anus over a period of years. Another of our patients performed his masturbatory movements always a little higher on his body until he finally reached his mouth. He claimed that he had a hundred penes and therefore could never finish. As his movements gradually approached

---

72. Cf. movements of the head; also "the rocking-horses in the patient's bed."

the mouth, he hit upon the notion that he had to fill his empty head. Thus the movements had two meanings; downward movements served the purpose of masturbation, and the movements toward the mouth the purpose of filling his head, or eating.

Such practices as the smearing of feces and urine are also sexual symbols, a fact which has been known for a long time. Many of these sick women urinate during their orgasms. It seems that in women the act of urination is linked closely with sexuality. Schizophrenics can also experience pleasurable feelings in connection with defecation (Schreber).

Other anomalies of the sexual drive can arise by way of displacement. Not every catatonic who seeks to have intercourse with his ward-mates has homosexual tendencies. In fact, the patient can simply disregard, or better yet hallucinate, the appropriate sexual partner. A man ran about looking for his (imaginary) wife. Then, for a long time he stared at the doctor whom he recognized as such, finally blurting out: "But you are really my beloved." Afterwards he asked one of the other doctors whether he was not his wife, unbuttoning his trousers as he spoke. On the following day the patient said to the same physician: "I don't know whether you are a representative of a young lady. Yesterday, I saw one here who looked very much like you." When his attention was called to the doctor's beard, he looked closely at the doctor and then said: "In the theater women often play the roles of men." Some time later he grasped the doctor's hand and exclaimed, filled with rapture: "Aren't you the young girl who took lessons from me?" Later, he approached other patients in the same way. Another catatonic transferred his love to men after he had been sexually aroused by a girl who did not permit his advances. But he was still quite capable of recognizing the true sex of his desired fellow patients and fellow workers.

The drawings of many patients also reveal the symbolism of love. They entwine different letters or circles; others draw genitals more or less openly. Whoever is a bit more skillful goes even further. A young married woman drew numerous knights with lances, and left no doubt as to their meaning when she drew two figures with the lances protruding from the trousers in the position of an erect penis. The woman who was in love with her priest ultimately identified her beloved with the Holy Ghost. This gave her the opportunity for a beautiful apotheosis: she drew herself as Mary, and the Holy Ghost as a sun with its rays where the genitals should be; to the right and left she placed two stylized praying angels. The drawing was repeated many times; ultimately it became so abbreviated as to be unrecognizable.

Though greatly condensed, the following example may serve as a concrete illustration of the process by which sexual feelings and ideas are formed into a system: A young servant girl felt herself bewitched by her employer who had "set up" a magic wand (she illustrates with her finger the position of an erect penis). The magic wand, or "a snake," is also drawn through her mouth. She has attacks in which she "arches her back" accompanied by coital movements and orgasm, without any active participation on her part. This occurred for the first time while she was sitting in the audience at the theater. One of the actors, a young teacher, sat with his legs spread apart. The patient had the feeling that he was looking at her in a very special way (previously she had had an affair with a teacher). When he knocked his elbows against a chair, she felt the thrust pass through her whole body. She heard him say to her that "she should do it for him." Her legs and then her labia were spread apart; she felt as if she were being hoisted into the air by her labia, culminating in sensations of intercourse. Subsequently, she developed similar attacks whenever she was sexually excited. While in the hospital, she even had an attack of this kind when a clothes brush which had a long handle (!) was placed on the table near her bed. The peculiar feeling that her labia were being spread apart and pulled up was to be explained by the fact that, years before, a faithless lover had satisfied himself and her by such manipulations with his fingers. Although she knew that these attacks were not true intercourse, nevertheless, once while she was straining at stool, she was not quite clear whether or not she had given birth to a child and was afraid to flush the toilet, for which she was reprimanded.

Not all the pathological manifestations of schizophrenia can be related directly to wishes and fears. When one patient declares that she is Switzerland, or when another wants to take a bunch of flowers to bed with her so that she will not awaken any more—these utterances seem to be quite incomprehensible at first glance. But we obtain a key to the explanation by virtue of the knowledge that these patients readily substitute similarities for identities and think in symbols infinitely more frequently than the healthy: that is, they employ symbols without any regard for their appropriateness in the given situation.

The most irrelevant and unessential part may be utilized to represent the whole idea. In the entire poem and story of the *Cranes of Ibykus*, the idea of "free" (that is, free of blame and error) plays a very minor role indeed. Nonetheless, it gave B. S. the occasion to identify herself with the cranes because, though not free, she should have been free.

This example also shows in another way how carelessly these patients form their associations. To be sure, the patient is not free; she only should be free. But that does not prevent her from identifying with the Cranes of Ibykus which are partially determined by the idea, "free." Even the plural is completely ignored; she is the cranes although she does not think of herself in the plural. What is more, she *is* the Cranes. (See the previous case of the patient who called her husband "black men.") This highly inappropriate use of the *copula* is quite common among the most varied types of patients. Frequently, however, a symbol "means" something very different to them. But the logical or grammatical form, in which the pathologically associated ideas are linked, is also a matter of indifference to them. In that case, it is very tempting to use the *copula* since, after all, what the patient wants to state is essentially an attribute of the subject. The patient wants to *be* free; he *is* big, etc. Thus the previously cited woman, who called herself the Bride of Jehovah, is "*die*[73] Jehova." Yet she is still capable of noticing the contradiction and correcting herself. Miss B. S., who is the Cranes of Ibykus, had seen the cranes on her entrance into the hospital. They were quite black which signified the mourning over her commitment to the hospital. She would like to be released. The symbol for passage into freedom is for her, as for many patients, the key. Therefore she would like to have the key. She is just as prone to say. "Declare the key," or that "she is the key." She also "possesses" Switzerland; and in the same sense she says, "I am Switzerland." She may also say, "I am freedom," since for her, Switzerland meant nothing else than freedom. In the same way, depressed schizophrenics say of themselves that they are sin. The difference between the use of such phrases in the healthy and in the schizophrenics rests in the fact that in the former it is a mere metaphor, whereas for the patients the dividing line between direct and indirect representation has become obscured. The result is that they frequently think of these metaphors in a literal sense.

Similarities of words play an especially great role. A patient finds a bit of linen thread (*Leinenfaser*) in his food. The sound "*lein*" also appears in the German word, *Feuerlein*; he used to know a Miss Feuerlein. Ergo, he was given to understand that he had an affair with her.

Many a word designates more than one idea. These different ideas may be mistaken for each other, or even identified with each other via the word. (Home as building and as a family; skirt as an article of clothing and as a verb "to avoid"; the symbolic "black" of sin and the color, black.)

---

73. *Die* is the feminine form of the article.

A religious paranoid is named Nägeli.[74] Christ was nailed to the Cross. Therefore, Nägeli is Christ; he has also been nailed. But nails are also required in love. He honors nails highly, but not the nail-hole (he has been separated from his wife). The nail is the symbol of virility; the nail-hole is the symbol of femininity and also of money. In the language of flowers he is called Nägeli as the representative of nails. The woman is represented by the rose, the fickle withering rose. That is the reason why the president of America is called Roosevelt, i. e., the rose of the world, in accord with present-day world philosophy which venerates women. The man is also Adam, or dawn (the slight similarity of these words is sufficient for the schizophrenic to equate them), i. e., King of the Day, or, in the flowery language, Nägeli. The rose is Eve (evening) and Queen of the Night. (Note the identification of not only evening and night, but also that of evening with Queen of the Night, which is an abstract concept.) The patient relates all these things quite spontaneously if one merely listens to him.

The same patient fought the practice of misusing the confederate cross for the purpose of advertising. Once he had to stay in bed for a few weeks because of a number of hypochondriacal complaints. He rather liked staying in bed, because "he was lying on the cross."

Everyday the metaphoric figures of speech, too, give the patients an occasion for the pathological use of symbolism since the metaphors are taken in their literal sense by the patients. A patient, very worried about the financial straits of his family, becomes in his better moods the great merchant, F., a veritable Rothschild around whom the whole world revolves. He actually sees the rotations of the earth and the trees. Another patient complains that the attendant has given him a slap on the face. Investigation did not reveal that the attendant had been at fault in any way. The patient justifies himself: if one is stripped like a skeleton to take a bath, it is a slap in the face. A patient dreams that someone "pulled" (i. e., bought) a mattress from her at a very low price. Then she says, "I shot." (One should also note the unconstrained change of the subject: It was she who sold and the buyer "pulled" the mattress from her. Thus, he should have been the person who shot—pulled the trigger.) A schizophrenic who was very anxious to get married was refused by a widow. This rejection angered him greatly; he built the delusion that it was a sin to have asked her to marry him. He then felt a heavy pressure on his chest as if someone were sitting on him. Possibly it was that woman. Later on he was convinced of it; it was certainly she. He

74. The word is a high German diminutive of *Nagel,* which means the flower *Nelke*= carnation, and also a small nail.

also felt how she, with the help of the devil and spiritists, compressed his body. Other patients hear black, frightful voices; they see their own fate as a black cloud coming down on them; they are all black, like sinners. They have sweet (pleasant) and sour (unpleasant) dreams. They have a taste in their mouths like the "grape-spray-thing" (slaked lime and copper sulphate); it is bitter, i. e., they feel compelled to curse. A paranoid "needs sugar as an antidote to the gall-bitter world complaints." A scholar believes that he is a charade because he cannot understand what is happening to him. A (latent) hebephrenic makes a terrible fuss when anything black is left lying about; he curses and buries it. He had wanted very much to marry a certain Catholic girl, but the black ones (the priests) had prevented it. Therefore he fiercely hates everything black. A catatonic saw the "Social-democracy as a passing phenomenon," going through the room.[75] A paranoid woman could not sleep because she had to carry her husband's mistress on her back. A hebephrenic complains that mail coaches starting from her heart drive around under her skin and then pass out on to the street only to meet with an accident. One coach is green; inside it is the Queen of England whom I had given her. (In the delusions of grandeur of women patients, the Queen of England often represents the highest attainable position for any woman on earth; as Mary signifies the highest in the religious and erotic spheres.) She hopes to become Queen of England; therefore the latter is forced to meet with an accident, and lies dead on the road. Two other coaches, in which the patient's false lovers are riding, are painted yellow. They meet with their accident in the churchyard and the false lovers lie dead there.

One woman claims that someone put money into her purse, i. e., "he reproached her with gold coins by figures of speech." At other times, she identified the coins with snow and the latter with sperm (Danae). A very religious patient had the delusion that the nurse stood on her head, that the nurse was upside down: the nurse was reversed, i.e., she was a convert which the patient herself desired to be. A drunkard's wife believes that she is in hell; she has to haul coals from the devil. A young girl attended a wedding and insisted she had certain claims on the bridegroom. During the ceremony, she saw the bride standing in front of the altar in the form of a dog. The priest who conducted the ceremony had given her something to eat in church so that now she was no longer able to work. As she left the church, she called out to persons passing by: "Both of us are still here"; whereby she obviously wanted to indicate the still existing connection with the bride-

75. Personal communications by Abraham.

groom. The second wife of a widower was convinced that the first wife of her husband was still alive, but she lived only in her husband's heart.

Often, the part idea which gave rise to the symbol is derived, not from the designation, but from the concept itself. For instance, a masturbating hebephrenic, who desired normal sexual intercourse, finds a high peak in a mountain range so shocking that he gets into a fight with his companion and has to return home. This is an analogy which can hardly be called pathological. But what is certainly pathological is the interpretation of the analogy in the sense of the real sexual organ and the correspondingly violent reaction. An analogy which was completely transformed into reality was seen in the case of a female paranoid. She was dissatisfied with her husband, felt cast off by him and therefore maintained she was Genevieve. The food parcels which a catatonic received from home signified freedom to her and were therefore good. The hospital food meant confinement and was, therefore, bad. A Swiss patient had some differences with his wife who was a native of Berlin. He generalized this conflict into the delusion that Switzerland was at war with Prussia. A German woman had married a Swiss citizen who then abandoned her. She proceeded to earn her living as a prostitute among the Italian laborers. This situation gave occasion to the delusion that various "nations" were at war with each other, the Italians protecting the Germans residing in Switzerland. A young girl misbehaved and was very much afraid of her parents' reproaches. She hallucinated that she was being beaten to death, at times by her mother, at other times by her father. A hebephrenic has relations with a Catholic woman. This affair induces him to interpret an unintelligible but earnest and impressive voice as a sign from God that he has been chosen to bridge the cleavage between the Catholics and Protestants by setting a model example (his actual conduct, however, was rather poor indeed). It sounds very much like a conscious allegory when a mathematician relates that the great giant, Think, appeared to him. God wished to kill the giant but could not; then the people tried to kill him. That he, the mathematician, was the giant could be deduced soon afterwards when the patient as the giant, Think, was to be slain by God. God "appeared to him very enormous." However, the patient was just as huge as God at that moment and subdued God, wrestling with him for four hours.

In this context we should also mention the delusion of poisoning. Although it occurs frequently, we have been able to trace its roots only in a few cases. The apparently simple logical explanations of unpleasant body sensations or the desire to leave the hospital ("where one is ruined," where the food is bad, and where the care is viewed as unsatisfactory and/or harmful) are not as helpful in understanding the schizophrenic as normal logic and normal explanations would lead one to believe. Up to now we have never found such ideas to be really at the root of the poisoning delusions. We know that an affective complex of some sort is necessary for the elaboration of a delusion, a complex which involves the patient's ego far more intensely than such ordinary discomforts would. Behind the obsessive thoughts and fears of being poisoned, we find the masturbation complex. It seems conducive to think of it in this connection, too. However, we also often hear such comments as: the patients have poisoned themselves by excessive masturbation, or "the body has been poisoned by abuse"; yet these patients do not show the least evidence of a delusion of poisoning.

The following cases have given us some insight into a few of the ways in which the poisoning delusion arises: A female paranoid is jealous of a woman physician. The patient is being poisoned by that doctor—however, as she expressly adds, not by the food, but by words. The jealousy, in this instance, contributes the affect; the symbol, "poisoned words," furnishes the material for the construction and elaboration of the delusion. Another woman patient had a quarrel with her daughter, just why we do not know. The daughter now "puts poison into her food because she has a salty mouth." This delusion originated in the same way as the delusion in the previous example, only here the patient has gone one step farther; she actually finds the poison in her food although the releasing symbolic figure of speech is still part of the delusion. A hebephrenic woman had a very dear friend whom she loved but could not marry. Later on, a desire for wealth was added to the love complex. She entertained the hope that a rich man, a coffee dealer, would marry her. Since he did not do so he became her persecutor. At this point she refused to drink any coffee. But soon she began to complain that the milk had been poisoned and also refused to drink milk. She gave two explanations: people are envious of her because now she can really marry the coffee dealer; and these people put poison in her milk which she can actually taste. They also made it impossible for her to marry the man she really loved by their poisonous gossip; they had poisoned her relationship (milk) with him. The patient, as was previously mentioned, gave us these explanations herself. She did not distinguish in any way between real and symbolic poisoning. Yet at the very same time, she was perfectly capable of working, could judge situations and people quite correctly as long as they were not connected with her delusions.

A man had an affair with his friend's wife and was called to account. Now he believes himself to be maligned everywhere and "sprayed with poison."

The poisoning delusion of another patient evolved in a more logical fashion. He had set up in business in direct competition with one of his relatives. The business failed; nevertheless he demanded that this relative support him but he did not receive enough. Then came the delusion that this relative had killed the patient's father, who had been dead for some years, because the father had known that the relative was a homosexual. The patient utilized his delusion to blackmail the man; however, he became afraid that the relative would counteract by resorting to arms or poison. In prison, he refused all food for fear of poison. The previously cited impotent man, who was keen on getting rid of his wife, claimed that his wife, among other things, wanted to poison him. But in this instance the choice of the means may have been accidental.

In the following case, we are again dealing with a poisoning delusion but in quite another sense from that of being poisoned by one's enemies. The case also demonstrates how the mechanism of displacement may conceal the meaning of an idea.

A married woman fell mentally ill after she had injected some sublimate of mercury into her vagina in the hope of interrupting a pregnancy. Since then she constantly maintained that she had been poisoned; that it was a terrible tragedy, that the druggist had given her poison, that he ought to be punished. She had read in an encyclopedia that in case of mercurial intoxications blood appeared in the rectum and stools. She then developed the "stereotypy" of continually boring the finger into her rectum in order to convince herself that there was no blood. Neither kindness nor restraint could modify this behavior. She could not prove that she had been poisoned nor could she think of a single symptom. Yet during her lengthy treatment, she could not be convinced that she had not been poisoned. She made her complaints in a completely stereotyped manner without extensive associations, although this educated woman could engage in very interesting and intelligent conversations about other topics. Also her affective expressions were not appropriate to the idea of poisoning; she just complained in certain definite words which did not seem to have any connections. It was quite different if one took several hours to talk to the patient. Her constant association to poisoning was her husband whom she praised in such high tones that one suspected her to have something against him. Her husband was a very good husband, a decent husband, the best of husbands—but the tone of voice in which these statements were uttered made one expect them to be followed by a "but." The "but," however, was never expressed. Instead, in completely indifferent tone, she threw in the remark: "My brother doesn't go out at night." The same train of thought was repeated many times in the same stereotyped fashion. But if one made her stick to this theme without suggesting anything, however, one could observe the following: what she stated negatively with good intentions about her brother she really desired to state positively and in derogatory sense about her husband. Finally, it came out that her husband recently stayed away from home a good deal of time and that she feared his having been unfaithful to her. This was the reason why she did not want to have his child and not, as she had claimed at first, because she was afraid of a difficult pregnancy. Once we succeeded in bringing this whole complex into her consciousness and in talking to her about it, her affect became entirely normal and appropriate and it became clear that fragments of its expression had been absorbed in her complaints about poisoning. Anyone who has ever made this experience and checked it several times can no longer doubt that the complex, which made the disease manifest and then dominated the symptomatology—that this complex was the anxiety about the husband's unfaithfulness. Behind this feeling we find another fear: that she was not pretty enough for her husband—a fear which had some justification. She had always considered him to be the most handsome man, whereas she herself was far from pretty. She had more or less forced him into marriage, perhaps with the assistance of her wealth. It is also conceivable that the attempted abortion weighed heavily on her conscience and that, for this reason, the after all not too far-fetched idea of poisoning received its affective charge which was necessary in order to elaborate such a senseless delusional idea; but I found no evidence for this assumption. The woman felt unhappy because she could not trust her husband. On the one hand, her doubts resulted in the desperate fear of a new pregnancy; on the other hand, the unbearable idea of his unfaithfulness usually remained inaccessible to her consciousness, while the affective charge had been displaced to the far more tolerable delusional idea of poisoning.[76]

In our schizophrenic, the "affective cathexis," to use Freud's term,

76. The genesis of this case is very similar to a previously published one: during her puerperium, a hysteric woman feared that her husband wanted to leave her. She then evolved the closely related delusional idea that her child had died; she concentrated her entire affect on this idea while the differences with her husband disappeared completely from her memory (72).

was "displaced" from the unfaithfulness of the husband to the sublimate injection; this shifting of affective cathexis permitted the elaboration of this incident into a delusional idea. The idea of poisoning was a "screen idea" for the idea of unfaithfulness.

By means of displacement, the content of delusions can often become removed a long way from the original idea. In most cases it would be quite impossible to recognize the point of departure if the patients did not always retain the original idea alongside of the new elaboration, or if one could not trace the development of the displacement. However, there are still a good many cases with severe associational disintegration in which we cannot trace the vicissitudes of affective displacement.

A patient had the unconscious wish to have sexual intercourse with her father. This wish found expression in the delusion that her father wanted to kill her. She associated the mother with the father, and ultimately substituted the mother for the father. Thus the original wish finally appeared as the delusion that the mother wanted to kill her. The displacement went much farther in the previously mentioned woman who thought she was a man and possessed testicles which meant that, via Christ, she was in love with a priest. Another patient had the same original delusion. But in place of the priest, there were successively substituted the Holy Ghost, God the Father, and Christ who in turn was represented by a lamb. Now a lamb belongs to a ram. Therefore, "I am a ram," in this case originally meant: "I have obtained my priest." We cannot always determine the extent to which these patients employ such expressions merely symbolically, as a means of designating their delusional idea. It is certain that they often take the new expression of the delusional ideas quite literally and so construct a new delusion (as a rule without surrendering the old). Furthermore, the interpretations of these new elaborations often change in these patients, so that at times the displaced phrase is employed as a symbolic expression of the original delusional idea and, at other times, it is employed in its literal sense as a new delusion. Yet the distinction between these two modes of thinking is not as sharply defined in the sick person as it would be in the healthy.

A rather frequent type of displacement occurs in the following form: in an erotic delusion various persons are substituted in terms of specific analogies. The patient is in love with the superintendent of the factory. In the hospital the patient substitutes the hospital "superintendent" for the factory "superintendent." However, since the former is a physician, all other hospital physicians can represent him. Generally, these different persons are simultaneously more or less condensed into a single person. Another illustration: A young woman was in love with a theological student who did not respond to her advances. Afterwards, she tried in vain to marry another theological student. Finally she married the brother of the first theological student loving her husband exclusively in his brother's image. It was only many years later that she became clearly schizophrenic.[77]

Emotional reasons usually determine the process of displacement inasmuch as less unpleasant ideas are frequently substituted for highly unpleasant ones. Unfortunately, however, the patient then transfers the original affect to the new idea, with the result that he obtains little benefit from the substitution. One of our catatonics became overtly ill after having jumped aboard a railway train which had already started to move. He now believes that he is persecuted by railways and interprets all railway signals as referring to him. However, it turned out that the patient also made certain self-reproaches which were far more important than his minor misdemeanor. He had engaged in sexual play with rabbits. The new, "auxiliary" trauma of the railway incident had merely awakened his slumbering sense of sin by way of an extremely superficial analogy, resulting in the substitution of the railroad persecution for the idea of having sinned. Naturally, such displacements may also occur after the actual outbreak of the disease. We are dealing with a very similar case when a patient believes that his hands are unclean instead of feeling that he is morally unclean.

Condensation is another means of disguising the delusional idea. We have already seen that the lover and his child can very easily be fused into one person. The mechanism may operate on a much wider scale inasmuch as some delusional notion may contain an entire delusional system. One of our patients was preoccupied intensely with women who wore their hair cut short. In the hospital, he saw a young girl with this hair-do who, in addition, was even more striking because she constantly shook her head in a stereotypied manner. In a short time, all his delusional persons and the entire delusional system which he had constructed within the past twenty years were condensed into that girl. She came to represent all those imaginary persons as well as the entire delusional complex.

The application of Freudian principles of interpretation is not as simple as the fragmentary examples which we have cited might lead

77. Such marriages due to displacement or such symbolic acts—in this context, there is little difference between them—are not at all rare among healthy persons.

one to believe. One of the complicating factors is, for instance, "overdetermination" of psychic formations. When a Swiss quarrels with his Prussian wife, he need not, under all circumstances, construct the delusion that Prussia is at war with Switzerland; there must be other codeterminants. If we want to determine the location of a point in space, we must define it in terms of the three dimensions. To determine a psychic formation in such a way that nothing else but that one phenomenon will be thought of, an infinitely larger number of determinants is required. The factor of "overdetermination" which necessitates multiple "interpretations" of the same symptom has brought a great deal of discredit to Freud's dream interpretations. This same factor will also constitute an obstacle to the acceptance of the explanation of the schizophrenic symptoms. Nevertheless, on closer examination, the concept of overdetermination is obviously self-evident. Many "constellations," dispositions, and occasions must be present before that particular thought which we now attempt to analyze was originally formed in all its nuances.[78]

In order to illustrate the phenomenon of overdetermination in all its ramifications, one would have to write monographs on individual case histories. Therefore, in addition to the few previously discussed instances where the same delusion had more than one root, I will here only refer to Jung's patient, B. S. She is the Cranes of Ibykus not only because the poem contains the word "free" but also because the phrase, "Free of sin and blemish is the pure child-like Soul." This phrase refers to herself. (In such cases, the patient may subsequently have added some of the new interpretations to the original idea.)

The tendency to symbolization may also manifest itself in the form of symbolic acts and, in view of the schizophrenic dissociation, these acts do not even have to express one of the patient's more important complexes. A patient wanted to climb over a fence. When she was forbidden to do so, she found various excuses enabling her at least, to touch the fence with her toe; she then laced and unlaced her shoe several times, etc.[79]

Another patient stands on the tips of her toes whenever she feels

---

78. I would like to call your attention to the manifold significance of Catholic symbolism. The patterns of medieval thought afford many points of comparison with schizophrenia. During that period, too, thought processes had autistically turned away from reality; the conclusions of thought processes were not the result of logical operations; rather, the conclusions were affectively predetermined judgments and logic was used to the extent only that it led to the desired end. Homo Dei in the image of mortals could just as well have been the brainchild of a modern schizophrenic.

79. Similar behavior can be observed in children who have been forbidden to do something.

that this or that person is just too common, that she is far too good for them, etc. A catatonic, who was admitted to the hospital from the investigation department of the courts, was very much afraid of me. Occasionally, she said that she was not afraid of me any more and moved a bit closer to me as she spoke. A catatonic returned from a vacation, greatly troubled because she had not been able to manage on the outside. When she was going back to her ward, she said goodbye to the doctor and the nurse instead of to her mother. A catatonic looked all over the ward for her change-purse. She declared that she must have it because the people had to travel by train. This symbolic act actually concealed an important complex which, moreover, was linked with a screen memory. But the real reason for her concern with money probably was the fact that her husband was seriously sick while she was taken care of in the hospital. A paranoid tore paper up into small pieces and threw them into the toilet bowl. She also had the habit of sewing tiny pieces of cloth: these were her thoughts.

The tendency to symbolic behavior can dominate the patient to such an extent that it becomes impossible for him to maintain himself outside an institution. One of our hebephrenics had to be returned to the hospital twice because, in addition to other things, she cut branches off a *Quittenbaum* (quince-tree) in order to signify that she was "quits" with the pastor. She threw these branches into the creek; they were her sins which would be carried down to the sea. She also ran singing through the village, carrying a stick to which she had tied a petticoat and other articles symbolizing the pastor's relationship to certain other women.

The Relation of Schizophrenia to Dreams

At various points of our studies, we have noted that in many respects the disease shows analogies to dreams, a phenomenon which cannot be without significance. In dreams, a similar dissociation of thinking occurs: symbolisms, condensations, predominance of emotions which often remain hidden hallucinations—all these can be found in both states and in the same way. The analogy becomes identity in those cases where the patients handle their dream-hallucinations as real ones, where delusions are formed in dreams, and maintained in the waking state.[80] We do not know how many dream-delusions occur in schizophrenics. We are only certain that delusional ideas—but not all of them

80. We have observed a schizophrenic who, for many years, produced hallucinations exclusively in dreams. The verification and uniform content of the hallucinations proved that they were pathological; later hallucinations of equal significance occurred in hypnagogic states; and only after many years did the patient produce them in his waking states.

—are developed in dreams and that, according to our present state of knowledge, thinking in dreams and schizophrenic autistic thinking are essentially identical.[81]

It should also be mentioned here that those dreams of schizophrenics which have been analyzed up to now differ in no way from the dreams of healthy persons. There is not sufficient space in this volume for detailed analyses of the dreams of schizophrenics, although it is possible to do them. I shall only mention the case of a hebephrenic who reacted in a very good-natured manner to the teasing he was subjected to by another patient. However, in the following night he dreamed that his annoying neighbor was beaten severely. In some cases, the patients were aware of the meaning of their dreams; they spontaneously supplied us with Freudian interpretations. Therefore, we see that such instances also present us with the pathological mixture of various trains of thought.

The only difference between schizophrenic manifestations and dreams which I have noted is the more pronounced split in the personality of the schizophrenic. The normal dreamer is usually entirely dominated by one of his complexes or by a homogeneous mixture of complexes. The schizophrenic, however, registers "doubly" or perhaps, if he has several independent constellations of complexes his registration may be manifested in the direction of reality as well as in that of his delusions. As far as we know, the healthy dreamer, on the other hand, does not register reality as such or he registers merely fragments of it. However, this difference is not necessarily a fundamental one since the very essence of sleep lies in the exclusion of as much reality as possible. Furthermore, the isolation from reality during sleep is not complete. Many individuals can register the passage of time better while they are asleep than when they are awake. A mother will awaken at the slightest movement of her sick child, but other louder noises will not disturb her; this proves that she is selective and that she differentiates between the events occurring in reality even while she sleeps.

Thus, in spite of the difference in genesis and in spite of other minor differences, it may yet be possible to show that the secondary symptomatology of schizophrenia is wholly identical with that of dreams.

Other deliria have also been compared with dreams. French psy-

---

81. It is strange that Pilcz and Lasègue find that "paranoiacs" (according to our classification, mostly schizophrenics) do not dream of their delusional ideas, whereas our findings are confirmed by Kahlbaum, Kraepelin, Sante de Santis, and von Krafft-Ebing. One of our patients spontaneously verbalized the fact which is also known to many other patients: "The human dream-life is identical with the sphere of the voices of the insane."

chiatrists, in particular, have established a specific class of "*oneiro-deliria*" and have considered them as an etiological group of psychoses. In France, delirium tremens, the prototype of this group, has been regarded as a prolonged dream for a long time. However, on closer scrutiny, delirium tremens cannot very well be compared with a dream although outwardly both phenomena are characterized by visual hallucinations. In typical cases of alcoholic delirium the symbolism is recognizable. Moreover, the delirious patient himself is too frequently merely a spectator, watching his hallucinations which interest him because of their strangeness but which do not concern him otherwise. This certainly does not happen in dreams. The various kinds of fever deliria seem to bear a closer resemblance to dreams; however, they have not been sufficiently investigated to be discussed here. The majority of fever deliria which I have observed could easily be differentiated from schizophrenia.

(h) *The Catatonic Symptoms*

1. General Remarks

As yet there exists no acceptable explanation for catatonic symptoms. However, it is easy to note analogies in the activities of healthy persons during states of concentrated attention. While listening to a speech we may twist a certain button on our coat or draw stereotyped figures ("doodles"). Newton is said to have remained sitting on his bed for a whole day with a stocking in his hand while brooding over a problem. We are inclined to obey simple commands automatically when our attention is concentrated on something else. Nevertheless we cannot explain these symptoms in schizophrenia on the basis of a simple disturbance of attention, if for no other reason, because it cannot always be demonstrated. We must mention Alter's extraordinary attempt to explain a portion of the catatonic symptoms as the result of "the diminishing effect of attention" (i. e., not of a decrease of attention). According to him, negativism, automatisms, and stereotypies are determined partly by psychic and partly by motor factors. The intra-psychic process is to be conceived of as follows: "On account of a sejunctive disturbance, the congruity (which is normally marked by considerable awareness) between the spatial components of the perception of a movement and the component of the will to execute this movement is not effected in certain cases. Consequently, the individual does not become aware of correct termination of the completed movement." Lundberg states that the psychic symptoms of a catatonia are due to thyroid insufficiency whereas the motor symptoms result from a parathyroid insufficiency. As far as I am concerned, I could never accept his theory as a possibility and even less as a probability. Schuele (680) relates the cataleptiform attacks (raptus, mutism, abstinence) to masturbation or uterine disturbances whereas Wernicke's school terms the hyperkinetic motility psychosis the most common type of menstrual psychosis. However, it is not improbable, though it has not been proven that the relationship of catatonic symptoms to sexuality is closer than that of other secondary manifestations of schizophrenia.

It may be assumed that the catatonic symptoms do not comprise a homogeneous group. Partly, they are probably only held together by the fact that most of them are signs of increased severity of the disease. However, compulsions, for example, also occur in very mild cases, yet we cannot very well separate them from the other catatonic automatisms.

Thus we are lacking a unitary viewpoint for the discussion of the genesis of all catatonic phenomena.

2. Stupor

Since we do not consider the external clinical picture of stupor as a homogeneous symptom, we refer the reader to our previous enumeration of its various sources. In addition, increased intro-cranial pressure, caused by edemas of the pia and the brain, and other cerebral swellings precipitate stuporous manifestations. However, the experiments of Gross mentioned above prove that general complications in the functions of the brain do not necessarily occur in stupor.

3. Negativism

I believe I have demonstrated that the present theories with respect to negativistic phenomena are either incorrect or inadequate.[82] For example, negativism cannot simply be explained on the basis of motility, aside from the fact that as yet we have no proof for the presence of primary motor disturbances in schizophrenia. At the present, therefore, a complete theory cannot be established but it is hoped that the following remarks may be of aid in developing such a theory.

In schizophrenia, the patient's relationship to the outside world has been altered; it has on the whole become a hostile one. The patients live in their autistic worlds. Thus it can be shown in many cases that the patients consider all stimuli emanating from the outside world, which they cannot block off, as unpleasant disturbances. As a result of this, negativistic attitudes develop.

In addition to the patient's autistic need to be alone with his

82. Psychiatr.-neurolog. Wochenschrift, 1910-1911.

thoughts and feelings, the sensitivity of the wound which every severe schizophrenic has received from life demands rejection of many external influences. If the complex is touched upon in analysis or in some other way, many patients become negativistic for a long period of time. Questions referring to the complex are at first answered in the negative much more frequently by these patients than by healthy persons. If we consider our own reactions when we are suffering from physical pain we can accept it as a matter of course that the patients fear not only the actual contact with their wound but also the possibility of such contact. This explains the persistence of negativism. We can also observe that healthy people and children, especially, assume an attitude of general negativism when they are suffering from pains which we are unable to alleviate.

The general relationship to and attitude of his environment is another incentive for the patient to defend himself. From his point of view this attitude is an entirely hostile one. (He is being locked up in an institution, his most important wishes are not being considered, etc.) For this reason, the intensity of negativism increases and decreases in proportion to the degree of resistance offered by the environment.

Moreover, the patients are unable to understand adequately the external world because of the disturbance in their thinking processes. Therefore, the reason for their blind resistance is identical with that of epileptics in twilight states, of frightened children or animals. This source of negativism is also evident in many cases.

If schizophrenic disturbances of motility actually exist, they would also serve to make contact with the outside world undesirable. It is certain, however, that many patients resist any approach because any form of thinking and acting is an effort for them.

Sexuality also plays an important role in negativism. Even under normal conditions, no other affect is as ambivalent as the sexual one (especially in the female species of both humans and animals). Therefore, negativistic patients, too, often produce distinctly sexual expressions. At times, these expressions convey anger; at other times, bashfulness depending upon the strength of the pleasure-component connected with the sensation of approach.

The difference between normal reserve and negativistic attitudes is not so considerable if one bears in mind that every positive drive has its negative component and vice-versa (cf. the theory of ambivalence). Thus, a relatively small preponderance of one or the other element will upset the balance.

In cases of pronounced positive suggestibility it will also be found that negative suggestibility is strongly developed, either by way of contrast or as a more or less conscious defense mechanism (children, hysterics, senile patients). The command-automatism of schizophrenics represents a pathological degree of suggestibility. Consequently, it is to be expected that in such patients the negative suggestibility is also of a high degree. However the frequent predominance of this negative suggestibility is due to the previously mentioned distortions of the patients' relations to the environment.

It is obvious that passive negativism is a transition to active negativism. One must be well aware of the extent of schizophrenic inertness in order not to find the common occurrence of simple passive negativism so remarkable. When someone resists an order to open his mouth, he will involuntarily clench his jaws tightly together. Even in more complicated situations one has very good reasons for doing just the opposite of what one is being forced to do. Active negativism in the sense of actual aggression is, of course, even easier to understand: the attack is considered instinctively and consciously the best defense.

Our theory readily permits interpretation of the fact that often negativism is expressed only toward certain persons. These usually include the doctors, attendants and perhaps those relatives who offer resistance, or with whom the complexes are connected. The other patients on the ward, with whom only superficial contact is maintained, do not provoke negativism except in cases where attempts at complete isolation from the environment are being made.

In the same way, as the break with the outside world produces external negativism, internal inner conflicts precipitate inner negativism. We can observe the symptom distinctly in healthy persons who are torn between their various drives. Considering the disrupted state of the schizophrenic psyche, this symptom must occur in such cases much more frequently and intensely. The patient may be split in such a way that he consumes, without inhibition, the meal prepared for another patient while protesting simultaneously that he is taking nothing at all.

Like others, we also have considered the possibility that purely intellectual negativism may be rooted in a general tendency to opposing associations. This, however, could not be demonstrated. But in our discussion of intellectual ambivalence we have noted the close relationship between thesis and antithesis. In view of the uneasiness with which many patients refer to their thoughts, of the vague nature of their inner processes, and of their need to regard and imagine things differently from the norm, it is obvious that often the exact opposite of the intended word or thought will be expressed. The previously discussed affective factors also favor expression of the opposite, in place of the primary notion. However, intellectual processes are not subjected to affective influences to the same degree as the will. It is understandable, therefore, that negativism of the intellect occurs much more rarely and, especially, is much less persistent than negativism of the will. Yet we still have to find an explanation, e.g., for the phenomenon that in dreams there is almost a preference for representing a certain idea by its very opposite.

It is evident that many delusions and hallucinations may lead, if not to negativism, at least to a negativistic attitude. Often, however, the relationships are reversed inasmuch as, for instance, hallucinations may be determined by negativism.

4. The Motor Symptoms

To date, observations which would prove conclusively that motor symptoms originate in specifically altered motor areas of the cortex or in even more peripheral spheres, have not been published. The numerous attempts at localization which were made in this field, especially, have not produced any final results. According to our present state of knowledge all motor symptoms are dependent upon psychic factors for their origin as well as their disappearance. The motor symptoms which we have been able to analyze could often be explained entirely on a psychic basis. However, the possibility must not be excluded that somewhere within the motor apparatus alterations take place which produce a portion of these symptoms or, at least, create the necessary predisposition to them (consider, e.g., increased muscular irritability). As yet we have not succeeded in detecting any evidence of such changes and to demonstrate for instance, primary disintegration of associations in motility.

In accordance with his theory of antagonism between the higher and the deeper centers, Meynert stated that disturbances which can be regarded as symptoms of irritation are the result of increased activity of the subcortical centers accompanied by cortical weakness (473). This theory was revived by F. Lehmann in 1898. By way of disagreement, I wish to point out that, aside from the weakness of Meynert's nutritional theory, up to the present we have had no reason whatever to assume that the activity of subcortical centers has any bearing on schizophrenia. Choreal, athetotic, and tetanic phenomena are entirely different from the motor symptoms which accompany schizophrenia. Neither can the movements of idiots be mistaken for catatonic ones. Apparently, the former fulfill their purpose in the movement as such, they are expressions of the pleasure that all of us derive from making motions. I am not implying that identical movements may sometimes not also occur in schizophrenia. In fact, many persons who are by no means mental defectives will show such stereotypies as turning their thumbs around each other continually. However, these movements are no more symptoms of schizophrenia than the rhythms. Our experience confirms the observation of Kraepelin (397) and Fauser that in catatonia the natural tendency for rhythmical movements can manifest itself free of control—but only in the sense that the catatonic utilizes rhythms on occasions where the healthy person would suppress them. The symptomatology very definitely indicates that there is no basis for the assumption that the large number of schizophrenic motor phenomena derive from innate mechanisms.

Schuele (679) has made the most exhaustive studies of disturbances of motility. But in spite of his excellent descriptions I am unable to agree with his differentiations. For example, I have only rarely noted anything resembling spasms in our patients. The compulsive movements which we observe do not comform with Schuele's definitions. We would consider most of the movements he describes as stereotypies. I am unable to differentiate between psychic reflex movements and cerebral reflex movements. As far as I am concerned, a simple tonic contraction represents by no means a "coarse muscular" symptom. Schuele also mentions that in flexibilitas cerea alterations occur in the molecular structure of the muscles; I am not aware of the basis for this assumption.

Schuele and Wernicke also attribute certain peculiarities of posture and similar symptoms to paresthesias or, specifically, to "distortions of somatic awareness." Usually, however, these paresthesias cannot be located. They may be the source of tic-like movements but these are not connected with catatonia.[83]

Wernicke cannot relate the persistent muscle tensions to volitional activity. He calls certain movements "pseudo-spontaneous," a term which can only connote a negative concept, i.e., something that is neither spontaneous nor automatic. For him, flexibilitas cerea represents the specific cortical reflex to passive movements. Anton (19) links catatonic rigidity to the rigidity resulting from extirpation of the cerebrum. Alter finds a special disease in patients with Storch's "stereopsyche."

Kleist differentiates various types of disturbances of movement associated with specific cerebral pathways. According to my analyses of catatonic disturbances of movement, they were always dependent upon psychic factors. But if, as happened occasionally, certain symptoms seemed to suggest a more definite localization of the process in a cer-

83. Kraepelin (388) noted that certain tics of phobic patients represented symbolic activities; the mechanisms of these tics are identical with those of catatonic stereotypies.

tain portion of the brain, these manifestations were never of the catatonic type but rather showed the usual focal symptomatology. Schizophrenic speech disturbances (such as verbigeration, mannerisms, mutism, neologisms, etc.), in particular, are basically different from aphasic disorders. At one time, I have also observed an alteration of the "frontal lobes—cerebellar system" in a catatonic; we found that the Purkinje cells had disintegrated and there was also atrophy of the caudate bodies. However, the resulting disturbances of movement differed sharply from those of the four hundred schizophrenic patients in the hospital. In my entire, intensive and extensive experience I have never seen "choreal" disturbances which belonged to schizophrenia. The reason why Wernicke's school assumes the presence of such disturbances, can only be that their concept of choreal movements extends far beyond anything which is actually seen in the various forms of chorea. The confinement of the movements to specific groups of muscles can be much better explained on a psychic than on an anatomic basis, aside from the fact that in some cases the psychic origin of the symptoms can be demonstrated. A *Schnauzkrampf* is more readily understood as an expression of contempt than as a localized tonic contraction of the muscles which control protusion of the lips. Moreover, this symptom is characterized by changes in intensity which, under psychic influences, may vary from zero to a maximum. The nature of these changes can only be understood if we consider at least their precipitations as a psychic process.

Attempts have been made to localize catalepsy in the muscles. Schuele (680) assumes that it is connected with pathological, if not infectious, conditions of the musculature; Kahlbaum, in a more obscure fashion, terms it a "cerebro-spinal" symptom. Rieger states that "the entire solution to the secret" of catalepsy lies in the fact that the antagonist muscles are as strongly innervated as the protagonists. The difficulty of carrying out spontaneous movements would lend support to Rieger's concept, if only this symptom were not missing so frequently. Absence of this symptom makes it difficult for us to see this antagonistic innervation unless its presence is determined by negativism.

For us there can be no doubt that catalepsy is precipitated by psychic factors on the basis of some unknown, generalized predisposition. Only such a concept can explain the rapid changes that occur under psychic influences. Unfortunately, this is about all we can say in this respect. Yet if we carefully examine the situations in which we find the physiological equivalent of catalepsy, it appears probable that the symptom is connected with the disturbance in the process of thinking. We notice suggestions of catalepsy in the attitudes of healthy persons when they are absorbed in something (Newton), or when they are unable to make any progress in their thinking, as in fatigue. Under such circumstances one may maintain for a considerable time some accidentally assumed positions of the body or of a limb. In other psychoses, catalepsy is also inevitably connected with a severe disturbance in the process of thinking. Riklin (612) assumes that there is a connection with monoideism.

There are certainly many causes for the genuine incapacity to move which is independent of the patient's conscious or unconscious volition or in direct contrast to his conscious wish, and which occurs in conjunction with, or without, cataleptic symptoms. In organic states of clouded consciousness, the difficulty in moving is probably part of the patient's general cerebral condition. In such cases we are dealing undoubtedly with an exclusion of motility analogous to that found in sleep; the patients may experience the symptom as in a nightmare or remain unaware of it as in an ordinary dream. Blockings and the influence of split-off complexes generally, often interfere with motility. Hallucinations, delusions, and autistic withdrawal from the environment also frequently do not permit execution of movements or reduce inclination to them. All or, at least, some of these factors may operate in the same patient. In that event, it is almost impossible to determine the share that each individual factor has in producing the symptom of immobility.

We consider the movements of agitated, active catatonics, their twisting, their grimaces, etc. psychically determined. Observation and discussion with the patients have given us no basis for assuming other causes for such motor activity.

With respect to echopraxia in catatonia, the explanation previously offered will also apply in this instance: every perception of movement stimulates us to a larger or smaller degree to imitate it. Under normal conditions, however, this stimulus is suppressed by other associations. In cases where associations have been eliminated or weakened, the stimulus may manifest itself and consequently the imitation is carried out. Thus echopraxia occurs chiefly in states of clouded consciousness or in similar conditions. However, the fact that sometimes it may occur independent of such states, indicates that as yet we are not acquainted with all its causes. On certain occasions, the visual or auditory fascination may be so great that the sensory impression becomes predominant and simultaneously suppresses other associations. Under different circumstances, the patient may believe, more or less consciously, that the gesture he perceives implies a command to imitate it. However, all these conjectures can hardly satisfy us.

Mutism[84] is frequently merely a partial phenomenon of the general motionlessness, regardless of whether this condition is the result of catalepsy or of tension. But in the main, chronic mutism is based on three fundamental causes which partly coincide with each other: in the lack of interest—the patients have nothing at all to say; in the autism —the patients have no wish for any contact with the outside world; and in the negativism—the patients do not want to do the very things that could normally be expected of them. Other causes, such as the difficulty of finding words, which is seen in the apraxia-like states of clouded consciousness, and also delusional ideas may be involved in individual cases.

It is probably significant for the understanding of this symptom that, in the process of recovery from stuporous states, it has the tendency to be the last one to disappear.

5. Catatonic Symptoms of Complexes

Automatisms: The nature of automatisms can be readily understood on basis of the isolation of the complexes. Under certain conditions, the split-off strivings of our psyche, which have remained active in the unconscious, become manifest in actions and thoughts.

If the patient is amenable to analysis, one can nearly always uncover the complex behind the automatisms. In cases where this connection cannot be discovered, it must be remembered that all kinds of accidental occurrences may be associated with the complex. In advanced cases, therefore, as in delusions, a generalization of this process may occur.

Moreover, it is possible that in certain stages of the schizophrenic process the disintegration of psychic activity may be so severe that even complexes which are only slightly emotionally charged may become independent.[85] (Such complexes may simply be connected with some accidental event, brought about by external circumstances.)

Naturally, actions emerging from the unconscious must appear as something strange to the thinking patient.[86] When these actions conflict with the actual content of consciousness and when they are associatively linked with it while, and immediately before, they are being carried out, the conscious personality will become resistant and will

84. Cf. Schuele (680).

85. Also in healthy persons, emotional stupor can result in catatonic postures, stereotypies, and even in verbigeration. "A healthy man who had just been calmly discussing oil-immersion, was most embarrassed about thirty minutes after that discussion when he noticed that his fly was open, just as he met a lady on the staircase. Afterwards he caught himself murmuring oil-immersion—oil-immersion—oil-immersion." Löwy, Zeitschr. f.d. ges. Neur. u. Psych., Orig 1., p. 339.

86. This results in the various types of "disturbances of the feeling of affectivity," etc., Pick (570).

perceive the drive as a compulsion. Depending on the strength of the resistance, compulsive acts or merely obsessive ideas may consequently develop.

Freud states that compulsive acts are invariably due to repression. Although in our patients complexes do not always seem to be repressed, I cannot claim without further study that Freud's dictum does not also apply to schizophrenia. I feel all the more inclined to reserve my opinion since Friedmann has arrived at rather similar conclusions by way of his theory of "incomplete ideas" which he regards as the basis of compulsions, whereas Newmann already recognized the connection between sexuality and mysophobia.

When the isolation is so marked that not even the execution of the compulsive act leads to an associative connection with the conscious personality, the result is an automatic action in which the patient functions like a third party as a spectator. In borderline cases, only the motor activity is connected with the personality. The patient believes that he is acting of his own volition but he does not give account to himself of the reasons for his action; nor does he offer any resistance to it.[87]

Thus automatisms must be placed alongside of hallucinations and delusions; they are hallucinations of thinking, striving and wanting, in the same way as there are hallucinations of memory. Consequently, confusing combinations and transitional forms of the different symptoms are common. A married man has sexual desires with respect to one of his relatives; after some time, voices accuse him of a sex crime; then they whisper that he is going to cause a disaster. He feels the compulsion to precipitate the disaster himself. However, it is only eleven years later that he commits a murderous attack, soon after the compulsion had been converted into commanding voices. Another patient had had obsessive thoughts for some time; then he felt "that a certain action was being driven towards him" (compulsive impulse); then he began to carry out compulsions, whereupon a "hyperkinetic motility psychosis" broke out. Following this, the patient felt better than previously for many years, although his catatonia could still be diagnosed. A hebephrenic was once rebuked because he insulted one of our staff physicians by calling him "a dirty Jew." As a result, the patient developed the obsessive idea that he had used the same vile phrase in his letters and he was obliged to read all of them aloud. Later on, he developed the compulsion to say those words out loud; and this compulsion was in

---

87. When the complex absorbs the entire personality, we speak of (hysteriform) twilight states.

time generalized until it turned into a more extensive coprolalia.

It is striking that some authors maintain (in contrast to others, such as Schuele) that obsessive-compulsive ideas are never combined with psychoses (Thomsen). The truth is that when compulsive ideas occur in conjunction with schizophrenia, the symptoms of the latter disease become manifest very early in the course of the illness and that they consequently assume a prominent position. It may also be true that, once schizophrenia has been ruled out, forms of pure obsessive-compulsive ideas are very rarely found in combination with genuine psychoses.

In this connection, it must be remembered that movements such as, e.g., climbing resulting from the patient's idea that he is a cat, may constitute transitions to automatisms but are by no means necessarily compulsive movements (Désci, 158). Similarly, there is a tendency to extend the concept of compulsions beyond its limits, particularly with respect to schizophrenia.

Many authors employ the term, "instinctual acts" for motor automatisms. The former term should be restricted to drives which express existing needs (the feeding instinct, the instinct of self-preservation or suicidal drives) and whose ultimate motives are conscious. Unfortunately, however, there are no other words in the English language to define such manifold symptom complexes as pyromania, kleptomania, and similar syndromes. But this inexactness of terminology is of no importance with respect to schizophrenia since its automatisms are more or less independent of the personality and, therefore, not "instinctual" acts in the previously defined sense.

Berze (59), in agreement with Wundt, emphasizes the fact that the content of consciousness has been altered in such a way that it does not manifest itself as "actively willed" but as "passively experienced;" this is a good description of automatic symptoms. However, the symptom described is not characteristic for some vaguely defined paranoia, as Berze states; it is a common occurrence in schizophrenia.

Up to the present, no evidence has been presented that would support a theory of localization of automatisms. An "*automatisme dans les centres de la langue*" (Arnaud) is, of course, an entirely inadequate explanation for phenomena of such great affective significance. Neither is there any basis for the theory classifying primary and secondary cerebro-spinal automatisms, advanced by Brugia and Marzocchi. From our point of view, we cannot argue with Schuele's very similar theories.[88]

---

88. By means of posthypnotic suggestion, the different types of automatisms can be experimentally produced.

It is relatively easy to prove with respect to some of the "peculiar ideas" that they suddenly emerge from the unconscious. The fragments of songs, or biblical quotations, etc., which the patients unexpectedly sing or cite often to their own and to the astonishment of others, are always connected with their complexes. This applies also to many other abrupt statements.[89]

Once, one of our patients said, entirely out of context: "It says in the Bible that one must go to the Samaritan woman at Jacob's Well." (John IV.) During her illness, the patient was troubled by the fact that —like the other woman in the Bible—she had had sexual relations with several men; two of them were her husbands, but she had not been married to the third.

The best-known manifestation of the activity of the complexes is the unmotivated laughter. Freud has called attention to the fact that often in analysis patients laugh when a complex is touched upon. We have seen this happen occasionally in schizophrenia and our observations indicate the same source for the ominous laughter of our patients. We must only add that in schizophrenics stimulation of the complex is by no means always provided by external factors but far more often by inner ones. Usually, the patients, themselves, do not know why they are laughing; they feel that they are being compelled to laugh. Thus, the behavior of the patients is the same in this instance as in other expressions of the complexes.

This interpretation is also supported by the example of a periodic hebephrenic for whom his compulsive laughter was a definite sign that another episode of his illness was on its way: at the approach of a new attack, the complexes became again active. A previously mildly imbecile patient had never laughed before his schizophrenia became manifest at the age of forty-five; at the beginning of his illness, his laughter was a striking symptom. In the following case, the connection with the complex is very clear: A patient converted an incubus that at one time oppressed her into "one or two rubber-dolls" which she identified with her lover. Now, the lover tortures her by means of these dolls; he presses and chokes her and causes her palpitation; he squeezes the sides of her head, and demands that she should be gay: now she must laugh all day long.

Naturally, the also not uncommon unmotivated crying spells have a similar origin.

---

89. These also occur in healthy people. Cf. Freud's *Psychopathology of Everyday Life,* and Jung (344).

6. Mannerisms

Mannerisms can be explained, not on the basis of isolation of the complexes, but rather on the basis of the persistent influence which these complexes exert; some of the stereotypies, at least, can also be interpreted in this way. Even normal persons tend to exaggerate or, at least, to put special emphasis on expressions which correspond to their wishes. The vain person will be recognized by his clothes and by his general behavior; the man who is proud of his physical strength expresses it in his gait and in every one of his movements. However, we notice not only those who are something but, even more, those who want to be something that they are not. In a truly distinguished person, the distinguished pose, the distinction of every movement is natural; distinction is an integral part of his personality. This is exactly the reason why he is not conspicuous. In the person who merely affects distinction, we notice the contradiction between his true nature and the affectation. Whereas a certain movement is in one case a part of the person, it appears as something foreign in the other man. A person who imitates the form without comprehending the content will be unable to adjust the form to the content. For instance, he will overemphasize conspicuous details: the truly cultured individual demonstrates the greater independence of his fingers from each other with every gesture of his hand. The person, who wants to create an impression of more culture than he actually possesses, will only notice how the other extends his little finger and will imitate this detail in an extreme manner at every opportunity.

Schizophrenics act in an identical way. However, because of the lack of control in these patients and because the complexes generally exert far greater tyranny in them than in normal individuals, the exaggeration will be even more marked. The results are the affectations of the catatonic, the boorish conduct of the hebephrenic, and the absurd decorum of the megalomanic.

This also explains the fact that the patients are entirely conscious of many of their mannerisms. A hebephrenic even presented to me some of his empty-sounding neologisms asking for my criticism—from which, however, he expected nothing but praise. The insolent behavior of many hebephrenics, together with their tendency to brag and to attack the most difficult problems has been regarded by some authors as a symptom complex which the patients have carried over from puberty. This may partly be true. It was certainly not the case in our patient who was representative of the worst characteristics of adolescence. As long as he was well he did not exhibit any of these traits. His illness only became manifest when he was about twenty years old and had been employed for a long time already; it was a distinct catatonia.

In the main, the symptomatological similarity between adolescence and schizophrenia depends on entirely different factors. In the same way as many schizophrenics, young people strive to appear socially and intellectually superior to what they actually are. They express this by ignoring conventions and by their desire to handle problems requiring a much higher degree of intelligence than they possess. This also partly explains their tendency to employ foreign words and to pronounce these in a special way. For example, Kraepelin has called attention to the fact that many catatonics accentuate the word "doctor," on the second syllable i.e., "doctór." Such peculiarities were always found to be connected with a complex concerning the quality of distinction and importance.

The tendency to the use of diminutives and the child-like conduct by which it is often accompanied can be explained in a similar way. In some cases, we were able to prove that this tendency was an expression of a child complex. At first, the patients talked to their imaginary children in this fashion, then they generalized this mannerism, particularly, when they identified the father of the child with the child. The patients may also reserve the use of diminutives exclusively for conversations with the child.[90] Hecker's case talked in an officer's jargon probably because his girl hoped to marry an officer.

It is not uncommon for patients to alter their mannerisms so as to conform with the complex that happens to be activated.

We can also find analogies to stereotypies in the healthy person who, not infrequently in a state of abstraction, executes stereotyped movements or drawings which betray the operations of a hidden complex.

The schizophrenic stereotypies which can be traced to their origin show very clearly that they are connected with a complex. The spinster who imitated the movements of a shoemaker at work had loved a shoemaker some thirty years ago. The girl who continually seemed to balance herself had met the man she adored at a dance. A patient's lover is announced as a visitor; she verbigerates, "This is, he is," until he actually comes, and retains this habit; later she verbigerates, "My dear one," and sometimes she also adds, "Our baby boy." A schizophrenic woman who is working as an attendant says on every occasion,

90. Bezzola has called my attention to the possibility that child-like behavior might also point to a dream or some other complex dating back to early youth. However, I have not come across an example of such a genesis in schizophrenics.

regardless of who it is she happens to be speaking to: "Isn't this so, Max?" Max had been her first sweetheart. Even suicidal attempts may be repeated in a stereotyped manner after the original affect has passed.

Almost every time I visit his ward, a patient hands me a note containing only four words which are supposed to indicate how badly he has been treated. Patients who are continuously twisting doorknobs, used to have an intense desire to get out, even though now they do not know what to do when the door is opened for them. Patients who kiss the shoes of other persons or the floor are under the influence of a complex of inferiority; occasionally they may also express their love for a person in this way. When patients rock an object they hold in their arms or when they make rocking movements without holding an object, the action is usually connected with a child complex.

A patient draws a number of stylized mouths; these mouths say, "Praise the Lord." Other associations reveal that the "Lord" is the priest she loves. A girl repeats stereotyped touching of the axilla, mouth, ears and genitals innumerable times every day; these symptoms are results of a masturbation complex. This complex is also the basis for the hand motions of a man which gradually moved farther and farther away from his genitals and closer to his mouth. Putting a finger into the mouth or the ear often has the same meaning. We have seen head movements develop as the result of displacements of coitus movements. We could prove in two patients that their *Schnauzkrampf* represented an expression of contempt for their environment, together with marked self-satisfaction.[91]

None of these interpretations are arbitrary. All of them were supplied by the patients themselves and, in part, were objectively verified; the patients associate the complex with the stereotypies and conversely, the stereotypies with the complex. It is, therefore, not unusual that access is gained to the patient by way of his stereotypies. The balancing catatonic, for instance, was completely rigid, mute, and unresponsive until someone joined her in her balancing act as if dancing. All of a sudden, she was transformed; one could hardly recognize her as the same patient. She told us everything we wanted to know about her love-affair and her life-story, with complete clarity, like any healthy person. We were able to repeat the experiment several times before the increasing severity of her catatonia made it impossible.

In the light of the schizophrenic peculiarities of association, it appears obvious that stereotypies associate themselves with thoughts

91. According to Darwin, the orangutan and the chimpanzee protrude their lips when they are dissatisfied (Dromard). This can also be seen in young children.

that were originally foreign to them. The fact that, as a rule, stereotypies are increasingly simplified in the course of time and that they also transform themselves in other ways, such as the displacement of sexual symptoms upwards, is connected with the general characteristics of our psyche.

Thus, it would appear that the theory of stereotypies has been established: they are symptomatic acts in the Freudian sense; they provide a means of expression for a complex which always continues its activity.

However, the question as to why the stereotypies are so persistent certainly demands a special explanation. Freud and Jung state that there is no decrease in the intensity of the repressed affects. Nevertheless, it must still be proven that this theory, resulting from findings in neurotics and healthy individuals, is also valid for schizophrenia. In schizophrenia, we note that stereotypies for many years may accompany complexes which apparently have not been repressed. Further, in the course of remissions, complexes often recede to such a degree that it becomes almost impossible to determine their affective tone. I am, therefore, not yet convinced that repression is the cause for the persistence of stereotypies; or that in schizophrenia, affective constellations may not diminish in intensity with the passage of time. On the other hand, I have repeatedly observed that the complexes and their affects may persist for decades without any changes in content or intensity.

However that may be, the definition of stereotypies as symptoms of complexes would suffice for the time being, if it were not for the fact that we can prove that the tendency to stereotypies occurs in schizophrenia also independent of the complexes.

It is not uncommon for patients to continue to verbigerate for a long time some accidentally snatched up word. In doing physical exercises some patients, who are not yet catatonic at all, find it difficult to stop promptly when it comes to repetitious exercises. I have often observed that a patient, who may be a very good pianist, gets stuck on a trill or on some other repeated musical figure. Dromard reports that the patients do not drop their arms when the support on which they had been resting them is suddenly removed, and that induced oscillatory movements do not cease with the cause. Perhaps it should be mentioned in this connection that very frequently facial expressions cannot keep pace with the changes of emotion. The first symptom of illness in a stage-prompter was the fact that he kept on prompting the same phrase three and four times in succession and that, in spite of good insight, he was unable to stop doing so. A patient rinses his mouth and cannot stop repeating the rinsing movements although he no longer has any water in his mouth. Another patient who has nodded his head in answer to a question, continues to nod while shaking out the same dust rag for a half-hour. Occasionally, when patients are asked to identify pictures, they demonstrate a perseveration similar to that seen in organic brain diseases; the same symptom can also be seen in writing. During a celebration at the hospital, a hebephrenic made a fairly adequate speech. Nine months later, he greeted a returning doctor with another speech employing many of the sentences he had used in his earlier speech, which were not at all appropriate to this occasion. Sommer (724) found that in solving arithmetical problems the patients made the identical errors a week later when the problems were again presented to them. Passively induced movements may also persist for a long time.[92] Wiersma suspects the presence of a prolonged aftereffect of stimuli in "paranoia."

In spite of the fact that the tendency to stereotypies is usually demonstrable in acute catatonic thrusts only (we have never noted them in the associations of chronic patients[93]), we cannot assume that this predisposition does not exert some influence on the development of stereotypies. We must conclude, therefore, that both factors are involved in their formation; thus, the general tendency to stereotypies would correspond to the patient's predisposition; the influence of the complex would be the precipitating factor and would also determine the content of the stereotypies.

Probably, a third element is also involved. Kraepelin called attention to the fact that in cases where the capacity for planned pursuit of definite goals is disturbed, secondary drives may assert themselves; in the absence of inhibitions provided by new aims, the patients will tend to continue whatever activities they had been practicing hitherto. From this viewpoint, therefore, stereotypies would represent acts of will whose purpose is determined by a preceding process. Indeed, during

---

92. Expressions, which originally had an affective meaning may become detached from the complex and subsequently appear as accidental stereotypies: during examination, a patient at first answered every question which touched upon the complex with the words, "Just that." As the examination proceeded, the patient utilized this phrase more and more often, until finally she answered with it any and all questions. It certainly also happens that accidental expressions are linked to a complex and that we cannot discover the connection. In the case of the balancing girl, the stereotypy was, after all, a rather arbitrary symbol for her lover. In accordance with the mechanism of schizophrenic associations, it is quite likely that, for example, a word which has been accidentally overheard is being definitely tied up with a complex. However, it would be somewhat difficult to assume that in all the above-mentioned instances, such accidental connections with the complex occasioned the development of stereotypies.

93. In repetition experiments, Pfenninger found a greater percentage of different reactions in chronic schizophrenics than in normal persons.

states of absorption, we see that even in healthy persons secondary activities are characterized by a marked monotony. Schiller, for example, filled many pages with drawings of little horses.

Many authors attempt to explain the nature of stereotypies in terms of the loss of the inhibiting functions of the cerebral cortex, i.e., the deterioration (e.g., Jastrowitz, 324; Fauser, 215).

Unfortunately, limited space does not permit any further discussion regarding the problem of stereotypies which is, of course, of paramount importance for the understanding of schizophrenia. I must refer the reader to the works of Neisser and of Heilbronner (293). For our purposes, we wish to add only the following significant details: the tendency of sub-conscious complexes to express themselves in stereotypies is also demonstrated in association-experiments (Riklin, 612a). Furthermore, Ziehen also points to the connection between stereotypies and "overcharged" ideas. Attempts have always been made to explain stereotypies of posture on the basis of sensory disturbances (correction of certain deficiencies, Wernicke; disturbances of body-image, Siemerling, etc.). Kahlbaum's interpretation of the stereotypies of speech is equally inadequate. We might, perhaps, consider the possibility that tonic spasms of muscles of the speech organs produce mutism, but it seems hardly plausible that clonic contractions should produce definite words and sentences and adapt these to the given occasion. Our observations have offered no evidence that would support some of the newer, more "psychic" theories of localization, such as Alter's (sejunction between stereo-psyche and patho-psyche, 10). However, many factors would argue against the presence of such simple disturbances.

Stereotypies have been linked and, in some cases, confused with similar phenomena. These are usually as complicated processes as the stereotypies themselves, and it is, therefore, quite likely that some partial manifestations of other syndromes coincide with some partial manifestations of stereotypy.

Some people still define it as a stereotypy when patients always repeat the same act or assume the same position, in response to "voices" or delusions. Naturally, this interpretation is incorrect if one agrees with most psychiatrists that delusions and hallucinations are independent of stereotypies. In that case, the anomaly would lie in an entirely different direction; the stereotypy would merely have the same psychological significance as movements which healthy persons (factory workers, for example) repeat frequently, for valid reasons; or, to draw another comparison, the situation would be identical to one where a senile, as the result of his memory defects, always repeats the same old tale. It approaches verbigeration when a patient continually expresses all his wishes in the same words: "Please be so kind," and when he exclaims this phrase every time a person enters the room, or a patient is moved, etc. In this case, the wish and the method of expression are sterotyped; but, since the patient really wants to say something, we cannot define this symptom as verbigeration.

The occupational motions which are not uncommonly observed in patients with organic brain disease, are a group of symptoms entirely different from those of schizophrenic stereotypies. In this connection, we wish to mention "perseverations" (i.e., the patient clings to some specific act or word, etc.) which, by some authors, are not clearly distinguished from the stereotypies, although the two phenomena are essentially different.

Heilbronner (293) states that perseveration and verbigeration are differentiated by the fact that, to form verbigeration, a drive to speak must be added to perseveration. This concept is only adequate when dealing with organic brain diseases since, in schizophrenic verbigeration, the influence of the complex is the primary factor.

Ragnar Vogt (786) has attempted to construct a psychological unit, consisting of perseveration, stereotypy, and Kraepelin's concept of excitation.

Masoin (455) and, particularly, Weygandt (816) relate schizophrenic stereotypies to the stereotyped movements of children and oligophrenics. Kraepelin, on the other hand, distinguishes two types of stereotypies, one of which, characterized chiefly by rhythmical movements, belongs with both of these groups. However, even on superficial observation, the automatic stereotypies of schizophrenia, which are essentially independent of the patients' moods, present a picture which is entirely different from the rocking and swaying movements of oligophrenics.

As a curiosity, it shall also be mentioned that Dromard (191) tries to differentiate the stereotypies of dementia praecox from those of secondary dementia. In appearance, tics may be sufficiently similar to stereotypies to cause confusion; all the more so, since tics also often represent symbolic actions.

Ziehen's theory of pseudo-stereotypies occurring in manics deficient of ideas often causes diagnostic difficulties. According to my observations, we are dealing in such cases usually with a combination of inhibition and flight of ideas.

Besides others, verbigeration is often one of the symptoms of the "onomatomania" of the French.

Many students have noted that there is some connection between stereotypies and complexes, e.g., Dromard, Ricci, Mondio. Schuele vividly terms certain postural stereotypies, "delusional ideas that have gained shape."

(i) General Viewpoints

In spite of the many details which psychoanalysis has explained for us, it is still too early to classify the entire symptomatology of schizophrenia from a single point of view. However, a tentative formulation of our present knowledge may be in order at this point.

In part, (possibly entirely) the overt symptomatology certainly represents the expression of a more or less unsuccessful attempt to find a way out of an intolerable situation. Aside from the purely hysteriform mechanisms, we know of three ways by which the patients try to help themselves.

1. The patient renders reality harmless by refusing to let it touch him (autism); he ignores it, isolates it, withdraws into his own thoughts. For these patients, autism has the same meaning as the walls of the monastery have for the monks, that the lonely desert has for some saints, and their studies for some scientists. In this respect, the difference between sickness and health is merely a quantitative one.

2. In the long run, however, this expedient rarely suffices: most of the patients who come to the hospital consider their wishes fulfilled, the obstacles overcome. This type of reaction can only succeed completely if, simultaneously, in conformance with autism, the isolation of reality is effected or if it has been transformed in accordance with the patient's wishes. This transformation of reality takes place in the twilight states; generally, however, these cannot be maintained indefinitely. Thus the patients try to help themselves in the same way as the daydreamers or the poets.

Even if the patients do not succeed entirely in altering the image of reality to correspond with the dictates of their wishes, they manage, at least, to change it in such a way that obstacles appear merely as accidental and, in principle, surmountable (delusions of persecution which convert obstacles into machinations of certain people).

3. Probably more frequently than we know at present, patients actually transform the accessible portion of reality; not, of course, in the sense of total wish fulfillment—when this is possible, there is no overt disease—but in the sense of escape: they become manifestly sick. The flight into disease is particularly striking in the Ganser syndrome,

in some of the hypochondriacal forms, and in the *Faxenpsychose* (75 a), [94] and certainly constitutes a decisive factor in other forms as well. For obvious reasons, it is most commonly seen when there are purely external conflicts: legal investigations, financial difficulties, undesired release from the hospital, etc.[95]

Not only the first two, but all three types of reaction can readily form manifold combinations. As in other psychic phenomena, there are nearly always several motives that contribute to the manifestations. Moreover, the mechanisms and results of this affective eudemonia are concealed and distorted by the other disturbances, chiefly, by the obscurity of thinking and the accessory symptoms.

CHAPTER II

THE THEORY OF THE DISEASE

A. The Concept of Schizophrenia

The differentiation made between primary and secondary symptoms provides the concept of the disease. *We assume the presence of a process, which directly produces the primary symptoms; the secondary symptoms are partly psychic functions operating under altered conditions, and partly the results of more or less successful attempts at adaptation to the primary disturbances.*

We must add, however, that it is not absolutely necessary to assume the presence of a physical disease process. It is conceivable that the entire symptomatology may be psychically determined and that it may develop on the basis of slight quantitative deviations from the normal, just as in some people the disposition to hysterical symptoms is so strong that they become hysterical when confronted with the ordinary diffi-

94. Translator's note: Lit. tr.: buffoonery psychosis.

95. It is not at all rare that the disease takes a turn for the worse when the patients are faced with the possibility of release from the institution, or sometimes even when they are to be transferred to a better ward. We have inevitably found that the reason for the aggravation in the patient's condition lies in his fear of having to return to the life outside the hospital. The woman does not want to recover because, as yet, she cannot tolerate the idea of returning to the husband she does not love; the governess wants to remain at the hospital because she hates her job; the man, because he finds the struggle for existence still too much for him. One of our catatonic women patients stated flatly that if we were to send her away from Switzerland (the home of her lover) and back to her own country, an acute attack would render this plan impossible; and she kept her word. However, this acute episode did not differ in any way from any of her previous ones. In the cases reported by Birnbaum, the gain from the disease is generally very clear.

culties of life, whereas, in the average person, hysteria can develop only in consequence of a very severe psychic trauma.

Thus, there has been no lack of attempts to explain this disease on a functional basis. Tiling actually parallels it with hysteria (and paranoia) and suggests that it develops in the congenitally mental defectives and in hesitant, ambivalent individuals. Stadelmann makes similar statements.

In addition to the fact that the anatomical findings do not correspond with the severity of the manifest symptoms, there are some other elements in favor of the theory that the genesis of this disease is a psychic one. Aggravations and improvements in the patient's condition are often psychically determined. Among the symptoms preceding the outbreak of schizophrenia, we find generally a disposition to introversion which may explain the appearance of autism and, indirectly, most of the other symptoms. The significance of the undeniable anatomical findings may be questioned on the basis of Schott's (667) interpretation of atrophy as the result of inactivity; or, according to Jung, by regarding them as the consequence of toxins produced by affects. The symptomatology of this disease differs bassically from that of any other known organic or toxic disorder.[96] On the other hand, differentiation from the functional neuroses is so vague, that a mild schizophrenic may give the impression of a hysteric or a neurasthenic for a long period of time. Furthermore, practically all schizophrenic manifestations may appear to represent merely exaggerations of well-known neurotic symptoms. Jung has shown how these neurotic symptoms may be explained on the basis of especially intense or intensely aroused affectivity, or, perhaps, on the basis of a primary tendency to introversion. Possibly, the tremors could be interpreted as psychic manifestations; in fact, it has even been attempted to explain manic and depressive symptoms in this manner. The fact that most are incurable, and that they are unable to find relief by means of abreactions, may be regarded as the outcome of the already existing exaggerated introversion which prevents a complete restitution of reality.

However, the pathological anatomical findings exist, and even though the nature of their relation to the psychosis remains enigmatic, the above interpretations of primary manifestations appear forced in this light. Furthermore, it is striking that in most cases close scrutiny of the anamneses will reveal evidence of the disease, prior to the psychic trauma accused of being its cause. The extent to which the associations have become disconnected has its equal only in the dreams of healthy and neurotic individuals, but never in ordinary affective reactions. The

---

96. Sommer has termed the symptoms of the disease "disturbances of conduction," by way of differentiating them from others.

other primary symptoms, such as the fine, relatively regular tremor, some of the pupillary disturbances, the manic-depressive symptoms which, when present, appear as integral parts of the disease process, the organic types of attacks—all these are not easily fitted into the functional concept of the disease. Introversion cannot very well serve as an explanation for everything, since patients who express their complexes and wish to act in accordance with them, are just as incurable as others who do not. In spite of some exceptions, the course of the disease itself appears in general as spontaneous and, to a considerable degree, independent of psychic influences. In functional disorders, there are no analogies to the basic incurability of all patients, and to the impossibility to influence the course of the disease in the majority of cases, that we find in schizophrenia. It is also significant that the incidence of this disease is as frequent among "primitive" peoples as it is among civilized ones although, according to Kraepelin, catatonia is less common among the former group.

Complete justice to all these factors can only be done by a concept of the disease which assumes the presence of (anatomic or chemical) disturbances of the brain; the course of the cerebral disorder is chronic, for the most part, but there are also phases of acute forward thrusts or of standstill; the disturbance of the brain determines the primary symptoms (disconnection of association, perhaps the disposition to hallucinations and stereotypies, a portion of the manic and the depressive syndromes and of the states of clouded consciousness, etc.). In more severe exacerbations, psychic symptoms, such as certain confusional and stuporous states, are direct consequences of the cerebral process. The rest of the psychic symptoms develop indirectly by way of abnormal mechanisms in the primarily disturbed psyche, inasmuch as the affectivity, in particular, gains pathological superiority over the weakened logical functions.

As a psychic process, the disease generally, if not always, begins surreptitiously. To start with, it remains latent until an acute pathological thrust produces prominent symptoms, or until a psychic shock intensifies the secondary symptoms.[97] The relationship between the acute thrust of the brain disturbance and the releasing psychic experience is, of course, not a mutually exclusive one. In the event of a slight, or a hardly progressing, brain alteration, not only a severe psychic trauma can release the manifest disease. However, in proportion to the rapidity with which the cerebral process advances and to the severity of the permanent changes, the occasions required to cause marked dis-

97. Often, we find a lengthy, latent period between the traumatic experience and the acute onset of the disease because the former is first subjected to elaboration.

turbances become increasingly smaller, until, finally, even everyday difficulties suffice to upset the delicate balance. Most frequently, therefore, both factors contribute their share to the formation of the psychotic symptom complexes.

Following an acute advance, the cerebral process may come to a standstill or it may even regress to some degree; the latter, e. g., is very likely the case in non-fatal cerebral edema. In that event, the psyche may also recover its power in considerable measure; or some of the disease symptoms may remain, forming a "residual state." However, at any given time, the disease process as well as the secondary symptoms may resume their progress, either at a slow or at a rapid rate.

Improvements in the patients' condition may also be accomplished by psychic factors. These may, partly, be connected with the outside world—some external change may have a beneficial effect on the patient's frame of mind—partly they may originate within the patient himself as he learns to live with his complexes, as a twilight state dissolves, or because the affect has exhausted itself. The nature of the healing effects of the psychic process is not as yet fully understood; it is certain, however, that some psychic self-healing processes must exist.

Therefore, the course of the symptoms and the course of the disease process need not run parallel to each other by any means.

Partly, at least, the significance of the adolescent period with respect to the outbreak of the disease, certainly lies in the fact that this point marks the beginning of the difficulties of life for the individual. In particular, at this time, the most powerful of all complexes—sexuality—asserts itself. Thus, in a large number of our patients, we see that the psychosis becomes overt between the ages of fifteen and twenty-five, although, in a more or less latent form, it had been present for a long time. It is not necessary to assume the operation of other factors favoring the manifestation of the disease in this particular age group. Still, we cannot exclude the possibility (hitherto accepted as a fact) that also the actual disease process may show a preference for the postpubescent period.

According to our concept of the disease, the outcome is not only inherent in the disease itself, but dependent upon many external and internal contingencies. With the identical cerebral disorder, one patient may recover, whereas another patient may deteriorate because of some difference in his psychic predisposition, because of insufficient stimulation, or because of the increased efficacy of his psychic trauma. However, we are as incapable of explaining the variations in disease courses and disease groups on the basis of the patients' psychic predispositions or their psychic experiences, as we are of explaining them on the basis of some assumed disease process.

The most important present-day theories, which attempt to interpret the individual symptoms, the symptom groups, or the total picture of the disease, are discussed in detail by Jung, in his *Psychology of Dementia Praecox*, to which I wish to refer my readers.[98]

Therefore, we note only the following: We must realize that it would be incorrect to assume that we are dealing with the fundamental disorder if we are content to state that "the highest psychic function" (Gross) or the identical "apperception" in Wundt's sense of the term (Weygandt), has been disturbed.

Necessarily, every generalized disturbance must do the greatest damage to the most complicated functions. Therefore, until we have demonstrated the mechanism which affects this "highest function," it will remain our duty to search for the primary symptoms.

It is no improvement of the situation, when only individual aspects of the "highest psychic function" are selected, such as the attention (Tschisch: according to Arndt, 24), the "function of the real," the "ego-synthesis," or the "realm of consciousness" (P. Janet).

Other terms, such as "weakness of mental images" (Sérieux), "diminution of volitional and intellectual activity," "incapacitation of the mental effort" (Masselon), or "*abaissement du niveau mentale,*" are meaningless for us, although they designate general disturbances. There is absolutely no evidence to support a purely quantitative-dynamic concept of the disturbance since, in some cases, we can establish that there is considerable expenditure of psychic energy. However, if one insists on the assumption of a "weakening of psychic activity" (Freusberg), then this hypothesis can explain everything, and consequently nothing: the concept is too general. If the phrase "*abaissement du niveau mentale,*" is intended to designate the "lowering" of conscious psychic activities to the level of functions which are ordinarily unconscious, it represents, not an explanation, but merely a definition of an important portion of our psychological observations on schizophrenia, in words, which can easily be misinterpreted, since they may also be understood dynamically.

All these terms represent pseudo-explanations which, however, are

---

98. In my estimation, however, Jung certainly handles his predecessors far too gently. Theories, which combine correct and false facts, are more dangerous to science than complete errors; and hypotheses, which are only "justified in a certain sense," always create confusion because the necessary reservations cannot always be stated. Clear-cut concepts can only be formed if we ruthlessly reject everything that does not belong to them, regardless of whether we are dealing with simple problems or with entire theories.

unquestionably valuable for purposes of discussion and as inspirations for new observations.

There are also theories with respect to the clinical pictures presented by schizophrenia, which localize the pathological process in certain portions of the brain or the psyche. Neisser's hypothesis, based on interference by deeper parts of the brain which do not transmit consciousness, is a very good observation rather than an explanation. In this case the hypothetical—and certainly incorrect—element consists only in the fact that the author places the unconscious psychic functions in deeper layers of the brain than the conscious ones.

Van Erp Taalman Kip asserts that, in contrast to all other psychoses, the chronic delusional insanity is a sub-cortical disease. In his description of a case exhibiting bizarre script, Pfister (564) attempts to relate this symptom to an injury of the first gyrus angularis. Lomer (423) considers contraction of the retinal vessels as the explanation for the case of a woman patient who experienced a murderous assault in her hallucinations, during which everything appeared to be colored by an ugly green. Had he thought, and investigated his case, more along psychological lines, he would probably have discovered the idea of unwelcome "hope" that the patient expressed "in green." [99]

DeBuck explains catatonia on the basis of disturbances of the will, and of the most superficial combination of accompanying emotions and their conversion into actions—functions, which he ascribes to the deep layers of the cerebral cortex.

Wernicke (804) establishes the transition to psychic localizations, when he states: "The so-called hypochondriacal paralyses prove that the exclusion of the will may manifest itself in localized muscle areas." However, our problem is not one of localized muscle areas, but one of ideas of localized areas, which is an entirely different matter.

Försterling's term, "auto-psychic disturbance of identity," represents, of course, not an explanation, but a designation for an isolated group of symptoms which relates to the personality.

B. The Disease Process

We do not know what the schizophrenic process actually is. In advanced cases, anatomical findings show a mild cerebral atrophy and

---

99. Translator's note:
The German phrase, "*etwas in grün ausdrücken,*" (lit.: "to express something in green") is used colloquially to indicate that a person is simply restating or confirming an already established fact in different words or actions. In addition, the color green is commonly used to represent hope.

certain histological changes.[100] However, the implications of these findings are unknown to us.

The cerebral atrophy cannot serve as an explanation for the schizophrenic symptoms since diffuse reduction of the cortex produces entirely different manifestations. Regarding the histological changes, we are unable to determine whether they are the causes of the psychosis, or whether they are merely phenomena paralleling the psychic symptoms, in the sense that, e.g., some toxic agent produces both the psychic symptoms and the histological changes.

Kahlbaum has related catatonia to cerebral edema. In isolated, fatal cases, we have also seen severe cerebral edema accompanied by extremely tense arachnoid; the symptomatology of certain confusional and clouded states appears to have some connection with this type of cerebral edema.[101]

Kiernau and Weber (797) found residuals of a generalized or toxic meningitis in dementia praecox. I also have frequently noted marked turbidity of the pia mater; in several cases, there were white nodules along the blood vessels, perhaps residuals of previous turberculous meningitides. However, these are certainly not constant findings.

In one case, Doutrebente and Marchand have found a thickening of the pia mater and conclude that we are dealing with a resultant inferiority of the cerebral *Anlage*. Ideler (1886) suggested that catatonia might be a protracted form of paresis. Klippel and L'Hermite, as well as others (Soc. de psychiatrie de Paris, 1909), have related the disease to cerebellar atrophy. Schuele (675a) and Ferrari consider the possibility of atavism; the former, on the basis of the formation of delusions and myths; the latter, because of the peculiarities of the patients' expressions in writing. Whitewell seeks the cause for stupors in a congenital hypoplasia of the vascular system; Meynert (473 and 474) ascribes stupor to hydrocephalus, closing of the commissures, and easily transuding blood vessels.

Many authorities consider schizophrenia the result of a congenital pathological disposition of the brain. The influence of heredity, the frequency of the disease among oligophrenics and after cerebral trauma, the abnormal character traits of many of the persons who subsequently later develop schizophrenia—all these factors would point in this direction. However, what is regarded as an abnormal *Anlage*, may already be an expression of the disease itself. When we consult the literature as to which types of brains tend to develop these mental diseases, we

---

100. Cf. The Anatomy of Psychoses in Alzheimer's textbook.
101. Cf. Tetzner, Reichardt, and Gianelli.

are confronted with utter confusion: distinctions are made between active and disabled brains, between degenerated and non-degenerated individuals, between psychopathic and normal persons, psychoneurotics and psychotics, etc. However, the remarkable fact is that one authority considers as positive what another calls negative evidence.[102] Thus, the diseases defined in accordance with these criteria do not correspond with each other. The worst aspect of this situation is the fact that tests of these theories on larger material reveal innumerable contradictions; these are certainly not clarified by acknowledging the fact that an almost infinite number of deviations from the normal actually exists, and that, at the present time, none of these deviations can be related to any of the known psychoses.

Therefore, the question as to which of the pre-Kraepelinian clinical pictures of disease are based on an abnormal brain *Anlage,* has not been answered; nor is it possible to find an answer to it if it is actually true that schizophrenia, comprising all these psychoses, constitutes a natural group. The problem, however, of the existence of a specific cerebral disposition to schizophrenia and of the manner in which it expresses itself, has as yet not even been attacked, so that, once again, we do not know whether the problem can be solved at all.

At present, there is a preference for the toxic theories. These may be divided into the auto-toxic group and the infectious group.

The only support for the first group is provided by Berger's (52) experiments. He discovered that the blood of catatonics contained a specific substance which had a stimulating effect on the cortical motor centers of dogs and which was not present in other diseases including the hallucinatory confusional states. Since, at present, catatonia cannot be differentiated from these confusional states and since the number of experiments made was far too small, these investigations are as yet entirely inconclusive. It is also questionable, whether the toxin was not of an accidental or secondary nature.

Otherwise, there is no basis at all for the auto-toxic theories of the disease. The thyroid gland has often been blamed for producing the schizophrenic toxin or for not neutralizing it; I know of no basis for this assumption. However, the ineffectiveness of thyroidin on the disease, and the fact that schizophrenia occurs with the same frequency in regions where goiter is prevalent and in seaboard areas, speaks decisively against this theory. We cannot exclude with the same certainty a possible connection of the disease with a hyperfunctioning of the thyroid

102. Of the many authors who ascribe some manifestations of schizophrenia to a congenital or to an inherited disability of the brain, we wish to make special mention of Ossipow (539 a), who defines catatonia as "an illness of the hitherto healthy brain."

gland (in the sense of Basedow's disease),[103] especially since most Basedow-psychoses—in spite of their fairly strong affectivity—resemble schizophrenia so closely that up to now it has not been possible to separate them. Of old, our disease has been related to the sexual function; in this connection, the reproductive glands were considered as responsible factors (Lomer, Tschisch). After all, the frequent onset of the disease during and immediately after puberty, its aggravation during the menses, the common incidence of masturbation in association with it, the predominance of sexual delusions—all these factors seem to indicate a connection with the genital function. However, castration does not cure the disease. Bornstein believes that it may involve an exaggeration of processes of puberty, since the oxygen metabolism is higher in children and lower in his schizophrenic patients than it is in healthy adults. Dide (173) was unable to discover any factor which could explain the psychosis. Haberkant sees a genetic relationship between dementia praecox and osteomalacia in the fact that both are dependent on the reproductive as well as on the thyroid glands.

French psychiatrists consider a great number of various deliria and confusional states, most of which belong to schizophrenia, as the result of intoxication. Dercum maintains that the confusional state is a symptom of intoxication, whereas systematization accompanied by organized behavior represents a sign of cerebral alterations.

When dealing with psychoses that belong to schizophrenia, it has often been attempted to ascribe to exhaustion or some other type of physical weakness considerable etiological significance. Stadelmann assumes that an "exhaustion *Anlage*" predisposes to catatonia. Krafft-Ebing stated that "hallucinatory delusional insanity" occurs when a brain, already afflicted with susceptible weakness as the result of a neuropathic, specifically hereditary constitution, is subjected to exhausting conditions. It may be argued that Tschisch, on the other hand, emphasizes the fact that he observed catatonia develop in physically strong, healthy, and hereditarily not predisposed individuals. The actual situation is, probably, that the condition of the patient's physical strength has absolutely nothing to do with the disease; neither does it appear that the patient's physical strength at the time of the outbreak, or abstinence or over-eating during the disease, will influence its course (Zablocka). The transition to the infectious theory of the disease is made by Dide's assumption that some infectious process, e. g., tuberculosis, forms the basis of the disease. He ascribes the insufficient detoxication to the fatty degen-

---

103. After completion of this work, I saw Berkley's report on cures affected by means of partial strumectomy and iodin-lecithin. This observation requires checking.

eration of the liver which he frequently found in catatonics and hebephrenics. According to him, paranoid forms of the disease, where he could not discover the changes in the liver, are, perhaps, secondary consequences of the "toxi-infectious processes."

Bruce has succeeded in lending the greatest degree of probability to the infectious theory. In diseases, which we must include in the acute episodes of schizophrenia, he not only found bacteria in the patients' blood stream, but, on the basis of the specific reactions of the leucocytosis, concluded that he was dealing with an infectious disease. Dide and Sacquépée have reported similar findings. This is a practical lead, but, as yet, the bacteriological and hematological findings are entirely inadequate. Furthermore, it must be remembered that several schizophrenic thrusts are often preceded by an acute infectious disease. Therefore, we cannot reject the idea that schizophrenia may be an aftermath of certain infections. However, it is also possible that the disease is produced by one or more specific infections, which may be of an acute or a chronic nature, or which may remain latent for a long time, and from which the body could free itself completely only in exceptional cases. If the current interpretation of the relationship between acute and chronic rheumatic arthritis is correct, these infections offer us an analogy to the course of schizophrenia. Arthritis deformans can occur either chronic or acute; frequently, after an acute attack, anatomical residuals remain in the joints. However, the same changes may also develop in a chronic fashion. The acute symptoms, the pains, may be mild or severe; they may manifest themselves merely as an occasional pinching sensation in the joints, or as paralyzing attacks of arthritis; they may be absent for many years at a time, or they may occur almost daily or weekly for many years. However, if the local processes are intense, they always, as time goes on, result in certain changes of the joints which, in severe cases, cripple the patient.

The course of schizophrenia is identical. However, the only conclusion to be drawn from this parallel is that the possibility of an analogous infection exists.

SECTION XI

THERAPY

Except for the treatment of purely psychogenic disorders, the therapy of schizophrenia is one of the most rewarding for the physician who does not ascribe the results of the natural healing processes of psychosis to his own intervention.

As yet we do not know of any real prophylaxis for this disease. Hereditary factors give us some indications that members of a severely tainted family should not marry. Children of alcoholic parents seem more endangered than others. This aspect constitutes one of the reasons for the fight against alcoholism. Whatever else could be said coincides with general prophylaxis of mental disease.

We can say even less with regard to prophylaxis in individual cases since we do not yet know the releasing factors in this disease. The avoidance of masturbation, of disappointments in love, of strain or frights are recommendations which can be made with a clear conscience because these are things which should be avoided under all circumstances. However, we cannot prove that such precautions have ever prevented the outbreak of schizophrenia.

We are in a slightly better position—theoretically, at least—as far as the prodromal phase of the disease is concerned. Once the diagnosis is established as probable or certain, no physician will neglect to take these general precautions: the best physical hygiene in which sufficient sleep and nourishment are especially important; avoidance of all toxic or psychic excitants. After all, we know that such injurious factors frequently make the disease overt or aggravate it. However, we can go a bit farther. Strong affects facilitate the outbreak of acute attacks; much opposition aggravates the disease. Idleness facilitates the predomination by the complexes over the personality; whereas regulated work maintains the activity of normal thinking. These recommendations cannot always be fulfilled since we are so often dealing with patients who are dependent on their parents and on others.

All ambitious plans must be given up. On the other hand one should induce the patients to perform lighter tasks. The occupations should be selected in such a way that an occasional interruption will not matter too much and we can avoid conflict with the patients if a hebephrenic mood prevents them from working. Farm work and gardening are of course, most suitable, especially because these occupations which are generally regarded as "healthy" are more readily accepted as being of therapeutic value. Therefore it is also less difficult to persuade the patients to take up this kind of work rather than some other occupation. For girls and women, housework can be recommended, of course, but under the proper supervision. Routine, mechanical officework can be helpful in some cases. However, we must caution against having the patients engage in independent, intellectual work which involves a certain degree of responsibility. Faultless performance can hardly be expected and the unavoidable rebukes can greatly endanger the entire pleasure that the patients take in their work. Affects, as such, cannot be avoided; all the more should situations be avoided which give occasion to emotional excitement. For unmarried persons, in particular, close friendships with members of the opposite sex are dangerous and for the married, any occasions for marital dissatisfaction. Pregnancy should be avoided by all means.

Unfortunately, it is necessary to discuss the recommendation that the patients marry. Not only are the patients' parents and relatives inclined to recommend such measures, but also physicians are prone to offer this piece of advice—and they do so even in cases where they do not have the "excuse" of the fallacious diagnosis of "nervousness." In one case, a doctor advised marriage because the patient's delusions were of a sexual nature. The consequences, of course, are most regrettable since a second family and, in addition, also perhaps the children (the hereditary factor cannot be excluded) are made unhappy. Under all circumstances, if the disease is diagnosed or suspected, marriage must be discouraged with the greatest emphasis.

With equal emphasis one should warn against all expensive therapies. Doctors and the laity constantly recommend all sorts of "nerve cures" for chronic patients. Close, and sometime even distant, relatives often sacrifice all they own for a totally incurable patient, only to fall, together with the patient, into the greatest poverty later on. A small farmer with some property ruined himself financially because, among other things, some doctor had prescribed two bottles of expensive champagne daily for his daughter. Even in wealthier families, the education and upbringing of the healthy children frequently suffers because everything is being sacrificed, quite uselessly, on the one sick member. Let us openly say to ourselves and to others that, *at present, we know of no measures which will cure the disease, as such, or even bring it to a halt.*

Even when the patient is brought to the hospital, every consideration should be given to the family's means. For many of the severer patients, it makes little difference whether they are being cared for in the ward or in private rooms. This information should be given to the family who out of love, pride, or fear of what their neighbors will say, is only too eager to sacrifice means which could be much more usefully applied in some other way.

Both for the prodromal stage, as well as for the overt disease, some remedies have been recommended which are supposed to cure, or at least ameliorate the illness. More recently organotherapy (Kraepelin, Hill, Sprague) has been tried; and in analogy to the use of thyroid in myxodemas, thyroid extracts have been administered; even parathyroid preparations (Pighini) have been given to these patients—without success. Iodine and thyroid extracts are being urged in catatonia.

Lommer and von Rohé have again recommended castration which, of course, is of no benefit to the patients themselves.[1] However, it is to be hoped that sterilization will soon be employed on a larger scale in these cases as in other patients with a pathological *Anlage* for eugenic reasons.

I have never seen any success with the gynecological treatment which is recommended by some authors; on the contrary, it usually has negative results. (This statement does not, of course, imply that women who are obviously suffering from diseases of the genital system should not be treated locally.) The corresponding treatment of men with sounds, bougies, etc., is, of course, equally unsuccessful, even though it is supposed to be directed against a definite symptom which is also considered by some as the cause: masturbation. As a palliative measure against this symptom, though not as a cure of the disease, we might mention bromide which, in some cases, really reduced the sexual drive and the onanism but, most significantly, has no effect on the disease itself. Hecker even claims to have reduced the sexual allusions in the conversation of one patient by the use of small doses of bromides. Under certain circumstances, particularly in private practice, one will not completely give up the

1. I recall very vividly four castrated schizophrenics. One of them had cut off his own testicles. Two had their ovaries removed for "nervous troubles;" i.e., in reality, because of the psychosis. A fourth had an ovariectomy because of an inflammatory process of the internal genitalia. In none of these cases could we detect a beneficial effect on the course of the disease. In two cases, castration was followed by the actual outbreak of the illness, giving rise to the patients' notion that they were no longer "complete" human beings, thus constituting an integral part of the disease symptoms. Unilateral castration was also of no help in another male case. These admittedly scant observations confirm the obvious consideration that sexual thoughts do not indicate that the disease originates in the sexual organs. After all, such thoughts occur also in the normal individual and their presence rather demonstrates the contrary; namely, that psychic and physical sexuality is normal, or at least active.

struggle against masturbation by dietary measures, and the recommendation of cool and not too soft sleeping facilities. However, I must add that all these measures are of very doubtful value in schizophrenia, and that, unless there are very special reasons, it is hardly worth the effort to undertake the rather futile battle against this bad habit.

Where a new attack of the disease appears to have been released by a pregnancy, one may have to consider abortion. One woman, in whom this was done for gynecological reasons and whose main complex was centered on the fear of having more children, was greatly improved directly following the intervention. But in view of the present legal aspects of the problems, I do not like to recommend this procedure for psychological reasons although I consider it a grave misfortune to have children raised by a schizophrenic mother.

As a means of combatting the disease itself all sorts of dietary cures have been advocated; in England, particularly, special emphasis is laid on fattening the patients. I have seen neither good nor bad results from such methods, except where the withdrawal of alcohol was concerned.

Carlo Livi recommended blood transfusions; saline infusions have also been tried but without success.

The observation, that remissions sometimes occurred after fevers, has led to attempts to induce artificial fever (W.v. Jauregg); even erysipelas and streptococci have been inoculated (Catala, Boeck). More recently, these experiments were made by less dangerous methods using tuberculin, inactivated bacterial cultures of pyocyaneus, and anti-streptococcus serum (Marr). So far it has not been established that these methods do not sometimes result in improvement.

Bruce, who regards schizophrenia and the related psychoses as primarily infectious, has recommended turpentine injections in order to increase the lymphocytic count and so raise the patient's resistance. The value of this kind of treatment is still very problematical.[2] Some authors have tried to explain conditions which certainly were schizophrenic, in terms of intestinal toxins; they gave laxatives and even tried to disinfect the bowels (Macpherson). There is no evidence whatsoever to substantiate the correctness of such a view.

Once the disease has been recognized, the question as to whether or not to institutionalize the patient must be decided. The institution as such does not cure the disease. However, it may be valuable from an educational viewpoint and it may alleviate acute, agitated states due to psychic influences. At the same time, it carries with it the danger that

---

2. Ittin has used nucleic acid in very severe cases with no success.

the patient may become too estranged from normal life, and also that the relatives get accustomed to the idea of the institution. For this reason, it is often extremely difficult to place even a greatly improved patient outside the institution, after he has been hospitalized for a number of years.

In general, it is preferable to treat these patients under their usual conditions and within their habitual surroundings. The patient should not be admitted to the hospital just because he suffers from schizophrenia, but only when there is a definite indication for hospitalization. The indication is, of course, given when the patient becomes too disturbing or dangerous, when restraint is necessary, when he presents a threat to the well-being of the healthy members of his family, or when it is no longer possible to influence him. In the latter event, the institution will attempt to educate the patient to act in a more acceptable manner, after which he will be released.

Release from the hospital follows the same principles. One should not wait for a "cure." One can consider it an established rule that earlier release produces better results. Often, apparently very severe cases may suddenly behave very well outside the hospital. However, all factors must be taken into consideration. In particular, we must consider the qualities of the patient's relatives; they may as easily ruin the patient as they may continue his education. If suitable work is available for the improved patient, one will, of course, have fewer doubts about releasing him than if this is not the case. It is difficult to state exactly which of the agitated patients are qualified for early release. The chances for release become smaller, the more "organic" and less "psychogenic" the picture of the disease appears. The only, and often very practical, criterion is the patient's capacity to react in a positive manner to changes in environment and treatment.[3]

I do not believe that a premature release as such is as harmful to the schizophrenic as it is to the manic-depressive. On the other hand, the outside situation may be such that it may produce a relapse (a meeting with a former lover, quarrels, family troubles; living with a happily married sister, which reminds the patient of her own failure to marry, etc.)

---

3. In bad, overcrowded institutions, which are fortunately becoming increasingly rare, schizophrenics who submit to it are soon turned into work-slaves by the hospital personnel who treat them as if they were merely obstinate, healthy persons. As soon as the patients are somewhat improved they must be released for want of space. In these institutions, the doctor releases the patients more readily than in others where he has closer contact with them and can consequently clearly recognize any pathological manifestations. Unwittingly, the patient is supported in his efforts to encase himself in his disease; and certain types of patients are being prevented from leaving "good" hospitals, whereas the same types are being released as "cured" from the poorer institutions.

If, upon release, the patient cannot be placed with his own family, the care he may receive from a strange family often serves as an adequate substitute. Of course, the latter situation demands supervision by a competent authority. Especially the inactivated cases, who have acquired some discipline in an institution where they had relative freedom of movement, are well suited for organized family care.

At the present time, the only type of therapy that can seriously be considered for schizophrenia as a whole is the psychic method. Unfortunately, however, we have barely passed the empirical stage in this field. Since the symptomatology of the disease is dominated by the complexes and since these often offer a starting point for us from which to penetrate the patient's psyche, it might also be expected that the disease could be influenced from this angle. Indubitably, improvement in response to psychic treatment occurs, but we are at a loss to state what must be done in each individual case in order to bring about that improvement. Therefore, we are forced to grope in the dark; indeed, it might be said that the only way is to offer chance itself a great many opportunities, so that it may seize one of them. If this is done at the right moment, a good deal can often be accomplished.

At present, there is nothing we can do at the peak of an active thrust of the disease. We are forced to wait for improvement. However, in many cases, it is difficult to recognize when the end of the acute stage has been reached. A catatonic may still appear very ill; he may appear negativistic, violent, and autistic to the greatest degree; yet he may already react to certain outside influences and on being transferred home may impress his family as being well. In these cases, we actually learn only through the result that the nature of the disease has changed. However, if we examine and observe our cases carefully, we will usually be able to detect precious indications that the patient has become accessible.

But there is an additional factor to be considered. In general, our handling of the case cannot influence such facts as that an acute episode has broken out, that it continues to persist, or that the disease process advances or comes to a standstill. However, when a certain patient wants to smash his own head, when he insists on smearing, breaks windows, tears his clothes, etc., his actions are not directly determined by the disease process itself, but constitute reactions of his complexes to inner and, particularly, to external circumstances. Therefore, potentially at least, the opportunity to influence the patient's symptoms is always given. It is difficult to make any statement as to the specific manner by which we can influence each individual case or the patients in general. There are some rules which are actually contradictory, but which are, nevertheless, valid, depending on the case and the circumstances. In particular, every effort should be made to avoid provocation of the patient's negativism; the less resistance and contradiction the patient encounters from those around him, the less inclination is there on his part to oppose them in terms of negativism. On the other hand, a great deal can be accomplished by issuing precise commands which render resistance useless. At the Rheinau Hospital, I once encountered a number of patients who appeared to be unmanageable. The nursing staff insisted that it was impossible, for instance, to comb or to wash them. Firm and unconditional adherence to the hospital rules in this respect resulted within a few days in obtaining the desired result in all cases; the patients gave up their resistance and the majority of them became, also in other respects, a good deal more accessible. Whereas a suicidal drive may certainly be eliminated by permitting the patient to act it out, the same result may also be obtained when the patient is made to realize that it is completely impossible for him to carry out his impulses. Many kinds of pathological misconduct can be eliminated by the refusal to tolerate them.

The general tasks or treatment, then, consist in educating the patient in re-establishing his contact with reality, i.e., in combatting autism. Often, neither tasks can be accomplished for a long time, until, finally the patient gives up his resistance and permits himself to be influenced. It is very important to make repeated attempts at gaining access to the patient. In no other disease, except in schizophrenia, is it essential that external circumstances be changed occasionally. If the patients are permitted to remain always in the same set of surroundings, they easily become more and more encased in their disease and proportionally less accessible. Avoidance of this danger represents the great advantage of transfer to another ward, another hospital, or even home —in general, to some other environment. Especially in chronic cases, transfers to other hospitals should be arranged more frequently (Riklin). Sometimes it is possible to make a sort of deal even with a disturbed patient, regarding his transfer to a better ward. For example, one of our patients had to be kept in isolation because of her constantly noisy and violent behavior, and consequently became much worse. She was transferred to a better ward on condition that she behave herself and with the promise of early release. She immediately became calm and eligible for release from the institution.

Occupational therapy represents the best means of meeting our demands. It provides an opportunity for exercising the normal psychic functions, for continual active and passive contact with reality, it stimulates the patients' capacity for adaptation, and forces them to think about normal life outside the hospital. Most important, occupational therapy offers the attendant personnel almost the only opportunity for close contact with the patients. After all, in the absence of some such external means, it is impossible for anyone to maintain for any length of time psychic contact with individuals with whom one does not have any spiritual rapport. Even in acute stages, occupational therapy proves often both practical and useful. Every mental institution should have the kind of set-up that will make it possible to offer every patient some kind of work at all times. In some cases, outdoor work has the most beneficient effect. For women, customary housework serves almost the same purpose. Transcribing and other mechanical clerical work proves useful for patients who were previously accustomed to such occupations. In the majority of cases, it is impossible to elicit mental efforts, and in other cases, such an effort may be most harmful. It is very important to organize the work in such a way that the patients can accept it as a matter of course. If that is done, the patients will merely have to fit themselves into an organism of which they are already a part, by virtue of their admission to the hospital. In that way, participation in the work will not demand anything resembling special obedience and, consequently, will not serve as a provocation for negavitism.

Only a trial will reveal in which cases occupational therapy cannot be applied. It must also be remembered that some patients are subject to abnormal feelings of fatigue; consequently, they should be encouraged to work only with the proper caution or, at times, not at all. In rare cases, occupational therapy contributes to hallucinations; in that event, it should be stopped but, if possible, only temporarily.

In cases of pseudo-distinction, where not only the patients, but occasionally their relatives, object in principle to any kind of work, artistic activity may be an alternative. In individual cases, it may be of good service but, because of the lack of need for contact with reality, it must be carefully supervised. Moreover, some danger is represented by the patients' tendency to play around, to indulge in bizarre activities, and particularly in the case of music, by their inclination to become absorbed in their own emotions. Regarding professional artists, it is advisable to make it possible for the patient to work in his field during the period of improvement.

Sports may also be considered as an inferior substitute for work. However, as an addition to work, it is of considerable value when dealing with people who are well acquainted with it. Otherwise, games such as cards, billiards, and bowling must serve the same purpose.

Social events of every type, including dances, and walks, are very beneficial to suitable patients. They help to maintain or to re-establish the contact with reality.[4] Chronically withdrawn patients' cases may often take a turn for the better on such social occasions.[5]

Special care should be taken to provide sufficient opportunity for entertainment on Sundays which is generally a bad day for our patients. Even on the disturbed wards, reading matter should be available. It is also of benefit, if local custom approves of it, that in this day the women patients do some work for their own advantage (such as crocheting lace, which provides them with a little spending money.)

The aim of the patients' education must be the development of self-control. This includes control of some disease symptoms. Many patients can be taught to suppress their agitation, to pay less attention to their hallucinations and not to become upset by them, and to give up asocial habits. Intelligent patients with good dispositions may, in some cases, accomplish an admirable degree of self-control. But even patients with less favorable dispositions can be taught to adapt their behavior to the normal as much as possible.

As in all other fields of education, the first goal should be the proper utilization of time. Since many schizophrenics have lost the capacity for feeling boredom, external stimulation must be substituted for it. However, those patients who are still bothered by boredom should be given the opportunity to banish it; otherwise, just like healthy persons in a similar situation, they will get into all kinds of mischief.

In sensitive individuals appeals to ethics or to their ambition may be effective during certain stages of their illness; at least, we may succeed in interesting them in some useful occupation. However, in more advanced cases and in persons whose disposition is not so sensitive, this is not possible. In such instances, we may have to resort to the proven correctives of "candy" and the "whip." However, punishments should not consist in hurting the patient, but rather in withholding the "candy" to which the patient is not actually entitled. Anyway, antisocial behavior necessarily leads to results that may constitute punishment; thus, for example, a patient may have to be transferred to another ward where the other inmates are equally antisocial and, therefore, unpleasant. However, I do not believe in renouncing disciplinary measures altogether, although, also in this respect, too little is far better than too much.

One should think that religious influences would serve as useful

4. It is, of course, important to avoid the use of alcohol at all social functions, since otherwise the disadvantages may outweigh the advantages.

5. In one of the hospitals, I encountered a violent woman patient who was regarded as so dangerous that no less than four attendants at a time were permitted in her room. One Christmas Eve, I took this patient along to the party at the hospital. On New Year's Day she introduced herself as a singer; some weeks later she was released. She has successfully maintained her improvement.

means of education but I have never seen any success due to them, in schizophrenia. Is it possible that those who handle patients in this manner cannot find the right way?

A special task of institutional education is that of helping the patients to get accustomed to freedom. In the hospital, the patients cannot direct their own activities. After a time, many patients lose the ability to do so, unless special attention is paid to this aspect. Therefore, they must be conditioned to self-reliance by granting them certain freedoms, such as passes, vacations, trial-releases, and, if possible, the opportunity to work independently in the hospital.[6] Most of the patients who remain in the institution can also be trained to take walks on Sundays[7]; after all, the situation appears far more humane when the patients are permitted to go out. However, I must add that, in some cases, I have often asked myself whether I was really doing a service to these patients in getting them accustomed to new needs.

The special attendant is also an important factor in education. He can separate the patient requiring special supervision from the others, and can provide him with work and entertainment. When dealing with cases of limited financial means, we often advise the relatives to transfer the patient to a less expensive class of the hospital and to use the difference to pay for a special attendant.

Close attention must be paid to the nature of the suggestion exerted by the patient's environment. Good surroundings have a very different influence on the patient than unpleasant and noisy ones. The secret of the success of many institutions lies in the fact that they have a great deal of space, numerous wards, and adequate facilities for separating antisocial patients from the others. The actual suggestive therapy accomplishes very little in schizophrenia. Some patients, however, are amenable to hypnosis; it is possible to suggest sleep to them; hallucinations may be eliminated for short periods of time, and the patients may be calmed down temporarily. However, the results are not permanent, except in patients whose conditions would improve any way. This type of therapy is, therefore, rarely worth the effort it requires. Nevertheless, I continued the suggestive therapy started by Forel in a patient with frequent, and evidently very severe hallucinatory excitements. I hypnotized the patient at the onset of every agitated attack, and eventually succeeded in definitely eliminating the periods of excitement. Consequently, the patient has now maintained himself outside a hospital for some fifteen years. Attempts at interrupting the treatments demonstrated

6. During trial-releases, the relatives are taught to assume the proper attitudes toward the patients.

7. This applies particularly to institutions which are not situated close to towns.

that the improvement was not purely coincidental.

On the other hand, the customary methods of suggestion should be utilized in schizophrenia to the same extent as in any other disease. Although far more rarely, we may still be able to alleviate certain complaints by disguised suggestion, to induce sleep by means of milk sugar, etc.

The method of uncovering the complexes and permitting abreaction is rarely as successful with severe schizophrenics as it is with neurotics. It does not change the patients. However, in milder cases which are more common in private practice than in institutions, this type of therapy results sometimes in distinct improvement which may persist for several years. In the event of relapse, the treatment may be successfully repeated. It happens that, only recently, we succeeded, by way of abreaction, in inducing normal sleep, within a few days, in a rather advanced schizophrenic who had been unable to get rid of his insomnia in rest-homes. (It is irrelevant for purposes of therapy whether there exists such a thing as actual abreaction, or whether we are dealing merely with a different form of disguised suggestion.) The transference of affection to the physician, which can be successfully utilized in hysteria, results in schizophrenia mostly in pathological "love," occasionally followed by sexual persecutory ideas.

I am unable to imagine in what manner a sytematic education of the thinking of these patients could be carried out. When we succeed in enabling the patient to control his complexes, we have usually accomplished the desirable result. Nevertheless, some authors have recommended "mental exercises," schooling, etc. (recently, Masselon); their success is probably not very great.

Many severe cases have demonstrated the impossibility of actual re-educating them to purposeful behavior. Yet even in these cases, some measure of success may still be achieved by a method which is correctly defined by the rather disreputable word, "drill." In this manner the patients can be brought to the point where they will do the correct thing, either mechanically or out of habit. They have some control over their pathological impulses; they do very little harm, if any; they feed, dress, and undress themselves, and are often capable of doing simple, mechanical work. Considering the antisocial behavior of the severe, negativistic patient, these therapeutic results are not to be underestimated.

The manner in which each individual case is handled, must be left to the physician. Consideration must be given, not only to the patient's personality but also to that of the physician himself. A method, which has proven valuable in the hands of one physician, may result in failure in the hands of another. The principal rule is that no patient must ever be completely given up, the doctor must always be prepared to take action, and to offer the patient the chance to abandon his pathological way of thinking. Sufficient funds and personnel should be available to give the patients the necessary care in the hospitals, especially, there should be adequate space, which should make it possible to provide every patient with appropriate surroundings and treatment, at the opportune time. These prime considerations must never be neglected.

Isolation and bed-care require special discussion. For many acute cases, bed-care is the best method of treatment. Some disturbed patients are best confined to bed. The very fact of being in bed and the absence of clothes represent important means of suggestion for a calm attitude. In addition, the bed itself, with its blankets and sheets, provides, in many instances, material for a harmless kind of occupation. In weak, abstinent patients, bed-rest is also necessary for physical reasons. However, I must emphasize that, on the whole, bed-care is in no way comparable to occupational therapy. Only patients who, for some reason, are unable to work should be confined to bed. Naturally, bed-care represents a distinct advance over the laissez-faire method, which used to be practiced in many places. It has the particular advantage that it contributes to closer contact between the nursing staff and the patients; it compels the attendants to concern themselves with the patients, a very important factor for both parties. However, occupational therapy serves the same purpose even better. Also, there are rarely patients who complain about the work they have to do; whereas, in the course of my twelve years in the institution, I was never able to get to the point where most patients did not consider confinement to bed as a severe punishment.[8]

More recently, bed-care in the open air has been advocated as a form of treatment. Naturally, this offers certain obvious advantages: change, the necessity of closer supervision, and the hygienic and psychic effects of sunlight and fresh air. Unfortunately, however, I have, as yet, no experience with this particular "therapeutic method."

Also with respect to isolation, my experiences do not wholly agree with the principles which contemporary psychiatric literature appears to advocate. Isolation is an evil, for many reasons; but in some cases it is a necessary, and, in many, the least of unavoidable evils. However, it also has some good sides. We must resort to isolation, if we are sympathetic with our patients; for example, when a single, agitated patient disturbs the sleep of the entire ward, annoys the other patients in day-

8. According to Schuele and Anton (20) bed-rest is liable to produce cramps in the legs. I have not observed this symptom.

time, and, in general, represents a disturbing element, which prevents the other inmates from calming down.

Moreover, isolation may represent an excellent means of education for the patient, not as much in the direction of the "whip," as in that of "candy;" removal of all sources of irritation is often appreciated as a relief by the schizophrenics. Patients, who are subject to sudden states of agitation and who have not yet learned to control themselves, react very favorably to immediate isolation at the onset of every attack, provided, proper care is taken to make the patients understand their removal as necessary precaution, and not as punishment. Many patients can be trained to the extent that they will demand isolation on their own account, when they feel the approach of an attack of agitation. At this stage, they have already acquired some degree of self-control; subsequently, it will be no problem to leave the door of the isolation-room open, so that the patients can decide themselves, when they are socially acceptable again. This represents another means of education, which enables many patients to regain full—or, at least, partial—self-control.[9] The fact, that many schizophrenics, just like healthy persons, prefer to sleep in a room of their own, rather than among a number of not exactly sociable patients, is, strangely enough, often overlooked. In fact, I have received far fewer complaints about isolation than about confinement to bed. Indeed, at the institution, I was often obliged to combine isolation with some unpleasant factor, so as to avoid being forced by certain patients to keep them constantly in isolation. However, in schizophrenia, isolation presents many dangers which do not apply to other psychoses. The schizophrenic, left to his own devices, very easily becomes increasingly enmeshed in his autism and develops all kinds of unpleasant habits, particularly, smearing.

If isolation is utilized properly, none of these disadvantages will occur. I am very well acquainted with the almost incorrigible products of the isolation-cells of many hospitals. However, I may also add that I have not seen any develop in our own institution, despite the fact that we still practice isolation to a large extent, though, in daytime much less than previously. Of course, isolation is never prolonged beyond the point where it is absolutely necessary. However, the most important rule is that, even with isolated patients, we must constantly seek to maintain as close a contact as possible. In this way, the patients' psychic isolation is limited and they can present their complaints. On the other hand, we are in the position to select the proper moment for terminating isolation, and can also influence the patients in other ways. If they

9. Roller's phrase, "Isolation often brings speedy relief to the disturbed patient," still holds true.

begin to show bad habits, another form of treatment must be started at once.

The acute episodes of the disease represent the most important, as well as the most difficult, problems for palliative therapy. Many schizophrenics are constantly and severely agitated during hallucinatory states; at the same time no other patients are as difficult to influence as they are. The self-inflicted injuries of these patients, their destruction of everything within their reach, their actual physical attack on attendants—actions, which they carry out with utmost cleverness and disregard for their environment—these are the strongest indications for the use of restraint. In most of these cases, not to restrain them would result in the destruction of everything destructible, including the hospital staff. Anyone who claims that he can handle such situations without the use of restraint, applies the word, restraint, in a sense different from that demanded by idiomatic speech.

The manner in which the necessary restraint is applied, depends on the hospital facilities, on the experience and, to some extent, on the personality of the physician in charge. At first it may be attempted to confine the patient to bed. If this fails, the use of continuous baths may be expected to yield good results. Naturally, occupational therapy can only be employed in milder cases, and then with caution. The percentage of patients who can be handled more easily will depend on the quality of the available equipment, on the nature of the other inmates, on the spirit prevailing in the institution, on the skill and tact of the physicians and the rest of the staff; and, moreover, on something indefinable, which is also related to personalities of the people attending the patients, and which is effective, in addition to skill and tact. Even agitated schizophrenics can be influenced by the environment, although temporarily many cases appear totally unimpressed by all existing methods of finding a systematic approach to them.

In the event that nothing can be accomplished in that way, a trial-isolation, with or without a special attendant, may reveal whether or not separation from the other patients would be of any help. If the result is positive, temporary isolation should be ordered, if the result of the trial-isolation is negative, there remains, as a last resort, the wet pack and sedatives, which may be used either separately, or combined. When the wet pack is applied to milder cases, the arms may often be left free. However, I rarely consider it necessary with such patients. The complete wet pack (arms included) is the most severe restraint, of which I know. Consequently, I often did not make use of it for many years. After all, it will hardly ever be needed in chronic cases. In the institutions, however, there were certain cases in which, unfortunately, I was unable to avoid this measure. But I know that, with more funds and more space I would hardly ever have had to resort to it.

In patients with an uncontrollable drive to inflict injury upon themselves, it is advisable to use a restraining sheet, which is more easily applied than the wet pack and which makes no pretense (recognized by the staff as well as by the patients) at constituting a medical measure. The success of this method proves that the calming effect of the wet pack is not due to the wet coverings, but rather to the physically enforced rest, which quickly induces sleep, even in the most severely agitated patient.

In contrast to what might be concluded from recent literature, I have found that physical restraint is not entirely harmful, but that it may have beneficial influence on certain, individual cases. The most severe agitation with suicidal drives may be alleviated within thirty minutes by application of the restraining sheet. Because of our great reluctance to resort to such measures of restraint, we, at one time, spent many months applying all other methods and wasting our staff and sedatives, in the effort to treat a girl who, after the actual acute episode had already passed, could not control her drive to inflict every possible injury upon herself. As soon as the restraining sheet had been securely fastened, so that any further attempts to injure herself appeared futile, the patient submitted at once, behaved normally, and was soon afterwards released, in excellent condition. This case also presents a typical illustration of how the psychic residues of the disease can stimulate the disease itself. Therefore, if no results can be obtained by means of kindness and greatest possible indulgence, I believe that it is preferable to experiment with the use of restraint rather than to permit the patient to destroy himself.

In schizophrenia, I consider enforcement by means of restraint better under all circumstances than holding the patient down by actual physical force. The latter method will challenge and increase the patient's negativism, and will also exhaust him far more physically, because of his continued efforts at resistance.

Sedatives are not only important as chemical restraint, but, in schizophrenia as in other diseases, they often constitute a means of alleviation which we must not withhold from the patients if for no other reason, than that of simple humaneness. Anyone who suffers mentally has as much claim to medication that will relieve his symptoms, within the limits of harmlessness, as anyone who suffers physically. Admittedly, it is difficult to define where exactly harmful use begins. However, one does not get the impression that even rather high doses of various sedatives encourage deterioration. Thus, we may conclude that reasonable administration of sedatives in the usual doses is harmless. In a great many cases, sedatives also have an educational value. Patients, who, otherwise could not get accustomed to work, to their bed, to bathing, and to normal conditions, may gradually be trained, while under the effect of mild sedation, and may owe their improvement to the medication. Of course, no sedative should be given continuously.

A third reason for using sedatives is consideration for the other patients. I prefer to drug the patient who disturbs the peace to having the others robbed of their sleep or become agitated.

I have not yet seen any actual harm result from the use of sedatives. The strongest contra-indication presents the fact that they are ineffective in more severe cases. The quantities of various sedatives, which, separately or combined, can be taken by some schizophrenics without any calming effect are really astonishing.[10]

Perhaps such cases require unusual doses, in order to be affected by sedatives. However, no one is likely to wish to make the test as to what happens first on increasing the doses: collapse, or sedation.

Apomorphine is a chemical restraint of a special type. Some acute agitated states can be interrupted immediately by an injection of an emetic dose of apomorphine. In attacks that have not lasted longer than a few days, the quieting effect may persist for some time, so that the excitement is often definitely eliminated. Simultaneously, apomorphine is effective as a tool of education, inasmuch as the patient remains fully conscious while he calms down, and in this way can practice better behavior. I must mention this remedy, although I cannot recommend it on ethical grounds; but then, again, I must ask whether it is not more unethical to permit a whole roomful of patients to be annoyed by a single agitated patient than to cause the offender to vomit. According to my observation, none of the patients complained about the use of this method, and, we have not lost contact with any of them. Generally, the patients themselves made fun of it, although they were rather impressed by its prompt effect. I have no experience with this drug in patients with complete confusional states who were no longer capable of discussing matters.[11]

Treatment of schizophrenia by medication does not exist. Ziehen

---

10. This applies to purely psychic agitations, as well as to those on an apparently organic basis. As far as I know, the theories of sleep and those concerning sedatives, continue to ignore this highly important fact.

11. In many places the drug has been condemned because of unfortunate experiences with it. It seems that it was not used only on suitable patients. Naturally, it can only be effective in the relatively rare cases with whom one has sufficient rapport to make them understand the reasons for this measure and who, at the same time, are still capable of reacting to such a restraining influence on the part of the physician in a positive way, and not with negativism.

believes that by the use of opium he has often prevented a "hypochondriacal neurasthenia" from developing into a "hypochondriacal melancholia." I am rather doubtful as to whether our prognostic knowledge would justify such a belief. All other assertions in this direction are not worth discussing.

Hitzig has recommended the use of atropine for cutting short attacks in periodic psychoses to which, according to his examples, our periodic schizophrenias would also belong. At first the drug really seems to give the desired result. However, I have used it only in a few cases because, after some time, the patients ceased to react to the drug, and subsequently made up for the disturbances that had been eliminated.

The individual symptoms of the disease are to be treated in accordance with the usual principles. We only wish to mention at this point that "blocking" may be eliminated or alleviated for a few hours by means of alcohol (this might be useful in an examination) and that it is advisable to suppress some of the peculiarities which the patients so readily adopt. The paper-crowns, the wooden swords and rag-dolls have disappeared from our hospitals, to the advantage of the patients. However, this does not imply that, in some cases, the patient should not be permitted to keep one of his possessions which may be connected with his complexes; but this should only be done with due consideration of all circumstances, because it may encourage the autism.

The situation is similar with respect to hypochondriacal and hysteriform complaints about physical difficulties. On the whole, it is best for the patient to get accustomed to the idea that it is up to him to come to terms with his symptoms and that ignoring them is often the only remedy for them. There are also cases where some suggestive drugs are used. In that event, it should be carefully avoided that the patient forms a habit of taking them. Once on taking charge of a ward, I noted that a certain woman patient had fallen into the habit of taking thirteen different remedies for various non-existent complaints. After these drugs had gradually been withdrawn it was much easier to get along with her.

Refusal to accept food can be handled in the usual way. Schizophrenics, particularly, may be induced to eat by permitting them to "steal" the food which is apparently intended for another patient, or by catering in some other way to their negativism or their delusions. However, I find it difficult to see what can be gained by this; in any event, chronic cases often lose much discipline and capacity for rapport by these methods. I believe that it is better—with the exception, perhaps, of very special cases—to insist on strict obedience to the hospital rules. If a patient really does not eat for a whole week, one must resort to tube-feeding. However, this should be interrupted repeatedly so as to give the patients an opportunity to feed themselves; in this way, the tube will hardly ever remain for any length of time. In private sanitoria, we may be compelled to violate this principle; not because of the patient, but because of his relatives, who, unfortunately, feel less pity with the patient when he has to be tortured by tube-feedings for a whole month, than when he goes hungry for a few days. I have not observed that either hunger or adequate nourishment have any influence on the course of the disease.

Also with respect to other unpleasant peculiarities, particularly, smearing, it will be necessary to intervene as early and as energetically as possible if one wants to avoid the gradually progressing development of incorrigible stereotypies. In this case, a great deal depends on the skill of the hospital staff. The mere order to see to it that the patient uses the toilet regularly or that he must be given an enema at a specific time every day, does not suffice with respect to smearing. In view of the negativism, it is in many cases advisable to have these regulations carried out as impersonally as possible, as physical necessity for the patient; in other patients, one may give in to a certain amount of bargaining. In any case, however, such individual symptoms also indicate that frequent changes in the external circumstances may be useful (transfer to another ward, etc.) Minor undesirable habits can often be combatted by very simple measures. Thus a catatonic woman, living at home, stuffed all the toilet paper she could find in the bathroom into the toilet. It was enough to move the paper-holder a half-foot higher to eliminate forever this inconvenient habit. It is also important that the patients are not offered any opportunities to indulge in their peculiarities. In cases of long standing, it is not always worthwhile to try to combat certain habits. Kahlbaum suggested that it was necessary to prevent the patients from the practice of pulling out their hair, in order to avoid permanent alopecia. However, we may permit a patient to pull out his hair for many years, without fear of such danger; as soon as the patient stops pulling it, the hair will grow back.

The most serious of all schizophrenic symptoms is the suicidal drive. I am even taking this opportunity to state clearly that our present-day social system demands great, and entirely inappropriate cruelty from the psychiatrist in this respect. People are being forced to continue to live a life that has become unbearable for them for valid reasons; this alone is bad enough. However, it is even worse, when life is made increasingly intolerable for these patients by using every means to subject them to constant humiliating surveillance. Most of our worst restraining measures would be unnecessary, if we were not duty-bound to preserve the patients' lives which, for them as well as for others, are only of negative value. If all this would, at least, serve some purpose! However, like Savage, I am convinced, that in schizophrenia it is this very surveillance which awakes, increases, and maintains the suicidal drive. Only in exceptional cases would any of our patients commit suicide, if they were permitted to do as they wished. And even if a few more killed themselves—does this reason justify the fact that we torture hundreds of patients and aggravate their disease? At the present time, we psychiatrists are burdened with the tragic responsibility of obeying the cruel views of society; but it is our responsibility to do our utmost to bring about a change in these views in the near future.

BIBLIOGRAPHY

Abbreviations

A.	= Archiv für Psychiatrie und Nervenkrankheiten. Berlin, Hirschwald.
Abst.	= Abstracted in.
Amps.	= Annales medico-psychologiques.
An.	= Archives de neurologie.
CBN.	= Centralblatt für Nervenheilkunde und Psychiatrie, Leipzig, Barth.
Dp. or d.	= Dementia praecox, démence précoce, déments précoces, demenza precoce.
Jahrb.	= Jahrbücher für Psychiatrie und Neurologie. Leipzig und Wien, Deuticke.
JB.	= Jahresbericht über die Leistungen und Fortschritte auf dem Gebiete der Neurologie und Psychiatrie. Berlin, S. Karger.
Jmsc.	= Journal of Mental Science.
Marh.	= Marhold.
MS.	= Monatsschrift für Psychiatrie und Neurologie, Berlin, S. Karger.
Münch med. WS.	= Münchner medizinische Wochenschrift, München, J. F. Lehman.
NCB.	= Neurologisches Centralblatt, Leipzig, Veit & Komp.
WS.	= Psychiatrisch-neurologische Wochenschrift. Halle a. S., Marhold.
Z.	= Allgemeine Zeitschrift für Psychiatrie. Berlin. Georg Reimer.

Numbers with asterisk indicate the page on which the year of publication of a book was reported in the review of literature in the *Allgemeine Zeitschrift für Psychiatrie.*

1. Abraham, Traum und Mythus. Leipzig und Wien, Deuticke, 1909.
2. ——— Über die Bedeutung sexueller Jugendtraumen für die Symptomatologie der Dp. CBN., 1907, p. 409.
3. ——— Die psychosexuellen Differenzen der Hysterie und der Dp. CBN., 1908, p. 521.

3 *a*) D'Abundo, Stati nevropatici consecutivi al terremoto del 28. XII. 1908. Riv. it. d. Neuropat. etc., II, 2, 1909. Abst.: CBN., 1909, p. 616.

4. Adam, A Case of Melancholia with Stupor and Catalepsy. Jmsc., 1884, p. 508.
5. Adler, Über die im Zusammenhang mit akuten Infektionskrankheiten auftretenden Geistesstörungen. Z., 1897, Vol. 53, p. 740.
6. Agostini, Über die Isotonie des Blutes bei Geisteskranken. Rivist. sper. di freniat., Vol. 18, 1893, 72 *.
7. Albrand, Okulistische Beiträge zur Wertung der Degenerationszeichen. A., 1908, Vol. 44, p. 121.
8. Albrecht, Zur Symptomatologie der Dp. Z., 1905, Vol. 62, p. 659.
9. Alt, Die Symptome der Personenverwechslung bei Geisteskranken. Z., 1888, Vol. 44, p. 50.
10. Alter, Zur Genese einiger Symptome in katatonen Zuständen. NCB., 1904, p. 8.
11. ——— Über eine seltenere Form geistiger Störung. MS., 1903, Vol. 14, p. 246.
12. ——— Stereopsychosen. MS., 1904, Vol. XVI, p. 297.

13. Alzheimer, Einiges zur pathologischen Anatomie der Geistesstörungen. NCB., 1900, p. 489.
14. Amadei e Tonini, Über die Paranoia und ihre Formen. Arch. it. per le mal. nerv., 1884, II. Halbjahr, 91 *.
15. Amerika, das diebische, und die geheime Polizei. Von einem Auswanderer. Falkenberg (Lothringen), Hirtzmann, 1905.
16. Anglade in Ballet, Traité de pathologie mentale. Paris, Doin, 1903.
17. Antheaume et Roger Mignot, Remarques sur la stéréotypie graphique. L'encéphale, 1906. Abst.: NCB., 1907, p. 725.
18. Anton, Nerven- und Geisteserkrankungen in der Zeit der Geschlechtsreife. Wiener klin. WS., 1904, p. 1161.
19. ——— Gehirnerkrankung und Katatonie. Mitteilungen des Vereines der Ärzte in Steiermark, 1902, No. 2, 97 *.
20. ——— in Näcke, Über Wadenkrämpfe. MS., 1906, Vol. XX, p. 570.
21. Arnaud in Ballet, Traité de pathologie ment. Paris, Doin, 1903.
21 *a*) Arndt (Diskussion über periodische Psychosen). Z., 1888, Vol. XLIV, p. 665.
22. Arndt R., Katalepsie und Psychose. Z., 1874, Vol. XXX, p. 28.
23. ——— Über Tetanie und Psychose. Z., 1874, Vol. XXX, p. 53.
24. Arndt E., Geschichte der Katatonie. CBN., 1902, p. 81.
25. Arnemann, Über Jugendirresein. Leipzig, Konegen, 1906.
26. Aschaffenburg, Initialdelirien beim Typhus. Z., 1896, Vol. LII, 1896, p. 75.
27. ——— Die Katatonie. Z., 1898, Vol. LV, p. 60.
28. ——— Die Katatoniefrage. Z., 1898, Vol. LIV, p. 1004.
29. ——— Diskussion über die Diagnose und Prognose der Dp. Z., 1899, Vol. LVI, p. 260.
30. ——— Klinische Formen der Wochenbettpsychosen. Z., 1901, Vol. LVIII, p. 346.
31. ——— Diskussion über die Puerperalpsychosen. Z., 1901, Vol. LVIII, p. 706.
32. ——— Stimmungsschwankungen der Epileptiker. Abhandlungen über Geisteskrankheiten, Halle, Marh, 1906. Vol. VII.
33. Astwazaturow, Über Negativismus der sprachlichen Äusserungen. Obosrenije psych., 1907. Abst.: NCB., 1908, p. 381.
34. Azémar, Deux cas de manie guérie à la suite d'une infection grave. Amps., 1901.
35. Baelz, Emotionslähmung. Z., 1901, Vol. LVIII, p. 717.
36. Baldwin, Entwicklung des Geistes. Berlin, 1898.
37. Ball, Das Pubertätsirresein oder die Hebephrenie. L'Encéphale, 1884, II, No. 1, u. p. 87 *.
38. Ballet, Traité de Pathologie ment. Paris, Doin, 1903.
39. ——— Der Verfolgungswahn mit systematischer Entwicklung. Progrès méd., 1892, p. 115 *.
40. Barbé, Refus d'alimentation dans la d. cat. An., 1906, XXI, No. 123. Abst.: NCB., 1906, p. 1014.
41. Bartels, Wortneubildungen bei Geisteskranken. Z., 1889, Vol. XLV, p. 598.
42. Bauer, Catalepsie symptomatique et rythme de Cheyne-Stokes. Revue neurol., 1903, p. 249.
43. Baugh, Some Observations on Confus. Insanity. Brit. Med. Journ., 1905, II. Abst.: JB., p. 949.
44. Bechterew, Über die Bedeutung der Aufmerksamkeit für Lokalisation und Entwicklung halluzinatorischer Bilder. CBN., 1905, Vol. XVI, p. 330.
45. Becker, Beitrag zur Lehre von den Störungen der Assoziationen. CBN., 1909, p. 269.
46. Bellamy, Hallucinations érotiques. Thèse Bord., 1900.
47. Bellot, Eine halluzinatorische Melancholie auf der Spitze eines Kirchturms. Amps., 1887, II, 77 *.

48. Bendix, Über Kinderpsychosen mit besonderer Berücksichtigung ihrer Frequenz und Prognose. Dissert. Rostock, 1906.
49. Bennecke, Dp. in der Armee. Dresden, 1907. Med. Abt. des königl. sächs. Kriegsministeriums. Abst.: CBN., 1908, p. 428.
50. Berger, Die Grübelsucht, ein psychopath. Symptom. A., VI, p. 217.
51. ——— Die Grübelsucht und Zwangsvorstellungen. A., VIII, p. 616.
52. ——— Studien zur Pathogenese der Geisteskrankheiten. Berl. klin. WS., 1903, p. 693, und MS., 1904, Vol. XVI, p. 1 und 213.
53. Bernhardt, Über pollutionsartige Vorgänge beim Weibe ohme sexuelle Vorstellungen und Lustgefühle. Ärztliche Praxis, 1903, No. 17. Abst.: NCB., 1905, p. 171.
54. Bernheim, Über kataleptiforme Stellungen bei Typhus abdominalis und in gewissen psych. Zuständen. Wien. klin. Rundschau, No. 1, 1896, p. 1, 59 *.
55. Bernstein, Über die Dp. Z., 1903, Vol. LX, p. 554.
56. Bertschinger, Verblödungspsychosen. Z., 1897, Vol. LVIII, pp. 269/305.
57. Berkley, An Abstract of the Results Obtained in the Treatment of Catatonia by Partial Thyroidectomy and Thyro-Lecithin. – Folia neur. biol. II. Vol., pp. 157-166.
58. Berze, Das Primärsymptom der Paranoia. Halle, Marh., 1903.
59. ——— Primärsymptom der Paranoia. CBN., 1906, p. 432.
60. Bessière, Stéréotypies démentielles. Amps., 1906, p. 206.
61. Bianchi, Trattato di Psichiatria. Napoli, 1905. Abst.: CBN., 1905, p. 198.
62. Bianchini, Observation sur les tableaux cliniques de paranoia et d. paranoide. Rev. neur., 1906, No. 14. Abst.: NCB., 1906, p. 1013.
63. Binder, Über motorische Störungen stereotypen Charakters bei Geisteskranken mit besonderer Berücksichtigung der Katatonie. A., 1889, Vol. XX, p. 628.
64. Binet et Féré, Recherches expérimentales sur la physiologie des mouvements chez les hystériques. Arch. de physiol., 1887, p. 323.
65. Binswanger, Über die Pathogenese und klinische Stellung der Erschöpfungspsychose. Berl. klin. WS., 1897, p. 496.
66. ——— Über den Symptomenkomplex der inkohärenten Erregung. NCB., 1904, p. 1067.
67. Binswanger und Berger, Zur Klinik und pathologischen Anatomie der postinfektiösen und Intoxikationspsychosen. A., 1901, Vol. 34, p. 107.
67 a) Binswanger und Siemerling, Lehrbuch der Psychiatrie. II. edition, Jena, Fischer, 1907.
68. Birt, On Certain Questions Relating to the Urinology of the Insane. Brain, IX, p. 362.
69. Bischoff, Über familiäre Geisteskrankheiten. Jahrb., 1905, Vol. XXVI, p. 109.
70. Birnbaum, Psychosen mit Wahnbildung und wahnhafte Einbildungen bei Degenerationen. Halle, Marh., 1908.
71. Bleuler, Affektivität, Suggestibilität und Paranoia. Halle, Marh., 1906.
72. ——— Freudsche Mechanismen in der Symptomatologie von Psychosen. WS. 1906, No. 35 und 36, Vol. VIII.
72 a) ——— Frühe Entlassungen. WS., Vol. VI, 1905.
73. ——— Die Prognose der Dp. (Schizophreniegruppe). Z., 1908, Vol. LXV.
73 a) ——— Bewusstsein und Assoziation. (Jungs diagnostische Assoziationsstudien.) Journal für Psychologie und Neurologie, Vol. VI, 1905, p. 126.
74. ——— Die negative Suggestibilität. WS., 1904, No. 27 und 28.
74 a) ——— Zur Theorie des schizophrenen Negativismus. WS., 1910/1911, No. 18-21.
75. ——— Extrakampine Halluzinationen. WS., 1903, No. 25.
75 a) Das Faxensyndrom. WS., 1910/1911, p. 375.
76. ——— Zur Ätiologie und Therapie der nichtpuerperalen Osteomalacie. Münch. med. WS., 1893, No. 15, p. 277.

77. Bleuler und Jung, Komplexe und Krankheitsursachen bei Dp. CBN., 1908, p. 220.
78. Blin, Les troubles oculaires dans la Dp. Rev. neur., 1906, p. 4, Abst.: NCB., 1906, p. 569.
79. ——— Manifestations oculaires de la Dp. et considérations sur la pathogénie de cette maladie. Thèse, Paris, 1905.
80. Boeck, Versuche über die Einwirkung künstlich erzeugten Fiebers bei Psychosen. Read Before the Society of Psychology and Neurology. Jahrb., 1896, Vol. XIV, p. 199.
81. Bogdanoff, Experimentelle Untersuchungen der Merkfähigkeit bei Gesunden und Geisteskranken. Sterns Beitrag zur Psychologie der Aussage. Vol. II, p. 1, 1905.
82. Boidard, Sur la Dp. Thèse, Paris, 1905. Abst.: Arch. gén. méd., 1906, p. 1068.
83. Bolton, Morbid Changes in d., Jmsc., 1901, p. 330.
84. ——— Amentia and Dementia. Jmsc., 1906, Vol. LI ff.
85. Bonhoeffer, Die akuten Geisteskrankheiten der Gewohnheitstrinker. Jena, 1901.
86. ——— Über ein eigenartiges, operativ beseitigtes katatonisches Zustandsbild. CBN., 1903, p. 15.
87. ——— Über den pathologischen Einfall. Deutsche med. WS., 1904, No. 39, p. 1420.
88. ——— Klinische Beiträge zur Lehre von den Degenerationspsychosen. Zwanglose Abhandlungen aus dem Gebiete der Nerven- und Geisteskranken. Vol. VII, No. 6, Halle, Marh., 1907.
89. Bornstein, Untersuchungen über die Atmung der Geisteskranken. MS., 1908, XXIV, p. 392.
90. Borsos, Vergrösserung der Schilddrüse im Anschlusse an epileptiforme Anfälle. Orvosi Hetilap, 1907. Abst.: NCB., 1908, p. 269.
90 *a*) Bostroem, Die Benennung optischer Eindrücke. Halle, Marh., 1909.
91. Boucher, Beitrag zur Lehre vom Delirium chronicum. An., II, 1884. Abst.: Z., Vol. 40, p. 88.
92. Bouman, Assoziationen bei Geisteskranken. (Sommers Klin. f. ps. u. nerv. Krankh., Vol. II, 1907, pp. 505/523.) Halle, Marh., 1907.
92 *a*) Brahm Otto, Karl Stauffer-Bern. Göschensche Verlagshandlung, Bern.
93. Brassert, Über sekundäre Paranoia. Z., 1896, Vol. LII, p. 772.
93 *a*) Bremer, Sur les névroses et psychoses dues aux cyclones. Rev. neurol., 1898, No. 11. Abst.: JB, p. 1138.
94. van Brero, Einiges über die Geisteskrankheiten des malaiischen Archipels. Z., 1897, Vol. LIII, p. 44.
95. Breuer und Freud, Über den psychischen Mechanismus hysterischer Phänomene. NCB., 1893, p. 4.
96. Breukink, Über Ermüdungskurven bei Gesunden und bei einigen Neurosen und Psychosen. Journ. Ps. u. N., 1904, Vol. IV, No. 2, p. 85.
97. ——— Über eknoische Zustände. MS., XIV, 1903, p. 97.
97 *a*) Brierre de Boismont, Des Hallucinations.
98. Brissard, Sur la fréquence du goitre chez les aliénés. Thèse, Genève, 1905. Rev. méd. de la Suisse rom., 1906, No. 11, p. 632.
99. Brissaud, Urémie cérébrale avec attitudes cataleptoïdes. Sem. méd. 1893, pp. 125/127.
100. Brissaud et Lamy, Attitudes cataleptiques chez un brightique délirant. Gaz. hebd. de méd. et de chir., 1890, p. 367.
101. Brosius, Die Katatonie. Z., 1876, Vol. XXXIII, pp. 770, 783, 802.
102. Bruce, Bacteriological and Clinical Observations on the Blood of Cases Suffering from Acute Continuous Mania. Appended discussion. Jmsc., 1903, p. 219.
103. ——— Further Clinical Observations in Case of Acute Mania Particularly Adolescent Mania. Appended discussion. Jmsc., 1903, p. 441.
104. ——— Studies in Clinical Psychiatry. Lond. Mc. Millan, 1906.
105. ——— The Symptoms and Etiology of Mania. Jmsc., 1908, p. 207.

106. Bruce and Peebles, Clinical and Experiment. Observ. on Katatonia. Jmsc., 1903, p. 614.
107. ——— Quantitative and Qualitative Leucocyte Counts in Various Forms of Ment. Disease. Appended discussion. Jmsc., 1904, p. 409.
108. Brugia e Marzocchi, Die Zwangsbewegungen bei einigen Formen geistiger Störung. Arch. ital. per le mal. nerv., 1887, Vol. 24, p. 50*
108 a) Bruyn, A Study of Emotional Expression in Dp. J. Abnormal Psychology, 1909, III, p. 378.
109. Bryant, Second Annual Report of the Manhattan State Hospitale for Year Ending. 30. IX. 1906.
110. de Buck, Quelques réflections à propos de la catatonie. Bull. de soc. méd. ment. Belgique, 1903, pp. 425-435. Abst.: CBN., 1905, p. 850.
111. Buccola, Dp. Thèse. Paris, 1905, p. 68.
112. Bumke, Die Pupillenstörungen bei Geistes- und Nervenkrankheiten. Jena, Fischer, 1904.
113. ——— Was sind Zwangsvorgänge? Halle, Marh., 1906.
114. Busch, Auffassung und Merkfähigkeit bei Dp. in Kraepelin: Psych. Arbeiten. Vol. V, p. 293, Leipzig, Engelmann, 1908.
115. Cahen, Contribution à l'étude des stéréotypies. An., 1901, p. 476.
116. Canger und Angiolella, Paranoische Wahnideen bei moralischem Irresein. Manicomio, 1895, No. 2 u. 3. Abst.: 1896, p. 89*.
117. Charpentier, Mémoires sur les dp. Congrès Rouen, 1890. Ballet, p. 808.
118. Chaslin, La confusion mentale primitive. Paris, Asselin, 1895.
119. Chastenet, Folie de la puberté. Amps., 1890, 84*.
120. Chatelain, Die Spätheilungen. Journ. d'alién. ment. etc., 1896. Abst.: Z., 1897, p. 62*.
121. Chenais, Recherches sur les symptomes physiques de la dp. à forme catat. Thèse, Paris, 1902.
122. Chenais et Dide, Urologie der Dp. und Reflexe der Fascia lata. In Masselon: Dp., Paris, 1902.
123. Chotzen, Kasuistischer Beitrag zur Frage der chronischen Alkoholhallucinosis. CBN., 1907, p. 1.
124. ——— Über atypische Alkoholpsychosen. A., Vol. XLI.
125. ——— Komplizierte akute und chronische Alkoholpsychosen. Z., 1909, Vol. 66, p. 42.
126. Christian, La Dp. des jeunes gens. Paris, Masson, 1899, und Amps., LVII.
127. ——— Étiologie de la Dp. Amps., 1899.
128. Chvostek, Beiträge zur Theorie der Halluzinationen. Jahrb., 1892, Vol. 10, p. 267.
129. Clarke, Diskussion über Dp. der brit. med. soc., 1906, in Toronto. Brit. med. Journ. II, p. 755.
129 a) Claude, Atrophie des Kleinhirns bei Dp. Soc. Psychiatrie, Paris, 21. I. 1909. NCB., 1909, p. 616.
130. Claus, Catatonie et stupeur. Congrès des alién. et neurol. de France Bruxelles, 1903, p. 101. An., XVI, p. 218.
131. Clouston, Presidential adress. Med. psych. assoc. Edinb., 1888, Jmsc. Abst.: Z., 1890, Vol. 46, p. 283.
132. Colucci, Metodi e criteri per la educabilità dei d. Ann. di nevrol., 1902, XX.
133. Conaghey, Adolescent Insanity. A Protest Against the Use of the Term "Dp." Jmsc., April 1905. Abst.: Z., p. 160.
134. Cotard, Du délire des négations. An., 1882, p. 561.
135. Cramer, Die Halluzinationen im Muskelsinn. Freiburg i. B., Mohr, 1889. Z., 1890, Vol. 46, p. 327*.
136. ——— Abgrenzung und Differenzialdiagnose der Paranoia. Z., 1895, p. 286. Diskussion dazu eod. lo. pp. 178 ff.

137. ——— Über Sinnestäuschungen bei geisteskr. Taubstummen etc. A., 1896, Vol. 28, p. 875.
138. ——— Entwicklungsjahre und Gesetzgebung. Göttingen, 1902. JB., 1902, p. 1221.
139. ——— Über Jugendirresein. NCB., 1905, p. 539.
140. ——— Gerichtliche Psychiatrie. II. Auflage, p. 216.
141. ——— Jahresversammlung des deutschen Vereines für Psychiatrie in München. Diskussion. WS., 1906, p. 73.
142. Crisafulli, Sulla istologia e patogenesi della dp. Il Morgagni, Jan. 1906, p. 52. Abst.: Arch. gén. de méd., p. 1068.
143. Crocq, Considérations sur la catatonie. Bull. soc. de méd. ment. de Belgique. Juni 1902, 101*.
144. ——— Fréquence et étiologie de la Dp. 1 bidem, 1904, pp. 282/302. Abst.: CBN., 1906, p. 822.
145. Cullerre, Délire aigu et urémie. An., 1901, XII, p. 449.
146. ——— De l'excitation sexuelle dans les psychopathies anxieuses. An., 1905, XIX, p. 81. Abst.: JB., p. 955.
147. ——— Über Pubertätspsychosen. XIIIième Congrès internat. de méd. Paris, 1900, p. 100, Section de psychiat.
148. Curschmann, Untersuchungen über die idiomuskuläre Übererregbarkeit. Deutsche Zeitschrift für Nervenheilkunde, Vol. XVIII, 1905. Abst.: NCB., p. 855.
149. Dagonet, Chronische Melancholie mit Angstzuständen. Verlust des Gefühls der Persönlichkeit. Bull. soc. méd. ment. Belgique. Juni, 1891. Z., Vol. 48, 1892, p. 77.
150. ——— Beobachtungen über Délires associés und die Transformationen des Deliriums. Amps., 1895, p. 110*.
151. Damsch und Cramer, Katalepsie und Psychose bei Ikterus. Berl. klin. WS, 1898, p. 278.
152. Daraszkiewicz, Über Hebephrenie, insbesondere deren schwere Form. Dissertation, Dorpat, 1892.
153. Darcanne, Contribution au diagnost. clinique de la Dp. Thèse, Paris, 1904.
154. Dawson, A Case of Hebephrenia. Jmsc., 1903, p. 303.
155. ——— Notes on Two Cases Illustrating the Difference Between Katat. and Mel. Atton. Jmsc., 1903, p. 686.
156. Damaye, Remarques sur l'action clinique de l'iode au cours des états de stupidité et de confusion mentale. Rev. de psych., 1907, pp. 448, 142*.
157. Désci, Ein Fall von Jugendirresein. Jahrb. der hauptstädtischen Spitäler in Budapest, 1903 (Hungarian), abst.: NCB., 1904, p. 867.
158. ——— Über die Zwangsbewegungen bei Geisteskranken. Orvosi Hetilap, No. 7, 1904. Abst.: JB., p. 985.
159. Delbrück, Die pathologische Lüge. Stuttgart, Enke, 1891.
160. ——— Über die forensische Bedeutung der Dp. VI. Hauptversammlung des deutschen medizinischen Beamtenvereins.
161. Deny, Les Dp. Journ. de méd. int. IX, 1905, p. 329.
162. ——— Les délires systématisés chroniques. Journ. méd. int. IX, 1905, p. 201.
163. ——— Les états anxieux et les idées délirantes de négation, leur pathologie. Rev. Internat. de méd. et de chir. XVI, 1905, pp. 269/271.
164. Deny et Camus, Délire d'interprétation et paranoia. Amps., 1906, II.
165. ——— Étude nosologique du délire de négation. Amps., No. 3, 1906, p. 423.
166. Deny et Roy, La dp. Paris, Baillière, 1903, p. 70. Gaz. des hôpit. No. 93.
167. ——— Les d. vésaniques. Août 1904. Compte rend: Sem. méd.
168. Dercum, The Heboid Paranoid Group (Dp.). Clinical Relations and Nature (Americ. Journ. of Insanity, 1906, IV, p. 541). Abst.: NCB., p. 1013.
169. Deroubaix, Réflexions à propos de cinq cas de psychose aiguë étudiés histologiquement. Journ. de neurol., 1904, No. 23, p. 443. Abst.: JB., p. 985.

170. ——— Stupeur mél. et stupeur catat. Journ. de neurol., 1905, No. 2, p. 35. Abst.: JB., p. 956.

171. van Deventer, Betrachtungen über traumatische Psychosen. Psych. Bladen, V., 1887, II., 82*.

172. ——— Heilung eines Falles von Paranoia persecutoria nach 15 jährigem Anstaltsaufenthalt. Psych. Bladen, 1896. 91*.

173. Dide, La Dp. un syndrôme mental toxiinfectieux subaigu ou chronique. Rev. neurol., 1905, p. 381, No. 7. Abst.: NCB., p. 819.

174. ——— Essai de classification des maladies ment. Congrès de Rennes, 1905. Gaz. des hôpit., p. 1077. Abst.: NCB., p. 1085.

175. Dide et Assicot, Signes oculaires dans la Dp. Gaz. des hôpit., p. 1077. Congrès de Rennes, 1905, abst.: NCB., p. 1086.

176. Dide et Chenais, Recherches urologiques et hématologiques dans la Dp. Amps., 1902. Abst.: NCB., 1903, p. 591.

177. Dide et Sacquépée, Microbes du sang dans la Dp. Soc. de neurol. de Paris, 1905 (16. VII.), Arch. gén. méd., p. 1850.

178. ——— Congrès de Rennes. NCB., 1905, p. 1086. Revue neurologique, 1905, No. 16, und Annales de neurol., 1905.

179. Dieckhoff, Die Psychosen bei psychopathisch Minderwertigen. Z., 98, Vol. LV, p. 215.

180. Diem, Die einfach demente Form der Dp. A. 1903, Vol. 37, p. 111.

181. ——— Die psycho-neurotische erbliche Belastung der Geistesgesunden und der Geisteskranken. Arch. f. Rassen- und Gesellsch.-Biologie, 1905, p. 215.

182. Doutrebente et Marchand, Considération sur l'anatomie patholog. de la Dp. à propos d'un cas. Rev. neurol. IV, 1905, p. 386. Abst.: NCB., p. 820.

183. Drapes, A Note on Psychiatric Terminology and Classific. Jmsc., 1906, LII, p. 75.

184. Dreifus, Ein Beitrag zur Kenntnis des hysterischen Irreseins. CBN., 1906, p. 875.

185. ——— Über Verkennung von geistigen Erkrankungen. Münch. med. WS., 1906, p. 1311.

186. ——— Über Tod im katatonischen Anfall bei Dp. CBN., 1907, p. 451.

187. ——— Melancholie, ein Zustandsbild des manisch-depressiven Irreseins. Jena, Fischer, 1907.

188. Dromard, De la dissociation de la mimique chez les aliénés. Journ. de ps. norm. et pathologique, 1907, pp. 417-438.

189. ——— Considérations pathogéniques sur le mutisme et la sitiophobie de Dp. CBN., 1905, p. 622.

190. ——— Les troubles de la mimique volontaire chez les aliénés. Journ. de ps. norm. et pathol., 1906, p. 1.

191. ——— Étude clinique sur les stéréotypies des Dp. An., 1905, XIX, p. 189.

192. ——— Étude psychologique et clinique sur l'échopraxie. Journ. de ps. norm. et path. II, 1905, pp. 385-403.

193. Ducosté, Les fugues dans les psychoses et les d. An., 1907, No. 2, pp. 38, 121. Abst.: NCB., p. 861.

193 *a*) Dufour, Cerebellarer Typus der Dp. Soc. de Psychiatrie de Paris, January 21, 1909. Abst.: NCB., 1909, p. 616.

194. Dumond de Monteux in Ballet, Traité de pathol. mentale, p. 148.

195. Dunkerlost, Über Ätiologie und Behandlung der Katatonie. Need. Ver. f. Psych., 1883.

196. Dunton, Some Points in the Diagnosis of Dp. Americ. Journ. of Insanity. July 1902, 94*.

197. Dupré, Diskussion über Délire d'interprétation et paranoia. Amps., 1906, II, p. 106.

198. Durocher et Leborgne, Diagnostic de la Dp. à forme paranoide et des psychoses à base d'interprétations délirantes sans évolutions démentielles. Congrès de Rennes, 1905. Rev. neurol. Abst.: CBN., p. 874.

199. Easterbrook, Diskussion zu Bruces Vortrag über Antistreptococcosserum. Jmsc., 1903, p. 446.
200. Ebbinghaus, Über eine neue Methode zur Prüfung geistiger Fähigkeiten und ihre Anwendung bei Schulkindern. Zeitschrift für Psychologie und Physiologie der Sinnesorgane, 1897, Vol. XIII, p. 401.
201. Eberschweiler, Untersuchungen über die sprachliche Komponente der Assoziationen. WS., 1855.
202. Eisath, Periodisch verlaufende Geistesstörungen. Z., 1903, Vol. LX, pp. 395-406.
203. ——— Frühform der D. paralytica, 1904. MS., Vol. 16, p. 549.
204. Elmiger, Über 49 Fälle von Pubertätsirresein. Z., 1900, Vol. 57, p. 490.
205. Elter, Querulanten mit Dp. Dissert., Zürich, 1903.
206. Elzholz, Akute Psychose geheilt nach 13 Jahren. Wien. med. WS., No. 39, Z., 1896, Vol. 52, p. 107.
207. Ennen, Zur Lehre von den periodischen Geistesstörungen. NCB., 1902, p. 50.
208. Ermes, Über die Natur der bei Katatonie zu beobachtenden Muskelzustände. Dissert., Giessen, 1903.
209. Eustace, H. M. A case of Dp. with discussion Leeper, Con. Normann. Jmsc., 1904, p. 516.
210. Evensen, Die psychologische Grundlage der katatonischen Krankheitszeichen. Neurologia (Japan.), Vol. II, No. 5. December 1903.
211. ——— Dp. Ugdom-saanmes Sindssygdomme. I Kristiania, Aschehoug & Co., 1904. Abst.: 1905, Vol. 62, p. 464.
212. ——— Grundträkkene det Norske Sindssygeväsens Udvikling i de Sidste 100 aar. Kristiania, Cammermeyer, 1905.
213. Falret, De la catalepsie. Arch. gén. de méd. Août 1857.
214. Fauser, Endogene Symptomenkomplexe bei exogenen Krankheitsformen. Z., 1905, Vol. 62, p. 165.
215. ——— Zur Psychologie des Symptoms der rhythmischen Betonung bei Geisteskranken. Z., 1905, Vol. 62, p. 687.
216. ——— Zur Kenntnis der Melancholie. NCB., 1906, p. 962.
217. Fels, Über den Symptomenkomplex der primären Inkohärenz mit Erregung. MS., 1906, XIX, p. 488.
218. Ferrari, Die Entartung der schriftlichen Ausdrucksweise bei der erotischen Paranoia. Rivist. sper. di freniat., 1893, Vol. 19, 121*.
219. Fink, Beitrag zur Kenntnis der Jugendirreseins. Z., 1880, Vol. 37, pp. 490-520.
220. Finzi e Vedrani, Contribuz. clinica alla dottrina della Dp. Riv. sper. di fren., 1899, Vol. XXV, 1.
221. Fischer, Über einige Veränderungen, welche Gehörshalluzinationen unter dem Einflusse des galvanischen Stromes erleiden. A., 1887, Vol. 18, p. 34.
222. ——— Über die Beziehungen zwischen der Schilddrüse und den weiblichen Geschlechtsorganen. Wien. med. WS., 1896, pp. 6-90.
223. Fitschen, Die Beziehung der Heredität zum periodischen Irresein. Diss. Zürich. Berlin, Karger, 1900, MS., 1900, Vol. 7, p. 127.
224. Foerster, Demonstration eines solitären Pons-Tuberkels, der anfänglich unter dem Bilde einer funktionellen Psychose verlief. Z., 1905, Vol. 62, p. 871.
225. ——— Stupor alkoholicus. Diskussion. Z., 1906, Vol. 63, p. 345.
226. ——— Über die klinischen Formen der Psychosen bei direkter Erblichkeit. Z., 1907, Vol. 64, p. 176.
227. Foersterling, Ein Fall von Motilitätspsychose mit vorwiegender Beteiligung der Sprache. MS., 1904, Vol. XV, pp. 282-301.
228. Forster, Über die Affekte. MS., 1906, Vol. XIX, p. 400.
229. Forel, Selbstbiographie eines Falles von Mania acuta. A., 1901, Vol. 34, p. 960.
229 *a*) ——— Rasches Weisswerden der Haare und schwarzer Nachwuchs. Zeitschrift für Hypnotismus, Vol. 7, 1898, p. 140.
230. Franke, Einseitige Halluzinationen. Diss. Freiburg, 1903.

231. Foville, Über den Grössenwahn oder Verrückheit mit überwiegenden Grössenideen. Amps., I, 1882. Z., 1883, Vol. 39, p. 388.
232. Freud, Analyse eines Falles von chronischer Paranoia. NCB., 1896, pp. 442-448.
233. ——— Psychopathologie des Alltagslebens. II. Auflage, Berlin, Karger, 1907.
234. ——— Traumdeutung. Wien und Leipzig, Deuticke, 1900.
235. ——— Der Witz und seine Beziehung zum Unbewussten. Ibidem, 1905.
236. ——— Drei Abhandlungen zur Sexualtheorie. Ibidem, 1905.
237. Freusberg, Über motorische Symptome bei einfachen Psychosen. A., Vol. 17, p. 757.
238. Friedmann, Zur Entstehung der Wahnideen und über die Grundlage des Urteils. MS., I, p. 455, and II, pp. 17 and 278.
239. ——— Über die logischen Werte der Zwangsvorstellungen. Verein süddeutscher Irrenärzte. Z., 1902, Vol. 59, p. 151.
240. Fritsch, Zur Frage der primären Paranoia. Jahrb. f. Psych., I, 79, p. 36.
241. ——— Zur Kenntnis der Melancholia attonita. Wien. med. Presse. 1878, p. 1477.
242. ——— Die Verwirrtheit. Jahrb. II, 1880, p. 27.
243. Fritsche, Über Beeinflussbarkeit der Halluzinationen und Wahnideen bei Geisteskranken durch Wachsuggestion. Dissert. Berlin, 1905.
244. Fuchs, Die Messung der Pupillengrösse und Zeitbestimmung der Lichtreaktionen der Pupillen bei einzelnen Psychosen und Krankheiten. Jahrb., 1904, Vol. 24, p. 326.
245. ——— Ungewöhnlicher Verlauf der "Katatonie." Z., 1904, Vol. 61, p. 241.
246. Fürstner, Über Schwangerschafts- und Puerperalpsychosen. A., 1875, Vol. V, p. 505.
247. Discussion of Krapelin's Lecture "Gegen die Manie" Concerning the Delimitation of Paranoia. Z., 1894, Vol. 50, p. 1081.
248. Fuhrmann, Über akute juvenile Verblödung. A., 1905, Vol. 40, p. 817.
249. de Fursac, Manuel de Psychiatrie. Paris, Alcan, 1903.
250. ——— Les écrits et les dessins dans les maladies nerveuses et mentales. Essai clinique. Paris, Masson, 1905. JB., 1906.
251. Gadziacki, Über Zucker und Eiweiss im Urin Geisteskranker. Wjestnik psych. Jahrg. IX, 1893. Z. 84 *.
252. Ganser, Über einen eigenartigen hysterische Dämmerzustand. A., 1898, Vol. 30, p. 633.
253. ——— Zur Lehre vom hysterischen Dämmerzustand. A., 1904, Vol. 38, p. 34.
254. Gatz, Über körperliche Symptome bei Dp. Diss. Zürich, 1907.
255. Gaupp, Zur prognostischen Bedeutung der katatonischen Erscheinungen. CBN., 1903, pp. 680 ff.
256. ——— Zur Frage der kombinierten Psychosen. CBN., 1903, p. 766.
257. ——— Die Depressionszustände des höheren Lebensalters. Münch. med. WS., 1905, No. 32, p. 1531.
258. ——— Die Besonderheiten des psychiatrischen Grosstadtmaterials. WS., 1906, Vol. 8, p. 77.
259. ——— Klinische Untersuchungen über Ursachen und Motive des Selbstmordes. Vierteljahrsschr. f. gerichtl. Med., 3. Folge, No. XXXIII.
260. Geist, Über Klassifikation der Psychosen, besonders der periodischen. Z., 1907, Vol. 64, p. 65.
261. Gianelli, Sulla morte improvvisa nella Dp. Riv. di patolog. nerv. e ment. 1908.
262. Gierlich, Über periodisch Paranoia und die Entstehung der paranoischen Wahnidee. A., 1905, Vol. 40, p. 19.
263. Gluszezewski, Die akute halluzinatorische Verwirrtheit als Initialstadium bei Melancholie. Diss. Marburg, Friedr., 1902.
264. Goldstein, Ein Beitrag zur Lehre von den Alkoholpsychosen. Z., 1907, Vol. 64, p. 240.

265. Gombault, La d. terminale dans les psychoses. Amps., 1900, p. 231. Abst.: NCB., p. 871.
266. Gonzales, Contributo allo studio della Dp. Riv. sper. di fren., 1904, Vol. 30, p. 765. JB., 1905.
267. Goodall, Bemerkungen über Katatonie. Jmsc., 1892, 111 *.
268. Graeter, Dp. mit Alkoholismus chronicus. Leipzig, Barth, 1909.
269. Gregor, Ein Beitrag zur Kenntnis des intermittierenden Irreseins. Z., 1906, Vol. 63. Abst.: NCB., 1906, p. 1056.
270. ——— Beitrag zur Psychopathologie des Gedächtnisses. MS., XXV, p. 362.
270 *a*) ——— Über die Diagnose psychischer Prozesse im Stupor. CBN., 1907, p. 953.
271. Gregor und Hänsel, Beiträge zur Kenntnis der Störung äusserer Willenshandlungen. MS., 1908 I, XXIII.
272. Gross Ad., Untersuchungen über die Schrift Gesunder und Geisteskranker in Kraepelins psychologischen Arbeiten. Leipzig, Engelmann, 1899, Vol. II, pp. 450 and 550.
273. Gross, Über Stupor. Jahressitzung des Vereines der deutschen Irrenärzte in Heidelberg. Z., 97, Vol. 53, p. 855.
274. Gross O., Die Affektlage der Ablehnung. MS., 1902, Vol. 12, p. 359.
275. ——— Beitrag zur Pathologie des Negativismus. WS., 1903, V. Jahrgang, p. 269.
276. ——— Zur Differentialdiagnostik negativistischer Phänomene. WS., 1904, Vol. VI, p. 345.
277. ——— Zur Nomenklatur "D. sejunctiva." NCB., 1904, p. 1144.
278. ——— Über Bewusstseinszerfall. MS., 1904, Vol. XV, p. 45.
279. Haberkant, Osteomalacie und Psychose. Z., 1906, Vol. 63, p. 148.
280. ——— Osteomalacie und Dp. A., 1909 I, 45, p. 1.
281. Haeschl, Discussion of Pötzl's Lecture (A Case of Catatonie). Wien. klin. WS., 1904, p. 1422.
282. Halbrey, Über das Symptom des Gedankensichtbarwerdens. Z., 1908, p. 307.
283. Hammond, Remarks on Cases of Katatonia. Am. Journ. Neur. and Psych., 1883, p. 302.
284. Hartmann, Über die hereditären Verhältnisse bei Verbrechern. Diss. Zürich, 1904. MS. für Kriminalpsychologie und Strafrechtsreform, I, p. 493.
285. Hecht, A Study of Dp. Journ. of Nerv. and Ment. Diseases. 1905, Vol. 32, No. 11, p. 689. Abst.: Jmsc., 1906, p. 797.
286. Hecker, Zur klinischen Diagnostik und Prognostik der psych. Krankheiten. Z., 77. Vol. 33, pp. 602 and 612.
287. ——— Die Hebephrenie. Virch. Arch. 71, Vol. 52, pp. 394 ff.
288. ——— Ursachen und Anfangssymptome der psychischen Krankheiten. Sammlung klin. Vorträge, No. 108, 77.
289. Hegar, Zur Frage der sogenannten Menstrualpsychosen. Z., Vol. 58, p. 357.
290. Heggi, Über die Formen der Dp. NCB., 1907, 26, p. 492.
291. Heilbronner, Sprachstörung bei funktionellen Psychosen mit Ausschluss der apathischen Störungen. 1906, CBN.
292. ——— Studien über eine eklamptische Psychose MS., 1905, XVII, p. 425.
293. ——— Über Haftenbleiben und Stereotypie. MS., 1906, XVII. und XVIII. Ergänz.-No., pp. 428 resp. 283 ff.
293 *a*) ——— Zur klinisch psychologischen Untersuchungstechnik. MS., 1905, Vol. XVII, p. 115.
294. ——— Über Residuärsymptome und ihre Bedeutung. CBN., 1907, Vol. 30, p. 369.
295. ——— Hysterie und Querulantenwahn. CBN., 1907, p. 769.
296. Heinicke, Über die ammoniakalische Reaktion des Harns bei Phosphaturien und über Phosphaturie und Ammoniurie als objektive Symptome von Psychosen. Münch. med. WS., 1904, Vol. 27, p. 1201.
297. Heller, Über D. infantilis. Zeitschrift für Erforschung und Behandlung des jugendlichen Schwachsinns. II. Abst.: NCB., 1908, p. 378.

298. Hellpach, Religiöse Wahnbildungen bei thyreogener Erregung. Zeitschrift für Religionspsych., I, p. 360.
299. Hertz, Wahnsinn, Verrücktheit, Paranoia? Z., Vol. 52, p. 701.
300. Herzer, Beitrag zur Klinik der Puerperalpsychosen (Generationspsychosen). Z., 1906, Vol. 63, p. 245.
301. Hess, Psychiatrisch-pädagogische Behandlung bei Jugendpsychosen. CBN., 1905, pp. 436/437.
302. ——— Über Heboidophrenie. CBN., 1906, p. 500.
303. Hey, Das Gansersche Symptom in seiner klinischen und forensischen Bedeutung. Berlin, Hirschwald, 1904, p. 37.
304. Hirschl, Dp. und Syphilis. Diskussion (Pilcz; v. Wagner). NCB., 1907, p. 871.
305. Hitchcock, A Case of Dp. of Med. Legal Interest. Americ. Journ. of Insanity, IV, 1906, Vol. 62, p. 615.
306. Hitzig, Über den Querulantenwahnsinn. Leipzig, Vogel, 1895.
307. Hoche, Das akute halluzinatorische Irresein (Amentia). Deutsche Klinik, Vol. VI, p. 197.
308. ——— Über Dp. Deutsche Klinik, Vol. VI, pp. 207/224. Abst.: CBN., 1902, p. 477.
309. Hoche in Binswanger und Siemerling. Psychiatrie, II. Auflage.
310. Holm, Om Temperat. ved psychopatiske tilstande og dens diagnostiske betydning. Norsk Magaz. f. Lägevidensk, XV., 1900. Abst.: NCB., 1901, p. 764.
311. Hoth, Statistischer Beitrag zur Dp. (Jugendirresein). Dissert. Rostock, 1906.
312. Hübner, Untersuchungen über die Erweiterung der Pupillen auf psychische und schmerzhafte Reize etc. WS., 1905/1906, p. 123. A., 1906, p. 1016.
313. ——— Beschreibung eines Apparates zur Untersuchung der Pupillen nebst Bemerkungen über einige Pupillenreaktionen. MS., XXII, p. 15.
314. ——— Untersuchungen über die Erweiterung der Pupillen. A., 1906, Vol. 41, pp. 1035 ff. Klinischer Teil.
315. Hüfler, Über die katatonischen Anfälle. Jahresversammlung des deutschen Vereines für Psychiatrie. Berlin 24./25. IV. 1908. Z., Vol. 65, p. 469.
316. Jahrmärker, Zur Frage der Dp. (Eine Studie.) Halle, Marhold, 1903. Abst.: NCB., p. 594.
317. ——— Vorstellung eines Dp.-Kranken. Münch. med. WS., 1907, p. 295.
318. ——— Endzustände der Dp. CBN., 1908, p. 489.
319. Janet P., État mental des hystériques. Paris, 1894.
320. ——— Névroses et idées fixes. Paris, 1898.
321. ——— Les obsessions et la psychasténie. Paris, Alcan, 1903.
322. Janet P. in Vogt, Die hysterische Dissoziation im Lichte der Lehre von der Energie-Absorption. CBN., 1906, p. 255.
323. Jastrowitz, Diskussion zu dem Cramerschen Referat über Paranoia. Z., 1895, Vol. 51, p. 179.
324. ——— Demonstration einiger Fälle von Dp. NCB., 1905, p. 175.
325. Ideler, Discussion of Knecht's Lecture: Über die katatonischen Erscheinungen in der Paralyse. Z., 1886, Vol. 42, p. 340.
326. Jendrássik, Über die Entstehung der Halluzination und des Wahnes. NCB., 1905, p. 1090.
327. Jensen, Die Katatonie. A. Encyclop. des W. und K. II. Section XXXIV, 1884, part 1, 52 *.
328. Ilberg, Die Bedeutung der Katatonie. Z., 1898, pp. 417 ff.
329. ——— Der akute halluzinatorische Alkoholwahnsinn. Festschrift zur Feier des 50 jährigen Bestehens des Stadtkrankenhauses Dresden-Friedrichstadt, 1899. Abst.: NCB., 1900, p. 360.
330. ——— Jugendirresein. Volkmanns Vorträge, No. 224, p. 20, Leipzig, 1898.
331. ——— Über Geisteskrankheiten in der Armee zur Friedenszeit. Halle, Marh., 1903.
332. Infeld, Beiträge zur Kenntnis der Kinderpsychosen. Jahrb., 1902, XXII, p. 326.
333. Jörger, Beitrag zur Kenntnis der Pseudologia phantastica. Vierteljahrsschrift für

gerichtliche Medizin und öffentliches Sanitätswesen, 3. Folge. 1904. 27. Suppl.-Heft, p. 52.
334. Joffroy et Dupony, Trois cas de fugues chez les aliénés. Congrès de Dijon, 1908. L'Encéphale, p. 421.
335. Joffroy et Gombault, Paralysie générale progressive chez un sujet ayant présenté auparavant du délire de persécution etc. XIIIième. Congrès internat. de méd. Paris, 1900. Sect. de psychiatrie, p. 220.
336. Johnstone, Dp. Jmsc., October 1905, p. 711.
337. Jolly, Akuter Alkoholismus. Z., 1895, Vol. 51, p. 192.
338. ——— Degenerationspsychose und Paranoia. Charitéannalen, Vol. XXVII, 1903, p. 465. Abst.: NCB., 1903, p. 596.
339. Jones, The Question of Dp. Jmsc., LIV, 1908. Abst.: NCB., 1909, p. 437.
340. Ireland, Rezension von Kaiser, Hyst. und Katat. Jmsc., 1902, p. 582.
341. Isserlin, Über Jungs "Psychologie der Dp." etc. CBN., 1907, p. 329.
342. ——— Psychologische Untersuchungen an Manisch-Depressiven. MS., 1907, XXII, p. 535.
343. Juliusburger, Über Pseudo-Melancholie. CBN., 1906, p. 216.
344. Jung, Über die Psychologie der Dp. Halle, Marh., 1907, p. 88.
344 *a*) ——— Diagnostische Assoziationsstudien. Journ. für Psychologie und Neurologie. Vol. III, 1904 ff.
344 *b*) ——— Ärztliches Gutachten über einen Fall von Simulation geistiger Störung. Schweiz. Zeitschrift für Strafrecht. 1904, p. 55.
345. Kahlbaum, Gruppierung der psychischen Krankheiten. Danzig, Kafemann, 1863.
346. ——— Die Katatonie oder das Spannungsirresein. Berlin, Hirschwald, 1874.
347. ——— Klinisch-diagnostische Gesichtspunkte der Psychopathologie. Sammlung klinischer Vorträge, No. 126, 1878.
348. ——— Über Heboïdophrenie. Z., 1890, Vol. 46, p. 461.
349. ——— Über einen Fall von Pseudoparanoia. Z., 1893, Vol. 49, p. 486.
350. ——— Zur Kasuistik der Katatonie. MS., 1902, XII, pp. 22 and 56.
351. Kaiser, Beiträge zur Differenzialdiagnose der Hysterie und Katatonie. Z., 1901, Vol. 58, pp. 957, 1126, and 1902, p. 67.
352. ——— Dp. oder Gehirntumor. Z., 1905, Vol. 62, p. 92.
353. Kandinsky, Sinnestäuschungen. Berlin, Friedländer, 1885, pp. 38/39 and 93.
354. Kazowsky, Zur Frage nach dem Zusammenhange von Träumen und Wahnvorstellungen. NCB., 1901, pp. 440 and 508.
355. Kelp, Über Verfolgungswahn. Z., 90, Vol. 46, p. 117.
355 *a*) Kent and Rosanoff, Study of Association in Insanity. Americ. Journ. Insanity. LXVII, 1910.
356. Keraval, Die unter dem Namen Paranoia zusammengefassten mehr oder weniger kohärenten Delirien. An., 1894. Abst.: Z., 1895, p. 109 *.
357. Kern, Drei Fälle von Herderkrankung des Gehirns mit Psychose. A., 1905, Vol. 40, pp. 848 and 867.
358. Kernéis, Les délires de zoopathie interne. Thèse Bordeaux, 1907.
359. Kiefer, Ein Fall von Hebephrenie. Z., 1892, Vol. 48, p. 389.
360. Kielholz, Die Alkoholiker in der Pflegeanstalt Rheinau. Dissert. Zürich, 1905.
361. Kiermann, Die Katatonie. Lancet, 1884, I. Z., 1885, Vol. 41, p. 52 *.
362. Kip, Van Erp Taalman. Kraepelins Klassifikation der Psychosen. Psych. neurol. Bladen, 1899. Abst.: 60 *.
363. ——— Chronische Waanzin. Psych. neurol. Bladen, 1899. Abst.: NCB., 1900, 672.
364. Kirn, Psychosen der Strafanstalt. Z., 1889, Vol. 45, p. 1.
365. Kleist, Über die Motilitätspsychosen Wernickes. WS., 1907/1908, p. 139.
366. ——— Untersuchungen zur Kenntnis der psychomotorischen Bewegungsstörungen bei Geisteskranken. Leipzig, Klinkhardt, 1908.
366 *a*) ——— Weitere Untersuchungen an Geisteskranken mit psychomotorischen Störungen, Leipzig, Klinkhardt, 1909.

367. Klien, Über die psychisch bedingten Einengungen des Gesichtsfeldes. A., 1907, Vol. 42, p. 359.
368. de Klippel, Anatomie pathologique et nature de la Dp. Rev. de psych., VIII, 1904, p. 420.
369. de Klippel et Lhermitte; Dp. Anatomie pathogique et pathologénie. Ibidem, VIII, 1904, p. 45.
370. ——— ——— Les lésions de la moelle dans la Dp. L'encéphale 1906, p. 113.
370 *a*) ——— ——— Atrophie des Kleinhirns bei der Dp. Soc. Psychiatr. de Paris. January 21, 1909. NCB., 1909, p. 616.
371. de Klippel et Trenannay, Délire systématisé de rêve à rêve. Revue de Psychiat., IV, p. 97. Abst.: JB., 1901, p. 884.
372. Klippstein, Über die hebephrenischen Formen der Dp. Kraepelins. CBN., 1906, p. 453.
373. Knapp, Körperliche Symptome bei funktionellen Psychosen. A., 1908, Vol. 44, p. 709.
374. ——— Confusional Insanity and Dp. J. Nerv. and Ment. Disease. October, 1908. Abst.: CBN., 1909, p. 265.
375. Knecht, Über die katatonischen Erscheinungen in der Paralyse. Z., 1886, Vol. 42, p. 331.
376. Koller, Jenny, Beitrag zur Erblichkeitsstatistik der Geisteskranken etc. A., 1895, Vol. XXVII, p. 268.
377. Kölpin, Klinische Beiträge zur Melancholiefrage. A., 1904, Vol. 39, p. 31.
378. ——— Dp. Z., 1908, p. 1.
379. Köppe, Gehörsstörungen und Psychosen. Z., 1867, Vol. 24, p. 34.
380. Köppen, Über akute Paranoia. Z., 1899, Vol. 56, p. 642 (with discussion).
381. ——— Über Albuminurie und Propeptonurie bei Psychosen. A., 1889, XX, p. 825.
382. Köttgen, Klinische Katatonien bei organischer Erkrankung des Schädelinhaltes. Diss. Zürich, 1899.
383. Kohnstamm, Beziehungen zwischen Zwangsneurose und Katatonie? CBN., 1908, p. 710.
385. Konrád, Zur Lehre von der akuten halluzinatorischen Verworrenheit. A., 1885, Vol. 16, pp. 522 and 533 ff.
386. ——— Über galvano-elektrische Reaktion an den Gehörs- und Gesichtsnerven bei Halluzinationen. Jahrb., 1886, Vol. VI, p. 148.
387. Kraepelin, Kompendium der Psychiatrie. Leipzig, 1883.
388. ——— Lehrbuch der Psychiatrie. Seventh Edition. Leipzig, Barth, 1903.
389. ——— Einführung in die psychiatrische Klinik. Second Edition, Leipzig, Barth, 1905.
390. ——— Psychologische Arbeiten. Leipzig, Engelmann.
391. ——— Über Verwirrtheit. Z., 1886, Vol. 42, p. 352.
392. ——— Über Erinnerungsfälschungen. A., 1886 and 1887, Vol. 17 and 18.
393. ——— Über Katalepsie. Z., 1892, Vol. 48, p. 170.
394. ——— Über Remissionen bei Katatonie. Z., 1896, Vol. 52, p. 1126.
395. ——— Zur Diagnose und Prognose der Dp. Heidelberger Versammlung 26./27. November 1898. Z., 1899, Vol. 56, pp. 254 and 262.
396. ——— Fragestellungen der klinischen Psychiatrie. CBN., 1905, pp. 573 ff.
397. ——— Diskussion über Fausers Vortrag über rhythmische Betonung. CBN., 1905, p. 630.
398. ——— Über Sprachstörungen im Traume. Psychologische Arbeiten, 1905, Vol. V, No. 1.
398 *a*) Krafft-Ebing, Psychopathia sexualis. Stuttgart, Enke., 1898, Tenth Edition, p. 154.
399. Krause, Über das Lautwerden der eigenen Gedanken. Charitéannalen, XXVIII, 1904. Abst.: NCB., 1904, p. 866.
400. Kretz, Bemerkungen zur akuten Verrücktheit. Z., 1884, Vol. 40, p. 281.

401. Kron, Die Basedowsche Krankheit und das Geschlechtsleben des Weibes. Berl. klin. WS., 1907, No. 50 and 51, pp. 1611 and 1651.
402. Lange, Hölderlin. Stuttgart, Enke, 1909.
403. Langès, La confusion mentale chronique et ses rapports avec la Dp. Thèse Bordeaux, 1907.
404. Lasègue in Pilcz, Über eine gewisse Gesetzmässigkeit in den Träumen. NCB., 1899, pp. 187.
405. Latron, Des états cataleptiques dans les infections et les intoxications. Thèse Paris, 1901.
406. Laubi, Die körperlichen Degenerationszeichen bei Geisteskranken. Diss. Basel, 1887.
407. Laufenauer, Über katatonische Verrücktheit. Orvosi Hetilap, 1882. Abst.: Z., Vol. 39, p. 388.
408. Legrain, Délire chez les dégénerés. 1886, Paris, Delahaye.
409. Lehmann F., Zur Pathologie der katatonen Symptome. Z., 1898, Vol. 55, p. 276.
410. Lehmann G., Zur Frage über den günstigen Einfluss akuter Krankheiten auf den Verlauf von Geistesstörungen. Z., 1887, Vol. 43, p. 200.
411. Leubuscher und Ziehen, Klinische Untersuchungen über die Salzsäureausscheidung des Magens bei Geisteskranken. Jena, 1892.
412. v. Leupoldt, Zur klinischen Bewertung pathologischer Wanderzustände. Z., 1905, Vol. 62, p. 303.
413. ——— Zur Symptomatologie der Katatonie. Sommers Klinik für psychische und nervöse Krankheiten. Halle, Marh., 1906, p. 39.
414. Levy-Bianchini, Sull età comparsa e sull' influenza dell' ereditarietà nella patogenesi della Dp. o primitiva. Riv. sper. di freniatria, 1903, XXIX, p. 558.
415. Levinstein-Schlegel, Pathologie und Therapie der psychischen Krankheiten. Berlin, Hirschwald, 1892.
416. Lewis, Bevan. A Text-Book of Mental Diseases. London, Griffin, 1889, p. 238.
417. Liebscher, Künstlich hervorgerufener "halbseitiger" Ganser. Jahrb. f. Psych., 1907, Vol. 28, p. 113.
418. ——— Die transkortikale motorische Aphasie in ihren Beziehungen zu den Psychosen. MS., 1908, XXVI, p. 107.
419. Liepmann, "Über Ideenflucht." Halle, Marh., 1904.
420. Lindenborn, Allgemein pathologische Betrachtungen über das Vorkommen und die Bedeutung der Unreinlichkeit der Geisteskranken. A., 1886, Vol. 17, p. 322.
421. Livi, La lipemania stupida e la transfusione sanguinae. Z., 1877, Vol. 33, p. 382.
422. Lobsien, Aussage und Wirklichkeit bei Schulkindern. In Stern's Psychologie der Aussage. II. Folge. No. II, p. 29, 1904.
423. Lomer, Zur Kenntnis des Farbensehens. Z., 1905, Vol. 62, p. 63.
424. ——— Untersuchungen über juvenile D. mit einem Heilvorschlag. Z., 1905, Vol. 62, pp. 387 ff.
425. ——— Über einige körperliche Begleiterscheinungen der Verblödung. WS., 1908/1909, p. 137.
426. ——— Das Verhältnis der Involutionspsychosen zur juvenilen Demenz. Z., 1905, Vol. 62, pp. 769/770.
427. Löwenstein, Beitrag zur Differentialdiagnose des katatonischen und hysterischen Stupors. Z., 1908, Vol. 65, p. 790.
428. Lugaro. L'ipocondria persecutoria una forma tardiva della D. paranoide. Riv. di pat. nerv. e ment., 1904, IX.
429. ——— Sulle allucinazioni unilat. dell' udito. Riv. di patolog. nerv. e ment., IX. 1904, p. 228. Abst.: Jmsc., p. 766.
430. Lugiato, Studio sulla morfologia dei Dp. Il Morgagni, 1907, No. 1. Abst.: NCB., 1908, p. 379.
431. Lukacs, Beiträge zur Pathologie und pathologischen Anatomie der Dp. Klinikai füzetek, 1907, No. 3. Abst.: NCB., 1908, p. 38.

432. Lundborg, Beitrag zur klinischen Analyse des Negativismus bei Geisteskranken. CBN., 1902, p. 554.
433. ——— Eine Hypothese betreffend die Natur des katatonischen Symptomenkomplexes. CBN., 1905, p. 289.
434. Lundvall, Blod undersök ningar pa sinnessynka Hygica, 1907, No. 11. Abst.: CBN., 1908, p. 481.
435. Luther, Zur Kasuistik der Geistesstörungen auf dem Boden des chronischen Alkoholismus. Z., 1902, Vol. 59, p. 26.
436. Mackie, Blutuntersuchungen. Jmsc., Jan. 1901. Abst.: WS., 1901, p. 225.
437. Macpherson, Bemerkungen über den Einfluss der Desinfektion des Darmes auf einige Formen akuten Irreseins. Jmsc., 1893, Z. 159 *.
438. ——— Dp. Review neur. and ps., 1907, p. 185, Vol. V, No. 3.
439. Maggiotto, Le cosi dette "stimate isteriche" e la D. precoce. Giorn. di psich. clin. e tecn. man., 1904. Abst.: CBN., 1905, p. 46.
440. Magnan, Leçons cliniques sur les maladies mentales. Paris, 1897.
441. ——— Von den systemisierten Wahnideen. Internat. klin. Rundschau, 1893, No. 51. Abst.: Z., 138 *.
442. ——— Psychiatrische Vorlesungen. Leipzig, Thieme, 1891.
443. Magnan et Sérieux, Délire chronique à évolution systématique. Paris, Masson.
444. Mairet, Pubertätsirresein. Amps., 1888/1889. Abst.: Z., 1888, 305 * und 89, 195 *.
445. Marandon de Montyel, Les formes de la Dp. Diskuss. Kongress zu Pau. NCB., 1904, p. 1152.
446. Marchand, Du rôle étiologique de la syphilis dans les psychoses. Rev. de psych., III, 1905, p. 405. Abst.: Arch. génér. de méd., 1906, IV, p. 1068.
447. Marguliés, Die primäre Bedeutung der Affekte im ersten Stadium der Paranoia. MS., 1901, Vol. 10, p. 283.
448. Marie, P., D. de la puberté. Congrès de Pau, 1904. Abst.: JB., 1906, p. 1002.
449. Marie, A., La D. Paris, Doin, 1906.
450. Marr, Discussion of Bruce's Lecture (Antistreptococcusserum). Jmsc., 1903, p. 446.
451. Marro, Les psichosi della pubertà. Torino, 1896.
452. ——— Les psychoses de la puberté. Pariser Kongressbericht, 1900, pp. 31 ff.
453. Maschenko, Über pathologisch-anatomische Veränderungen der Grosshirnrinde beim sekundären Schwachsinn. NCB., 1900, p. 988.
454. Masoin, Remarques sur la catatonie. Journ. de neurol., Belg., 1902, p. 61.
455. ——— Observations sur la Dp. et la catatonie. Bull. soc. méd. ment. Belge. December, 1902. Z., 1903, Vol. 60, p. 162 *.
456. Masselon, Psychologie des Dp. Thèse Paris, Boyer, 1902. Abst.: CBN., 1903, p. 422.
457. ——— La dp. Paris, Joanin, 1904.
458. ——— Un cas fruste de dp. An., XVII, 1904. Abst.: CBN., 1905, p. 132.
459. Mayer bei Meynert, 16 Fälle von Halbtraumzustand. Jahrb., 1892, Vol. 11, p. 236.
460. Mayr, E., Die Sekretion des Magensaftes und ihre Beziehungen zu psychopathologischen Zustandsbildern. Wien. klin. WS., 1907, p. 1285.
461. Mayser, Zum sogenannten halluzinatorischen Wahnsinn. Z., 1886, Vol. 42, pp. 114 and 133.
462. Meeus, La Dp. chez les jeunes gens. Bull. soc. méd. ment. Belgique, 1902. Mars/juin et sept.
463. ——— Considérations générales sur la signification clinique de la Dp. Amps., 1904, Vol. XX, p. 207. Abst.: NCB., 1905, p. 83.
464. Meschede, Über krankhafte Fragesucht, Phrénolepsia erotematica, eine bisher wenig bekannte Form partieller Denkstörung. Z., 1872, Vol. 28, p. 390.
465. Meyer, Ad., Fundamental Conceptions of Dp. Brit. Méd. J., 1906, Sept.
466. Meyer, E., Beitrag zur Kenntnis der akut entstandenen Psychosen und der katatonischen Zustände. A., 1899, Vol. 32, p. 780.

467. ——— Klinik der Puerperalpsychosen. Berl. klin. WS., 1901, p. 8075.
468. ——— Zur prognostischen Bedeutung katatonischer Erscheinungen. Münch. med. WS., 1903, p. 1369.
469. ——— Über akute und chronische Alkoholpsychosen etc. A., 1904, Vol. 38, p. 331.
470. ——— Über psychische Infektion. Berl. klin. WS., 1905, p. 669.
471. ——— Die Ursachen der Geisteskrankheiten. Jena, Fischer, 1907.
472. Meyer, L., Intentionspsychosen. A., 1889, Vol. 20, p. 1.
473. Meynert, Klinische Vorlesungen über Psychiatrie. Wien, 1890.
474. ——— Die akuten halluzinatorischen Formen des Wahnsinns und ihr Verlauf. Jahrb. II, 1881, p. 181.
475. ——— Amentia, die Verwirrtheit. Jahrb., IX, 1890, p. 1.
476. Mignot, Étude des troubles pupillaires dans quelques maladies mentales. Thèse, Paris, 1902.
476 *a*) Miyake Koichi, Jugendirresein (in Tokio). From the Neurological Institute, University of Vienna, XVI, p. 315, Wien, Deuticke, 1908.
477. ——— Les troubles phonétiques dans la Dp. Amps., 1907, p. 5. Abst.: NCB., 1908, p. 380.
477 *a*) Mickle, Katatonie. Brain, 1889, Vol. XII, p. 503.
478. Möbius, Über Scheffels Krankheit. Halle, Marh., 1907.
479. ——— Geschlechter der Tiere, II, p. 24.
480. Möller, Beitrag zur Lehre von dem im Kindesalter entstehenden Irresein. A. 1882, Vol. 13, p. 188.
481. Mönkemöller, Kombinierte Psychosen? Z., 1901, Vol. 58, p. 639.
482. ——— Zur Lehre von der periodischen Paranoia. Z., 1905, p. 638.
483. ——— Haftpsychosen. MS. für Kriminalpsychologie, Vol. I, p. 686.
484. Mönkemöller und Kaplan, Eine neue Methode der Fixierung von Fusspuren zum Studium des Ganges. NCB., 1900, p. 798.
485. Mohr, Über Zeichnungen von Geisteskranken und ihre diagnostische Verwertbarkeit. CBN., 1906, p. 702.
485 *a*) Moll, Konträre Sexualempfindung. Third Edition, Berlin, Fischer, 1899, p. 353.
486. Mondio, Allucinazioni e frenosi sensoria. Riv. sper. d. freniat. Vol. 29, No. 1 and 2. Z., 1903, 102 *.
487. ——— Eredità e degenerazione nello sviluppo della D. consecutiva etc. Riv. mensile di Neuropat. e Psich., 1900, No. 4 e 5. Abst.: NCB., 1901, p. 133.
488. Monod, Les formes frustes de la Dp. Thèse, Paris, 1905.
489. Moravcsik, Über Katatonie. Orvosi Hetilap, 1905. No. 27, Beilage. Abst.: JB., 1045/1046 and NCB., 1905, p. 875.
491. ——— Künstlich hervorgerufene Halluzinationen. CBN., 1906, p. 215.
492. ——— Über einzelne motorische Erscheinungen Geisteskranker. Z., 1907, Vol. 64, p. 733, and CBN., 1907. pp. 137/138.
494. Morawitz, Klinische Mischformen von Katatonie und Epilepsie. Diss. Zürich, 1900.
495. Morel, Traité des maladies mentales. 1860, pp. 491, 560, 712.
496. Mouratoff, Etudes sur la D. catatonique. An., 1904, II, No. 97, Vol. XVII. Abst.: JB., 1055.
497. Mucha, Beiträge zur Kenntnis der Katatonie. Z., 1898, Vol. 55, p. 429.
498. ——— Ein Fall von Katatonie im Anschlusse an die erste Menstruation. NCB., 1902, p. 937.
499. Müller, A., Periodische Katatonie. Dissert. Zürich, 1900.
499 *a*) Müller, H., Beiträge zur Kenntnis der Hyperemesis gravidarum. WS., 1908/1909, p. 93.
500. Münzer, Ein Beitrag zur Lehre der Puerperalpsychosen. MS., 1906, XIX, pp. 362 and 375.
501. Muggia, Appunti sperimentali sulle condizioni organiche dei Dp. Est. d. Rif. med., XXII, p. 26.

502. v. Muralt, Katatonische Krankheitsbilder nach Kopfverletzungen. Z., 1900, Vol. 57, p. 457.
502 a) Muthmann, Zur Psychologie und Therapie neurotischer Symptome. Halle, Marhold, 1907.
503. Näcke, Die Menstruation und ihr Einfluss bei chronischen Psychosen. A., 1896, Vol. 28, p. 169.
504. ——— Über katatonische Symptome in Verlauf der Paralyse bei Frauen. Z., 1893, Vol. 49, p. 51.
505. ——— Raritäten aus der Irrenanstalt. Z., 1894, Vol. 50, p. 630.
506. ——— Rezidiv oder nicht? Irrenfreund, 1900. Abst.: Z., 57*.
507. ——— Wahnidee und Irrtum. WS., 1905, No. 48/49.
508. ——— Die Spätepilepsie im Verlaufe chronischer Psychosen. Z., 1905, Vol. 62, p. 610.
509. ——— Der Kuss bei Geisteskranken. Z., 1906, Vol. 63, p. 106.
510. Näcke und Steinitz, Sieben Tage lang anhaltende, völlige und plötzlich nach Chloroformasphyxie eingetretene Aufhellung des Geistes bei einer sekundär verwirrten Geisteskranken. Irrenfreund, 1901. Abst.: NCB., 1902, p. 84.
511. Nasse, Über die plötzliche Umbildung einer klinischen psychischen Krankheitsform in eine neue. Z., 1888, Vol. 44, p. 434.
512. Neisser, Katatonie. Stuttgart, Enke, 1887.
512 a) ——— Über die originäre Verrücktheit. A., 1888, Vol. 19, p. 491.
513. ——— Über das Symptom der Verbigeration. Z., 1890, Vol. 46, p. 168.
514. ——— Erörterungen über die Paranoia vom klinischen Standpunkt. CBN., 1892, p. 1.
515. ——— Residualwahn. Sitzung des Vereines ostdeutscher Irrenärzte zu Leubus. June 1892, Z., 1893, Vol. 49, pp. 486 ff.
515 a) ——— Mitteilungen über vorausgegangene Psychosen bei Paralytikern. Berl. klin. WS., 1894, No. 38.
516. ——— Über die Sprachneubildungen Geisteskranker. Z., 1898, Vol. 55, p. 443.
517. ——— Beitrag zur Ätiologie der periodischen Psychosen. Vgl. A., 1903, Vol. 36, pp. 144/146.
518. ——— Discussion of Cramer's: Krankhafte Eigenbeziehung und Beobachtungswahn. CBN., 1903, p. 236.
519. ——— Diskussion. Sitzung der Berliner Gesellschaft für Psychiatrie und Nervenkrankheiten. NCB., 1905, p. 487.
519 a) Zur klinischen Beurteilung der Konfabulation. NCB., 1905, p. 738.
520. ——— Individualität und Psychose. Vortag in der Gesellschaft der Naturforscher, 1905. Berlin Hirschwald, 1906. Abst.: NCB., p. 722.
521. ——— Klinische Mitteilungen über das Dominieren und Andauern bestimmter Vorgänge bei Geisteskranken. Münch. Psych. Kongr., 1896, p. 302; WS., 1905/1906, p. 123.
522. ——— Zur Dp.-Frage. WS., 1909/1910, p. 8.
523. Nissl, Kritische Bemerkungen zu Ziehens Aufsatz: "Über einige Lücken und Schwierigkeiten der Gruppierung der Geisteskrankheiten". CBN., 1904, p. 171.
524. ——— Hysterische Symptome bei einfachen Seelenstörungen. NCB., 1902, p. 89.
525. Nolau, Ist die Katatonie eine besondere Form der Geistesstörung? Jmsc., 1892, 111*.
526. Norman Conolly, Notes on Hallucinations. Jmsc., 1903, pp. 272 ff.
527. Obersteiner, Über Psychosen in unmittelbarem Anschlusse an die Verheiratung. Nuptiales Irresein. Jahrb. Vol. 22, 1902, p. 313.
528. Obici, Intorno ai rapporti fra le "psichosi isteriche" e la D. primitiva. Giorn. di psich. clin. e tecn. manic. 1904. Abst.: CBN., 1905, p. 46.
529. Obici e Bonon, Richerche intorno alla resistenza dei globuli rossi nei malati di monte. Ann. di neurol., 1900. Vol. XVIII, p. 1.
529 a) Oppenheim, Nervenkrankheiten etc. Berlin, Karger, 1907, Second Edition.

530. Oekonomakis, Dp. (primitiva), Hebephrenie, Katatonie, Paranoia. Athen, 1907 (Greek). Abst.: NCB., 1907, p. 1177.
531. D'Ormea, Trauma al capo e Dp. Giorn. di psich. clin. e tecn. manic., 1905, Vol. XXXIII, pp. 135/146.
532. ——— Calcio e magnesio delle urine nei Dp. Giorn. di psich. clin. e tecn. manic., 1906. Abst.: NCB., 1906, p. 723.
533. ——— Il potere riduttore delle urine nei Dp. Riv. sperim. di freniatr., 1906, Vol. 32, p. 79.
534. D'Ormea e Maggioto, La eliminazione del bleu di metilene e del ioduro di potassio per via renale. Ricerche sul ricambio materiale nei Dp. Prima nota 1904. Giorn. di ps. Vol. 33, pp. 73-94.
535. ——— Ricerche sul ricambio materiale nei Dp. Ricerche urologiche. Secunda nota. Ibidem. Ferrara 1904. 32 pp. 209/234.
536. ——— Ricerche urologiche e ricerche comparative sulla eliminazione del bleu di metilene per via renale negli stati di depressione e di eccitamento, Dp. e di altre psicosi. Ricerche sul ricambio materiale nei Dp. Ferrara, 1905. Terza e quarta nota.
537. Orschansky, Über Bewusstseinsstörungen und deren Beziehungen zur Verrücktheit und D. A., 1889, Vol. 20, pp. 309/342.
538. Osske, Zur Prognose der Hebephrenie. Diss. Jena, 1906.
539. Ossipow, Die Schlangenbesessenheit und ihre Stellung in der Klassifikation der Psychosen. Obosrenje psychiatrii. Abst.: NCB., 1906, p. 365.
539 *a*) ——— Zur Ätiologie der Katatonie. Abst.: NCB., 1909, p. 382.
540. Ostermayer, Beiträge zur Kenntnis der Katatonie. Deutsch. Arch. f. klin. Med., Vol. 48, 1890/1891, p. 481.
541. Pactet, La folie dans les prisons. Rev. de ps., 1905, IX, p. 133.
542. Palmore, Observations on the Classification of Insanity. Jmsc., 1899, Jan. Z., 59*.
543. Paris, Contribution à l'étude de la catatonie et Dp. An., 1903, XVI, p. 409.
544. Pascal, Les ictus dans la Dp. Congrès de Lille, 1906. Abst.: NCB., p. 1080.
545. ——— Les remissions dans la Dp. Rev. de psychiat. mars et avril, 1907.
546. ——— Formes mélancoliques de la Dp. An., 1907. Abst.: CBN., pp. 956-958.
547. ——— Pseudo-Neurasthénie prodromique de la Dp. Paris, Masson, 1907. Abst.: La presse méd., No. 6.
548. Patin et Madia, Contribution clinique et critique à l'étude de la catatonie. (Italian.) Ann. di neurol., 1903. Abst.: Amps., 1906, p. 469.
549. Peeters-Gheel, Troubles intellectuels et catatonie. Bullet. d. soc. méd. ment. Belgique. June 1902, Z. 101*.
550. Pelletier, L'association des idées dans la manie aiguë et dans la débilité mentale. Thèse Paris, 1903.
551. Peretti, Zur Kasuistik der plötzlichen Genesungen bei Psychosen. Z., 1890, Vol. 46, p. 62.
552. Peterson, Katatonia. Rev. des Journ. améric., 1896.
553. Peterson and Jung, Psycho-physical Investigations With the Galvanometer and Pneumograph in Normal and Insane Individuals. Brain, p. 153, Vol., 30, 1907.
554. Peterson and Langdone, Katatonia. Proceedings of the Americ. Med. Psych. Association, 1897. Abst.: Z., 1898, p. 126*.
555. Petrén, Spätheilung von Psychosen. Diss. Stockholm, Norstedt, 1908. Nord. med. Arkiv. Afd., II (Jnre med.).
556. Pfeifer, Über das Krankheitsbild der "zirkumskripten Autopsychose auf Grund einer überwertigen Idee". MS., 1906, Vol. XIX, p. 49.
556 *a*) Pfenninger, Untersuchungen über die Konstanz und den Wechsel der psychologischen Konstellation. Jahrb. für psychoanalytische Forschung, III, 1911.
557. Pfersdorff, Über intestinale Wahnideen im man.-depr. Irresein. CBN., 1904, p. 161.
558. ——— Der Wahn der körperlichen Beeinflussung. MS., 1905, Vol. 17, pp. 158/169.

559. ——— Die Remissionen der Dp. Zeitschrift für klinische Medizin, 1904. Vol. 55, pp. 488 ff. Abst.: CBN., 1906, p. 79.
560. Pfersdorff, Über eine Form der Depression in der Dp. CBN., 1905, pp. 733 ff.
561. ——— Die Prognose der Dp. WS., 1905/1906, p. 199, A., 1905, Vol. 40, p. 1058. Wanderversammlung der südwestdeutschen Neurologen und Irrenärzte in Baden-Baden, V., 1905.
562. ——— Über Rededrang bei Denkhemmung. MS., Vol. XIX, 1906, p. 108.
563. ——— Mischzustände bei Manisch-Depressiven. NCB., 1908, p. 1142.
564. Pfister, Zur Ätiologie und Symptomatologie der Katatonie. Z., 1906, Vol. 63, p. 275.
565. ——— Über Verbigeration. Lecture. Z., 1906, Vol. 63, p. 548.
566. Pförringer, Verhalten des Körpergewichtes bei zirkulären und anderen Psychosen. MS., Vol. 23, Suppl. 124.
567. Pianetta, Caso di alluzinationi unilaterali. Manicomio, XIX. Abst.: Jmsc., 1904, p. 556.
568. Pichon, Gleichzeitiges Vorkommen verschiedener Delirien bei demselben Individuum. L'encéphale No. 4, 5 and 6. Abst.: Z., 87, p. 55*.
569. Pick, Psychiatrische Beiträge zur Psychologie des Rhythmus und Reimes. Zeitschrift für Psychologie und Physiologie der Sinnesorgane, XXI, p. 401.
570. ——— Zur Pathologie des Ich-Bewusstseins. A., 1904, Vol. 38, p. 22.
570 *a*) ——— Über pathologische Träumerei und ihre Beziehung zur Hysterie. Jahrb., 1896, XIV, 280.
571. ——— Über Hyperästhesie der periodischen Retinaabschnitte; zugleich ein Beitrag zur Lehre von den katatonen Bewegungen. MS., 1908, Vol. 211, p. 382.
572. ——— Über sogenannten Transitivismus bei Geisteskranken. Prag. med. WS., 1905, pp. 259 and 275.
573. ——— Über primäre Demenz. Wandervorträge, 1891.
574. ——— Über primäre progressive Demenz bei Erwachsenen. Prager med. WS., 1904, p. 417.
575. Pieraccini in Ballet. Traité de Pathologie mentale, p. 148 (fuite de la pensée).
576. Pieraccini, Periodisches Stummsein einer Geisteskranken. Rivist. sperim. di fren., 1893, Vol. 19, p. 1, 121*.
577. Pighini, Contribuzione allo studio della Dp. Riv. sper. di fren., 1905, Vol. 31, p. 156*.
578. ——— Il ricambio organico nella Dp. Rivist. di fren., 1907. Abst.: NCB., 1908, p. 379.
579. Pighini e Paoli, Di una speciale forma del globulo rosso nella Dp. Rivist. di fren. e med., XXXII. Abst.: NCB., 1907, p. 913.
580. Pilcz, Über eine gewisse Gesetzmässigkeit in Träumen. NCB., 1899, p. 187.
580 *a*) ——— Lehrbuch der speziellen Psychiatrie. Leipzig und Wien, Deuticke, 1904.
581. Pobiedin, Zur Lehre von den akuten halluzinatorischen Psychosen. Z., 1902, Vol. 59, p. 481.
582. Popoff, Recherches hématologiques chez les aliénés. Thèse Lyon, 1908. Lyon, Rey.
583. Pötzl, Fall von Katatonie. Wien. klin. WS., 1904, p. 1422.
584. Probst, Über das Gedankenlautwerden und über Halluzinationen ohne Wahnideen. MS., 1903, Vol. 13, p. 401.
585. Pugh, The Alkalinity of Blood in Mental Disease. Jmsc., 1903, p. 71.
586. Raecke, Über Erschöpfungspsychosen. Z., 1900, Vol. 57, p. 39.
587. ——— Zur Lehre von den Erschöpfungspsychosen. MS., 1902, Vol. 11, pp. 12 and 120.
588. ——— Über hysterische Schlafzustände. Berl. klin. WS., 1904, p. 1323.
589. ——— Verkannte Geisteskranke. MS. f. Kriminalpsych., 1907, Vol. 3, p. 472.
590. ——— Katatonie im Kindesalter. A., 1909, Vol. 45, p. 245.

591. ——— Zur Prognose der Katatonie. Deutsch. Ver. f. Psych., Berlin, 1908. Abst.: WS., 1908/1909, p. 115.
592. Raggi, Psychische Kontrasterscheinungen bei einer Geisteskranken. Arch. ital. per le malatie nerv., Vol. 24, No. 4 and 6. Abst.: Z., 1887, p. 58*.
593. Rathmann, Über die nach Schädeltrauma auftretenden psychischen Störungen. Vierteljahrsschrift für gerichtliche Medizin, 1901, Vol. 22, p. 1.
594. Rauch, Über die katatonen Symptome. Diss. Leipzig, 1906.
595. Rauschke, Begleitdelirien. NCB., 1905, p. 673.
596. ——— Ein Fall von Paranoia acuta simplex. Münch. med. WS., 1906, p. 1378.
597. Rebizzi, La causa tonica in alcune malatie mentale.
598. Redepenning, Der geistige Besitzstand von sogenannter D. MS., 1908, 23. Suppl. p. 139.
599. Régis in Marie, p. 7. Notes à propos de la Dp. Revue de psych., 1904, Vol. VIII, p. 150.
600. ——— La confusion mentale. Amps., 1905. Abst.: NCB., p. 1154.
601. Régis et Lalanne, Catatonie et insuffisance rénale. Congrès de Limoges, 1907.
602. Rehm, Weitere Erfahrungen auf dem Gebiete der Lumbalpunktion. CBN., 1905, pp. 798 ff.
603. Reichhardt, Über Todesfälle bei funktionellen Psychosen. CBN., 1905, p. 1.
604. ——— Leitfaden für die psychiatrische Klinik. Fischer, Jena, 1907.
605. Reis, Über einfache psychologische Versuche an Gesunden und Geisteskranken. Kraepelins psychologische Arbeiten. Leipzig, Engelmann, 1899, Vol. II, p. 587.
606. Reuter, Ein Fall von "extrakampiner" Halluzination. Orvosi Hetilap, No. 7 (Hungarian), 1904. Abst.: JB., p. 1017.
607. Ricci, Le stereotypie nelle d. e spezialmente nelle d. consecutive. Rivist. sperim. di freniatr., XXV. Abst.: NCB., 1899, p. 996.
608. Ricksher and Jung, Further Investigations on the Galvanic Phenomenon and Respiration in Normal and Insane Individuals. J. of Abnorm. Psych., II, p. 189, December 1907.
609. Rieger, Über normale und kataleptische Bewegungen. A., 1882, Vol. XIII, pp. 427/481.
610. Riklin, Zur Psychologie hysterischer Dämmerzustände und des Ganserschen Symptoms. WS., 1904, No. 21/22.
611. ——— Über Versetzungsbesserungen. WS., 1905/1906, p. 154.
612. ——— Beitrag zur Psychologie der kataleptischen Zustände bei Katatonie. WS., 1906/1907, No. 32/33.
612 *a*) ——— Analytische Untersuchung der Symptome und Assoziationen eines Falles von Hysterie. WS., 1905, No. 46.
613. ——— Über Gefängnispsychosen. WS., 1907/1908, No. 30–37.
614. ——— Wunscherfüllung und Symbolik im Märchen. Wien und Leipzig, Heller, 1908.
615. v. Rinecker, Über die Bedeutung von Hebephrenie als klinisches Krankheitsbild. Vortrag. Z., 1881, Vol. 37, p. 570.
616. Risch, Über die Verwechslung von Denksperrung mit angeborenem Intelligenzdefekt in den Haftpsychosen. CBN., 1908, p. 249.
617. ——— Beitrag zum Verständnis der psychogenen Zustände. Z., 1908, p. 171.
618. ——— Die Gehirnsperrung, eine Schutzmassregel des Zentralnervensystems. CBN., 1908, p. 563.
619. ——— Symptomenkomplex der frischen Haft etc. MS., 1909, Vol. XXV, p. 305.
620. Rizor, Jugendirresein. A., 1908, Vol. 43.
621. Robertson in Ballet, p. 139. Reflexsprache.
622. ——— Unilateral Hallucinations, Their Relative Frequency, Associations and Pathology. Jmsc., 1901.
623. Rohé, Beziehungen zwischen Erkrankungen der Beckenorgane und Geistesstö-

rungen beim Weibe. Ninty-fifth Annual Report of the Maryland Hospital for the Insane, 1894, 127*.
624. Roller, Motorische Störungen beim einfachen Irresein. Z., 1886, Vol. 42, p. 1.
625. Rorie, Notes on Adolescent Insanity in Dorset, with discussion. Jmsc., Vol. 50, p. 226. Abst.: JB., 1904, p. 1020.
626. Rosenfeld, Über Herdsymptome bei den zur Verblödung führenden Psychosen. Zeitschrift für klinische Medizin, Vol. 56. Abst.: CBN., 1905, pp. 323 and 471.
627. ——— Über Partialdefekte bei Endzuständen der Katatonie. NCB., 1905, p. 631.
628. ——— Psychische Störungen bei vasomotorischer Neurose. CBN., 1908, p. 137.
629. ——— Über Einfluss psychischer Vorgänge auf den Stoffwechsel. Z., 1906, Vol. 63, p. 367.
630. Rousseau, De la folie à l'époque de la puberté. Thèse Paris, 1857.
630 *a*) Roubinowitch et Levaditi, Rôle de la syphilis dans l'étiologie de la Dp. Gaz. des hôpit., 1909, June.
631. Rowe, Is Dp. the "New Peril" in Psychiatry? Americ. Journ. of Insanity. Vol. 63, No. 3. Abst.: CBN., 1908, p. 444.
632. Rudolphson, Zur Kenntnis und klinischen Bedeutung der idiomuskulären Wulstbildung. A., 1889, Vol. 20, p. 473.
633. Rüdin, Über die klinischen Formen der Gefängnispsychosen. Diss. Berlin, 1901.
634. ——— Eine Form akuten halluzinatorischen Verfolgungswahns in der Haft ohne spätere Weiterbildung des Wahns und ohne Korrektur. Z., 1903, Vol. 60, p. 852.
635. ——— Über die klinischen Formen der Seelenstörungen bei zu lebenslänglicher Zuchthausstrafe Verurteilten. Habil.-Schr. München, 1909.
636. Rust, Über die Katatonie oder das Spannungsirresein. Diss. Berlin, 1879.
637. Sachs B., Referat zur Eröffnung der Diskussion der Americ. neurol. assoc. September 1904. Journ. Nerv. and Ment. Diseases, 1905. Abst.: NCB., p. 866.
638. Salerni, Le oscillazioni periodiche mensili della temperatura, del polso e del respiro nelle alienate menstruate e nelle amenorroiche. Riv. sperim. di freniatr. 30, p. 323. Abst.: JB., 1904, p. 1022.
639. Sandberg, Zur Psychopathologie der chronischen Paranoia. Z., 1896, Vol. 52, p. 627.
640. Sander, Über eine spezielle Form der primären Verrückheit. A., 1868, Vol. I, pp. 387 ff.
641. Sandri, La formola emo-leucocitaria nella Dp. Riv. di Patolog. nerv. e ment. X. Abst.: NCB., 1907, p. 913.
642. Sano et Heilporn, Un cas de catatonie. Bullet. de la soc. méd.-ment. Belgique, September 1901.
643. de Sanctis, Sante, Negativismo vesanico e allucinazioni antagonist. Bull. della soc. Lancisiana degli osped. di Roma, XVI. 1896. Abst.: Zeitschrift für Psychiatrie und Physiologie der Sinnesorgane, Vol. 13, p. 397.
644. ——— D. praecocissima catatonica oder Katatonie des früheren Kindesalters. 1908, No. 1.
645. ——— Psicopatologia della idea di negazione. Manic. moderno, XVI, 1900. Abst.: NCB., 1902, p. 28.
646. ——— Intorno alla psichopatologia dei neologismi. Annali di nevrol., XX, p. 597. Abst.: NCB., 1904, p. 226.
647. ——— Sopra alcune varietà della Dp. Rivist. sper. di freniatr. 32, p. 141. Abst.: NCB., 1907, p. 181.
647 *a*) ——— Die Träume. Übersetzung. Marhold, Halle, 1901.
648. Sartorius, Die forensische Bedeutung der Dp. Z., 1908, p. 666.
649. Savage, Lettsonian-Lectures on the Mental Disorders of Decay. Lancet, 1905, No. 42, pp. 625, 913.
650. ——— Lettsonian-Lectures on Functional Mental Disorders. Lancet, Febr. 1905, p. 409.

651. Schäfer, Ein Fall von Dp. katatonischer Form (Kraepelin), der nach 15 jähriger Dauer in Genesung ausging etc. MS., 1907, XXII. Suppl., pp. 72–80.
652. ——— Katatonisches Krankheitsbild bei Hirnabszess. Mitteilungen aus den Hamburger Staatsirrenanstalten. Abst.: NCB., 1906, p. 878.
653. ——— Der moralische Schwachsinn. Halle, Marh., 1906. Abst.: NCB., p. 568.
654. Scheffer, Melancholie met katatonische verschijnselen na negenjarigen duur plotselijk genesen. Psych. and neur. Bladen, 1899, I, 27. Abst.: CBN., 1900, p. 672.
655. Schermers, Over katatonie. Psych. and neur. Bladen, 1901, p. 253. Abst.: NCB., 1903, p. 552.
656. v. Schleiss-Löwenfeld, Fälle von Hebephrenie etc. Dissert. München, Wolf, 1904.
657. Schlöss, Über die Beziehungen zwischen Melancholie und Verrücktheit. Jahrb., XIV, 1896, p. 114.
658. Schmidt, Hirnabszess bei katatonischem Krankheitsverlauf. Z. 1904, Vol. 61, p. 679.
659. Schneider, Ein Beitrag zur Lehre von der Paranoia. Z., 1903, Vol. 60, p. 65.
660. Schoenthal, Beiträge zur Kenntnis der im frühen Lebensalter auftretenden Psychosen. A., 1892, Vol. 23, p. 799.
661. Scholl, Versuche über die Einführung von Komplexen in die Assoziation von Gesunden und Geisteskranken. Klinik für psych. und nerv. Krankheiten. Published by Sommer, III. Vol., 1908, p. 197.
662. Scholz, Über Pubertätsschwachsinn. Z., 1897, Vol. 53, p. 912 ff.
663. ——— Eine irre Verbrecherin. Z., 1899, Vol. 56, p. 603.
664. Schott, Beitrag zur Lehre von der sogenannten originären Paranoia. MS., 1904, Vol. 15, No. 5.
665. ——— Beitrag zur Lehre von der Ideenflucht in der Manie. CBN., 1904, p. 519.
666. ——— Beitrag zur Lehre von der katatonischen Verrücktheit. Z., 1905, Vol. 62, p. 257.
667. ——— Klinischer Beitrag zur Lehre von der Dp. Kraepelins. MS., 1905, Vol. 17. Suppl., p. 118.
668. ——— Mord beziehungsweise Totschlag und Dp. Vierteljahrsschrift für gerichtliche Medizin, XXX, 1905, p. 76*.
669. Schreber, Denkwürdigkeiten eines Nervenkranken. Leipzig, Mutze, 1903.
670. Schreiber, Ein Fall von zirkulärem Irresein mit täglich alternierendem Typus. Pester medizinische Presse, 1901. Abst.: NCB., 1902, p. 83.
671. Schröder, Die Katatonie im höheren Lebensalter. NCB., 1902, p. 638. Abst.: MS., Vol. 12, p. 79.
672. ——— Ein Beitrag zur Frage der Kombination von Psychosen und Morbus Basedowii. Festschrift zum 25 jährigen Jubiläum des Direktors Dr. Tiling, Riga, Grothuss, 1909.
673. ——— Chronische Alkoholpsychosen. Hoche, Sammlung zwangloser Abhandlungen, 1905, Halle, Marhold.
674. Schubert, Alternierende Psychose. Z., 1893, Vol. 49, p. 498.
675. Schuele, Chirurgische Erlebnisse bei Geisteskranken. Z. 83, Vol. 39, p. 1.
675 *a*) ——— Zur Paranoiafrage. Z., 1894, Vol. 50, p. 301 ff.
676. ——— Handbuch der Geisteskrankheiten. Leipzig, Vogel, 1880.
677. ——— Klinische Pychiatrie. Spezielle Pathologie und Therapie bei Geisteskrankheiten. Leipzig, Vogel, 1886.
679. ——— Zur Katatoniefrage. Z., 1898, Vol. 54, p. 515.
680. ——— Klinische Beiträge zur Katatonie. Z., 1901, Vol. 58, pp. 221 ff.
681. Schultz, Über das Verhalten der Alkaleszenz des Blutes und der weissen und roten Blutkörperchen bei Nerven- und Geisteskrankheiten. MS., XX, 1907, p. 21.
682. Schultze, Bemerkungen zur Paranoiafrage. Deutsche med. WS., 1904, No. 3, p. 89. Abst.: JB., p. 1056.
683. ——— Über epileptische Äquivalente. Münch. med. WS., 1900, p. 465/466.

684. ——— Dp. Deutsche med. WS., 1907, Vol. 33.
685. Schultze, Über Psychosen bei Militärgefangenen. Z., 1904, Vol. 61, p. 602.
686. ——— Weitere psychiatrische Beobachtungen an Militärgefangenen. Jena, Fischer, 1907.
687. Schuster, Psychische Störungen bei Hirntumoren. Stuttgart, Enke, 1902.
688. Séglas, La paranoia. An., 1887.
689. ——— Ein Fall von kombiniertem Irresein. Amps., 1888, I, 91*.
690. ——— Une observation de mélancholie cataleptic. Nouv. Inconogr. de la Salpêtrière, 1889.
691. ——— Les troubles du langage chez les aliénés. Paris, Rueff, 1892. Abst.: CBN., p. 526.
692. ——— Die Halluzination und die Verdoppelung der Persönlichkeit bei der Paranoia (folie systématique). Die Besessenen und die psychomotorische Varietät des systematischen Verfolgungswahns. Amps., 1893. Abst.: Z. 1895, Vol. 51, 116*.
693. ——— Leçons cliniques sur les maladies mentales et nerveuses. Paris, Asselin, 1895.
694. ——— La d. paranoide. Amps., 1900, Vol. 58, p. 232. Abst.: JB., 960.
695. ——— Dp. et catatonie. Nouv. Inconogr. de la Salpêtrière, 1902, p. 4. Abst.: CBN., 1903, p. 416.
696. ——— Des hallucinations antagonistes unilatérales et alternantes. Amps., 1903. Abst., NCB., p. 1026.
697. ——— Symptomes catatoniques au cours de la paralysie générale. Nouv. Inconogr. de la Salpêtrière, 1907, No. 1. Abst.: NCB., p. 824.
698. Séglas in Ballet, Séméiologie des affections mentales.
699. Séglas et Chaslin, La catatonie. An., 1888, I, 91*, et Brain, Vol. XII, 1890, p. 191.
700. Séglas et Darconne, Le dermographisme chez les aliénés. Amps., 1901.
701. Seiffer, Gedächtnisuntersuchungen. Ps. Verein Berlin, 14. März 1908. CBN., p. 417.
702. Serbski, Formen psychischer Störung, die unter dem Namen der Katatonie beschrieben sind. Gesammelte Abhandlungen. Moscow, 1890 (Russian). Z., 1892, 256*.
703. ——— Über die unter dem Namen Katatonie geschilderten Psychosen. CBN., 1891, p. 145.
704. ——— Über die akuten Formen der Amentia und Paranoia. Z., 1892, Vol. 48, p. 328.
705. ——— Contribution à l'étude de la Dp. Amps., 1903/1904. Abst.: NCB., 1905, p. 83.
706. ——— On the question of Dp. Journ. of Ment. Pathology, II, 1902, p. 175.
707. Sérieux, Dp. Gaz. hebdomadaire de méd. et chir. 1901.
708. ——— Dp. Rev. de psych., 1902, No. 6, p. 241.
709. Sérieux et Masselon, Signes physiques de la Dp. Soc. méd. psych. June 30, 1902.
710. Siefert, Beitrag zur Paranoiafrage. A., 1905, Vol. 39, p. 783.
711. ——— Über die Geistesstörungen der Strafhaft etc. Halle, Marhold, 1907.
712. Siemerling, Diskussion zu Kraepelin. Z., 1899, Vol. 56, p. 260.
713. Sioli, Über direkte Vererbung von Geisteskrankheiten. A., 1885, Vol. XVI, pp. 113 ff.
714. Sklarek und van Vleuten. Abst.: JB., 1904, p. 1025.
715. Smith, Ely, Jeliffe, The Signs of Pre-Dp.: Their Signification and Pedagogic Prophylaxis. Americ. Journ. Med. Sc. VIII, 1907, p. 956.
716. Smith Percy, Presidential Address on Paranoia. Jmsc., 1904, p. 607. Abst.: NCB., 1906, p. 329.
717. Snell, Über eine besondere Art von Zwangsvorstellungen mit entsprechenden Bewegungen und Handlungen bei Geisteskranken. Z., 1874, Vol. 30, p. 651.
718. ——— Die Überschätzungsideen der Paranoia. Z., 1890, Vol. 46, p. 447.
719. ——— Hypothermie bei Geisteskranken. Z., 1898, Vol. 55, p. 305.

720. Sölder, Über Preseveration, eine formale Störung im Vorstellungsablauf. Jahrb., 1899, Vol. 18, p. 508.
720 a) Sollier, Psychologie de l'idiot et de l'imbecille. Paris, 1891. Translation. Hamburg und Leipzig, Voss. 1891.
721. Soltmann in Gerhardts Handbuch der Kinderkrankheiten. Vol. V, p. 1.
722. Sommer, Beiträge zur Kenntnis der kriminellen Irren. Z., 1888, Vol. 40, p. 117.
723. ——— Diskussion. Versammlung südwestdeutscher Irrenärzte. Z., 1899, Vol. 56, p. 261.
724. ——— Zur Lehre von der "Hemmung" geistiger Vorgänge. Z., 1894, Vol. 50, p. 234.
725. ——— Diagnostik der Geisteskrankheiten. Wien und Leipzig, 1894, pp. 260/261. Abst.: Z., 1895, Vol. 51, p. 1028.
726. ——— Objektive Darstellung katatonischer Muskelzustände. NCB., 1903, p. 1160.
727. ——— Klinische Psychiatrie. Halle, 1906, p. 161.
728. Soukhanoff, Sur la pathogénie des obsessions morbides. Congrès Bruxelles 1903. Abst.: NCB., 1904, p. 237.
729. ——— Sur les associations psychiques obsédantes de contraste dans les états mélancoliques. An., XVIII, p. 305. Abst.: JB., 1904, p. 1026.
730. Soutzo, fils, La psychiatrie moderne et l'oeuvre du prof. Kraepelin. Amps., 1906, pp. 243 and 402.
731. Specht, Über den pathologischen Affekt in der chronischen Paranoia. Festschrift, Erlangen, 1901.
732. ——— Über Hysteromelancholie. CBN., 1906, p. 545.
733. ——— Zur Analyse einiger Schwachsinnsformen. NCB., 1906, pp. 1133/1134.
734. Spitzka, Über masturbatorisches Irresein. Jmsc., 1888. Abst.: Z., 1889, p. 90*.
735. Sprague, Primary D. of Puberty (The British Med. Journ., 1898). Americ. Journ. of Ins. Vol. 57, No. 2. Abst.: Z., 1900, 179*.
736. Sprague and Hill, Primary D. and Dp. Trans-Americ. Med. Ps. Assoc. May 1900. Abst.: Jmsc., 1901, p. 808.
737. Stadelmann, Das Wesen der Psychose auf. Grundlage moderner naturwissenschaftl. Anschauung. No. IV, die Katatonie. München, Otto Gmelin, 1905. Abst.: JB., p. 423.
738. ——— Erlebnis und Psychose. Versammlung deutscher Naturforscher, Dresden, 1907. NCB., p. 924.
739. Stauffer s. Brahm.
740. Stawitz, Über den Schwachsinn als Folgezustand ungeheilter Psychosen. Diss. Würzburg, 1889.
740 a) Steele Whitmore, Das Blut der Melancholischen und der Erfolg systematischer tonischer Behandlung. Jmsc., 1893, 158*.
741. Steinheil, Catalepsie symptomatisch bei Intoxikations- und Infektionskrankheit. Rev. neurol., 1901, No. 18.
742. Stekel, Nervöse Angstzustände und deren Behandlung. Berlin und Wien, Urban & Schwarzenberg, 1908. Abst.: CBN., p. 766.
743. Stelzner, Analyse von 200 Selbstmordfällen. Berlin, Karger, 1906.
744. Stern, Beitrag zur Psychologie der Aussage. Vol. II, p. 9.
745. Sterz, Über psychische Störungen im Pubertätsalter. Jahrb., I, 1879, p. 94.
746. Stoddart, A Study of Emotions. Brain, 1904, pp. 509-521.
747. Stransky, Zur Kenntnis gewisser erworbener Blödsinnsformen, spez. der Dp. "Wiener klinische Rundschau," 1903. Jahrb., 1904, Vol. 24, pp. 1, 79, 95 ff.
748. ——— Zur Auffassung gewisser Symptome der Dp. NCB., 1904, pp. 1074 and 1140.
749. ——— D. tardiva. Ein Beitrag zur Klinik der Verblödungspsychosen. MS., 1905, Vol. 18. Suppl.
750. ——— Über die Dp. in ihrer Bedeutung für die ärztliche Praxis. Vortrag. Wien, Urban & Schwarzenberg, 1905. Wiener medizinische Presse, No. 29, p. 1379.
751. ——— Zur Lehre von den kombinierten Psychosen. NCB., 1905, p. 970.

752. ——— Zur Lehre von der Amentia. Wiener med. WS., 1905, No. 1 and Journal f. Ps. und Neur., Vol. IV, No. 4, Vol. V, No. 1, Vol. VI, 1–4.
753. ——— Zur Amentiafrage. CBN., 1907.
754. Strohmayer, Zur Klinik, Diagnose und Prognose der Amentia. MS., XIX, p. 417.
755. Svetlin, Ein Beitrag zur Lehre von der Katalepsie, A. Vol. VIII, p. 548.
756. Swoboda, Studien zur Grundlegung der Psychologie. Leipzig und Wien, Deuticke, 1905.
757. Tahier, Stupeur catatonique et stupeur mélancolique. Thèse Bordeaux, 1904. No. 132.
758. Tamburini, Fälle von Katatonie, Irrenfreund, 1887, 8 and 9. Abst.: Z., 1888, Vol. I, p. 90 and Riv. sper. di fren., 1886.
759. Tanzi und Riva, Paranoia. Beitrag zur Theorie der psychischen Degeneration. Riv. sper. di fren., 1884, II, 1885 I, Abst.: Z., 92*.
760. Taube, Über hypochondrische Verrücktheit. Diss. Dorpat, 1886. II. Semester, 53*.
761. Tetzner, Tod durch gehäufte Krampfanfälle bei Katatonie. WS., 1905/1906, pp. 225, 236.
762. Thomsen, Klinisches über Zwangsvorstellungen. CBN., 1904, p. 773.
763. Thwaites, Dp. and Mental Degeneracy in Syria. Jmsc., 1908, p. 511.
764. Tigges, Kahlbaums Katatonie. Z., 78, Vol. 34, p. 753.
765. Tiling, Individuelle Geistesartung und Geistesstörung. Wiesbaden, Bergmann, 1904. pp. 35/36, CBN., XV. p. 408.
766. Tintemann, Querulatorische Psychosen im Zusammenhang mit Arbeiterversicherung. Münch. med. WS., 1907, p. 1479.
767. Tonnini, Die sekundäre Verrücktheit. Riv. sper. di fren. XIII 1, 1887, II, 84*.
768. Tomaschny, Der Kopfschmerz bei Dp. Z., 1908, Vol. 65, p. 778.
769. Toulouse et Damaye, La démence vésanique est-elle une d.? Rev. de psych., 1903.
770. Towbridge, The Insanity of Pubescence. Alienist and Neurol., 91, July, p. 341.
771. Trépsat, Altération trophique chez des Dp. catatoniques. Nouv. iconogr. de la Salp., 1904, p. 465.
772. ——— Étude des troubles physiques dans la Dp., hébéphréno-catatonique. Thèse Paris, 1905, p. 17.
773. Trömner, Über jugendliche Verblödungsprozesse. NCB., 1899, p. 1066.
774. ——— Das Jugendirresein. Halle, Marh., 1900. Sammlung zwangloser Abhandlungen aus dem Gebiete der Nerven- und Geisteskrankheiten, III. Vol. No. 5.
775. Tschisch, Über Geisteskrankheiten bei Prostituierten. Obosrenije psichiat., 1906, No. 12, NCB., 1907, p. 825.
776. ——— Die Katatonie (Monograph). Neurol. Westnik., 1897/1898. Abst.: Z., 1899, p. 138*.
777. Tuczek, Über Zwangsvorstellungen. Berl. klin. WS., No. 6, Vol. 36, 1899, p. 213.
778. Urstein, Ein Beitrag zur vergleichenden Psychiatrie. CBN., 1906, p. 629.
778 *a*) ——— Dp. Urban & Schwarzenberg, Wien, 1909.
779. Ullmann, Über protrahierte hysterische Dämmerzustände. Dissert. Berlin, 1907.
780. Urquhart, Nomenclature of Mental Diseases. Jmsc., 1903, p. 236.
781. Veraguth, Das psychogalvanische Reflexphänomen. Berlin, Karger, 1909.
782. Vieregge, Versuche über die Merkfähigkeit für Zahlen an Gesunden und Geisteskranken. Vortrag. Abst.: Z., 1908, Vol. 65, p. 207.
783. Vigouroux et Juquelier, Contribution clinique à l'étude des délires du rêve. Journ. de ps. norm. et pathol. 1908, p. 131.
784. Vogt, Ragnar, Zur Psychologie der katatonen Symptome. CBN., 1902, pp. 433/434.
785. ——— Zur Psychophysiologie des Negativismus. CBN., 1903, p. 85.
786. ——— Über den Begriff "Anregung" beziehungsweise "Perseveration" der kortikalen Vorgänge. CBN., 1904, p. 29.
787. Voisin, Les psychoses de la puberté. Compte rendu du XIII Congrès internat. de méd., 1900. Section de psychiat., pp. 49, 63-73.

788. ——— Notes sur un cas de mélancolie avec stupeur à forme cataleptique. An., 1877, XIII, p. 354.
789. Vorkastner, Über pseudomelancholische Zustände. MS., 1905, XVII, p. 133.
790. Vorster, Über das Verhalten des spezifischen Gewichtes des Blutes bei Geisteskranken. Z., 1894, Vol. 50, p. 1081.
791. ——— Über die Vererbung endogener Psychosen in Beziehung zur Klassifikation. MS., 1901, Vol. IX, p. 161.
792. Wagner v. Jauregg, Einiges über erbliche Belastung. Wien. klin. WS., 1906, p. 1.
793. Wagner in Lettres d'Autriche, De l'influence des affections fébriles sur les psychoses. Sem. méd., 1887, p. 280.
794. Wassermeyer, Zur Pupillenuntersuchung bei Geisteskranken. A., 1908, Vol. 43, p. 124.
795. Weber, L. W., Über Psychosen unter dem Bilde der reinen primären Inkohärenz. Münch. med. WS., 1903, p. 1417.
796. ——— Akute primäre Inkohärenz. Z., 1903, Vol. 60, p. 755.
797. ——— Über akute tödlich verlaufende Psychosen. MS., 1904, Vol. 16, p. 81.
798. ——— Fortschritte in der psychiatrischen Diagnostik. Deutsche med. WS., 1904, p. 922, Vol. 25.
799. ——— Traumatische Psychosen. NCB., 1905, p. 539.
800. ——— Posttraumatische Psychosen. Deutsche med. WS., 1905, p. 1183. Abst.: JB., p. 1014.
801. Weiler, Pupillenuntersuchungen bei Geisteskranken, 1906, p. 475.
802. Weininger, Geschlecht und Charakter. Wien und Leipzig, Braumüller, 1903.
802 *a*) ——— Gedanken über Geschlechtsprobleme. Second edition. Berlin, Concordia, 1907.
803. Werner, Über die psychiatrische Nomenclatur "Verrücktheit" und "Wahnsinn". Z., 1890, Vol. 46, p. 524.
804. Wernicke, Grundriss der Psychiatrie. Leipzig, Thieme, 1900.
805. ——— Krankenvorstellungen. Breslau, 1899.
806. ——— Über Halluzinationen, Ratlosigkeit und Desorientierung in ihren wechselseitigen Beziehungen. NCB., 1900, p. 1131. Abst.: JB., 1901, p. 849.
807. ——— Report of Discussions, Society of German Psychiatrists, Z., 1899, Vol. 56, p. 642.
808. ——— Discussion of E. Meyer's: Zur Klinik der Puerperalpsychosen. Z., 1901, Vol. 58, pp. 701/702.
809. Westphal, C., Zwei Krankheitsfälle. A., 1877, Vol. 7, pp. 622-631.
810. ——— Über die Verrücktheit. Z., 1878, Vol. 34, p. 252.
811. ———, A., Über bisher nicht beschriebene Pupillenerscheinungen im katatonischen Stupor mit Krankendemonstrationen. Autoref: CBN., 1907, p. 736.
812. ——— Über ein im katatonischen Stupor beobachtetes Pupillenphänomen. Deutsche med. WS., No. 27, 1907. JB., p. 1127.
812 *a*) ——— Weitere Beobachtungen über im katatonischen Stupor beobachtete Pupillenphänomene etc. Deutsche med. WS., 1909, No. 23.
813. Weygandt, Atlas und Grundriss der Psychiatrie. Lehmanns Atlanten, 1902 (p. 392).
814. ——— Alte Dp. CBN., 1904, p. 613.
815. ——— Über leicht abnorme Kinder. CBN., 1905, p. 25.
816. ——— Dp. und Idiotie. CBN., 1905, p. 600 und Zeitschrift für Erforschung und Behandlung des jugendlichen Schwachsinns, 1907.
817. Wherry, Is Delusional Insanity Due to Disease of the Brain? Alienist und Neurolog. 1905. Abst.: JB., p. 1044.
819. Whitwell, Zur Pathogenese des Stupors. Brain, 1895, 124*.
820. Wideröe, Primary d. of Puberty. The British. Med. Journ., 1898. Abst.: JB., p. 1163.

821. ——— Primär pubertets. d. Norsk Mag. f. Lägevidensk. 1898, p. 367. Abst.: JB., p. 1227.
822. Wiersma, Die Sekundärfunktion bei Psychosen. Journ. f. Ps. u. Neurol., 1906/1907, Vol. VIII, p. 1.
823. Wiglesworth, On the Pathology of Certain Cases of Melancholia Attonita or Acute d. Jmsc., 1883, p. 355.
824. Wille, C., Die Lehre von der Verwirrtheit. A., 1888, Vol. 19, p. 328.
825. ——— Die Psychosen des Pubertätsalters. Leipzig und Wien, Deuticke, 1898.
826. Wilmanns, Zur Psychopathologie des Landstreichers. Eine klinische Studie. Leipzig, Barth, 1906.
827. ——— Zur Differenzialdiagnostik der "funktionellen" Psychosen. CBN., 1907.
828. ——— Über Gefängnispsychosen. Halle, Marh., 1908.
829. Wintersteiner, Augenspiegelbefunde bei Psychosen. NCB., 1907, p. 1103.
830. Wise, Genesung chronischer Geistesstörung. Journ. of Insanity, April 1886, I, 180*.
831. Wolf, Weitgehende Besserungen beziehungsweise Genesungen an Geisteskranken unter spezieller Bezugnahme auf § 1569 d. B. G. B. Heidelberger Diss., 1899.
832. Wolff, Zur Frage der Benennung der Dp., CBN., 1908, p. 856.
833. Wolfsohn, Die Heredität bei Dp., Z., 1907, Vol. 64, pp. 347 ff.
834. Wollenberg in Binswanger und Siemerling, First edition, p. 310.
835. Wollny, Über Telepathie, Leipzig, Wigand, 1888.
836. ——— Sammlung von Aktenstücken in Sachen der gemeingefährlichen Einwirkungen durch Magnetisation auf telepathischem Wege. Leipzig, Wigand, 1888.
837. Würth, Über Bettbehandlung bei chronischen Psychosen. Z., 1902, Vol. 59, p. 57.
838. Yennaropoulos, Folie quérulante. Diss. Genève, 1905.
839. Zablocka, Prognosestellung bei der Dp. Diss. Berlin, Reimer, 1908.
840. Ziehen, Psychiatrie. Quotations from the Second Edition. Leipzig, Hirzel, 1902.
841. ——— Pubertätspsychose. XIII. Congrès Paris. Compte rendu. pp. 11 and 27.
842. ——— Über Störungen des Vorstellungsablaufes bei der Paranoia. A., 1892, Vol. 24, pp. 112, 365 and 1120. Abst.: CBN., 1891, p. 443.
843. ——— Tagesschwankungen der Körpertemperatur bei funktionellen Psychosen. Z., 1894, Vol. 50, p. 1042.
844. ——— Über die Affektstörung der Ergriffenheit bei akuten Psychosen. MS., 1901, Vol. 10, pp. 310-319.
845. ——— Die Geisteskrankheiten des Kindesalters. Berlin, Reuther, 1902.
846. ——— Zur Differentialdiagnose der Hebephrenie. Psych. en neurol. Bladen, No. 1, 1902, pp. 7 ff. Abst.: CBN., p. 478.
847. ——— Rückläufige Assoziationen bei Geisteskrankheiten. NCB., 1904, p. 1065.
848. ——— Über einige Lücken und Schwierigkeiten der Gruppierung der Geisteskrankheiten. MS., XV, p. 147.
849. ——— Über seltenere Menstrualpsychosen. CBN., 1906, pp. 651/652. Abst.: NCB., p. 729
850. Zweig, Dp. jenseits des 30. Lebensjahres. A., 1908, Vol. 44, p. 1015.

SELECTED BIBLIOGRAPHY
1911–1948

The translator has endeavored to establish, below, a selected bibliography of books, monographs and articles for the period between 1911 and 1948, which in his opinion indicates the trend of the work in the field of schizophrenia during the past thirty years. It consists of works which are outstanding either for their originality or their traditional value. Many of these have been selected also from the point of view of including valuable bibliographies, useful to the student who is investigating the field. A complete bibliography would consist of many thousands of books, monographs and papers.

BOOKS AND MONOGRAPHS

Abraham, K., *Selected Papers,* Institute of Psychoanalysis and Hogarth Press, London, 1927.

Alexander, F., *Psychoanalysis of the Total Personality,* Nervous and Mental Disease Publishing Co., New York, 1930.

———, and French, T. M., *Psychoanalytic Therapy,* Ronald Press Co., New York, 1946.

Alzheimer, A., *Contributions to the Pathological Anatomy of Dementia Praecox,* Deutsche Ver. f. Psych., Breslau, 1913.

Association for Research in Nervous and Mental Disease: Vol. 5, *Schizophrenia,* P. Hoeber, New York, 1928.

Association for Research in Nervous and Mental Disease: Vol. 10, *Schizophrenia,* Williams and Wilkins Co., Baltimore, 1931.

Baruk, H., *Medical Psychiatry,* Masson & Co., Paris, 1938.

Beck, S. J., *Personality Structure in Schizophrenics,* Nervous and Mental Disease Monographs, New York, 1931.

———, *Rorschach's Test,* Grune and Stratton, New York, 1944. (2 vols.)

Bellak, L., *Dementia Praecox; The Past Decade's Work and Present Status: A Review and Evaluation,* Grune and Stratton, New York, 1948.

Berze, J., and Gruhle, H., *Psychology of Schizophrenia* (Monograph on dem. ges. der Neurol. u. Psychiat.), J. Springer, Berlin, 1929.

Bleuler, E., *The Theory of Schizophrenic Negativism,* Nervous and Mental Disease Monograph Series No. 11, New York, 1912.

———, *Affectivity, Suggestibility and Paranoia,* "N. Y. State Hosp. Bulletin," Feb., 1912.

———, *Textbook of Psychiatry* (trans. by A. A. Brill), Macmillan & Co., New York, 1924.

———, *Affectivity, Suggestibility, Paranoia,* Marhold, Halle, 1926 (2nd edition).

———, *Natural History of the Soul and Its Coming into Consciousness,* J. Springer, Berlin, 1932.

Board of Control (England and Wales): *Results in 1000 Leucotomies,* H. M. Stationery Office, London, 1947.

Boisen, A. T., *The Exploration of the Inner World; A Study of Mental Disorder and Religious Experience,* Willet, Clark & Co., Chicago, New York, 1936.

Bradley, C., *Schizophrenia in Childhood,* Macmillan, New York, 1941.

Braunmuhl, A. von, *Insulin Shock Treatment of Schizophrenia (Including Cardiazol Convulsion),* J. Springer, Berlin, 1938.

Brickner, R. M., *The Intellectual Functions of the Frontal Lobes*, Macmillan, New York, 1946.
Bumke, O., editor, *Handbook of Mental Diseases* (Vol. 9 on Schizophrenia), J. Springer, Berlin, 1932.
Burrow, T., *The Structure of Insanity*, Paul, Trench, Trubner, London, 1932.
Cameron, E. D., *Objective and Experimental Psychiatry*, Macmillan Co., New York, 1941 (2nd edition).
Campbell, C. M., *Destiny and Disease in Mental Disorders*, W. W. Norton, New York, 1935.
Cannon, W. B., *Bodily Changes in Pain, Hunger, Fear and Rage*, Appleton, New York, 1929.
———, *The Wisdom of the Body*, W. W. Norton, New York, 1932.
Claude, H., and Rubenovitch, H., *Biologic Therapy in Mental Diseases*, Masson & Co., Paris, 1940.
Dayton, N., *New Facts in Mental Disorders*, C. C. Thomas, Springfield, Ill., 1940.
Delay, J., *Derangements of the Humors*, Presses Universitaires de France, Paris, 1946.
———, *Electroshock and Psycho-physiology*, Masson & Co., Paris, 1946.
Delmond, J., *Essay on Schizophasia*, Le François, Paris, 1935.
Dunbar, F., *Emotions and Bodily Changes*, Columbia University Press, New York, 1938.
Fenichel, O., *The Psychoanalytic Theory of Neurosis*, W. W. Norton & Co., New York, 1945.
Ferenczi, S., *Contributions to Psychoanalysis*, Richard C. Badger, Boston, 1916.
———, *Further Contributions to the Theory and Technique of Psychoanalysis*, Institute of Psychoanalysis and Hogarth Press, London, 1926.
Freeman, W., and Watts, J. W., *Psychosurgery*, C. C. Thomas, Springfield, Ill., 1942.
Freud, S., *Collected Papers*, L. Woolf and the Institute of Psychoanalysis, London, 1925. 4 vols. (as well as the other works of Freud translated into English).
Frostig, J., *Schizophrenic Thinking*, Georg Thieme, Leipzig, 1929.
Halstead, W. C., *Brain and Intelligence*, University of Chicago Press, Chicago, 1947.
Hanfmann, E., and Kasanin, J., *Conceptual Thinking in Schizophrenia*, Nerv. & Ment. Dis. Monograph Series No. 67, New York, 1942.
Hinsie, L. E., *Treatment of Schizophrenia*, Williams and Wilkins Co., Baltimore, 1930.
Hoch, A., *Benign Stupors*, Macmillan, New York, 1924.
Hoch, P. H., *Failures in Psychiatric Treatment*, Grune and Stratton, New York, 1948.
Hoskins, R. G., *The Biology of Schizophrenia*, W. W. Norton, New York, 1946.
Jessner, L., and Ryan, V. G., *Shock Treatment in Psychiatry; A Manual*, Grune and Stratton, New York, 1941.
Jong, H. de and Baruk, H., *Experimental Catatonia by Means of Bulbocapnine*, Masson and Co., Paris, 1931.
Jong, H. de, *Experimental Catatonia*, Williams and Wilkins, Baltimore, 1945.
Jung, C. G., *Psychological Types*, Harcourt, Brace and Co., New York, 1923.
———, *Psychology of Dementia Praecox*, Nervous and Mental Disease Monographs, New York, 1936. (1st edition, 1909.)
Kahn, E., *Schizoid and Schizophrenia in Relation to Heredity*, J. Springer, Berlin, 1923.
Kalinowsky, L. B., and Hoch, P. H., *Shock Treatments and Other Somatic Procedures in Psychiatry*, Grune and Stratton, New York, 1946.
Kallmann, F. J., *The Genetics of Schizophrenia*, J. J. Augustin, New York, 1938.
Kanner, L., *Child Psychiatry*, C. C. Thomas, Springfield, Ill., 1935.
Kasanin, J. S., editor, *Language and Thought in Schizophrenia*, University of California Press, Los Angeles, 1944.
Kehrer, F., and Kretschmer, E., *Predisposition to Mental Disorders*, J. Springer, Berlin, 1924.
Kempf, E. J., *Psychopathology*, C. V. Mosby Co., St. Louis, 1920.

Kendig, I., and Richmond, W. V., *Psychological Studies in Dementia Praecox,* Edwards Bros., Ann Arbor, Michigan, 1940.

Klopfer, B., and Kelley, D. M., *The Rorschach Technique,* World Book Co., Yonkers-on-Hudson, 1942.

Kraepelin, E., *Textbook of Psychiatry,* 8th edition, Ambrosius Barth, Leipzig, 1913.

———, *Dementia Praecox,* Chicago Medical Book Co., Chicago, 1919.

———, *Dementia Praecox and Paraphrenia* (from 8th German edition), Livingstone, Edinburgh, 1925.

Kretschmer, E., *Physique and Character,* Harcourt, Brace, New York, 1925.

———, *Textbook of Medical Psychology,* Grune and Stratton, New York, 1948.

Lange, J., *Catatonic Phenomena Appearing in Manic Disorders,* J. Springer, Berlin, 1922.

Langfeldt, G., *Prognosis in Schizophrenia and Factors Influencing Course of Disease, Katamnestic Study, Including Individual Re-examinations in 1936. With Some Considerations Regarding Diagnosis, Pathogenesis and Therapy,* "Acta Psychiat. et Neurol.," (Supp. 13), pp. 1-228, 1937.

Lessing, O., *Internal Secretions and Dementia,* Karger, Berlin, 1920.

Lewis, N. D. C., *Constitutional Factors in Dementia Praecox,* Nervous and Mental Disease Publishing Co., New York, 1923.

———, *Research in Dementia Praecox,* The National Committee for Mental Hygiene, 1936.

Lutz, J., *Schizophrenia in Childhood,* Art. Institut Orell Fussli, Zurich, 1937.

Malzberg, B., *Social and Biological Aspects of Mental Disease,* State Hospitals Press, Utica, N. Y., 1940.

Minkowski, E., *Schizophrenia,* Payot et Cie, Paris, 1927.

Moniz, E., *Surgical Attempts in the Treatment of Certain Psychoses,* Masson & Co., Paris, 1936.

Mourgue, R., *Neurobiology of Hallucinations,* M. Lamertin, Brussels, 1932.

Murray, H. A., *Explorations in Personality,* Oxford University Press, New York, 1938.

Nodet, C., *The Groups of Hallucinatory Psychoses,* Doin & Co., Paris, 1938.

Nunberg, H., *Practice and Theory of Psychoanalysis,* Nervous and Mental Disease Monographs, New York, 1948.

Pavlov, I., *Lectures on Conditioned Reflexes,* International Publishers, New York, 1928.

Pavlov, I. P., *Conditioned Reflexes and Psychiatry,* International Publishers Co., New York, 1941.

Pollock, H. M., and Malzberg, B., *Hereditary and Environmental Factors in the Causation of Manic-Depressive Psychoses and Dementia Praecox,* State Hospitals Press, Utica, N. Y., 1939, (with R. G. Fuller).

Prinzhorn, H., *Plastic Art of the Psychotic,* J. Springer, Berlin, 1923.

Rapaport, D., *Diagnostic Psychological Testing,* Yearbook Publishing Co., Chicago, 1946, 2 vols.

Rorschach, H., *Psychodiagnostics,* E. Bircher Verlag, Bern and Leipzig, 1921.

———, *Psychodiagnostics,* Grune and Stratton, New York, 1947.

Rudin, E., *Studies in Heredity and Origin of Mental Diseases,* J. Springer, Berlin, 1916.

Sakel, M., *The Pharmacological Shock Treatment of Schizophrenia,* Nervous and Mental Disease Monographs, New York and Washington, 1936.

Sargant, W., and Slater, E., *Introduction to Somatic Methods of Treatment in Psychiatry,* Williams and Wilkins, Baltimore, 1944.

Schilder, P., *Hallucination and Perception,* J. Springer, Berlin, 1918.

———, *The Image and Appearance of the Human Body,* Kegan, Paul, London, 1935.

———, *Introduction to a Psychoanalytic Psychiatry,* Nerv. and Ment. Dis. Monograph Series, No. 50, 1928.

Sears, R. B., *Survey of Objective Studies of Psychoanalytic Concepts,* Social Science Research Council Bulletin, No. 5, New York, 1943.

Shakow, D., *The Nature of Deterioration in Schizophrenic Conditions*, Nervous and Mental Disease Monographs, Coolidge Foundation, New York, 1946.
Sheldon, W. H., Stevens, S. S., and Tucker, W. B., *The Varieties of Human Physique*, Harper Bros., New York, 1940.
Skalweit, W., *Constitution and Process in Schizophrenia*, Georg Thieme, Leigzig, 1934.
Slavson, S. R., ed., *The Practice of Group Psychotherapy*, International Universities Press, New York, 1947.
Storch, A., *Primitive Archaic Forms of Inner Experience and Thought in Schizophrenia*, Nervous and Mental Disease Monograph Series, No. 36, New York, 1924.
Sullivan, H. S., *Conceptions of Modern Psychiatry*. William A. White Psychiatric Foundation, Washington, D. C., 1945.
Tompkins, S. S., *The Thematic Apperception Test*, Grune and Stratton, New York, 1947.
Tramer, H., *Textbook of Child Psychiatry*, Karger, Basel, 1945.
Wertheimer, F., and Hesketh, F., *Significance of the Physical Constitution in Mental Disease*, Williams and Wilkins, Baltimore, 1926.
White, W. A., *Outlines of Psychiatry*, Nervous and Mental Disease Publishing Co., Washington, 1926.
Wilmanns, K., *Schizophrenia.* (In Bumke's "Handbook of Mental Diseases," Vol. 9, Special part, part 5.), J. Springer, Berlin, 1932.
Wolberg, L. B., *Hypnoanalysis*, Grune and Stratton, New York, 1945.
Zilboorg, G., and Henry, G. W., *A History of Medical Psychology*, W. W. Norton, New York, 1941.

ARTICLES AND PAPERS

Accornero, F., and Bini, L., *Insulin Shock at the Neuropsychiatric Clinic in Rome*, "Am. J. Psychiat.," (Suppl.), 94, 209-213, 1938.
Alexander, F., *Schizophrenic Psychoses; Critical Considerations of Psychoanalytic Treatment*, "Arch. Neurol. and Psychiat.," 26, 815-828, 1931.
Alexander, F. A., and Himwich, H. E., *Nitrogen Therapy for Schizophrenia; Preliminary Report on Technic.*, "Am. J. Psychiat.," 96, 643-655, 1939.
Alexander, G. H., *Therapeutic Efficacy of Electro-Convulsive Therapy*, "J. Nerv. and Ment. Dis.," 102, 221-230, 1945.
Alpers, B. J., and Hughes, J., *Changes in the Brain After Electrical Convulsions in Cats*, "Arch. Neurol. & Psychiat.," 47, 385-390, 1942.
Angyal, A., *Experience of Body-Self in Schizophrenia*, "Arch. Neurol. and Psychiat.," 35, 1047-1053, 1936.
Angyal, A., and Blackman, N., *Vestibular Reactivity in Schizophrenia*, "Arch. Neurol. and Psychiat.," 44, 611-620, 1940.
Angyal, A., Freeman, H., and Hoskins, R. G., *Psychologic Aspects of Schizophrenic Withdrawal*, "Arch. Neurol. Psychiat.," 44, 621-626, 1940.
Angyal, L., *Periodic Schizophrenia and Schizophrenic Twilight States*, "Allg. Ztschr. f. Psychiat.," 102, 185-216, 1934.
———, *Insulin Shock; Motor and Tonic Manifestations; Physiology and Pathology of Frontal Lobe After Insulin Shock in Schizophrenia*, "Ztschr. f. d. ges. Neurol. u. Psychiat.," 157, 35-80, 1937.
———, *Insulin Shock*, "Arch. f. Psychiat.," 106, 662-680, 1937.
Arieti, S., *Primitive Habits and Perceptual Alterations in the Terminal Stage of Schizophrenia*, "Arch. Neurol. and Psychiat.," 53, 378-384, 1945.
Ashby, W., *The Pattern of Distribution of Carbonic Anhydrase in the Cerebrum of Man Compared with that of Certain Lower Animals*, "J. Bio. Chem.," 156, 323-329, 1944.

———, *On the Distribution of Carbonic Anhydrase in the Cerebrum,* "J. Bio. Chem.," 156, 331-341, 1944.

Atkin, I., *Triazol 156 in Chronic Schizophrenia,* "Lancet," 1, 435-437, 1939.

Bak, R., *Regression of Ego-Orientation and Libido in Schizophrenia,* "Internat. J. Psychoanalysis," 20, 65-71, 1939.

———, *Dissolution of Ego, Mannerism and Delusion of Grandeur,* "J. Nerv. and Ment. Dis.," 98, 457-463, 1943.

Barbara, D. A., *Positive Transference in Schizophrenia; Case,* "Psychiatric Quart.," 18, 674-686, 1944.

Barrera, S. E., Lewis, N. D. C., Pacella, B. L. and Kalinowsky, L. B., *Brain Changes Associated with Electrically Induced Seizures,* "Tr. Am. Neurol. A.," 31-35, 1942.

Baruk, H., *Experimental Catatonia Due to Colon Bacilli,* "Presse Med.," 41, 1588-1589, 1933.

———, *Mental State During Catatonic Attack,* "Ann. Med.-Psychol.," 92, pt. 1, 317-346, 1934.

———, and Laurent, D., *Somatic Prodromal Phase of Dementia Praecox,* "Sem. de hop. de Paris," 9, 437-448, 1933.

———, and Massaut, C., *Physiologic Action of Scopolamine-Chloralose; Bulbocapnine and Scopolamine-Chloralose; Application to Certain Problems of Experimental Catatonia,* "Ann. Med.-Psychol.," (pt. 2), 94, 702-712, 1936.

Beiglbock, W., and Dussik, K. T., *Physiology of Hypoglycernic Shock in Schizophrenia,* "Am. J. Psychiat.," Suppl., 94, 50-59, 1938.

Bellak, L., and Parcell, B., *The Prepsychotic Personality in Dementia Praecox, A study of 100 Cases,* "Psychiatric Quart.," 20, 627-637, 1946.

Bender, L., *Principles of Gestalt in Copied Forms in Mentally Defective and Schizophrenics,* "Arch. Neurol. and Psychiat.," 27, 661-686, 1932.

———, *Anal Component in Persecutory Delusions,* "Psychoanalytic Rev.," 31, 1934.

———, *Clinical Study of 100 Schizophrenic Children,* "Am. J. Orthopsychiat.," 17, 40, 1947.

Bennett, A. E., *Curare, a Preventive of Traumatic Complications in Convulsive Shock Therapy,* "Am. J. Psychiat.," 97, 1040-1045, 1941.

———, *An Evaluation of "Shock" Therapies,* "Psychiat. Quart.," 19, 465-477, 1945.

Bennett, C. R., and Miller, T. K., *Observation on Treatment of Mental Cases with Sub-Shock Doses of Insulin,* "Am. J. Psychiat.," vol. 96, 4, 961-966, 1940.

Benon, R., *Mania in Dementia Praecox,* "Schweiz. Arch. f. Neurol. u. Psychiat.," 12, 166-169, 1923.

Berger, H., *Dementia Praecox,* "Med. Klinik," 19, 101-103, 1923.

Bergler, E., and Eidelberg, L., *The Mechanism of Depersonalization,* "Internat. Ztschr. f. Psychoanal.," 31, 1935.

Berkwitz, N. J., *Faradic Shock in Treatment of Functional Mental Disorders,* "Arch. Neurol. and Psychiat.," 44, 760-766, 1940.

Berlin, B. M., *Experimental Treatment of Schizophrenia with Antireticular Cytotoxic Serum,* "Med. Zhur.," 10, 1297-1302, 1940.

Berze, J., *Insulin Shock,* "Wien. Med. Wchnschr.," 83, 1365-1369, 1933.

———, *Study of Schizoids,* "Ztschr. f. d. ges. Neurol. u. Psychiat.," 153, 600-621, 1935.

Bibring, E., *Psychology of Fear of Death in Paranoiac Schizophrenia,* "Internat. Ztschr. f. Psychoanal.," 14, 508-517, 1928; also 15, 1928.

Billig, O., and Freeman, W. T., *Fatal Catatonia,* "Am. J. Psychiat.," 100, 633-638, 1944.

Binswanger, L., *Psychoanalysis and Clinical Psychiatry,* "Internat. Ztschr. f. Psychoanal.," 7, 1921.

———, *Concerning the Problem of Frequency of Schizophrenia in Childhood,* "Ztschr. Kinderpsychiat.," 156, 694-712, 1936.

Bjerre, P., *Radical Treatment of Chronic Paranoia,* "Jahrb. f. Psychoanalyt. Forsch.," 3, 1911.

Bleckwenn, W. J., *The Use of Sodium Amytal in Catatonia*, "A. Res. in Nerv. and Ment. Dis.," 1929.

Bleuler, E., *Disturbances of Association as a Primary Symptom of Schizophrenia; an Hypothesis*, "Allg. Ztschr. Psychiat.," 74, 1-21, 1918.

———, *Dementia Praecox*, "Rev. Neurol.," 2, 474, 1926.

———, *Syntonia, Schizoidia and Schizophrenia*, "J. f. Psychiat. u. Neurol.," 38, 47-57, 1929.

———, *Physiogenic and Psychigenic in Schizophrenia*, "Am. J. Psychiat.," 10, 203-211, 1930.

———, *Primary and Secondary Symptoms of Schizophrenia*, "Ztschr. f. d. ges. Neurol. u. Psychiat.," 124, 601-646, 1930.

———, *Psyche and Psychoid*, "Psychiat. Quart.," 4, 35, 1930.

Bleuler, M., *Schizophrenia; Review of Work of Prof. Eugen Bleuler*, "Arch. Neurol. and Psychiat.," 26, 610-627, 1931.

———, *Hereditary Prognosis in Schizophrenia; Review of Literature for 1939-1940*, "Fortschr. d. Neurol., Psychiat.," 13, 49-63, 1941.

Boisen, A. T., *Schizophrenia and Religious Experience, Coll. and Contrib. Papers*, Elgin State Hosp., 70-83, 1929.

———, *Form and Content of Schizophrenic Thinking*, "Psychiatry," 5, 23-33, 1942.

Bolles, M., and Goldstein, K., *Impairment of "Abstract Behavior" in Schizophrenic Patients*, "Psychiatric Quart.," 12, 42-65, 1948.

Bond, E. D., and Hughes, S., *Insulin Shock Therapy After Seven Years*, "Am. J. Psychiat.," 101, 62-63, 1944.

Bonhoeffer, K., *Significance of Exogenous Factors in Schizophrenia*, "Monatsschr. f. Psychiat. u. Neurol.," 88, 201-215, 1934.

Boss, M., *The Psychic Dynamics of Prolonged Narcosis (Klasi) Treatment of Schizophrenia*, "Schweiz. Arch. f. Neurol. u. Psychiat.," 36, 209, 1935.

———, *Psychopathology of Dreams in Schizophrenic Psychosis*, "Ztschr. f. d. ges. Neurol. u. Psychiat.," 162, 459-494, 1938.

Bourguignon, G., *Chronaxia and Disorders of Facial Expression in Catatonia*, "Am. Med.-Psychol.," 89 (pt. 1), 461-471, 1931.

Bowman, K. M., *Prepsychotic Personality*, "Am. J. Orthopsychiat.," 4, 473-498, 1934.

———, and Kasanin, J., *Constitutional Schizophrenia*, "Am. J. Psychiat.," 13, 645-658, 1933.

Braatöy, T., *Prognosis in Schizophrenia*, "Acta Psychiat. et Neurol.," 11, 63-102, 1936.

Bradley, C., and Bowen, M., *Behavior Characteristics of Schizophrenic Children*, "Psychiatric Quart.," 15, 296-315, 1941.

Braun, E., *Analysis of 716 Cases in Munich Psychiatric Clinic*, "Arch. f. Psychiat.," 80, 131-171, 1927.

Braunmuhl, A. von, *"Zig-Zag Method"; Technic and Use*, "Nervenarzt," 10, 545-553, 1937.

Brill, A. A., *Psychological Factors in Dementia Praecox; An Analysis*, "J. Abnorm. Psychol.," 3, 1908.

———, *Schizophrenia and Psychotherapy*, "Am. J. Psychiat.," 9, 519-541, 1929.

Bruetsch, W. L., *Chronic Rheumatic Brain Disease As Possible Factor On Causation of Some Cases*, "Am. J. Psychiat.," 97, 276-296, 1940.

Bullard, D., *Experiences in the Psychoanalytic Treatment of Psychotics*, "Psychoanalyt. Quart.," 9, 1940.

Bumke, O., *Pupillary Disturbances in Dementia Praecox*, "Munch. Med. Wochn.," 57, 2688, 1910.

———, *Disintegration of Dementia Praecox*, "Klin. Wchschr.," 3, 437-440, 1924. (Ab. J.A.M.A. 82, 1308, 1924).

Burger, H., *Psychopathology of Schizophrenic Terminal States*, "Ztschr. f. d. ges. Neurol. u. Psychiat.," 102, 719-747, 1926.

Burkhardt, H., *Schizophrenic Paralogia; Study of Problem of Autoism,* "Ztschr. f. d. ges. Neurol. u. Psychiat.," 145, 99-111, 1933.

Burlingame, C. C., *Editorial Comment On Metrazol,* "Digest of Neurol. and Psychiat.," 13, 1945.

Buscaino, V. M., *Production of Hallucinosis, Catatonia and Parkinsonism by Action of Amines,* "Riv. di. pat nerv.," 34, 162-165, 1929.

———, *Recent Research,* "Encéphale," 25, 48-56, 1930.

———, *Toxicity of Amines; Study of Buscaino Reaction,* "Rassegna di studi psichiat.," 28, 792-804, 1939.

Bychowski, G., *Schizophrenic Stupor,* "Ztschr. f. d. ges. Neurol. u. Psychiat.," 140, 30-50, 1932.

———, *Physiology of Schizophrenic Thinking,* "J. Nerv. and Ment. Dis.," 98, 368-386, 1943.

Cameron, N., *Thinking in Senile Deterioration and Schizophrenic Disorganization,* "Am. J. Psychol.," 51, 650-664, 1938.

———, *Deterioration and Regression in Schizophrenic Thinking,* "J. Abnorm. and Social Psychol.," 34, 265-270, 1939.

———, *Schizophrenic Thinking in a Problem-Solving Situation,* "J. Ment. Sci.," 75, 1939.

———, and Hoskins, R. G., *Insulin-Hypoglycernia Treatment of Schizophrenia,* "Am. J. Psychiat.," Suppl., 94, 265-269, 1938.

Campbell, C. M., *Form and Content of the Psychoses; the Role of Psychoanalysis in Psychiatry,* "Cornell U. Med. Bull.," 5, 1915.

———, *Two Cases Illustrating Combination of Affective and Schizophrenic Symptoms,* "Am. J. Psychiat.," 6, 243-257, 1926.

———, *Definition or Delimitation of Schizophrenic Type of Reaction,* "A. Res. Nerv. and Ment. Dis. Proc.," (1925), 5, 16-30, 1928.

———, *Schizophrenic Maladjustment,* "J. Neurol. and Psychopath.," 10, 237-241, 1930.

———, *Clinical Studies in Schizophrenia (Schizophrenic Surrender),* "Am. J. Psychiat.," 99, 475-483, 1943.

Carlisle, C. L., and Hecker, C. H., *Benzedrine Sulfate (and Ephedrine Sulfate) in Catatonic Stupors,* "M. Bull. Vet. Admin.," 13, 224-227, 1937.

Cerletti, U., and Bini, L., *Electroshock,* "Arch. Gen. Di. Neurol., Psychiat. e. Psicoanal.," 19, 266, 1938.

Chase, L. S., *Analysis of Criteria in 150 Schizophrenics Treated with Metrazol or Insulin,* "J. Nerv. and Ment. Dis.," 98, 464-473, 1943.

———, and Silverman, S., *Criteria in Schizophrenia; Critical Survey of Literature,* "Am. J. Psychiat.," 98, 360-368, 1941.

Cheney, C. O., and Clow, H. E., *Prognostic Factors in Insulin Shock Therapy,* "Am. J. Psychiat.," 97, 1029-1039, 1941.

———, and Drewry, P. H., Jr., *Results of Nonspecific Treatment,* "Am. J. Psychiat.," 95, 203-217, 1938.

Clark, L. P., *Practical Remarks on the Use of Modified Psychoanalysis in Borderline Neuroses and Psychoses,* "Psychoanalyt. Rev.," 6, 1919.

Claude, H., *Catatonia,* "Paris Med.," 2, 303-306, 1924.

———, *Relation of Hysteria to Schizophrenia,* "Ann. Méd.-Psychol.," (pt. 2), 95, 1-14, 1937.

———, Borel, A., and Robin, G., *Schizoid Versus Cycloid Personality,* "Encéphale," 19, 209-216, 1924.

———, ———, and ———, *Ether Mental Test in Diagnosis of Dementia Praecox,* "Encephale," 19, 419-421, 1924.

———, Dublineau, J., Ey, H., and Rubinovitch, P., *Schizophrenia,* "Ann. Méd.-Psychol.," 92, (pt. 1), 557-566, 1934.

———, and Levy-Valensi, J., *Schizophrenia in Balzac's "Comédie Humaine,"* "Progrès Méd.," 585-590, 1934.

———, Minkowski, E., and Tison, *Analysis of Bleuler's Dementia Praecox,* "Encéphale," 20, 1-13, 1925.

Cloetta, M., and Maier, H. W., *Improvement of Psychiatric "Prolonged Sleep" Treatment (Use of Cloetta Mixture),* "Am. J. Psychiat.," 91, 1409-1412, 1935.

Cohen, L. H., *Imagery and Its Relations to Schizophrenic Symptoms,* "J. Ment. Sc.," 84, 284-346, 1938.

Cohen, R. A., *Management of Anxiety in a Case of Paranoid Schizophrenia,* "Psychiatry," 10, 143-157, 1947.

Coleman, S. M., *Prepsychotic Schizoid; Character Study,* "J. Ment. Sci.," 77, 804-818, 1931.

Collins, R. T., *Affect in Schizophrenic Reaction Types,* "J. Ment. Sc.," 89, 21-41, 1943.

Conn, J., *An Examination of the Clinical-Pathological Evidence for the Concept of Dementia Praecox as a Specific Disease Entity,* "Am. J. Psychiat.," 90, 1039-1082, 1934.

Coriat, I. H., *Treatment of Dementia Praecox by Psychoanalysis,* "J. Abnorm. Psychol.," 12, 1917.

———, *Dynamic Interpretation of Kretschmer's Types,* "Am. J. Psychiat.," 6, 259-266, 1926.

———, *Psychoanalytic Theory of Hallucinations,* "Psychoanalyt. Rev.," 21, 1934.

Cossa, P., and Bougeant, H., *Insulin; Late Results of Shock Therapy in Schizophrenia,* "Ann. Med.-Psych.," (pt. 2), 199, 42-46, 1942.

Cotton, H. A., *Fatty Degeneration of the Cerebral Cortex in Psychoses with Special Reference to Dementia Praecox,* "J. Exper. Med.," 22, 442, 1915.

Darrah, L., *Shall We Differentiate Between Schizophrenia and Dementia Praecox?* "J. Nerv. and Ment. Dis.," 91, 323-328, 1940.

Davidson, M., *Study of Schizophrenic Performance on Stanford-Binet Scale,* "Brit. J. M. Psychol.," 17, 93-97, 1937.

Davis, P. A., and Davis, H., *The E.E.G. of Psychotic Patients,* "Am. J. Psychiat.," 95, 1007, 1939.

———, and ———, *Evaluation of Electroencephalograms of Schizophrenic Patients,* "Am. J. Psychiat.," 96, 851-860, 1940.

———, *Comparative Study of Electroencephalograms of Schizophrenic and Manic-Depressive Patients,* "Am. J. Psychiat.," 99, 210-217, 1942.

Dedichen, H. H., *A Comparison of 1459 Shock-Treated and 969 Non-Shock-Treated Psychoses in Norwegian Hospitals,* "Acta Psychiat. et Neurol.," Suppl., 1946.

Delmas-Marsalet, P., *Postural Reflexes in Catatonia: A Phase of Psychic Negativism,* "Compt. rend. Soc. de Biol.," 95, 1351-1354, 1926.

Demole, V., *Dementia Praecox, Hypoglycernia, Insulin, Vitamin* B_1, "Am. J. Psychiat.," Suppl., 94, 59-66, 1938.

Despert, J. L., *Schizophrenia in Children,* "Psychiatric Quart.," 12, 366-371, 1938.

———, *Comparative Study of Thinking in Schizophrenic Children and in Children of Preschool Age,* "Am. J. Psychiat.," 97, 189-213, 1940.

———, *Thinking and Motility Disorder in Schizophrenic Child,* "Psychiatric Quart.," 15, 522-536, 1941.

———, *Early Recognition of Childhood Schizophrenia,* "Am. J. Psychiat.," 104, 36, 1947.

Deutsch, H., *Forms of Emotional Disturbance; Relationship to Schizophrenia,* "Psychoanalyt. Quart.," 11, 301-321, 1942.

Devereux, G., *Sociologic Theory of Schizophrenia,* "Psychoanalyt. Rev.," 26, 315-342, 1939.

Domarus, E. von, *Pre-Logical Thinking in Schizophrenia,* "Ztschr. ges. Neurol. u. Psychiat.," 87, 84-93, 1923.

———, *A Theory of Schizophrenic Thinking,* "Ztschr. ges. Neurol. u. Psychiat.," 108, 703-714, 1927.

———, *Hallucinations of Schizophrenics*, "Ztschr. f. d. ges. Neurol. u. Psychiat.," 112, 636-638, 1928.
Dunlap, C. B., *Dementia Praecox – Some Preliminary Observations on Brains*, "Am. J. Psychiat.," 3, 403, 1924.
———, *The Pathology of the Brain in Schizophrenia*, "Res. Publ. Assoc. Res. Nerv. Ment. Dis.," 5, 371-381, 1928.
Dussik, K. T., *Three and a Half Years of Hypoglycernic Therapy of Schizophrenia*, "Am. J. Psychiat.," Suppl., 94, 269-276, 1938.
Eidelberg, L., *Psychoanalysis of a Case of Paranoia*, "Psychoanalyt. Rev.," 32, 373, 1945.
Eissler, K., *Limitations to the Psychotherapy of Schizophrenics*, "Psychiatry," 6, 1943.
Evensen, H., *Studies Made of 800 Patients After Their Discharge from Psychiatric Hospital at Gaustad During Years 1915 to 1929*, "Acta Psychiat. et. Neurol.," 11, 799-816, 1937.
Ewald, G., *Dementia Praecox and Schizophrenia: Discussion of Terminology*, "Ztschr. f. d. ges. Neurol. u. Psychiat.," 123, 465-471, 1930.
Ewalt, J. R., and Bruce, E. I., *Newer Concepts of Schizophrenia*, "Texas Reports on Biol. and Med.," 6, 97-107, 1948.
Fairbarn, W. R. D., *Endopsychic Structure Considered in Terms of Object-Relationships*, "Internat. J. Psychoanal.," 25, 70-93, 1944.
———, *Object-Relationships and Dynamic Structure*, "Internat. J. Psychoanal.," 27, 30-37, 1946.
Falstein, E. I., *Dementia Praecox in Infants and Children*, "Illinois M. J.," 76, 271-281, 1939.
Faris, R. E. L., *Incidence of Schizophrenia in Primitive Societies*, "J. Abnorm. and Social Psychol.," 29, 30-31, 1934.
Federn, P., *Narcissism in the Structure of the Ego*, "Internat. J. Psychoanalysis," 9, 1928.
———, *The Analysis of Psychotics*, "Internat. J. Psychoanal.," 15, 1934.
———, *Psychoanalysis of Psychoses*, "Psychiat. Quart.," 17, nos. 1, 2, 3, Jan., April, July, 1943.
———, *Principles of Psychotherapy in Latent Schizophrenia*, "Am. J. Psychotherapy," 1, 129-144, 1947.
Feigenbaum, D., *Analysis of a Case of Paranoia Persecutoria; Structure and Cure*, "Psychoanalyt. Rev.," 17, 1930.
Ferraro, A., *Insulin; Neuropathologic Findings in Three Additional Cases of Schizophrenia*, "J. Neuropath. and Exper. Neurol.," 1, 188-199, 1942.
Fiamberti, A. M., *Mechanism of Therapeutic Action of "Vascular Shock" Produced by Acetycholine and Choline Derivatives*, "Géor. de. psychiat. e di neuropat.," 67, 270-280, 1939.
Finesinger, J. E., Cohen, M. E., and Thonson, K. J., *Velocity of Blood Flow in Schizophrenia*, "Arch. Neurol. and Psychiat.," 39, 24-36, 1938.
Fisher, V. E., *Psychic Shock Treatment in Early Schizophrenia*, "Am. J. Orthopsychiat.," 14, 358-367, 1944.
Flournoy, H., *Meyer's Viewpoint on Dementia Praecox*, "Encéphale," 21, 180-194, 1926.
Forstmeyer, W. M., *Insulin Shock; Influence on Permeability of Barrier Between Blood and Cerebrospinal Fluid in Schizophrenia*, "Am. J. Psychiat.," Suppl., 94, 133-139, 1938.
Foxe, A. N., *Omnipotence as a Defense*, "Psychoanalyt. Rev.," 25, 1938.
Freeman, W., *Prefrontal Lobotomy; the Problem of Schizophrenia*, "Am. J. Psychiat.," 101, 739-748, 1945.
———, *Transorbital Lobotomy*, "Digest of Neurol. and Psychiat.," Series 15, 398, 1948.
———, and Watts, J. W., *Results of Lobotomy Over a 10 Year Period*, "Med. Ann. District of Columbia," 16, 355-360, 1947.

———, and ———, *Schizophrenia in Childhood: Its Modification by Pre-Frontal Lobotomy*, Institute of Living, Series No. 15, April, 1947.

French, T. M. and Kasanin, J., *Psychodynamic Study of Recovery of 2 Schizophrenic Cases*, "Psychoanalyt. Quart.," 10, 1-22, 1941.

Freudenberg, R., *Insulin Shock in Schizophrenia; Behavior of Blood Sugar During Therapy*, "Am. J. Psychiat.," Suppl., 94, 139-142, 1938.

Fromm-Reichmann, F., *Transference Problems in Schizophrenics*, "Psychoanalyt. Quart.," Vol. 8, No. 4, Oct., 1939.

———, *Preliminary Note on Emotional Significance of Stereotypies in Schizophrenics*, "Bull. Forest San.," 1, 17-21, April, 1942.

———, *Psychoanalytic Psychotherapy with Psychotics*, "Psychiatry," 6, 1943.

———, *Problems of Therapeutic Management in a Psychiatric Hospital*, "Psychoanalyt. Rev.," 34, 259-273, 1947.

———, *Notes on the Development of Treatment of Schizophrenics by Psychoanalytic Psychotherapy*, "Psychiatry," 11, 263-273, 1948.

Frostig, J., *Insulin Shock in Schizophrenia with Reference to Clinical Problems*, "Am. J. Psychiat.," Suppl., 94, 220-226, 1938.

Frostig, J. P., van Harreveld, A., Tyler, D. B., and Wiersma, C. A., *Electro-Narcosis in Animals and Man*, "Arch. Neurol. and Psychiat.," 51, 232, 1944.

Galant, J. S., *Catatonic Contractures*, "Monatsschr. f. Psychiat. u. Neurol.," 72, 68-77, 1929.

———, *Natural History of Schizophrenia*, "Jour. Nerv. and Ment. Dis.," 78, 128, 1933.

Garma, A., *Reality and "id" in Schizophrenia*, "Internat. Ztschr. f. Psychoanal.," 18, 183-200, 1932.

Georgi, F., *Problem of Convulsions and Insulin Therapy*, "Am. J. Psychiat.," Suppl., 94, 67-74, 1939.

Geroff, W., *Pathogenesis and Prognosis of Schizophrenia (Catatonia, Hebephrenia, Dementia Simplex)*, "Arch. f. Psychiat.," 106, 585-598, 1937.

Gibbs, C. E., *Relation of Puberty to Behavior and Personality in Patients with Dementia Praecox*, "Am. J. Psychiat.," 3, 121-129, 1923.

Gillespie, R. D., *Psychotherapy of the Psychoses*, "Brit. J. Med. Psychol.," 30, 1943.

Glover, E., *Psychoanalytic Approach to the Classification of Mental Disorders*, "J. Ment. Sci.," 78, 819, 1932.

Goitein, P. L., *Significance of Ambivalency for Schizophrenic Dissociation; Clinical Study*, "J. Clin. Psychopath.," 6, 37-59, July, 1944.

Goldstein, K., *Significance of Special Mental Tests in Schizophrenia*, "Am. J. Psychiat.," 96, 575-588, 1939.

———, *Significance of Psychologic Research in Schizophrenia*, "J. Ment. Dis.," 97, 261-279, 1943.

Gosline, A., *Treatment of the Prepsychotic Schizoid Personality*, "Psychiat. Quart.," 10, 454, 1936.

Gottlieb, J. S., and Hope, J. M., *Prognostic Value of Intravenous Administration of Sodium Amytal in Cases of Schizophrenia*, "Arch. Neurol. and Psychiat.," 46, 86-100, 1941.

———, and Huston, P. E., *Treatment of Schizophrenia; Follow-up Results in Cases of Insulin Shock Therapy and in Control Cases*, "Arch. Neurol. and Psychiat.," 49, 266-271, 1943.

Gralnick, A., *Seven Year Survey of Insulin Treatment in Schizophrenia*, "Am. J. Psychiat.," 101, 449-452, 1945.

Grebelskaje-Albatz, E., *Schizophrenia of Early Childhood in its Clinical Aspects*, "Schweiz.," 34, 244-253, 1934; 35, 30-40, 1935.

Greenacre, P., *Content of Schizophrenic Characteristics Occurring in Affective Disorders*, "Am. J. Insanity," 75, 197, 1918.

Gullota, S., *Use of Sodium Amytal in Interruption of Catatonic Syndrome,* "Riv. de Pat. Nerv.," 40, 241-257, 1932.

Gurry, J., and Chasen, M., *Preliminary Survey of the Results of Group Therapy of Psychoses,* "Dis. Nerv. Syst.," 9, 52, 1948.

Halberstadt, G., *Dementia Praecox of Melancholic Type,* "Rev. Neurol.," 2, 18-27, 1925.

———, *Late Schizophrenia,* "Encéphale," 20, 655-662, 1925.

———, *Remissions, Intermissions and Circular Evolution in Course of Dementia Praecox,* "Paris Méd.," 2, 312-315, 1926.

———, *Dementia Praecox Accompanied by Obsessions: Three Cases,* "Encéphale," 23, 128-133, 1928.

Hall, G., and Neymann, C. A., *Studies of Schizophrenic Reactions,* "J. Nerv. and Ment. Dis.," 56, 433, 1922.

Halloran, R. D., Corwin, W., and Semrad, E. V., *Adaptation of Total Push Treatment Principle to State Hospital at Large,* "Dis. Nerv. Syst.," 3, 371-374, 1942.

Halpern, F. G., *Insulin; Rorschach Interpretation of Personality Structure of Schizophrenics Who Benefit from Therapy,* "Psychiat. Quart.," 14, 826-833, 1940.

Hanfman, E., *Analysis of Thinking Disorder in Case of Schizophrenia,* "Arch. Neurol. and Psychiat.," 41, 568-579, 1939.

Harms, E. (editor), *Schizophrenia in Childhood. The Nervous Child,* 1, 139-289, 1942.

———, *Childhood Schizophrenia and Childhood Hysteria,* "Psychiatric Quart.," 19, 242-257, 1945.

Harris, M. M., Horwitz, W. A., and Milch, E. A., *Sodium Amytal as Prognostic Aid in Insulin and Metrazol Shock Therapy of Dementia Praecox,* "Am. J. Psychiat.," 96, 327-333, 1939.

Harrison, R., *Studies in the Use and Validity of the Thematic Apperception Test with Mentally Disordered Patients,* "Char. and Person.," 9, No. 2, 1940.

Hartmann, H., *Case of Depersonalization,* "Ztschr. f. ges. Neurol. u. Psychiat.," 74, 1922.

Heath, R. G., and Pool, J. L., *Bilateral Fractional Resection of Frontal Cortex for the Treatment of Psychoses,* "J. Nerv. and Ment. Dis.," 107, 411-429, 1948.

Hemphill, R. E., *Hyperthyrotic Catatonia; Schizophrenic Symptom-Complex,* "J. Ment. Sc.," 88, 1-30, 1942.

Hilfiker, K., *Critique of Freud's View on Ideation of Schizophrenic Patients and Primitive Peoples,* "Allg. Ztschr. f. Psychiat.," 89, 97-108, 1928.

Hill, J., *Hallucinations in Psychosis,* "J. Nerv. and Ment. Dis.," 83, 405-421, 1936.

Hinsie, L. E., *Malaria Therapy in Schizophrenia,* "Psychiat. Quart.," 1, 210, 1927.

———, *Catatonic Syndrome,* "Psychiat. Quart.," 6, 457-468, 1932.

———, *Clinical Manifestations of Catatonic Form,* "Psychiat. Quart.," 6, 469-474, 1932.

Hitschmann, E., *Paranoia Homosexuality and Anal Eroticism,* "Internat. Ztschr. f. Psychoanal.," 1, 1913.

Hoch, A., *Personality and Psychosis,* "State Hosp. Bull.," 6, 220, 1913-1914.

———, *Acute Psychoses with Symptoms Resembling Dementia Praecox,* "Am. J. Psychiat.," 1, 356-372, 1922.

Hoch, P. H., *Prolonged Narcosis in Schizophrenia,* "Psychiat. Quart.," 9, 386-391, 1935.

———, *Clinical Biologic Interrelations Between Schizophrenia and Epilepsy,* "Am. J. Psychiat.," 99, 507-512, 1943.

Hoff, H., and Potzl, O., *Effects of Heat Puncture of Thalamus and Corpus Striatum in Advanced Schizophrenia,* "Psychiat.-Neurol. Wchnschr.," 34, 110-113, 1932.

Hofstatter, L., Smolek, E. A., and Busch, A. K., *Prefrontal Lobotomy in Chronic Psychoses with Special Reference to Section on Orbital Areas Only,* "Arch. Neurol. and Psychiat.," 53, 125-130, 1945.

Hollos, I., *Psychoanalytic Explanation of a Case of Dementia Praecox,* "Internat. Ztschr. f. Psychoanal.," 2, 1914.

Hoop, J. H. van der, *Concerning Projection and its Content*, "Internat. Ztschr. f. Psychoanal.," 10, 1924.

———, *Psychology of Schizophrenia*, "Psychiat. en Neurol. Bl.," 32, 457-483, 1928.

Hoskins, R. G., and Jellinek, E. M., *Schizophrenic Personality with Special Regard to Psychologic and Organic Concomitants*, "A. Res. Nerv. and Ment. Dis. Proc.," 14, 211-233, 1933.

Huber, K., *Alcohol Hallucinosis and its Relations to Schizophrenia*, "Schweiz. Arch. f. Neurol. u. Psychiat.," 44, 43-68, 1939.

Hunt, R. C., and Appel, K. E., *Prognosis in Psychoses Lying Midway Between Schizophrenia and Manic-Depressive Psychoses*, "Am. J. Psychiat.," 93, 313-339, 1936.

———, Feldman, H., and Fiero, R. P., *"Spontaneous" Remissions*, "Psychiatric Quart.," 12, 414-425, 1938.

Imber, I., *Hysteriform Mechanism in Schizophrenia; Clinical Study*, "Gior. d. r. Accad. di Med. di Torino," pt. 2, 98, 260-263, 1935.

———, *Pupillary Disturbances in Schizophrenia; Clinical Study*, "Riv. di Neurol.," 9, 133-162, 1936.

Impastato, D. J., *Study of Over 2,000 Cases of Electrofit-Treated Patients*, "N. Y. State J. Med.," 43, 2057, 1943.

Isaacs, S., *Special Mechanism in Schizoid Boy*, "Internat. J. Psychoanalysis," 20, 333-339, 1939.

Janet, P., *Dementia Praecox*, "J. de Psychol. Norm. et Path.," 24, 477-492, 1927.

Jasper, H. H., Fitzpatrick, C. P., and Solomon, P., *Analogies and Opposites in Schizophrenia and Epilepsy; Electroencephalographic and Clinical Studies*, "Am. J. Psychiat.," 95, 835-851, 1939.

Jelgersina, G., *Delusions in Schizophrenia*, "Nederl. Tijdschr. v. Geneesk.," 2, 4076-4085, 1928.

Jelliffe, S. E., *Mental Pictures in Schizophrenia and in Epidemic Encephalitis*, "Am. J. Psychiat.," 6, 413-465, 1927.

———, *Vigilance, Motor Pattern and Inner Meaning in Some Schizophrenic Behavior*, "Psychoanal. Rev.," 17, 305-330, 1930.

Jong, H. de, and Baruk, H., *Pathogenesis of Catatonic Syndrome and Experimental Catatonia*, "Encéphale," 25, 180-189, 1930.

———, *Experimental and Clinical Catatonia*, "Nederl. Tijdschr. v. Geneesk.," 1, 640-648, 1929.

Jung, C. G., *On the Psychogenesis of Schizophrenia*, "J. Ment. Sci.," 85, 999-1011, 1939.

Kallman, F. J., *Scientific Goal in Prevention*, "Proc. Internat. Genet. Cong.," (1939), 7, 172, 1941.

Kallman, F., *Twin Index Studies in Schizophrenia*, "Am. J. Psychiat.," 103, 309, 1946.

Kallman, F. J., Barrera, S. E., Hoch, P. H., and Kelley, D. M., *Role of Mental Deficiency in Incidence of Schizophrenia*, "Am. J. Ment. Deficiency," 45, 514-539, 1941.

Kamm, B. A., *Technical Problem in Psychoanalysis of Schizoid Character*, "Bull. Menninger Clin.," 1, 275-284, 1937.

———, *Schizophrenia and Compulsion Neurosis*, "Bull. Menninger Clin.," 2, 1938.

Kant, O., *Sense of Compulsion in Schizophrenics*, "Ztschr. f. d. ges. Neurol. u. Psychiat.," 111, 417-441, 1927.

———, *Dynamic Analysis of Delusions of Schizophrenics; 2 Cases*, "Ztschr. f. d. ges. Neurol. u. Psychiat.," 150, 272-304, 1934.

———, *Differential Diagnosis of Schizophrenia in Light of Concept of Personality Stratification*, "Am. J. Psychiat.," 97, 342-357, 1940.

———, *Types and Analyses of Clinical Pictures of Recovered Schizophrenics*, "Psychiatric Quart.," 14, 676-700, 1940.

———, *Comparative Study of Recovered and Deteriorated Schizophrenic Patients*, "J. Nerv. and Ment. Dis.," 93, 616-624, 1941.

———, *Dreams of Schizophrenic Patients*, "J. Nerv. and Ment. Dis.," 95, 335-347, 1942.

———, *Problem of Psychogenic Precipitation in Schizophrenia*, "Psychiatric Quart.," 16, 341-350, 1942.

———, *Clinical Analysis of Schizophrenic Deterioration; Investigation Aided by Sodium Amytal Interviews*, "Psychiat. Quart.," 17, 426-445, 1943.

———, *Evaluation of Prognostic Criteria in Schizophrenia*, "J. Nerv. and Ment. Dis.," 100, 598-605, 1944.

Karpman, B., *Hebephrenic Fancies; Relation to Two Basic Crime Trends; Incest and Parricide*, "J. Nerv. and Ment. Dis.," 100, 48-506, 1944.

Kasanin, J., *Pavlov's Theory of Schizophrenia*, "Arch. Neurol. and Psychiat.," 28, 210-218, 1932.

———, *Acute Schizo-Affective Psychoses*, "Am. J. Psychiat.," 13, 97-126, 1933.

———, and Kaufman, M. R., *Dementia Praecox in Infants and Children*, "Am. J. Psychiat.," 9, 307-384, 1929.

———, and Veo, L., *The Early Recognition of Mental Diseases in Children*, "Am. J. Orthopsychiat.," 1, 406-429, 1932.

Katan, M., *Understanding of Schizophrenic Speech*, "Internat. J. Psychoanalysis," 20, 353-362, 1939.

———, *Role of the Word in Schizophrenia*, "Internat. Ztschr. f. Psychoanal. u. Imago," 25, 138-173, 1940.

Katzenelbogen, S., *Pharmacologic (Insulin and Metrazol) Shock Therapy*, "Internat. Clinics," 1, 105-114, 1940.

———, *Formulation of Dementia Praecox by Kraepelin, Bleuler and Meyer*, "Psychiatric Quart.," 16, 439-453, 1942.

Kaufman, M. R., *Religious Delusions in Schizophrenia*, "Internat. J. Psychoanalysis," 20, 363-376, 1939.

Kempf, E. J., *Psychoanalytic Treatment of Dementia Praecox; Report of a Case*, "Psychoanal. Rev.," 6, 15, 1919.

Kerschbaumer, L., *Poetry in Schizophrenia*, "J. Nerv. and Ment. Dis.," 91, 141-156, 1940.

Klasi, J., *Concerning the Therapeutic Use of "Prolonged Narcosis" by Means of Somnifene in Schizophrenics*, "Ztschr. f. d. ges. Neurol. u. Psychiat.," 74, 557, 1922.

Kleist, K., *Classification of Atypical Psychoses; Diagnosis of Schizophrenia*, "Schweiz. Arch. f. Neurol. u. Psychiat.," 23, 3-37, 1928.

Knight, R. P., *Psychotherapy in Acute Paranoid Schizophrenia with Successful Outcome; Case*, "Bull. Menninger Clin.," 3, 97-105, 1939.

———, *Relationship of Latent Homosexuality to the Mechanism of Paranoid Delusions*, "Bull. Menninger Clin.," 4, 1940.

Koester, A., *Frequency of Loss of Pupillary Reflexes*, "Arch. f. Psychiat.," 81, 601-605, 1927.

Kogan, I. M., *Manifestations of Oedipus Complex*, "Internat. Ztschr. f. Psychoanal.," 14, 518-528, 1928.

———, *End of World and Rebirth; Schizophrenic's Phantasy*, "Internat. Ztschr. f. Psychoanal.," 18, 86-104, 1932.

Kolb, L., and Vogel, V. H., *The Use of Shock Therapy in 305 Mental Hospitals*, "Am. J. Psychiat.," 99, 90, 1942.

Kopeloff, L. M., Kopeloff, N., Hinsie, L. E., and Etchells, J. L., *Tuberculous Bacillemia and Dementia Praecox*, "J. Bact.," 30, 49-59, 1935.

Kosawa, H., *Schizophrenic Hallucinations Concerning Face*, "Internat. Ztschr. f. Psychoanal.," 19, 434-439, 1933.

Kraepelin, E., *Signs of Mental Disorder*, "Alienist and Neurologist," 40, 85, 1919.

Krapf, E., *Rare Occurrence of Symptomatic Epilepsy with Schizophrenia*, "Arch. f. Psychiat.," 83, 547-586, 1928.

Kronfeld, A., *Changes of Views on Schizophrenia*, "Monatsschr. f. Psychiat. u. Neurol.," 73, 140-166, 1929.

———, *Conception of Schizophrenia in Modern French Psychiatry,* "Allg. Ztschr. f. Psychiat.," 92, 173-191, 1929.

Kubie, L. S., *Modifications in Schizophrenic Reactions with Psychoanalytic Treatment,* "Arch. Neurol. and Psychiat.," 37, 874-880, 1937.

Laforgue, R., *Schizophrenia, Schizomania and Schizonoia,* "Ztschr. f. d. ges. Neurol. u. Psychiat.," 105, 448-458, 1926.

———, *Scotomatization in Schizophrenia,* "Internat. J. Psychoanalysis," 8, 473-478, 1927.

———, *Study of Schizophrenia,* "Internat. J. Psychoanalysis," 17, 147-162, 1936.

Lang, T., *Studies on Male Homosexuals and Their Families; Relationship Between Homosexuality and Schizophrenia,* "Ztschr. f. d. ges. Neurol. u. Psychiat.," 171, 651-679, 1941.

Lange, J., *Schizophrenic Reaction,* "Munchen. Med. Wnschr.," 73, 1152-1155, 1926.

Langenstrasse, K. H., *Treatment of Stupor (Loevenhart Method of Carbon-Dioxide-Oxygen Inhalation),* "Am. J. Psychiat.," 11, 447-455, 1932.

Langfeldt, G., *Schizophrenic Psychoses; 4 Cases,* "Encéphale," 2, 183-201, 1937.

Lehmann-Facius, H., *The Sulfur Treatment of Schizophrenia,* "Arch. f. Psychiat.," 105, 103, 1936.

Lehrman, S. R., *Schizophrenic "Deterioration,"* "Psychiatric Quart.," 14, 140-156, 1940.

Lemke, R., *Social Prognosis of Schizophrenia on Basis of Encephalography,* "Arch. f. Psychiat.," 104, 89-136, 1935.

Lengyel, B. A., *Remission and Mortality Rates in Schizophrenia,* "Am. J. Hyg.," (Sec. A), 33, 16-32, 1941.

Levering, I., *Nursing Care in Schizophrenia,* "Am. J. Nursing," 40, 1077-1083, 1940.

Levin, M., *Transitory Schizophrenias Produced by Bromide Intoxication,* "Am. J. Psychiat.," 2, 103, 1946.

Levine, A., and Schilder, P., *Catatonic Pupil,* "J. Nerv. and Ment. Dis.," 96, 1-12, 1926.

———, and ———, *Motor Phenomena During Nitrogen Inhalations,* "Arch. Neurol. and Psychiat.," 44, 1009-1017, 1940.

Levy, E., *Schizophrenic Formal Disturbances of Thought,* "Psychiatry," 6, 55-69, 1943.

Lewis, N. D. C., *Pathology of Dementia Praecox,* "J. Nerv. and Ment. Dis.," 62, 225-260, 1925.

———, *Graphic Art Productions in Schizophrenia,* "A. Res. Nerv. and Ment. Dis. Prac.," (1925), 5, 344-368, 1928.

———, *Mechanisms in Certain Cases of Prolonged Schizophrenia,* "Am. J. Psychiat.," 9, 543-552, 1929.

———, and Blanchard, E., *Clinical Findings in "Recovered" Cases of Schizophrenia,* "Am. J. Psychiat.," 11, 481-492, 1931.

Liberson, W. T., and Wilcox, P. H., *Electro-Convulsive Therapy: a Comparison of "Brief Stimuli Technic" with the Friedman-Wilcox-Reiter Technic,* "Digest of Neurol. and Psychiat.," 13, 292, 1945.

Libertson, W., *Critical Analysis of Insulin Therapy at Rochester State Hospital,* "Psychiat. Quart.," 15, 635-647, 1941.

Lindemann, E., *Psychological Changes in Normal and Abnormal Individuals Under Influence of Sodium Amytal,* "Am. J. Psychiat.," 11, 6, 1932.

Lurie, L. A., Tietz, E. B., and Hertzman, J., *Functional Psychoses; Analysis of Findings in 20 Cases of Psychotic Children Studied at Child Guidance Home,* "Am. J. Psychiat.," 92, 1169-1184, 1936.

Lutz, J., *Dementia Praecox in Infants and Children,* "Schweiz. Arch. f. Neurol. u. Psychiat.," 39, 335-372, 1937.

———, *Dementia Praecox in Infants and Children,* "Schweiz. Arch. f. Neurol. u. Psychiat.," 40, 141-163, 1937.

Malamud, W., and Miller, W., *Psychotherapy in Schizophrenia,* "Am. J. Psychiat.," 88, 457-480, 1931.

———, and Render, N., *Course and Prognosis in Schizophrenia*, "Am. J. Psychiat.," 95, 1039-1057, 1939.

Malzberg, B., *Insulin Treatment; Outcome in 1,000 Patients*, "Psychiat. Quart.," 12, 528-553, 1938.

———, *A Follow-Up of Those Treated in N. Y. Civil Hospitals*, "Ment. Hyg.," 23, 641-646, 1939.

May, J., *The Dementia Praecox-Schizophrenia Problem*, "Am. J. Psychiat.," 88, 401-466, 1931.

Mayer-Gross, W., *History of Dementia Praecox*, "Klin. Wchnschr.," 3, 1075-1077, 1924.

———, *Primary and Secondary Symptoms of Schizophrenia*, "Ztschr. f. d. ges. Neurol. u. Psychiat.," 124, 647-672, 1930.

Meduna, L. von, *Experiments on Biological Control of Outcome of Schizophrenia by Producing Epileptic Attacks with Injections of Camphor and Metrazol*, "Ztschr. f. d. ges. Neurol. u. Psychiat.," 152, 235-262, 1935.

———, *Metrazol Convulsions in Schizophrenia*, "Schweiz. Arch. f. Neurol. u. Psychiat.," Suppl., 39, 32-38, 1937.

———, *Cardiazol (Metrazol) Therapy – General Discussion*, "Am. J. Psychiat.," Suppl., 94, 40-50, 1938.

———, *Common Factors in Shock Therapies*, "Dis. Nerv. System," 6, 283-285, 1945.

Meduna, L. J., Braceland, F. J., and Vaechules, J., *Biochemical Disturbances in Mental Disorders; Anti-Insulin Effect of Blood in Schizophrenia*, "Arq. Serv. Nac. doen. ment.," pt. 2, 443-461, 1943.

Meduna, L., and Friedman, E., *Convulsive Therapy of Psychoses; Survey of More Than 3,000 Cases*, "J.A.M.A.," 112, 501-509, 1939.

Meduna, L. J., and McCulloch, W. S., *Modern Concept of Schizophrenia*, "M. Clin. North America," 29, 147-164, 1945.

Menninger, K. A., *Schizophrenic Syndrome as Product of Acute Infectious Disease*, "A. Res. Nerv. and Ment. Dis. Proc.," (1925), 5, 182-203, 1928.

Menninger von Lerchenthal, E., *Handwriting in Schizophrenia*, "Ztschr. f. d. ges. Neurol. u. Psychiat.," 107, 27-50, 1927.

Meyer, A., *Fundamental Conceptions of Dementia Praecox*, "Brit. M. J.," 2, 757, 1906.

———, *Constructive Formulations of Schizophrenia*, "Am. J. Psychiat.," 1, 355, 1922.

———, *Evolution of Dementia Praecox Concept*, "A. Res. Nerv. and Ment. Dis. Proc.," (1925), 5, 3-15, 1928.

Milici, P., *Psychology of Dementia Praecox*, "Psychiat. Quart.," 17, 87-111, 1943.

Miller, W. R., *Psychogenic Factors in Polyuria of Schizophrenia*, "J. Nerv. and Ment. Dis.," 84, 418-426, 1936.

Minkowski, E., *Autodescription of Schizophrenia*, "Medicine," 5, 377-381, 1924.

———, *Bergson's Conceptions as Applied to Psychopathology*, "J. Nerv. and Ment. Dis.," 63, 553-568, 1926.

———, *Autism and Schizophrenic Attitudes*, "J. de psychol. norm. et path.," 24, 465-476, 1927.

Minski, L., *Vasomotor Disturbances in Schizophrenia*, "J. Ment. Sc.," 83, 437-439, 1937.

Mira, E., *Myokinetic Psychodiagnosis*, "Proc. Roy. Soc. Med.," 33, 173-194, 1940.

Moniz, E., *Prefrontal Leucotomy in Treatment of Mental Disorders*, "Am. J. Psychiat.," 93, 1379-1385, 1937.

———, and Furtado, D., *Prefrontal Leukotomy in Schizophrenia; Cases*, "Ann. Med.-psychol.," pt. 2, 95, 298-309, 1937.

Monakow, C. von, and Kitabayashi, S., *Schizophrenia and the Choroid Plexes*, "Schweiz. Arch. f. Neurol. u. Psychiat.," 4, 363, 1919.

Morel, F., *Surgical Treatment of Schizophrenia*, "Am. J. Psychiat.," Suppl., 94, 309-314, 1938.

Morgan, C. D., and Murray, H. A., *A Method for Investigating Fantasies; the Thematic Apperception Test*, "Arch. Neurol. and Psychiat.," 34, 289-306, 1935.

Morgenthaler, W., *Dogma of Incurability of Dementia Praecox*, "Ztschr. f. d. ges. Neurol. u. Psychiat.," 100, 668-677, 1926.

Mott, E., *The Reproductive Organs in Relation to Mental Disorders*, "Brit. Med. J.," Pt. 1, 463-467, 1922.

Mott, F. W., *Pathology of Dementia Praecox*, "Proc. Roy. Soc. Med.," 13, 25, 1920.

———, and Prados y Such, M., *Pathological Studies in Dementia Praecox in Relation to Interstitial Cells of Leydig*, "Proc. Roy. Soc. Med.," 15, 1-4, 1922.

Muehlig, W. A., *Schizophrenia; Neurologic Signs*, "J. Michigan M. Soc.," 39, 116-117, 1940.

Muller, M., *Insulin in Schizophrenia*, "Am. J. Psychiat.," Suppl., 94, 5-23, 1938.

Muralt, A. V., *Psychoanalysis of Schizophrenia*, "Schweiz. Arch. f. Neurol. u. Psychiat.," 14, 216-237, 1924.

Murphy, G., *Types of Word-Association in Dementia Praecox, Manic-Depressives and Normals*, "Am. J. Psychiat.," 2, 539-571, 1923.

Myerson, A., *Theory and Principles of "Total Push" Method in Chronic Schizophrenia*, "Am. J. Psychiat.," 95, 1197-1204, 1939.

Notkin, J., and De Natale, F. S., *Statistical Comparisons Between Pre-Insulin and Insulin Eras; Recoveries and Improvements*, "Psychiat. Quart.," 12, 423-443, 1938.

Oberndorf, C. P., *A Theory of Depersonalization*, "Tr. A. N. A.," 1933.

Ophuijsen, J. H. W. van, *On the Origin of the Feeling of Persecution*, "Internat. J. Psychoanal.," 1, 1920.

Osborne, R. L., *Palaeophrenia: Revaluation of Concept of Schizophrenia*, "J. Ment. Sc.," 86, 1078-1085, 1940.

Palmer, H. A., *Scheid's Cyanotic Syndrome (Case Record and Summary of Original Monograph of K. Scheid)*, "J. Ment. Sc.," 87, 635-638, 1941.

Pappenheim, E., and Kris, E., *The Function of Drawings and the Meaning of the Creative Spell in a Schizophrenic Artist*, "Psychoanal. Quart.," 15, 6-31, 1946.

Parker, S., *Character of Modern Psychiatry: Synthetic Presentation of Work of Paul Schilder*, "J. Nerv. and Ment. Dis.," 63, 313-342, 1926.

Paskind, H. A., and Brown, M., *Diagnosis, Psychoses Resembling Schizophrenia Occurring with Emotional Stress and Ending in Recovery*, "Am. J. Psychiat.," 96, 1379-1388, 1940.

Pfeffer, A. Z., and Pescor, M. J., *Multiple Transfusions for Schizophrenia*, "Arch. Neurol. and Psychiat.," 52, 131-134, 1944.

Pfister, O. E., *Therapy, Amytal Test Before Shock Therapy of Schizophrenia*, "Monatschr. f. Psychiat. u. Neurol.," 107, 102-106, 1943.

Piowtrowski, Z. A., *Test Behavior of Schizophrenic Children*, "Proc. Am. A. Ment. Deficiency," 57, 332-347, 1933.

———, *Insulin; Rorschach Manifestations of Improvement in Treated Schizophrenics*, "Psychosom. Med.," 1, 508-526, 1939.

———, *Rorschach Method as Prognostic Aid in Insulin Shock Treatment of Schizophrenics*, "Psychiat. Quart.," 15, 807-822, 1941.

———, *Experimental Psychological Diagnosis of Mild Forms of Schizophrenia*, "Rorschach Research Exchange," 9, 189-200, 1945.

Polatin, P., and Hoch, P., *Diagnostic Evaluation of Early Schizophrenia*, "J. Nerv. and Ment. Dis.," 105, 221, 1947.

———, and Spotnitz, H., *Insulin: Ambulatory Shock Technique in Schizophrenia*, "J. Nerv. & Ment. Dis.," 97, 567-575, 1943.

Pollock, H. M., *Frequency of Schizophrenia in Relation to Sex, Age, Environment, Nativity and Race*, "A. Res. Nerv. and Ment. Dis. Proc.," 5, 47-64, 1928.

———, *Metrazol; Statistical Study of 1140 Patients*, "Psychiat. Quart.," 13, 558-573, 1939.

———, and Malzberg, B., *Hereditary and Environmental Factors in Causation of Manic-Depressive Psychoses and Dementia Praecox,* "Am. J. Psychiat.," 96, 1227-1244, 1940.

Potter, R. W., *Schizophrenia in Children,* "Am. J. Psychiat.," 12, 1254, 1933.

Proctor, L. D., *Indications for Shock Therapy in Mental Illness,* "Canad. M. A. J.," 52, 130-136, 1945.

———, and Godwin, J. E., *Clinical and Electro-Physiological Observations Following Electroshock,* "Am. J. Psychiat.," 101, 797-805, 1945.

Rachlin, H. L., *Statistical Study of Benign Stupor in 5 New York Hospitals,* "Psychiatric Quart.," 11, 436-444, 1937.

Reiter, P. J., *Examination of Theory of Toxic Origin,* "Bibliot. f. laeger," 129, 287-309, September, 1937; also, "Ztschr. f. d. ges. Neurol. u. Psychiat.," 160, 598-614, 1938.

Rennie, T. A. C., *Prognosis, Follow-Up Study of 500 Patients with Schizophrenia Admitted to Hospital from 1913 to 1923,* "Arch. Neurol. and Psychiat.," 42, 877-891, 1939.

———, *Prognosis, Analysis of 100 Cases of Schizophrenia with Recovery,* "Arch. Neurol. and Psychiat.," 46, 197-229, 1941.

———, *Present Status of Shock Therapy,* "Psychiatry," 6, 127-132, 1943.

———, *Prognosis in Schizophrenic Conditions Following Shock Treatment,* "Psychiatric Quart.," 17, 642-654, 1943.

Rickers-Ovsiankina, N., *Rorschach Test as Applied to Normal and Schizophrenic Subjects,* "Brit. J. M. Psychol.," 17, 227-257, 1938.

Rickman, J., *A Survey; the Development of the Psychoanalytic Theory of the Psychoses (1894-1927),* "Brit. J. Med. Psychol.," 7, 321-357, 1927.

Rivers, T. D., and Bond, E. D., *Follow-Up Results in Insulin Shock Therapy after One to Three Years,* "Am. J. Psychiat.," 98, 328-384, 1941.

———, and Rome, H. P., *Insulin; Prolonged Coma in Schizophrenia,* "Arch. Neurol. and Psychiat.," 51, 550-556, 1944.

Rizatti, E. M., *Clinical Concept of Schizophrenia,* "Schizofrenie," 1, 37-66, 1931.

Roenau, E., *Ambivalence; Use of the Term for Last 25 Years in Discussion of Dementia Praecox,* "Ztschr. f. d. ges. Neurol. u. Psychiat.," 157, 153-165, 1937; comment by Bleuler, 157, 166-168, 1937.

Romano, J., and Ebaugh, F. G., *Schizophrenia; Preliminary Report,* "Am. J. Psychiat.," 95, 583-596, 1938.

Rosen, J. N., *A Method of Resolving Acute Catatonic Excitement,* "Psychiat. Quart.," 20, 2, 1946.

———, *The Treatment of Schizophrenic Psychosis by Direct Analytic Therapy,* "Psychiat. Quart.," 21, 3-37, 1947.

Rosenzweig, S., and Shakow, D., *Play Technic in Schizophrenia,* "Am. J. Orthopsychiat.," 7, 36-47, 1937.

Ross, J. R., and Malzberg, B., *Review of Results of Pharmacological Shock Therapy and Metrazol in New York State,* "Am. J. Psychiat.," 96, 297-316, 1939.

———, and others, *Pharmacologic Shock Treatment of Schizophrenia; Two-Year Follow-Up Study from New York State Hospitals with Some Recommendations for Future,* "Am. J. Psychiat.," 97, 1007-1023, 1941.

Rubin, M. A., Malamud, W., and Hope, J. M., *Electroencephalogram and Psychopathic Manifestations in Schizophrenia as Influenced by Drugs,* "Psychosom. Med.," 4, 355-361, 1942.

Rudolf, G. de M., *Experimental Treatments of Schizophrenia,* "J. Ment. Sci.," 77, 767-791, 1931.

Rupp, C., and Fletcher, E. K., *Five to Ten Year Follow-Up Study of 641 Schizophrenic Cases,* "Am. J. Psychiat.," 96, 877-888, 1940.

Sakel, M., *Insulin Hypoglycernic Shock in Schizophrenia,* "Wien. Med. Wchnschr.," 84, 1211; 1265; 1299; 1326; 1353; 1383; 1401; 85, 35; 68; 94; 121; 152; 179, 1934.

———, *Significance of Epileptic Seizures as a Therapeutic Factor in Medicinal Shock*

Therapy of Schizophrenia, "Klin. Wchnschr.," 16, 1277-1282, 1937.
———, *New Treatment of Schizophrenia*, "Am. J. Psychiat.," 93, 829-841, 1937.
———, *Origin of Insulin Shock Treatment of Schizophrenia*, "Encéphale," 1, 153-164, 1938.
Scheidegger, W., *Deaths from Catatonia at Psychiatric Clinic of Zurich from 1900 to 1928*, "Ztschr. f. d. ges. Neurol. u. Psychiat.," 120, 587-649, 1929.
Schilder, P., *Psycology of Dementia Praecox*, "Deutsche Med. Wchnschr.," 49, 1433-35, 1923.
———, *Psychology of Schizophrenia from Psychoanalytic View Point*, "Ztschr. f. d. ges. Neurol. u. Psychiat.," 112, 279-282, 1928.
———, *Effect of Hypnosis on Schizophrenics*, "Ztschr. f. d. ges. Neurol. u. Psychiat.," 120, 700-707, 1929.
———, *Scope of Psychotherapy in Schizophrenia*, "Am. J. Psychiat.," 11, 1181-1187, 1932.
———, *Clinical Studies on Particular Types of Depressive Psychoses — Their Differential Diagnosis from Schizophrenic Processes*, "J. Nerv. and Ment. Dis.," 80, 501; 658, 1934.
———, *Psychology of Metrazol Treatment*, "J. Nerv. and Ment. Dis.," 89, 133-144, 1939.
———, *Psychology of Schizophrenia*, "Psychoanalyt. Rev.," 26, 380-398, 1939.
———, and Sugar, N., *Schizophrenic Speech Disturbances*, "Ztschr. f. d. ges. Neurol. u. Psychiat.," 104, 689-711, 1926.
Schmideberg, M., *Contribution to the Psychology of Persecutory Ideas and Delusions*, "Internat. J. Psychoanal.," 12, 1931.
Schneck, J. M., *Pyknolepsy, with Report of Its Occurrence in Case of Schizophrenia*, "J. Nerv. and Ment. Dis.," 102, 276-279, 1945.
Schneider, A., *Disorders of Speech in Schizophrenia*, "Ztschr. f. d. ges. Neurol. u. Psychiat.," 108, 491-524, 1927.
Schulz, B., *Study of Offspring of Schizophrenic Parents*, "Ztschr. f. d. ges. Neurol. u. Psychiat.," 168, 332-381, 1940.
Shapiro, L. B., *Prior to Introduction of Shock Therapy*, "Elgin State Hosp. Papers," 3, 9-12, 1939.
———, and Read, C. F., *Fever Treatment with Sulfur-in-Oil, Especially with Reference to Acute Cases*, "J. Nerv. and Ment. Dis.," 86, 162-165, 1937.
Shipley, W. C., and Kant, F., *The Insulin Shock and Metrazol Convulsant Shock Therapy of Schizophrenia with Emphasis on Psychological Aspects*, "Psychol. Bull.," 37, 259-284, 1940.
Skalweit, W., *Schizophrenia, a Review of Literature*, "Fortschr. d. Neurol., Psychiat.," 7, 143-161, 1935.
Spielmeyer, W., *Problem of Anatomy of Schizophrenia*, "J. Nerv. and Ment. Dis.," 72, 241-244, 1930.
Sprague, G. S., *Regression in Catatonia*, "J. Nerv. and Ment. Dis.," 91, 566-578, 1940.
Starcke, A., *Mentality of Schizophrenics*, "Psychiat. en neurol. bl.," 32, 484-490, 1928.
Steinfeld, J., *Therapeutic Results on "Treatment-Resistant" Schizophrenics*, "Bull. Forest San.," 1, 1942.
Stengel, E., *Significance of Compulsive Neurotic Personality in Schizophrenia*, "Arch. f. Psychiat.," 106, 509-553, 1937.
Stockings, G. T., *Etiology, Pathogenesis and Clinical Study of Mescaline Psychosis, with Special Reference to Mechanism of Genesis of Schizophrenia*, "J. Ment. Sc.," 86, 39-47, 1940.
———, *Schizophrenia in Military Psychiatric Practice*, "J. Ment. Sci.," 91, 110-112, 1945.
Storch, A., *Psychobiologic Architecture of Schizophrenia*, "Neurol. u. Psychiat.," 10, 748-769, 1926.
Stransky, E., *Nature of Schizophrenia*, "Jahrb. f. Psychiat. u. Neurol.," 46, 217-254, 1929.

———, *Progress in Knowledge of Schizophrenia*, "Wien. Klin. Wchschr.," 45, 1446; 1479, 1932.

Strauss, H., and Rahm, W. E., *Metrazol; Effect on E.E.G.*, "Psychiat. Quart.," 14, 43-48, 1940.

Strecker, E. A., *Preliminary Study of Precipitating Situation in 200 Cases of Mental Disease*, "Am. J. Psychiat.," 1, 503-536, 1922.

———, and Palmer, H. D., and Grant, F. C., *Prefrontal Lobotomy*, "Am. J. Psychiat.," 98, 524-532, 1942.

———, and Willey, G. F., *Prognosis in Schizophrenia*, "J. Ment. Sci.," 73, 9-39, 1927.

Sukhareva, G. E., and Kogan, E. I., *Prognosis of Schizophrenia of Childhood and Puberty*, "Sovet. psikhonevrol.," No. 6, 120-131, 1933.

Sullivan, H. S., *Schizophrenia: Its Conservative and Malignant Feature, Preliminary Communication*, "Am. J. Psychiat.," 4, 77-91, 1924.

———, *Peculiarity of Thought in Schizophrenia*, "Am. J. Psychiat.," 5, 21-86, 1925.

———, *Affective Experience in Early Schizophrenia*, "Am. J. Psychiat.," 6, 467-483, 1927.

———, *Onset of Schizophrenia*, "Am. J. Psychiat.," 7, 105-134, 1927.

———, *Affective Experience in Early Schizophrenia*, "A. Res. Nerv. and Ment. Dis. Proc.," (1925), 5, 141-158, 1928.

———, *Tentative Criteria of Malignancy in Schizophrenia*, "Am. J. Psychiat.," 7, 759-787, 1928.

———, *Research in Schizophrenia*, "Am. J. Psychiat.," 9, 553-567, 1929.

———, *Socio-Psychiatric Research; Implications for Schizophrenia Problem*, "Am. J. Psychiat.," 10, 977-991, 1931.

———, *Modified Psychoanalytic Treatment of Schizophrenia*, "Am. J. Psychiat.," 11, 519-540, 1931.

———, *Therapeutic Investigations in Schizophrenia*, "Psychiatry," 10, 121-125, 1947.

———, *Notes on Investigation, Therapy and Education in Psychiatry and Their Relations to Schizophrenia*, "Psychiatry," 10, 271-280, 1947.

Tauber, C. G., *Hallucinations in Process of Healing of Schizophrenia*, "Schweiz. Arch. f. Neurol. u. Psychiat.," 32, 376-381, 1933.

Tausk, V., *Origin of the "Influencing Machine" in Schizophrenia*, "Psychoanalyt. Quart.," 2, 519-556, 1933.

Taylor, J. H., *Returns of Schizophrenics Following Shock Therapy; Report on Patients Released 5 to 7 Years Ago*, "Dis. Nerv. System," 6, 28-29, 1945.

Tidd, C. W., *Treatment of Schizophrenia by Psychotherapy*, "Bull. Menninger Clin.," 2, 89-93, 1938.

Tietz, E. B., Thompson, G. N., van Harreveld, A., and Wiersma, C. A. G., *Electronarcosis – a Therapy in Schizophrenia*, "Am. J. Psychiat.," 101, 821, 1945.

Tillotson, K. J., *Practice of "Total Push" Method in Treatment of Chronic Schizophrenia*, "Am. J. Psychiat.," 95, 1205-1213, 1939.

Tomlinson, P. J., and Ozarin, L. D., *Ambulatory Insulin Therapy; Report of 52 Cases*, "Psychiat. Quart.," 16, 167-173, 1942.

Tramer, M., *Dangers of Psychoanalysis in Dementia Praecox*, "Schweiz. Med. Wchnschr.," 54, 273-275, 1924.

———, *Record of Day-by-Day Development of Child from Birth to Fifth Year; Early Manifestation of Infantile Schizophrenia*, "Ztschr. f. Kinderpsychiat.," 2, 17, 86, 115, 1935.

———, *Further Record of Case of Early Manifestation of Infantile Schizophrenia*, "Ztschr. f. Kinderpsychiat.," 10, 115-121, 1943.

Verbrugge, E. M., *In Connection with Pavlov's Laws of Inhibition and Excitation*, "Schweiz. Med. Wchnschr.," 70, 59-62, 1940.

Vigotsky, L., *Thought and Speech*, "Psychiatry," 2, 29-54, 1930.

———, *Thought in Schizophrenia*, "Arch. Neurol. and Psychiat.," 31, 1063-1077, 1934.

Walder, R., *Schizophrenic and Creative Thinking,* "Internat. J. Psychoanal.," 7, 366-376, 1926.

Washburne, A. C., and Hodgson, E. R., *Regression Neuroses and Schizophrenia; Analysis of 40 Cases,* "Am. J. Psychiat.," 97, 1073-1085, 1941.

Wechsler, D., Halpern, F., and Jaros, E., *Insulin; Psychometric Study of Treated Schizophrenics,* "Psychiat. Quart.," 14, 466-476, 1940.

Weigert-Vowinckel, E., *Contribution to Theory of Schizophrenia,* "Internat. J. Psychoanalysis," 17, 190-201, 1936.

Weininger, B. I., *Psychotherapy During Convalescence from Psychosis,* "Psychiatry," 1, 257-264, 1938.

Wespi, H., *Schizophrenia in Uniovular Twins; Discussion of Problem of "Endogenous-Exogenous" Factors in Pathogenesis,* "Schweiz. Arch. f. Neurol. u. Psychiat.," 48, 110-128, 1941.

White, W. A., *Some Considerations Bearing on Diagnosis and Treatment of Dementia Praecox,* "Am. J. Psychiat.," 1, 193, 1921.

———, *Comparative Method in Psychiatry,* "J. Nerv. and Mental Dis.," 61, 1-17, 1925.

———, *Language of Schizophrenia,* "Arch. Neurol. and Psychiat.," 16, 395-413, 1926.

———, *Language of Schizophrenia,* "A. Res. Nerv. and Ment. Dis. Proc.," (1925), 5, 323-343, 1928.

Whitehead, D., *Prognosis in Dementia Praecox,* "Psychiatric Quart.," 11, 383-390, 1937.

Whitehorn, J. C., and Zipf, G. K., *Schizophrenic Language,* "Arch. Neurol. and Psychiat.," 49, 831-851, 1943.

Wigers, F., *Uniovular Twins with Schizophrenia Appearing in One,* "Acta Psychiat. et Neurol.," 9, 541-556, 1934.

Wittels, F., *Psychology and Treatment of Depersonalization,* "Psychoanalyt. Rev.," 27, 1940.

Wittman, M. P., and Russell, J. T., *Mental Efficiency Levels Before and After Shock Therapy,* "Elgin State Hosp. Papers," 4, 70-81, 1941.

Wohlfahrt, S., *Histopathology of Schizophrenia,* "Acta Psychiat. et Neurol.," 11, 687-707, 1937.

Wolff, S. C., *Thought Content in Catatonic Dementia Praecox,* "Psychiat. Quart.," 6, 504-512, 1932.

Wooley, L. F., *Studies in Obsessive-Ruminative Tension States; Exploration of Psychoneurotic-Psychotic Borderland,* "Psychiatric Quart.," 11, 74-93, 1937.

Wyrsch, J., *Emotional Rapport with Schizophrenics,* "Schweiz. Arch. f. Neurol. u. Psychiat.," 37, 139-148, 1936.

———, *Schizophrenia Associated with Manic-Depressive Psychosis ("Mixed Psychoses"),* "Ztschr. f. d. ges. Neurol. u. Psychiat.," 159, 668-693, 1937.

———, *Schizophrenic Hallucinosis,* "Allg. Ztschr. f. Psychiat.," 108, 231-253, 1938.

———, *Psychopathology of Simple Schizophrenias,* "Monatsschr. f. Psychiat. u. Neurol.," 102, 75-106, 1940.

———, *Theory and Clinical Aspects of Paranoid Schizophrenia,* "Monatsschr. f. Psychiat. u. Neurol.," 106, 57-101, 1942.

———, *Psychotherapy and Schizophrenia,* "Monatsschr. Psychiat.," 110, 237-244, 1945.

Yates, I., *Schizophrenia Beginning at About 3 Years of Age (?); Case for Diagnosis,* "Proc. Roy. Soc. Med.," 31, 560-562, 1938.

Yoder, O. R., *Socialization Program (Occupational and Recreational Therapy),* "Occup. Therapy," 17, 107-115, 1938.

Zilboorg, G., *Post-Partum Schizophrenias,* "J. Nerv. and Ment. Dis.," 68, 370-383, 1928.

———, *Dynamics of Schizophrenic Reactions Related to Pregnancy and Childbirth,* "Am. J. Psychiat.," 8, 733-767, 1929.

———, *Deeper Layers of Schizophrenic Psychoses,* "Am. J. Psychiat.," 11, 493-511, 1931.

———, *Ambulatory Schizophrenia,* "Psychiatry," 4, 149-155, 1941.

INDEX